The Case-Tutor™ Courseware for Students

Accompanying this textbook is a Microsoft® Excel-based software package called Case-Tutor™. This optional supplement consists of (1) study questions for each of the 27 cases in this book and (2) custom-designed case preparation exercises for 12 of the cases that walk you through the needed analysis, tutor you in appropriate use of the concepts and tools, and provide number-crunching assistance. The 12 cases for which there's a case preparation exercise on Case-Tutor™ are indicated by the Case-Tutor™ logo in the Table of Contents.

The study questions for each of the 27 cases serve as a guide for what to think about and what to analyze in preparing the assigned cases for class. You'll find the 12 custom-designed case preparation exercises valuable in learning how to think strategically about a company's situation, applying the tools and concepts of strategic management, and arriving at sound recommendations about what actions management should take to improve the company's performance.

Case-Tutor™ can be used with any Windows-based PC loaded with Microsoft® Excel (either the Office 97 version or the Office 2000 version).

How to Obtain the Software. If use of the Case-Tutor™ software supplement intrigues you, click on the E-Learning Center at the Web site for the textbook—www.mhhe.com/thompson. You can use a credit card to purchase the software and immediately download the files to diskettes or to your own PC's hard drive.

A SPECIAL NOTE TO STUDENTS

Unlike other business courses that concentrate narrowly on a particular function or piece of the business—accounting, finance, marketing, production, human resources, or information systems—strategic management is a big picture course. It cuts across the whole spectrum of business and management. The center of attention is the *total enterprise*—the industry and competitive environment in which it operates, its long-term direction and strategy, its resources and competitive capabilities, and its prospects for success.

Throughout the course, the spotlight will be trained on the foremost issue in running a business enterprise: What must managers do, and do well, to make the company a winner in the game of business? The answer that emerges and the theme of the course is that good strategy making and good strategy execution are always the most reliable signs of good management. The task of this course is to explore why good strategic management leads to good business performance, to present the basic concepts and tools of strategic analysis, and to drill you in the methods of crafting a well-conceived strategy and executing it competently.

You'll be called on to probe, question, and evaluate all aspects of a company's external and internal situation. You'll grapple with sizing up a company's standing in the marketplace and its ability to go head-to-head with rivals, learn to tell the difference between winning strategies and mediocre strategies, and become more skilled in spotting ways to improve a company's strategy or its execution.

In the midst of all this, another purpose is accomplished: to help you synthesize what you have learned in prior business courses. Dealing with the grand sweep of how to manage all the pieces of a business makes strategic management an integrative, capstone course in which you reach back to use concepts and techniques covered in previous courses. For perhaps the first time you'll see how the various pieces of the business puzzle fit together and why the different parts of a business need to be managed in strategic harmony for the organization to operate in a winning fashion.

The journey ahead is exciting, fun, and immensely worthwhile. No matter what your major is, the content of this course has all the ingredients to be the best course you've taken—best in the sense of learning a great deal about business, holding your interest from beginning to end, and enhancing your powers of business judgment. As you tackle the subject matter, ponder Ralph Waldo Emerson's observation, "Commerce is a game of skill which many people play, but which few play well." What we've put between these covers is aimed squarely at helping you become a savvy player. Good luck!

Arthur A. Thompson
A. J. Strickland

Cases in
Strategic | Management

Cases in
Strategic | Management

A. J. Strickland III

University of Alabama

Arthur A. Thompson, Jr.

University of Alabama

John Gamble

University of South Alabama

Twelfth Edition

Boston   Burr Ridge, IL   Dubuque, IA   Madison, WI   New York   San Francisco   St. Louis
Bangkok   Bogotá   Caracas   Kuala Lumpur   Lisbon   London   Madrid   Mexico City
Milan   Montreal   New Delhi   Santiago   Seoul   Singapore   Sydney   Taipei   Toronto

McGraw-Hill Higher Education ✖️

*A Division of The **McGraw-Hill** Companies*

CASES IN STRATEGIC MANAGEMENT

Published by McGraw-Hill/Irwin, an imprint of The McGraw-Hill Companies, Inc. 1221 Avenue of the Americas, New York, NY, 10020. Copyright © 2001, 1998, 1995, 1992, 1988, 1985, 1982, by The McGraw-Hill Companies, Inc. All rights reserved. No part of this publication may be reproduced or distributed in any form or by any means, or stored in a data base or retrieval system, without the prior written consent of The McGraw-Hill Companies, Inc., including, but not limited to, in any network or other electronic storage or transmission, or broadcast for distance learning. Some ancillaries, including electronic and print components, may not be available to customers outside the United States.

This book is printed on acid-free paper.

2 3 4 5 6 7 8 9 0 VNH/VNH 0 9 8 7 6 5 4 3 2 1

ISBN 0-07-231978-X

Vice president/Editor-in-chief: *Robin J. Zwettler*
Publisher: *John E. Biernat*
Senior sponsoring editor: *John Weimeister*
Senior developmental editor: *Laura Hurst Spell*
Senior marketing manager: *Ellen Cleary*
Project manager: *Kelly L. Delso*
Senior production supervisor: *Lori Koetters*
Coordinator freelance designer: *Mary L. Christianson*
Senior supplement coordinator: *Becky Szura*
Media technology producer: *Burke Broholm*
Freelance cover and interior designer: *Design Solutions*
Cover image: © *Guy Crittenden/SIS*
Compositor: *GAC Indianapolis*
Typeface: *10/12 Times Roman*
Printer: *Von Hoffmann Press, Inc.*

Library of Congress Cataloging-in-Publication Data

Strickland, A. J. (Alonzo J.)
    Cases in strategic management / A. J. Strickland III, Arthur A. Thompson, Jr., John Gamble. — 12th ed.
        p. cm.
    Includes biographical references and index.
    ISBN 0-07-231978-X
    1. Strategic planning—United States—Case studies. 2. Industrial management—United States—Case studies. I. Title: Strategic management. II. Thompson, Arthur A., 1940– III. Gamble, John (John E.) IV. Title.

HD30.28 .S755 2001
658.4'012—dc21   00-056107

www.mhhe.com

about the | authors

Arthur A. Thompson, Jr., earned his BS and PhD degrees in economics from the University of Tennessee in 1961 and 1965, respectively; spent three years on the economics faculty at Virginia Tech; and served on the faculty of the University of Alabama's College of Commerce and Business Administration for 24 years. In 1974 and again in 1982, Dr. Thompson spent semester-long sabbaticals as a visiting scholar at the Harvard Business School.

His areas of specialization are business strategy, competition and market analysis, and the economics of business enterprises. He has published over 30 articles in some 25 different professional and trade publications and has authored or co-authored five textbooks and four computer-based simulation exercises.

Dr. Thompson is a frequent speaker and consultant on the strategic issues confronting the electric utility industry, particularly as concerns the challenges posed by industry restructuring, re-regulation, competition, and customers' freedom of choice. He spends much of his off-campus time giving presentations to electric utility groups and conducting management development programs for electric utility executives all over the world.

Dr. Thompson and his wife of 39 years have two daughters, two grandchildren, and two dogs.

Dr. A. J. (Lonnie) Strickland, a native of North Georgia, attended the University of Georgia, where he received a bachelor of science degree in math and physics in 1965. Afterward he entered the Georgia Institute of Technology, where he received a master of science in industrial management. He earned a PhD in business administration from Georgia State University in 1969. He currently holds the title of Professor of Strategic Management in the Graduate School of Business at the University of Alabama.

Dr. Strickland's experience in consulting and executive development is in the strategic management area, with a concentration in industry and competitive analysis. He has developed strategic planning systems for such firms as the Southern Company, BellSouth, South Central Bell, American Telephone and Telegraph, Gulf States Paper, Carraway Methodist Medical Center, Delco Remy, Mark IV Industries, Amoco Oil Company, USA Group, General Motors, and Kimberly Clark Corporation (Medical Products). He is a very popular speaker on the subject of implementing strategic change and serves on several corporate boards.

He has served as director of marketing for BellSouth, where he had responsibility for $1 billion in revenues and $300 million in profits.

In the international arena, Dr. Strickland has done extensive work in Europe, the Middle East, Central America, Malaysia, Australia, and Africa. In France he developed a management simulation of corporate decision making that enables management to test various strategic alternatives.

In the area of research, he is the author of 15 books and texts. His management simulations, Tempomatic IV and Micromatic, were pioneering innovations that enjoyed prominent market success for two decades.

Recent awards for Dr. Strickland include the Outstanding Professor Award for the Graduate School of Business and the Outstanding Commitment to Teaching Award for the University of Alabama, in which he takes particular pride. He is a member of various honor leadership societies: Mortar Board, Order of Omega, Beta Gamma Sigma, Omicron Delta Kappa, and Jasons. He is past national president of Pi Kappa Phi social fraternity.

John E. Gamble is Assistant Professor of Management at the University of South Alabama. He received his PhD from the University of Alabama in 1995. Dr. Gamble also received his bachelor of science and master of arts degrees from the University of Alabama.

Dr. Gamble teaches strategic management to undergraduates, graduates, and executives in management development programs. His consulting activities center on strategic planning and strategy implementation. Dr. Gamble's research has been published in *Journal of Business Venturing, Journal of Labor Research, Health Care Management Review,* and *Labor Studies Journal.*

the | preface

The use of cases to drive home key concepts and principles and to engage students in managerial decision making continues to be a core component of today's courses in strategic management. We think this collection of 27 cases is appealing to students, stimulating to teach, and on target with respect to the leading problems and issues in strategic management. Supplementing the case lineup in this edition is a new e-collection of over 30 proven, preselected cases at the Web site for the text that instructors can draw on for additional case assignments; plus, there is a companion courseware package called Case-Tutor™ designed to help students do a better job of case preparation.

THE CASE COLLECTION IN THE 12TH EDITION

The 27 cases in this edition include 19 new cases not appearing in any of our previous editions, 7 updated cases from the 10th and 11th editions, and 1 carry-over case—the now-classic two-page Robin Hood case. According to our custom, we have grouped the cases under five chapter-related, topical headings to highlight the close links between the cases and strategic management concepts.

In the Section A grouping are four cases spotlighting the manager as chief strategy maker and chief strategy implementer; these cases—Steve Case, America Online, and Time Warner; The DaimlerChrysler Merger (A) and (B); and Giuseppe's Original Sausage Company—demonstrate why the strategy-making, strategy-executing role of managers is relevant to a company's long-term market success. Section B contains 13 cases (including 6 cases on dot-com companies) whose central issues deal with analyzing industry and competitive situations and crafting business-level strategy. In Section C are cases on Campbell Soup and Black & Decker (both of which are updated from previous editions) that illustrate the issues of strategy making in diversified companies. The six cases in Section D all revolve around the managerial challenges of implementing and executing strategy. Section E contains two cases—one on Motorola and one on Levi Strauss—highlighting the links between strategy, ethics, and social responsibility.

THE NEW COLLECTION OF E-CASES

As a way to make it simple and convenient for instructors to supplement the 27 cases included in the text, we've assembled an e-collection of 31 of the best and most popular cases from our 10th and 11th editions, giving you a total of nearly 60 cases from which to choose in making case assignments. However, *the e-collection will be expanded on an ongoing basis as fast as we are able to secure freshly written cases, get them satisfactorily formatted, and secure the rights to post them for classroom use.* We believe that the cases from our continually updated e-collection will prove valuable as supplements to the cases in the text and keep case assignments current. We hope that the e-case collection will eventually consist of 60 to 70 cases eminently suitable for strategic management courses and that you can be confident are of a caliber paralleling those in our texts over the years. The e-case collection, which instructors can browse in the "instructor center" at the Web site for the text (www.mhhe.com/thompson), is organized to make it easy and convenient for instructors to identify and select the cases that best meet their course needs. Teaching notes for all the e-cases are also available in downloadable or viewable form for instructor perusal and use.

The Value-Added Contribution of an E-Case Collection   The option of delivery cases to students in electronic form is intended to give instructors more flexibility and variety in assembling the best possible package of case assignments for their courses and to take advantage of the speed and economies that the Internet and e-commerce now provide. Providing materials to students in electronic rather than in printed form or on disks and CDs is substantially more cost efficient, thus reducing the prices that students have to pay utilizing traditional campus bookstore channels and simplifying the process of putting together a customized case assignment package. Students can download the desired files of assigned cases not in this casebook directly to the hard disks of their own computers or to floppy disks if they are working in a university PC lab.

The 27 cases in the 12th edition plus the initial 31 cases in the e-library all reflect our steadfast preference for cases that feature interesting products and companies and that are capable of sparking both student interest and lively classroom discussions. Over 40 of the 58 cases involve high-profile companies, products, or people that students will have heard of, know about from personal experience, or can easily identify with. The six dot-com company cases, plus several others, will provide students with insight into the special demands of competing in industry environments where technological developments are an everyday event, product life cycles are short, and competitive maneuvering among rivals comes fast and furious. At least 25 of the cases involve situations where company resources and competitive capabilities play as much a role in strategy making and strategy implementing as do industry and competitive conditions. Indeed, we made a special effort to ensure that the cases selected for the text and for the e-library vividly demonstrate the relevance of the resource-based view of the firm. Scattered throughout the lineup are over a dozen cases concerning non-U.S. companies, globally competitive industries, and/or cross-cultural situations; these cases, in conjunction with the globalized content of the text chapters, provide ample material for linking the study of strategic management tightly to the ongoing globalization of the world economy—in proper keeping with the standards of the American Assembly of Collegiate Schools of Business (AACSB). You'll also find cases where the central figures are women and cases dealing with the strategic problems of family-owned or relatively small entrepreneurial businesses. Eighteen of the 27 printed cases in the text involve public companies about which students can do further research in the library or on the Internet, and 7 have videotape segments that are available from the publisher. Several cases in the e-case collection on the Web site have accompanying video segments.

THE NEW E-LEARNING CENTER AT THE WEB SITE

A new feature of this edition's Web site is the creation of an "e-learning center" that functions as an electronic bookstore where students can use a credit card to purchase and immediately obtain:

- The Case-TUTOR courseware that is a companion to this edition.
- Downloadable portable document format (PDF) files of most of the cases in this 12th edition and selected cases from the 10th and 11th editions, plus files of freshly written cases that have become available since publication of this edition.
- A digitally delivered version of both the Player's Manual and software for *The Business Strategy Game.*

The addition of the e-learning collection of products is intended to give instructors not only more flexibility and variety in selecting the package of case assignments for their courses but also the advantage of the Internet's speed and economies. Providing materials to students in electronic form is substantially more cost-efficient than providing them in printed form or on disks and CDs. Students can download the desired files directly to the hard disks of their own computers or to floppy disks if they are working in a university PC lab.

Our new e-learning library is a first step in what we suspect will eventually become a universal practice of delivering learning materials via the Internet. We would be delighted for you to share with us any ideas and suggestions for helping the e-learning library concept better meet the needs of both students and instructors.

THE GUIDE TO CASE ANALYSIS AND USE OF THE INTERNET

Prior to Case 1, we have once again included a section called "A Guide to Case Analysis," which gives students positive direction in what the case method is all about and offers suggestions for approaching case analysis. As an integral part of this discussion, there's a section on how to use the Internet to (1) do further research on an industry or company, (2) obtain a company's latest financial results, and (3) get updates on what has happened since the case was written. The amount of information available on the Internet has increased at such a rapid-fire pace that the challenge now is to sort quickly through all that is available to find what is really pertinent to the topic at hand. We think students will find our list of suggested Web sites to be a time-saving and valuable assist in running down the information they need. And to further facilitate student use of the Internet, many of the cases include company Web site addresses.

THE CASE-TUTOR SOFTWARE OPTION

We've all experienced poor and uneven student preparation of cases for class discussion. Sometimes it's because of inadequate effort but more often it's because of inexperience in using the tools of strategic analysis to arrive at solid recommendations and/or uncertainty over exactly what analysis to do. To give students some direction in what to think about in preparing a case for class, Case-TUTOR provides study questions for all 27 cases in the 12th edition. To help them learn how to use the concepts and analytical tools properly, we've created interactive study guides (not a solution!) for students to use in preparing 12 of the cases. Each of the 12 study guides has been custom-designed to fit the specific issues and analytical problems posed by that case. We scrupulously avoided creating one generic study guide because cases in strategic management cut across a broad range of issues and require diverse analytical approaches. (Strategy analysis in single-business situations is fundamentally different from strategy analysis of diversified companies; cases where the spotlight is on developing a strategy are fundamentally different from cases where the main issues revolve around strategy implementation and execution.)

The custom-designed case preparation guides on Case-Tutor provide:

- *Study questions* to trigger the process of thinking strategically and to point students toward the analysis needed to arrive at sound recommendations.
- A series of *interactive screens organized around the study questions* that coach students in the use of whatever analytical tools are appropriate—whether it be five-forces analysis, strategic group mapping, identification of key success factors, SWOT analysis, value chain analysis, competitive strength assessments, construction of business portfolio matrixes, industry attractiveness assessments, or strategic fit matchups. These screens are intended to help students arrive at substantive, reasoned, supportable answers to the study questions.
- *Assistance in performing calculations related to the analysis.* This can include statistics useful in evaluating industry data and company operating performance, measures of profitability, growth rates, and assorted financial ratios.
- *What-if exercises* (where appropriate) that allow students to readily develop projections of company financial performance (when such projections are germane to the case, and when data in the case permit such projections to be made).
- *Questions* specifically aimed at helping students create a set of analysis-based, supportable action recommendations.
- *The capability to make printouts* of the work done (to serve as notes students can use in the class discussion or as hand-in assignments to be checked or graded).

The interactive design of the case preparation guides keeps the ball squarely in the student's court to do the analysis, to decide what story the numbers tell about a company's situation and performance, and to think through the options to arrive at recommendations. The Case-Tutor software supplement is thus not a crutch or "answer file" for the cases; rather, it is a vehicle for using the personal computer to tutor students in strategic thinking and helping them learn to correctly apply the tools and concepts of strategic management. We endeavored to design the case preparation guides to coach students in how to think strategically about business problems and issues, to drill them in the methods of strategic analysis, and to promote sound business judgment. Instructors can be assured that the case notes students develop with the aid of Case-Tutor will represent their work, not ours.

THE BUSINESS STRATEGY GAME OPTION

An extensively revised and upgraded version of *The Business Strategy Game* makes an interesting and exciting companion to this 12th edition.

About the Simulation

We designed *The Business Strategy Game* around producing and marketing athletic footwear because students can readily understand the footwear industry and because the market displays the characteristics of many globally competitive industries—fast growth, worldwide use of the product, competition among companies from several continents, production in low-wage locations, and a marketplace where a variety of competitive approaches and business strategies can coexist. The simulation allows the imaginary companies to manufacture and sell their brands in North America, Asia, Europe, and Latin America, plus the option to compete for supplying private-label footwear to North American chain retailers. Branded sales can be pursued through any or all of three distribution channels—independent footwear retailers, company-owned and operated retail stores, and direct sales made online at the company's Web site.

Competition is head-to-head—each team of students must match their strategic wits against the other company teams. Companies can focus their branded marketing efforts on one geographic market or two or three or all four. They also can compete aggressively or de-emphasize branded sales and specialize in private-label production (an attractive strategy for low-cost producers). They can establish a one-country production base or they can manufacture in all four of the geographic markets to avoid tariffs and mitigate the risk of adverse exchange rate fluctuations. Low-cost leadership, differentiation strategies, best-cost producer strategies, and focus strategies are all viable competitive options. Companies can position their products in the low end of the market or the high end, or they can stick close to the middle on price, quality, and service; they can have a wide or narrow product line, small or big dealer networks, extensive or limited advertising. Company market shares are based on how each company's product attributes and competitive efforts stack up against those of rivals. Demand conditions, tariffs, and wage rates vary from geographic area to geographic area. Raw materials used in footwear production are purchased in a worldwide commodity market at prices that move up or down in response to supply-demand conditions. If a company's sales volume is unexpectedly low, management has the option to liquidate excess inventories at deep discount prices.

Each student-managed company has plants to operate; a workforce to compensate; distribution expenses and inventories to control; capital expenditure decisions to make; marketing and sales campaigns to wage; a Web site to operate; sales forecasts to consider; and ups and downs in exchange rates, interest rates, and the stock market to take into account. Students must weave functional decisions in production, distribution, marketing, finance, and human resources into a cohesive action plan. They have to react to changing market and competitive conditions, initiate moves to try to build competitive advantage, and decide how to defend against aggressive actions by competitors. And they must endeavor to maximize shareholder wealth via increased dividend payments and stock price appreciation. Each team of students is challenged to use their entrepreneurial and strategic skills to become the next Nike or Reebok and ride the wave of growth to the top of the worldwide athletic footwear industry. The whole exercise is representative of a real-world competitive market where companies try to outcompete and outperform rivals—things are every bit as realistic and true to actual business practice as we could make them.

There are built-in planning and analysis features that allow students to (1) craft a three-year strategic plan, (2) evaluate the economics of expanding capacity, (3) draw strategic group maps, (4) quickly prepare and print out an assortment of charts and graphs showing various performance trends, and (5) build different competitive strategy scenarios. Calculations at the bottom of each decision screen provide instantly updated projections of sales revenues, profits, return on equity, cash flow, and other key outcomes as each decision entry is made. The sensitivity of financial and operating outcomes to different decision entries is easily observed on the screen and on detailed printouts of projections. With the speed of today's personal computers, the relevant number-crunching is done in a split second. The game is designed throughout to lead students to decisions based on analysis.

The Business Strategy Game runs on any PC loaded with Microsoft Excel (either the Office 97 version or the Office 2000 version) and is suitable for both senior-level and MBA courses. The game can be installed to run on a network and has a new e-mail feature to facilitate use in distance-learning situations.

The mostly new seventh-generation version of *The Business Strategy Game* has a raft of features that we think users will find appealing and that take the simulation to a much-higher plateau of capability than in previous editions. The changes we've instituted are the product of valuable feedback and suggestions from users, several new ideas on our part, and an ongoing effort on our part to continuously improve the simulation.

What Sets This Simulation Apart

The Business Strategy Game has five features that make it an uncommonly effective teaching/learning aid for strategic management courses: (1) *the product and the industry*—as we noted earlier, students can readily identify with and understand the athletic footwear industry; (2) *the global environment*—students gain up-close exposure to what global competition is like and the kinds of strategic issues that managers in global industries have to address; (3) *the realistic quality of the simulation exercise*—we've designed the simulation to be as faithful as possible to real-world markets, competitive conditions, and revenue-cost-profit relationships; (4) *the wide degree of strategic freedom students have in managing their companies*—we've gone to great lengths to make the game free of bias as concerns use of one strategy versus another; and (5) *the long-range strategic planning and analysis capabilities it incorporates as an integral part of the exercise of running a company*.

These features, wrapped together as a package, provide an exciting and valuable bridge between concept and practice, the classroom and real-life management, and reading a textbook and learning by doing. Instructors will find opportunity after opportunity to use examples and happenings in *The Business Strategy Game* in their lectures on the text chapters.

The Value a Simulation Adds

Our own experiences, along with hours of discussions with users, have convinced us that simulation games are *the single best exercise available* for helping students understand how the functional pieces of a business fit together and giving them an integrated experience. First and foremost, the exercise of running a simulated company over a number of decision periods helps develop students' business judgment. Simulation games provide a live case situation where events unfold and circumstances change as the game progresses. Their special hook is an ability to get students personally involved in the subject matter. *The Business Strategy Game* is very typical in this respect. In plotting their competitive strategies each decision period, students learn about risk taking. They have to respond to changing market conditions, react to the moves of competitors, and choose among alternative courses of action. They get valuable practice in reading the signs of industry change, spotting market opportunities, evaluating threats to their company's competitive position, weighing the trade-offs between profits now and profits later, and assessing the long-term consequences of short-term decisions. They chart a long-term direction, set strategic and financial objectives, and try out different strategies in pursuit of competitive advantage. They become active strategic thinkers, planners, analysts, and decision makers. And by having to live with the decisions they make, they experience what it means to be accountable for decisions and responsible for achieving satisfactory results. All this serves to drill students in responsible decision making and to improve their business acumen and managerial judgment.

Second, students learn an enormous amount from working with the numbers, exploring options, and trying to unite production, marketing, finance, and human resource decisions into a coherent strategy. They begin to see ways to apply knowledge from prior courses and figure out what really makes a business tick. The effect is to help students integrate a lot of material, look at decisions from the standpoint of the company as a whole, and see the importance of thinking strategically about a company's competitive position and future prospects. Since a simulation game is, by its very nature, a hands-on exercise, the lessons learned are forcefully planted in students' minds—often with lasting impact. Third, students' entrepreneurial instincts blossom as they get caught up in the competitive spirit of the game. The resulting entertainment value helps maintain an unusually high level of student motivation and emotional involvement in the course throughout the term.

Features of the New Version

- *An easy-to-use e-mail feature that makes the simulation ideal for use in distance-learning situations.* This addition is a response to requests from numerous users. The e-mail feature allows company members to click on a built-in e-mail button that will send their decision file to the instructor/game administrator, lets instructors open e-mailed files and direct them into the processing sequence with a few clicks, and then lets instructors/game administrators readily e-mail the results back to company members for use in the next round of decision making.

- *A revised and integrated demand forecasting tool.* There's a new screen that allows each footwear company to develop sales projections for the number of pairs it is likely to sell in each market segment, given its contemplated marketing effort and given the overall competitive effort it expects to encounter from rival companies. Company members can use these projections as the basis for production and plant operations decision, for shipping decisions to the various distribution centers, and for crafting a marketing strategy that will produce the desired sales and market share. However, the accuracy of the sales projections will be no better than students' ability to anticipate changes in market conditions and rivals' competitive effort.

- *The addition of Latin America as a new geographic region of the global market.* We've added Latin America to the list of geographic regions constituting the global footwear market. Companies can now locate plants and sell their footwear products in any or all of four regions—North America, Asia, Europe, and Latin America. The simulation begins with a tariff of $4 on footwear imported into Europe, a $6 tariff on footwear imported into Latin America, and an $8 tariff on footwear imported into Asia. All companies start the simulation with a 1-million pair plant in North America and a 3-million pair plant in Asia. Exchange rate fluctuations are tied to the U.S. dollar, the euro, the Japanese yen, and the Brazilian real.

- *The Internet marketing and online sales feature.* Companies now compete online to sell direct to consumers based on three global factors (comparative selling prices, the number of models and styles offered at the Web site, and speed of delivery) and three region-specific factors (product quality, image rating, and advertising). As might be expected, there is some channel conflict between online sales and a company's attempt to secure sales through brick-and-click retail outlets; company co-managers have to address the conflict and cannibalization issues if they elect to pursue a "bricks-and-mortar" strategy (a situation that many real-world companies have to contend with).

- *The option to open a chain of company retail stores.* Companies now have the option of investing in building a chain of company-owned and operated retail "mega-stores" in major shopping centers to supplement or substitute for selling at wholesale through independent retail dealers. However, just as is the case with online sales, company-owned stores pose some distribution channel conflict because independent retailers see them as cannibalizing their own sales. Company members thus now have to wrestle with which of three distribution channels to emphasize—independent dealers, company-owned stores, and online sales—and they have to cope with whatever channel conflicts result.

- *New production options.* In this new version, decision entries have been added that allow plants to produce private-label footwear of a specified quality and product line breadth and to produce branded footwear of a different specified quality and product line breadth. In former versions of the simulation, all production at a plant had to be of the same quality and involve the same number of models and styles—there was no distinction between producing private-label and branded footwear. The flexibility to produce both types of footwear and specify the quality and models of each gives companies a much richer and more realistic set of strategy options. We've also increased the number of plant upgrade options from three to six in order to provide more ways to match production strategy and production costs to fit the needs of a company's pricing and marketing strategy and its production capacity requirements. All these plant-related changes give company managers more ways to utilize plant assets and to deal with high-cost plants; they also serve to dampen the tendency that existed in prior editions for companies to invest in more plant capacity than was really needed and thus create excess supply conditions.

- *The use of Microsoft Excel and PC requirements.* This new seventh edition requires that the simulation be played on PCs loaded with Microsoft Excel—the version on Office 97 or Office 2000. Moreover, the PCs must have a Windows-based operating system (Windows 95, Windows 98, Windows NT, or Windows 2000) and preferably 64 MB of RAM and a 233-MHz or faster chip (the program will run on lesser-equipped machines, but at slower-than-desired speeds). If your class does not have access to PCs with a Windows-based operating system and a recent version of Microsoft Excel, then you will need to use the sixth edition version of *The Business Strategy Game.*

- *New screen designs and support calculations.* We used the reprogramming of the simulation as an opportunity to greatly improve screen layouts, to incorporate more instructions for use of the software and of the rules directly on the screen (so as to minimize the need for students to look up things in the Player's Manual), and to provide a far richer set of onscreen calculations to guide decision making. While the screens contain a lot more information and take a bit longer to digest, players will find most all of the information they need is either directly on the screens or is readily accessible on the menu bar guide at the top of each screen. If students forget some of the information in the Player's Manual, they can quickly access the information online by clicking on the Help button—the Help button takes them directly to screens displaying the related information in the Player's Manual, thus bypassing the need to look up rules and procedures in the manual.

- *A revamped Player's Manual.* The changes we've made in this edition necessitated a fundamental rewrite of the Player's Manual. So we took the opportunity to recast the whole presentation around demand forecasting, plant operations, warehousing and shipping, sales and marketing, and the financing of company operations—the very things that are the central focus of the decision screens and the overall strategy-making process. The discussion of the decisions in each area of the company's operations is integrated with the reports concerning each area of company operations. We think you'll find that the new presentation of the Player's Manual, coupled with the information-rich screen designs, will make playing of the simulation easier for students and dramatically reduce the number of questions about rules and procedures.

- *Software downloads at the McGraw-Hill/Irwin Web site for the text.* In past editions, users have encountered problems with getting the latest version of the software and with defective disks. Beginning with this edition, all of the key software that students need to play the simulation must be downloaded directly from the Web site, thus ensuring that the correct and latest version is always readily available and detouring many of the annoying problems of defective disks. Students who wish to do so can bypass the use of a printed version of the manual and, using a credit card, purchase an electronic version of the entire Business Strategy Game package at the Web site. Similarly, all the necessary software for instructors/game administrators is posted on the Web site for immediate availability; electronic files of the Player's Manual and the Instructor's Manual are available to instructors for immediate inspection and use.

There are numerous lesser changes and refinements that do their part to make this edition a truly next-generation product. But, while much is new, users of prior editions will still find much that is familiar; the effort to gear up for this new edition is quite modest and the overall time it takes to process and administer the game has been significantly reduced. As before, instructors have numerous ways to heighten competition and keep things lively as the game progresses. There are options to raise or lower interest rates, alter certain costs up or down, and issue special news flashes announcing new tariff levels, materials cost changes, shipping difficulties, or other new considerations to keep business conditions dynamic and "stir the pot" a bit as needed. And the built-in scoreboard of company performance keeps students constantly informed about where their company stands and how well they are doing. Rapid advances in PC technology have cut the processing time to under 5 minutes—it should take no more than 20 minutes for you or a student assistant to turn the decisions around for an entire industry once you have processed a few decisions and learned the routine.

A separate Instructor's Manual for *The Business Strategy Game* describes how to integrate the simulation exercise into a course, provides pointers on how to administer the game, and contains step-by-step processing instructions. In the case of difficulties, technical personnel at McGraw-Hill/Irwin can provide instructors with quick assistance via a toll-free number. Assistance is also available directly from the co-authors and at the Web site.

THE 12TH EDITION INSTRUCTOR'S PACKAGE

The instructor's package for the 12th edition of *Cases in Strategic Management* includes an Instructor's Manual containing:

- An introductory section of suggestions for structuring the course and making the best use of the 27 cases in this edition, a grid showing the broad issues and problems that each case involves, and some suggestions for sequencing the cases.
- A comprehensive teaching note for each of the 27 cases.
- Periodic updates for the epilogues at the end of each teaching note that are posted in the "instructor center" at the Web site for this text (www.mhhe.com/thompson). The updates provide the latest information we have on anything of significance that has happened at the company since the case was written.

Videotape segments are available from the publisher for 7 of the 27 cases, and there are accompanying video segments for several cases in the e-case collection on the Web site.

CASE RESEARCH ACKNOWLEDGMENTS

We are much indebted to the case researchers who have contributed their work to this volume and to the companies whose cooperation made the cases possible. To each one goes a very special thank-you. The importance of timely, carefully researched cases cannot be overestimated in contributing to a substantive study of strategic management issues and practices. From a research standpoint, cases in strategic management are invaluable in exposing the generic kinds of strategic issues companies face, in forming hypotheses about strategic behavior, and in drawing experience-based generalizations about the practice of strategic management. Pedagogically, cases about strategic management give students essential practice in diagnosing and evaluating strategic situations, in learning to use the tools and concepts of strategy analysis, in sorting through various strategic options, in crafting strategic action plans, and in figuring out successful ways to implement and execute the chosen strategy.

Without a continuing stream of fresh, well-researched, and well-conceived cases, the discipline of strategic management would quickly fall into disrepair, losing much of its energy and excitement. There's no question, therefore, that first-class case research constitutes a valuable scholarly contribution.

Any comments you wish to make about the mix of cases or a specific case will be most welcome, as will your calling our attention to specific errors. Please e-mail us at astrickl@cba.ua.edu and/or athompso@cba.ua.edu, fax us at (205) 348-6695, or write us at P.O. Box 870225; Department of Management and Marketing; The University of Alabama; Tuscaloosa, Alabama 35487-0225.

A. J. Strickland
Arthur A. Thompson
John Gamble

table of contents

Handwritten note: 2 groups present on same day

---

 *Cases for which there are case preparation exercises on Case-TUTOR.™

*Cases for which there are case preparation exercises on Case-TUTOR.™

Cases in
Strategic
Management

A Guide to Case Analysis

I keep six honest serving men
(They taught me all I knew);
Their names are What and Why and When;
And How and Where and Who.
—Rudyard Kipling

In most courses in strategic management, students use cases about actual companies to practice strategic analysis and to gain some experience in the tasks of crafting and implementing strategy. A case sets forth, in a factual manner, the events and organizational circumstances surrounding a particular managerial situation. It puts readers at the scene of the action and familiarizes them with all the relevant circumstances. A case on strategic management can concern a whole industry, a single organization, or some part of an organization; the organization involved can be either profit-seeking or not-for-profit. The essence of the student's role in case analysis is to diagnose and size up the situation described in the case and then to recommend appropriate action steps.

WHY USE CASES TO PRACTICE STRATEGIC MANAGEMENT?

A student of business with tact
Absorbed many answers he lacked.
But acquiring a job,
He said with a sob,
"How does one fit answer to fact?"

The above limerick was used some years ago by Professor Charles Gragg to characterize the plight of business students who had no exposure to cases.[1] The truth is that the mere act of listening to lectures and sound advice about managing does little for anyone's management skills. Accumulated managerial wisdom cannot effectively be passed on by lectures and assigned readings alone. If anything had been learned about the practice of management, it is that a storehouse of readymade textbook answers does not exist. Each managerial situation has unique aspects, requiring its own diagnosis, judgment, and tailor-made actions. Cases provide would-be managers with a valuable way to practice wrestling with the actual problems of actual managers in actual companies.

The case approach to strategic analysis is, first and foremost, an exercise in learning by doing. Because cases provide detailed information about conditions and problems of different industries and companies, your task of analyzing company after company and situation after situation has the twin benefit of boosting your analytical skills and exposing you to the ways companies and managers actually do things. Most college students have limited managerial backgrounds and only fragmented knowledge

---

[1]Charles I. Gragg, "Because Wisdom Can't Be Told," in *The Case Method at the Harvard Business School,* ed. M. P. McNair (New York: McGraw-Hill, 1954), p. 11.

about companies and real-life strategic situations. Cases help substitute for on-the-job experience by (1) giving you broader exposure to a variety of industries, organizations, and strategic problems; (2) forcing you to assume a managerial role (as opposed to that of just an onlooker); (3) providing a test of how to apply the tools and techniques of strategic management; and (4) asking you to come up with pragmatic managerial action plans to deal with the issues at hand.

OBJECTIVES OF CASE ANALYSIS

Using cases to learn about the practice of strategic management is a powerful way for you to accomplish five things:[2]

1. Increase your understanding of what managers should and should not do in guiding a business to success.
2. Build your skills in sizing up company resource strengths and weaknesses and in conducting strategic analysis in a variety of industries and competitive situations.
3. Get valuable practice in identifying strategic issues that need to be addressed, evaluating strategic alternatives, and formulating workable plans of action.
4. Enhance your sense of business judgment, as opposed to uncritically accepting the authoritative crutch of the professor or "back-of-the-book" answers.
5. Gaining in-depth exposure to different industries and companies, thereby acquiring something close to actual business experience.

If you understand that these are the objectives of case analysis, you are less likely to be consumed with curiosity about "the answer to the case." Students who have grown comfortable with and accustomed to textbook statements of fact and definitive lecture notes are often frustrated when discussions about a case do not produce concrete answers. Usually, case discussions produce good arguments for more than one course of action. Differences of opinion nearly always exist. Thus, should a class discussion conclude without a strong, unambiguous consensus on what do to, don't grumble too much when you are *not* told what the answer is or what the company actually did. Just remember that in the business world answers don't come in conclusive black-and-white terms. There are nearly always several feasible courses of action and approaches, each of which may work out satisfactorily. Moreover, in the business world, when one elects a particular course of action, there is no peeking at the back of a book to see if you have chosen the best thing to do and no one to turn to for a provably correct answer. The only valid test of management action is *results.* If the results of an action turn out to be good, the decision to take it may be presumed right. If not, then the action chosen was wrong in the sense that it didn't work out.

Hence, the important thing for a student to understand in case analysis is that the managerial exercise of identifying, diagnosing, and recommending builds your skills; discovering the right answer or finding out what actually happened is no more than frosting on the cake. Even if you learn what the company did, you can't conclude that it was necessarily right or best. All that can be said is "Here is what they did . . . "

---

[2]Ibid., pp. 12–14; and D. R. Schoen and Philip A. Sprague, "What Is the Case Method?" in *The Case Method at the Harvard Business School,* ed. M. P. McNair, pp. 78–79.

The point is this: *The purpose of giving you a case assignment is not to cause you to run to the library or surf the Internet to discover what the company actually did but, rather, to enhance your skills in sizing up situations and developing your managerial judgment about what needs to be done and how to do it.* The aim of case analysis is for *you* to become actively engaged in diagnosing the business issues and managerial problems posed in the case, to propose workable solutions, and to explain and defend your assessments—this is how cases provide you with meaningful practice at being a manager.

PREPARING A CASE FOR CLASS DISCUSSION

If this is your first experience with the case method, you may have to reorient your study habits. Unlike lecture courses in which you can get by without preparing intensively for each class and have latitude to work assigned readings and reviews of lecture notes into your schedule, a case assignment requires conscientious preparation before class. You will not get much out of hearing the class discuss a case you haven't read, and you certainly won't be able to contribute anything yourself to the discussion.

To get ready for class discussion of a case, you must study the case, reflect carefully on the situation presented, and develop some reasoned thoughts. Your goal should be to end up with a sound, well-supported analysis of the situation and a sound, defensible set of recommendations. The Case-TUTOR software package that accompanies this edition will assist you in preparing the cases—it contains a set of study questions for each case and step-by-step tutorials to walk you through the process of analyzing and developing reasonable recommendations.

To prepare a case for class discussion, we suggest the following approach:

1. *Skim the case rather quickly to get an overview of the situation it presents.* This quick overview should give you the general flavor of the situation and indicate the kinds of issues and problems you will need to wrestle with. If your instructor has provided you with study questions for the case, now is the time to read them carefully.

2. *Read the case thoroughly to digest the facts and circumstances.* On this reading, try to gain full command of the situation presented in the case. Begin to develop some tentative answers to the study questions from your instructor or in the Case-TUTOR software package, which you can download at the Web site for the text. If your instructor has elected not to give you assignment questions or has not recommended regular use of the Case-TUTOR, then start forming your own picture of the overall situation being described.

3. *Carefully review all the information presented in the exhibits.* Often, there is an important story in the numbers contained in the exhibits. Expect the information in the case exhibits to be crucial enough to materially affect your diagnosis of the situation.

4. *Decide what the strategic issues are.* Until you have identified the strategic issues and problems in the case, you don't know what to analyze, which tools and analytical techniques are called for, or otherwise how to proceed. At times the strategic issues are clear—they are either stated directly in the case or easily inferred from it. At other times you will have to dig out the issues from all the information

given; if so, the study questions and the case preparation exercises provided in the Case-TUTOR software will guide you.

5. *Start your analysis of the issues with some number crunching.* A big majority of strategy cases call for some kind of number crunching—calculating assorted financial ratios to check out the company's financial condition and recent performance, calculating growth rates of sales or profits or unit volume, checking out profit margins and the makeup of the cost structure, and understanding whatever revenue-cost-profit relationships are present. See Table 1 on the next page for a summary of key financial ratios, how they are calculated, and what they show. If you are using Case-TUTOR, some of the number crunching has been computerized and you'll spend most of your time interpreting the growth rates, financial ratios, and other calculations provided.

6. *Apply the concepts and techniques of strategic analysis you have been studying.* Strategic analysis is not just a collection of opinions; rather, it entails applying the concepts and analytical tools described in Chapters 1 through 13 to cut beneath the surface and produce sharp insight and understanding. Every case assigned is strategy related and presents you with an opportunity to usefully apply what you have learned. Your instructor is looking for you to demonstrate that you know *how* and *when* to use the material presented in the text chapters. The case preparation guides on Case-TUTOR will point you toward the proper analytical tools needed to analyze the case situation.

7. *Check out conflicting opinions and make some judgments about the validity of all the data and information provided.* Many times cases report views and contradictory opinions (after all, people don't always agree on things, and different people see the same things in different ways). Forcing you to evaluate the data and information presented in the case helps you develop your powers of inference and judgment. Resolving conflicting information comes with the territory because a great many managerial situations entail opposing points of view, conflicting trends, and sketchy information.

8. *Support your diagnosis and opinions with reasons and evidence.* Most important is to prepare your answers to the question "Why?" For instance, if after studying the case you are of the opinion that the company's managers are doing a poor job, then it is your answer to "Why do you think so?" that establishes just how good your analysis of the situation is. If your instructor has provided you with specific study questions for the case or if you are using the case preparation guides on Case-TUTOR, by all means prepare answers that include all the reasons and number-crunching evidence you can muster to support your diagnosis. Work through the case preparation exercises on Case-TUTOR *conscientiously,* or, if you are using study questions provided by the instructor, *generate at least two pages of notes!*

9. *Develop an appropriate action plan and set of recommendations.* Diagnosis divorced from corrective action is sterile. The test of a manager is always to convert sound analysis into sound actions—actions that will produce the desired results. Hence, the final and most telling step in preparing a case is to develop an action agenda for management that lays out a set of specific recommendations. Bear in mind that proposing realistic, workable solutions is far preferable to casually tossing out top-of-the-head suggestions. Be prepared to explain why your recommendations

table 1   Key Financial Ratios, How They Are Calculated, and What They Show

Ratio	How Calculated	What It Shows
Profitability ratios		
1. Gross profit margin	$\dfrac{\text{Sales} - \text{Cost of goods sold}}{\text{Sales}}$	An indication of the total margin available to cover operating expenses and yield a profit.
2. Operating profit margin (or return on sales)	$\dfrac{\text{Profits before taxes and before interest}}{\text{Sales}}$	An indication of the firm's profitability from current operations without regard to the interest charges accruing from the capital structure.
3. Net profit margin (or net return on sales)	$\dfrac{\text{Profits after taxes}}{\text{Sales}}$	Shows after-tax profits per dollar of sales. Subpar profit margins indicate that the firm's sales prices are relatively low or that costs are relatively high, or both.
4. Return on total assets	$\dfrac{\text{Profits after taxes}}{\text{Total assets}}$ or $\dfrac{\text{Profit after taxes} + \text{interest}}{\text{Total assets}}$	A measure of the return on total investment in the enterprise. It is sometimes desirable to add interest to the after-tax profits to form the numerator of the ratio since total assets are financed by creditors as well as by stockholders; hence, it is accurate to measure the productivity of assets by the returns provided to both classes of investors.
5. Return on stockholders' equity (or return on net worth)	$\dfrac{\text{Profits after taxes}}{\text{Total stockholders' equity}}$	A measure of the rate of return on stockholders' investment in the enterprise.
6. Return on capital employed	$\dfrac{\text{Profits after taxes} - \text{Preferred stock dividends}}{\text{Total stockholders' equity} + \text{total debt} - \text{Par value of preferred stock}}$	A measure of the rate of return on the total capital investment in the enterprise.
7. Earnings per share	$\dfrac{\text{Profits after taxes and after preferred stock dividends}}{\text{Number of shares of common stock outstanding}}$	Shows the earnings available to the owners of each share of common stock.
Liquidity ratios		
1. Current ratio	$\dfrac{\text{Current assets}}{\text{Current liabilities}}$	Indicates the extent to which the claims of short-term creditors are covered by assets that are expected to be converted to cash in a period roughly corresponding to the maturity of the liabilities.
2. Quick ratio (or acid-test ratio)	$\dfrac{\text{Current assets} - \text{Inventory}}{\text{Current liabilities}}$	A measure of the firm's ability to pay off short-term obligations without relying on the sale of its inventories.
3. Inventory to net working capital	$\dfrac{\text{Inventory}}{\text{Current assets} - \text{Current liabilities}}$	A measure of the extent to which the firm's working capital is tied up in inventory.
Leverage ratios		
1. Debt-to-assets ratio	$\dfrac{\text{Total debt}}{\text{Total assets}}$	Measures the extent to which borrowed funds have been used to finance the firm's operations. Debt includes both long-term debt and short-term debt.
2. Debt-to-equity ratio	$\dfrac{\text{Total debt}}{\text{Total stockholders' equity}}$	Provides another measure of the funds provided by creditors versus the funds provided by owners.

table 1 (*concluded*)

Ratio	How Calculated	What It Shows
Leverage ratios (*cont.*)		
3. Long-term debt-to-equity ratio	$\dfrac{\text{Long-term debt}}{\text{Total stockholders' equity}}$	A widely used measure of the balance between debt and equity in the firm's long-term capital structure.
4. Times-interest-earned (or coverage) ratio	$\dfrac{\text{Profits before interest and taxes}}{\text{Total interest charges}}$	Measures the extent to which earnings can decline without the firm becoming unable to meet its annual interest costs.
5. Fixed-charge coverage	$\dfrac{\text{Profits before taxes and interest} + \text{Lease obligations}}{\text{Total interest charges} + \text{Lease obligations}}$	A more inclusive indication of the firm's ability to meet all of its fixed-charge obligations.
Activity ratios		
1. Inventory turnover	$\dfrac{\text{Sales}}{\text{Inventory of finished goods}}$	When compared to industry averages, it provides an indication of whether a company has excessive or perhaps inadequate finished goods inventory.
2. Fixed assets turnover	$\dfrac{\text{Sales}}{\text{Fixed assets}}$	A measure of the sales productivity and utilization of plant and equipment.
3. Total assets turnover	$\dfrac{\text{Sales}}{\text{Total assets}}$	A measure of the utilization of all the firm's assets; a ratio below the industry average indicates the company is not generating a sufficient volume of business, given the size of its asset investment.
4. Accounts receivable turnover	$\dfrac{\text{Annual credit sales}}{\text{Accounts receivable}}$	A measure of the average length of time it takes the firm to collect the sales made on credit.
5. Average collection period	$\dfrac{\text{Accounts receivable}}{\text{Total sales} \div 365}$ or $\dfrac{\text{Accounts receivable}}{\text{Average daily sales}}$	Indicates the average length of time the firm must wait after making a sale before it receives payment.
Other ratios		
1. Dividend yield on common stock	$\dfrac{\text{Annual dividends per share}}{\text{Current market price per share}}$	A measure of the return to owners received in the form of dividends.
2. Price-earnings ratio	$\dfrac{\text{Current market price per share}}{\text{After-tax earnings per share}}$	Faster-growing or less-risky firms tend to have higher price-earnings ratios than slower-growing or more-risky firms.
3. Dividend payout ratio	$\dfrac{\text{Annual dividends per share}}{\text{After-tax earnings per share}}$	Indicates the percentage of profits paid out as dividends.
4. Cash flow per share	$\dfrac{\text{After-tax profits} + \text{Depreciation}}{\text{Number of common shares outstanding}}$	A measure of the discretionary funds over and above expenses that are available for use by the firm.

Note: Industry-average ratios against which a particular company's ratios may be judged are available in *Modern Industry and Dun's Reviews* published by Dun & Bradstreet (14 ratios for 125 lines of business activities), Robert Morris Associates' *Annual Statement Studies* (11 ratios for 156 lines of business), and the FTC-SEC's *Quarterly Financial Report* for manufacturing corporations.

are more attractive than other courses of action that are open. You'll find Case-Tu-TOR's case preparation guides helpful in performing this step, too.

As long as you are conscientious in preparing your analysis and recommendations, and have ample reasons, evidence, and arguments to support your views, you shouldn't fret unduly about whether what you've prepared is "the right answer" to the case. In case analysis there is rarely just one right approach or set of recommendations. Managing a company and crafting and executing strategies are not such exact sciences that there exists a single provably correct analysis and action plan for each strategic situation. Of course, some analyses and action plans are better than others; but, in truth, there's nearly always more than one good way to analyze a situation and more than one good plan of action. So, if you have carefully prepared the case using either the Case-TUTOR case preparation guides or your instructor's assignment questions, don't lose confidence in the correctness of your work and judgment.

PARTICIPATING IN CLASS DISCUSSION OF A CASE

Classroom discussions of cases are sharply different from lecture classes. In a case class students do most of the talking. The instructor's role is to solicit student participation, keep the discussion on track, ask "Why?" often, offer alternative views, play the devil's advocate (if no students jump in to offer opposing views), and otherwise lead the discussion. The students in the class carry the burden of analyzing the situation and of being prepared to present and defend their diagnoses and recommendations. Expect a classroom environment, therefore, that calls for *your* size-up of the situation, *your* analysis, what actions *you* would take, and why *you* would take them. Do not be dismayed if, as the class discussion unfolds, some insightful things are said by your fellow classmates that you did not think of. It is normal for views and analyses to differ and for the comments of others in the class to expand your own thinking about the case. As the old adage goes, "Two heads are better than one." So it is to be expected that the class as a whole will do a more penetrating and searching job of case analysis than will any one person working alone. This is the power of group effort, and its virtues are that it will help you see more analytical applications, let you test your analyses and judgments against those of your peers, and force you to wrestle with differences of opinion and approaches.

To orient you to the classroom environment on the days a case discussion is scheduled, we compiled the following list of things to expect:

1. Expect the instructor to assume the role of extensive questioner and listener.

2. Expect students to do most of the talking. The case method enlists a maximum of individual participation in class discussion. It is not enough to be present as a silent observer; if every student took this approach, there would be no discussion. (Thus, expect a portion of your grade to be based on your participation in case discussions.)

3. Be prepared for the instructor to probe for reasons and supporting analysis.

4. Expect and tolerate challenges to the views expressed. All students have to be willing to submit their conclusions for scrutiny and rebuttal. Each student needs to learn to state his or her views without fear of disapproval and to overcome the hesitation of speaking out. Learning respect for the views and approaches of others is an integral part of case analysis exercises. But there are times when it is OK to

swim against the tide of majority opinion. In the practice of management, there is always room for originality and unorthodox approaches. So while discussion of a case is a group process, there is no compulsion for you or anyone else to cave in and conform to group opinions and group consensus.

5. Don't be surprised if you change your mind about some things as the discussion unfolds. Be alert to how these changes affect your analysis and recommendations (in the event you get called on).

6. Expect to learn a lot in class as the discussion of a case progresses; furthermore, you will find that the cases build on one another—what you learn in one case helps prepare you for the next case discussion.

There are several things you can do on your own to be good and look good as a participant in class discussions:

- Although you should do your own independent work and independent thinking, don't hesitate before (and after) class to discuss the case with other students. In real life, managers often discuss the company's problems and situation with other people to refine their own thinking.

- In participating in the discussion, make a conscious effort to contribute, rather than just talk. There is a big difference between saying something that builds the discussion and offering a long-winded off-the-cuff remark that leaves the class wondering what the point was.

- Avoid the use of "I think," "I believe," and "I feel"; instead, say, "My analysis shows—" and "The company should do . . . because—" Always give supporting reasons and evidence for your views; then your instructor won't have to ask you "Why?" every time you make a comment.

- In making your points, assume that everyone has read the case and knows what it says; avoid reciting and rehashing information in the case—instead, use the data and information to explain your assessment of the situation and to support your position.

- Bring the printouts of the work you've done on Case-TUTOR or the notes you've prepared (usually two or three pages' worth) to class and rely on them extensively when you speak. There's no way you can remember everything—especially the results of your number crunching. To reel off the numbers or to present all five reasons why, instead of one, you will need good notes. When you have prepared thoughtful answers to the study questions and use them as the basis for your comments, *everybody* in the room will know you are well prepared, and your contribution to the case discussion will stand out.

PREPARING A WRITTEN CASE ANALYSIS

Preparing a written case analysis is much like preparing a case for class discussion, except that your analysis must be more complete and put in report form. Unfortunately, though, there is no ironclad procedure for doing a written case analysis. All we can offer are some general guidelines and words of wisdom—this is because company situations and management problems are so diverse that no one mechanical way to approach a written case assignment always works.

Your instructor may assign you a specific topic around which to prepare your written report. Or, alternatively, you may be asked to do a comprehensive written case analysis, where the expectation is that you will (1) *identify* all the pertinent issues that management needs to address, (2) perform whatever *analysis* or *evaluation* is appropriate, and (3) propose an *action plan* and *set of recommendations* addressing the issues you have identified. In going through the exercise of identify, evaluate, and recommend, keep the following pointers in mind.[3]

Identification

It is essential early on in your paper that you provide a sharply focused diagnosis of strategic issues and key problems and that you demonstrate a good grasp of the company's present situation. Make sure that you can identify the firm's strategy (use the concepts and tools in Chapters 1–10 as diagnostic aids) and that you can pinpoint whatever strategy implementation issues may exist (consult the material in Chapters 11–13 for diagnostic help). Consult the key points we have provided at the end of each chapter for further diagnostic suggestions. Review the study questions for the case on Case-Tutor. Consider beginning your paper with an overview of the company's situation, its strategy, and the significant problems and issues that confront management. State problems/issues as clearly and precisely as you can. Unless it is necessary to do so for emphasis, avoid recounting facts and history about the company (assume your professor has read the case and is familiar with the organization).

Analysis and Evaluation

This is usually the hardest part of the report. Analysis is hard work! Check out the firm's financial ratios, its profit margins and rates of return, and its capital structure, and decide how strong the firm is financially. Refer back to Table 1, which contains a summary of various financial ratios and how they are calculated. Use it to assist in your financial diagnosis. Similarly, look at marketing, production, managerial competence, and other factors underlying the organization's strategic successes and failures. Decide whether the firm has valuable resource strengths and competencies and, if so, whether it is capitalizing on them.

Check to see if the firm's strategy is producing satisfactory results and determine the reasons why or why not. Probe the nature and strength of the competitive forces confronting the company. Decide whether and why the firm's competitive position is getting stronger or weaker. Use the tools and concepts you have learned about to perform whatever analysis or evaluation is appropriate. Work through the case preparation exercise on Case-Tutor if one is available for the case you've been assigned.

In writing your analysis and evaluation, bear in mind four things:

1. You are obliged to offer analysis and evidence to back up your conclusions. Do not rely on unsupported opinions, overgeneralizations, and platitudes as a substitute for tight, logical argument backed up with facts and figures.

---

[3]For some additional ideas and viewpoints, you may wish to consult Thomas J. Raymond, "Written Analysis of Cases," in *The Case Method at the Harvard Business School,* ed. M. P. McNair, pp. 139–63. Raymond's article includes an actual case, a sample analysis of the case, and a sample of a student's written report on the case.

2. If your analysis involves some important quantitative calculations, use tables and charts to present the calculations clearly and efficiently. Don't just tack the exhibits on at the end of your report and let the reader figure out what they mean and why they were included. Instead, in the body of your report cite some of the key numbers, highlight the conclusions to be drawn from the exhibits, and refer the reader to your charts and exhibits for more details.

3. Demonstrate that you have command of the strategic concepts and analytical tools to which you have been exposed. Use them in your report.

4. Your interpretation of the evidence should be reasonable and objective. Be wary of preparing a one-sided argument that omits all aspects not favorable to your conclusions. Likewise, try not to exaggerate or overdramatize. Endeavor to inject balance into your analysis and to avoid emotional rhetoric. Strike phrases such as "I think," "I feel," and "I believe" when you edit your first draft, and write in "My analysis shows," instead.

Recommendations

The final section of the written case analysis should consist of a set of definite recommendations and a plan of action. Your set of recommendations should address all of the problems/issues you identified and analyzed. If the recommendations come as a surprise or do not follow logically from the analysis, the effect is to weaken greatly your suggestions of what to do. Obviously, your recommendations for actions should offer a reasonable prospect of success. High-risk, bet-the-company recommendations should be made with caution. State how your recommendations will solve the problems you identified. Be sure the company is financially able to carry out what you recommend; also check to see if your recommendations are workable in terms of acceptance by the persons involved, the organization's competence to implement them, and prevailing market and environmental constraints. Try not to hedge or weasel on the actions you believe should be taken.

By all means state your recommendations in sufficient detail to be meaningful—get down to some definite nitty-gritty specifics. Avoid such unhelpful statements as "The organization should do more planning" or "The company should be more aggressive in marketing its product." For instance, do not simply say, "The firm should improve its market position" but state exactly how you think this should be done. Offer a definite agenda for action, stipulating a timetable and sequence for initiating actions, indicating priorities, and suggesting who should be responsible for doing what.

In proposing an action plan, remember there is a great deal of difference between, on the one hand, being responsible for a decision that may be costly if it proves in error and, on the other hand, casually suggesting courses of action that might be taken when you do not have to bear the responsibility for any of the consequences. A good rule to follow in making your recommendations is: *Avoid recommending anything you would not yourself be willing to do if you were in management's shoes.* The importance of learning to develop good managerial judgment is indicated by the fact that, even though the same information and operating data may be available to every manager or executive in an organization, the quality of the judgments about what the information means and which actions need to be taken does vary from person to person.[4]

---

[4]Gragg, "Because Wisdom Can't Be Told," p. 10.

It goes without saying that your report should be well organized and well written. Great ideas amount to little unless others can be convinced of their merit—this takes tight logic, the presentation of convincing evidence, and persuasively written arguments.

PREPARING AN ORAL PRESENTATION

During the course of your business career it is very likely that you will be called on to prepare and give a number of oral presentations. For this reason, it is common in courses of this nature to assign cases for oral presentation to the whole class. Such assignments give you an opportunity to hone your presentation skills.

The preparation of an oral presentation has much in common with that of a written case analysis. Both require identification of the strategic issues and problems confronting the company, analysis of industry conditions and the company's situation, and the development of a thorough, well-thought-out action plan. The substance of your analysis and quality of your recommendations in an oral presentation should be no different than in a written report. As with a written assignment, you'll need to demonstrate command of the relevant strategic concepts and tools of analysis, and your recommendations should contain sufficient detail to provide clear direction for management. The main difference between an oral presentation and a written case is in the delivery format. Oral presentations rely principally on verbalizing your diagnosis, analysis, and recommendations and visually enhancing and supporting your oral discussion with colorful, snappy slides (usually created with Microsoft's PowerPoint software).

Typically, oral presentations involve group assignments. Your instructor will provide the details of the assignment—how work should be delegated among the group members and how the presentation should be conducted. Some instructors prefer that presentations begin with issue identification, followed by analysis of the industry and company situation analysis, and conclude with a recommended action plan to improve company performance. Other instructors prefer that the presenters assume that the class has a good understanding of the external industry environment and the company's competitive position and expect the presentation to be strongly focused on the group's recommended action plan and supporting analysis and arguments. The latter approach requires cutting straight to the heart of the case and supporting each recommendation with detailed analysis and persuasive reasoning. Still other instructors may give you the latitude to structure your presentation however you and your group members see fit.

Regardless of the style preferred by your instructor, you should take great care in preparing for the presentation. A good set of slides with good content and good visual appeal is essential to a first-rate presentation. Take some care to choose a nice slide design, font size and style, and color scheme. We suggest including slides covering each of the following areas:

- An opening slide covering the "title" of the presentation and names of the presenters.
- A slide showing an outline of the presentation (perhaps with presenters' names by each topic).
- One or more slides showing the key problems and strategic issues that management needs to address.
- A series of slides covering your analysis of the company's situation.

● A series of slides containing your recommendations and the supporting arguments and reasoning for each recommendation—one slide for each recommendation and the associated reasoning has a lot of merit.

You and your team members should carefully plan and rehearse your slide show to maximize impact and minimize distractions. The slide show should include all of the pizzazz necessary to garner the attention of the audience, but not so much that it distracts from the content of what group members are saying to the class. You should remember that the role of slides is to help you communicate your points to the audience. Too many graphics, images, colors, and transitions may divert the audience's attention from what is being said or disrupt the flow of the presentation. Keep in mind that visually dazzling slides rarely hide a shallow or superficial or otherwise flawed case analysis from a perceptive audience. Most instructors will tell you that first-rate slides will definitely enhance a well-delivered presentation but that impressive visual aids accompanied by weak analysis and poor oral delivery still add up to a substandard presentation.

RESEARCHING COMPANIES AND INDUSTRIES VIA THE INTERNET AND ONLINE DATA SERVICES

Very likely, there will be occasions when you need to get additional information about some of the assigned cases, perhaps because your instructor has asked you to do further research on the industry or company or because you are simply curious about what has happened to the company since the case was written. These days it is relatively easy to run down recent industry developments and to find out whether a company's strategic and financial situation has improved, deteriorated, or changed little since the conclusion of the case. The amount of information about companies and industries available on the Internet and through online data services is formidable and expanding rapidly.

It is a fairly simple matter to go to company Web sites, click on the investor information offerings and press release files, and get quickly to useful information. Most company Web sites are linked to databases containing the company's quarterly and annual reports and 10K and 10Q filings with the Securities and Exchange Commission. Frequently, you will find mission and vision statements, values statements, codes of ethics, and strategy information, as well as charts of the company's stock price. The company's recent press releases typically contain reliable information about what of interest has been going on—new product introductions, recent alliances and partnership agreements, recent acquisitions, and other late-breaking company developments. Some company Web pages also include links to the home pages of industry trade associations where you can find information about industry size, growth, recent industry news, statistical trends, and future outlook. Thus, an early step in researching a company on the Internet is always to go to its Web site and see what's available.

Online Data Services

Lexis-Nexis, Bloomberg Financial News Services, and other online subscription services available in many university libraries provide access to a wide array of business reference material. For example, the Web-based Lexis-Nexis Academic Universe contains business news articles from general news sources, business publications, and industry trade publications. Broadcast transcripts from financial news programs are also available through Lexis-Nexis, as are full-text 10-Ks, 10-Qs, annual reports, and company profiles for more than 11,000 U.S. and international companies. Your business librarian should be able to direct you to the resources available through your library that will aid you in your research.

Public and Subscription Web sites with Good Information

In addition to company Web pages and online services provided by your university library, almost every major business publication has a subscription site available on the Internet. *The Wall Street Journal Interactive Edition* not only contains the same information that is available daily in its print version of the paper but also maintains a searchable database of all *Wall Street Journal* articles published during the past few years. The newspaper's online subscription site also has a Briefings Books section that allows you to conduct research on a specific company and track its financial and market performance in near–real time. *Fortune* and *Business Week* also make the content of the most current issue available online to subscribers as well as provide archives sections that allow you to search for articles related to a particular keyword that were published during the past few years.

The following Web sites are particularly good locations for company and industry information:

Securities and Exchange Commission EDGAR database (contains company 10-Ks, 10-Qs etc.)	www.sec.gov/cgi-bin/srch-edgar
NASDAQ	www.nasdaq.com
CNNfn: The Financial Network	www.cnnfn.com
Hoover's Online	www.hoovers.com
The Wall Street Journal Interactive Edition	www.wsj.com
Business Week	www.businessweek.com
Fortune	www.fortune.com
MSN Money Central	www.moneycentral.msn.com
Yahoo! Finance	www.quote.yahoo.com
Individual News Page	www.individual.com

Some of these Internet sources require subscriptions in order to access their entire databases.

Using a Search Engine

Alternatively, or in addition, you can quickly locate and retrieve information on companies, industries, products, individuals, or other subjects of interest using such Internet search engines as Lycos, Go, Excite, Snap, and Google. Search engines find articles and other information sources that relate to a particular industry, company name, topic, phrase, or keyword of interest. Search engine technology is becoming highly intuitive in retrieving Web pages related to your query and will likely direct you to the company Web site and other sites that contain timely and accurate information about the company. However, keep in mind that the information retrieved by a search engine is unfiltered

table 2   The 10 Commandments of Case Analysis

To be observed in written reports and oral presentations, and while participating in class discussions.

1. Go through the case twice, once for a quick overview and once to gain full command of the facts; then take care to explore the information in every one of the case exhibits.

2. Make a complete list of the problems and issues that the company's management needs to address.

3. Be thorough in your analysis of the company's situation. Either work through the case preparation exercises and/or study questions on Case-Tutor or make a minimum of one to two pages of notes detailing your diagnosis.

4. Use every opportunity to apply the concepts and analytical tools in the text chapters—all of the cases in the book have very definite ties to the concepts/tools in one or more of the text chapters and you are expected to apply them in analyzing the cases.

5. Do enough number crunching to discover the story told by the data presented in the case. (To help you comply with this commandment, consult Table 1 in this section to guide your probing of a company's financial condition and financial performance.)

6. Support any and all opinions with well-reasoned arguments and numerical evidence; don't stop until you can purge "I think" and "I feel" from your assessment and instead are able to rely completely on "My analysis shows."

7. Prioritize your recommendations and make sure they can be carried out in an acceptable time frame with the available resources.

8. Support each recommendation with persuasive argument and reasons as to why it makes sense and should result in improved company performance.

9. Review your recommended action plan to see if it addresses all of the problems and issues you identified—any set of recommendations that does not address all of the issues and problems you identified is incomplete and insufficient.

10. Avoid recommending any course of action that could have disastrous consequences if it doesn't work out as planned; therefore, be as alert to the downside risks of your recommendations as you are to their upside potential and appeal.

and may include sources that are not reliable or that contain inaccurate or misleading information. Be wary of information that is provided by authors who are unaffiliated with reputable organizations or publications or that doesn't come from the company or a credible trade association—be especially careful in relying on the accuracy of information you find posted on various bulletin boards. Articles covering a company or issue should be copyrighted or published by a reputable source. If you are turning in a paper containing information gathered from the Internet, you should cite your sources (providing the Internet address and date visited); it is also wise to print Web pages for your research file (some Web pages are updated frequently).

The Learning Curve Is Steep

With a modest investment of time, you will learn how to use Internet sources and search engines to run down information on companies and industries quickly and efficiently. And it is a skill that will serve you well into the future. Once you become familiar with the data available on the different Web sites mentioned above and with one or more search engines, you will know where to go to look for the particular information that you want. Search engines nearly always turn up too many information sources that match your request rather than too few; the trick is to learn to zero in on those most relevant to what you are looking for. As with most things, once you get a little experience under your belt on how to do company and industry research on the Internet, you will find that you can readily find the information you need.

THE 10 COMMANDMENTS OF CASE ANALYSIS

As a way of summarizing our suggestions about how to approach the task of case analysis, we have compiled what we like to call "The 10 Commandments of Case Analysis." They are shown in Table 2 on the previous page. If you observe all or even most of these commandments faithfully as you prepare a case either for class discussion or for a written report, your chances of doing a good job on the assigned cases will be much improved. Hang in there, give it your best shot, and have some fun exploring what the real world of strategic management is all about.

case | 1 Steve Case, America Online, and Time Warner

Arthur A. Thompson
The University of Alabama

John E. Gamble
University of South Alabama

Every day, millions of people across the world log on to America Online to check their e-mail, track their stock portfolios, visit their favorite spots on the Internet, and send instant messages to friends on their buddy lists. In early 2000 AOL had 22 million subscribers and handled 110 million e-mails, 200 million stock quotes, and 562 million instant messages daily. Many subscribers used AOL features to create online photo albums, online calendars, and electronic jukeboxes. The company's members could also use AOL to purchase an airline ticket, reserve a car or hotel, or get a map from the airport to the hotel. They could purchase an unlimited variety of merchandise and services through Shop@AOL and pay their bills with an AOL Visa or through electronic banking provided by AOL and Intuit.

Other AOL brands brought the company millions more sets of eyeballs each day. Netscape Netcenter had 27.5 million registrants; Digital City, the number one local online network, had more than 6 million visitors each month from 60 U.S. cities; and ICQ, the number one communication community, had 53.1 million registrants and averaged 8 million daily users. Over 150 million movie tickets were purchased from AOL's MovieFone Web site each year. This combined traffic made AOL the leading interactive Internet medium, with more than $4.7 billion in 1999 revenues, nearly $400 million in net earnings, and a market capitalization of nearly $200 billion at year-end 1999. Exhibit 1 presents selected financial and operating highlights for America Online during the 1992–99 period. The performance of the company's stock price is shown in Exhibit 2.

Much of the company's success through 1999 was attributable to CEO and chairman Stephen Case's visionary leadership and his efforts to make AOL an essential and ubiquitous component of everyday life. During the last half of the 1990s, Case's entrepreneurship, his strategic vision for AOL, and AOL's undeniably significant market impact had made him one of the most prominent and influential top executives in the United States. His views on the Internet economy were paid close attention in industry *exhibit 1*   Selected Financial and Operating Highlights, America Online, Inc., 1992–99

	Year Ended June 30				
	1999	1998	1997	1996	1995
Statement of operations data					
Subscription services	$3,321	$2,183	$1,478	$1,024	$ 352
Advertising, commerce, and other	1,000	543	308	111	50
Enterprise solutions	456	365	411	188	23
Total revenues	4,777	3,091	2,197	1,323	425
Income (loss) from operations	458	(120)	(485)	64	(41)
Net income (loss)	$ 762	$ (74)	$ (485)	$ 35	$ (55)
Income (loss) per common share					
Net income (loss) per share—diluted	$ 0.60	($ 0.08)	($ 0.58)	$ 0.04	($0.09)
Net income (loss) per share—basic	$ 0.73	($ 0.08)	($ 0.58)	$ 0.05	($0.09)
Weighted average shares outstanding					
Diluted	1,277	925	838	944	587
Basic	1,041	925	838	751	587
Net cash provided by operating activities	$1,099	$ 437	$ 131	$ 2	$ 18
Earnings before interest, taxes, depreciation and amortization (EBITDA)	968	302	111	138	11
Balance sheet data					
Working capital (deficiency)	$ 254	$ 108	($ 40)	$ 72	$ 18
Total assets	5,348	2,874	1,501	1,271	459
Total debt	364	372	52	25	24
Stockholders' equity	3,033	996	610	707	242

Source: America Online 1999 annual report.

circles and by the news media. Then on January 10, 2000, AOL stunned the business world with an announcement of potentially far-reaching consequences for business. Steve Case, Time Warner co-chairmen Gerald Levin and Ted Turner, and other America Online and Time Warner executives held a joint press conference describing plans to merge the two companies. The new company, to be named AOL Time Warner, would combine one of the largest "old-economy" media companies with the world's largest "new-economy" media company to create a company positioned, they said, to lead the second Internet revolution and capitalize on the convergence of entertainment, information, communications, and online services. Combined sales of the two companies would approach $33 billion.

America Online's brands included AOL, AOL.com, AOL MovieFone, ICQ, CompuServe, Netscape, Digital City, iPlanet, Spinner, Winamp, and AOL Instant Messenger. Time Warner's brands included *Time, Fortune, Sports Illustrated, People, Money, Southern Living, Parenting, Entertainment Weekly,* Book-of-the-Month Club, Warner Bros., CNN, TBS, TNT, Turner Classic Movies, World Championship Wrestling, Cartoon Network, HBO, Cinemax, Warner Music Group (five studios and over 70 artists), and Looney Tunes; in addition, Time Warner was the second largest provider of cable TV services, serving 12.4 million homes in over 34 areas of the country. Top executives at the

exhibit 2   Monthly Performance of America Online, Inc.'s Stock Price,
1992 to March 2000

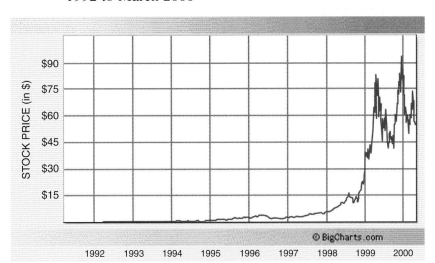

two companies believed the merger would allow Time Warner to bring its entertainment
brands to consumers in a digital environment, in addition to traditional formats, while
AOL could use Time Warner's broadband cable resources and satellite television capabilities to deliver online content to consumers at speeds much greater than possible over
telephone lines. If approved by shareholders and regulators, the merger would convert
each company's shares to AOL Time Warner shares at a fixed ratio. Each Time Warner
share was to be exchanged for 1.5 shares of the new company's shares, and each AOL
share was to be exchanged for 1 share of the new company's stock. The new stock would
be traded under the symbol AOL on the New York Stock Exchange.

Steve Case would become chairman of AOL Time Warner, and Gerald Levin
would serve as CEO. Case believed the merger was so important to securing AOL's future that he was willing for Levin to function as AOL Time Warner's CEO in order to
win the support of Time Warner management for the merger. The impetus for the
merger had come from Steve Case and AOL—it was Case's vision for the merged
company that had prompted him to initiate merger discussions, and he was the person
most responsible for sparking the excitement of Time Warner executives and leading
the effort to pull the deal together.

STEPHEN M. CASE: CHAIRMAN, PRESIDENT, AND CEO OF AMERICA ONLINE

Steve Case was born and raised in Honolulu, Hawaii, where his father was a lawyer
and his mother a teacher. Case's entrepreneurial spirit surfaced at an early age. When
Case was six, he and his brother opened a juice stand and charged 2 cents a cup, but
many of their customers gave them a nickel and let them keep the change—an experience that taught the boys the value of high margins. A few years later, the two brothers

started a business selling a variety of products door-to-door and by mail. Then they began selling ad circulars and, in addition, shared a newspaper route.

Case attended Williams College, in Williamstown, Massachusetts, where he majored in political science and was the lead singer in two rock groups. After graduating in 1980, he accepted a marketing position at Procter & Gamble and worked to promote Lilt, a home permanent kit, after unsuccessfully attempting to obtain a position with Time, Inc.'s HBO. Unhappy with managing a mature business, Case left after two years to join Pizza Hut as manager of pizza development. The job involved a lot of travel, and he often spent evenings exploring his new laptop computer. He joined an early online service called The Source, and even though the service provided only text messages at a painfully slow rate, Steve Case became fascinated by the possibilities.

In 1983, Case's brother, then an investment banker, introduced him to the founders of Control Video; they offered him a job as a marketing assistant on the spot, and he accepted. When the company's video game business soured, the board of directors brought in entrepreneur Jim Kimsey as CEO, who proceeded to groom Case to take over the top spot. Kimsey and Case convinced venture capitalists to put up $5 million to back their idea of forming an online service for users of Commodore computers, and Control Video became Quantum Computer Services. It was Case who engineered Quantum's deals with Apple Computer and Tandy (although he used up much of the $5 million in capital in the process and had some of the venture capital board members calling on Kimsey to fire him). And it was Case who, when the Apple deal fell through, helped turn the basis for it into America Online.

When he was made CEO of America Online in 1992, Case quickly fashioned a growth-at-any-cost strategy and charged ahead. Despite industry observers' numerous predictions over the years that AOL would stumble or that its membership growth would soon slow to a crawl, Steve Case kept making new acquisitions, forging new alliances, adjusting the company's marketing strategies, and adapting AOL's services and content to fast-paced changes in the marketplace.

When Microsoft announced that it would bundle its new Microsoft Network software in with its Windows 95 operating system software, Steve Case was a leader in urging the Justice Department to block the move as an unfair advantage. Microsoft, however, was allowed to proceed. Later, in March 1996, Case negotiated a head-turning pact with Microsoft whereby AOL would integrate Microsoft's Internet Explorer (a Web browser) into its online software; Microsoft, in return, would include AOL software in every copy of its Windows 95 operating system. Case explained the reasons for choosing Microsoft's Internet Explorer over Netscape's Navigator, the market share leader in Web browsers:

> . . . there were a number of reasons we went with Microsoft. We think the Internet Explorer technology is evolving at a rapid rate and its modular design will enable us to plug it in to AOL quickly. Strategically, we thought it would be smart for us to make sure there were two strong providers of Web technology in the marketplace. We didn't want anyone, whether Microsoft or Netscape, to have the kind of monopoly in Web technology that Microsoft has in operating systems.[1]

Within four years as CEO, Case had led AOL in becoming the largest online service, with more than 5 million users. In 1998, Case stated that the mission of AOL was

---

[1]As quoted in "AOL CEO Steve Case," *Forbes,* October 7, 1996, p. 95.

"to build a global medium as central to people's lives as the telephone or television . . . and even more valuable."[2] In 2000, AOL's 22 million subscribers easily made it the world's largest online service.

Because of his success in transforming AOL into what many observers believed was the most potent force in cyberspace, Case was often asked to speak at PC-related conventions, usually drawing packed audiences. His views were widely sought by business reporters, industry analysts, and executives from Internet-related companies. He discussed the growth of AOL's subscriber base and the Internet revolution at one such event during the fall of 1999 as follows:

> Today, the Internet is becoming as central to everyday life as the phone and the TV. Right now, 53 percent of U.S. households own a PC—up from 39 percent in 1995. Already, 37 percent of households have online access—when just eight or nine years ago, most Americans didn't know what online access was. At AOL, it took us about a decade to get our first 1 million members. Now we add an additional million members every few months. When we started, 90 percent of AOL users were men. Today, more than half are women—about the same proportion as the overall U.S. population. The Internet is becoming a mass medium. I knew this for sure a few years ago when my parents finally understood what I did for a living.[3]

Even before AOL's success was evident, those who knew Steve Case were impressed by his vision and his ability to forge success in an emerging industry. Although Case functioned as an ardent and visible spokesman for AOL and had fashioned a hard-charging image for the company, he displayed a low-key, non-egotistical management style in his relationships with AOL executives and employees. Case was also a hands-on manager who stayed on top of how things were going. In 1996, former U.S. general Alexander Haig, an AOL board member, said that Case "borders on genius. If you look at how this young fella has positioned this company, he has ventures with every big player in the business. Instead of being beaten to death by Microsoft, as everyone predicted, they came courting him."[4] "When I met Steve," recalled another AOL board member, "he was 30 years old, and he already had a messianic vision of a connected world where the Internet was going to be part of daily life in every way imaginable. AOL is about being the leader in making this medium all that it has the potential to be."[5] Another close observer of Case and AOL said, "Every time people ask 'How is he going to survive?' he makes the right moves."[6]

Nonetheless, Case had taken a number of potshots from critics. Ned Brainard of *HotWired*, for example, labeled Case a "shameless self-promoter." Disgruntled AOL members had, from time to time, posted messages on AOL bulletin boards "flaming" Steve Case and AOL for policies and practices they disagreed with, long wait times for customer support, excessive busy signals at peak hours (which spurred such labels as America On Hold), and assorted other grievances.

---

[2]As stated in America Online's 1998 annual report.

[3]Speech given to the National School Boards Association, 13th Annual Technology and Learning Conference, Dallas, Texas, November 11, 1999.

[4]As quoted in "The Online World of Steve Case," *Business Week,* April 15, 1996, p. 80.

[5]"These Guys Want It All," *Fortune,* February 7, 2000, p. 72.

[6]Ibid.

COMPANY HISTORY AND BACKGROUND

Control Video Corporation was founded in the early 1980s with the business purpose of creating an online service that specialized in video games for users of Atari computer-game machines. At the time, two brands of home computers, the Apple II and the Commodore 64, dominated the market for playing online computer games. But because of maddeningly slow modems and modest processing power, playing video games online was not popular, and thus Control Video soon failed. The company was reorganized by James Kimsey and Steve Case as Quantum Computer Services in 1985; the new company focused its energies on developing customized online services for other companies. Quantum created a service for Commodore, then a leading computer company, called Q-Link. Commodore ended up selling millions of its home computers, and Q-Link was a hit with Commodore users. Quantum generated enough revenues to keep the company going. During the next several years, Quantum expanded to serve other computer users. Steve Case made a deal with Apple Computer in 1987 to create software packages for its Apple II and Macintosh models, and in 1988 he convinced Tandy Corporation to support a new online service, PC-Link, for purchasers of its DOS-based Radio Shack computers. Then in 1989 Apple withdrew from its deal at the last minute. Frustrated by the turn of events with Apple, Quantum decided to introduce the software service it designed for Apple under the name America Online.

Quantum's promotional strategy for its online service was to blanket home computer users with diskettes containing the America Online software. It gave the disks away at trade shows, got them included in magazine subscription mail-outs, had them attached to magazine covers at newsstands, and mailed them to selected households. By 1990, management had decided to bring all of its segmented online services together under one overall service. Quantum changed its name to America Online in 1991 and went public in 1992, raising $66 million to fund its expansion. Steve Case was named CEO shortly thereafter.

When Case took over as CEO, America Online, with only 200,000 subscribers and 250 employees, was well behind CompuServe and Prodigy, the two leading online services. In early 1993, AOL cut its monthly fee well below what CompuServe and Prodigy were charging and began mailing out massive numbers of diskettes with free trial offers. The company also made its start-up disks available to United Airlines passengers with their meals, inserted AOL CDs in boxes of cereal, and even included AOL disks with deliveries of Omaha Steaks. AOL's membership growth accelerated to the point where it had trouble handling the influx of new subscribers. Users would get abruptly disconnected, and logging on in peak periods sometimes took over an hour. Numerous complaints led Case to issue a letter of apology and to promise network improvements. Case proceeded to initiate agreements with NBC, the *New York Times,* CNN, *Time,* and others to provide AOL with content for its service. AOL made investments to handle a bigger volume of users; acquired new companies to boost its network and multimedia expertise and its software development capabilities; and continued to solicit new members with aggressive marketing.

By early 1995, America Online had 1 million subscribers but still trailed Prodigy (which had 1.5 million subscribers) and industry leader CompuServe (which had over 2 million subscribers). The company then began offering members Internet and World Wide Web access and kept flooding the market with diskettes, running arresting ads and come-ons, and offering consumers first 10 then 15 free hours to try the service, all the while improving the breadth and quality of the content of its services. AOL launched AOL Germany in 1995 through a joint venture with Bertelsmann AG, the world's third largest publisher. AOL UK, AOL Canada, and AOL France were all launched in early 1996. By mid-1996 the company's enhanced services, international expansion, and aggressive marketing built its membership to more than 6 million subscribers.

AOL's Setbacks during 1996

In July 1996 AOL, pressured by inquiries from the Federal Trade Commission and several state attorneys general, settled a class-action lawsuit concerning its billing practices by agreeing to give members free time online. The agreement cost AOL about $8 million. On August 7, AOL's system crashed during an equipment upgrade and the network went dead for 19 hours; the failure made headlines in newspapers and on TV and users complained about being deprived of e-mail and World Wide Web connections. In an apology to subscribers, Steve Case wrote, "I would like to be able to tell you this sort of thing will never happen again, but frankly, I can't make that commitment."

AOL encountered additional problems in August 1996, when the National Basketball Association sued the company in federal court, charging it with misappropriating proprietary data and violating intellectual property laws by providing real-time updates on NBA games in progress, not only giving the scores as each point was made but also providing summaries of player performance. AOL claimed that it was exercising its constitutional right to free speech and that the NBA didn't own the underlying facts about its basketball games. The three other major professional sports leagues (for baseball, football, and ice hockey) filed briefs supporting the NBA's lawsuit. AOL subsequently altered its practice of reporting on games in progress by delaying its updates.

In October 1996, the company's shares fell 10 percent the day following its 10-K filing with the Securities and Exchange Commission that noted its difficulties in retaining subscribers. AOL management attributed its problems with customer retention (referred to as "customer churn") to an increased number of lower-priced competitors and to the flat-rate monthly service pricing of many Internet service providers. In the October–December 1995 quarter, AOL signed up 1.8 million new subscribers but 950,000 members canceled, for a net gain of 850,000. Analysts estimated that in the January–March 1996 quarter AOL signed up 2.3 million new users and 1.4 million users quit. One analyst estimated that up to 45 percent of AOL's subscriber base canceled service each year; the same analyst observed that AOL spent more than $300 million in marketing in 1996 to add a net of 3.2 million subscribers to its membership base.[7] Steve Case indicated in the fall of 1996 that AOL's cost to acquire a subscriber averaged about $45 and that the company's customer churn was running under 40 percent.

Later in October, reacting to mounting criticism that the manner in which it accounted for its marketing expenses resulted in greatly overstated profits, America Online announced that it was changing its accounting practice of amortizing its marketing expenditures for acquiring new subscribers. Whereas the typical company charged marketing expenses against earnings as the expenses were incurred, it was AOL's practice

---

[7]*The Wall Street Journal,* October 2, 1996, p. B5.

to spread those costs over a 24-month period; AOL's accounting methods (agreed to by its auditors, Ernst & Young) had the effect of increasing the company's reported short-term profits—an outcome that critics said was misleading to investors. AOL's decision to switch to a practice of charging subscriber acquisition costs as a current operating expense resulted in an immediate charge against prior earnings of $350 million—an amount over 50 times greater than the company's total profits in the five preceding years combined (see again Exhibit 1).

AOL's Move to Flat-Rate Pricing

In November 1996, AOL announced that starting in December it would give members the option to switch to unlimited usage for $19.95 per month instead of paying $9.95 for basic service of five hours per month and $2.95 for each additional online hour. It also offered several other pricing plans, including advance renewal rates of $14.95 per month for customers paying two years in advance, advance renewal rates of $17.95 for customers paying one year in advance, and a light usage program of 3 hours per month for $4.95 (with additional time at $2.95 per hour). In addition to its new pricing options, America Online sought to further spur new subscriber sign-ups in November by boosting its trial offer from 15 free hours to 50 free hours.

The response to these marketing initiatives was overwhelming, greatly exceeding what AOL had expected and prepared for. Over 1.2 million new members signed on in the last quarter of 1996, and an estimated 75 percent of existing members switched to the new flat-rate, unlimited-use pricing plan. Virtually overnight, usage of AOL's service jumped dramatically (especially during the peak hours of 8 PM until midnight), straining existing capacity and causing members to get busy signals when they tried to sign on. In November 1996, the month before the unlimited use pricing plan went into effect, AOL members spent 66 million hours collectively online, more than double the 30 million hours they averaged during the summer months of 1996 and 50 percent more than the 44 million hours logged in September. In December 1996, the total soared to more than 100 million hours and rose further to about 125 million hours in January 1997. The number of daily sessions rose from 6.2 million in October to more than 10 million in January 1997 and over 11 million in February. AOL users averaged more than 32 minutes per day in January 1997, compared to 14 minutes per day in September 1996. And the number of simultaneous users increased from 185,000 in November 1996 to more than 260,000 in January 1997. Member complaints about busy signals and congested network traffic escalated, even though AOL had added about 20,000 modems to its network to accommodate increased call-ins and was adding thousands more weekly. One member's experience was typical: "It's literally impossible to get on AOL at night. I do business on the Internet and this has really hurt me."

In January 1997, five AOL members filed a class-action lawsuit in a state court in Los Angeles, alleging they were not getting the promised services due to repeated busy signals; similar suits were filed in three other states as well. State attorneys general from 36 states quickly joined in, reacting to a chorus of customer complaints. AOL responded by announcing it would spend $350 million to upgrade its network over the next five months by adding 150,000 modems, building new data centers, hiring 600 additional customer service representatives, adding 1-800 access numbers, and cutting back on the recruitment of new members. In an open letter to members, Steve Case said:

Last fall, you told us you wanted an unlimited use plan, and we delivered. Naturally, we anticipated more usage, and prepared for it, but we seriously underestimated the surge in demand that actually occurred. We know that you are having problems getting online and we are working day and night to improve the situation . . .

The events of the past few weeks have vividly reminded us of the responsibilities we have, as the service that 8 million members rely on each day. We take these responsibilities seriously, and I can assure you we will do everything in our power to meet them.

AOL'S EVOLVING STRATEGY, 1997–99

In early 1997 America Online, under mounting pressure of legal action, formally agreed to issue refunds or credit toward future service to cover network access and service problems during December 1996 and January 1997. Under terms of the agreement, customers could choose whether to receive credit for a free month of service or qualify for cash rebates up to $39.90. By March 1997, AOL had a total of 250,000 modems in place, was handling more than 11 million connections per day, and was distributing 10.5 million e-mail messages daily. On an average day, AOL members were, collectively, spending just over 4 million hours online and accounting for 225 million Web hits daily.

Steve Case saw the move to flat-rate pricing and the ensuing system overloads as hard evidence that Internet users were adopting his vision of the future and AOL's role in their lives: "What was happening, for really the first time, was that we impacted people's daily lives in a significant way. Suddenly, almost overnight, we became part of their everyday life. That's why there was this national outrage and tremendous passion and frustration, because people needed us, and many of them loved us, and we had disappointed them. It was a coming of age for the medium."[8]

AOL's Use of Alliances and Acquisitions to Enhance the Online Experience

America Online began making acquisitions to build its capabilities to deliver interesting online content in 1994. The company's acquisitions added expertise in creating multimedia experiences, improving the performance of its software, bringing new functionality to AOL's service, and improving the performance of AOL's network. Exhibit 3 presents AOL's acquisitions from August 1994 through December 1999. Through the company's acquisitions and its own internal product development efforts, it was able to offer a richer interactive experience than most of its online and Internet rivals.

In 1997 AOL launched its version 4.0 software that built on the resources gained through the company's numerous acquisitions and alliances and was faster, more responsive, and more interactive than its 3.0 predecessor. AOL 4.0 allowed members to send other members e-mail with embedded color photographs, custom backgrounds, multiple attachments, and different fonts. On the chat side, members could display a photograph, graphic image, or live video camera footage while they were chatting. Users could also click on a button and request an AOL phone conversation with the person they were chatting with. Another new feature was Driveway, an automated offline information option that could be customized by members to retrieve particular content from e-mail, newsgroups, the Web, and other places. Other new features included e-mail spelling and grammar checking, greeting card creation, address book enhancements,

---

[8]"The Internet Is Mr. Case's Neighborhood," *Fortune,* March 30, 1998, p. 72.

exhibit 3　America Online's Acquisitions, August 1994–December 1999

Date	Price in Stock	Company Acquired
August 1994	$34 million	Redgate Communications, Ted Leonis's company, which made multimedia CD-ROMs with online links
November 1994	$6 million	Navisoft, a maker of software for creating Web sites
December 1994	$41 million	BookLink Technologies, which provided AOL's first browser
February 1995	$35 million	ANS, creator of the Internet network
May 1995	$30 million	Medior, interactive media developer
May 1995	$15 million	WAS, developer of Web server software
June 1995	$11 million	Global Network Navigator, which provided the foundation for AOL's new Internet browser
September 1995	$15 million	Ubique, maker of software for 3-D worlds
February 1996	$59 million	Johnson-Grace, provider of data compression
August 1996	Not disclosed	ImagiNation Network, producer of online multiplayer games
March 1997	Not disclosed	Lightspeed Media, online program developer
January 1998	Not disclosed	PLS, developer of information indexing and search technologies
February 1998	$1.3 billion deal involving AOL's ANS, H&R Block, and WorldCom	CompuServe
June 1998	$29 million	NetChannnel, a Web-enhanced television company
June 1998	$287 million	Mirabilis, producer of ICQ instant communications technology
November 1998	Not disclosed	PersonaLogic, maker of online decision tree software
March 1999	$10.2 billion	Netscape
April 1999	Not disclosed	When, Inc., an Internet calendar developer
May 1999	Not disclosed	MovieFone, Inc.
June 1999	$400 million	Winamp, Spinner.com, and SHOUTcast music brands
June 1999	$15 million	Digital Marketing Services, online marketing research and online incentive marketing

Source: America Online press releases and *Business Week,* April 15, 1996, p. 82.

16-character screen names, additional security and control, and streaming video and multimedia enhancements for the World Wide Web.

In 1997, AOL began an alliance with Tel-Save, a small long-distance company, that allowed the company to offer its customers long-distance service at 9 cents per minute. AOL furthered its global reach in 1997 with the launch of AOL Japan and AOL Australia to gain more than 1 million international subscribers by the end of the year. AOL also announced an "AOL Anywhere" initiative in December 1997 that would ultimately make the company's services available beyond PCs through alliances and investments in interactive television, handheld connected devices, and broadband technology.

In 1998 AOL expanded its paying membership to 14.5 million through its continued aggressive marketing and the acquisition of CompuServe. Steve Case saw the interactive experience not as separate online and Internet markets but as a seamless product; he therefore made acquisitions to ensure that AOL would become a notable Internet destination. The company expanded its content available to AOL.com non-subscribers and acquired both instant communication provider ICQ and Web community Digital City. AOL's combined brands were visited by tens of millions of different people in 1998.

AOL also acquired a Web-enhanced television company called NetChannel and PLS, the leading developer of information indexing and search technologies, to improve the functionality of upcoming versions of AOL's software. AOL entered into an alliance with Sun Microsystems in November 1998 to build end-to-end electronic solutions and to help other companies put their businesses on the Internet. The company created a number of other alliances in 1998 with companies such as eBay to improve the diversity of its content, and added a mixture of e-commerce sites through alliances with 1-800-FLOWERS, J. Crew, Barnes & Noble, Preview Travel, DLJ Direct, E*Trade, Intuit, and others. AOL also created an investment unit in 1998 to examine interactive investment opportunities related to the Internet. The company expanded its international presence in 1998 with the launch of AOL Austria with the help of Bertelsmann AG.

AOL's Acquisition of Netscape

During 1999 AOL acquired Netscape for $10.2 billion in AOL stock. The Netscape acquisition provided AOL with the browser technology necessary to enhance its product development resources and provided the company with a West Coast location for job candidates unwilling to move to Virginia, but more importantly it gave AOL the resources necessary to provide electronic commerce services to business customers. Even though AOL customers could buy goods and services through the company's online service, prior to the Netscape acquisition AOL's e-commerce capabilities were primarily restricted to its efforts to offer an online shopping mall to Internet retailers.

In 1996, AOL attempted to develop the computer software and services necessary for companies to put their business online, but firms were hesitant to contract with AOL for their e-commerce requirements. AOL's senior vice president of its enterprise solutions group said that the company's failure in landing commercial accounts was largely attributable to the "psychic clash" encountered by business executives considering purchasing software from a consumer online service—many companies thought that it "bordered on a joke" that AOL's technology could reliably handle their mission-critical operations.[9]

The Netscape acquisition, along with AOL's existing agreement with Sun Microsystems, allowed the company to offer e-commerce solutions under a brand that would appeal to the business customer. Furthermore, the addition of Netscape to AOL's brands brought more daytime visitors to AOL sites and added a highly talented pool of workers needed to develop newer generations of AOL's software and browser capabilities. Steve Case commented on the importance of the addition of Netscape to AOL's portfolio of brands shortly after the company had been reorganized to fully capture the strategic fit benefits of the acquisition:

---

[9]"AOL's New State: Firm Faces Challenge Selling Software, Services to Business," *Washington Post,* November 29, 1998, p. H01.

This acquisition will greatly accelerate our business momentum by advancing our multiple-brand, multiple-product strategy and helping us take e-commerce to a new level. We are especially excited about adding Netscape's talented-people—highly regarded in Silicon Valley and elsewhere—to our team. We will continue to build Netscape's successful businesses, including expanding the audience for popular Netscape NetCenter and extending both the Navigator and Communicator browsers to the emerging market of next-generation Internet devices.[10]

Some industry analysts suggested that America Online should integrate the Netscape Navigator and Communicator browsers into the upcoming versions of its online software in lieu of using Microsoft's Internet Explorer.

Other Recent Acquisitions and Alliances

In 1999 AOL acquired When.com and PersonaLogic, the developers of Web-based calendar services; online music brands Spinner.com, Winamp, and SHOUTcast; and MovieFone, the premier movie information and ticketing brand. Also in 1999, the company acquired online incentive marketing and marketing research firm Digital Marketing Services, Inc.

AOL signed an alliance with CBS to become its exclusive provider of broadcast news, formed alliances with Bell Atlantic, SBC, Ameritech, and GTE to provide high-speed digital subscriber line (DSL) access to AOL customers, forged an advertising partnership with First USA, and formed alliances with Gemstar DIRECTV, Hughes Network Systems, Philips Electronics, and Liberate Technologies to create a television-based online service. In addition, AOL and 3Com Corporation created an alliance that would allow AOL subscribers to access their e-mail with their PalmPilots; AOL and Motorola began to develop wireless applications for AOL's Instant Messenger; and the company partnered with Gateway to introduce a family of specialized Internet appliances that would automatically launch AOL when the device was switched on. The new appliances would be a low-cost alternative to PCs and would come in countertop, desktop, or wireless handheld models.

Many of America Online's alliances were accompanied by equity investments in the company's partners. AOL had made investments in more than 70 publicly and closely held companies that were valued at more than $2 billion in early 2000. In addition, America Online had invested $1.5 billion in Hughes Electronics and $800 million in Gateway. A list of AOL's content and e-commerce partners is presented in Exhibit 4.

America Online's Strategy to Finance Its Growth

The company's rapid growth had been financed largely through new issues of common stock. The company had raised nearly $1.5 billion from the issue of new shares of common and preferred stock in fiscal years 1993–99 to pay for the costs of attracting new subscribers; new product development; and investments in modems, servers, and other equipment needed to operate and expand its online network capability. America Online had also generated the more than $12 billion needed for its many acquisitions through the issuance of new shares. The company's cash flows from operations had remained

---

[10]"America Online Announces New Organization to Integrate Netscape and Extend Industry Leadership," *Business Wire,* March 24, 1999.

exhibit 4　America Online's Content and E-Commerce Partners

Auto, Travel American Airlines Norwegian Cruise Line Budget Rent-a-Car Preview Travel The Hertz Corporation AutoTrader.com **Babies, Children, and Toys** Gymboree.com eToys Healthtex BabyCenter iBaby Sesame Street Toysrus.com KBKids.com Americasbaby.com **Books, Videos, Movies, Music,** **Electronics and Computers** DIRECTV barnesandnoble.com Amazon.com CDNow DVD Express New Line Cinema Beyond.com 800.COM Onsale **Cards, Office Supplies, Gifts, Art,** **and Collectibles** americangreetings.com eBay 1-800-FLOWERS.com Godiva Chocolatier Art.com Sharper Image	Office Max Red Envelope.com **Clothing, Apparel, Fashion,** **and Accessories** J. Crew Fossil JCPenney bluefly.com eBags Brooks Brothers Guess Steve Madden Levi Strauss **Educational Programming** Nickelodeon MamaMedia New York Times Learning Network Cartoon Network Time for Kids **Food, Cooking, and Consumer** **Products** OmahaSteaks.com Procter & Gamble Cooking.com Hickory Farms Tavolo **Health, Pharmacy, Beauty,** **and Fitness** PlanetRx.com Drugstore.com Healthquick HealthAxis.com AmericasDoctor.com Avon	**News, Sports, Entertainment,** **and General Interest** CBS News CBS SportsLine The Weather Channel iVillage Oxygen Media Inc. People Online E! Online MTV Bloomberg **Insurance, Real Estate, Banking,** **and Financial Services** E*Trade TD Waterhouse The Motley Fool Ameritrade Century 21 Real Estate Corporation Realtor.com First USA Intuit DLJdirect iOwn.com Bank of America BankOne Citibank Scudder Investments The Kaufmann Fund Union Bank of California **Pets, Hobbies, and Outdoors** Chipshot.com PetSmart Eastman Kodak Company L. L. Bean Mammoth Golf

Source: AOL Web site.

negative until 1997, when America Online generated $131 million from its operating activities. AOL began to record investment gains from many capital investments in strategic allies after those companies had later gone public. At year-end 1999 the company had not yet paid a dividend to its shareholders. Exhibits 5, 6, and 7 show America Online's income statements, balance sheets, and cash flow statements for 1994–99.

The Costs of Marketing, Acquiring New Subscribers, and Developing New Products

Acquiring new subscribers absorbed a sizable fraction on America Online's financial resources. In 1999 AOL's current marketing expenses were $808 million, up from $77 million in 1995. The company's marketing expenditures had amounted to as much as 28

exhibit 5   Consolidated Statements of Operations, America Online, Inc., 1994–99
(In Millions, Except Per Share Data)

	Year Ended June 30					
	1999	1998	1997	1996	1995	1994
Revenues						
Subscription services	$3,321	$2,183	$1,478	$ 992	$ 334	$ 98
Advertising, commerce and other	1000	543	308	102	50	17
Enterprise solutions	456	365	411	—	—	—
Total revenues	4,777	3,091	2,197	1,094	394	116
Costs and expenses						
Cost of revenues	2,657	1,811	1,162	627	230	69
Sales and marketing	808	623	608	213	77	24
Write-off of deferred subscriber acquisition costs	—	(385)	—	—	—	—
Product development	286	239	195	54	14	5
General and administrative	408	328	220	110	43	14
Amortization of goodwill and other intangible assets	65	24	6	7	2	—
Acquired in-process research and development	—	94	9	17	50	—
Merger, restructuring and contract termination charges	95	75	73	—	—	—
Settlement charges	—	17	24	—	—	—
Total costs and expenses	4,319	3,211	2,682	1,029	416	112
Income (loss) from operations	458	(120)	(485)	65	(21)	4
Other income, net	638	30	10	(2)	3	2
Income (loss) before provision for income taxes	1,096	(90)	(475)	62	(21)	6
(Provision) benefit for income taxes	(334)	16	(10)	(33)	(15)	(4)
Net income (loss)	$ 762	($ 74)	($ 485)	$ 30	($ 36)	$ 2
Earnings (loss) per share						
Earnings (loss) per share—diluted	$ 0.60	($ 0.08)	($ 0.58)	$ 0.28	($0.51)	$0.03
Earnings (loss) per share—basic	$ 0.73	($ 0.08)	($ 0.58)	$ 0.28	($0.51)	$0.03
Weighted average shares outstanding—diluted	1,277	925	838	108	70	69
Weighted average shares outstanding—basic	1,041	925	838	108	70	69

Source: America Online annual reports.

percent of revenues in prior years but totaled less than 20 percent in 1999. Prior to 1997, these expenses did not include all that the company actually spent in soliciting new members. As noted earlier, AOL employed an accounting practice whereby it treated a large portion of the solicitation costs of new subscribers (including the costs of printing, producing, and shipping starter kits; obtaining mailing lists of qualified prospects; and creating direct response advertising) as a capital investment rather than a current expense; it then depreciated these "capital investments" over the next 12 to 18 months. In 1996, AOL spent approximately $275 million on subscriber acquisition efforts that it classified as capital investment. Moreover, company accountants opted in 1996 to increase the time frame over which AOL amortized subscriber acquisition costs from 12 and 18 months to 24 months, a change that had the effect of increasing the company's reported 1996 earnings by $48 million (actions and outcomes that were described in the *exhibit 6*   Consolidated Balance Sheets, America Online, Inc., 1998–99 (In Millions)

	June 30	
	1999	1998
Assets		
Current assets		
Cash and cash equivalents	$ 887	$ 677
Short-term investments	537	146
Trade accounts receivable, less allowances of $54 and $34, respectively	323	192
Other receivables	79	93
Prepaid expenses and other current assets	153	155
Total current assets	1,979	1,263
Property and equipment at cost, net	657	503
Other assets		
Investments including available-for-sale securities	2,151	531
Product development costs, net	100	88
Goodwill and other intangible assets, net	454	472
Other assets	7	17
Total assets	$5,348	$2,874
Liabilities and Stockholders' Equity		
Current liabilities		
Trade accounts payable	$ 74	$ 120
Other accrued expenses and liabilities	795	461
Deferred revenue	646	420
Accrued personnel costs	134	78
Deferred network services credit	76	76
Total current liabilities	1,725	1,155
Long-term liabilities		
Notes payable	348	372
Deferred revenue	30	71
Other liabilities	15	7
Deferred network services credit	197	273
Total liabilities	2,315	1,878
Stockholders' equity		
Preferred stock, $.01 par value; 5 million shares authorized, no shares issued and outstanding at June 30, 1999 and 1998, respectively	—	—
Common stock, $.01 par value, 1.8 billion shares authorized; 1,100,893,933 and 973,150,052 shares issued and outstanding at June 30, 1999 and 1998, respectively.	11	10
Additional paid-in capital	2,703	1,431
Accumulated comprehensive income—unrealized gain on available-for-sale securities, net	168	145
Retained earnings (accumulated deficit)	151	(590)
Total stockholders' equity	3,033	996
Total liabilities and stockholders' equity	$5,348	$2,874

Source: America Online annual reports.

***exhibit* 7**   Consolidated Statements of Cash Flows, America Online, Inc., 1997–99
(In Millions)

	June 30		
	1999	**1998**	**1997**
Cash flows from operating activities			
Net income (loss)	$762	($74)	($485)
Adjustments to reconcile net income (loss) to net cash provided by operating activities			
Write-off of deferred subscriber acquisition costs	—	—	385
Non-cash restructuring charges	7	32	22
Depreciation and amortization	298	191	93
Amortization of deferred network services credit	(76)	(32)	—
Charge for acquired in-process research and development	—	94	9
Compensatory stock options	20	33	2
Deferred income taxes	334	(18)	(1)
Gain on sale of investments	(564)	(28)	—
Amortization of subscriber acquisition costs	—	—	59
Changes in assets and liabilities, net of the effects of acquisitions and dispositions			
Trade accounts receivable	(123)	78	(122)
Other receivables	12	(67)	2
Prepaid expenses and other current assets	(63)	28	(50)
Deferred subscriber acquisition costs	—	—	(130)
Other assets	4	(5)	(15)
Investments including available-for-sale securities	(16)	(40)	(30)
Accrued expenses and other current liabilities	319	141	130
Deferred revenue and other liabilities	185	104	262
Total adjustments	337	511	616
Net cash provided by operating activities	1,099	437	131
Cash flows from investing activities			
Purchase of property and equipment	(301)	(384)	(230)
Product development costs	(49)	(51)	(57)
Proceeds from sale of investments	769	87	26
Purchase of investments, including available-for-sale securities	(2,289)	(166)	(208)
Maturity of investments	133	103	83
Net (payments) proceeds for acquisitions/dispositions of subsidiaries	30	(98)	30
Other investing activities	(69)	(22)	(11)
Net cash used in investing activities	(1,776)	(531)	(367)
Cash flows from financing activities			
Proceeds from issuance of common and preferred stock, net	836	141	251
Proceeds from sale and leaseback of property and equipment	8	70	20
Principal and accrued interest payments on line of credit and debt	(22)	(2)	(22)
Proceeds from line of credit and issuance of debt	65	371	1
Net cash provided by financing activities	887	580	250
Net increase in cash and cash equivalents	210	486	14
Cash and cash equivalents at beginning of year	677	191	177
Cash and cash equivalents at end of year	$887	$677	$191
Supplemental cash flow information			
Cash paid during the year for interest	$17	$10	$2

Source: America Online annual reports.

notes to the company's financial statements in its 1996 annual report). This change came on the heels of AOL's having agreed a few months earlier, following a review by the Securities and Exchange Commission, to reduce the portion of member-acquisition expenses it capitalized. An article in *Business Week* indicated that the company's practice of treating subscriber acquisition expenses as a capital investment instead of as a current expense allowed the company to report a loss of only $35.8 million in 1995 instead of a loss of $84.5 million.[11]

In 1999, America Online's product development expenses were more than $400 million, up from $14.3 million in 1995. These costs included amortization charges for software development (e.g., for AOL 5.0), new content features, and other R&D activities relating to improving the content and functionality of the company's online services. AOL was endeavoring to position itself as a catalyst of innovation, not only investing in original content but also promoting new kinds of interactive programming and building previously unimagined services.

Even though AOL promoted innovation, its central focus in the development of new software was ease of use. AOL was very careful to design its service for people with modest computer skills rather than those who were technically oriented. In fact, most programmers and other computer professionals used a service other than AOL to connect to the Internet. Bob Pittman, the company's chief operating officer, commented on AOL's philosophy concerning innovation in its software: "Well, ours has never been a technology service. AOL always has been focused on the mass market. I think that was the genius of Steve Case. Very early on, when it was just computer users online, he said, 'You know what, we're going to build a service for the mass market.' Now that the mass market is coming, AOL is the obvious choice. It's easy to use, understandable, and things are there that real people are interested in, not just people interested in computers."[12]

AOL's Efforts to Become Profitable

Beginning in 1996, AOL investors began to call for the company to earn a profit. The company's revenues had grown at a dramatic rate, to more than $1 billion, but AOL was still recording significant losses. Steve Case saw that he was having difficulty reining in expenses (the company was adding about 200 new employees on average each month) while trying to increase the company's services and chose to bring in someone to help him keep AOL's daily operations under control. He recruited an executive from FedEx, William Razzouk, to become the company's president and chief operating officer (COO) in April 1996. However, Razzouk's command-and-control management style clashed with Case's style and with AOL's laid-back, collegial culture, and Razzouk abruptly resigned after four months on the job.

In October 1996, Case recruited Robert W. Pittman to pursue Wall Street's vision of a profitable AOL. Pittman had been a college dropout who, at age 24, helped develop The Movie Channel and co-founded MTV shortly after The Movie Channel merged with Showtime. Pittman later helped launch VH-1 and Nick at Nite before turning around Time Warner's Six Flags theme-park business. Pittman met Case in 1995, when as head of Century 21 Realty he began discussions with AOL to provide an online site for the company's real estate listings.

---

[11]Ibid., p. 81.

[12]Interview with CNNfn, *In the Game,* March 31, 1998.

With Pittman as COO, the company scaled back its growth-at-any-price strategy and launched a reorganization that put Pittman in charge of AOL, CompuServe, and AOL Studios, the unit that developed AOL's proprietary content. With all three of AOL's operating units reporting to him, Pittman concentrated on improving efficiencies throughout the company while growing revenues beyond subscription fees. Pittman quickly cut costs by cutting back the company's mailings of sign-up disks and called for the sale of the company's data network to WorldCom. The result was a decrease in the cost to sign up a new customer from $375 in 1996 to $77 in 1998. The sale of AOL's data network reduced the cost of connecting a member from 90 cents per hour prior to the sale to 45 cents per hour in 1998.

Pittman also brought in substantial new revenues from e-commerce ventures and advertising. Much of AOL's e-commerce revenue came not from goods sold by AOL, but from fees charged to companies wanting to sell their merchandise or services to AOL subscribers. Tel-Save paid AOL a $100 million up-front fee plus ongoing commissions for the exclusive right to offer long-distance services to AOL customers, and eBay paid AOL a $75 million fee to link its online auctions to AOL's online service. Some companies offered AOL an equity stake in their company in lieu of up-front fees. Pittman was named as one of *Business Week*'s "25 Top Executives" in 1998.

AOL's Principles Regarding the Internet

Since the use of the Internet and online services was growing at dramatic rates and the interactive medium was growing in very unpredictable ways, AOL managers believed that it was important for the company to develop principles to guide public policy regarding the Internet. The company stated four basic principles: (1) Internet policy should foster individual choice and empowerment in the economic and social dimensions; (2) public policies should be led by the market and the industry rather than by a government gatekeeper; (3) where government involvement was determined to be necessary, policies should be technologically neutral and nondiscriminatory; and (4) policies should be designed to ensure that all segments of society and all countries of the world had access to the potential of the new medium.

AOL believed that adherence to these principles was essential if society was to realize the full benefit of the Internet. AOL believed too that there were sizable economic incentives to promote restrained public policy related to the Internet. In 2000, 200 million people were connected to the Internet and some estimates suggested that there might eventually be 1 billion Internet users worldwide. U.S. consumers purchased $13.6 billion in goods and services online in 1998, and the U.S. Commerce Department projected that the Internet would account for $300 billion worth of business-to-business commerce and that 500,000 small businesses would use the Internet by 2002. The U.S. Chamber of Commerce projected that by 2006 almost one-half of U.S. workers would be employed by industries that produce information technology or are intensive users of it. AOL also pointed to educational benefits of the Internet and its use to promote citizen involvement in the political process as reasons to support its principles guiding public policy concerning interactive services.

Steve Case believed that companies like AOL could police themselves and could shape the interactive medium to serve the public interest:

> Many of the policy issues are ultimately centered on creating a better environment for online consumers. Safeguarding children, protecting privacy, enforcing security and ensuring fair tax treatment of online purchases are just some of the issues on which America Online

has led coalitions of industry representatives, consumer advocates, and government officials to build effective, mediumwide solutions.

At the same time, we are working hard to maximize the medium's positive impact. For example, we will soon introduce exciting new tools that will enable people to donate their time or money online and connect to hundreds of thousands of nonprofit organizations and charities. We are also working to use this medium to reinvigorate the political process and help more people connect more easily with government services, and have invested significantly in learning achievement. Perhaps the most important is our work on bridging the "digital divide" between the information technology "haves" and "have-nots" so the interactive revolution does not leave behind the very populations who need the empowerment of these tools the most.[13]

In a speech to the National School Boards Association, Case discussed how the Internet presented a challenge to educators and how it could improve the delivery of education:

Kids live in Internet time. They want to learn in Internet time. Which means we have to teach classes and run schools in Internet time. And that's not easy. In fact, it's exhausting. This new medium is pushing us faster and further than anything we've ever confronted.

The good news is that we have time to respond, because we're only at the very beginning stages in the development of this interactive world. But even in its early days, this medium holds the promise of reforming education and giving our kids the tools to learn throughout their lives. It can help us make the transition from classroom-centered, location-specific, age-based schooling . . . to anytime, anywhere, any-age lifelong learning that's continuous, customized, and connected.

Such a transition is a major break from the past. For most of this century, schools have run on the same principles that guided the Industrial Age—mass production, standardization, and one best way.

That system worked well in its time, but it just won't do anymore. The world moves too fast. Along with passing on the substance of the lesson, we've got to sharpen the very skill of learning.

The Internet can help us forge this broader reform in education. It can help us transition from childhood schooling that begins and ends . . . to lifelong learning that goes and goes.

From an education system with the institution at the center . . . to a system where learning is flexible enough to be truly centered on the child. From the old regime of command and control . . . to a new interactive ethic of nurture and guide. We can use the Internet to do some amazing things, to stretch our kids' minds, expand their possibilities, and prepare them for life in a connected society.[14]

The AOL Foundation

America Online created the AOL Foundation in October 1997 with a $150 million endowment from Steve Case. The foundation's mission was to leverage the power of the emerging global medium to improve the lives of families and children and to empower the disadvantaged. In 1998 and 1999 the foundation addressed the "digital divide" through research initiatives, partnerships, and projects. The AOL Foundation saw that it was necessary to work with others in the industry, the policy community, and the nonprofit community to ensure that Americans of all backgrounds had the opportunity

---

[13]America Online, Inc., 1999 annual report.

[14]Speech given to the National School Boards Association, 13th Annual Technology and Learning Conference, Dallas, Texas, November 11, 1999.

to share in the economic and social benefits of the Internet. The foundation believed that such collaborative efforts could expand entrepreneurial opportunities in communities that lack access to capital; foster better understanding of cultural and religious differences; and provide rural citizens with greater access to goods, information, and medical services. The foundation also focused on using online services to foster civic engagement, educational applications, health care information, and philanthropy.

In an April 2000 speech to newspaper executives from around the country, Steve Case commented on the need for organizations like the AOL Foundation to address the digital divide:

> There has always been a gap between the "haves" and the "have-nots" in our society. The question we face today is whether the Internet is going to widen that gap or close it. As you know, there is a growing divide between people who have access to the new technology and those who don't—a divide that breaks along many fault lines, including education, income, race, and geography.
>
> Seventy-five percent of households with incomes over $75,000 own computers, yet only 10 percent of our poorest families do—an unacceptable situation when more than 60 percent of all new jobs will require high-tech skills by 2002.
>
> But we can do something about it. Giving young people the tools to reach their dreams is not a job any one person or entity can or should do alone—not parents, not teachers, not community leaders, not businesses, not government. It's something we have to do together—joining our resources and expertise, sharing the things we know can work and applying those ideas to existing programs—working from the top down and the bottom up.
>
> I am especially proud of the role we are playing at AOL to help launch PowerUp, a unique public-private partnership to create a network of community technology centers that teach young people the skills they need—and that give them the guidance they need—to make the most of their potential.
>
> We have to keep asking ourselves: What are the concrete steps we must take to ensure that the benefits of the Internet Revolution are equally shared, leaving no community or country behind in the Internet Century?[15]

STEVE CASE'S VISION FOR THE INTERNET AND INTERACTIVITY BEYOND 2000

Steve Case believed that the Internet and interactivity had already created a great deal of change in the way people communicated, conducted business, stayed abreast of the latest news around the world, and spent leisure hours. In a letter to AOL shareholders, published in the company's 1999 annual report, Steve Case made the following comments about the future of the Internet and interactivity:

> The interactive medium has already changed our lives in remarkable ways, and it will become even more central to people and businesses around the world with the dawn of the new millennium.
>
> The interactive experience is becoming increasingly embedded in consumers' everyday routines—everything from communicating, shopping, and keeping informed to investing, learning and just having fun. And nearly every company already has, or will, put its business online—seeking the benefits of the medium's efficiencies, convenience and reach.

---

[15]Speech given at ASNE Conference, April 14, 2000.

Today, we are seeing the next wave of Internet growth on the horizon. Interactivity is fast moving beyond PCs tethered to narrowband telephone lines. Consumers will have the ability to connect anytime from anywhere, as well as enjoy robust new high-speed online services, from interactive TV and handheld devices to broadband access.

This new world of interactivity is driving several significant trends that we believe will define the future of the medium.

First, online consumers are demanding new interactive tools and features to enhance their online experience and make it even more convenient and valuable to everyday life.

Second, many Internet consumers are seeking to extend their interactive experience beyond the PC in an integrated, affordable, and simple way.

Third, doing business and shopping online will become even more efficient and convenient as e-commerce reaches the next level of success.

Fourth, Internet use worldwide will explode with the increasing availability of connected devices.

Finally, as the medium becomes more central to people's lives, it will become increasingly critical that we build public trust and ensure that the medium serves the public interest.

Case went on to summarize what the company had done to position itself to be interactivity leader of the future. He listed the following AOL actions to improve and enhance consumers' online experiences:

Central to fulfilling these demands are the diverse acquisitions we made over the past year to broaden and enhance our offerings. Several of our newly acquired companies are helping us build usage around key functions or categories, creating deeper and stickier relationships with our members and other Internet consumers.

We have moved quickly to maximize Netscape's talent and technologies. For example, Netscape's expertise has enabled the development of an enhanced Web-based Quick Checkout "wallet" technology. And, with more than 17 million registrants, the addition of Netscape Netcenter to our portfolio of brands now gives the company the #1 reach in the work and home audiences.

We have positioned CompuServe as our value brand to enlarge the overall online audience by attracting price-sensitive consumers. We are continuing to grow ICQ and extend its communications functionality with services like free Web-based e-mail and ICQ-branded Internet telephony for its 38 million registrants. Also, Digital City offers local content in 60 markets nationwide, and has more than five million unique visitors monthly.

Steve Case went on to describe AOL's extension of interactivity beyond the PC:

We believe consumers are looking to AOL to pull all these interactive experiences together into a seamless and convenient package that requires, for example, just one e-mail address for any device or network. Over the past year, we extended our "AOL Anywhere" strategy with critical alliances and investments in interactive television, handheld connected devices and broadband connectivity.

Making real progress toward developing AOL TV for launch in the coming year, we concluded key partnering agreements with Philips Electronics for advanced set-top boxes enabled for AOL TV's Liberate Technologies for a comprehensive software platform; and Gemstar International for electronic programming guides, which will be the cornerstone of the AOL TV experience. We also formed a strategic alliance with Hughes Electronics to offer AOL TV to Hughes's DIRECTV subscribers.

Taking the first step to extend AOL-branded interconnectivity to handheld devices, we are making AOL e-mail available via personal organizers and we are exploring ways to develop a more full-featured version of AOL software for other portable devices.

Case also discussed how the company was becoming a key player in e-commerce solutions and generating revenues from its own e-commerce initiatives:

During fiscal 1999, we signed 58 multiyear advertising and commerce agreements, each worth in excess of $1 million. In the Internet's largest ever advertising and marketing partnership, we reached a five-year agreement worth up to $500 million with First USA.

Designed to enhance the shopping experience across our brands, our Shop@AOL initiative is setting a new industry standard for consumer convenience. Shop@AOL provides seamless integration to our commerce partners' sites and new Web-based tools to help them promote their products even more effectively on the service.

The Netscape-Sun Alliance has introduced "iPlanet" as its new product brand for its comprehensive, easy-to-deploy Internet infrastructure and e-commerce solutions. By fiscal year's end, more than 300 companies, including over half of the Fortune 100, turned to the Alliance to help put their businesses online.

AMERICA ONLINE IN 2000

In 2000, AOL was growing closer (1) to being able to offer its services worldwide because of the alliances forged in 1999 with satellite, telecommunications, and technology firms and (2) to realizing its mission of building "a global medium as central to people's lives as the telephone or television . . . and even more valuable." AOL was accessible to subscribers and Internet users through its Interactive Services Group, Interactive Properties, Netscape Enterprise Group, and AOL International.

Interactive Services Group

AOL was America Online's flagship online service and the world's leading interactive service. AOL's content allowed members to spend 56 million hours collectively each month connecting in 15,000 chat rooms devoted to topics like politics, parenting, travel, the arts, romance, finance, and sports. AOL also provided its members with up-to-the-minute, in-depth news coverage. Subscribers could also read the latest entertainment and sports news on AOL. The company's news-related content partners included CBS, National Public Radio, the Associated Press, the *New York Times, Time* magazine, *People* magazine, and E! Online.

AOL's personal finance content allowed members to receive stock quotes, obtain the latest business news from Bloomberg News and *Financial Times,* and review financial analysis reports from TheStreet.com, The Motley Fool, and Morningstar. AOL customers could also trade stocks with DLJdirect, E*Trade, TD Waterhouse, and Ameritrade and could use the banking services of Bank of America, Citibank, Wells Fargo, Union Bank of California, and BankOne.

AOL also provided extensive health care information to its subscribers through partnerships with drkoop.com, the Mayo Clinic, AmericasDoctor.com, and other medical information services. Travel information and booking could be done online with AOL. AOL also had a special Kids Only section and hosted live events with such special guests as General Colin Powell, Mick Jagger, Rosie O'Donnell, and Michael Jordan.

AOL's e-mail service was thought to be among the easiest to use and was featured in a 1998 Warner Bros. film, *You've Got Mail.* Members could conduct spelling and grammar checks and customize e-mails with a variety of fonts and colors, photos, or hyperlinks. AOL's Instant Message feature allowed users to tell when friends, family members, or co-workers were online to receive and send real-time private messages. AOL members could also shop at what Forrester Research called the "Internet's Miracle Mile" via the Shop@AOL feature. AOL 5.0, introduced in 1999, allowed AOL subscribers to keep an online calendar, customize their AOL Welcome screen, and send and receive photos with "You've Got Pictures."

CompuServe, AOL's value-priced online service, had approximately 2 million members worldwide in early 2000. CompuServe lacked many of the features offered with AOL, but did offer subscribers 30 content channels, a Shop@CompuServe site that included many of the same partners found at Shop@AOL, and up to 100 free real-time stock quotes per day.

America Online's Netscape NetCenter came about through its acquisition of Netscape in 1999 and significantly increased AOL's daytime traffic by capturing complementary audiences and broadening AOL's reach both at home and at work. NetCenter was one of the most visited sites on the Internet during daytime hours, and 74 percent of NetCenter visitors went online every day. NetCenter featured a customizable My Netscape start page, numerous search engines, AOL's Instant Messenger, WebMail, a Web calendar, a Web site creation service, an address book, and an Internet telephony service. All NetCenter features were available to registrants free of charge. Netscape Communicator 4.7 also included an integrated Shop@Netscape button that linked users with hundreds of merchants.

AOL.com offered all Internet users, whether or not they were AOL subscribers, content, search tools like AOL NetFind, AOL NetMail, and a personalized news service AOL Instant Messenger (AIM), also available at AOL.com, was the most widely used instant messaging system on the Internet. AIM 2.0 also allowed users to search the Web and yellow and white pages, and to complete file transfers. AIM was also available through co-branding agreements with Apple Computer, Mindspring Enterprises, Earthlink Network, and Juno Online services.

Interactive Properties Group

America Online's Interactive Properties Group included the company's brands that operated across multiple platforms. Digital City, which provided content of local interest for 60 U.S. cities, was accessible through AOL's online service, AOL.com, NetCenter, MCI WorldCom Internet, and its Web site (www.digitalcity.com). Digital City partnered with leading local media companies to deliver interesting local content and was named "1999's Best City Guide" by an independent panel of judges.

ICQ (short for "I seek you") was an easy-to-use combination of e-mail, chat, and Internet telephony. Like e-mail, ICQ allowed users to exchange messages with other ICQ users, and like chat, ICQ messages appeared instantly. But ICQ users claimed that the service was more like using a telephone than using e-mail or chat. When ICQ users logged on, they would be immediately notified who among their correspondents was online. All of a user's correspondents would see any typed instant messages unless a private message was requested with a single correspondent. ICQ was most popular with Internet users seeking communications that were faster and more efficient than e-mail. ICQ was used by college students to exchange notes in Internet-wired classrooms, and some companies used ICQ for online training exercises for their employees. More than two-thirds of ICQ users were under the age of 35 and lived outside the United States.

MovieFone users could purchase movie tickets through a telephone service or by visiting www.moviefone.com. The Web site also provided extensive movie information, including reviews, movie trailers, theater locations, and show times. MovieFone services covered approximately 27,000 screens in 1,000 cities and had been used by 20 percent of U.S. moviegoers. AOL also could make music available over the Internet with its 1999 acquisition of Spinner Networks and Nullsoft. Spinner's Web site featured over 100 music channels, containing more than 175,000 songs, and allowed listeners to read information about a song while it was playing. The Spinner Web site also provided links for real-time listener feedback and allowed users to purchase music online. Nullsoft was the producer of the Winamp MP3 player and ShoutCast, a streaming MP3 system that allowed users to broadcast their own music programs over the Internet.

The Netscape Enterprise Group

America Online's Sun-Netscape alliance allowed the company to provide e-commerce solutions for the Internet economy. America Online offered end-to-end solutions, including hardware, software, operating system, consumer access, and content through its iPlanet branded products. Its e-commerce software provided calendar and message services, security services such as certificate management and firewalls, remote access, online business-to-business transactions, procurement, and sales and billing processing. In early 2000 more than one-half of Fortune 100 firms and 40 to 50 percent of the highest-traffic sites on the Internet were powered by America Online's e-commerce services.

AOL International

America Online had entered more than 100 international markets in Europe, Asia, Latin America, and Australia. America Online had entered into strategic alliances as part of its international strategy to acquire the resources necessary to provide local content in each specific country market. Its relationship with Bertelsmann allowed it to bring AOL Europe and CompuServe Europe to the United Kingdom, Australia, Austria, Germany, the Netherlands, Sweden, and Switzerland, and to provide local content to its customers in those countries. AOL Europe intended to enter more European markets in 2000, and America Online also planned to launch a new Netscape Online service in the United Kingdom in 2000.

In 1999 America Online began service in Hong Kong through a distribution agreement with China Internet Company, which was responsible for producing both Chinese and English-language content for the Hong Kong market. AOL also purchased an equity interest in China.com to expand its commitments in the region. AOL's joint venture with the Cisneros Group, a Latin American publisher, allowed it to bring service to Latin American markets in 1998. AOL Brazil was launched at the end of 1999.

AOL'S PROPOSED MERGER WITH TIME WARNER, INC.: A NEW ERA AND A NEW DIRECTION

The January 10, 2000, announcement by America Online and Time Warner executives of a $156 billion agreement to merge AOL's Internet franchises, technology and infrastructure, and e-commerce capabilities with Time Warner's vast array of media, entertainment, and news brands and broadband delivery systems stunned the business world. The *exhibit 8*   Selected Financial and Operating Highlights, Time-Warner, Inc., 1995–99 (In Millions, Except Per Share Data)

	Year Ended June 30				
	1999	1998	1997	1996	1995
Income statement data					
Total revenues	$27,333	$14,582	$13,294	$10,064	$8,067
Business segment operating income	6,035	1,496	1,271	966	697
Net income	1,948	168	246	(191)	(166)
Preferred dividend requirements	(52)	(540)	(319)	(257)	(52)
Income (loss) per common share					
Net income (loss) per share—diluted	$1.43	($0.31)	($0.13)	($1.04)	($0.57)
Net income (loss) per share—basic	$1.51	($0.31)	($0.13)	($1.04)	($0.57)
Weighted average shares outstanding					
Diluted	1,398.3	1,194.7	1,135.4	431.2	383.8
Basic	1,267.0	1,194.7	1,135.4	431.2	383.8
Balance sheet data					
Total assets	$51,239	$31,640	$34,163	$35,064	22,132
Total debt	18,105	17,528	11,841	12,724	9,941
Stockholders' equity	9,713	8,852	9,356	9,502	3,667

Note: Since 1993, Time Warner had not consolidated certain parts of its entertainment operations because Media One, which owned a portion of these properties, had rights that allowed it to participate in the management of Time Warner Entertainment's businesses; these rights were subsequently modified as part of Media One's completion of its acquisition by AT&T. Thus, starting in 1999, Time Warner consolidated the Entertainment Group into its financial statements. This is what accounts for the substantial difference in revenues and income between 1998 and 1999.

Source: Time Warner, Inc., annual reports.

agreement to create AOL Time Warner represented the largest merger in history to date and would create the world's first fully integrated media and communications company. Exhibit 8 presents a summary of Time Warner, Inc.'s financial performance between 1995 and 1999. Exhibit 9 presents an overview of Time Warner's company history, its business operations, and a brief biographical sketch of its key officers. Statistics related to the size and scope of AOL Time Warner's operations are presented in Exhibit 10.

America Online and Time Warner executives made the following comments regarding the benefits of the proposed merger.

- **Steve Case:**

  This is an historic moment in which new media has truly come of age. We've always said that America Online's mission is to make the Internet as central to people's lives as the telephone and television, and even more valuable, and this is a once-in-a-lifetime opportunity to turn this promise into reality. We're kicking off the new century with a unique new company that has unparalleled assets and the ability to have a profoundly positive impact on society. By joining forces with Time Warner, we will fundamentally change the way people get information, communicate with others, buy products, and are entertained—providing far-reaching benefits to our customers and shareholders.

exhibit 9   Profile of Time Warner, Co-Chairman and CEO Gerald Levin, and Co-Chairman R. E. (Ted) Turner.

Company History

In 2000 Time Warner, Inc.'s portfolio of businesses included cable television networks, cable movie channels, movie production, magazines, book publishing, syndicated television production, cartoon production, music production, local news channels, and cable systems. The company's history dated to *Time* magazine's founding in 1923 by Henry Luce. Time, Inc., expanded beyond print publications in 1989 when it acquired Warner Bros. film production and cable assets in 1989 and was renamed Time Warner. Time Warner acquired Ted Turner's Turner Broadcasting System, Inc., for $7 billion; Turner's company consisted of a variety of cable television channels (TBS SuperStation, CNN, TNT, the Cartoon Network, and Turner Classic Movies); MGM's extensive library of 3,700-plus films; and New Line and Castle Rock movie production companies.

Time Warner struggled throughout most the 1990s, not earning a profit until 1997. However, the company's cash flows and earnings before interest, taxes, depreciation, and amortization (EDITDA) were strong enough for the company to fund its portfolio and improve its competitive strength in most of its businesses. Time Warner's culture prior to its merger with Turner Broadcasting System in 1996 placed little emphasis on cost controls with the company's executives and entertainment personalities enjoying such lavish perks as private jet travel to almost any desired destination. Upon the completion of the merger, Ted Turner became the Time Warner's vice chairman; he reportedly pushed to cut Time Warner's expenses and continued to exercise influence over the Turner Entertainment division of Time Warner. Most analysts believed that Turner's influence had contributed greatly to Time Warner's improved financial performance and growing strength in its entertainment brands.

Time Warner had attempted to make publishing and entertainment content available to online audiences as early as 1994, when it launched its Pathfinder Web site. Plans called for putting its entire library of magazine and book titles online, but constant strategy changes, Web page designs, and personnel shifts made Pathfinder a fiasco. Later, Time Warner launched an interactive TV set-top service through its cable TV subsidiary called Road Runner, but it was still in the early stages and was unprofitable. At the time of the AOL–Time Warner merger announcement, Time Warner's president Richard Parsons remarked, "We could work for a decade and maybe still not get up to a level [with AOL]."*

Time Warner Co-Chairman and CEO Gerald Levin

In 1972, Gerald Levin began his career with Time, Inc., where he helped launch HBO in 1975 and was a chief architect of the company's merger with Warner Bros. in 1989. Levin became the company's CEO in 1992 upon the death of his predecessor, Steven Ross. Time Warner experienced lackluster financial and market performance during Levin's first years as CEO, largely as a result of the fiercely competitive environment of the U.S. cable industry. Analysts and investors saw Time Warner's cable business as a drag on earnings and made repeated calls for Levin to divest the business. Gerald Levin stubbornly clung to the business, which by the late 1990s was thought to be among the most valuable assets in the company's portfolio after new legislative and technological changes had made the industry highly attractive. Levin was considered a hardworking, resilient manager with good strategy-making skills.

Time Warner Co-Chairman R. E. (Ted) Turner

R. E. (Ted) Turner began his media career in 1960 when, after leaving college without a degree, he went to work for his father's Georgia-based outdoor advertising company. At age 24, Turner found himself in charge of the business that was short of cash and $6 million in debt after his father had a breakdown and committed suicide. Within two years, Turner successfully turned around the company that sold advertising on billboards and beginning in 1970, Turner began making acquisitions. Turner first acquired two Chattanooga radio stations and an Atlanta UHF television station before launching Turner Broadcasting in 1976. Turner later launched CNN in 1979 and CNN Headline News in 1982 before purchasing the MGM's and RKO's libraries of films, television programs, and cartoons. He also purchased the Atlanta Braves Major League Baseball franchise and the Atlanta Hawks (a National Basketball Association franchise). Turner Broadcasting System's newly acquired programming allowed it to broadcast live sports programs and TV reruns, cartoons, and movies on TBS, charge royalties for broadcasts of the programs by other networks, and provide content for the launch of the Cartoon Network, TNT, and Turner Classic Movies. When Turner Broadcasting System was acquired by Time Warner in 1996, Ted Turner became Time Warner's largest shareholder, holding approximately 12 percent of the company's shares. Ted Turner was also named co-chairman of Time Warner and was involved in key management decisions at the company.

exhibit 9   (*continued*)

Composition of Time Warner's Business Units

1999 Financial Performance Summary, by Business Segment

Business Segment	Revenues	Operating Income	EBITDA
Cable networks	$ 6.1 billion	$ 1.2 billion	$ 1.4 billion
Publishing	4.7 billion	627 million	679 million
Music	3.8 billion	179 million	452 million
Filmed entertainment	8.1 billion	796 million	997 million
Broadcasting (WB Network)	384 million	(96) million	(92) million
Cable systems	5.4 billion	3.4 billion	3.9 billion

Turner Entertainment Group

TBS Superstation (most-watched cable TV network)

TNT (available in 75 percent of U.S. homes)

Cartoon Network (50 million-plus U.S. subscribers, plus 20 million foreign subscribers in 120 countries)

Turner Classic Movies (30 million U.S. subscribers)

Atlanta Braves (Major League baseball franchise)

Atlanta Hawks (NBA franchise)

Atlanta Thrashers (NHL franchise)

World Championship Wrestling

Goodwill Games

New Line Cinema

Fine Line Features

CNN News Group (more than 75 million U.S. subscribers; reaches nearly 150 million households in 212 countries; more than 1 billion people worldwide have access to a CNN service)

Home Box Office (34.6 million U.S. subscribers and 12 million foreign subscribers)

HBO

Cinemax

Publishing Business Segment

Magazines (32 publications with combined readership of 130 million)

Time

Fortune

Sports Illustrated

People

Entertainment Weekly

Life

Money

Southern Living

Southern Accents

Cooking Light

Parenting

Health

20 others

Book-of-the-Month Club

(*continued*)

exhibit 9   (*concluded*)

Warner Books
Time-Life Books
Sunset Books (a publisher)
Oxmoor House (a publisher)

Filmed Entertainment Business Group
Warner Bros. motion pictures (5,700 full-length and feature films and 13,500 animated titles)
Warner Bros. television series (32,000 episodes of various programs)
Castle Rock motion pictures
New Line Cinema
Telepictures Productions
Warner Bros. Television Animation
The WB Network
Hanna-Barbera Studios

Music Business Segment
Warner Music Group (5 studios, over 1,000 recording artists, 1 million music copyrights, 20 percent market share of U.S. album sales, world's most diversified and vertically integrated music company)
The Atlantic Group music production
Elektra Entertainment Group
Sire Records Group
Warner Bros. Records
Warner Music International
Columbia House Records (joint venture with Sony)

Cable Systems Business Segment
Time Warner Cable (this division had 100,000-plus subscribers in each of 34 areas of the United States and served 12.4 million homes)
Road Runner (a jointly owned high-speed online service with 320,000-plus customers and approximately 10,000 new customers being added weekly)
Local news channels (a total of 4)

*"AOL, Time Warner Set Plan to Link in Mammoth Merger," *The Wall Street Journal Interactive Edition,* January 11, 2000.

- **Gerald Levin, Chairman and CEO of Time Warner:**
  This strategic combination with AOL accelerates the digital transformation of Time Warner by giving our creative and content businesses the widest possible canvas. The digital revolution has already begun to create unprecedented and instantaneous access to every form of media and to unleash immense possibilities for economic growth, human understanding, and creative expression. AOL Time Warner will lead this transformation, improving the lives of consumers worldwide.

- **Bob Pittman, AOL's president:**
  The value of this merger lies not only in what it is today but in what it will be in the future. We believe that AOL Time Warner will provide companies worldwide with a convenient, one-stop way to put advertising and commerce online as well as take advantage of the best in traditional marketing. We will accelerate the development of Time Warner's cable broadband assets by bringing AOL's hallmark ease-of-use to this platform. We expect America Online to help drive the growth of cable broadband audiences, and we will use our combined infrastructure and cross-promotional strengths to enhance the growth and development of both America Online and Time Warner brands around the world.

exhibit 10   Combined AOL–Time Warner Statistics

Selected financials*	
Revenue	$32.8 billion
EBITDA	7.5 billion
Net income	2.4 billion
Cash and cash equivalents	3.7 billion
Long-term debt	19.8 billion
Employees	82,100
Customer relationships	
Online subscribers	24 million
Magazine subscribers	25.4 million
Cable TV network subscribers	73 million
ICQ, AOL Instant Messenger, and Netscape NetCenter registrants	107 million

*Based on the combined year-end 1999 financials of each company.
Source: "The Men Who Would Be King," *Fortune,* February 7, 2000.

● **Richard Parsons, Time Warner's president:**

This is a defining event for Time Warner and America Online as well as a pivotal moment in the unfolding of the Internet age. By joining the resources and talents of these two highly creative companies, we can accelerate the development and deployment of a whole new generation of interactive services and content. The heightened competition and expanded choices this will bring about will be of great benefit to consumers. For the creative and innovative people who are the lifeblood of our companies, it means a truly exciting range of new opportunities to explore and give shape to. For our shareholders, it means we'll be able to grow in ways we couldn't have as separate companies, producing superior returns in both the short and long term.

Steve Case later further discussed the benefits of the merger and how AOL Time Warner would be positioned to lead the second Internet revolution:

One thing the last few years have made crystal clear is that in such a rapidly changing, Internet-charged economy, companies must constantly reinvent themselves to attract new customers. And today, it's not how many assets your company has, it's how you connect those assets and constantly innovate to better serve consumers.

In this new environment, it is critical to integrate the new technologies for consumers. Whether in wireless or other new markets, both individual companies and industries must build bridges between platforms, mediums, content and services—capitalizing on new synergies, creating new businesses, and taking advantage of transforming business opportunities.

That, in fact, is our game plan for AOL Time Warner. And we believe we are uniquely positioned to put it into play, for a number of reasons.

First, our combined assets are unrivaled—not only because of their range and value, but because of the way they fit together like pieces of a puzzle. From the world's most popular media, Internet and communications brands and properties, to our technological expertise and infrastructure, we are poised to lead the next wave of growth.

Second, we have strong, sticky relationships with our customers, including more than 110 million paying subscribers between the two companies. In fact, our combined brands touch consumers more than 2.5 billion times monthly, all around the world.

Third, our combined resources give us the strength to take full advantage of new opportunities. With significant revenues, critical strategic partnerships, a world-class operational team, management vision, and a deep talent pool, we will drive strong and consistent growth.

Finally, we are committed to putting the interests of both our customers and shareholders first. AOL and Time Warner have always believed that the best way to return shareholder value is to bring new value into the lives of consumers.

That's what we'll do as a combined company. Just as *Time* has been a part of people's lives for 75 years, and CNN for 20, we plan to entwine our brands into the fabric of society, improving our customers' lives . . . and becoming the most valuable company in the world.[16]

Preliminary Plans of How the Merged Companies Would Operate

As part of the merger agreement announcement, the two companies said they would begin new marketing, commerce, content, and promotional agreements that would immediately expand various relationships already in place. Subsequently, AOL's online service added Time Warner content that included *InStyle* magazine, *People, Teen People,* and *Entertainment Weekly.* Time Warner's CNN.com and Entertaindom.com programming was prominently featured on various America Online services, and AOL members were given access to a wide range of Time Warner promotional music clips from Time Warner's selection of popular artists. In addition, Time Warner and AOL MovieFone participated in online–offline cross-promotion of Time Warner movies and related content, including live events.

AOL also planned to use Time Warner's broadband capabilities and content to help launch AOL Plus, AOL's broadband service scheduled for a spring 2000 release. Time Warner began making a series of special offers exclusively to AOL members that included discounts on magazine subscriptions, premium cable subscriptions, and movie passes. Time Warner began aiding AOL in building its online membership by distributing AOL disks in its Warner Bros. retail stores and including AOL trial-offer disks in promotional mailings and product shipments. AOL services such as Instant Messenger, Digital City, AOL Search, and MovieFone were to be made available to the subscribers of Road Runner, Time Warner's broadband service.

Other specific opportunities that AOL and Time Warner executives identified as revenue- and profit-enhancing synergies between the two companies included the following:

1.   Combining Time Warner's music labels with America Online's online marketing and e-commerce capacities presented opportunities for growing Time Warner's music revenues.

2.   Combining America Online's AOL TV and MovieFone with Time Warner's cable networks and Warner Bros. movies and television offered valuable programming, cross-promotional, and e-commerce opportunities.

3.   AOL's ability to use Time-Warner's broadband capabilities could expedite Internet access at high speeds via cable modem, DSL, wireless, or satellite.

4.   AOL could enhance its online news offering with content from CNN, *Time,* and local all-news channels such as NY1 News.

5.   AOL Time Warner could develop and leverage technology across all of the businesses, creating new opportunities to expand services and share infrastructure.

---

[16]Speech given at CS First Boston Global Telecom Conference, March 8, 2000.

6. AOL Time Warner could offer businesses and consumers a communications platform that combined America Online's popular instant messaging products with Time Warner's ability to offer local telephony over cable.

7. AOL could devote a large percentage of its advertising budget to Time Warner publications and broadcast media outlets.

Planned Roles of AOL Time Warner's Top Executives   Steve Case's role as AOL Time Warner's chairman of the board was to oversee the new company's technological developments and global expansion initiatives. As CEO, Gerald Levin would set the company's strategy and oversee its management. Ted Turner would have the title of vice chairman of the new company. AOL president and COO Bob Pittman and Time Warner president Richard Parsons would act as co-chief operating officers of the new company. When questioned by analysts and business reporters about whether AOL Time Warner would be top heavy, with highly-talented executives whose egos and management styles might conflict, Steve Case responded, "There's a big meal to serve."[17] He and Levin expressed the opinion that a deep, talented senior management team was a strong asset, given the ambitious objectives of the new company; the broad range of products, brands, and services to be integrated; and the fast-paced changes occurring in the marketplace.

Reaction to the Merger

Reactions to the proposed merger were quite mixed. Some analysts were unconvinced that the merger made good sense for AOL, arguing that the combined companies could not increase net income and cash flows at rates sufficient to keep AOL's stock price at its former levels, much less keep it rising. Other analysts saw the merger as beneficial, making comments like "The merger of America Online with Time Warner is one of the greatest strategic alliances in the history of the Internet."[18] Merger proponents saw very little downside risk in the merger and great potential for the new company to be a global leader in interactive communications. One communications industry analyst commented, "They don't stand to lose much. And what they stand to gain is enormous." Another characterized the merger benefit as "one plus one equals four."[19]

Skeptics predicted that AOL Time Warner would have difficulty integrating AOL's technology-oriented culture with the celebrity-based culture of Time Warner's entertainment business and the no-nonsense culture of its cable business. Negative analysis centered on the price AOL had agreed to pay for Time Warner's shares and the level of cash flows needed to justify the rising stock price to which AOL investors had become accustomed. While there were obvious synergies between the two companies (like AOL's ability to offer broadband service over Time Warner cable's cable lines, which served 20 percent of all U.S. cable subscribers), there were concerns that AOL's proposed buyout price gave Time Warner shareholders a far-too-rich 71 percent premium over its market valuation at the time of the merger agreement. The premium would

---

[17]"Investors Puzzle as AOL, Time Warner Integration Begins," The Associated Press State & Local Wire, January 12, 2000.

[18]"Fletcher and Faraday Announce Investment Opinion," PR Newswire, January 14, 2000.

[19]"AOL: You've Got Content, but Is Content Still King?" *Investors Business Daily,* January 13, 2000.

create a $150 billion goodwill charge resulting from the difference between the company's purchase price and book value that AOL would be required to write off over the next 10 years—the $15 billion per year goodwill writeoff would result in the company's reporting a loss each year for an indefinite time. This was why AOL executives and some Wall Street analysts were arguing that the profitability of the combined companies had to be viewed from the perspective of earnings before interest, taxes, depreciation, and amortization (EBITDA) rather than net earnings. But even using this measure, many analysts believed that the new AOL Time Warner would need to increase EBITDA to approximately $11 billion soon after the merger to maintain the growth of its share price.

Analysts were additionally concerned that the market would have trouble choosing earnings multiples to set a price on the new company's shares. Prior to the merger, Time Warner shares traded at a multiple of 14 times EBITDA, which was consistent with many old-economy firms, while AOL traded at 55 times EBITDA, which was consistent with the multiples of most growing new-economy firms. Some analysts were concerned that the new AOL Time Warner would become an old-economy company rather than a more competitively powerful new-economy company, since Time Warner's media properties accounted for about 80 percent of the combined company's 1999 cash flow. An analyst for J. P. Morgan Securities remarked, "That's what everyone is trying to get their arms around now: what this new entity is, and how to value it. This is going to continue to evolve. I think we need to take some time and see how things settle out."[20] Investment company Edward Jones's chief market strategist said that he no longer considered AOL a high-flying Internet company that could "grow 40 or 50 percent per year."[21]

An analyst for Merrill Lynch stated that if the new AOL could achieve $11 billion in EBITDA and a multiple of 40, the company's shares could trade as high as $90 within a year of the merger. If the market saw the company as less of an Internet company and more of a traditional media company, then an EBITDA multiple of 25 might be more realistic. The Merrill Lynch analyst stated that under the latter valuation scenario, AOL's message to shareholders would be "You've got losses."[22] AOL's shares, trading in the $90 to $95 per share range in the weeks prior to the merger, subsequently drifted downward to trade in the $55 to $65 range in March–April 2000.

In a speech given in April 2000, Steve Case reflected on AOL's growth and discussed how convergence would affect the future of the interactive medium:

> The average AOL user has gone from being online one hour a week to one hour a day. And while that's been gratifying for us and a sign of real progress, it's just scratching the surface. Having gotten a taste of interactivity, people are starting to say, "Why can't my PC be as simple and visually compelling as my TV—and why can't my TV be as powerful and flexible as my PC?" They're starting to ask, "Why can't I send instant messages from my cell phone?" And, "Why can't all these new devices work together in a way that's simple and easy to understand?"
>
> These days, we call it convergence—and it is turbo-charging a second Internet Revolution that will make the first one look almost quaint by comparison.
>
> Just think about the four devices we rely on the most in our homes: the television, the PC, the telephone, and the stereo. Already, the distinctions between these four devices are

---

[20]"Investors Puzzle as AOL, Time Warner Integration Begins.

[21]"Wall Street Doubts AOL's Staying Power after Its Merger with Time-Warner," *St. Louis Post-Dispatch,* January 15, 2000, p. B1.

[22]"Welcome to the 21st Century," *Business Week,* January 24, 2000, p. 39.

blurring—and interactivity is starting to connect all of them—giving people access to the Internet wherever they are and whenever they want.

Soon, televisions will come equipped with interactive program guides, and people will be able to bookmark their favorite programs like they bookmark their favorite Web sites. They will even be able to access interactive services like e-mail and Instant Messaging while they're watching TV—and trade comments on breaking stories or sports events.

The role of the PC will change, too. Just as the TV has evolved in many houses from a single console in the living room, people will have interactive devices all through the house. A recent AOL survey found that 52 percent of people online are already rearranging the furniture for the PC.

The fact is, the first steps of convergence already are driving consumers' expectations—and the more they get, the more they want.

The Internet has already changed the landscape of our lives. Ten years ago, the Internet was the exclusive province of researchers. Just five years ago, the World Wide Web barely existed, there was no talk about a "new economy," and, hard though it may be to believe, "e" was just the fifth letter in the alphabet.

Today, more than 200 million people are online worldwide, and if projections hold true—as I think they will—that number will more than double in the next three years. There are around 800 million Web pages, covering everything from world markets to world wrestling. And "e" has become the prefix for a massive social and economic transformation.[23]

---

[23]Speech given at ASNE Conference, April 14, 2000

case 2 The DaimlerChrysler Merger (A)

Gaining Global Competitiveness

George Rädler

International Institute for Management Development

> In interviews, the men who run Detroit's Big 3 auto companies squinted at the horizon and offered similar descriptions of the future they see, one dominated by fewer car companies and smarter, more demanding customers. Perhaps the agreement is surprising, but it is based on the certainty that what once was a comfortable, predictable, nationalistic industry is gone forever. It's a clear sign that global reach and critical mass are needed to survive the ferocious future envisioned by the auto chiefs.
> —*USA Today*, September 29, 1998

The car industry is the world's largest manufacturing industry, and the most global. Many car companies consider the world market their home market; they have production sites around the globe and produce "global cars."

However, the surprise was big when Daimler-Benz AG and Chrysler Corporation announced on May 7, 1998, their coming together in a "merger of equals." The first true transatlantic merger, the DaimlerChrysler fusion created a company with revenues of $132 billion and approximately 440,000 employees. An international union of this size was without precedent, and it set the stage for more mergers. Previously unthinkable deals, such as Ford's acquisition of Volvo and the Renault–Nissan connection, were suddenly concluded in a matter of weeks.

How could an industry of former national champions change so fast?

Car Industry at Another Breakpoint?

Since Henry Ford's invention of the conveyor belt, the automotive industry has been shaped by breakpoints. Each signals a dramatic change in the industry. After World War II, for example, Japanese carmakers were able to provide fuel-efficient cars with good price/performance ratios during the oil crises of both 1973 and 1979. Within 15 years, Japanese car companies had secured about 30 percent of the American market and a considerable share of the European market (although protectionistic measures hindered the penetration). To a lesser extent, Korean manufacturers replicated this success.

Prepared under the supervision of Professor Ulrich Steger as a basis for class discussion rather than to illustrate either effective or ineffective handling of an administrative situation.

exhibit 1   Value Chain (as a Percent of Total Price to the Consumer)

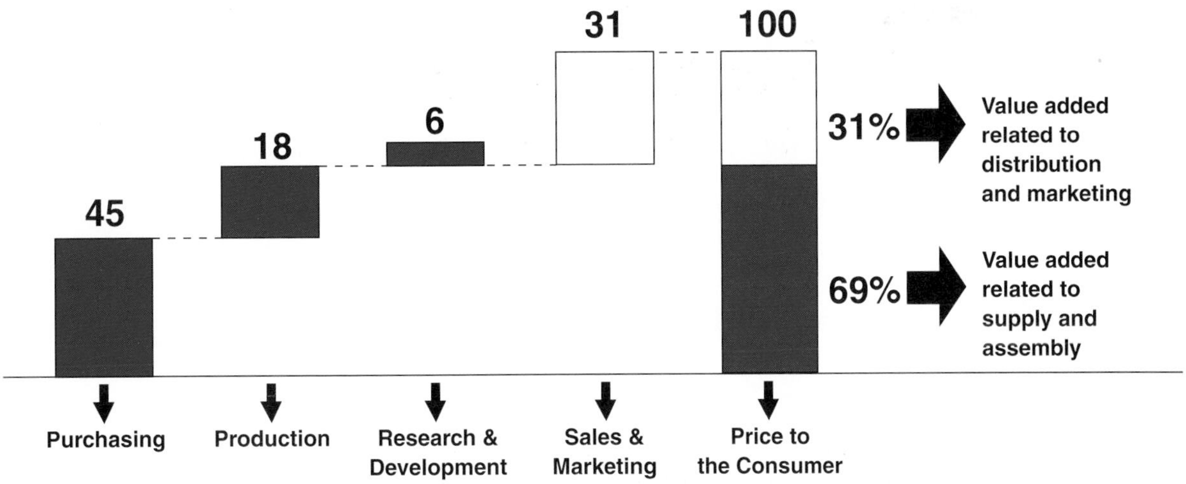

Source: McKinsey, A. T. Kearney, DaimlerChrysler, IMD Research.

Another breakpoint was the arrival of "lean manufacturing systems" around the globe. A 1990 study revealed that, in production hours per vehicle and inventory control, respectively, Japanese car plants were more than twice to more than 10 times as efficient as their European competitors. In order to survive, car companies optimized their operations within a few years. (Refer to Exhibit 1 for the value chain of a typical car company.)

The global drive for rationalization led to an estimated overcapacity of 20 to 30 percent and decreasing price levels. This overcapacity was one of the drivers of consolidation in the industry. Already, some industry experts expected only six car companies to survive this round of megamergers. They referred to this scenario as the end game.

THE WORLDWIDE MARKET FOR CARS AND COMMERCIAL VEHICLES

During the past five decades, the world population has doubled; at the same time, the number of cars on the road has increased tenfold to 500 million units (which is in addition to almost 300 million trucks and motorbikes). The global market for motor vehicles as measured by the number of registrations of both cars and commercial vehicles has grown from 46.4 million units in 1993 to 50.9 million units in 1998. (Refer to Exhibit 2 for an overview of new car registrations.)

The three main regions (North America, Western Europe, and Japan) accounted for 75 percent of all vehicles sold in 1998 and are still the most important markets. These traditional markets in the industrialized countries were saturated, and growth was expected from expansion in developing countries in Asia and Latin America. Nevertheless, economic difficulties resulted in large idle capacity in these formerly promising markets, too. Moreover, due to currency volatility, high inflation, and competitive pressure, developing markets have proven difficult.

exhibit 2 The Worldwide Market for Cars (in 000s of Units)

New registration of cars and commercial vehicles by region							Forecast	
	1993	1994	1995	1996	1997	1998	1999	2000
Cars								
Western Europe	11,451	11,934	12,021	12,790	13,408	14,341	13,800	12,700
NAFTA	9,656	10,154	9,424	9,390	9,333	9,358	8,930	8,335
South America	1,485	1,737	1,898	1,938	2,215	1,703	1,120	1,460
Japan	4,200	4,210	4,444	4,669	4,492	4,093	4,200	4,450
Asia (excluding Japan)	2,700	2,972	3,267	3,533	3,599	2,468	2,743	3,098
Eastern Europe	1,879	1,560	1,533	1,729	1.906	1,820	1,534	1,580
Other markets	988	880	1,072	1,150	1,208	1,268	1,289	1,345
Total	**32,358**	**33,447**	**33,658**	**35,199**	**36,161**	**35,051**	**33,616**	**32,968**
% change	−3.6	3.4	0.6	4.6	2.7	−3.1	−4.1	−1.9
Commercial vehicles								
Western Europe	1,328	1,421	1,528	1,647	1,766	1,958	1,854	1,750
NAFTA	6,315	7,118	7,056	7,623	8,086	8,617	8,230	8,160
South America	451	478	485	558	590	576	370	480
Japan	2,267	2,316	2,421	2,409	2,233	1,781	1,995	2,276
Asia (excluding Japan)	2,448	2,550	2,850	2,830	2,450	2,050	2,270	2,550
Eastern Europe	625	350	310	360	395	405	420	490
Other markets	634	535	618	625	632	442	450	460
Total	**14,068**	**14,767**	**15,267**	**16,052**	**16,152**	**15,829**	**15,589**	**16,166**
% change	4.5	5	3.4	5.1	0.6	−2	−1.5	3.7
Total cars and commercial vehicles	**46,426**	**48,214**	**48,925**	**51,251**	**52,313**	**50,880**	**49,205**	**49,134**
% change	−1.3	3.9	1.5	4.8	2.1	−2.7	−3.3	−0.1

Source: The Economist Intelligence Unit, April 1999.

Although Western markets were very competitive, a few profitable market niches existed; some of the highest growth rates were found in the segment for light trucks. This segment has been extremely successful in North America and to a lesser extent in Europe and Japan. (Refer to Exhibit 3 for more detailed descriptions of new segments in the U.S. auto market.) The light truck segment included:

- *Pickup trucks*—accounted for 19.1 percent of the American market, with Ford as the market leader.
- *Multipurpose vehicles (MPVs)—minivans*—invented by Chrysler; the flexibility of MPVs (spaciousness, good handling) made them extremely popular among American families (market share: 10.5 percent in 1998).
- *Sport utility vehicles (SUVs or 4 × 4s)*—represented the fastest growing segment of the U.S. market for automobiles. They reached a record market share of 18 percent of all newly sold vehicles in 1998.
- *Minicars*—mainly popular in Europe.

exhibit 3　New Segments in the U.S. Auto Market

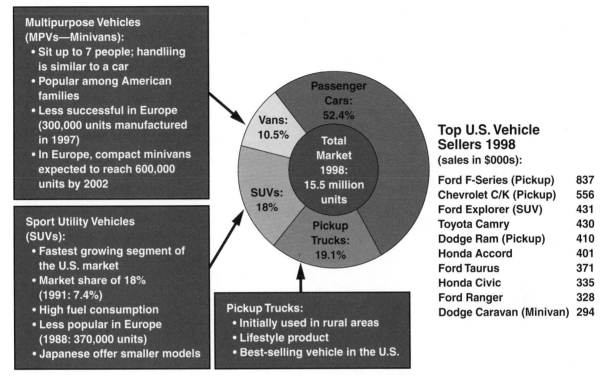

Multipurpose Vehicles (MPVs—Minivans):
- Sit up to 7 people; handliing is similar to a car
- Popular among American families
- Less successful in Europe (300,000 units manufactured in 1997)
- In Europe, compact minivans expected to reach 600,000 units by 2002

Sport Utility Vehicles (SUVs):
- Fastest growing segment of the U.S. market
- Market share of 18% (1991: 7.4%)
- High fuel consumption
- Less popular in Europe (1988: 370,000 units)
- Japanese offer smaller models

Pickup Trucks:
- Initially used in rural areas
- Lifestyle product
- Best-selling vehicle in the U.S.

Vans: 10.5%
Passenger Cars: 52.4%
SUVs: 18%
Pickup Trucks: 19.1%
Total Market 1998: 15.5 million units

Top U.S. Vehicle Sellers 1998
(sales in $000s):

Ford F-Series (Pickup)	837
Chevrolet C/K (Pickup)	556
Ford Explorer (SUV)	431
Toyota Camry	430
Dodge Ram (Pickup)	410
Honda Accord	401
Ford Taurus	371
Honda Civic	335
Ford Ranger	328
Dodge Caravan (Minivan)	294

Source: IMD Research.

The number of available models has also increased considerably over the past two decades. In 1981, 60 brands with a total of 268 models were available on the German market. By 1998, the number of brands had gradually increased to 67; however, the number of models had increased sharply to over 550. Many car manufacturers had switched to a so-called platform design, and they could produce several models on the same platform. Volkswagen optimized this system and was planning to use only four platforms for its annual production capacity of over 4.2 million units, thus combining economies of scale with model scope. (Refer to Exhibit 4 for more about Volkswagen's platform strategy.)

However, lowering production costs was not enough to satisfy customers. Increasingly, customers were demanding features at no extra cost. Features such as power windows, power locks, and air conditioning were included in the base package or were available at reduced prices.

THE AUTO INDUSTRY—SURVIVAL OF THE FITTEST

Trends in the Industry

Overcapacity　Overcapacity in this high-fixed-cost industry was not distributed equally around the globe. Already in the 1980s, America's Big Three started removing

exhibit 4   Volkswagen's Platform Strategy

Each platform consists of:
- **bottom part of the chassis**
- **various modules of:**
  - **– steering**
  - **– power train**

60% of manfacturing cost

In 1996, Volkswagen started its concept of four platforms. The platforms are used for the Volkswagen, Seat, Audi, and Skoda brands. The number in parentheses () indicates the 1999 retail price range of each model sold in Switzerland (prices in 000s of Swiss francs, including value-added tax).

Platform	Volkswagen	Seat	Audi	Skoda	Capacity
Compact Class	Polo (16-26) Lupo (15-20)	Arosa (14-19) Cordoba (19-28)		Felicia (15-21)	Over 1 million
Golf Class	Golf (22-36) Jetta (26-38) Beetle (30)	Toledo (24-36)	A3 (28-38) TT (46-54)	Octavia (21-41)	Over 2 million
Middle Class	Passat (31-47)		A4 (37-72) A6 (43-67)		Over 1.2 million
Luxury			A8 (78-125)		Over 15,000

Models of the Golf Class Platform:

Seat Toledo   Audi TT   VW Golf   Skoda Octavia   VW Bora   VW Beetle   Audi A3

Note: Exchange rate: 1 U.S.$ = 1.5 Swiss francs.

Source: Volkswagen AG, HypoVereinsbank Research.

overcapacity by closing a total of 30 plants in the United States and Canada. American market research companies expected North American utilization to remain above 80 percent and Western European around 70 percent. Asian utilization was a concern as Japanese companies expanded recklessly in the late 1980s and had idle capacity. Mazda, for example, was running at a utilization rate of 60 percent during most of the 1990s.

Continuing overcapacity has decreased the number of car companies. In 1960, a total of 42 independent car manufacturers existed; by 1999, only 17 remained. (See Exhibit 5 for an overview of consolidation in the auto industry.) However, although mergers and acquisitions often made sense on paper, their implementation frequently proved to be more difficult and expensive than expected. It took Ford more than five years to see a profit from its Jaguar acquisition. For BMW's acquisition of Rover, optimistic forecasts expected a profit by 2001—seven years after the company was acquired.

Changing Role of Suppliers   Components accounted, on average, for 45 percent of the value chain. Instead of merely supplying batches of parts to order, component suppliers increasingly had to manufacture very complex modules, from complete suspension packages to ready-to-build-in driver cockpits. Suppliers were required to design, develop, and produce the modules according to strict quality standards. Moreover, they needed to be able to manage the complex system of subassemblies. In return, car manufacturers granted suppliers long-term supply contracts, in many cases as the sole supplier. In some of the most modern factories, suppliers already accounted for 80 percent of the value, leaving manufacturers the role of running "systems integrators" and marketing functions. The surviving companies were becoming systems integrators, establishing closer relationships with the manufacturers.

exhibit 5   Consolidation in the Automotive Industry

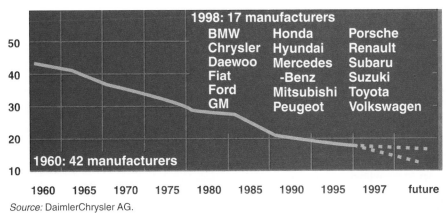

Source: DaimlerChrysler AG.

Large suppliers with the necessary capital backing had a better chance of offering their products globally. Pressure to reduce prices and to establish a global presence had forced many suppliers to merge or to exit the industry. Even heavyweight ITT, one of the five largest American component suppliers in 1995, decided in early 1998 to leave the automotive industry altogether. Overall, the effect of "lean manufacturing" and heavy concentration was changing the structure in the auto industry—only two suppliers remained for producing fuel injection systems (Lucas and Robert Bosch) and sunroofs (Rockwell and Webasto). The situation was similar for seats, clutches, and windscreens. Experts believed that the profit margins of these powerful suppliers could increase from their current 6 percent of sales.

Marketing and Brand Image Is Key   The distribution channel, including marketing expenses, accounted for up to 30 percent of a vehicle purchase price. Manufacturers had started streamlining this channel by reducing excessive stocks and the number of dealers. Dealers, already struggling because of a heavy reliance on after-sales service (40 percent of the dealer's revenue, but 90 percent of profits), were facing new competitors:

- In 1997, Auto-by-Tel, a General Electric (GE) subsidiary, sold 750,000 cars over the Internet (1995: 50,000 units). Microsoft and Dell have also entered this retail sector.

- GE had entered the financing market and financed around 850,000 vehicles in Europe.

- "Megadealer" companies such as CarMax successfully entered the market for used cars by opening large superstores. They offered a wide variety and good consultation at attractive prices.

- AutoNation, a megadealer, created a new business concept based on selling, renting, leasing and servicing. The company already owned around 200 car dealerships in North America. This consolidation strengthened the position of the surviving dealers vis-à-vis the manufacturers. In an attempt to limit the power of dealers, the manufacturers had taken legal action to prevent megadealers from buying more independent sales outlets.

On the marketing side, the traditional market segmentation became more difficult and in some cases obsolete due to overlapping segments. (See Exhibit 6 for an *exhibit 6*   Market Segmentation in the European Market in 1997

Social Status		Traditional	Materialistic, status-oriented	Materialistic, consumption-oriented	Hedonistic and fun-oriented	Postmaterialistic, environmentally conscious	Postmodern, want to feel, own and enjoy

Value orientation

Source: *Manager Magazine*, Marketing Systems, IMD Research.

overview of the market segmentation in Europe.) Hence, car manufacturers were forced to focus more on the power of brands. The power of brands could be clearly seen in the case of the New United Motor Manufacturing, Inc. (NUMMI) plant in California. Since 1989, the plant has produced two almost-identical cars: the Toyota Corolla and the GM Geo Prizm. The Toyota car sold at $9,000 in 1989, about 10 percent higher than its American counterpart. Over five years, the Corolla depreciated more slowly; its secondhand value was 18 percent higher than GM's Geo Prism. This difference accounted for the strength of Toyota's brand name.

Impact of Technology

- On average, R&D expenses accounted for around 6 percent of sales, but Daimler-Benz spent 8 percent on R&D in 1997. Ford's Mondeo world car set records for development costs—a total of $6 billion—but Ford boasted an average profit margin of around $1,000 per vehicle sold in 1997. The auto industry had become knowledge-intensive, and R&D was a crucial aspect of differentiating cars (which have become a lot more similar due to the usage of platforms, and aerodynamic and regulatory constraints). Since the time-to-market of cars has gotten shorter (from 60 months in 1988 to 24 months in 1998), even large manufacturers have decided to cooperate to reduce R&D expenses per vehicle. Overall, about 500 cooperation agreements existed in the automotive industry.

- Traffic jams had become a reality in almost all urban areas. Authorities took various approaches for reducing overcongestion. One of the most promising was using computers to help increase the flow of traffic ("telematics"). Computers calculated the optimal speed for maintaining a flow of traffic and then adjusted the maximum posted speed limit on roadside digital screens. The European market was estimated to grow from DM 1 billion in 1998 to over DM 10 billion in 2004.

- Dealing with heavy pollution, the California Air Resources Board made a directive to increase the proportion of cars with lower emissions. Although this directive sanctioned the use of electric vehicles, their market potential was still limited due to high cost, limited reach, and safety problems. As a result, many car companies started to invest in fuel cells. Mercedes-Benz was expected to introduce a fuel cell car in 2003.

DAIMLER-BENZ: SHAKE OR BE SHAKEN

With good reason, Daimler-Benz AG (DB) was perceived as the incarnation of German engineering competence. Its luxury cars were regarded as the best-engineered cars (overengineered, some would say) with a constant stream of innovations in safety, quality, electronic features, comfort, and design. DB cars sold in more than 200 countries, and Mercedes was one of the strongest global brands.

However, in the early 1990s, Daimler-Benz took several hits: Its ambitious diversification process into a "technology concern" did not produce the anticipated synergies. The European truck division produced heavy losses. And Japanese rivals pressed DB's luxury cars with similar quality and technology, but at much lower prices.

DB staged a thunderous turnaround, especially after Jürgen Schrempp took over as CEO in early 1995. In an operation called "stop the bleeding," all unprofitable business units were restructured, closed, or sold, very much in a U.S. style never before seen in Germany. Although DB reversed the diversification process so that it remained a kind of "transportation company" (cars, trucks, buses, railway, aerospace, telecommunications, and related services), DB still covered a much broader range than its competitors (and Chrysler).

How to Survive in a Consolidating Industry

Once the restructuring got on its way, Schrempp started to think about the future of Daimler-Benz and the car industry. Schrempp saw the writing on the wall. He noticed that:

- Except for niche players (e.g., BMW, Porsche, Volvo), none of the luxury car brands was still independent. Big global players owned most brands: Ford Motors controlled Jaguar, and GM sat in the driver's seat at Saab.
- Since the mid-1980s, the number of brands competing in the luxury segment had increased from 9 to 19.
- The world economy was experiencing the longest expansion cycle in several decades. Overcapacity was estimated at 20 to 30 percent, and what would happen during the next downturn?
- Mercedes-Benz's attempts to expand outside its traditional target segment met with more obstacles than expected. The most visible experience was the "moose test," a cornering test performed by journalists, where a Mercedes A-class subcompact model tipped. As a result, the model had to be redesigned. The establishment of the "Smart" brand (initially a joint venture with Swatch) for "city cars" was also challenging. Mercedes-Benz invested over DM 2 billion, but the development took longer than expected. The market introduction had to be delayed by six months.
- Mercedes-Benz's 8 percent R&D cost-on-turnover was far above the industry average (and nearly three times the Chrysler figure). Due to the small production volume, suppliers had to be given permission to transfer innovations to competing

exhibit 7   The Global Players in the Automotive Industry:
Annual 1997 Sales of Passenger Cars (in Millions of Units)

GM	8.8
Ford	6.9
Toyota	4.5
Volkswagen	4.3
Chrysler	2.9
Nissan	2.6
Fiat	2.6
Honda	2.3
PSA	2.1
Renault	1.9
BMW	1.2
Mitsubishi	1.1
Mercedes	0.7

MILLIONS OF VEHICLES

Source: Deutsche Bank AG.

car brands within six months. (Refer to Exhibit 7 for annual global sales of passenger cars.) Hence, the advantage of technological superiority was becoming difficult to communicate to customers.

- Although Mercedes-Benz was trying to become a global player (e.g., the new M-class production site in Alabama or the E-Class assembly in India and South Africa), it was basically still a German company (some would even insist, *Swabian*) with huge factories (e.g., the Sindelfingen plant outside Stuttgart still employed around 30,000 people in the late 1990s).

- The acquisition of Freightliner Trucks in the United States went smoothly. The company almost tripled its sales within a decade; however, it was run as a completely separate entity, with little interference from Stuttgart.

Schrempp and his team knew that more change was needed in order to remain in the top league of global players in the automotive industry. Otherwise they could be shaken by the industry consolidation. So in 1997, Schrempp commissioned, in addition to internal studies, a study by an investment bank identifying possible partners.

HOW TO AVOID THE THREAT OF ANOTHER BANKRUPTCY AT CHRYSLER

If DB was run by blue-ribbon engineers, Chrysler had to adopt more of a street-fighter mentality. Being the smallest and the most vulnerable of the U.S. Big Three, Chrysler had been to the edge of the cliff of bankruptcy twice in the last two decades. Moreover, it was the target of a hostile takeover battle by its largest shareholder, Kirk Kerkorian.

When Bob Eaton took over as CEO in 1994, he had a clear message: "I want to be the first CEO who does not lead the company back from bankruptcy."

exhibit 8   1997 Financial Performance of Selected Automakers
(All Annual Data in Billions of U.S. Dollars)

	Daimler-Benz AG	Chrysler Corp.	General Motors	Ford
Domestic sales	$ 23.0	$ 57.0		
International sales	46.6	4.2		
Total Sales	**$ 69.6**	**$ 61.2**	**$ 178.0**	**153.6**
Net Earnings	**$ 1.8**	**$ 2.8**	**$ 6.7**	**6.9**
Domestic employees	225,266			
International employees	74,802			
Total Employees	**300,068**	**121,000**	**608,000**	**360,000**

Note: Chrysler's domestic sales include sales in Canada.

Exchange rate: $1 = DM 1.78 (this rate was used in the combination agreement).

Net earnings of Daimler-Benz AG does not include tax benefits (around $2.8 billion in 1997).

Source: Annual reports.

After diversification had led to a dramatic cash drain in the late 1980s, Chrysler focused only on cars and light trucks. It was praised for developing the new markets for minivans (market share of almost 50 percent in the United States), sport utility vehicles (sales of the Jeep brand more than doubled between 1990 and 1997), and pickup trucks.

But fighting for survival had turned Chrysler into a strong competitor during the 1990s. Its time-to-market design and development times (due to conventional platform models) set world standards and were still widely considered best for cost-effectiveness. Overall, Chrysler was the leanest manufacturer of the Big Three. Compared to GM, Chrysler had one-third the sales but only one-fifth of the employees. (Refer to Exhibit 8 for GM, DB, and Chrysler financial results and employee numbers.) Cost effectiveness became an obsession. As a result, the profitability per employee stood at around $23,000, more than double the value for GM.

Although Chrysler was characterized to be a "fast follower" in technology and mostly bought technology from suppliers, trendy and fashionable design has been instrumental in the market success in recent years.

Chrysler—the Smallest of the Big Three

Although Chrysler was doing very well in the late 1990s, Bob Eaton was also concerned about the future:

- Any decline in the U.S. economy could hit Chrysler harder than the larger Big Three rivals and the Japanese competitors.
- Competition was also catching up in the market segments for minivans and sport utility vehicles, where Chrysler was the leader.
- Chrysler's position in the car segment was weakening. Between 1990 and 1997, its U.S. production rate of passenger cars fell by 40 percent to 440,000 units, while GM and Ford had decreases of less than 20 percent.
- Chrysler's plans to expand the company beyond the North American Free Trade Area (NAFTA) were stagnating due to a lack of management depth and products suited to non-NAFTA markets. The company sold less than 10 percent of its cars outside NAFTA.

- The rapid dissemination of electronic systems in cars (e.g., global positioning system) raised a question about the company's strategy of buying most car technology from suppliers. Might this approach erode Chrysler's core competencies to the degree that it risked becoming more of an assembler than a manufacturer, which could result in a weakened position in the value creation chain?

- The emerging distribution systems in the U.S. car industry (megadealers, e-commerce, car management companies) with their higher retailer power could affect Chrysler more deeply than competitors because of its smaller market share.

In light of these facts, Schrempp approached Eaton in January 1998. Given the circumstances of the industry, Eaton was very responsive to Schrempp's proposal to discuss a merger. Within four months and under strict secrecy, a team of only 20 to 30 managers from both companies worked out the details of this merger. The merger of Daimler-Benz AG and Chrysler Corporation was announced on May 7.

THE MERGER FOR GROWTH AND THE MERGER OF EQUALS: RHETORIC OR REALITY?

In communicating the merger to the boards, investors, employees, customers and the public, Schrempp and Eaton constantly stressed the following themes:

- This was a merger of equals, not an acquisition. The U.S. press in particular doubted this claim, noting that the 58:42 distribution of shares represented a significant premium for Chrysler. Although Chrysler was relatively more profitable, its price-earnings ratio was much lower, in the range of 13.5; Daimler-Benz, in contrast, tracked with a price-earnings ratio of approximately 21.5.

- This was a "merger for growth"—no layoffs, no plant closures, no scrapping of brands or products. Both brands were kept separate, and financial analysts were quick to point out that this strategy limited the potential synergies that the merged companies might otherwise have reaped. Overall, the combined company expected cost savings of $1.4 billion in its first year of operation.

- The merger was going to be the "best-implemented merger." The integration phase was expected to last for three years. The "merger of equals" philosophy was also expected to lead to the "best of two worlds" state, where the strength and best practices of Daimler and Chrysler would combine to form a stronger new entity, outpacing competition. Every process was reviewed in order to pick the best solution. For more details refer to Case 3, "The DaimlerChrysler Merger (B): Shaping a Transatlantic Company."

The geographic spread and product portfolio showed very little overlap between both companies, due to the simple fact that Mercedes-Benz was only in the upper market segments, whereas the Chrysler brands were more mid-market and stronger in specialized segments like minivans, SUVs or pickups. (Refer to Exhibits 9 and 10 for the geographic spread and market segments of the two companies.) Some financial analysts were fast to point out the difficulty of achieving cost savings in purchasing due to a lack of overlapping products.

For most of Daimler-Benz's other activities (heavy trucks, aerospace, etc.), no similar Chrysler division existed. Even in financial services, Chrysler was much more focused on captive customers (e.g., dealers) than the Debis subsidiary of Daimler-Benz.

exhibit 9　Geographic Sales and Production Volume of Chrysler Corporation and Daimler-Benz AG, 1997

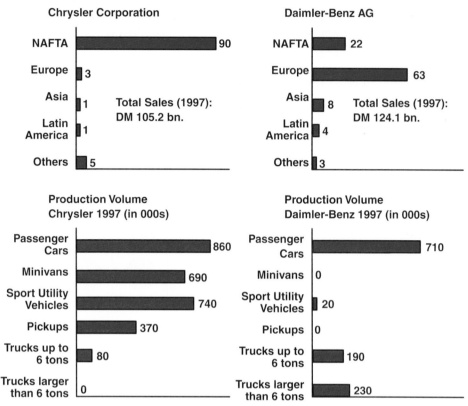

Source: DaimlerChrysler AG.

However, the complementarity of products didn't mean that there were no bumps on the road to the merger agreement. One was the price premium for Chrysler. Even more contentious were the questions of where and how to incorporate the new company, and what to name it. In order to discuss these delicate questions, the representatives from DB and Chrysler considered three options for the incorporation of the new company:

- A U.S. company.
- A German company.
- A neutrally incorporated company (e.g., in the Netherlands).

The team agreed to let the facts speak for the decision (and it was clear that the facts were mainly monetary). The exchange rate for the stocks was decided three weeks before the merger announcement. However, other issues proved to be more complex. For American managers it was difficult to imagine operating with a German two-tier board system (management board and supervisory board) with co-determination (having labor representation on the supervisory board). Nevertheless, DB's loss-carry forward and a tax-free solution for Deutsche Bank, DB's major shareholder, and other shareholders led to the establishment of DaimlerChrysler in Germany. After that, the slogan "Let the facts speak for the solution" became a model for conflict resolution in the merger process.

exhibit 10 Geographic Spread of Daimler-Benz AG and Chrysler Corporation

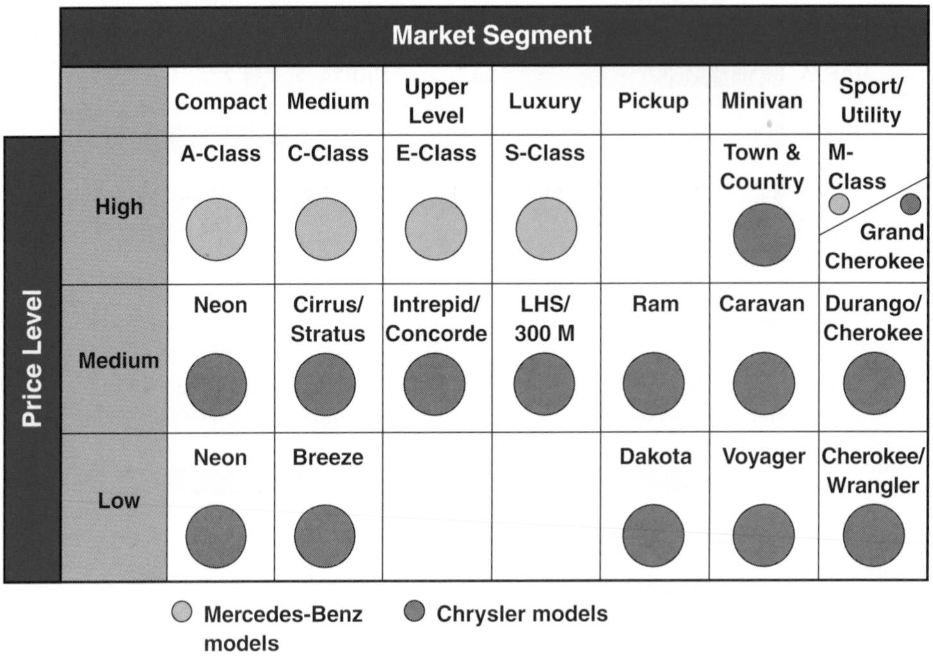
Market Segment
Compact
Medium
Upper Level
Luxury
Pickup
Minivan
Sport/ Utility
Price Level
High
Medium
Low
A-Class
C-Class
E-Class
S-Class
Town & Country
M-Class
Grand Cherokee
Neon
Cirrus/ Stratus
Intrepid/ Concorde
LHS/ 300 M
Ram
Caravan
Durango/ Cherokee
Neon
Breeze
Dakota
Voyager
Cherokee/ Wrangler
Mercedes-Benz models
Chrysler models

Source: DaimlerChrysler AG.

Triggering a New Round of Consolidation

The DaimlerChrysler merger sent shock waves through the global automobile industry, issuing in a new round of consolidation. Ford bought the Volvo car division and was forming a premium brand division called Premier Automotive, run by BMW's former number two manager, Wolfgang Reitzle. DaimlerChrysler showed a strong interest in acquiring Nissan, the second largest player in Japan. Only a few weeks after DaimlerChrysler decided not to bid for Nissan, Renault joined forces with Nissan. Within one year, the number of Korean manufacturers fell from five to two—Hyundai and Daewoo.

A Recession Just around the Corner?

The portents for an economic slowdown on the horizon were numerous:

- Although the North American market was currently not showing any indications of a slowdown, analysts had become increasingly nervous about the long expansion cycle in the United States. Moreover, Chrysler's most profitable cars (SUVs, pickups, and minivans) were being attacked by new models from Honda, Toyota, and BMW.
- Europe's business outlook was uncertain—growth was slower than expected, and a weakening Euro was a good indicator of this uncertainty.
- Growth expectations had been considerably dampened, not only in emerging countries in Asia and Latin America but also in Japan, the third largest market in

the world. Japanese car and truck sales had fallen by 12 percent in 1998—the worst sales decline in two decades.

Was the DaimlerChrysler merger solid enough to stand a recession in an industry that had a global capacity of 71 million units but sold only 52 million at the peak of the cycle? What would happen in a downturn? Said Thomas Stallkamp, the president of DaimlerChrysler:

> I wouldn't want to hope for a crisis, but sometimes it brings people together even faster.

Thinking about the industry, Schrempp wanted to shake things up, rather than be shaken. But the end game in the global auto industry has more than one round. . . .

case 3

The DaimlerChrysler Merger (B)

Shaping a Transatlantic Company

George Rädler
International Institute for Management Development

> Since the announcement of the merger, we have not only kept our promises, we have exceeded them. As a result, your company shines more brightly than even we dared to imagine.
> —Bob Eaton, co-chairman of DaimlerChrysler, to shareholders

> Our merger has become a model for others throughout the entire business world. DaimlerChrysler has been named the most respected company in Europe by the Financial Times.
> —Jürgen Schrempp, co-chairman of DaimlerChrysler

In late May 1999, one year after the initial merger announcement, the two co-chairmen and other board members of DaimlerChrysler AG (DCX) met in Stuttgart to review the progress of the merger. The mood was good because the General Assembly on May 18 had gone very well. Despite some criticism of the few small dark spots (surprising losses from the new Smart "city-car"), the results for the first year of consolidated operations were better than expected: sales had risen by 12 percent to $146.5 billion, and the operating profit had grown by 38 percent to $9.6 billion. Overall, DCX was the world's most profitable car company in 1998 and, on top of that, over 19,000 new employees had been hired. Other divisions (aerospace, Debis/Chrysler Financial Services) had achieved record results. (Refer to Exhibit 1 for an overview of DCX.)

The board members were proud of their achievements so far, but there were numerous challenges for the future. Increasingly, financial analysts were questioning whether DCX had gone too far with its strict brand separation: Was the company running the risk of hindering anticipated cost savings?

The board members were well aware that in today's volatile world, neither the shareholders, the financial analysts, nor the media, who were following the merger closely, would give any credit for past successes. Some critical voices remained.

Although the integration plan was clearly working, the wear and tear on the organization was becoming visible. Indeed, some top managers complained about spend-

Prepared under the supervision of Professor Ulrich Steger as a basis for class discussion rather than to illustrate either effective or ineffective handling of an administrative situation.

Copyright © 1999 by IMD—International Institute for Management Development, Lausanne, Switzerland. Used with permission.

exhibit 1 Financial Overview of DaimlerChrysler AG, Financial Year 1998

	Mercedes-Benz Passenger Cars, Smart	Chrysler, Plymouth, Jeep, Dodge	Commercial Vehicles Mercedes-Benz, Freightliner, Sterling, Setra	Chrysler Financial Services	Debis Services (Financial Services, IT, Telecom)	DaimlerChrysler Aerospace	Others
Revenue (in $ million)	**38,234**	**66,101**	**27,175**	**3,376**	**11,232**	**10,290**	**4,019**
Growth in % over 1997	*18.3%*	*8.5%*	*15.7%*	*19.5%*	*21.5%*	*12.1%*	*(12.1%)*
Operating profit (in $ million)	**2,338**	**4,942**	**1,110**	**765**	**460**	**731**	**(171)**
Growth in % over 1997	*15.7%*	*25.1%*	*176.6%*	*11.3%*	*59.3%*	*119.4%*	—
Unit sales	**922,795**	**3,093,716**	**489,680**	—	—	—	—
Growth in % over 1997	*29%*	*7.2%*	*17.3%*	—	—	—	—
Employees	**95,158**	**123,180**	**89,711**	**3,513**	**20,221**	**45,858**	**32,581**

Note: Due to double counting, the revenue figure is larger than $146.5.

Source: Annual report.

exhibit 2   Share Price of DaimlerChrysler AG, April 1997–June 1999

Source: Reuters.

ing up to 40 percent of their time on merger activities, rather than running their day-to-day operations. Notes Dr. Rüdiger Grube, senior vice president of corporate strategy:

> After the honeymoon is over, you sort out the easy things first. Then you come to the more difficult items—and here comes the real test for the merger of equals. Do you work things out and look for the best solutions, wherever you find it? Or do you go on war for your system? The pressure does not allow you to play politics but forces a constructive attitude, because you have to deliver results. There is no place to hide, and this sometimes causes stress. But the complexity makes it difficult to keep everything on a speedy track.

Although the first year of the merger was indeed successful in many respects, the board members were debating how to improve the performance of the stock and how to continue in increasingly uncertain times. (See Exhibit 2 for the development of the stock.)

Implementation Is Everything

From research, DCX executives knew that most mergers fail. (Refer to Exhibit 3 for an overview of why mergers fail.) Many unsuccessful mergers are not ill-designed from the beginning; failure occurs during implementation. That was perhaps why Schrempp

exhibit 3   Why Do Mergers Fail?

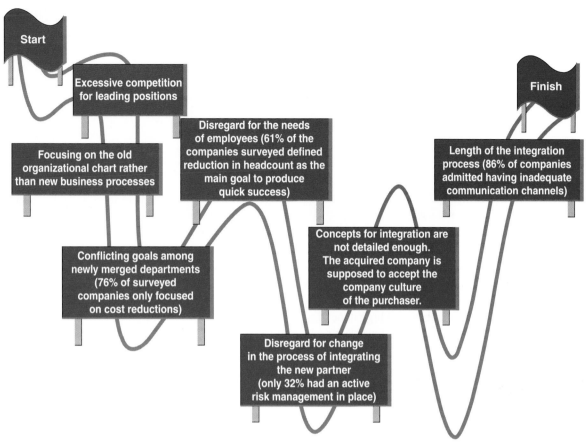

Source: A. T. Kearney, IMD Research.

had committed himself to making the DaimlerChrysler merger the best strategically, and the best-implemented and communicated. As Dr. Christoph Walther, head of communications, noted:

> We always try to raise issues before we were asked.

For Dr. Alexander Dibelius, managing partner of Goldman Sachs and one of the leading bankers behind the merger, one issue stood out above all others:

> Lack of speed is the single most important reason for failure. What you don't achieve in the beginning, you never see materialized.

Knowing this, the key players in the DCX merger had set the internal goal of concluding the merger in two years (abandoning the former official goal of three years)—the maximum time Bob Eaton would serve as co-chairman. Eaton stated publicly that he was going to retire in 2001.

But speed was not an eminent characteristic of the German model of corporate governance. Not only was the strict division of supervisory board and management

exhibit 4   Co-determination—German Model of Corporate Governance

Management board versus supervisory board
Management board: runs day-to-day operations
Supervisory board: hires and controls the management board

Supervisory board
- 20 members for companies >20,000 employees
- The members of the board are divided equally between representatives from shareholders and employees
  - Representatives from the employee side are voted in
  - At least two union members have to be on the supervisory board
  - At least one blue-collar worker has to be on the supervisory board
  - One senior manager (white collar) also has to be on the supervisory board
- Shareholders elect members of the supervisory board for the capital side
- Chairman (always from the capital side) has two votes in case of a 50/50 split

board slowing down decisions, but the necessary consensus with the workers' councils and workers' representative on the supervisory board also had to be built on all important issues of employment. (Refer to Exhibit 4 for an overview of co-determination.) Given both the high dependency on public contracts in aerospace and railways and the regulatory framework for cars and trucks, other stakeholders couldn't be ignored either. Schrempp didn't see this as a disadvantage:

> It takes more time to come to a decision, but you can implement faster, because everybody is on board. However, you have to communicate intensively—both internally and externally.

Speed, Speed, Speed—and Monitoring Results

The so-called proxy statement of the merger specified the financial targets, and included savings of $1.4 billion in the first year of combined operations, as well as annual benefits of approximately $3 billion within three to five years of the merger agreement. Soon after signing the merger agreement, co-chairmen Schrempp and Eaton clearly defined a framework for the postmerger integration phase. Speed was priority number one, followed by accountability and transparency. In the integration effort, it was important to have all of top management involved in the process.

The Chairmen's Integration Council (CIC) was founded in order to monitor the integration. The CIC was co-chaired by both Eaton and Schrempp. (Refer to Exhibit 5 for an overview of the Postmerger Integration Structure.) Further members included two executives from Chrysler and four from Daimler-Benz. The integration process was divided into 12 clusters, which were called Issue Resolution Teams (IRTs). Twelve IRTs were grouped around functional areas (e.g., purchasing) and identified and realized the synergies between the two companies. For example, one team analyzed the various e-mail systems and came up with a proposal for the board. Daimler-Benz used to have a different e-mail system for each division while Chrysler just had one e-mail system. Subsequently the team proposed to have only one e-mail system for DaimlerChrysler. Each IRT was jointly run by one management board

exhibit 5   Postmerger Integration at DaimlerChrysler AG

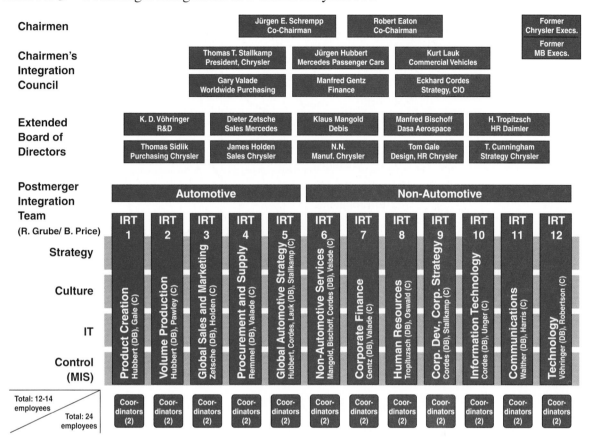

member from Chrysler and one from Daimler; they reported directly to the CIC. Due to the board members' heavy workloads, each IRT had two coordinators who stayed in close contact with their counterparts from other IRTs. In addition to a dedicated team of around 10 individuals, these coordinators formed the Postmerger Integration (PMI) Team. The PMI Team supported and helped monitor the integration process. Altogether, this PMI structure was referred to as distributed leadership and included around 50 dedicated individuals. This relatively small coordination structure, in turn, oversaw around 80 integration projects involving hundreds of managers across the organization.

The "war room" was the center for aggregating and monitoring the progress of the different PMI projects. Located in Stuttgart, the war room was equipped with the most modern information technology equipment. The project coordinators had to input their progress on a weekly basis. Each project was constantly monitored by a set of "traffic lights." A green light signaled that everything was on track; a yellow light indicated a few delays; and a red light implied serious difficulties. Top executives could access this system from any computer. In case of a red light, members of the CIC normally sent an e-mail to the team leader asking for reasons for the slow progress.

exhibit 6   Brand Profiles of Chrysler and Mercedes

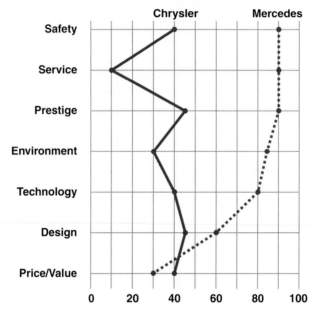

Source: Marketing Systems.

Combining a Luxury Brand with a Mass-Volume Producer

The brand value of both Mercedes-Benz and Chrysler was undisputed. Before the merger, Mercedes-Benz was ranked as one of the world's 10 most powerful brands, and Chrysler had an established position in North America. However, the perception of both brands was very different. (Refer to Exhibit 6 for brand profiles.) As the brands were often considered the most valuable asset, both brands even had their own members on the board, James Holden (former Chrysler vice president of sales and marketing) and Dr. Dieter Zetsche (former Mercedes-Benz vice president of sales and marketing). They also headed the IRT sales and marketing. This committee discussed a broad range of issues. The guidelines for both brands were listed in the "Guidelines for DaimlerChrysler Brand Management." This book (internally it was referred to as the "bible") outlined the clear separation of both brands. The bible prohibited a common platform strategy for the Mercedes-Benz/Chrysler brands as well as the establishment of combined Mercedes-Benz/ Chrysler dealers in Europe. However, financial analysts started to wonder where the financial savings would be found if there were so few common parts. In addition, critics pointed out that Chrysler was lacking appropriate products for the European market and developing countries.

Beyond the Figures and Organization Charts

The cultural issues, the "soft" feature of the merger, were discussed intensively, particularly in the media. Many American journalists didn't buy into the "merger of equals" concept at all—they referred to DaimlerChrysler as an acquisition of the Chrysler Corporation. They eagerly tried to find signs of a takeover, especially when executives from Chrysler were leaving. But as one observer stated:

> These reports are missing the point. In Detroit, there has always been a fluctuation of executives among the Big Three. In every merger, there are winners and losers. Not only that some functions double, more important: some made it to the new headquarters and others were downgraded to becoming brand managers.

Top management reminded the employees that this was a merger of equals and encouraged them to pay close attention to cultural issues. Moreover, managers were expected to first identify the changes that would have a large impact on the organization.

In Europe, the public focused on differences in compensation. Bob Eaton's salary in 1997 ($16 million) was estimated to be eight times that of Jürgen Schrempp, who was one of the best-paid executives in Germany. By American standards, even Eaton's salary looked small—Alex Trotman, ex-CEO of Ford, had received a total salary of $73.1 million in 1998. However, these high salaries did not sell well in the more egalitarian German society. Hilmar Kopper, the chairman of the supervisory board, tried to steer a middle ground for the compensation of the board:

> There won't be an Americanization of the German executive pay system.

As part of the business combination agreement, all Chrysler employees' salaries were guaranteed for two years. For the future executive salaries, Kopper proposed four elements: a base salary depending on the executive's responsibilities, an annual bonus payment, stock-option plans, and phantom share payouts linked to certain key earnings targets. Some employees saw this as a move towards the U.S. model, with higher performance-related pay for members of the management board and executives. Kopper also had to deal with salary differences in other parts of the organization. In order to retain the most capable managers, the new company would pay its 200 top managers a globally competitive salary.

Dividend payments were also Americanized. DCX adopted a dividend similar to former Chrysler payments rather than the much lower payment by Daimler-Benz. However, the U.S. media was not convinced by these moves, because DCX decided not to release a proxy statement (includes details on top executive compensation) with the 1998 annual report. DCX, incorporated in Germany, was legally not required to file the proxy statement but could have supplied it voluntarily. Being incorporated in Germany also led to DCX's removal from the Standard & Poor 500 Index (S&P 500). Because many American investment funds were limited to investing their money in the S&P 500, a major shift in shareholder structure took place. After the merger, American shareholders accounted for only 25 percent of the shareholders, compared to 44 percent at the announcement. (Refer to Exhibit 7 for the changing structure of shareholders.)

In order to convince critics and lessen internal concerns and uncertainties, DCX created a vision and mission statement. It was developed by a working group and presented for discussion at the first DCX top management meeting (executive board and vice presidents) in Seville in December 1998. Then it was rolled out in the spring of 1999 in a trickle-down process. Management had to explain the mission/vision, outlining the goals of DaimlerChrysler to their direct reports. (Refer to Exhibit 8 for the main goals.) Videos, overhead slides, and a proposed schedule for each session supported the rollout.

exhibit 7   Shareholder Structure of DaimlerChrysler AG

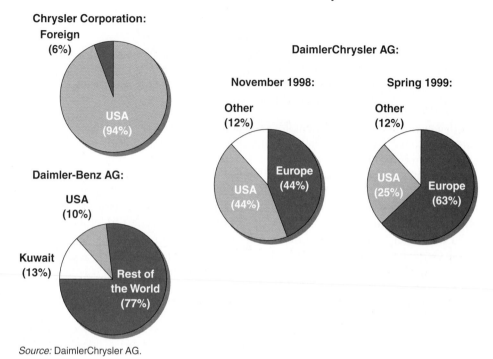

Source: DaimlerChrysler AG.

What Next?

Critics pointed out that integration of processes and brand separation might not be the right way for two companies as diverse as Daimler and Chrysler. To make their point, they referred to the example of the U.S. Freightliner and Sterling divisions, which were U.S. market leaders in heavy trucks despite not being integrated with the Mercedes truck division.

Other critics argued that because there was little overlap between Daimler and Chrysler, there were also few synergies to reap. As the Economist Intelligence Unit wrote: "Current harmony is little surprise—but complementarity reduces potential for synergies."[1] Financial analysts, ever hard to satisfy, pointed out that $1.4 billion in savings for year one of the merger, and $3 billion in years three to five, was not much for a sales volume of approximately $146 billion.

One huge synergy, the use of Mercedes' European and global distribution system, could not be leveraged, because as Tom Stallkamp, number two after Schrempp/Eaton, admitted:

> Chrysler does not yet have the right product for the markets.

---

[1]EIU Motor Business Europe, 1st Quarter 1999. London: The Economist Intelligence Unit Limited, 1999, pp. 74–102.

exhibit 8   DaimlerChrysler's Mission, Goals, and Values

OUR PURPOSE
Our purpose is to be a global provider of
automotive and transportation products and services, generating
superior value for our customers, our employees and our shareholders.

OUR MISSION
Our mission is to integrate two great companies to become a world enterprise that by 2001 is the
most successful and respected automotive and transportation products and services provider.
We will accomplish this by consistently delighting our customers with the quality and innovation of our products and services,
resulting from the excellence of our processes, our people, and our unique portfolio of strong brands.

OUR GOALS

Delighted Customers	Superior Profitability	Unique Portfolio	Sustained Growth	Integrated Enterprise	Globalization

OUR SHARED BELIEFS AND VALUES

• Customer Focus   • Innovation   • Teamwork   • Inspiration   • Openness   • Agility
• Quality   • Speed   • Excellence   • Profitability   • Responsibility

Source: DaimlerChrysler AG.

How to move forward was therefore very much on the CIC agenda. As Schrempp stated:

> The DaimlerChrysler merger was only the necessary precondition to remaining a player in the global automobile industry.

Although the first year of integration was successful, the members of the CIC wondered whether they were still well positioned for the future challenges.

case | 4 Giuseppe's Original Sausage Company

Michael T. Smith
Christian Brothers University

Jana F. Kuzmicki
Mississippi University for Women

As Joseph Cotrone, president and CEO of Giuseppe's Original Sausage Company, drove back to his office after conducting a promotion at a Seessel's grocery store in East Memphis, he wondered what the recently announced sale of Seessel's to the much larger Albertson's chain of grocery stores meant to his business. This was the second time within two years that Cotrone's first, and most important, customer was undergoing a change in ownership. Even though his seven-year-old company had finally broken even, Cotrone could not escape the feeling that he was just spinning his wheels, that he had yet to fulfill the dreams he had for the business he had started in 1991.

Cotrone pondered the issues he felt were hindering the success of his company: time involved in developing and establishing new accounts, lack of consistency in sales volume, inability to develop long-term relations with major customers, and financial instability. While sales continued to increase, the company did not have a core group of customers it could count on year in and year out. Cotrone's vision was to grow the business to a stage where he could afford to hire the necessary staff to run the day-to-day operations. Then he could spend his time in the kitchen creating new varieties of sausages—culinary works of art—which was his long-term goal.

COMPANY BACKGROUND AND HISTORY

When Joe Cotrone relocated to Memphis, Tennessee, in the late 1980s, he had a vision of operating a sausage company in which he could create a variety of different sausages using exotic meats and spices. Having moved from New Jersey, Cotrone missed the various types of high-quality sausages available in the Northeast. In the South, sausage (only links or patties) was viewed primarily as a meat to be served with breakfast. Cotrone was used to a much broader selection of sausages, typically featured as the main meat for breakfast, lunch, or dinner. In the Northeast, sausage often took center stage at meals other than breakfast, in both restaurants and homes.

The art of making sausage came naturally to Cotrone. He began by making custom sausages out of the kitchen in his home in the early 1990s. His original customers included friends, associates, and patrons at the restaurant where he worked as a bartender. In addition to serving his specialty sausages at the bar, Cotrone also sold them from a cooler he kept in his car. Customer demand soon exceeded Cotrone's production capabilities (maximum of 100 pounds per week), so he made plans to open a full-scale sausage company outside his home.

Giuseppe's Original Sausage Company began to take shape in late 1991. On November 1, 1991, Cotrone signed a six-month lease for space in a commercial building. This marked the beginning of a long journey, filled with numerous challenges, for Cotrone's gourmet sausage company. Although the space leased had once been used as a facility to manufacture sandwiches, it required additional renovations in order to meet the U.S. Department of Agriculture (USDA) regulations to produce sausage on a commercial scale. The regulations required the interior of the facility to be modified with new freezers, floors, walls, plumbing, and doors. Delays in construction and government-mandated renovations pushed back the scheduled opening (late March 1992) of Giuseppe's Original Sausage Company. Demands of the USDA, the Health Department, and various other government agencies exacted a toll on Cotrone's financial resources. As his personal capital dwindled, Cotrone had no choice but to initiate a search for external investors.

In the midst of regulation-driven renovations and the search for capital, Cotrone grabbed an opportunity, Memphis in May, to market his fledgling company. Memphis in May was an annual month-long series of cultural, social, and entertainment events that had a unifying theme of honoring a specific country. Fortunately for Cotrone, the 1991 Memphis in May festival spotlighted Italy and thus presented an ideal opportunity to introduce and market his newly formed company. Cotrone rented a booth from which to sell his specialty sausages to festival attendees. Sales were brisk, and Cotrone received a lot of very favorable comments from the festival participants.

In late 1992, Giuseppe's opened its doors to business, with sales to Seessel's (a local upscale grocery chain) and local restaurants. Sales were slow during the initial years. Sales to local restaurants quickly took priority over those to Seessel's. The sales projections that Cotrone had originally forecasted proved to be too optimistic. The outside investors Cotrone had recruited kept Giuseppe's afloat through the lean times before sales began to slowly increase by the mid-1990s. While Cotrone focused the majority of his attention on sales to local restaurants, Seessel's, and Kroger (a national retail grocery chain) during the mid-1990s, he also developed a flyer that featured his specialty sausages and could be sent or given to his ever-expanding individual customers.

By late 1997, Giuseppe's had sales of over $250,000 due to larger-order quantities from an expanding customer base, including the newly established Tunica, Mississippi, casinos. Giuseppe's staff included a plant manager, a full-time sausage maker, and a part-time salesperson. While a computer and basic business software (Microsoft Office, Small Business Edition) had been purchased, neither Cotrone nor his newly hired staff had been able to invest the necessary time to operationalize the computer system's potential contributions.

THE SPECIALTY SAUSAGE INDUSTRY

The results of an A. C. Nielsen study indicated that consumers nationwide purchased almost 462 million pounds of dinner sausage during 1997. According to a 1996 USDA study, the projected average total meat and poultry weight per capita was 208.8 pounds per year. The specialty dinner sausage market consisted of two segments: retail (supermarket) and food service (restaurants; institutions such as hospitals, schools, and nursing homes; and other establishments). In 1997, the retail segment exceeded $2 million

exhibit 1 Meals Purchased at Commercial Restaurants per Person, 1984–1996

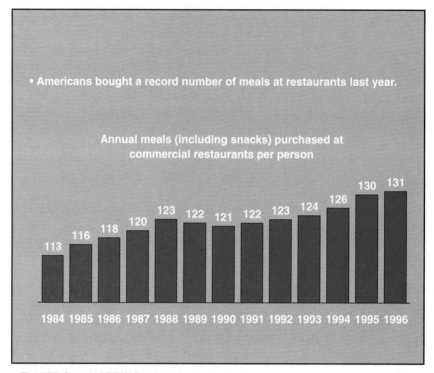

Source: The NPD Group's CREST Service.

in sales, and the industry as a whole had grown at a rate of 18.3 percent from 1996. The most popular flavor was the "smoked flavor" sausage (45.7 percent). Other popular flavors included Polish flavor (21.3 percent), hot flavor (7.7 percent), and Italian flavor (4.3 percent). There was significant variation in the growth rates according to the flavor of sausage. Italian flavor sausage had experienced the most growth, at 31.2 percent from 1996 to 1997, followed by Polish flavor sausage at 24 percent, and smoked flavor sausage at 15.6 percent.

Restaurants were critical customers of the sausage industry. According to a 1996 Crest report from the NAPD Group (the seventh largest research consulting firm in the United States), the average number of meals eaten in U.S. restaurants by individuals had steadily increased since 1990 (see Exhibit 1). The study's results also indicated that 72 percent of households purchased a processed meat product every month.

There had also been an explosion of interest in ethnic specialty foods. In 1992, a survey conducted by Research Advantage to monitor dining-out habits revealed that 84 percent of the surveyed customers ate Italian foods other than pizza, 40 percent of the consumers enjoyed Cajun foods, and 32 percent had a taste for French cuisine.

One significant characteristic that was likely to affect the sausage industry in the near future was revealed in a 1998 study conducted by the NAPD Pantry Check. The study's results indicated the average time taken to prepare meals in the U.S. household was decreasing. The study stated that "70 percent of households spend no more than 45 minutes preparing a typical meal." This finding was likely to affect the amount of time people would spend preparing dinner sausages. If buyers felt sausage took too long to cook, they might bypass dinner sausages for a less time-intensive alternative.

Health and Nutrition Issues   Numerous studies had been conducted on the nutritional value of all types of food products. Government regulations specified that nutrition facts were to be included on almost every food product. This encouraged consumers to be more knowledgeable about the nutritional value of the foods they were purchasing and eating. For some food companies, the regulations tended to be damaging because they exposed the high fat content of their food items. According to a U.S. Food and Drug Administration study conducted in 1996, nutrition labels were 91 percent accurate, up 4 percent from 1994. Companies that elected to enter the low-fat segments of the sausage market had created a shift in marketing techniques by creating niche segments. While most sausages ranged from 15 to 25 grams of fat per pound, low-fat varieties ranged between 1.5 and 5 grams. Although reducing fat content had the notorious reputation of altering taste, low-fat sausages did present alternatives to regular sausage products.

Competition in the Specialty Sausage Industry

The dinner sausage industry was a competitive market. For example, approximately 25 to 30 major brands were sold in the Memphis retail market. In the retail segment, the major competitors included Bryan, Jimmy Dean, and Johnsonville. Exhibit 2 contains a profile of the major competitors and information regarding their sausage products. Many of these companies competed on a national scale. While competition among the companies often centered on price, other competitive features included special promotions, advertising, and the variety of product offerings. Shelf space and competitive interbrand pricing were keys to success in this market. Opportunities did exist for specialty sausage companies to market unique, high-quality products at premium prices. Price competition in the food-service segment was probably more severe because sausage typically lost its brand identity as it was prepared and served. Upscale restaurants might be willing to pay premium prices for high-quality, unique sausage that they could promote to their clientele, but institutions were going to be much more concerned about average taste and quality and below-average prices. Specialty sausage products had the potential to generate somewhat higher margins, but competitive copying and interbrand price comparisons served to limit the premium that could be realized on a consistent basis.

Large supermarkets (Piggly Wiggly, Kroger, Seessel's, Megamarket, and Jitney Premier) controlled over 50 percent of the available supermarkets in the Memphis area. This level of concentration was typical of most major metropolitan areas and was forcing many small grocers out of business. Thus, ever-increasing numbers of consumers were shopping at the large supermarkets. Nontraditional outlets of grocery products were also playing an increasing role in grocery sales. Companies such as Kmart with its Super Kmart, Wal-Mart with its Super Wal-Mart, and Sam's Club represented new retail grocery outlets. Large organizations with centralized buying and professional buyers made business more difficult for the small sausage producer.

exhibit 2   Major Competitors in the Sausage Industry

Manufacturer	Product	Price	Weight	Package	Fat Content	Characteristics
Johnsonville	Mild Italian sausage	$3.99	1.24 lb.	Tray	25 g	Instructions inside package; no sell-by date
	Bratwurst	3.99	1.24 lb.	Tray	25 g	
	Beer-n-bratwurst	3.99	1.24 lb.	Tray	25 g	
Dino's	Garlic Italian	N/A	3.29/lb.	Tray	N/A	Instructions on package; sell-by date
	Italian sausage	N/A	3.29/lb.	Tray	N/A	
	Cajun style charice	N/A	3.29/lb.	Tray	N/A	
King Cotton	Reduced fat smoked sausage	$1.99	1 lb.	Vacuum sealed	15 g	No instructions on package; no sell-by date
	Cajun style smoked sausage	1.99	1 lb.	Vacuum sealed	15 g	
	Smoked sausage	1.99	1 lb.	Vacuum sealed	16 g	
Jimmy Dean	Polska kielbasa	$2.59	1 lb.	Vacuum sealed	15 g	No instructions on package; no sell-by date
Bryan	Smoked bratwurst	$3.39	1 lb.	Vacuum sealed	22 g	No instructions on package; no sell-by date
	Smoked sausage	2.19	1 lb.	Vacuum sealed	16 g	
	Beef smoked sausage	3.29	1 lb.	Vacuum sealed	17 g	
	Polska kielbasa	3.29	1 lb.	Vacuum sealed	17 g	
	Cajun style smoked	3.29	1 lb.	Vacuum sealed	17 g	
John Morrell	Skinless Polish	$1.39	1 lb.	Vacuum sealed	22 g	Instructions on package; sell-by date
	Skinless Smoked	$1.39	1 lb.	Vacuum sealed	22 g	
Mr. Turkey	Turkey Polish kielbasa	$2.84	1.15 lb.	Vacuum sealed	5 g	No instructions on package; sell-by date
	Turkey smoked	2.84	1.15 lb.	Vacuum sealed	5 g	
	Italian style turkey Smoked sausage	2.84	1.15 lb.	Vacuum sealed	5 g	
Healthy Choice	Smoked	$2.94	.875 lb.	Vacuum sealed	1.5 g	Instructions on package; sell-by date
Giuseppe's	Chorizo	$3.99	1 lb.	Vacuum sealed	N/A	Instructions on package; sell-by date
	Bratwurst	3.99	1 lb.	Vacuum sealed	N/A	
	Cajun style Andouilles	2.79	.5 lb.	Vacuum sealed	N/A	
	Chaurice	2.79	.5 lb.	Vacuum sealed	N/A	
	Hot Italian	3.99	1 lb.	Vacuum sealed	15 g	
	Mild Italian	3.99	1 lb.	Vacuum sealed	15 g	
	Turkey Italian	3.99	1 lb.	Vacuum sealed	7 g	
	Hot turkey Italian	3.99	1 lb.	Vacuum sealed	7 g	

The retailers controlled shelf space, and food-service operations controlled menus as well as specific ingredients in the meals they prepared. The willingness of distributors to carry a manufacturer's product could mean the difference between ultimate market success or failure, especially for the small sausage makers. It was highly unlikely that consistent volume and profits were possible without the support of distributors. The implication was that downstream channel members had the ability to reduce profits that might be realized by sausage manufacturers.

As the market for dinner sausage continued to grow, new entrants were expected. As evidenced by Giuseppe's, it was possible for a new company to enter the industry in a relatively short time. Government regulations erected some barriers to entry, but the major barrier came from the ability of the large companies to wage significant marketing campaigns. Large meatpackers not currently in the sausage business also represented a potential threat if they decided to enter this market on a major scale.

Suppliers provided meats, spices, and packaging materials; they had relatively little ability to extract higher-than-normal profits from manufacturers. Sausage manufacturers could potentially improve their purchasing position and costs as their volume increased.

The Specialty Sausage Industry in Memphis

The retail segment of the dinner sausage industry in Memphis was a 6.1-million-pound, $12.25 million market as of 1997. The total market had grown at a rate of 15.4 percent from 1996. There were significant variations in the growth rate based on the flavor of sausage; growth rates ranged from a low of 3.9 percent for Polish-flavor sausage to a high of 45.8 percent for Italian-flavor sausage. The potential customer base for the sausage industry was growing as more people in the Mid-South gained experience with dinner sausages. Not only were new varieties of sausages being introduced on a regular basis, but the notion that sausages were cooked only for breakfast was being replaced with the idea that sausage represented an attractive alternative dinner meat. This represented a change that the Memphis area had not previously witnessed. The changing view of the role of sausage presented new opportunities and challenges for both large and small sausage manufacturers.

The larger regional and national companies, such as Bryan, Jimmy Dean, and Johnsonville, had a difficult time competing with the specialty dinner sausage products from small local producers such as Giuseppe's. Small companies could offer a wider variety of specialty sausages in smaller volumes, whereas large companies tended to concentrate on fewer varieties and a larger volume of sales per variety. Conversely, smaller companies confronted obstacles such as the much larger production volume and the marketing campaigns waged by the large companies. Specialty sausage makers were more likely to maintain their primary volume of sales in their local regions, whereas national competitors were able to generate sales over a wider geographical area.

As Memphis grew larger, so did communities and cities in the surrounding area. Over the past decade, the establishment of casinos in Tunica, Mississippi, located only 20 miles from Memphis, had had an incredible economic impact on the Mid-South. The growth of this small Mississippi town had caused significant changes in the local and surrounding economies by introducing the tourism industry on a much grander scale than in the past. According to the Memphis Community Network, an estimated 16 million people traveled to Memphis every year. The casinos were responsible for the large size of that number. The connection with sausage was that tourists, as well as Memphis citizens, wanted to enjoy the same types of food they were familiar with at home. Thus, the casinos were inclined to serve foods such as dinner sausages to the people in their establishments. For example, Giuseppe's Original Sausage generated nearly 19 percent of its total sales from just one casino, the Sheraton Casino, in 1997. There were eight other casinos in Tunica that did just as much, if not more, business. The casinos were willing to do whatever it took to attract people; serving quality dinner products was a nice extra.

GIUSEPPE'S ORIGINAL SAUSAGE COMPANY

Giuseppe's Original Sausage Company prided itself on producing high-quality premium sausages in a variety of different forms and flavors. Cotrone was committed to producing exceptional, distinctive-tasting sausages, many of which were made individually to suit his customers' preferences. His strategy involved purchasing only top-of-the-line ingredients, requiring employees to take extra precautions when producing the various types of sausage, and insisting that every aspect of the production process follow a specific set of procedures he had personally developed.

Giuseppe's product line consisted of more than 80 different sausage-related products. There were four primary markets for Giuseppe's sausage: supermarkets, restaurants, casinos, and mail-order/individual call-in. Three of these customer groups were consolidated into two categories: retailers and food services. Retail sales consisted of supermarkets, and food-service sales consisted of restaurants and casinos. Mail-order/individual call-ins did not represent a significant portion of sales. It was common for individual orders not to be picked up or paid for. Giuseppe's did not currently have the ability to handle credit card sales to individuals.

One of Cotrone's primary objectives was to generate enough sales in a given week to cover expenses and overhead. Cotrone aspired to expand his volume, thereby increasing both sales and profits. He also wanted to assure his customers that Giuseppe's sausage had the reputation of being the best in the industry. Customer satisfaction was another primary concern. Giuseppe's also took pride in keeping its work facility and sausage-making areas above the required standards stipulated by the USDA and local health department regulations.

The price of Giuseppe's sausage was pegged at the upper end of the spectrum, usually averaging a few cents above competitors' prices. While this approach established the company's position as a leader in the market, it was problematic in that no one knew how much, or even if, profits were being realized on the different varieties of sausage, let alone on individual orders. Methods for establishing prices lacked consistency. An accurate product costing system did not exist. Consequently, Cotrone was unable to determine the exact costs for the individual batches and varieties of sausage that were produced. Prices for the standard products were based on competitors' current prices. Prices for the specialty products were based on Cotrone's instinct—a general feel for what he thought his costs were for making the specialty sausage.

The Sausage-Making Process at Giuseppe's

Giuseppe's Original Sausage Company operated on the basis of a weekly production schedule due to the small size and unique nature of the company. Giuseppe's customers placed orders through either their distributor or direct contact with the company. This weekly scheduling placed unusual but manageable constraints on the company.

The meats used in the sausages were ordered weekly; the majority of the other sausage ingredients were kept in stock. This approach to ordering was required to maintain the quality standards that Cotrone had established for his sausage. Freshness was ensured with the weekly arrival of meats; however, production delays could occur if the deliveries did not arrive at the scheduled time. Dry ingredients were stored in separate containers in a moisture-controlled room to ensure freshness. Vegetables and fruits were stored in separate containers in refrigerators for freshness and taste considerations. The various types of meats used in the sausages were stored at freezing temperatures in temperature-controlled refrigeration units until needed for production. Meats for the next day's production were defrosted the previous night; this approach allowed production to begin with a thawed and pliable meat product. Exhibit 3 presents an overview of the process used in making the various sausage products.

The defrosted meats for each day's production schedule were removed from the refrigeration units in the morning and were then moved to the sausage production facility. The plant manager gathered the necessary spices and other ingredients, while the sausage maker prepared the meat for grinding. Regular (branded) sausage had the fat

exhibit 3 The Art of Sausage-Making: Process Flow Chart

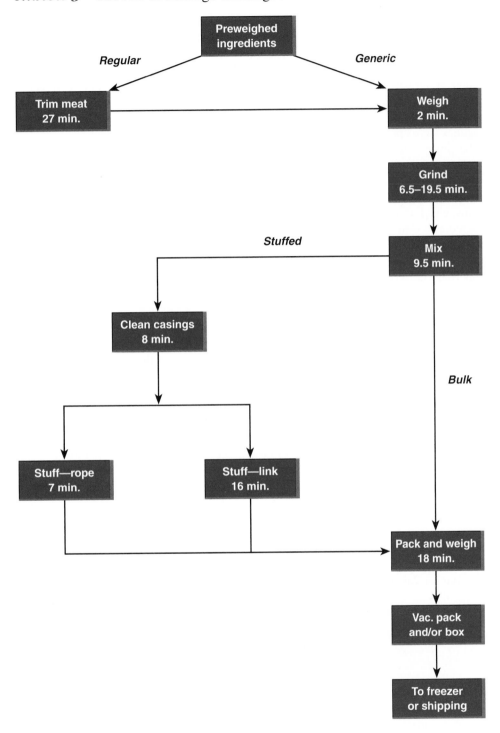

trimmed from the meat, whereas the generic (unbranded) sausage did not. The prepared meat was put in the grinder, where, depending on the type of sausage being produced, it could be ground up to three times. The various meats were ground in batches of up to 120 pounds, based on the size of the sausage order being manufactured. As soon as the meat was ground to the desired consistency, it was moved to the mixer.

The mixer was where the ground meats and other required ingredients were combined. Water was usually added to the ingredients to ensure proper and thorough blending. The thoroughness of the mix was the prime factor for the dependable taste of Giuseppe's sausages. The mixer had a capacity of 150 pounds, although the majority of batches were approximately 130 pounds (120 pounds of meat and about 10 pounds of other ingredients). During the mixing process, the plant manager and sausage maker prepared either the stuffing or the bulk packaging of the sausage. Sausages that were sold in nonbulk form were transferred to the stuffer for stuffing. The stuffer had the ability to stuff up to 50 pounds of sausage at a time into the natural casings. The natural skins, which were used for taste considerations, had to be thoroughly cleaned before the ingredients were injected into them. The stuffing process required a minimal amount of time due to the efficiency of the stuffer. The packaging process usually followed the stuffing process right away. Once the sausage was stuffed, it was either left in a straight rope stage or twisted into a link stage before being packaged. Packaging and labeling of the finished sausage product was custom-tailored to the specific customer's order.

Sausage that was either prepared for individuals or left in the bulk stage was vacuum sealed and labeled as individual packages, whereas sausage for restaurants and other institutional customers was placed in bulk plastic bags and boxed before labels were applied. Vacuum-sealed packaging ensured freshness of the sausage purchased by individual customers either at supermarkets or via UPS/FedEX shipment. The boxed rope and linked sausage was not vacuum packaged because it was either immediately shipped to the customer for prompt use or frozen for future shipment. Both freezing and immediate shipment ensured the freshness of the sausage without the added cost of vacuum packaging.

When the packaging process was finished, the sausage products were moved to the walk-in refrigeration units, where they were inventoried and stored until shipment occurred. The sausage-making process required 46 to 97 minutes per batch depending on both the product type (regular or generic) and the product form (bulk, rope, or link). There could also be up to 10 minutes of downtime between the end of one sausage batch and the beginning of the next to allow for equipment cleaning. Whenever possible, batches were sequenced to either avoid or minimize the time required for cleaning. As shown in the table below, current capacity ranged from 603 to 1,271 pounds of sausage per day depending on the type of product.

Production Capacity per Day (Excluding Cleanouts)			
Product	Minutes/Batch	Batches/Day (7.5 hours/day)	Pounds/Day (130 pounds/batch)
Generic			
Bulk	46	9.78	1,271
Rope	61	7.38	959
Regular			
Bulk	75	6.00	780
Rope	88	5.11	664
Link	97	4.64	603

exhibit 4   Meat Marketing and Distribution Channels

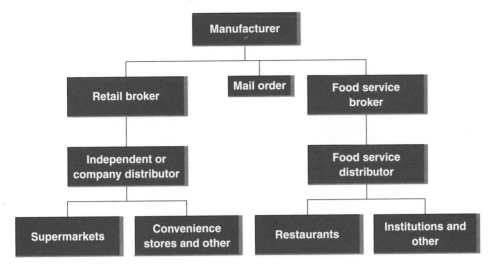

Marketing and Distribution

Food products, specifically meats, were normally marketed through a broker and distributor intermediary system to the retailer or ultimate end user. There were two distinct market segments served by different brokers and distributors: the retail market and the food-service market. Exhibit 4 portrays an overview of the distribution system.

The retail market segment consisted of retailers such as supermarkets and convenience stores. In 1997, there were 23 multistore grocery chains in the Memphis area. The notable multistore grocery store chains included Piggly Wiggly (27 stores), Kroger (25 stores), Seessel's (11 stores), Megamarket (4 stores), and Jitney Premier (4 stores). Giuseppe's had significant sales potential in the major supermarket chains, particularly in the large upscale markets located in the more affluent geographic areas of Memphis. If Giuseppe's decided to market its sausages to these supermarkets, it would have to deal with their distributors. Several supermarkets purchased their products from affiliated distributors such as Flemming, Kroger, and Albertson's. However, there were some independent distributors that provided additional products. Primary brokers, including Empire/Pyramid, Bud Mayer Company, and Sales Mark, handled sausage products in the Memphis area.

The food-service segment consisted of restaurants, education facilities, and large food-preparation companies. Potential customers were restaurants (> 300), hospitals (42), educational institutions (259), and nursing homes (29). Although there were over 300 restaurants in the Memphis metropolitan area, their significance as potential outlets for Giuseppe's sausage varied significantly depending on menu, image, and location. For example, there were about 100 Italian restaurants that could be potential customers. Other potential customers in this segment were primarily concerned with the price of the sausage, since sausage was not a featured item in their menu offerings.

The majority of food-service operators in Memphis purchased their product primarily from Alliant or Sysco. Combined, these two companies controlled over 80 percent of the Memphis food-service market. Brokers serving this market segment included Norbert, Delta Brokerage, and Sales Marketing Consultants.

exhibit 5   Major Customers of Giuseppe's Original Sausage Company

Company Name	Total Sales
Sheraton	$ 48,155
American Seafood	45,735
Nanda	8,192
Seessel's #1	5,158
Garibaldi's	4,402
Kroger	3,576
Seessel's #10	3,121
Seessel's #2	3,013
Flying Saucer	3,008
Seessel's #6	2,688
Seessel's #5	2,392
Seessel's #3	1,595
Seessel's #8	843
Seessel's #4	817
Seessel's #9	752
Methodist	730
Seessel's #7	356
Total of found invoices	$134,534
Total pounds from invoices	39,659
Total 1997 sales	$257,625

Difficulties in building volume were likely to occur if a company did not use the established distribution system. There were obviously efficiencies to be realized by supermarkets and food-service operators, as it was their common practice to consolidate purchasing and delivery with the distributors. The broker's primary role was to serve as the manufacturer's local sales force and assume responsibility for a major part of the manufacturer's local marketing efforts. A company that elected to work on a direct basis was unlikely to secure enough time with the final purchaser or a distributor's sales staff to significantly influence sales. For example, Sysco indicated it would consider a new specialty product, especially on a regional basis, only if it was offered by a broker. Due to their expertise, brokers were a valuable source of market information and marketing ideas that were not easily accessible to small manufacturers. At the present time, the majority of Giuseppe's sales did not originate from using the broker/distributor channel. Exhibit 5 contains information regarding 1997 sales to Giuseppe's major customers.

Financial Performance

Giuseppe's was a subchapter S corporation; Cotrone owned 60 percent and outside investors (primarily friends and acquaintances) owned the remaining 40 percent. While sales had continued to increase each year, profits remained elusive. In 1997, Cotrone was extremely pleased to have finally broken even, but he wondered what 1998 would bring. Much remained to be accomplished if he wanted to earn a reasonable income.

exhibit 6a   Income Statement of Giuseppe's Original Sausage
Company, 1994–1997

	Year			
	1994	1995	1996	1997
Sales	$139,821	$166,655	$210,686	$257,625
Cost of goods	81,348	74,891	107,964	155,918
Gross profit	58,473	91,764	102,722	101,707
Wages and salaries	60,388	33,288	42,188	44,659
Professional services	825	1,175	1,200	1,075
Auto and truck	17,364	2,387	3,234	5,486
Insurance	2,263	1,306	5,022	3,058
Travel and entertainment	1,153	206	1,018	1,130
Office expense	2,991	2,528	2,915	3,636
Telephone	1,927	2,626	2,830	3,834
Advertising	3,137	9,939	9,378	2,801
Repair and maintenance	2,407	4,434	4,918	1,342
Rent	13,016	13,939	16,959	10,913
Taxes and licenses	4,799	5,185	5,269	939
Interest	—	119	1,128	8,400
Depreciation	6,471	4,652	4,652	4,550
Utilities	6,817	6,889	7,435	2,18
Other	2,543	2,459	2,752	5,641
Total Operating Expenses	26,101	91,132	110,898	99,648
Operating income	(67,628)	632	(8,176)	2,059
Other income	(2,282)	(2,650)	(3,478)	(2,235)
Net income	$ (69,910)	$ (2,018)	$ (11,654)	$ (176)

One of Cotrone's primary goals was to hire additional staff to handle the daily operations so he could spend more of his time in the kitchen developing new sausage varieties. Exhibits 6 and 7 present recent financial data.

Cotrone decided a useful starting place to evaluate the company's financial soundness was to review sales and costs for 1997. He looked in his files for materials invoices to review the costs of the products sold in 1997 but did not find invoices for some of the materials needed to produce the products shown in Exhibit 8. Using the financial statements, he developed an analysis of cost of goods sold (see Exhibit 9) and estimated overhead costs per pound of sausage (see Exhibit 10). Next, he pulled out his box of sales invoices and reviewed them to see what he could learn. On further examination of the financial data, Cotrone realized that the sales invoices he found in the box represented only slightly more than 50 percent of his total 1997 sales—where were the remainder of the invoices?

The Future

While Joe Cotrone was proud of what Giuseppe's had accomplished over the past seven years, he knew the company's market and financial position was tenuous.

exhibit 6b   Giuseppe's Percentage Composition of Income Statement, 1994–1997

	Year			
	1994	1995	1996	1997
Sales	100.00%	100.00%	100.00%	100.00%
Cost of goods	58.18	44.94	51.24	60.52
Gross profit	41.82	55.06	48.76	39.48
Wages and salaries	43.19	19.97	20.02	17.33
Professional services	0.59	0.71	0.57	0.42
Auto and truck	12.42	1.43	1.53	2.13
Insurance	1.62	0.78	2.38	1.19
Travel and entertainment	0.82	0.12	0.48	0.44
Office expense	2.14	1.52	1.38	1.41
Telephone	1.38	1.58	1.34	1.49
Advertising	2.24	5.96	4.45	1.09
Repair and maintenance	1.72	2.66	2.33	0.52
Rent	9.31	8.36	8.05	4.24
Taxes and licenses	3.43	3.11	2.50	0.36
Interest	0.00	0.07	0.54	3.26
Depreciation	4.63	2.79	2.21	1.77
Utilities	4.88	4.13	3.53	0.85
Other	1.82	1.48	1.31	2.19
Total Operating Expenses	90.19	54.68	52.64	38.68
Operating income	−48.37	0.38	−3.88	0.80
Other income	−1.63	−1.59	−1.65	−0.87
Net income	−50.00%	−1.21%	−5.53%	−0.07%

Intense competition, ambiguous policies and procedures surrounding product costing and product pricing, uncertain distribution of Giuseppe's sausage products, combined with investor uncertainty, presented unique challenges to Giuseppe's future. For Giuseppe's Original Sausage Company to be successful over the long term, the company would need a sound strategy, ample capital, and more formal procedures related to its operations.

exhibit 7   Balance Sheet of Giuseppe's Original Sausage Company, 1994–1997

	Year			
	1994	1995	1996	1997
Assets				
Cash	$ 3,773	$ 1,364	$ 135	$ 6,400
Accounts receivable	9,163	14,194	18,360	30,153
Inventory	4,995	7,700	11,900	17,105
Building and assets	45,615	45,615	45,615	47,985
Less depreciation	−20,952	−25,037	−29,689	−36,609
Intangibles	4,469	4,469	4,469	4,469
Less amortization	−1,936	−3,427	−4,321	−4,469
Other expenses	75	75	75	75
Loans to shareholders	22,623	25,665	27,729	0
Total assets	$ 67,825	$ 70,618	$ 74,273	$ 65,109
Liabilities and Equity				
Accounts payable	$ 10,965	$ 12,075	$ 14,988	$ 7,416
Mortgages/notes/bonds—1 year			10,153	2,194
Other current liabilities	1,382	1,589	1,614	11,040
Loans from shareholders	14,000	17,600	14,000	14,000
Long-term debt			6,252	
Capital stock	155,500	155,500	155,500	160,000
Retained earnings	−114,022	−116,146	−128,234	−129,541
Total liabilities and equity	$ 67,825	$ 70,618	$ 74,273	$ 65,109

exhibit 8 Sales by Product Line for Giuseppe's Original Sausage
Company, 1997

Product	Amount	Pounds	Cost/Pound (Ingredients only)
Original Italian	$17,630	7,567	$1.29
Chicken	12,933	2,281	2.40
Cajun Andouille	8,547	2,546	1.20
Bratwurst	8,202	3,479	1.18
Turkey	7,190	2,933	1.06
Boudin	6,609	1,256	1.24
Lamb	5,647	953	2.46
Duck & Bacon	4,648	811	2.92
Sicilian	3,937	1,691	1.18
Santa Fe	3,364	634	1.54
Chorizo	2,955	1,231	1.19
Knackwurst	2,772	781	?
Smoky Catfish & Tail	2,730	408	?
Kielbasa	2,708	863	?
Jerked Pork & Banana	2,528	384	?
Cajun Style	2,460	1,535	.55
Seafood Boudin	2,136	430	3.51
Duck	1,845	264	2.92
Bangers	1,380	355	?
Crawfish Boudin	1,337	235	2.65
Boudin Blanc	1,325	541	.83
Items with sales between $500 and $1,000: 11	8,713	3,147	
Items with sales between $100 and $500: 16	4,258	2,115	
Items with sales below $100: 28	1,126	525	
One-time items	13,445	945	
Nonsausage Items			
Potato Salad	2,408		
Kraut	1,955		

exhibit 9   Cost of Goods Sold for Giuseppe's Original Sausage
Company, 1994–1997

	Year			
	1994	1995	1996	1997
Inventory—beginning	$ 2,600	$ 4,995	$ 7,700	$ 11,900
Purchases	69,955	66,523	97,970	156,573
Labor	62,169	34,991	44,344	44,659
Depreciation			12,038	4,550
Total	136,718	108,504	164,048	219,679
Inventory—ending	4,995	7,700	11,900	17,105
Cost of goods sold	$131,723	$100,804	$152,148	$202,574

exhibit 10   Estimated Overhead per Pound of Sausage for Giuseppe's
Original Sausage Company, 1997

Overhead Item	Expenses	Cost per Pound
Wages and salaries	$44,659	$0.59
Professional services	1,075	0.01
Auto and truck expense	5,486	0.07
Insurance	3,058	0.04
Travel and entertainment	1,130	0.01
Office expense	3,636	0.05
Telephone	3,834	0.05
Advertising	2,801	0.04
Repairs and maintenance	1,342	0.02
Rent	10,913	0.14
Taxes and licenses	939	0.01
Interest	8,400	0.11
Depreciation	4,550	0.06
Utilities	2,184	0.03
Other	5,641	0.07
Total	$99,648	$1.32

Total Pounds Produced = 75,562

case 5 The Chinese Fireworks Industry

IVEY

Ruihua Jiang
The University of Western Ontario

Paul Beamish
The University of Western Ontario

In February 1999, Jerry Yu was spending the Chinese New Year holidays in Liuyang (lee-ou-yang), a small city known as "the home of firecrackers and fireworks," located in Hunan Province in China. Jerry was an ABC (America-Born-Chinese). With an MBA, he was now running a small family-owned chain of gift stores in Brooklyn, New York. Liuyang was his mother's hometown. During his visit, his relatives invited him to invest in a fireworks factory that was owned by a village. Mr. Yu had been impressed by the extravagant fireworks shows he had seen during the festival; however, he wanted to assess how attractive the Chinese fireworks industry was before he even looked at the financial details of the factory.

HISTORY OF FIREWORKS AND FIRECRACKERS

Fireworks referred to any devices designed to produce visual or audible effects through combustion or explosion. The art of making fireworks was formally known as pyrotechnics. Firecrackers were a special kind of fireworks, usually in the form of a noisemaking cylinder. Firecrackers were often strung together and fused consecutively, a staple of Chinese New Year celebrations, weddings, grand openings, births, deaths and other ceremonial occasions.

The main ingredient of fireworks was the black powder: a ground-up mixture of potassium nitrate (saltpetre), sulfurs, and charcoal. The proportions of its ingredients had remained almost the same over the past thousand years: 75 parts-by-weight potassium

Ruihua Jiang prepared this case under the supervision of Professor Paul Beamish solely to provide material for class discussion. The authors do not intend to illustrate either effective or ineffective handling of a managerial situation. The authors may have disguised certain names and other identifying information to protect confidentiality.

nitrate, 15 parts charcoal, and 10 parts sulfur. It burned briskly when lighted, but did not erupt or make any noise. When it was found that a projectile could be thrust out of a barrel by keeping the powder at one end and igniting it, black powder became known as gunpowder. Today, smokeless powder has replaced black powder as the propellant in modern weaponry, but black powder remains a main ingredient in fireworks, both as a propellant and as a bursting charge.

It was generally believed that the Chinese were the first makers of fireworks. The Chinese made war rockets and explosives as early as the sixth century. One legend said that a Chinese cook, while toiling in a field kitchen, happened to mix together sulfur, charcoal, and saltpetre, and noticed that the pile burned with a combustible force when ignited. He further discovered that when these ingredients were enclosed in a length of bamboo sealed at both ends, it would explode rather than burn, producing a loud crack. This was the origin of firecrackers. In fact, the Chinese word for firecrackers—*bao-zhu*—literally means "exploded bamboo."

The loud reports and burning fires of firecrackers and fireworks were found to be perfect for frightening off evil spirits and celebrating good news at various occasions. For more than a thousand years, the Chinese had been seeing off past years and welcoming in new ones by firing firecrackers.

Fireworks made their way first to Arabia in the seventh century, then to Europe sometime in the middle of the 13th century. By the 15th century, fireworks were widely used for religious festivals and public entertainment. Most of the early pyrotechnicians in Europe were Italians. Even today, the best-known names in the European and American fireworks industry were Italian in origin. From the 16th to the 18th century, Italy and Germany were the two best known areas in the European continent for fireworks displays, representing two different styles. The Italians tended to display their fireworks with elaborate, ornamental structures—the "machines" that were often known as "temples." The Germans, on the other hand, tended to rely more on fireworks themselves. Referred to as the Northern School, most of these pyrotechnicians were from Nürnberg.

In 1777, the United States used fireworks in its first Independence Day celebration, and fireworks have became closely associated with July Fourth celebrations ever since. Today, most of the fireworks sales in the United States are made around July Fourth. Fireworks' popularity was highlighted and enhanced through memorable fireworks extravaganzas at the 400-year celebration of Columbus' landing in 1892, the Bicentennial Celebration in 1976, and Inauguration Day celebrations in 1997.

Up until the 1830s, the colors of the early fireworks were limited to the amberlike shades produced from the burning of charcoal and iron filings. After that, color advancement was swift, with blue being the last color added to the spectrum. In 1999, there were six basic colors used in fireworks: white, produced by magnesium or aluminum; yellow, by sodium salts; red, by strontium nitrate or carbonate; green, by barium nitrate or chlorate; blue, by copper salts in the presence of a volatile chlorine donoe; and orange or amber, by charcoal or iron.

LIUYANG—THE HOMETOWN OF FIRECRACKERS AND FIREWORKS

According to historical records in China, firecrackers and fireworks "emerged during the Tang dynasty (618–907 AD), flourished during the Song Dynasty (960–1279 AD), and originated in Liuyang." For more than a thousand years, Liuyang had been known

exhibit 1   Liuyang Firecrackers and Fireworks: Total Revenue and Export Sales (In U.S. $000)

	1992	1993	1994	1995	1996
Total revenue	49,639	55,542	86,747	126,506	134,940
Tax revenue	5,099	7,010	11,829	15,422	18,434
Export sales	15,100	30,200	51,240	84,030	85,560

Source: Liuyang Firecrackers and Fireworks Exhibition, 1998.

as the "hometown of firecrackers and fireworks of China," a title that was officially conferred to Liuyang by the State Council of China in 1995.

As early as 1723, Liuyang fireworks were chosen as official tributes to the imperial family and were sold all over the country. Exports started early: by 1875, firecrackers and fireworks were being shipped to Japan, Korea, India, Iran, Russia, Australia, England, the U.S., and other countries. In China, the name Liuyang had become almost synonymous with firecrackers and fireworks. Liuyang-made firecrackers and fireworks won numerous awards over its long history of fireworks making. In 1929, Liuyang fireworks won first place in the China National Commodity Exhibition; in 1933, they won an "Award of Excellence" at the Chicago World's Fair; in 1986, they won the first prize in the 21st Monaco International Fireworks Competition; and they also won several prizes in the "International Music-Fireworks Competition" held annually in Canada.

The long history and tradition had made fireworks more than just a livelihood for the Liuyang people. Almost every native person in the area knew something about fireworks making, or had actually made firecrackers or fireworks in their lifetime. As a result, Liuyang claimed an impressive pool of skilled labor.

Firecrackers and fireworks had become the pillar industry of Liuyang, employing more than 400,000 people in peak seasons, about one-third of the total population in the Liuyang District (including Liuyang City and the surrounding counties). Liuyang had more than 500 fireworks manufacturers. Among them, only one was a state-owned enterprise (SOE) with more than 1,000 workers. The rest were owned either by villages or families. Among them, about a dozen or so were medium to large factories with employment between 100 to 500 workers. The rest were small workshops employing anywhere from 10 to 50 people, depending on market demand.

Liuyang was the top fireworks exporter in the world, accounting for 80 percent of fireworks export sales of Hunan Province and 60 percent of those of China (see Exhibit 1 for information on revenue and export sales of Liuyang fireworks). The trademarked brand "Red Lantern" had become well known to fireworks-lovers around the world.

The Product

Fireworks could be classified into two categories: display fireworks and consumer fireworks. The display fireworks, such as aerial shells, maroons, and large Roman candles, were meant for professional (usually licensed) pyrotechnicians to fire during large public display shows. They were devices that were designed to produce certain visual or audio effects at a greater height above the ground than the consumer fireworks, which the general public could purchase in convenience stores and enjoy in their own backyards. Roughly, the display fireworks were known as Explosives 1.3 (Class B prior to 1991) in the U.S. The consumer fireworks belonged to Explosives 1.4 (Class C prior to 1991). The difference lay mainly in the amount of explosive components contained in the product. Canada had a similar classification system. In the U.K., it was more carefully divided into four categories: category one was indoor fireworks; category two was garden fireworks; category three was display fireworks; and category four was display fireworks for professionals only.

There were many varieties of fireworks. Liuyang made 13 different types with more than 3,000 varieties. The major types included fountains, rockets, hand-held novelties, nail and hanging wheels, ground-spinning novelties, jumping novelties, floral shells, parachutes, and firecrackers.

Historically, firecrackers made up 90 percent of the total production and sales. Over the past 50 years or so, however, there had been a shift away from firecrackers to fireworks. In 1999, firecrackers made up only about 20 percent of the total sales. The skill levels of fireworks-making had been greatly improved. For instance, the old-time fireworks could reach no more than 20 metres into the sky, while the new ones could go as high as 400 metres.

Not much had changed in fireworks-making. Over the last few decades, numerous novelties were added to the fireworks family. However, innovation had never reached beyond product variations. The ingredients had remained more or less the same. The process technology had not changed much either, although some manual processes, such as cutting the paper, rolling the cylinders, mixing powder, and stringing the cylinders could now be done by machines.

Safety Issues

The fact that fireworks were made with gunpowder and listed under explosives brought up the issue of safety. Numerous accidents involving fireworks had resulted in tragic human injuries and considerable property damages. As a result, fireworks had become heavily regulated in most countries.

According to the manufacturers, fireworks were the most dangerous during the production process. Powder mixing and powder filling, in turn, were the two most dangerous procedures. The workers had to abide by strict safety measures. Even a tiny spark caused by the dropping of a tool on the floor or the dragging of a chair could start a major explosion. The quality of the ingredients was also of significant importance. Impure ingredients could greatly increase the possibility of accidents. In Liuyang, almost every year, there would be one or more accidents that resulted in deaths and damages.

Once the fireworks were made, they were relatively safe to transport and store. Even in firing, good quality fireworks rarely caused any problems if everything was done properly. Most of the fireworks-related accidents occurred during private parties or street displays, and quite often involved children playing with fireworks that needed to be handled by adults, or laymen firing shells that required professional expertise. It was also often the case that illegal and/or inferior fireworks were used in the accidents. Most accidents were linked to consumer backyard events rather than to public displays.

According to the United States Consumer Products Safety Commission's (CPSC) data, injuries related to fireworks had declined by 44 percent, even though their use had increased (see Exhibit 2). For 1997, there were an estimated 8,300 fireworks-related injuries, 32 percent of which were caused by firecrackers. Of all the injuries related to firecrackers, 42 percent involved illegal firecrackers.

Children from ages 5 to 14 were the most frequently involved in fireworks-related injuries. However, fireworks were not the only consumer product that might cause injuries to this age group. According to a 1997 CPSC Injury Surveillance Report, fireworks

exhibit 2   Total Fireworks Consumption and Estimated Fireworks-
Related Injuries in the U.S.: 1990 to 1998

Year	Fireworks Consumption, Millions of Pounds	Estimated Fireworks-Related Injuries	Injuries per 100,000 Pounds
1990	67.6	12,100	17.8
1991	73.7	11,000	14.9
1992	87.1	12,600	14.5
1993	101.9	12,300	12.0
1994	117.0	12,500	10.7
1995	115.0	10,900	9.4
1996	118.0	7,800	6.2
1997	132.8	8,300	6.2
1998	112.6	7,000	6.2

Source: American Pyrotechnics Association.

were actually safer than some much more benign-looking products, like baseballs, pens and pencils (see Exhibit 3).

However, fireworks-related injuries were usually the most dramatic and the most widely publicized accidents, which partly explained the fact that fireworks was the only category among the products listed in Exhibit 3 for which prohibition, instead of education and adult supervision, was often urged.

In the United States, multiple government agencies were involved in regulating fireworks. The Bureau of Alcohol Tobacco and Firearms (BATF) controlled the manufacture, storage, sales and distribution of explosives, i.e., Class B fireworks. The CPSC regulated Class C consumer fireworks, and the Department of Transportation dealt with the transportation of fireworks.

Although at the federal level, fireworks and firecrackers were allowed as long as the safety features were up to the standard, local governments had their own different regulations regarding fireworks consumption. Out of the 50 states, 10 would not allow any fireworks, 5 would allow novelty fireworks, 18 would allow "safe and sane" fireworks, while the remaining 17 would allow essentially all consumer fireworks. For display fireworks, permits would have to be obtained from federal and local authorities and fire departments.

All legal consumer fireworks offered for sale in the United States had been tested for stability by the Bureau of Explosives and approved for transportation by the U.S. Department of Transportation. Because of the limited amount of pyrotechnic composition permitted in each individual unit, consumer fireworks would not ignite spontaneously during storage, nor would they mass-explode during a fire. Therefore, no special storage was required.

In most of Europe, similar regulations were in place for safety considerations, only the requirements were regarded as less stringent. In Canada, however, regulations were extremely restrictive. The Explosives Research Department under the Ministry of Natural Resources was in charge of regulating fireworks as one type of explosives. The Canadian Explosives Research Laboratory was responsible for setting standards and testing products. On the list of fireworks companies that were allowed to sell fireworks to Canada, no Chinese companies were found.

exhibit 3   Estimated Emergency Room Treatment per 100,000 Youths
(Ages 5 to 14)

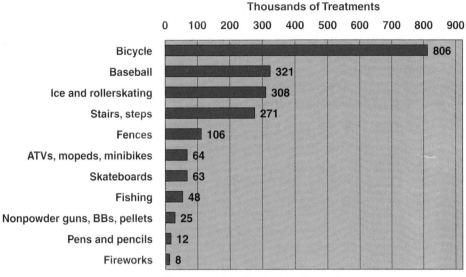

Thousands of Treatments

Bicycle	806
Baseball	321
Ice and rollerskating	308
Stairs, steps	271
Fences	106
ATVs, mopeds, minibikes	64
Skateboards	63
Fishing	48
Nonpowder guns, BBs, pellets	25
Pens and pencils	12
Fireworks	8

Source: American Pyrotechnics Association.

THE FIRECRACKERS AND FIREWORKS INDUSTRY IN CHINA

The firecrackers and fireworks industry in China was dominated by small family-owned-and-operated workshops. It was essentially a low-tech, highly labor-intensive industry. After 1949, government-run factories replaced the family-owned workshops. The increased scale and government funds made possible the automation of some processes. However, the key processes such as installing powder, mixing color ingredients, and putting in fuses were still manually done by skilled workers.

The factories themselves were made up of small workshops that stood away from each other, so that in case of an accident the whole factory would not explode. For the same safety consideration, the workshops were usually located near a water source and in sparsely populated rural areas, to reduce the noise and explosion hazard.

After the reform toward a market economy started in 1979, most of the factories were broken up and became family-run units of production again. It was hoped that this privatization might help to motivate people better, to increase their productivity, and consequently raise the output. However, this move also served to restrict further technological innovations. There were hardly any research and development (R&D) facilities nor human and capital resources allocated to R&D in most fireworks companies. The few resources that were available were all spent on product varieties. Even in Liuyang, out of the 400,000 or so people working in the industry, only four were engineers with advanced professional training and titles. The approximately 40 research facilities scattered in the Liuyang area were poorly funded and equipped.

In fact, the majority of the workers were regular farmers who had learned how to make fireworks just by watching and following their elders. They would come to work in fireworks workshops when there were jobs to be done, and return to till their fields if there were none. In Liuyang, for instance, only four to five factories were operating year-round. The rest of the 500-plus workshops would operate as orders came in. Since the fireworks-making communities were very concentrated geographically and had lasted for generations, only a few places (like Liuyang) came to claim a large pool of skilled fireworks-makers.

Although Liuyang was by far the most well-known place for making fireworks in China, it faced increasing competition within the country. Also located in Hunan Province, Liling was another major manufacturing community of fireworks. Liling fireworks might not enjoy the same reputation and variety as Liuyang products, but they were fierce in price competition. In the neighboring Jiangxi Province, Pingxiang and Wanzai fireworks had become strong competitors both in price and quality, especially on the low- and medium-priced market. In the high-end product market, especially in large display fireworks and the export market, Dongguan in Guangdong Province had taken advantage of its closeness to Hong Kong and more sophisticated management and marketing practices and snatched market share from Liuyang.

The initial capital requirement for starting a fireworks-manufacturing facility was relatively low. To set up a factory with the necessary equipment for making large display shells would require RMB 1,000,000.[1] However, setting up a small family workshop making consumer firecrackers and fireworks would require less than RMB 100,000. Consequently, the number of small manufacturers mushroomed after the government started to encourage private business ventures.

The labor cost was low in the area. Skilled workers engaged in major processes would earn an average of RMB 800 to RMB 1,000 per month. A nonskilled worker would be paid only RMB 300 to RMB 400 every month. Therefore, the labor cost took no more than 20 percent of the total cost. For the small private workshops, the percentage would be around 10 percent.

The main raw materials for fireworks were gunpowder, color ingredients, paper, fuse and clay soil. None would be difficult to procure. The prices and supply were both quite stable. The one possible problem in supply was quality. Major manufacturers would usually establish long-term relationships with their suppliers to guarantee the quality of materials. The small workshops would often go with the lowest prices, sometimes at the cost of quality, which could lead to fatal results.

The emergence of the small companies intensified competition. The private workshops were flexible and quick in responding to market demand. They did not entail much administrative cost. Compared to government-owned or some collectively owned factories, they did not have the social responsibilities of health care, retirement benefits, and housing. They usually did not do any product research or design. Oblivious to intellectual property protection, they would copy any popular product design and sell it for much less. The resulting price drop had become a serious problem for the whole industry. As the profit margin kept shrinking, some workshops would hire cheap unskilled workers, and use cheap equipment and raw materials to cut down on cost. The results could be disastrous. Low-quality-fireworks-related damages and injuries as well as factory accidents were reported every year, pushing the authorities to impose stricter regulations regarding fireworks.

THE DOMESTIC MARKET

Firecrackers and fireworks had long been an integral part of any ceremonies held in China. Firecrackers had to be fired for grand openings, weddings, funerals, festivals or

---

[1]In 1999, the exchange rate was around 8.30 yuan per U.S. $1.00.

any special occasions, both for good luck and to attract public attention. Until recently, demand had been stable, and on the rise in the past two decades because of increased economic development and living standards. Economically, market reform and unprecedented growth had given rise to the daily appearance of multitudes of new companies and new stores. As people's income level and living standards kept rising, fancier and pricier fireworks and firecrackers were desired over the cheap simple firecrackers, thereby creating more profit opportunities for fireworks manufacturers. Almost every household would spend at least a couple of hundred yuan on firecrackers and fireworks during the Spring Festival.

However, since the beginning of the 1990s, increased concerns over environmental pollution and safety of human life and property led more and more cities to regulate the consumption of fireworks and firecrackers. Every year, high profile fireworks-related accidents that led to human injuries or property damages were reported and emphasized on mass media before and after the traditional Spring Festival. Some articles even condemned firecrackers and fireworks as an old, uncivilized convention that created only noise, pollution, and accidents. In a wave of regulations, city after city passed administrative laws regarding the use of fireworks. By 1998, one-third of the cities in China had completely banned the use of firecrackers and fireworks. Another one-third had partially banned their use, allowing fireworks only in designated places. This led to a decline in domestic market demand.

In the meantime, domestic competition grew intensely. The reform toward a market economy made it possible for numerous family-run workshops to appear. They competed mainly on price. Almost every province had some fireworks-making workshops or factories, many set up and run with the help of skilled worked who had migrated from Liuyang. These small establishments usually were located in rural, underdeveloped areas where labor cost was minimal. The manufacturing was done manually, sometimes without safety measures, using cheap raw materials and simplified techniques. The products were sold locally at low prices, making it difficult for Liuyang fireworks to sell in those areas. To make things worse, these products would often copy any new or popular product designs coming out of Liuyang or other traditional fireworks communities, even using their very brand names.

Within the Liuyang area, similar small workshops bloomed in the past few years. The number of the workshops could exceed 500 in peak time and drop to half that number in a slow period. Since their cost was very low, they could be extremely flexible in price. To create sales, they would underprice each other, thereby bringing down the overall profit margin of the industry.

In the past, fireworks were sold through the government-run general merchandise companies. Eventually, private dealers took over a large part of the business. Overall, the distribution system was rather fragmented and messy. The old government-run channels were not very effective any more, especially for general merchandise. The new distribution channels were still rather chaotic. It was necessary to be close to the market to make any sense of it. Usually, wholesale dealers would get shipments directly from the manufacturers, and then resell to street peddlers and convenience stores.

In the countryside, wholesale markets would appear in focal townships, with wholesale dealers and agents of the manufacturers setting up booths promoting their products. Small peddlers in the surrounding areas would get supplies from the market and then sell them in small towns or villages. The wholesale markets in China were important outlets for distributing general merchandise like fireworks.

In the display fireworks market, the buyers were often central and local governments, who would purchase the product for public shows on national holidays or special celebrations. Obviously, a local company would have advantages in supplying to local government in its area. Large fireworks shows usually would use invited bidding to decide on suppliers. The amount of fireworks used could range from RMB 100,000 to several million yuan, depending on the scale of a fireworks show.

Another serious issue, account receivables and bad debt control, was a problem not just for fireworks manufacturers, but for all businesses operating in China. Bad debts and lack of respect for business contracts had created a credit crisis in the business world in China. The bad debt problem greatly increased transaction costs, slowed down the cash turnover, and had become a headache for fireworks manufacturers. Some had chosen to withdraw from selling in the domestic market, although the profit margin was higher than in the export market.

Legal restrictions, local protectionism, cutthroat price competition, hard-to-penetrate distribution channels, and bad debt were impacting negatively on the domestic sales of Liuyang fireworks. In 1997, seeing the decline of its fireworks sales, Liuyang Firecrackers and Fireworks Industry Department, the government agency in charge of the overall development of the pillar industry, decided to start an offensive strategy. First, it opened local offices in most of the 29 provinces, major cities, and regions to promote Liuyang fireworks. Second, it regulated the prices that Liuyang fireworks companies could quote and sell in export sales. Third, it resorted to a government-to-government relationships in order to secure contracts for large public fireworks displays in each province. One year after introducing the offensive strategy, Liuyang fireworks sales had increased.

The next two years would be big years for the fireworks industry in China. In October 1999, China would celebrate the 50th anniversary of the founding of the People's Republic; the central government, each province, and each city would hold its own celebration. Then, the turn of the millennium would certainly be celebrated with extravagant fireworks displays, both public and private.

THE EXPORT MARKET

Since the opening of the Chinese economy in 1979, exporting had become a major market for the Chinese fireworks industry. As one of the most celebrated products out of China, export sales of fireworks had risen between 1978 and 1998. According to government statistics, the recorded export sales of firecrackers and fireworks reached U.S.$143 and U.S.$172 million in 1994 and 1995, respectively. The estimate for 1998 was about U.S.$200 million.

The general belief was that China-made fireworks actually made up about 80 percent to 90 percent of the world's fireworks market. The products from China were rich in variety and low in price, but also had a lower reputation in quality control, packaging, and timing control, compared to the products made in Japan and Korea. China-made fireworks also would wholesale for much lower prices, usually 80 percent lower than similar products made in Japan or Korea.

Due to the lack of technology and management input, the Chinese fireworks industry had not made much progress in advancing the fireworks-making and packaging techniques, nor in quality control and marketing capabilities. There was little overall coordination of the export sales. As more and more companies were allowed to export directly, the competition kept intensifying and the profit margin of the export sales kept slipping. Some manufacturers would even sell at or below cost, just looking to get the tax refund that the government set aside to encourage export, which could sometimes reach 20 percent. As a result, underpricing each other became a common practice. Therefore, despite its dominant share of the world market, the Chinese fireworks export

exhibit 4   Comparison of FOB Import Prices from China and
Wholesale Prices of Chinese Fireworks in the U.S.

Name	Packing	FOB China[1] (U.S.$)	Wholesale in U.S.[2] (U.S.$)
Consumer Fireworks			
Thunderbombs	12/80/16	$12.40	$ 42.00
Tri-Rotating Wheel	24/12	15.50	48.50
Changing Color Wheel	72/1	20.70	57.60
Jumping Jack	20/48/12	16.70	60.00
Cuckoo	24/6	14.50	50.40
Ground Bloom Flower	20/12/6	16.50	62.40
Color Sparkler	24/12/8	16.40	66.74
Moon Traveller	25/12/12	9.20	40.00
Crackling Whips	72/12	16.99	50.40
Aerial Display	4/1	19.40	68.00
Evening Party	12/1	12.60	60.00
Assorted Fountain	18/4	10.30	64.20
Assorted Rockets	36/12	24.20	68.00
Display Fireworks			
4" Display Shell w/Tail	36/1	52.65	165.00
6"	10/1	41.82	160.00
8"	6/1	54.53	190.00
12"	2/1	60.95	190.00

[1]FOB major ports in South China. Cost, insurance, freight to major ports in the U.S. would be $3.00 to $4.00 more per carton.

[2]U.S. import duty rate for fireworks from China was 12.5 percent.

industry enjoyed limited profitability. Exhibit 4 provides a comparison of the free on board (FOB) prices quoted by the Chinese companies to U.S. markets versus the prices quoted by the U.S. importers and wholesalers to the retailers and end users on some consumer and display fireworks items. The importers enjoyed a high markup even after paying the 12.5 percent U.S. import duty. Of course, the importers had to absorb the cost of getting permits, shipping, storing and carrying the inventory for three to four months before making the sales.

Besides suffering from low profit margin, the Chinese fireworks makers were also risking losing their brand identities. Given the low cost and reasonably good quality of the Chinese fireworks, many large fireworks manufacturers and dealers in the West started to outsource the making of their brand-name fireworks. Failing to see the importance of brand equity, the Chinese fireworks manufacturers were sometimes reduced to mere manufacturing outfits for foreign companies, gradually losing their own brands.

There were also fireworks merchants in Korea, Japan, or Spain, who would buy the products from China, and then repackage them, or replace the fuses with better quality ones, then resell them for much higher prices.

The export market was usually divided into five blocks: Southeast Asia, North America, Europe, South America, and the rest of the world. The most popular market had been Europe, where the regulations on fireworks were less stringent, and orders were of larger quantities and better prices. The United States was considered a tough market because of complex regulations and high competition, nevertheless a necessary one if a company wanted to remain a viable world-player. The Canadian market was virtually closed to Chinese fireworks due to its regulations, although most of the fireworks consumed in Canada were imported, and had probably originated in China before being repackaged in other countries. The result of the stricter regulations in Canada was higher prices for consumers. It was estimated that a fireworks display that cost less than $3,500 in the U.S. would cost Canadians $8,000.

The foreign importers were powerful buyers for several reasons. First, they were very well informed, both through past dealings with China and the Internet. Second, they were able to hire agents who were very familiar with the industry in China. Third, they could deal directly with the factories that were willing to take lower prices. Fourth, there were basically no switching costs, so they could play the suppliers against each other.

The diversity of the cultures in the destination countries greatly reduced the seasonality of the fireworks production and sales. As a result, orders evened out throughout the year. However, the peak season was still toward the end of the year. For the U.S., it was before July 4. Usually, the importers would receive the shipment two or three months beforehand.

The Internet was gradually becoming a marketing outlet for Chinese fireworks. According to a fireworks company's office in Shenzhen, 20 percent to 30 percent of the business inquiries they got were through the Internet. However, export sales were still made mainly through foreign trade companies or agents.

In recent years, foreign investments were also funneled into the fireworks industry. In Liuyang, four of the large fireworks factories had foreign investments, made mainly by the fireworks trading companies in Hong Kong.

In 1999, out of the 5,000 or so containers of fireworks exported from China annually, about four-fifths were consumer fireworks. However, the demand for display fireworks was growing at a faster pace. It was predicted that the demand for display fireworks would increase as organized public shows grew more popular; at the same time, demand for consumer fireworks was expected to decline as regulations were getting stricter. Fireworks shows were increasingly being used in promotional campaigns, and were finding customers among amusement parks, sports teams, and retailers (for store openings, anniversaries and holiday celebrations). The massive annual Fourth of July fireworks put on by Macy's in New York City was one well-known example.

The Future of the Fireworks Industry in China

The managers of the Chinese fireworks companies that Jerry Yu talked to expressed mixed feelings toward the future outlook of their industry. One pessimistic view was that this was a sunset industry. This view held that regulations were killing the industry. Moreover, as people in general became more environmentally conscious and more distracted by the endless diversities of modern entertainment, traditional celebrations using firecrackers and fireworks would die a gradual death. As to the function of attracting public attention for promotional purposes, fireworks also faced challenges from new technologies, such as laser beams combined with sound effects.

In fact, make-believe "firecrackers" already appeared as substitutes in China. These make-believe firecrackers were made of red plastic tubes strung together like firecrackers. Electric bulbs were installed inside the tubes. When the power was turned on, the lights would emit sparks, accompanied by crackling reports that sounded like firecrackers. These were being used at weddings and grand openings in cities where firecrackers and fireworks were banned. More interesting substitutes were spotted at some weddings in Beijing, where people paved the road with little red balloons, and made the limousine carrying the bride and groom run over the balloons to make explosive cracking sounds as well as leave behind red bits and pieces of debris. On the other hand, more and more young couples were getting married in Western styles, in a church or a scenic green meadow outdoors, where serene and quiet happiness prevailed over the traditional noisy way of celebrating. Therefore, some managers believed that firecrackers and fireworks were doomed to fade off into history.

The more optimistic view, however, was that the industry would not die at all. If the right moves were made by the industry, it could even grow. Some said that tradition would not die so easily. It was in their national character for the Chinese to celebrate with an atmosphere of noisy happiness. Moreover, even in the West, the popularity of fireworks was not suffering from all the regulations. No real substitutes could replace fireworks, which combined the sensual pleasures of visual, audio, and emotional stimuli. For instance, the U.S. Congressional resolution in 1963 to use bells to replace fireworks in celebrating Independence Day never really caught on.

Fireworks were also being combined with modern technologies like laser beams, computerized firing, and musical accompaniment to make the appeal of fireworks more irresistible. The safety problem was not really as serious as people were made to believe, and would only improve with new technological innovations like smokeless fireworks.

However, both sides agreed that the Chinese fireworks industry would have to change its strategy, especially in international competition, to stay a viable and profitable player.

THE DECISION

Meanwhile, Jerry had to decide whether it was worthwhile to invest in the fireworks industry. He wondered whether he could apply the industry analysis framework he had studied in his MBA program.

The Richard Ivey School of Business gratefully acknowledges the generous support of The Richard and Jean Ivey Fund in the development of this case as part of the RICHARD AND JEAN IVEY FUND ASIAN CASE SERIES.

case 6 Competition in the U.S. Automotive Retailing Industry

Janet Parish
University of Alabama

Arthur A. Thompson
University of Alabama

Two perhaps interrelated revolutions are under way in the business of selling cars. One is the Web. The other is the consolidation of traditional dealers into national organizations like Wayne Huizenga's AutoNation or into manufacturer-controlled retail chains.
—From an article in *Forbes,* October 25, 1999

In early 2000, the automotive retailing industry seemed on the front edge of fundamental change. For a number of years, there had been rumblings of dissatisfaction among vehicle buyers with their purchasing experiences at local franchised dealerships. Apart from all the jokes about car salesmen, many customers reportedly found price haggling and high-pressure sales tactics distasteful or intimidating. Moreover, industry analysts believed there were many inefficiencies in the sales, marketing, and distribution of automobiles through the present franchised dealer networks of the major vehicle manufacturers, owing to costs that were believed to add as much as 30 percent to the sales prices of new vehicles. Automakers were looking at ways to overhaul their franchised dealer networks to squeeze some of these distribution inefficiencies out of the industry value chain. At the same time, hometown dealers were facing unprecedented competition from megaretailers, like AutoNation, and from a host of enterprising dot-com car-buying services that threatened to reshape the role and function of franchised dealers.

Increasingly, when shoppers went to local dealers to look for a new vehicle, they were armed with information gathered from the Internet concerning the invoice prices paid by dealers, the markups and margins that dealers had on each model and each option, the trade-in value of their present model, and perhaps price quotes from the new breed of dot-com auto retailers. Over 60 percent of car buyers were said to be using the Internet for research and price comparisons. Interested shoppers could go to hundreds of Internet sites to get free, detailed information on the various brands and models, read reviews of vehicle performance, and check out prices, rebates, and financing.

There were three types of Internet firms racing to get a slice of the budding market for online vehicle sales:

- *Lead generators* like Microsoft's CarPoint, cars.com, Autoweb.com, and car-club.com. The Web sites of lead generators let customers peruse all the various manufacturers' brands and models and make side-by-side model comparisons. They also provided base sticker prices and the prices of all the various options, and allowed visitors to check the models, colors, and optional equipment they wanted. Shoppers could fill out a simple form online requesting a price quote; the lead generator forwarded the customer requests for price quotes to nearby participating dealers, who followed up with an e-mail price quote and perhaps a telephone contact if a phone number was provided on the site form.

- *Direct sellers* like CarsDirect.com, carOrder.com, DriveOff.com, and Green light.com. The Web sites of direct sellers went a step further than lead generators, providing an immediate price quote and letting shoppers place an order online, then partnering with area franchised dealers to deliver the vehicle ordered.

- *Hybrid sites,* like Autobytel.com, that provided content for research, generated leads for participating dealers, took orders online, and used their franchised dealer networks for order fulfillment. Autobytel.com and some other hybrid sites also conducted auctions and provided online classified advertising that customers could use to sell a vehicle through online channels.

Online sales accounted for approximately 2.7 percent of the 15.5 million new vehicles sold in the United States in 1999.[1]

Meanwhile, manufacturers had launched Internet sites where vehicle buyers could get information, compare models and features, and be referred to nearby dealers for price quotes; visitors to Toyota's Web site could order custom-built cars and receive delivery within a week. As of mid-2000, more than 85 percent of the franchised dealers had launched Internet sites of their own to display their inventories and prices and to allow customers to fill out financing applications and request service appointments. In addition to their own sites, more than 50 percent of the 22,400 U.S. dealerships subscribed to one or more third-party Internet shopping services such as CarPoint (a service of the Microsoft Network), car.com, Autoweb.com, and Autobytel.com, which referred shoppers to nearby dealers to get price quotes on vehicles they were interested in. At the same time, thousands of franchised dealers had joined the dealer networks of the direct sellers and were providing the vehicles sold online. These developments reflected a growing understanding among both manufacturers and franchised dealers that the Internet had changed the dynamics of automotive retailing.

THE U.S. MOTOR VEHICLE RETAILING MARKET

Since Henry Ford's first Model T, more than 670 million new vehicles had been sold in the United States as of early 2000. Automotive retailing in the United States was nearly a $700 billion market in 2000, with annual sales of new cars and trucks running close to 15.5 million units in 1998 and 1999 and annual sales of used vehicles equal to

---

[1]Based on information compiled by J. D. Power and Associates.

exhibit 1   Number of Franchised Dealerships, 1978–99 (Beginning of Year)

Year	Number of Dealerships	Year	Number of Dealerships
1978	29,000	1989	25,000
1979	28,500	1990	24,825
1980	27,900	1991	24,200
1981	26,350	1992	23,500
1982	25,700	1993	22,950
1983	24,725	1994	22,850
1984	24,725	1995	22,800
1985	24,725	1996	22,750
1986	24,825	1997	22,700
1987	25,150	1998	22,600
1988	25,025	1999	22,400

Source: NADA Industry Analysis Division.

about 40 million units. There were an estimated 205 million vehicles in operation in the United States as of 1999.

Automotive retailers in the United States consisted of some 22,400 franchised dealers, who accounted for virtually 100 percent of new-car sales ($370 billion in revenues) and about 30 percent of the used-car sales ($120 billion in revenues). In addition, there were close to 35,000 independent used-car lots accounting for annual sales of $270 billion and close to 22 million used vehicles, plus a handful of blossoming online car sellers with sales of about 500,000 vehicles in 1999. Private-party sales of used vehicles were estimated to run close to 5 million units annually. Used vehicles had gained greater acceptance over the past 15 years due to improved vehicle quality and upward creep in the prices of new vehicles.

The Plight of the Small-Town Dealers

The number of new-car dealerships had declined gradually over the last three decades of the 20th century (see Exhibit 1). Dealer mergers and acquisitions, combined with manufacturers' efforts to weed out weak dealerships and reduce the overall number of dealer locations, were responsible for much of the decline. As shown in Exhibit 2, it was small-volume dealerships that were disappearing; dealerships selling more than 400 units annually were on the increase. In 1979 there were 11,500 dealer locations with sales of less than 150 new vehicles per year; in 1999, there are only 4,256 such dealerships. In contrast, in 1999 there were over 5,800 dealerships that sold more than 750 new units per year, compared to only 4,100 in 1979. Small-town dealers, lacking the scale of operation and market base of dealers in larger cities and towns, had found it hard to remain price-competitive and were either closing their doors or being acquired. Mounting price competition among both manufacturers anxious to build market share and dealers anxious to clear out inventories had made the retailing of new vehicles a low-margin, high-volume business in the 1990s. With the prices of new vehicles rising steadily, buyers had become quite price-sensitive and were shopping harder for the best

exhibit 2   Annual New-Unit Sales

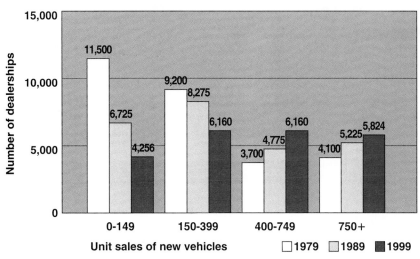

Source: NADA Industry Analysis Division.

deal, often driving 50 or 100 miles to shop at metropolitan dealers who were willing to accept bigger discounts off the sticker price. Small-volume dealers in mostly rural areas could not match the deeper discounts of high-volume dealers on new-vehicle sales and still cover their operating costs, hence the steady decline in the number of low-volume dealers. Those small-town dealers that were able to survive in the 1990s did so by taking on additional brands, both foreign and domestic, to build up their sales volume of both new and used vehicles.

By 2000, it was commonplace for dealers in most geographic locations, both rural and urban, to handle more than one manufacturer's brand. The National Automobile Dealers Association reported that its 19,500 members held nearly 40,000 separate franchises from domestic and foreign manufacturers. Exhibit 3 shows unit sales by dealership and average unit selling prices during the 1988–98 period.

The Emergence of Large-Volume, Multilocation Dealerships

Since the late 1980s and early 1990s, there had been a pronounced trend in auto retailing toward megadealerships offering not only a big selection of new models but also a wider variety of brands from multiple manufacturers. A number of aggressive, growth-minded dealers went on the acquisition trail, purchasing dealerships in several different cities and expanding their geographical reach. Then, in 1997, AutoNation, Inc., shook up the local dealer-dominated industry by acquiring hundreds of existing dealers and opening huge megalots to display and sell a variety of brands at a single metropolitan location. In less than three years, AutoNation had become the world's largest retailer of motor vehicles, boosting its revenues from $9 billion in 1997 to over $16 billion in 1998 to over $20 billion in 1999. Going into 2000, AutoNation had more than 400 automotive franchises in 23 states, representing 39 manufacturer brands. It also operated or

exhibit 3   Average Number of New Vehicles Sold per Dealership and
Average Retail Selling Prices, 1988–98

Year	New Vehicles Sold per Dealership	Average Retail Selling Price
1988	617	$14,100
1989	584	15,400
1990	567	15,900
1991	517	16,050
1992	555	17,100
1993	608	18,200
1994	661	19,200
1995	648	20,450
1996	664	21,900
1997	668	22,650
1998	691	23,600

Source: NADA Industry Analysis Division.

franchised 42 AutoNation USA used-vehicle megastores in 13 states. In 1999, Auto-
Nation sold approximately 1 million vehicles, the equivalent of two vehicles per minute,
24 hours a day, seven days a week.

Dealer Marketing and Sales Strategies

Franchised dealers relied heavily on advertising to attract the attention of people who
were in the market for a new vehicle and especially to draw price-sensitive customers
to their showrooms and lots. Dealer ads tended to emphasize the wide selection of
models and styles, discounts off sticker prices, special manufacturer rebates and promotions, low-cost financing, and low monthly payments. When shoppers drove onto
the lot, they were usually quickly greeted by a salesperson who inquired about their interests and guided them to the selection of models in inventory. Salespeople normally
strived to build a relationship with customers and win their confidence, touting the features of various models and offering test drives of those models that buyers found most
appealing. Most dealerships worked at making the buying experience pleasant and
paid considerable attention to delivering good after-the-sale service so that customers
would be loyal in returning for their next purchase.

Dealer Revenue-Cost-Profit Economics

Combined revenues of the 22,400 new-car dealers in the United States in 1998 were
a record $533.6 billion. Exhibit 4 shows the composition of dealer revenues. New-
vehicle department sales were up 7 percent in 1998 over 1997, used-vehicle sales up 4
percent, and service and parts sales up 2 percent. Pretax profits at the typical dealership
averaged $403,000. Exhibit 5 shows profit trends for new-car sales, used-car sales, and
service and parts sales. Exhibit 6 shows the trends in revenues and expenses for the average U.S. dealership for the 1988–98 period. The biggest expense dealers incurred
was for labor:

Payroll	$1,766,000
Advertising	234,800
Rent and equivalent	225,300
Floor-plan interest	87,700

In 1999, franchised dealers collectively spent $5.7 billion for advertising; this total included $2.9 billion for newspaper ads, $900 million for TV spots, $800 million for radio ads, and $272 million for Internet advertising. Advertising costs amounted to an average of $209 per new vehicle sold and $217 per used vehicle sold.

Dealer Pricing of New Vehicles   Dealers stocked their showrooms and lots with models they ordered directly from manufacturers. Dealers placed orders for specific models and styles based on the experience of what their customers liked and what styles, colors, and equipment options were selling best. However, as part of the bargain of filling dealer orders, manufacturers pressured dealers to take delivery of slow-selling, less-popular models and styles that they needed to move out of their own inventories of freshly produced models. The price that dealers paid manufacturers (called the dealer invoice cost) was usually 10 to 18 percent below the manufacturer's suggested retail price (MSRP)—the so-called sticker price customarily fixed to the rear window; the percentage markup over dealer invoice varied by make and model and was usually bigger for luxury makes and models than for low-end makes and models. However, it was standard practice for manufacturers to give dealers a small discount—termed a *holdback*—from the official invoice price for meeting certain sales targets. Dealers received the holdbacks at the end of the year; the size of each holdback varied from make to make and model to model, but was typically between 2 and 3 percent of the sales price. Because of the holdback, dealers anxious to make added sales often ran highly advertised "special clearance sales" at $100 (or some similarly small amount) over dealer invoice price. Many vehicle buyers did not know about the existence of holdbacks.

Dealers had discretion over the actual price at which they could sell a vehicle; some discount off the MSRP was typical. High-volume dealers generally operated on a lower margin over dealer invoice than did low-volume dealers; normally, dealers were unwilling to grant as large a discount off the MSRP on fast-selling vehicles in short supply from manufacturers. Traditionally, the size of the discount off the MSRP was the subject of back-and-forth bargaining between the dealer and the customer—a process

exhibit 4   Dealer Revenue Percentages, by Department, 1988 and 1998

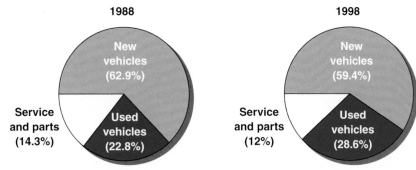

Source: NADA Industry Analysis Division.

exhibit 5   Profit Trends of Franchised Dealers, by Department, 1984–98

NEW-VEHICLE DEPARTMENT NET PROFIT
Average dealership, in thousands of dollars

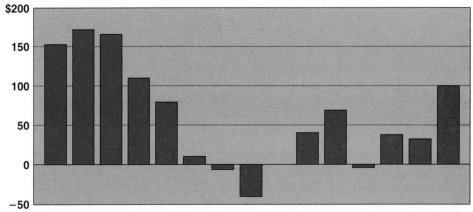

SERVICE AND PARTS DEPARTMENT NET PROFIT
Average dealership, in thousands of dollars

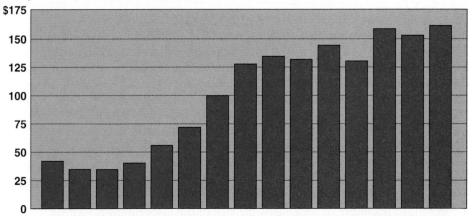

USED-VEHICLE DEPARTMENT NET PROFIT
Average dealership, in thousands of dollars

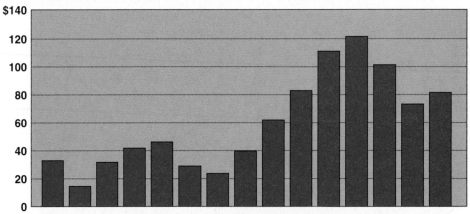

Source: NADA Industry Analysis Division.

exhibit 6 Selected Financial Statistics of Average Automotive Dealership, 1992–98

	1992	1993	1994	1995	1996	1997	1998	% Change 1997–1998
Total dealership sales	$14,372,487	$16,457,502	$18,865,279	$20,029,989	$21,562,332	$22,407,329	$23,712,667	5.8%
Total dealership gross	$ 1,983,403	$ 2,207,717	$ 2,471,352	$ 2,583,869	$ 2,788,010	$ 2,861,416	$ 3,058,934	6.9%
As % of total sales	13.8%	13.4%	13.1%	12.9%	12.9%	12.8%	12.9%	
Total dealership expense	$ 1,783,626	$ 1,944,109	$ 2,131,777	$ 2,303,449	$ 2,458,106	$ 2,554,435	$ 2,655,819	4.0%
As % of total sales	12.4%	11.8%	11.3%	11.5%	11.4%	11.4%	11.2%	
Net profit before taxes	$ 199,778	$ 263,608	$ 339,575	$ 280,420	$ 392,904	$ 306,980	$ 403,115	31.3%
As % of total sales	1.4%	1.6%	1.8%	1.4%	1.5%	1.4%	1.7%	
Net pretax profit in constant 1982 dollars	$ 137,409	$ 176,043	$ 221,113	$ 177,562	$ 198,926	$ 184,571	$ 238,508	29.2%
New-vehicle department sales	$ 8,609,119	$ 9,885,301	$11,375,763	$11,737,574	$12,527,715	$13,130,695	$14,085,324	7.3%
As % of total sales	59.9%	60.0%	60.3%	59.6%	59.1%	58.6%	59.4%	
Used-vehicle department sales	$ 3,650,612	$ 4,349,533	$ 5,074,760	$ 5,808,697	$ 6,360,888	$ 6,498,125	$ 6,781,823	4.4%
As % of total sales	25.4%	26.4%	25.9%	29.0%	29.5%	29.0%	29.6%	
Service and parts sales	$ 2,112,756	$ 2,240,668	$ 2,414,756	$ 2,483,719	$ 2,673,729	$ 2,778,509	$ 2,845,520	2.4%
As % of total sales	14.7%	13.6%	12.8%	12.4%	12.4%	12.4%	12.0%	
New-vehicle average selling price	$ 17,100	$ 18,200	$ 19,200	$ 20,450	$ 21,900	$ 22,650	$ 23,600	4.2%
Used-vehicle average selling price	$ 8,310	$ 9,130	$ 10,140	$ 11,050	$ 11,850	$ 12,100	$ 12,500	3.3%
Average net worth (as of 12/31)	$ 965,244	$ 1,022,053	$ 1,131,690	$ 1,220,597	$ 1,330,257	$ 1,389,052	$ 1,490,451	7.3%
Net profit as % of net worth	20.7%	25.8%	30.0%	23.0%	24.8%	22.1%	27.0%	

Source: NADA Industry Analysis Division.

that could consume hours and sometimes extend over several days. Most customers felt they were not getting a good deal unless they were able to negotiate what they considered a big discount off sticker price; some went from dealer to dealer in search of the best price. Many buyers were using the Internet to research dealer invoice costs and the value of the vehicle they wanted to trade in so that they could do a better job of negotiating. As part of their negotiating strategy, dealers tried to disguise the discount they were granting by presenting their offer to sell in terms of the difference between the sticker price and the trade-in allowance on the customer's used vehicle.

Used-Car Sales   Franchised new-car dealers sold 12 million used vehicles at retail in 1998 and 1999. Another 7.5 million used vehicles were wholesaled at auction or to other dealers. Franchised dealers acquired about 70 percent of their used-car inventories through trade-ins; the remaining 30 percent came from auction purchases, street purchases, and other sources. During the 1990s, the percentage of used cars obtained from auctions rose steadily from 10 percent in 1988 to 31 percent in 1998. Throughout the 1990s, the average retail price of used vehicles rose steadily from $7,400 in 1990 to $10,600 in 1995 to $12,500 in 1998.

The Service Department   Dealers considered after-the-sale service as one of the keys to building a strong relationship with the customers to whom they sold new and used vehicles. Vehicle owners who were highly satisfied with a dealer's repair and maintenance services and service department personnel were more likely to return to the dealership to purchase their next vehicles. Moreover, the service department was a dealer's biggest contributor to the bottom line (see Exhibit 5).

National Automobile Dealers Association

Approximately 19,500 of the 22,400 franchised dealers were members of the National Automobile Dealers Association (NADA), which fought vigorously to represent the best interests of its members. In recent years, NADA had spent considerable time and energy fighting both the Internet car-selling firms and the attempts of manufacturers to integrate forward into manufacturer-owned dealerships.

While NADA officials anticipated that growing buyer use of the Internet would affect motor vehicle retailing, they took comfort in the fact that the laws of most states prevented anyone other than a franchised dealer from selling directly to new-vehicle buyers—an obstacle that online car sellers were busily strategizing to get around. Moreover, NADA and most of its dealer members believed that the majority of buyers would want to personally look at the vehicle, check out the exterior and interior, and take a test drive before committing to a purchase that was typically the second-largest purchase they made (after buying a home).

In a keynote speech at the National Automobile Dealers Association 2000 Convention, James A. Willingham, NADA chairman, said:

> It's important to understand that dealers do much more than simply "sell" cars and trucks. We hire and train skilled sales and service professionals. We perform safety recalls and consumer education, such as the proper installation of child safety seats. We invest millions in technology, training, and facilities. In short, we bring tangible value to the transaction—dealer-added value.[2]

---

[2]www.nada.org.

Willingham suggested that while the Web was a great way to reach a new generation of consumers, it was not a replacement for traditional dealers. He expressed the view that there was more to motor vehicle retailing than agreeing on a price and delivering the vehicle:

> Most importantly, there's the feeling that someone—a real person—is standing behind the product. Now, combine a well-designed, dealer-based Web presence with the personal customer service of a top dealership, and you have a powerful "click-and-mortar" auto retailing strategy for the 21st century.[3]

Nonetheless, NADA felt compelled to look for ways to take advantage of the Internet on behalf of its 19,500 member dealers and to counter the emerging competition of online car-buying services. In 1999, NADA launched a Web site that fielded leads for member dealerships. The site was developed to offer shoppers the largest online new- and used-vehicle inventory of any automobile Web site. In April 2000, NADA launched its own car-shopping Web site (NADAdealers.com), providing consumers with:

- Access to the invoice prices of new vehicles. (However, the site did not reveal the incentives or holdbacks that manufacturers rebated to dealers for meeting sales targets—information that was available on some independent Internet sites.) NADA's move to disclose invoice prices was a radical departure from its long-standing opposition to disclosing dealers' costs for new cars and trucks, but observers felt it was necessary if dealers were to counter the e-challenge from dot-com companies.
- An online inventory of new and used vehicles at the 6,000 participating dealers. (Other dealers could post their inventories of new and used cars for $150 per month.)
- Links to used-car trade-in values and dealer sites.

NADA hoped that eventually all 19,500 of its dealer-members (about 90 percent of the 22,400 franchised dealers) would be accessible through its portal.[4] The NADA site provided shoppers with the names of three dealers in their geographic area that carried the brands they wanted to buy and made those referrals at no charge to the dealer, thus undercutting the referral sites that charged fees either to buyers or dealers for acting as middlemen in a transaction. NADA also began a program in which members could get software packages enabling them to set up their own Web sites or upgrade existing sites. NADA said it developed the site to reduce dealers' Internet marketing costs and to give dealers a direct relationship with online customers. NADA believed that its new initiatives would encourage dealers to affiliate with the NADA site and eventually allow consumers to search dealer inventories at all its members' locations.

AUTOMOBILE BUYER DEMOGRAPHICS

Exhibit 7 shows the demographic makeup of U.S. households in 1998, with projections to 2008. Whereas in the 1970s married couples with children under 18 accounted for close to 50 percent of all U.S. households, in 1998 this group made up only 25 percent, or about 25 million households. That number is not expected to increase in the next decade. More than 30 percent of the 102 million U.S. households were comprised of people either living alone or with nonfamily members; their numbers were expected to

---

[3]www.nada.org.

[4]"Auto Dealers to Launch a Web Site," *The Wall Street Journal,* March 16, 2000, p. A3.

exhibit 7   Selected U.S. Population Statistics, 1998, with Projections to 2008

	1998	2008	Change	1998 to 2008 Percent Change
All households	102,022,000	112,433,000	10,411,000	10.20%
Family households, total	70,938,000	77,864,000	6,926,000	9.80
Married couples without children < 18	28,977,000	34,335,000	5,458,000	18.80
Married couples with children < 18	25,166,000	25,155,000	−11,000	0.00
Female householder, no husband	12,917,000	14,061,000	1,144,000	8.90
Male householder, no wife	3,878,000	4,213,000	335,000	8.60
Nonfamily households, total	31,084,000	34,569,000	3,485,000	11.20
Living alone, total	25,637,000	28,780,000	3,089,000	12.00
Females living alone	15,154,000	17,255,000	2,101,000	13.90
Males living alone	10,537,000	11,525,000	988,000	9.40
Living with nonrelatives	5,393,000	5,789,000	396,000	7.30
Female householder	2,124,000	2,334,000	210,000	9.90
Male householder	3,269,000	3,455,000	186,000	5.70

Source: TGE Demographics.

increase 11 percent by 2008. Married couples without children at home accounted for 28 percent of all households and were expected to grow 19 percent by 2008, the strongest growth among all household types. One of the fastest-growing age groups was people over 65. During the 1998–2008 period, African American households were expected to grow to 14.3 million, a 16.6 percent growth rate. Hispanic households were expected to grow 36 percent, or to 11.6 million by 2008. The number of Asian American households will also increase to 36.5 percent by 2008. Children will be a large component of these numbers. Nearly 35.7 percent of Hispanic married couple households had children under 18 at home in 1998, followed by 32 percent of Asians, 25 percent of whites, and 18.3 percent of blacks. Market research indicated that the type of new vehicle purchased was strongly affected by whether or not children were present in a vehicle buyer's household and, if so, by their numbers and ages (see Exhibit 8).

Market research showed that used-vehicle buyers tended to be somewhat younger and less affluent than new-vehicle buyers. However, used vehicles were becoming more appealing to buyers between the ages of 35 and 49 with annual incomes ranging between $50,000 and $75,000. This was partly attributable to the widespread availability of low-mileage, nicely equipped vehicles in good condition that were coming off two-year and three-year lease programs.

Types of Vehicle Shoppers

A recent study by J. D. Power and Associates, a leading research authority on buyer experiences with motor vehicles, classified vehicle shoppers into four categories—armed unfriendlies, relationship seekers, low-involved pragmatists, and highly involved deal seekers.[5]

> *Armed unfriendlies* (33 percent) were said to be a relatively antagonistic group of shoppers. They tended to be precise and systematic, and came equipped with

---

[5] J. D. Power and Associates, Press Release, June 24, 1999. Posted at www.jdpower.com.

exhibit 8   Share of New Vehicle Purchase by Family Type, July 1998–June 1999

	Married Couples with Children	Married Couples without Children	Multiple Adults with Children	Multiple Adults without Children	One Adult with Children	One Adult, Living Alone
Small car	11.8%	11.1%	14.8%	13.5%	17.4%	15.9%
Midsize car	18.4	21.3	19.1	21.6	21.0	22.7
Large car	1.3	4.0	1.4	2.9	0.9	2.4
Sports car	4.2	4.5	4.8	5.0	4.5	5.6
Luxury car	7.0	10.1	6.7	9.2	6.7	9.0
Minivan	14.6	7.5	10.6	5.5	11.5	4.6
Sport utility vehicle	22.0	19.4	19.9	18.8	21.2	19.5
Pickup truck	19.6	21.3	21.6	22.7	15.9	19.8
Full-size van	1.4	0.8	1.1	0.8	0.9	0.5
Total	100.0%	100.0%	100.0%	100.0%	100.0%	100.0%

Source: The Polk Company.

information in order to better negotiate with sales personnel. This group of shoppers consisted of the youngest and most educated of the four groups of buyers.

Relationship seekers (25 percent) tended to be outgoing and loyal to brands and dealerships. They enjoyed the process of shopping and negotiating for a new vehicle.

Low-involved pragmatists (24 percent) were said to be private, reserved, and convenience-minded. Approximately 45 percent were female. Members of this group believed that shopping around for the perfect vehicle was not the best use of their time and were somewhat indifferent to the kind of car they drove.

Highly involved deal seekers (18 percent) were 73 percent male, younger than the average new-vehicle shopper, and usually shopped many dealerships before making a final selection. They tended to gather a significant amount of information before shopping. These buyers were said to be strong-willed, direct, and competitive. They enjoyed shopping for a new vehicle and were generally friendly toward dealerships and salespeople.

Growing Buyer Use of the Internet to Shop for Vehicles

More and more consumers were using the Internet as a tool to gather information about various models, to compare the features of one vehicle against another in trying to decide what to buy, to learn dealer invoice prices and rebate incentives, to search out the best prices from various dealers, and to avoid the high-pressure sales tactics that salespeople sometimes employed. One newspaper reported the experience of a buyer who had used the Internet to shop for a new vehicle as follows:

> Beth Trane knew she wanted to buy a new sport utility vehicle. But after visiting car dealerships near her home in Orlando, Fla., Trane knew she didn't want to buy her new SUV there.
>
> While researching options and prices on the Internet, Trane started to feel the Orlando dealerships were not offering her a good deal. She returned to the Internet, which pointed her to Miracle Toyota in Winter Haven, Fla.
>
> A few e-mails to that dealership helped her decide what to buy and what to pay for it. That prompted Trane, 38, to call Miracle Toyota to seal the deal. The first time she set foot on the lot was to pick up her 1999 Toyota 4Runner Limited.

exhibit 9   Example of Pricing Data Available from Online
                    Vehicle Sellers

2000 Dodge
Durango
Sport 4WD Sport Utility
Vehicle

select a new make, model, or trimline

	Invoice	MSRP	carOrder
My Total Price:	$26,571	$29,425	$27,371

Payment Estimator:	finance (edit):	$643.79
disclaimer	lease (edit):	$453.51

Source: www.carorder.com, April 2000.

"I was not happy with the shopping experience in Orlando," Trane said. "It's very pressured. Over the Internet, we were able to work out the numbers very easily. I just felt more comfortable."[6]

J. D. Power and Associates estimated that the share of new-car buyers using the Internet to help them with their car purchases had grown from 25 percent in 1998 to 60 percent during the last quarter of 1999, and projected that at least 65 percent would make use of the Internet by the end of 2000. The Internet sales manager of a suburban dealership in Birmingham, Alabama, said, "I'd say about 50 percent of the people who come onto our lot have gotten information off the Internet before they come here. Folks who use the Web are some of the most educated customers we have—they're sharp."[7] J. D. Power also reported that more than 60 percent of new-vehicle buyers believed they were able to find out the dealer invoice price during the shopping process.[8] Exhibit 9 illustrates the pricing information available from carOrder.com. According to Forrester Research, 8 million customers were expected to use the Internet for car buying by 2003 (up from an estimated 5 million in 1999), resulting in 500,000 vehicles sold over the Internet and sales totaling $12 billion. Some observers and executives of Internet car-buying companies, however, believed online vehicle sales would grow much more quickly.

J. D. Power's 1999 New Autoshopper.com Study predicted that the growing influence of the Internet would hit domestic manufacturers the hardest:

> The more time a person spends online, the less likely he or she is to purchase a domestic vehicle. Overall, domestic manufacturers currently have approximately 70 percent market share; however, this share drops to 58 percent among Internet shoppers. Furthermore, only half the shoppers who submit a purchase request to an online buying service purchase a domestic vehicle.[9]

MANUFACTURER EFFORTS TO ENTER THE AUTOMOTIVE RETAILING MARKET

Since 1998 Ford and General Motors had been trying to acquire franchised dealers in certain markets to begin setting up their own retail distribution network—a practice forbidden by the franchising laws in a number of states and a move vigorously opposed by

---

[6]Chris Brennan, "Will the Web Lure Buyers to Dealerships or Drive Them Away?" *The Tuscaloosa News* (a New York Times Regional Newspaper), January 23, 2000, p. D1.

[7]As quoted in "Kicking Tires in Cyberspace," *The Birmingham News,* February 6, 2000, p. D6.

[8]www.jdpower.com.

[9]1999 New Autoshopper.com Study, J. D. Power and Associates.

franchised dealers. In 1999 GM announced a controversial plan to buy up to 10 percent of its 7,000-plus dealerships; dealers complained loudly and bitterly, prompting GM to agree to consult with dealers in the future on such moves. Daewoo, a South Korean car maker that had entered the U.S. market in late 1998, had recently opened several factory-owned retail locations. Daewoo's retail distribution strategy for the U.S. market was to have a mix of 25 percent company-owned stores and 75 percent dealer-owned stores. Its plan had led to legislation in some states limiting or banning manufacturer-owned retail distribution. Ford had formed co-owned companies with local dealers in Tulsa, Oklahoma City, San Diego, Salt Lake City, and Rochester, New York, whereby participating dealers either sold their franchise rights to Ford or partnered with Ford at a newly open location. Either way, several dealership locations in the area were closed. Several manufacturers were also said to be developing or pursuing plans to begin advertising and selling used cars coming off company-leasing programs directly over the Internet.

Dealer Efforts to Combat Manufacturer-Owned Dealerships

Dealers had lobbied state lawmakers and regulators to block manufacturer-owned dealerships and also to prevent online sales of new cars by dot-com companies; they had put pressure on government officials in many states to strictly uphold existing franchise laws that made it all but impossible for anyone other than a franchised dealer to sell a new car to a customer—even the U.S. employees of Ford, GM, and other U.S.-based automakers had to buy through dealers rather than buying factory-direct. In 1999 franchised dealers in North Carolina successfully lobbied the state legislature to ban manufacturer-owned dealerships within 45 miles of a franchised dealer selling the same brand; dealers arguing in favor of the restriction expressed a fear that factory-owned franchises would get special treatment, such as a bigger supply of the best-selling models and easy credit approval for vehicle buyers.[10] Other dealers complained that entry of manufacturer-owned stores into the automotive retailing business created an unlevel playing field for dealers because it put them into direct competition with their suppliers. Opposing consumer groups argued that manufacturers wanted to get into retailing to consolidate and eliminate dealerships so they could get better control over pricing. Strong dealer opposition, coupled with restrictive legislation in certain states, was prompting car manufacturers to rethink their strategies and begin to cooperate more with dealers to ward off the dot-com car-buying services.

DEALER–MANUFACTURER ALLIANCES TO BLOCK MARKET INVASION BY THE DOT-COM COMPANIES

To combat the challenge of Internet car-buying services, dealers and manufacturers—despite their many acrimonious battles with each other over the years and the recent flap over manufacturer entry into automotive retailing—were cooperating to try to minimize buyers' use of dot-com companies in finding or buying a new or used vehicle. Dealers were lobbying state legislatures to maintain and enforce the laws that prohibited anyone other than a franchised dealer from selling a new vehicle within their borders—and so far they had been successful.

A strong manufacturer–dealer alliance put independent Web sites at a disadvantage. The strategy of Internet sites such as CarsDirect.com was to guarantee shoppers

---

[10]"Car Sellers, Automakers Haggle over Dealerships," *USA Today,* November 15, 1999, p. 10B.

a price for a vehicle, arrange to buy it from a dealer at a relatively modest markup over dealer cost, then deliver it to the buyer's home. Dot-com companies could not buy vehicles directly from the manufacturer and, so far, manufacturers had refused to do business with wholesale brokers who wanted to make a business of providing vehicles to dot-com sellers. Most observers believed that until online car sellers like CarsDirect.com and Autobytel.com had their own factory-direct source for vehicles it would be difficult for them to satisfy customers and capture more than a token share of the market for new-vehicle sales.

THE RESPONSES OF DEALERSHIPS TO BUYER USE OF THE INTERNET

Dealer-operated Web sites were growing in importance from the standpoint of providing a new source of leads and sales. While the majority of dealer sites received an average of 50 hits per month during the last quarter of 1999, 14 percent received more than 500 hits per month. And the numbers were trending upward each quarter. More than 50 percent of the dealers had partnered with lead-generating Internet sites like Microsoft's CarPoint, cars.com, and Autoweb.com by agreeing to pay monthly or per-hit fees for steering buyers to their dealerships.

Virtually all dealers had begun actively courting sales generated from Internet leads and e-mail inquiries from customers and had hired a new breed of salesperson—one who was computer and Internet savvy and could respond promptly and effectively to customer inquiries without scaring the customer away with high-pressure sales tactics. Over 95 percent of the dealers with Web sites had salespeople specifically assigned to handle Internet-generated leads. And most all dealers and their Internet salespeople were working on how to perfect their Internet sales techniques. So far, it was clear that a very quick response was critical; people wanted to know their message had been received and was being taken seriously. A good Internet rapport and knowledgeable, forthcoming answers to questions could often lead to sales, sometimes without any contact other than the Internet. Close to 50 percent of dealer Web sites allowed customers to fill out financing applications and request service appointments, as well as view inventories and prices.

Miracle Toyota in Winter Haven, Florida, was selling 35–40 cars per month through Internet contacts, most of which turned out to be comparison-shopping buyers in Tampa and Orlando. Lute Riley Honda in suburban Dallas sold nearly 100 cars a month from online contacts.[11] King Acura in Birmingham, Alabama, generated 325 leads in October 1999 from 45 different Internet sites ranging from www.acura.com (the manufacturer's site) to Yahoo! In January 2000, a slow month for vehicle sales, King Acura got 507 referrals from 62 sites.[12]

E-COMMERCE STRATEGIES OF VEHICLE MANUFACTURERS

Exhibit 10 shows the current market share trends for vehicle sales, by manufacturer. While manufacturers were developing a presence online, they were cognizant of the fact that their dealers were the ones who were in contact with the customers. They realized

---

[11]"Car Dealers Say: Follow the Mouse," *Business Week,* April 10, 2000, p. 110.
[12]"Kicking Tires in Cyberspace."

exhibit 10   New-Vehicle Sales in the United States and Market Share by Manufacturer, 1988–98

Year	Chrysler	Ford	GM	Toyota	Honda	Nissan	Volkswagen	Other Imports	Total
1988	2,208,100	3,751,900	5,511,400	936,000	769,000	642,500	197,200	1,359,000	15,374,900
	14.36%	24.40%	35.85%	6.09%	5.00%	4.18%	1.28%	8.84%	
1989	2,004,000	3,579,900	5,106,200	945,400	783,100	664,200	154,900	1,302,700	14,540,500
	13.78%	24.62%	35.12%	6.50%	5.39%	4.57%	1.07%	8.96%	
1990	1,698,100	3,317,100	4,934,300	1,058,000	854,900	621,600	157,500	1,216,300	13,857,700
	12.25%	23.94%	35.61%	7.63%	6.17%	4.49%	1.14%	8.78%	
1991	1,507,700	2,867,400	4,319,700	1,010,500	803,400	583,400	109,000	1,109,000	12,310,000
	12.25%	23.29%	35.09%	8.21%	6.53%	4.74%	0.89%	9.01%	
1992	1,713,000	3,192,500	4,397,500	1,023,600	768,800	585,500	90,500	1,089,000	12,860,600
	13.32%	24.82%	34.19%	7.96%	5.98%	4.55%	0.70%	8.47%	
1993	2,014,800	3,562,400	4,667,000	1,033,200	717,400	687,700	62,100	1,118,400	13,896,000
	14.74%	25.64%	33.59%	7.44%	5.16%	0.05%	0.45%	8.05%	
1994	2,204,000	3,818,100	5,015,900	1,088,100	788,200	774,300	109,600	1,260,400	15,058,600
	14.64%	25.35%	33.31%	7.23%	5.23%	5.14%	0.73%	8.37%	
1995	2,164,300	3,801,000	4,841,600	1,083,400	794,600	770,300	106,600	1,166,300	14,728,000
	14.70%	25.81%	32.87%	7.36%	5.40%	5.23%	0.72%	7.92%	
1996	2,450,800	3,843,400	4,743,600	1,159,700	843,900	749,800	163,200	1,142,700	15,097,200
	16.23%	25.46%	31.42%	7.68%	5.59%	4.97%	1.08%	7.57%	
1997	2,303,800	3,807,100	4,734,100	1,230,100	940,400	728,400	172,000	1,214,400	15,130,200
	15.23%	25.16%	31.29%	8.13%	0.06%	4.81%	1.14%	8.03%	
1998	2,510,000	3,860,200	4,570,100	1,361,000	1,009,600	624,600	267,200	1,342,300	15,541,900
	16.15%	24.84%	29.41%	8.76%	6.50%	4.00%	1.72%	8.64%	
Average	**2,073,782**	**3,581,909**	**4,803,764**	**1,084,455**	**824,845**	**675,391**	**144,545**	**1,210,955**	**14,399,600**
1988–98	**14.40%**	**24.88%**	**33.36%**	**7.53%**	**5.73%**	**4.69%**	**1.00%**	**8.41%**	

Source: NADA Industry Analysis Division.

the potential risk of channel conflict if the dealers felt threatened by their online presence. Until early 2000, manufacturers' Web sites served mainly to provide information for consumers and a referral service for dealerships. Virtually all of the leading manufacturers had Web sites that provided information about their various models and allowed consumers to configure the vehicles they were interested in—including optional equipment, exterior colors, and interior trim. This information was then transmitted to nearby dealers, whose salespeople would promptly be in touch with the prospect by e-mail or phone with a price quote and follow-up sales information. From there, visits to the dealer for a test drive or on-site inspection of the vehicles matching the buyer's preferences and negotiation and haggling over price proceeded in much the same fashion that it had prior to the advent of the Internet. In addition to the product information that was available on these sites, the manufacturers offered information to vehicle owners relating to service, financing, and safety issues.

However, in recent months there had been some new developments on the part of manufacturers.

Toyota Motor Corporation

In the fall of 1999, Toyota Motor Corporation announced that it would begin producing its Camry Solara coupe to customer order in only five days. Toyota planned to include other models in its five-day order-to-production-to-delivery strategy as soon as it perfected the process for the Camry. The move was seen as a possible first step in shifting from a build-for-dealer-inventory business model in North America to a build-to-order business model, which was already relatively common in Japan and Europe. Surveys of car buyers indicated that close to 50 percent were unable to find the model, color, or equipment configuration they preferred when shopping dealer lots. Traditionally, dealers made educated guesses as to what model, color, and equipment options buyers would prefer, placed their orders with manufacturers, and hoped that car buyers would find what they wanted from the array of vehicles they had in stock. To induce customers to compromise if what they wanted was not in stock, manufacturers offered rebates and dealers made price concessions. Custom-ordered vehicles could be obtained, but delivery times often ranged from 30 to 60 days.

Industry observers believed Toyota's competitive move to five-day delivery on custom orders was intended not only to better satisfy car buyers and encourage brand loyalty but also to gain the benefits of tighter supply chain management and reduce reliance on costly promotions to push sales of slow-selling models. A build-to-order business model permitted tighter just-in-time delivery of parts and components to Toyota assembly plants, plus a reduced need for profit-eroding rebates and discounts on unpopular models and configurations. It also paved the way for dealers to drastically cut the number of vehicles kept in stock (thus driving down their inventory-financing costs). If the build-to-order approach caught on with vehicle buyers, a dealership would have to stock only a minimal number of showroom models for inspection and test-drives, and a limited number of vehicles for immediate delivery; it would function mainly as a pickup point for custom orders. Dealer investments in acres of prime expensive real estate at visible, high-traffic locations would be less necessary. A build-to-order model would also work to the advantage of Internet car-buying services. It would be easy for car shoppers to do their research online, make price comparisons, and place their order.[13] According to one estimate, build-to-order assembly could reduce average vehicle costs by over $1,500.[14]

Ford Motor Company

In April 2000, Ford was in the midst of embracing the Internet and e-commerce on a number of fronts. In mid-1999, an internal team made a presentation to senior executives that envisioned (1) factories that built cars to customers' orders, (2) dealers that reported repair and maintenance problems on particular models or components via the Internet as vehicles came in for service so that assembly plants and suppliers could make corrective adjustments promptly, (3) suppliers that controlled inventories at Ford assembly plants and delivered most parts and components on a just-in-time basis, (4) links to suppliers and assembly plants such that when a customer hit the button to order a custom-equipped Ford Explorer online, all the relevant information would be instantaneously transmitted to suppliers providing the parts and components, to assembly plants building the vehicle, to the dealer who would deliver it, to the finance and insurance companies doing the underwriting, and to the Ford designers doing the brainstorming for new SUV models. Ford's CEO and other senior executives were impressed and began a series of initiatives called CustomerConnect to make the vision a reality and link buyers, parts suppliers, assembly plants, dealers, finance companies, and designers. In early 2000, Ford put in place a new online trading market for the company's 30,000 suppliers worldwide and began using the Internet to arrange for purchases and to communicate and coordinate more closely with its suppliers.

---

[13]"An Automaker Tries the Dell Way," *The Wall Street Journal,* August 30, 1999.
[14]"Detroit Goes Digital," *Fortune,* April 17, 2000, p. 172.

To pacify its dealers, Ford had pledged at the 2000 convention of the National Automobile Dealers Association to continue to partner with its franchised dealers in executing its e-commerce strategy and refrain from selling vehicles directly to buyers via the Internet. While Ford had eased back on its initiatives to acquire dealer franchises, its long-term strategic intent regarding forward integration into automotive retailing via acquiring dealerships remained unclear.

General Motors

General Motors launched an e-GM initiative in mid-1999 to link its suppliers and dealers and to forge closer ties to consumers via the Internet. Established as a separate venture within the company, e-GM had set up 150 consumer Web sites around the world to help buyers pick the vehicles they wanted to buy and to try to build relationships with prospective buyers. It had plans to integrate these sites, make them much easier to navigate (in response to complaints), and streamline the process of doing transactions online. GM's U.S. Web site, www.gmbuypower.com, had software that allowed shoppers to configure the vehicle they wanted and a locator service to determine whether any nearby dealers had that vehicle in stock. GM's TradeXchange initiative to move to online procurement with all of its suppliers was expected to cut the administrative costs of filling a purchase order from $100 to $10. During mid-1999, GM had moved to begin selling cars coming off lease programs to consumers in an Internet-based business in Houston, Texas, but Texas refused to issue a business license for GM's venture because of prevailing franchise laws; GM was forced to find a Texas dealership to function as a partner in its venture.

In the fall of 1999 GM began studying what it would have to do to take orders online, custom-produce the vehicles, and deliver them on a promised date. The internal changes were rather dramatic and far-reaching. By early 2000, a team of 100 GM executives and experts from all over the world had forged a plan to put custom-order manufacturing capabilities in place by at least 2003. The key time frames and capabilities that were needed included:[15]

- Reducing times from order to manufacture from 10 days (the minimum) in 1999 to 3 days.
- Reducing normal shipping times from the 11-day average in 1999 to 1–8 days. (Most vehicles were shipped by rail, then transferred to trucks for delivery to dealers.)
- Creating the capability to achieve shipping times of 1–4 days for "premium" orders or special delivery requests.
- Reducing the present elapsed order-to-delivery time from as much as 8 weeks to 4–11 days.

Top executives speculated that as many as 70 percent of GM's customers would take advantage of the opportunity to order custom-equipped vehicles by 2003. In addition, GM executives believed that a well-executed custom-order system could result in a 50 percent reduction in the $40 billion in inventories that dealers stocked and that GM maintained in parts inventories at its assembly plants. GM hoped that capturing information as consumers configured their cars online would help GM designers reduce the number of possible combinations, simplifying parts procurement and assembly. GM's plans included linking suppliers into its Web site so that they could track what was needed and so that the necessary components could be ordered in real time as customers

---

[15]"GM Retools to Sell Cars Online," *The Wall Street Journal,* February 22, 2000, p. B23.

submitted vehicle orders. Harold Kutner, GM's executive in charge of the new plan said, "I envision one day having a 'war room' crammed with computers and monitors where we could track any customer's order anywhere in the world."[16]

GM believed that offering customers quick delivery of custom vehicles would give it a significant competitive advantage over independent Internet sites. Internet car-buying services could not offer custom-built vehicles given the present restrictive franchising laws; their only option was to search through dealer stocks to find vehicles in nearby dealer inventories that closely matched what an individual buyer wanted. Like Ford, GM had pledged that it would stay out of the Internet retail business and would not undermine dealers with Internet-direct factory sales.

Ford-GM-DaimlerChrysler Online Purchasing Alliance

In early 2000, Ford, General Motors, and DaimlerChrysler announced the formation of an unprecedented alliance to build an online network to jointly handle the procurement of the $240 billion in materials, parts, components, and supplies that they used world-wide each year. The venture was expected to result in the creation of the world's largest business-to-business Internet company in terms of revenues and scale of operation. The purpose of the venture was to bring together all their suppliers, allowing them to transact purchases at a single Internet site and thereby streamline their entire supply chain. The three automakers had an equal ownership stake in the venture, which was expected to operate independently. Plans called for the supplier exchange site to be opened to other automakers and to offer them ownership stakes in the new company. Several analysts expected that online parts purchasing would ultimately cut the costs of the average vehicle by about $1,100.[17]

BUSINESS MODELS AND STRATEGIES OF THE DOT-COM COMPETITORS IN AUTOMOTIVE RETAILING

The first generation of automotive-related Internet sites began as pure information providers. They sought to attract site traffic by providing credible and useful information on brands and models, dealer invoice prices (always of great interest to buyers desirous of bargaining hard with dealers), the latest incentive and rebate offers from manufacturers, vehicle performance reviews, and other such topics of interest to vehicle shoppers. The business model of information providers called for covering the costs of the site by selling advertising. These early information providers quickly concluded that their strategy was too revenue-constrained and, seeing larger revenue-growth opportunities, transitioned to lead generators or direct sellers. One of the best sites for research and information was Edmunds.com, but starting in 2000 Edmunds.com expanded into lead generation and referrals, leaving no pure information providers among the major high-traffic automotive-related sites.

The Business Model of Lead Generators

A number of entrepreneurial companies saw early on that the Internet presented considerable opportunities in automotive retailing beyond just providing information. The

---

[16]Ibid.
[17]"Detroit Goes Digital," *Fortune*, April 17, 2000. p. 172.

first generation of online car services acted as content providers and dealer referral services. They developed sites with a wealth of information that car shoppers could peruse in the course of researching what to buy, and they also incorporated links to the Web sites of providers of auto-related products and services. Typically, the content at their sites consisted of both original information developed internally by their own editorial staffs and information assembled from a wide variety of outside sources. The leading outside source was Chrome Data, a company based in Portland, Oregon, that had pioneered the technology of online vehicle configuration and that collected and maintained a database of production specifications for all makes and models, descriptions of standard and optional equipment, vehicle photographs, and manufacturers' suggested retail prices (MSRPs). Chrome Data had incorporated all this information into software products that it sold commercially. Most of the online content providers used Chrome Data's software products as primary tools for giving site visitors the ability to configure custom-equipped models and check out the resulting sticker prices. Chrome Data was the only independent provider of such information, and its vehicle and pricing information precisely matched manufacturers' data, thus providing vehicle shoppers with very accurate product and pricing information.

Most sites had features that allowed shoppers to compare several different models side-by-side. When site visitors decided on a vehicle type equipped the way they wanted it, they could fill out a brief form containing an e-mail address, a zip code, and perhaps other information and click on a button requesting a price quote. The requests for price quotes were then forwarded to area dealers who had signed on with the online car-buying service to provide quotes; dealers either paid the online car-buying service a monthly fee for all such lead referrals or a fixed fee per referral. Competition was active among the growing number of lead generators to sign up dealers and gain the capability to provide quotes to shoppers nationwide.

The business model of car-buying sites that specialized in providing content and generating lead referrals was to cover costs and make a profit by (1) selling advertising and sponsorships to companies wishing to promote their own goods and services to the Web site audience, and (2) signing up dealerships as affiliates and charging them a fee for lead referrals. Such sites had shied away from trying to sell cars directly to car shoppers because of the barriers posed by state franchise laws, the costs of getting the vehicle to the buyer's home without having a number of local distribution points, and a general belief that only a very few shoppers would be willing to complete an entire transaction online without first having test-driven or seen the vehicle or talked to a salesperson.

The Business Model of Online Direct Sellers

The second generation of online car-buying services elected to go a step beyond referring leads to local franchised dealers and take on the task of brokering the entire transaction. Their strategy was to immediately quote customers a price for vehicles as shoppers configured their choices of makes, models, and optional equipment online. The price quotes typically included a total cash price for the vehicle, the monthly payment if the car was leased, and the monthly payment if the car was financed; shoppers could select from any of several leasing or monthly payment plans. Along with these quotes, shoppers were shown the dealer invoice cost and the MSRP. Once customers were ready to place an order, they could enter their credit card number authorizing a deposit of around $250 (usually refundable) to start the transaction rolling and get information as to the time and place of delivery. Online sellers filled customer orders by prearranging with area franchised dealers to supply particular makes and models and function as the actual seller (to comply with state franchise laws). Online sellers were able to provide instantaneous price quotes because they had already negotiated discounts from the vehicle's MSRP with participating area dealers; online brokers added a fee (usually in the neighborhood of $250) to the dealer's discounted price to arrive at the price quoted to online shoppers.

In effect, the business model of online direct sellers was to function as middleman or broker in making the sale. They had two primary revenue sources: (1) the fee earned from brokering the transaction, and (2) the sales of advertising and site sponsorship—especially ad sales to partners interested in providing financing or vehicle insurance or companies selling automotive-related goods and services. Their value added in the transaction was twofold—providing the area dealer with an additional sale and sparing the customer the time-consuming experience of visiting dealer showrooms and the nuisance of negotiating and haggling with dealers. However, like referral services, the strategies of direct sellers were currently constrained by the need to make the sale through franchised dealers and by an inability to source vehicles directly from manufacturers. Virtually all direct sellers were busily putting together nationwide dealer networks that would give them the capability to deliver all makes and models to customers in all geographic locations. A few direct sellers had signed on several thousand franchised dealers, giving them close to total national coverage; others had less than 100 participating dealers and were rushing to woo additional dealers and expand their geographic coverage. Direct sellers also relied on dealers to provide local support for the car-buying process not completed online, serve as a place where shoppers could test-drive vehicles, and potentially handle after-the-sale service of the automobile. The most ambitious and well-funded direct sellers were moving to expand their online buying service to shoppers in foreign countries; several had launched foreign Web sites and begun recruiting foreign dealers to function as distribution outlets for online sales in the targeted country markets.

The discounts off sticker price that direct sellers quoted to online shoppers were typically a function of a model's popularity—slow-selling makes and models carried bigger discounts, and popular makes and models carried smaller discounts. Most franchised dealers were reluctant to supply direct sellers with the best-selling models that were in short supply from the factory at much below MSRP because these could be sold right off their own lots without the added cost of paying a fee to the online broker to win an incremental sale. On the other hand, dealers were usually quite willing to supply makes and models that were readily available from the factory to direct sellers at big discounts from MSRP, allowing direct sellers, in turn, to quite lower prices to online shoppers. Shoppers in different zip codes or states were frequently quoted slightly different prices due to varying destination charges and to differences in the sizes of the discounts from MSRP that direct sellers had been able to negotiate with local dealers. It was not unusual for the prices quoted to online shoppers located in metropolitan areas to be somewhat lower than those quoted to shoppers located in outlying towns and rural areas where dealer competition was weaker and direct sellers could not negotiate as favorable terms.

All things considered, selling vehicles online was considered to cost less than using franchised dealer networks. If franchised dealers could be eliminated from the equation, some analysts estimated that about $1,050 could be trimmed off the $26,000 average price of a new vehicle.[18]

Price competition was becoming a factor among online sellers. Exhibit 11 shows the prices quoted by selected direct sellers for three representative makes and models.

---

[18]Ibid.

exhibit 11   Comparative Prices of Selected Online Vehicle Retailers, Standard Equipped
Models, April 2000

	MSRP	Dealer Invoice	carOrder.com Price	CarsDirect.com Price	Greenlight.com Price
2000 Toyota Camry 4dr Sedan LE	$20,843	$18,304	$19,216	$18,572	$18,004
Monthly payment if leased			$300.36	$308	$245.98
Monthly payment if purchased			$444.70	$371	$370.77
2000 Jeep Grand Cherokee 2x2 Laredo w/26E	$27,465	$24,937	$26,142	$25,180	$24,892
Monthly payment if leased			$442.81	$434	$356.56
Monthly payment if purchased			$613.79	$502	$513.37
2000 Mercedes-Benz ML320 Base	$35,945	$33,474	$35,816	$35,896	$35,177
Monthly payment if leased			$750.49	$566	$532.33
Monthly payment if purchased			$898.78	$715	$811.24

Source: Company Web sites.

PROFILES OF SELECTED ONLINE COMPETITORS IN AUTOMOTIVE RETAILING

Brief profiles of selected lead generators and direct sellers are presented below.

Microsoft's CarPoint

Among the automotive websites, CarPoint had drawn the most traffic as of fall 1999. CarPoint was one of the main features on the Microsoft Network portal. The site was widely praised for its ease of use and its depth of national content (said to be six times as much as some sites). It offered good side-by-side comparisons of models, rebate reports, maintenance reminders, personalized car pages with special offers, chat, and such services as financing and insurance. CarPoint had more than 50 "surround" video clips that let users take a 360-degree tour of a vehicle's exterior and interior. CarPoint had over 2,500 dealer members to whom it forwarded leads. CarPoint had transitioned its strategy from being a content provider to being a lead generator early on in its existence; starting in 2000, CarPoint seemed to be in the early stages of changing its strategy to become a direct seller.

Cars.com

The cars.com site was a comprehensive car information Web site that provided users with extensive local and national inventories of new and used vehicles. Vehicle shoppers could search the inventory listing by zip code, make, model, and year and easily submit quote requests to dealers by e-mail, fax, or telephone. Cars.com had more than 130 local newspaper affiliates that supplied classified ads for used vehicles; it displayed inventories in 26 of the top 30 U.S. metropolitan markets and was the only service that updated dealer inventories daily. It was the second most visited automotive retailing site during the September 1999–February 2000 period, according to Media Metrix.

Tom and Ray Magliozzi (the hosts of the popular "Car Talk" program on National Public Radio) and their award-winning CarTalk Web site were an integral part of the cars.com site. The site also offered rich editorial content on such topics as how to purchase a vehicle and tips for parents of young drivers, plus over 3,500 independent reviews on various makes and models going back to 1983.

Cars.com was a subsidiary of Classified Ventures, based in Chicago. Classified Ventures was formed by eight leading media companies: Gannett Co. (the published of *USA Today* and a number of local newspapers), Knight Ridder (another newspaper chain), the New York Times Co., the Washington Post Co., the Tribune Company, the Times Mirror Company (which was being acquired by the Tribune Company), and the McClatchy Company. Classified Ventures provided nationally branded online services for e-commerce opportunities relating to the market for classified advertising. In addition to the cars.com Web site, Classified Ventures operated four other national Web sites—Apartments.com, auctions.com, MovingCenter.com, and NewHomeNetwork.com; it also operated HomeHunter, a local resale real estate service.

CarsDirect.com

CarsDirect.com was a privately held company founded by Scott Painter, a former marketing vice president of 1-800-Dentist, and Internet entrepreneur Bill Gross, head of idealab!; the company had a number of corporate and institutional backers that included Goldman Sachs, Morgan Stanley Dean Witter, Michael Dell's MSD Capital, Oracle, Hambrecht & Quest (a prominent investment bank that specialized in helping finance Internet companies), Primedia Ventures (affiliated with the largest U.S. publisher of automotive publications, one of whose brands was IntelliChoice) and eight other venture capital firms. Nationally launched in May 1999, CarsDirect operated a research-rich Web site, covering more than 2,500 makes and models, and sold vehicles online. Shoppers could look at vehicle specifications, equipment options, safety features, value ratings, pricing data compiled by IntelliChoice, and IntelliChoice reports on vehicle performance. They could custom-configure a vehicle, compare CarsDirect's price against dealer invoice costs and MSRP, make side-by-side model comparisons, buy the vehicle of their choice online, and have it delivered to their home. By fall 1999, CarsDirect.com was selling about 1,000 vehicles per month and by March 2000 the company had over 2,000 participating dealers.

To arrive at the price it quoted shoppers, the company polled the more than 1,700 dealerships it did business with and created a bell-shaped curve of the dealer prices of every vehicle it offered for sale. It was the company's practice to price the vehicle in the bottom 10th percentile of the bell-shaped curve. According to Scott Painter, "We can guarantee that nine times out of ten, a car bought on our site is cheaper than if a consumer went to a dealership."[19] There was no price negotiation, and the price was consistent for all buyers. CarsDirect had teamed with Bank One, the fifth largest U.S. bank and a major automotive lender, to provide online financing for purchases and leases. They could also purchase vehicle insurance and extended warranties equal to double or triple the standard manufacturers' warranties. In March 2000, CarsDirect introduced a new "zero driveoff" leasing option whereby qualified buyers in 39 states could lease a new vehicle with no down payment.

CarsDirect had recently entered into strategic alliances with Autoweb, a major lead referral service, and cars.com. The alliance with Autoweb provided for the launch of a co-branded direct new-car-buying service on Autoweb.com, placement of exclusive links between the company's sites, and licensing of data content and tools. CarsDirect

---

[19]As quoted in "CarsDirect.com Cuts Auto-Buying Hassles," *Information Week,* November 8, 1999, p. 48.

customers were given the opportunity to list their used cars for sale on Autoweb's site. To signal long-term commitment to the alliance, the two companies each bought ownership stakes in the other. CarsDirect's alliance with cars.com provided a link on cars.com's site where shoppers who wanted to buy a vehicle direct could click directly to CarsDirect's site.

Gomez Advisors, a specialist in rating numerous types of online companies, had given CarsDirect top honors as the best overall car buying site on the Internet for three consecutive quarters (the latest being in March 2000). Gomez gave CarsDirect accolades for its customer service, up-front pricing, online leasing programs, the functionality of its new site design, and the attractive features of its financial calculator tool.

StoneAge.com

Headquartered in Detroit, StoneAge.com's mission was "to eliminate the hassle and stress of the car buying and selling experience." To try to make the whole process easier, more convenient, and worry free, StoneAge's Web site offered comprehensive information and three ways to buy a vehicle: a free service that provided a quote from an affiliated dealer along with invoice information; a $250-deposit service in which StoneAge conducted a search for the best price possible on a customer-specified vehicle; and an auction service in which shoppers sent a quote request to multiple dealers (at a cost of $1 per dealer) and dealers returned a bid via e-mail. Shoppers interested in used vehicles could search through the company's database of over 200,000 vehicles compiled from Internet and newspaper classified ads; StoneAge was putting in place the capability to list over 2 million used vehicles for sale in locations all across the United States. The service also had loan and lease payment calculators, as well as tools to apply for financing, insurance, and leasing. StoneAge had an extensive network of what it termed "top-rated" dealer affiliates; it strived to recruit dealer affiliates that had high customer satisfaction ratings in their locales. Its Web site attracted approximately 500,000 visitors per month.

CarPrices.com

CarPrices.com sought to differentiate its car buying service by *guaranteeing* customers the best purchases prices on the Internet or paying them double the difference in cash. Using its New Car PriceWar feature, customers specified their vehicle of choice (make, model, optional equipment, and colors), then sat back and waited while multiple dealers placed the bids to fill the order. The bid process typically took about 24 hours, and customers could log back on to CarPrices.com to view the bid comparison screen for their custom-equipped vehicle. CarPrices.com provided shoppers with dealer invoice cost and MSRP to help them evaluate the bids. According to CarPrices.com's promotional advertising, consumers who visited dealer showrooms to make their purchase bought cars from dealers, on average, at 8 percent above dealer invoice while the average online purchase was a 6 percent above invoice cost. Consumers who bought through CarPrices.com's PriceWar paid on average only 2 percent over invoice.

While the PriceWar feature was available only to residents of the San Diego area in the spring of 2000, CarPrices.com had recruited a sufficient number of participating dealers to roll out the feature in Los Angeles, Miami, Chicago, and Washington/Baltimore by mid-2000 and was expecting to have a national rollout sometime in 2001.

Like most of its rivals, CarPrices.com had a feature-rich site that provided a broad variety of information, news about new models, used-car prices and a search of used-car classified ads, special articles on automotive-related topics, insurance and financing options, calculators, a "lemon" check, manufacturers' rebates, and reviews of models.

DriveOff.com

DriveOff.com offered shoppers the ability to finalize all the terms and conditions of buying a vehicle online. Shoppers could research detailed specifications, standard and optional equipment, and safety features, and compare multiple vehicles side-by-side. Articles from USAutoNews.com were available for review. Once shoppers had configured the vehicle they wanted and selected which options were essential and which they would be willing to forgo, DriveOff.com provided a binding price and monthly payment (exclusive of state and local taxes and transportation charges, which varied according to the shopper's location). Shoppers still interested provided contact information, completed a credit application, and entered a credit card number to make a fully refundable $250 cash deposit on the vehicle. When DriveOff located a list of vehicles matching the shopper's preferences, the shopper was notified by e-mail to go to his or her Personal Auto Center on DriveOff's Web site to view the information. A shopper who accepted one of the matches could track every step of the transaction as it unfolded. Buyers were e-mailed a Deal Kit containing all the documents necessary to close the transaction and take delivery from a participating DriveOff dealer affiliate. All that remained was for the customer to pick up the vehicle at the dealership at the scheduled time, sign the closing documents, get a quick tutorial on how to operate the vehicle, and then drive off. If DriveOff could not find an acceptable match and the customer did not want to place a factory order for the vehicle, the credit card deposit was immediately refunded.

Greenlight.com

Greenlight.com was formed in 1999 by entrepreneurs with experience in both e-commerce and the automotive industry who saw an opportunity to improve the car-buying experience and put customers in control. The new company had received financial backing from a prominent Silicon Valley venture capital firm and from Asbury Automotive, a privately held U.S. group of 100-plus franchised automobile dealers representing virtually all makes and models. In January 2000, Amazon.com acquired 5 percent of the outstanding shares of Greenlight.com and contracted to make Greenlight its exclusive partner in the market for online car-buying. Under the agreement, Amazon provided Greenlight exclusive exposure to its 16 million-plus online shoppers; in return, Greenlight agreed to pay Amazon $82.5 million over five years and give Amazon warrants to increase its ownership stake to as much as 30 percent. In February 2000, Greenlight.com and AutoTrader.com announced a strategic partnership whereby Greenlight would become the exclusive online car-buying service offered by AutoTrader. AutoTrader.com had one of the largest selections of used cars for sale in the United States, with more than 40,000 listings from 40,000 U.S. auto dealers and more than 250,000 private sellers. The site had 5 million unique visitors in February 2000. AutoTrader.com was a venture of Trader Publishing Company, the publisher of *AutoTrader* and *AutoMart* magazines, which were distributed in more than 136,000 retail locations and had an estimated weekly circulation of 2.5 million copies. One of the investors in AutoTrader.com was the same Silicon Valley venture capital firm that had invested in Greenlight.com.

Greenlight was a direct seller of new vehicles; its site used vehicle configuration software and had a tool for helping shoppers choose a vehicle based on price range, body type, engine, or transmission. When shoppers selected the customized vehicle they wanted, Greenlight provided a no-haggle price; the company claimed that its everyday-low-pricing approach resulted in prices that were "low (often at invoice!)." Greenlight provided the vehicle's MSRP and the dealer invoice cost as a basis for comparison. Greenlight asked for a $200 refundable deposit to guarantee its price, reserve the vehicle, and process an order. Customer service representatives were available 24 hours a day to help with a purchase. The company provided home delivery, except where it was prevented from doing so by state franchise laws or manufacturers. In April 2000, Greenlight's service was available only in seven cities but the company planned to have national coverage before Fall 2000.

CarOrder.com

Headquartered in Austin, Texas, carOrder.com was launched in January 1999 as a spin-off business of Trilogy Software, also an Austin-based company. One of Trilogy's new products was software that allowed consumers to buy cars online. CarOrder.com's strategy was to acquire approximately 100 small, rural, typically underperforming dealerships with about 200 new-car franchises and turn them into what it termed "e-dealerships"—distribution centers for its Internet car buyers. The company was particularly interested in acquiring the worst-performing dealerships with the worst customer satisfaction ratings so that it could hold dealer acquisition costs down to around $1 million each. To finance its acquisitions, carOrder.com completed arrangements for $100 million in funding from Trilogy in September 1999. Company officials indicated they expected to raise another $500 million from private investors and a public stock offering in 2000.

Management's plan was to acquire the 100 dealerships region by region across the United States and turn them into e-dealers, eventually building national distribution and direct-delivery capability for its online sales. The strategy was for the company's Web site to attract vehicle shoppers and tie down the sales of new vehicles online. Vehicles sold online would be routed through the national chain of local dealers, thus allowing carOrder.com to comply with state franchise laws. The primary function of the acquired local dealerships was to provide a place where online shoppers could test-drive vehicles and where truckloads of new vehicles arriving from manufacturer assembly plants could be unloaded onto dealer lots. Newly unloaded vehicles would be run through the service department and made ready for either buyer pickup or for loading onto carOrder.com flatbed trucks for home delivery to the buyer.

The newly acquired dealerships would still handle local walk-in traffic and perhaps stock a small new-vehicle and used-vehicle inventory for local customers, but 60–90 percent of their sales volume was expected to eventually originate from Internet-generated sales at carOrder.com's Web site. Costs of operating the dealership would be smaller because they would need a minimal sales force and would need to keep smaller numbers of vehicles in inventory. Since carOrder.com could order directly from manufacturers, the company planned to give customers the opportunity to order custom-equipped vehicles, thus promoting wider use of a build-to-order business model. CarOrder.com's management believed that a build-to-order configured value chain could eventually cut $2,000 to $4,000 out of the cost of getting a new vehicle to a consumer, producing a significant pricing advantage over traditional dealers.

When NADA learned of carOrder.com's strategy, it immediately put pressure on manufacturers to sign agreements saying that they would not transfer any franchises to dot-com companies. So far, NADA's efforts had not derailed carOrder.com's strategy. In commenting on the challenges to carOrder.com's strategy, its CEO remarked, "We may be one of the only Internet companies with more lawyers than software engineers."[20]

Exhibit 12 shows carOrder.com's home page.

---

[20] As quoted in Fara Warner, "Web Auto Retailer CarOrder.com Receives Funds to Buy Dealerships," *The Wall Street Journal,* September 29, 1999, p. B4.

exhibit 12   carOrder.com's Home Page, April 2000

Source: www.carorder.com

Autobytel.com

Autobytel.com was a hybrid site. It began as a content provider and lead-referral service but its strategy had recently evolved to include direct sales at its new AutobytelDirect.com site. The company offered shoppers three ways to buy a vehicle: (1) shoppers could search the inventories of dealers, find a car that suited them, and, for a refundable credit card deposit, submit a purchase request to bid on vehicles at the Autobytel.com Auction; (2) they could buy direct online through the "Click and Buy" on posted inventory at AutobytelDirect; or (3) if customers wished, they could use the services of a personal shopper in locating and buying a vehicle. Autobytel also had auto auction and classified ad features for car owners who wanted to sell a vehicle. Autobytel's dealer affiliates had an online searchable inventory of over 50,000 vehicles. Customers could get real-time insurance quotes from any of three sources, purchase extended warranties, get free service quotes, check out vehicle recall, and check the value of their present vehicle.

Autobytel was launched in March 1995 and had served over 4 million customers since its inception. In 1999, Autobytel reported revenues of $40.3 million and losses of $23.3 million; its year-end cash balance was $85.5 million. It generated 1.06 million purchase requests in the last half of 1999, resulting in sales averaging about 50,000 vehicles per month. Autobytel received a fee of $100 to $300 from a dealer upon the completion of a sale, depending on the gross selling price of the vehicle.

In the first quarter of 2000, Autobytel's market share of vehicle sales on the Internet was about 45 percent. Its sales volume was bigger than the next two direct sellers combined. Autobytel completed its acquisition of CarSmart.com, a leading online buying site for new and used vehicles, in March 2000, giving it a database of over 6.5 million customers, a network of over 4,800 dealer affiliates, established relationships with over 200 credit unions, and strategic marketing agreements with 10 of the top Internet portals, including AOL, AltaVista, and Snap.com. The company generated vehicle sales totaling more than $3.4 billion through participating dealers (equal to vehicle sales of $1.6 million per hour) in the first quarter of 2000 and had a record-breaking 3 million site users.

Autobytel was aggressively pursuing international expansion. In addition to the United States, Autobytel had Web sites in Sweden, Australia, the United Kingdom, Japan, and Canada. Autobytel Europe was formed in January 2000 as a platform for expanding across Europe and partnering with strong vehicle distribution firms in Europe. Autobytel's strategic objective was to become the largest Internet car dealer in the world.

AUTONATION'S BRICK-AND-CLICK STRATEGY

Going into the new millennium, AutoNation was the world's largest automotive retailer, with 406 franchises in 21 states, 41 multiacre AutoNation USA used-vehicle megastores in 13 states, 350 Web sites, 1999 revenues of $20.1 billion and 1999 earnings of $283 million. AutoNation also owned Alamo Rent-a-Car and National Car Rental. The company (formerly named Republic Industries, with business interests extending beyond the automotive business) was formed in 1995 by corporate entrepreneur and billionaire H. Wayne Huizenga, a founder of Blockbuster and owner of the Miami Dolphins National Football League franchise. Huizenga's vision was to make AutoNation the Home Depot of the car-retailing business and build the first national automotive retail brand. The company's initial strategy had been to acquire strong franchised dealerships, build them into a national retail network, and then redefine the customer's vehicle-buying experience by changing the sales and services processes to better please customers and meet their expectations. The prices of all new and used vehicles at AutoNation's dealerships were posted on the vehicles and fixed—there was no price haggling. Salespeople were trained to be courteous and helpful. The company's multiacre used-car superstores located throughout a given metropolitan area were all served by a central used-car reconditioning center.

But the strategy so far had met with only modest success, partly because the dealerships could not achieve a large enough unit volume to justify the capital investment and operating costs associated with superstores. AutoNation's strategy had gone through several revisions to try to find the right combination. One revision involved buying Alamo Rent-a-Car and National Car Rental to serve as sources for funneling late-model used cars into AutoNation's inventory and avoid having to compete with other dealers for attractive late-model car inventory. But buyers were not excited about the "plain-vanilla" models that rental car companies favored. Starting in early 1999 Huizenga took the string of dealerships in the Denver area acquired earlier and renamed them all John Elway AutoNation USA. (AutoNation had purchased six John Elway dealerships in the Denver area in 1998.) To promote the one-price concept, a major advertising campaign was launched to saturate the Denver market. Salespeople were put through 60 days of training to learn how to deal with customers and sell a vehicle without getting into price haggling. Sales commissions were based on volume, as opposed to the normal practice of tying commission size to the amount of gross profit on each sale. The strategy boosted market share from 19 percent to 28 percent, but profit margins suffered. Huizenga commented, "There are a lot of moving parts in this business. It isn't just a simple thing like renting a video or picking up the trash. It is difficult, but you just have to keep working at it."[21] In September 1999, Huizenga relinquished his position as CEO and to fill the spot, brought in Michael Jackson, a former car dealer who had been the head of Mercedes-Benz's sales and marketing operations in North America.

In February 2000, with AutoNation's stock price languishing in single digits (down from a high of $46 in 1997), Michael Jackson announced that the company was putting new acquisitions on hold and shelving plans to make the AutoNation brand a household name for car buying.[22] Instead, Jackson said the company was shifting its focus to leverage its scale of operations to be the low-cost provider and concentrating on expanding the reach of its AutoNationDirect.com e-commerce site. He indicated that greater use of the Internet to reach prospective vehicle buyers would allow the company to grow its market share without spending heavily to acquire brick-and-mortar dealerships. AutoNation's new strategy was to market its Web site nationally and use its existing franchises as distribution points for delivering vehicles to customers. To serve buyers in cities where it did not already own franchises, the strategy was to license non-AutoNation dealers to serve as distribution and service locations for buyers. In addition to its own Web site, AutoNation announced plans to sell thousands of cars through Internet companies that steered leads to dealers to meet its goal of generating $1.5 billion in online cars sales in 2000 and $3 billion in 2001; toward this end, it signed national contracts with four lead-referral dot-com car services—Autoweb.com, AutoVantage.com, StoneAge.com, and CarPoint. AutoNation also expected to cooperate with dot-com companies that sold vehicles to buyers online; several had approached AutoNation to serve as a source for new and used vehicles (AutoNation maintained online listings of some 90,000 vehicles on the lots of its dealers which could easily be searched). To boost the sales that it was getting from lead-referral companies and from hits on its own Web sites, AutoNation had begun using its newly installed software capability to track which lead generators had the highest sales closures and which car brands sold best through which referral services; its software also tracked buyer requests sent to other AutoNation dealers, helping salespeople know what other types of vehicles the buyer was considering. Management believed such information would allow AutoNation to be more effective in selling vehicles from Internet contacts.

To further drive down costs and streamline operations, Michael Jackson announced that AutoNation would shut down its megastores for used cars, cut the size of AutoNation's workforce, and curtail corporate spending. Management was implementing efforts to use the Internet to combine and streamline back-office operations in its 400-plus dealerships and to let its dealers go online to search its inventory and bid for any of the 45,000 used cars in its inventory—actions that were expected to boost profit margins. Jackson's goal was to boost profit margins at the company's dealerships from 3.3 percent in the fourth quarter of 1999 to 3.8 percent in 2000—the industry average in 1999 was 2.8 percent. He called a halt to the plan of prior management to replace local dealership brands such as John Elway AutoNation in Denver with just the AutoNation brand.

It remained to be seen whether Jackson would alter AutoNation's one-price, no-haggle strategy. Many auto industry executives believed that the one-price, no-haggle

---

[21]As quoted in Alex Taylor, "Would You Buy a Car from This Man?" *Fortune,* October 25, 1999, p. 166.

[22]"AutoNation Goes Back to Basics with an Internet Twist," *The Wall Street Journal,* February 25, 2000, p. B4.

system was fundamental to reforming the automotive retailing business. Others, however, saw a one-price strategy as flawed because it put a dealer at a disadvantage to cross-town competitors who were willing to make a sale for $50 less, especially in an industry ruled by overcapacity in manufacturing and dealers who always had the incentive to make an additional sale. When Michael Jackson was running Mercedes-Benz's sales and marketing operation for North America, he had installed a system he called credible pricing, which involved reducing the sticker price to such a small margin over dealer invoice that it was uneconomical for dealers to trim much off the sticker price in negotiating price with customers.

AutoNationDirect.com   AutoNation launched AutoNationDirect.com in June 1999. Shoppers could explore product specifications for all makes and models of new vehicles, check sticker prices, view interior and exterior photographs, and see descriptions of standard and optional equipment. The site offered the largest inventory of new and used vehicles in the United States, featuring every major manufacturer, make, and model and covering all of AutoNation's dealerships. Shoppers could conduct their own searches for vehicles using the site's "Tour the Lot" feature. All prices were fixed, with no haggling. Buyers could reserve a vehicle with a credit card. If customer wished, they could arrange financing with Giggo.com, a financing division of DaimlerChrysler, and purchase car insurance from Progressive Insurance Co. without ever leaving the site. Buyers could pick up their vehicle at an AutoNation dealership or make arrangements for home delivery. The site offered shoppers the ability to study and compare reviews and independent commentary on all vehicle makes and models, and site visitors could write and share their own reviews. Over 600 dedicated Internet sales guides were available to assist customers in the selection and purchase process. In 1999 AutoNation-Direct's "Tour the Lot" feature along with AutoNation's 200-plus individual dealership Web sites contributed to more than $1 billion in vehicle sales via the Internet.

In March 2000 AutoNationDirect.com introduced two new features on its Web site called "Build Your Dream Car" and "Let Us Find It for You." The Dream Car feature recorded a shopper's preferences—make, model, optional equipment, trim levels, and interior and exterior colors—and instantly e-mailed the profile to one of AutoNation's Internet sales guides; the sales guide searched the entire online inventory of 100,000 new and used vehicles for a match. If a match was not available, the sales guide could order the desired vehicle from the manufacturer or through a secondary source. The Let Us Find It feature offered shoppers a short form they could use to have the Internet sales guides conduct similar searches including searches of vehicles leaving manufacturers' assembly plants en route to nearby AutoNation-owned dealerships. AutoNation management believed that the positive customer reaction to the AutoNationDirect.com site and its new features made it likely the company would achieve its target of $1.5 billion in online sales in 2000.

case | 7   Dell Computer Corporation: Strategy and Challenges for the 21st Century

Arthur A. Thompson
The University of Alabama

John E. Gamble
University of South Alabama

You don't ever really know whether you've come up with the right plan until much later—when it either works or it doesn't. What is the right plan? It's the one that helps you identify what you need to do to ensure success. It's the one that rallies your employees around a few common goals—and motivates them to achieve them. It's one that involves your customers' goals and your suppliers' goals and brings them altogether in a unified focus.
—Michael Dell

In 1984, at the age of 19, Michael Dell founded Dell Computer with a simple vision and business concept—that personal computers could be built to order and sold directly to customers. Michael Dell believed his approach to the PC business had two advantages: (1) Bypassing distributors and retail dealers eliminated the markups of resellers, and (2) building to order greatly reduced the costs and risks associated with carrying large stocks of parts, components, and finished goods. While the company sometimes struggled during its early years trying to refine its strategy, build an adequate infrastructure, and establish market credibility against better-known rivals, Dell's build-to-order, sell-direct approach proved appealing to growing numbers of customers worldwide during the 1990s as global PC sales rose to record levels. And, as Michael Dell had envisioned, the direct-to-the-customer strategy gave the company a substantial cost and profit margin advantage over rivals that manufactured various PC models in volume and kept their distributors and retailers stocked with ample inventories.

DELL COMPUTER'S MARKET POSITION IN EARLY 2000

Going into 2000, Dell Computer was the U.S. leader in PC sales, with nearly a 17 percent market share, about 1 percentage point ahead of second-place Compaq. Gateway was third with 8.9 percent, followed by Hewlett-Packard with 8.8 percent and IBM with 7.2 percent. Dell overtook Compaq as the U.S. sales leader in the third quarter of 1999, and it had moved ahead of IBM into second place during 1998 (see Exhibit 1). Worldwide, Dell Computer ranked second in market share (10.5 percent) behind Compaq (14.0 percent). IBM ranked third worldwide, with an 8.2 percent share, but this share was eroding. Since 1996, Dell had been gaining market share quickly in all of the world's markets, growing at a rate more than triple the 18 percent average annual increase in global PC sales. Even though Asia's economic woes in 1997–98 and part of 1999 dampened the market for PCs, Dell's PC sales across Asia in 1999 were up a strong 87 percent. Dell was also enjoying strong sales growth in Europe.

Dell's sales at its Web site (www.dell.com) surpassed $35 million a day in early 2000, up from $5 million daily in early 1998 and $15 million daily in early 1999. In its fiscal year ending January 31, 2000, Dell Computer posted revenues of $25.3 billion, up from $3.4 billion in the year ending January 29, 1995—a compound average growth rate of 49.4 percent. Over the same time period, profits were up from $140 million to $1.67 billion—a 64.1 percent compound average growth rate. Since its initial public offering of common stock in June 1988 at $8.50 per share, the company had seen its stock price split seven times and increase 45,000 percent. Dell Computer was one of the top 10 best-performing stocks on the NYSE and the NASDAQ during the 1990s. In recent years, Dell's annual return on invested capital had exceeded 175 percent.

Dell's principal products included desktop PCs, notebook computers, workstations, servers, and storage devices. It also marketed a number of products made by other manufacturers, including CD-ROM drives, modems, monitors, networking hardware, memory cards, speakers, and printers. The company received nearly 3 million visits weekly at its Web site, where it maintained 50 country-specific sites. It was a world leader in migrating its business relationships with both customers and suppliers to the Internet. In 1998 the company expanded its Internet presence with the launch of www.gigabuys.com, an online source for more than 30,000 competitively priced computer-related products. Sales of desktop PCs accounted for about 65 percent of Dell's total systems revenue; sales of notebook computers generated 20–25 percent of revenues, and servers and workstations accounted for 10–15 percent of revenues. Dell products were sold in more than 170 countries. In early 2000, the company had 33,200 employees in 34 countries, up from 16,000 at year-end 1997; approximately one-third of Dell's employees were located in countries outside the United States, and this percentage was growing.

COMPANY BACKGROUND

When Michael Dell was in the third grade, he responded to a magazine ad with the headline "Earn Your High School Diploma by Passing One Simple Test." At that age, he was both impatient and curious—always willing to try ways to get something done more quickly and easily. Early on, he became fascinated by what he saw as "commercial opportunities." At age 12, Michael Dell was running a mail-order stamp-trading business, complete with a national catalog, and grossing $2,000 per month. At 16, he was selling subscriptions to the *Houston Post*, and at 17 he bought his first BMW with the more than $18,000 he had earned. He enrolled at the University of Texas in 1983 as a pre-med student (his parents wanted him to become a doctor) but soon became immersed in the commercial opportunities he saw in computer retailing and started selling PC components out of his college dormitory room. He bought random-access memory (RAM) chips and disk drives for IBM PCs at cost from IBM dealers, who often had excess supplies on hand because they were required to order large monthly quotas from *exhibit 1*   Leading PC Vendors Worldwide and in the United States, Based on Factory Shipments, 1996–99

A. Worldwide Market Shares of the Leading PC Vendors*

1999 Rank	Vendor	1999 Market Shipments of PCs	1999 Market Share	1998 Market Shipments of PCs	1998 Market Share	1997 Market Shipments of PCs*	1997 Market Share	1996 Market Shipments of PCs*	1996 Market Share	Compound Growth Rate, 1996–99
1	Compaq Computer	15,732,000	14.0%	13,266,000	14.5%	10,064,000	12.6%	7,211,000	10.4%	29.7%
2	Dell Computer	11,883,000	10.5	7,770,000	8.5	4,648,000	5.8	2,996,000	4.3	58.3
3	IBM	9,287,000	8.2	7,946,000	8.7	7,239,000	9.1	6,176,000	8.9	14.6
4	Hewlett-Packard	7,577,000	6.7	5,743,000	6.3	4,468,000	5.6	2,984,000	4.3	36.4
5	Packard Bell/NEC	5,989,000	5.3	5,976,000	6.5	4,150,000	5.2	4,230,000	6.1	12.1
6	Gateway	4,685,000	4.2	3,540,000	n.a.	n.a.	n.a.	n.a.	n.a.	n.a.
	Others	57,573,000	55.2	50,741,000	55.5	49,369,000	61.8	45,727,000	66.0	10.8
	All vendors	112,726,000	100.0%	91,442,000	100.0%	79,938,000	100.0%	69,324,000	100.0%	17.6%

B. U.S. Market Shares of the Leading PC Vendors, 1998–99

1999 Rank	Vendor	1999 Market Shipments of PCs*	1999 Market Share	1998 Market Shipments of PCs*	1998 Market Share	Percent Growth 1998–99
1	Dell Computer	7,492,000	16.6%	4,799,000	13.2%	56.1%
2	Compaq Computer	7,222,000	16.0	6,052,000	16.7	19.3
3	Gateway	4,001,000	8.9	3,039,000	8.4	31.6
4	Hewlett-Packard	3,955,000	8.8	2,832,000	7.8	39.6
5	IBM	3,274,000	7.2	2,983,000	8.2	9.8
	Others	19,248,000	42.6	16,549,000	45.6	16.3
	All vendors	45,192,000	100.0%	36,254,000	100.0%	24.7%

*Includes branded shipments only and excludes OEM sales for all manufacturers.

Source: International Data Corp.

IBM. Dell resold the components through newspaper ads (and later through ads in national computer magazines) at 10–15 percent below the regular retail price.

By April 1984 sales were running about $80,000 per month. Michael Dell at age 18 dropped out of college and formed a company, PCs Ltd., to sell both PC components and PCs under the brand PCs Limited. He obtained his PCs by buying retailers' surplus stocks at cost, then powering them up with graphics cards, hard disks, and memory before reselling them. His strategy was to sell directly to end users; by eliminating the retail markup, Dell's new company was able to sell IBM clones (machines that copied the functioning of IBM PCs using the same or similar components) at about 40 percent below the price of an IBM PC. The price-discounting strategy was successful, attracting price-conscious buyers and producing rapid growth. By 1985, with a few people working on six-foot tables, the company was assembling its own PC designs. The company had 40 employees, and Michael Dell worked 18-hour days, often sleeping on a cot in his office. By the end of fiscal 1986, sales had reached $33 million.

During the next several years, however, PCs Limited was hampered by growing pains—a lack of money, people, and resources. Michael Dell sought to refine the company's business model; add needed production capacity; and build a bigger, deeper management staff and corporate infrastructure while at the same time keeping costs low. The company was renamed Dell Computer in 1987, and the first international offices were opened that same year. In 1988 Dell added a sales force to serve large customers, began selling to government agencies, and became a public company—raising $34.2 million in its first offering of common stock. Sales to large customers quickly became the dominant part of Dell's business. By 1990 Dell Computer had sales of $388 million, a market share of 2 to 3 percent, and an R&D staff of over 150 people. Michael Dell's vision was for Dell Computer to become one of the world's top three PC companies.

Thinking its direct-sales business would not grow fast enough, in 1990–93, the company began distributing its computer products through Soft Warehouse Superstores (now CompUSA), Staples (a leading office products chain), Wal-Mart Stores, Sam's Club, and Price Club (now Price/Costco). Dell also sold PCs through Best Buy stores in 16 states and through Xerox in 19 Latin American countries. But when the company learned how thin its margins were in selling through such distribution channels, it realized it had made a mistake and withdrew from selling to retailers and other intermediaries in 1994 to refocus on direct sales. At the time, sales through retailers accounted for only about 2 percent of Dell's revenues.

Further problems emerged in 1993, when Dell reportedly lost $38 million in the second quarter from engaging in a risky foreign-currency hedging strategy; had quality difficulties with certain PC lines made by the company's contract manufacturers; and saw its profit margins decline. Also that year, buyers were turned off by the company's laptop PC models. To get laptop sales back on track, the company took a charge of $40 million to write off its laptop line and suspended sales of those products until it could get redesigned models into the marketplace. The problems resulted in losses of $36 million for the company's fiscal year ending January 30, 1994.

Because of higher costs and unacceptably low profit margins in selling to individuals and households, Dell Computer did not pursue the consumer market aggressively until sales on the company's Internet site took off in 1996 and 1997. Management noticed that while the industry's average selling price to individuals was going down, Dell's was going up—second- and third-time computer buyers who wanted powerful computers with multiple features and did not need much technical support were choosing Dell. It became clear that PC-savvy individuals liked the convenience of buying direct from Dell, ordering exactly what they wanted, and having it delivered to their door within a matter of days. In early 1997, Dell created an internal sales and marketing group dedicated to serving the individual consumer segment and introduced a product line designed especially for individual users.

By late 1997, Dell had become the global industry leader in keeping costs down and wringing efficiency out of its direct-sales, build-to-order business model. Going into 2000, Dell Computer had made further efficiency improvements and was widely regarded as having the most efficient procurement, manufacturing, and distribution process in the global PC industry. The company was a pioneer and acknowledged world leader in incorporating e-commerce technology and use of the Internet into its everyday business practices. The goal was to achieve what Michael Dell called "virtual integration"—a stitching together of Dell's business with its supply partners and customers in real time such that all three appeared to be part of the same organizational team.[1] The company's mission was "to be the most successful computer company in the world at delivering the best customer experience in the markets we serve."[2]

Exhibits 2–5 contain a five-year review of Dell Computer's financial performance and selected financial statements.

Michael Dell

Michael Dell was widely considered one of the mythic heroes of the PC industry, and was labeled "the quintessential American entrepreneur" and "the most innovative guy for marketing computers in this decade." In 1992, at the age of 27, Michael Dell became the youngest CEO ever to head a Fortune 500 company; he was a billionaire at the age of 31. Once pudgy and bespectacled, Michael Dell at the age of 35 was physically fit, considered good-looking, wore contact lenses, ate only health foods, and lived in a three-story 33,000 square-foot home on a 60-acre estate in the Austin, Texas, metropolitan area. In early 2000 Michael Dell owned about 14 percent of Dell Computer's common stock, worth about $12 billion. The company's glass-and-steel headquarters building in Round Rock, Texas (an Austin suburb), had unassuming, utilitarian furniture, abstract art, framed accolades to Michael Dell, laudatory magazine covers, industry awards plaques, bronze copies of the company's patents, and a history wall that contained the hand-soldered guts of the company's first personal computer.[3]

In the company's early days Michael spent a lot of his time with the engineers. He was said to be shy, but those who worked with him closely described him as a likable young man who was slow to warm up to people.[4] Michael described his experience in getting the company launched as follows:

> There were obviously no classes on learning how to start and run a business in my high school, so I clearly had a lot to learn. And learn I did, mostly by experimenting and making a bunch of mistakes. One of the first things I learned, though, was that there was a relationship between screwing up and learning: The more mistakes I made, the faster I learned.
>
>   I tried to surround myself with smart advisors, and I tried not to make the same mistake twice. . . . Since we were growing so quickly, everything was constantly changing.

---

[1]Michael Dell used the term "virtual integration" in an interview published in the *Harvard Business Review.* See Joan Magretta, "The Power of Virtual Integration: An Interview with Dell Computer's Michael Dell," *Harvard Business Review,* March–April 1998, p. 75.

[2]Information posted on www.dell.com, February 1, 2000.

[3]As described in *Business Week,* March 22, 1993, p. 82.

[4]"Michael Dell: On Managing Growth," *MIS Week,* September 5, 1988, p. 1.

exhibit 2 Financial Performance Summary, Dell Computer, 1995–2000 (In Millions, Except Per Share Data)

	January 28, 2000	January 29, 1999	February 1, 1998	February 2, 1997	January 28, 1996	January 29, 1995
Results of operations data						
Net revenue	$25,265	$18,243	$12,327	$7,759	$5,296	$3,475
Gross margin	5,218	4,106	2,722	1,666	1,067	738
Operating income	2,263	2,046	1,316	714	377	249
Income before extraordinary loss	$ 1,666	1,460	944	531	272	149
Net income	$ 1,666	$ 1,460	$ 944	$ 518	$ 272	$ 149
Income before extraordinary loss per common share[a][b]						
Basic	$0.66	$0.58	$0.36	$0.19	$0.09	$0.06
Diluted	$0.61	$0.53	$0.32	$0.17	$0.08	$0.05
Number of weighted average shares outstanding[a]						
Basic	2,536	2,531	2,631	2,838	2,863	2,473
Diluted	2,728	2,772	2,952	3,126	3,158	3,000
Balance sheet data						
Working capital	$ 2,644	$ 2,644	$ 1,215	$1,089	$1,018	$ 718
Total assets	$11,471	6,877	4,268	2,993	2,148	1,594
Long-term debt	508	512	17	18	113	113
Total stockholders' equity	5,308	2,321	1,293	806	973	652

[a]All share and per share information has been retroactively restated to reflect the two-for-one splits of common stock.

[b]Excludes extraordinary loss of $0.01 basic per common share for fiscal year 1997.

Source: Dell Computer Corporation 2000 annual report.

exhibit 3 Dell Computer's Consolidated Statements of Income, Fiscal Years 1997–2000 (In Millions, Except Per Share Data)

	Fiscal Year Ended			
	January 28, 2000	January 29, 1999	February 1, 1998	February 2, 1997
Net revenue	$25,265	$18,243	$12,327	$7,759
Cost of revenue	20,047	14,137	9,605	6,093
Gross margin	5,218	4,106	2,722	1,666
Operating expenses				
Selling, general and administrative	2,387	1,788	1,202	826
Research, development and engineering	374	272	204	126
Purchased research and development	194	—	—	—
Total operating expenses	2,955	2,060	1,406	952
Operating income	2,263	2,046	1,316	714
Financing and other	188	38	52	33
Income before income taxes and extraordinary loss	2,451	2,084	1,368	747
Provision for income taxes	785	624	424	216
Income before extraordinary loss	1,666	1,460	944	531
Extraordinary loss, net of taxes	—	—	—	(13)
Net income	$ 1,666	$ 1,460	$ 944	$ 518
Basic earnings per common share (in whole dollars)				
Income before extraordinary loss	$ 0.66	$ 0.58	$ 0.36	$ 0.19
Extraordinary loss, net of taxes	—	—	—	(0.01)
Earnings per common share	$ 0.66	$ 0.58	$ 0.36	$ 0.18
Diluted earnings per common share (in whole dollars)	$ 0.61	$ 0.53	$ 0.32	$ 0.17
Weighted average shares outstanding				
Basic	2,536	2,531	2,631	2,838
Diluted	2,728	2,772	2,952	3,126

Source: Dell Computer Corporation's annual reports.

exhibit 4   Dell Computer's Consolidated Statements of Financial Position, Fiscal Years 1999 and 2000 (In Millions of Dollars)

	January 28, 2000	January 29, 1999
Assets		
Current assets		
Cash and cash equivalents	$ 3,809	$1,726
Short term investments	323	923
Accounts receivable, net	2,608	2,094
Inventories	391	273
Other	550	791
Total current assets	7,681	5,807
Property, plant, and equipment, net	765	523
Other	3,025	547
Total assets	$11,471	$6,877
Liabilities and Stockholders' Equity		
Current liabilities		
Accounts payable	$ 3,538	$2,397
Accrued and other	1,654	1,298
Total current liabilities	5,192	3,695
Long-term debt	508	512
Other	463	349
Commitments and contingent liabilities	—	—
Total liabilities	6,163	4,556
Stockholders' equity		
Preferred stock and capital in excess of $.01 par value; shares issued and outstanding: none	—	—
Common stock and capital in excess of $.01 par value; shares issued and outstanding: 2,543 and 2,575, respectively		1,781
Retained earnings		606
Other		(66)
Total stockholders' equity	5,308	2,321
Total liabilities and stockholders' equity	$11,471	$6,877

Source: Dell Computer Corporation's 2000 annual report.

We'd say, "What's the best way to do this?" and come up with an answer. The resulting process would work for a while, then it would stop working and we'd have to adjust it and try something else. . . . The whole thing was one big experiment.

From the beginning, we tended to come at things in a very practical way. I was always asking, "What's the most efficient way to accomplish this?" Consequently, we eliminated the possibility for bureaucracy before it ever cropped up, and that provided opportunities for learning as well.

Constantly questioning conventional thinking became part of our company mentality. And our explosive growth helped to foster a great sense of camaraderie and a real "can-do" attitude among our employees.

exhibit 5 Geographic Area Information, Dell Computer, Fiscal 1998–2000 (In Millions of Dollars)

	Americas	Europe	Asia Pacific and Japan	Eliminations	Consolidated
Fiscal year 2000					
Net revenue from unaffiliated customers	$17,879	$5,590	$1,796	—	$25,265
Transfers between geographic segments	48	5	2	(55)	—
Total net revenue	$17,927	$5,595	$1,798	$ (55)	$25,265
Operating income	$ 2,173	$ 403	$ 97	$(194)	$ 2,479
Corporate expenses					(216)
Total operating income					$ 2,263
Depreciation and amortization	$ 82	$ 41	$ 14	—	$ 137
Corporate depreciation and amortization					19
Total depreciation and amortization					$ 156
Identifiable assets	$ 2,456	$1,147	$ 413	—	$ 4,016
General corporate assets					7,455
Total assets					$11,741
Fiscal year 1999					
Net revenue from unaffiliated customers	$12,420	$4,674	$1,149	—	$18,243
Transfers between geographic segments	33	5	1	−39	—
Total net revenue	$12,453	$4,679	$1,150	($39)	$18,243
Operating income	$ 1,802	$ 446	$ 78	—	$ 2,326
Corporate expenses					−(280)
Total operating income					$ 2,046
Depreciation and amortization	$ 59	$ 29	$ 8	—	$ 96
Corporate depreciation and amortization					7
Total depreciation and amortization					$ 103
Identifiable assets	$ 1,640	$1,017	$ 234	—	$ 2,891
General corporate assets					3,986
Total assets					$ 6,877
Fiscal year 1998					
Net revenue from unaffiliated customers	$ 8,531	$2,956	$ 840	—	$12,327
Transfers between geographic segments	67	17	—	−84	—
Total net revenue	$ 8,598	$2,973	$ 840	($84)	$12,327
Operating income	$ 1,152	$ 255	$ 33	—	$ 1,440
Corporate expenses					−(124)
Total operating income					$ 1,316
Depreciation and amortization	$ 42	$ 16	$ 5	—	$ 63
Corporate depreciation and amortization					4
Total depreciation and amortization					$ 67
Identifiable assets	$ 1,363	$ 605	$ 172	—	$ 2,140
General corporate assets					2,128
Total assets					$ 4,268

Source: Dell Computer Corporation's 1998 and 2000 annual reports.

We challenged ourselves constantly, to grow more or to provide better service to our customers; and each time we set a new goal, we would make it. Then we would stop for a moment, give each other a few high fives, and get started on tackling the next goal.[5]

In 1986, to provide the company with much-needed managerial and financial experience, Michael Dell brought in Lee Walker, a 51-year-old venture capitalist, as president and chief operating officer. Walker had a fatherly image, came to know company employees by name, and proved to be a very effective internal force in implementing Michael Dell's ideas for growing the company. Walker became Michael Dell's mentor, built up his confidence and managerial skills, helped him learn how to translate his fertile entrepreneurial instincts into effective business plans and actions, and played an active role in grooming him into an able and polished executive.[6] Under Walker's tutelage, Michael Dell became intimately familiar with all parts of the business, overcame his shyness, learned the ins and outs of managing a fast-growing enterprise, and turned into a charismatic executive with an instinct for motivating people and winning their loyalty and respect. Walker also proved instrumental in helping Michael Dell recruit distinguished and able people to serve on the board of directors when the company went public in 1988. When Walker had to leave the company in 1990 because of health reasons, Dell turned for advice to Morton Meyerson, former CEO and president of Electronic Data Systems. Meyerson provided guidance on how to transform Dell Computer from a fast-growing medium-sized company into a billion-dollar enterprise.

Though sometimes given to displays of impatience, Michael Dell usually spoke in a quiet, reflective manner and came across as a person with maturity and seasoned judgment far beyond his age. His prowess was based more on having a pragmatic combination of astute entrepreneurial instincts, good technical knowledge, and marketing savvy rather than on being a pioneering techno-wizard. By the late 1990s, he was a much-sought-after speaker at industry and company conferences. (He received 100 requests to speak in 1997, 800 in 1998, and over 1,200 in 1999.) He was considered an accomplished public speaker and his views and opinions about the future of PCs, the Internet, and e-commerce practices carried considerable weight both in the PC industry and among executives worldwide. His speeches were usually full of usable information about the nuts and bolts of Dell Computer's business model and the compelling advantages of incorporating e-commerce technology and practices into a company's operations. A *USA Today* article labeled him "the guru of choice on e-commerce" because top executives across the world were so anxious to get his take on the business potential of the Internet and possible efficiency gains from integrating e-commerce into daily business operations.[7]

Michael Dell was considered a very accessible CEO and a role model for young executives because he had done what many of them were trying to do. He delegated authority to subordinates, believing that the best results came from "[turning] loose talented people who can be relied upon to do what they're supposed to do." Business associates viewed Michael Dell as an aggressive personality and an extremely competitive risk-taker who had always played close to the edge. Moreover, the people Dell hired had similar traits, which translated into an aggressive, competitive, intense corporate culture with a strong sense of mission and dedication. Inside Dell, Michael was

---

[5]Michael Dell, *Direct from Dell* (New York: HarperBusiness, 1999), pp. 17–20.

[6]"The Education of Michael Dell," *Business Week,* March 22, 1993, p. 86.

[7]"E-Commerce's Guru of Choice," *USA Today,* April 15, 1999, p. 3B.

noted for his obsessive, untiring attention to detail—a trait which employees termed "Michaelmanaging."

Michael Dell's Business Philosophy   In the 15 years since the company's founding, Michael Dell's understanding of what it took to build and operate a successful company in a fast-changing, high-velocity marketplace had matured considerably. His experience at Dell Computer and in working with both customers and suppliers had taught him a number of valuable lessons and shaped his leadership style. The following quotes provide insight into his business philosophy and practices:

> Believe in what you are doing. If you've got an idea that's really powerful, you've just got to ignore the people who tell you it won't work, and hire people who embrace your vision.
>
> It is as important to figure out what you're not going to do as it is to know what you are going to do.
>
> We instituted the practice of strong profit and loss management. By demanding a detailed P&L for each business unit, we learned the incredible value of facts and data in managing a complex business. As we have grown, Dell has become a highly data- and P&L- driven company, values that have since become core to almost everything we do.
>
> For us, growing up meant figuring out a way to combine our signature, informal style and "want to" attitude with the "can do" capabilities that would allow us to develop as a company. It meant incorporating into our everyday structure the valuable lessons we'd begun to learn using P&Ls. It meant focusing our employees to think in terms of shareholder value. It meant respecting the three golden rules at Dell: (1) Disdain inventory, (2) Always listen to the customer, and (3) Never sell indirect.
>
> I've always tried to surround myself with the best talent I could find. When you're the leader of a company, be it large or small, you can't do everything yourself. The more talented people you have to help you, the better off you and the company will be.
>
> A company's success should always be defined by its strategy and its ideas—and it should not be limited by the abilities of the people running it . . . When you are trying to grow a new business, you really need the experience of others who have been there and can help you anticipate and plan for things you might have never thought of.
>
> For any company to succeed, it's critical for top management to share power successfully. You have to be focused on achieving goals for the organization, not on accumulating power for yourself. Hoarding power does not translate into success for shareholders and customers; pursuing the goals of the company does. You also need to respect one another, and communicate so constantly that you're practically of one mind on the most important topics and issues that face the company.
>
> I have segmented my own job twice. Back in 1993–1994, it was becoming very clear to me that there was far too much to be done and far more opportunities than I could pursue myself . . . That was one of the reasons I asked Mort Topfer to join the company (as vice-chairman) . . . As the company continued to grow, we again segmented the job. In 1997, we promoted Kevin Rollins, who had been a key member of our executive team since 1996, to what we now call the office of the chairman. The three of us together run the company.
>
> Beyond winning and satisfying your customer, the objective must be to delight your customer—not just once but again and again. I spend about 40 percent of my time with customers . . . Customers know that I am not looking for insincere praise, or an affirmation of our strengths. They know by the quantity of the time that I spend and the kinds of questions that I ask that I want to hear the truth, and that I want to walk away with a list of ideas about how we can work to make a valued partnership that much more significant . . . When you delight your customers—consistently—by offering better products and better services, you create strong loyalty. When you go beyond that to build a meaningful, memorable total experience, you win customers for life. Our goal, at the end of the day, is for our customers to say, "Dell *is* the smarter way to buy a computer."

The pace of decisions moves too quickly these days to waste time noodling over a decision. And while we strive to always make the right choice, I believe it's better to be first at the risk of being wrong than it is to be 100 percent perfect two years too late. You can't possibly make the quickest or best decisions without data. Information is the key to any competitive advantage. But data doesn't just drop by your office to pay you a visit. You've got to go out and gather it. I do this by roaming around. I don't want my interactions planned; I want anecdotal feedback. I want to hear spontaneous remarks . . . I want to happen upon someone who is stumped by a customer's question—and help answer it if I can . . . I show up at the factory to talk to people unannounced, to talk to people on the shop floor and to see what's really going on. I go to brown-bag lunches two or three times a month, and meet with a cross-section of people from all across the company.[8]

Developments at Dell in Early 2000

Dell's unit shipments in the fourth quarter of 1999 were 3.36 million units, compared to 2.3 million units in the fourth quarter of 1998. In laptop PCs, Dell moved into second place in U.S. sales and fourth place worldwide in 1999. In higher-margin products like servers and workstations running on Windows NT, Windows 2000, and Linux, Dell ranked number two in market share in the United States and number three worldwide. In Europe, Dell ranked first in market share in Great Britain, third in market share in France, and second overall behind Compaq Computer. In Asia, Dell's sales were up 87 percent over 1998, despite sluggishness in the economies of several important Asian countries.

In 1999, about half of the industry's PC sales consisted of computers selling for less than $1,000. Dell's average selling price was $2,000 per unit in 1999, down from $2,500 in the first quarter of 1998. The company had recently introduced a line of WebPCs that was intended mainly for browsing the Internet. To counter the decline in the average selling prices of PCs, the company was placing increased emphasis on its line of PowerEdge servers and its Precision line of workstations, where average selling prices were $4,000 and higher, depending on the model.

MARKET CONDITIONS IN THE PC INDUSTRY IN 2000

There were an estimated 350 million PCs in use worldwide in 2000. Annual sales of PCs were approaching 130 million units annually (see Exhibit 6). About 50 million of the world's 350 million PCs were believed to have Intel 486 or older microprocessors with speeds of 75 megahertz or less. The world's population was over 6 billion people. Many industry experts foresaw a time when the installed base of PCs would exceed 1 billion units, and some believed the total would eventually reach 1.5 billion—a ratio of one PC for each four people. Forecasters also predicted that there would be a strong built-in replacement demand as microprocessor speeds continued to escalate past 1,000 megahertz. A microprocessor operating at 450 megahertz could process 600 million instructions per second (MIPS); Intel had forecast that it would be able to produce microprocessors capable of 100,000 MIPS by 2011. Such speeds were expected to spawn massive increases in computing functionality and altogether new uses and applications for PCs and computing devices of all types.

---

[8]Dell, *Direct from Dell,* pp. 29, 57, 50, 59, 60, 64, 65, 69, 139–40, 168–69, and 116.

exhibit 6   Actual and Projected Worldwide Shipments of PCs

Year	PC Volume (Millions)
1980	1
1985	11
1990	24
1995	58
1996	69
1997	80
1998	91
1999	113
2000	130 (projected)
2003	190 (projected)

Source: International Data Corp.

At the same time, forecasters expected demand for high-end servers carrying price tags of $5,000 to over $100,000 to continue to be especially strong because of the rush of companies all across the world to expand their Internet and e-commerce presence. Full global build-out of the Internet was expected to entail installing millions of high-speed servers.

Declining PC Prices and Intense Competition

Sharp drops in the prices of a number of PC components (chiefly, disk drives, memory chips, and microprocessors) starting in late 1997 had allowed PC makers to dramatically lower PC prices—sales of PCs priced under $1,500 were booming by early 1998. Compaq, IBM, Hewlett-Packard, and several other PC makers began marketing sub-$1,000 PCs in late 1997. In December 1997, the average purchase price of a desktop computer fell below $1,300 for the first time. It was estimated that about half of all PCs sold in 1998 were computers carrying price tags under $1,500; by 1999, close to half of all PCs sold were units under $1,000. Growth in unit volume was being driven largely by sub-$1,000 PCs. The low prices were attracting first-time buyers into the market and were also causing second- and third-time PC buyers looking to upgrade to more powerful PCs to forgo top-of-the-line machines priced in the traditional $2,000–$3,500 range in favor of lower-priced PCs that were almost as powerful and well-equipped. Powerful, multifeatured notebook computers that had formerly sold for $4,000 to $6,500 in November 1997 were selling for $1,500 to $3,500 in December 1999. The profits at Compaq, IBM, and several other PC makers began sliding in early 1998 and continued under pressure in 1999. Declining PC prices and mounting losses in PCs prompted IBM to withdraw from selling desktop PCs in 1999.

However, unexpected shortages of certain key components (namely, memory chips and screens for notebook computers) drove up prices for these items in late 1999 and moderated the decline in PC prices somewhat. But the shortages were expected to last only until suppliers could gear up production levels.

Continuing Economic Problems in Parts of Asia

Economic woes in a number of Asian countries (most notably, Japan, South Korea, Thailand, Indonesia, and to some extent, China) had put a damper on PC sales in Asia starting in 1997 and continuing through much of 1999. Asian sales of PCs in 1998 grew minimally (though sales were fairly robust in China); sales improved in 1999 but remained depressed in Thailand, Indonesia, and several other countries. China began experiencing some economic problems in 1999. In addition, sharp appreciation of the U.S. dollar against Asian currencies had made U.S.-produced PCs more expensive in terms of local currency to Asian buyers. In contrast, sales growth in the United States and Europe in 1999 remained strong, despite all the Y2K fears, mainly because of lower PC prices.

Disk-drive manufacturers and the makers of printed circuit boards, many of which were in Asia, were feeling the pressures of declining prices and skimpy profit margins. Industry observers were predicting that competitive conditions in the Asia-Pacific PC market favored growing market shares by the top four or five players and the likely exit of PC makers that could not compete profitably.

The Uncertain Near-Term Outlook for PC Industry Growth

While few industry observers doubted the long-term market potential for PC sales, there were several troubling signs on the near-term horizon, along with differences of opinion about just how fast the market for PCs would grow. A number of industry observers were warning of a global slowdown in the sales of PCs in 2000 and beyond, partly due to the economic difficulties in several Asian countries and partly due to approaching market maturity for PCs in the United States, Japan, and parts of Europe. Consequently, some analysts were forecasting gradual slowing of the industry growth rates from the 20–25 percent levels that characterized the 1990s down to the 10–12 percent range by 2005. However, U.S. shipments of PCs in the 1997–99 period had grown 20–25 percent annually, a much higher rate than most industry analysts had expected. Some 45 million new PCs were sold in the United States alone in 1999. Sales of servers, along with low-end PCs and workstations, were the fastest-growing segments of the PC industry in 1999 and were expected to be the segment growth leaders in 2000 and beyond.

On the positive side, some analysts expected that worldwide computer hardware sales in 2000–2003 period would grow at a compound annual rate of 15 to 20 percent, following cautious corporate buying in the second half of 1999 in preparation for meeting Y2K deadlines. Their expectations for 15–20 percent growth were based on (1) the introductions of Windows 2000 and Intel's new 64-bit Itanium microprocessors, (2) rapidly widening corporate use of the Internet and e-commerce technologies, (3) wider availability of high-speed Internet access, and (4) growing home use of PCs—as first-time purchasers succumbed to the lure of reasonably equipped sub-$1,000 PCs and as more parents purchased additional computers for use by their children. The three most influential factors in home ownership of PCs were education, income, and the presence of children in the household.

COMPETING VALUE CHAIN MODELS IN THE GLOBAL PC INDUSTRY

When the personal computer industry first began to take shape in the early 1980s, the founding companies manufactured many of the components themselves—disk drives, memory chips, graphics chips, microprocessors, motherboards, and software. Subscribing to a philosophy of "We have to develop key components in-house," they built expertise in a variety of PC-related technologies and created organizational units to produce components as well as to handle final assembly. While certain "noncritical" items were typically outsourced, if a computer maker was not at least partially vertically integrated and an assembler of some components, then it was not taken seriously as a manufacturer.

But as the industry grew, technology advanced quickly in so many directions on so many parts and components that the early personal computer manufacturers could not keep pace as experts on all fronts. There were too many technological innovations in components to pursue and too many manufacturing intricacies to master for a vertically integrated manufacturer to keep its products on the cutting edge. As a consequence, companies emerged that specialized in making particular components. Specialists could marshal enough R&D capability and resources to either lead the technological developments in their area of specialization or else quickly match the advances made by their competitors. Moreover, specialist firms could mass-produce a component and supply it to several computer manufacturers far cheaper than any one manufacturer could fund the needed component R&D and then make only whatever smaller volume of components it needed for assembling its own brand of PCs.

Thus, in recent years, computer makers had begun to abandon vertical integration in favor of a strategy of outsourcing most all components from specialists and concentrating on efficient assembly and marketing their brand of computers. Exhibit 7 shows the value chain model that such manufacturers as Compaq Computer, IBM, Hewlett-Packard, and others used in the 1990s. It featured arm's-length transactions between specialist suppliers, manufacturer/assemblers, distributors and retailers, and end users. However, Dell, Gateway, and Micron Electronics employed a shorter value chain model, selling direct to customers and eliminating the time and costs associated with distributing through independent resellers. Building to order avoided (1) having to keep many differently equipped models on retailers' shelves to fill buyer requests for one or another configuration of options and components and (2) having to clear out slow-selling models at a discount before introducing new generations of PCs. Selling direct eliminated retailer costs and markups. (Retail dealer margins were typically in the 4 to 10 percent range.) Dell Computer was far and away the world's largest direct seller to large companies and government institutions, while Gateway was the largest direct seller to individuals and small businesses. Micron Electronics was the only other PC maker that relied on the direct-sales, build-to-order approach for the big majority of its sales.

DELL COMPUTER'S STRATEGY

Dell management believed it had the industry's most efficient business model. The company's strategy was built around a number of core elements: build-to-order manufacturing, partnerships with suppliers, just-in-time components inventories, direct sales to customers, award-winning customer service and technical support, and pioneering use of the Internet and e-commerce technology. Management believed that a strong

exhibit **7** Comparative Value Chains of PC Manufacturers

Traditional PC industry value chain (utilized by Compaq Computer, IBM, Hewlett-Packard, most others)

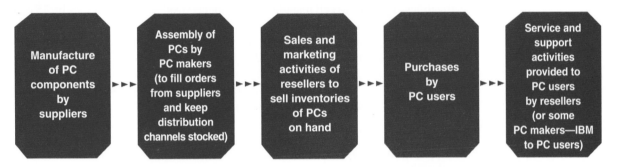

Build-to-order/direct sales value chain (employed by Dell Computer, Gateway, and Micron Electronics)

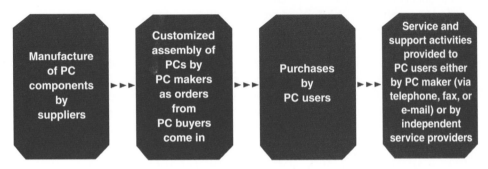

first-mover advantage accrued to the company from its lead over rivals in making e-commerce a centerpiece in its strategy.

Build-to-Order Manufacturing

Dell built its computers, workstations, and servers to order; none were produced for inventory. Dell customers could order custom-built servers and workstations based on the needs of their applications. Desktop and laptop customers ordered whatever configuration of microprocessor speed, random access memory (RAM), hard disk capacity, CD-ROM drive, fax/modem, monitor size, speakers, and other accessories they preferred. The orders were directed to the nearest factory. In 2000, Dell had PC assembly plants in Austin, Texas; Nashville/Lebanon, Tennessee; Limerick, Ireland; Xiamen, China; Penang, Malaysia; and El Dorado do Sul, Brazil. All six plants manufactured the company's entire line of products.

Until 1997, Dell operated its assembly lines in traditional fashion, with each worker performing a single operation. An order form accompanied each metal chassis across the production floor; drives, chips, and ancillary items were installed to match customer specifications. As a partly assembled PC arrived at a new workstation, the operator, standing beside a tall steel rack with drawers full of components, was instructed what to do by little red and green lights flashing beside the drawers containing the components the operator needed to install. When the operator was finished, the drawers containing the used components were automatically replenished from the other side, and the PC chassis glided down the line to the next workstation. However, Dell had reorganized its plants in 1997, shifting to "cell manufacturing" techniques whereby a team of workers operating at a group workstation (or cell) assembled an entire PC according to customer specifications. The shift to cell manufacturing reduced Dell's assembly times by 75 percent and doubled productivity per square foot of assembly space. Assembled computers were tested, then loaded with the desired software, shipped, and typically delivered within five to six business days of the order placement.

Dell's build-to-order, sell-direct strategy meant, of course, that Dell had no in-house stock of finished goods inventories and that, unlike competitors using the traditional value chain model (Exhibit 7), it did not have to wait for resellers to clear out their own inventories before it could push new models into the marketplace—resellers typically operated with 60 to 70 days' inventory. Equally important was the fact that customers who bought from Dell got the satisfaction of having their computers customized to their particular liking and pocketbook.

Quality Control Programs   All assembly plants had the capability to run testing and quality control processes on components, parts, and subassemblies obtained from suppliers, as well as for the finished products Dell assembled. Suppliers were urged to participate in a quality certification program that committed them to achieving defined quality specifications. Quality control activities were undertaken at various stages in the assembly process. In addition, Dell's quality control program included testing of completed units after assembly, ongoing production reliability audits, failure tracking for early identification of problems associated with new models shipped to customers, and information obtained from customers through its service and technical support programs. All of the company's plants had been certified as meeting ISO 9002 quality standards.

Partnerships with Suppliers and Just-in-Time Inventory Practices

Michael Dell believed it made much better sense for Dell Computer to partner with reputable suppliers of PC parts and components rather than integrate backward and get into parts and components manufacturing on its own. He explained why:

> If you've got a race with 20 players all vying to make the fastest graphics chip in the world, do you want to be the twenty-first horse, or do you want to evaluate the field of 20 and pick the best one?[9]

A central element of Dell Computer's strategy, therefore, was to evaluate the various makers of each component, pick the best one or two as suppliers, and partner with them for as long as they remained leaders in their specialty. Management believed long-term partnerships with reputable suppliers yielded several advantages. First, using name-brand processors, disk drives, modems, speakers, and multimedia components enhanced the quality and performance of Dell's PCs. Because of varying performance of different brands of components, the brand of the components was as important or more important to some end users than the brand of the overall system. Dell's strategy was to partner with as few outside vendors as possible and to stay with them as long as they maintained their leadership in technology, performance, and quality. Second, because Dell's partnership with a supplier was long term and because it committed to purchase a specified percentage of its requirements from that supplier, Dell was assured of getting the volume of

---

[9]As quoted in Magretta, "The Power of Virtual Integration," p. 74.

components it needed on a timely basis even when overall market demand for a particular component temporarily exceeded the overall market supply. Third, Dell's formal partnerships with key suppliers made it feasible to have some of their engineers assigned to Dell's product design teams and for them to be treated as part of Dell. When new products were launched, suppliers' engineers were stationed in Dell's plant, and if early buyers called with a problem related to design, further assembly and shipments were halted while the supplier's engineers and Dell personnel corrected the flaw on the spot.[10]

Fourth, Dell's long-run commitment to its suppliers laid the basis for just-in-time delivery of suppliers' products to Dell's assembly plants. Many of Dell's vendors had plants or distribution centers within a few miles of Dell assembly plants and could deliver daily or even hourly if needed. To help suppliers meet its just-in-time delivery expectations, Dell openly shared its daily production schedules, sales forecasts, and new-model introduction plans with vendors. Using online communications technology, Dell communicated inventory levels and replenishment needs to vendors on a daily or even hourly basis. Michael Dell explained what delivery capabilities the company expected of its suppliers:

> We tell our suppliers exactly what our daily production requirements are. So it's not, "Well, every two weeks deliver 5,000 to this warehouse, and we'll put them on the shelf, and then we'll take them off the shelf." It's, "Tomorrow morning we need 8,562, and deliver them to door number seven by 7 AM."[11]

Dell also did a three-year plan with each of its key suppliers and worked with suppliers to minimize the number of different stock-keeping units of parts and components in designing its products. Current initiatives included using the Internet to further improve supply chain management and achieve still greater manufacturing and assembly efficiencies.

Why Dell Was Committed to Just-in-Time Inventory Practices   Dell's just-in-time inventory emphasis yielded major cost advantages and shortened the time it took for Dell to get new generations of its computer models into the marketplace. New advances were coming so fast in certain computer parts and components (particularly microprocessors, disk drives, and modems) that any given item in inventory was obsolete in a matter of months, sometimes quicker. Having a couple of months of component inventories meant getting caught in the transition from one generation of components to the next. Moreover, it was not unusual for there to be rapid-fire reductions in the prices of components—in 1997 and early 1998, prices for some components fell as much as 50 percent (an average of 1 percent a week). Intel, for example, regularly cut the prices on its older chips when it introduced newer chips, and it introduced new chip generations about every three months. The prices of hard disk drives with greater and greater memory capacity had dropped sharply in recent years as disk drive makers incorporated new technology that allowed them to add more gigabytes of hard disk memory very inexpensively.

The economics of minimal component inventories were dramatic. Michael Dell explained:

> If I've got 11 days of inventory and my competitor has 80 and Intel comes out with a new 450-megahertz chip, that means I'm going to get to market 69 days sooner.
>
> In the computer industry, inventory can be a pretty massive risk because if the cost of materials is going down 50 percent a year and you have two or three months of inventory

---

[10]Ibid.

[11]Ibid.

versus 11 days, you've got a big cost disadvantage. And you're vulnerable to product transitions, when you can get stuck with obsolete inventory.[12]

Collaboration with suppliers was close enough to allow Dell to operate with only a few days of inventory for some components and a few hours of inventory for others. Dell supplied data on inventories and replenishment needs to its suppliers at least once a day—hourly in the case of components being delivered several times daily from nearby sources. In a couple of instances, Dell's close partnership with vendors allowed it to operate with no inventories. Dell's supplier of monitors was Sony. Because the monitors Sony supplied with the Dell name already imprinted were of dependably high quality (a defect rate of fewer than 1,000 per million), Dell didn't even open up the monitor boxes to test them.[13] Nor did it bother to have them shipped to Dell's assembly plants to be warehoused for shipment to customers. Instead, using sophisticated data exchange systems, Dell arranged for its shippers (Airborne Express and UPS) to pick up computers at its Austin plant, then pick up the accompanying monitors at the Sony plant in Mexico, match up the customer's computer order with the customer's monitor order, and deliver both to the customer simultaneously. The savings in time, energy, and cost were significant.

The company had, over the years, refined and improved its inventory tracking capabilities, its working relationships with suppliers, and its procedures for operating with smaller inventories. In fiscal year 1995, Dell averaged an inventory turn ratio of 32 days. By the end of fiscal 1997 (January 1997), the average was down to 13 days. The following year, it was 7 days, which compared very favorably with Gateway's 14-day average, Compaq's 23-day average, and the estimated industrywide average of over 50 days. In fiscal year 1999, Dell operated with an average of 6 days' supply in inventory. The company's long-term goal was to get its inventories down to a 3-day average supply.

Direct Sales

Selling direct to customers gave Dell firsthand intelligence about customer preferences and needs, as well as immediate feedback on design problems and quality glitches. With thousands of phone and fax orders daily, $35 million in daily Internet sales, and daily contacts between the field sales force and customers of all types, the company kept its finger on the market pulse, quickly detecting shifts in sales trends and getting prompt feedback on any problems with its products. If the company got more than a few of the same complaints, the information was relayed immediately to design engineers, who checked out the problem. When design flaws or components defects were found, the factory was notified and the problem corrected within a matter of days. Management believed Dell's ability to respond quickly gave it a significant advantage over rivals, particularly PC makers in Asia, that operated on the basis of large production runs of standardized products and sold them through retail channels. Dell saw its direct-sales approach as a totally customer-driven system, with the flexibility to change quickly to new generations of components and PC models.

Despite Dell's emphasis on direct sales, industry analysts noted that the company sold perhaps 10 percent of its PCs through a small, select group of resellers.[14] Most of

---

[12]Ibid.

[13]Ibid.

[14]"Dell Uses Channel to Move System Inventory," *Computer Reseller News,* January 12, 1998.

exhibit 8   Rapid Expansion of Dell Computer's Target Customer Segments, 1994–2000

Target Customer Segments			
1994	**1996**	**1997**	**2000**
• Large customers (both corporate and governmental buyers) • Small customers (both small businesses and individuals)	• Large companies • Midsize companies • Government agencies and educational institutions • Small customers (both small businesses and individuals)	• Global enterprise accounts • Large companies • Midsize companies • Federal agencies • State and local government agencies • Educational institutions • Small companies • Individual consumers	• Global enterprise accounts • Large and midsize companies (over 400 employees) • Health care businesses (over 400 employees) • Federal government • State and local government • Education—K–12 and higher education institutions (including special programs for personal-use purchases by faculty, staff, and students) • Small companies (under 400 employees) • Home and home office

Source: Joan Magretta, "The Power of Virtual Integration: An Interview with Dell Computer's Michael Dell," *Harvard Business Review,* March–April 1998, p. 78, and www.dell.com, February 1, 2000.

these resellers were systems integrators. It was standard for Dell not to allow returns on orders from resellers or to provide price protection in the event of subsequent declines in market prices. From time to time, Dell offered its resellers incentive promotions at up to a 20 percent discount from its advertised prices on end-of-life models. Dell was said to have no plans to expand its reseller network, which consisted of 50 to 60 dealers.

Dell's Use of Market Segmentation   To make sure that each type of computer user was well served, Dell had made a special effort to segment the buyers of its computers into relevant groups and to place managers in charge of developing sales and service programs appropriate to the needs and expectations of each market segment. Until the early 1990s, Dell had operated with sales and service programs aimed at just two market segments: (1) corporate and governmental buyers who purchased in large volumes and (2) small buyers (individuals and small businesses). But as sales took off in 1995–97, these segments were subdivided into finer, more homogeneous categories (see Exhibit 8).

In 1999, 65 percent of Dell's sales were to large corporations, government agencies, and educational institutions. Many of these large customers typically ordered thousands of units at a time and bought at least $1 million in PCs annually. Dell had hundreds of sales representatives calling on large corporate and institutional accounts. Its customer list included Shell Oil, Sony, Exxon-Mobil, MCI, Ford Motor, Toyota, Eastman Chemical, Boeing, Goldman Sachs, Oracle, Microsoft, Woolwich (a British bank with $64 billion in assets), Michelin, Unilever, Deutsche Bank, Wal-Mart, and First Union (one of the 10 largest U.S. banks). However, no one customer represented more than 2 percent of total sales.

Dell's sales to individuals and small businesses were made by telephone, fax, and the Internet. It had a call center in the United States with toll-free phone lines; customers could talk with a sales representative about specific models, get information faxed or mailed to them, place an order, and pay by credit card. Internationally, Dell had set up toll-free call centers in Europe and Asia.[15] The call centers were equipped with technology that routed calls from a particular country to a particular call center. Thus, for example, a customer calling from Lisbon, Portugal, was automatically directed to the call center in Montpelier, France, and connected to a Portuguese-speaking sales rep. Dell began Internet sales at its Web site (www.dell.com) in 1995, almost overnight achieving sales of $1 million per day. In 1997 sales reached an average of $3 million daily, hitting $6 million on some days during the Christmas shopping period. Dell's Internet sales averaged nearly $4 million daily in the first quarter of 1997, reached $14 million daily by year-end 1998, and climbed sharply to $35 million daily at the close of 1999. In early 2000, visits to Dell's Web site for information and order placement were approaching 2.5 million weekly, about 20 times more that the number of phone calls to sales representatives. In early 2000, about 43 percent of Dell's sales were Web-enabled and the percentage was increasing.

Dell in Europe   In fiscal year 1999, $6.6 billion of Dell's $18.2 billion in sales came from foreign customers. Europe, where resellers were strongly entrenched and Dell's direct sales approach was novel, was Dell's biggest foreign market, accounting for sales of $4.7 billion, up from $3.0 billion the prior year. Dell's European revenues were growing over 50 percent annually, and unit volume was increasing at nearly a 35 percent annual rate. Sales of PCs in Europe were 19.7 million units in 1997, 25.4 million units in 1998, and 29.9 million units in 1999. Expectations were for continued growth of 18 to 22 percent for the next several years. Europe's population and economy were roughly the same as those of the United States, but computer usage was only half that of the United States in 1999. Germany led Europe in sales of PCs, with 6.6 million units in 1999 (up 21.6 percent over 1998); Great Britain was second, with unit sales of 5.5 million (up 25.2 percent over 1998); and France was third, with 1999 unit sales of 4.4 million (up 26.7 percent over 1998). According to Dataquest, the top five market leaders in PCs in Europe were as follows:

Company	1999 Shipments	1999 Market Share (%)	1998 Shipments	1998 Market Share (%)	Percent Growth
Compaq	4,675,400	15.6	4,123,900	16.2	13.4
Fujitsu Siemens	3,471,600	11.5	2,615,000	10.3	32.8
Dell	2,612,200	8.7	1,943,600	7.7	34.4
IBM	2,340,300	7.8	2,107,400	8.3	11.1
Hewlett-Packard	1,897,600	6.3	1,482,900	5.8	28.0
Others	14,934,800	49.9	13,128,700	51.7	13.8
Totals	29,931,900	100.0	25,401,500	100.0	17.8

---

[15]"Michael Dell Rocks," *Fortune*, May 11, 1998, p. 66.

Fujitsu and Siemens had merged their PC operations in 1999 to move ahead of Dell in the ratings in Europe during 1999 (based on the combined market shares of the two brands); based on individual brand, however, Dell ranked second in Europe, ahead of both the Fujitsu brand and the Siemens brand.

Dell in China   Dell Computer entered China in 1998 and by 2000 had achieved a market share close to 2 percent. China was the fifth largest market for PCs in the world, behind the United States, Japan, Germany, and Britain. But with unit volume expanding 30 percent annually and a population of 1.2 billion people, the Chinese market for PCs was expected to become the second largest in the world by 2005 (with annual sales of $25 billion) and to become the world's largest PC market sometime thereafter. The market leader in China was Legend, a local company; other major local PC producers were Founder (ranked fourth) and Great Wall (ranked sixth). IBM, Hewlett-Packard, and Compaq were among the top five market share leaders in China—all three relied on resellers to handle sales and service. Other companies among the top 10 in market share in China included Toshiba, NEC Japan, and Acer (a Taiwan-based company). Dell, ranked eighth in market share in 1999, was the only market contender that employed a direct-sales business model. Dell's sales in China in 1999 were up 87 percent over 1998 levels.

Dell management believed that in China, as in other countries around the world, the company could be very price-competitive by cutting out middlemen and selling direct via the Internet, telephone, and a sales force that called on large customers. Dell's primary market target in China was large corporate accounts. Management believed that many Chinese companies would find the savings from direct sales appealing, that they would like the idea of having Dell build PCs to their requirements and specifications, and that—once they became Dell customers—they would like the convenience of Internet purchases and telephone orders. Dell recognized that its direct-sales approach would temporarily put it at a disadvantage in appealing to small-business customers and individual consumers. According to an executive from rival Legend, "It takes two years of a person's savings to buy a PC in China. And when two years of savings is at stake, the whole family wants to come out to a store to touch and try the machine."[16] But Dell believed that over time, as Chinese consumers became more familiar with PCs and more comfortable with making online purchases, it would be able to attract growing numbers of small-business customers and consumers through Internet and telephone sales.

IBM was the market leader in 1999 in the entire Asia-Pacific region, with an estimated 8.4 percent share, up from 8.1 percent in 1998.[17] Compaq had a second-place 7.3 percent share but was the market leader in a number of individual countries within the region. China-based Legend had a 7.1 percent share, most all of which came from sales in China. Samsung had the fourth largest market share, followed by Hewlett-Packard.

Dell in Latin America   In 2000, PC sales in Latin America were approaching 5 million units annually. Latin America had a population of 450 million people. Dell management believed that in the next few years use of PCs in Latin America would reach 1 for every 30 people (one-tenth the penetration in the United States), pushing annual sales up to 15 million units. The company's new plant in Brazil, the largest market in Latin America, was opened to produce, sell, and provide service and technical support for customers in Brazil, Argentina, Chile, Uruguay, and Paraguay.

---

[16]As quoted in Neel Chowdhury, "Dell Cracks China," *Fortune*, June 21, 1999, p. 121.

[17]According to data compiled by International Data Corporation and provided to the case researchers by IDC.

Customer Service and Technical Support

Service became a feature of Dell's strategy in 1986 when the company began providing a year's free on-site service with most of its PCs after users complained about having to ship their PCs back to Austin for repairs. Dell contracted with local service providers to handle customer requests for repairs; on-site service was provided on a next-day basis. Dell also provided its customers with technical support via a toll-free phone number, fax, or e-mail. Dell received close to 40,000 e-mail messages monthly requesting service and support and had 25 technicians to process the requests. Bundled service policies were a major selling point for winning corporate accounts. If a customer preferred to work with its own service provider, Dell supplied that provider with the training and spare parts needed to service the customer's equipment.

Value-Added Services   Selling direct allowed Dell to keep close track of the purchases of its large global customers, country by country and department by department—information that customers found valuable. And its close customer relationships resulted in Dell being quite knowledgeable about what each customer needed and how its PC network functioned. Aside from using this information to help customers plan their PC needs and configure their PC networks, Dell used it to add to the value it delivered to its customers. For example, Dell could load a customer's software at the factory, thereby eliminating the need for the customer's PC personnel to unpack the PC, deliver it to an employee's desk, hook it up, place asset tags on the PC, then load the needed software from an assortment of CD-ROMs and diskettes—a process that could take several hours and cost $200 to $300.[18] Dell's solution was to load the customer's software onto large Dell servers at the factory and, when a particular version of a customer's PC came off the assembly line, to use its high-speed server network to load whatever software the customer had specified onto the PC's hard disk in a few seconds. If the customer so desired, Dell would place the customer's asset tags on the PC at the factory. Dell charged customers only $15 or $20 for the software-loading and asset-tagging services—the savings to customers were thus considerable. One large customer reported savings of $500,000 annually from having Dell load its software and place asset tags on its PCs at the factory.[19] In 1997, about 2 million of the 7 million PCs Dell sold were shipped with customer-specific software already loaded on the PCs.

In late 1997, in another effort to add value for its customers, Dell, following Compaq's lead, created a financial services group to assist customers with financing their PC networks.

Premier Pages   Dell had developed customized, password-protected Web sites (called Premier Pages) for 40,000 corporate, governmental, and institutional customers worldwide. Premier Page sites gave customer personnel online access to information about all Dell products and configurations the company had purchased or that were currently authorized for purchase. Employees of Dell's large customers could use Premier Pages to (1) obtain customer-specific pricing for whatever machines and options they wanted to consider, (2) place an order online that would be electronically routed to higher-level managers for approval and then on to Dell for assembly and delivery, and (3) seek advanced help desk support. Customers could also search and sort all invoices and obtain purchase histories. These features eliminated paper invoices, cut ordering time, and reduced the internal labor customers needed to staff corporate purchasing and

---

[18]Magretta, "The Power of Virtual Integration," p. 79.
[19]"Michael Dell Rocks," p. 61.

accounting functions. A customer's Premier Pages also contained all of the elements of its relationship with Dell, including who the Dell sales and support contacts were in every country where the customer had operations, what software Dell loaded on each of the various types of PCs the customer purchased, and service and warranty records for each machine. So far, customer use of Premier Pages had boosted the productivity of Dell salespeople assigned to these accounts by 50 percent. Dell was providing Premier Page service to thousands of additional customers annually and adding more features to further improve functionality.

www.dell.com   At the company's Web site, which underwent a global redesign in late 1999 and had 50 country-specific sites in local languages and currencies, prospective buyers could review Dell's entire product line in detail, configure and price customized PCs, place orders, and track those orders from manufacturing through shipping. The closing rate on sales coming through www.dell.com were 20 percent higher than sales inquiries received via telephone or fax. The company was adding Web-based customer service and support tools to make a customer's online experience pleasant and satisfying. Already the company had implemented a series of online technical support tools:

- *Support.Dell.com*—This Web-based feature allowed customers to create a customized support home page; review technical specifications for Dell systems; obtain information and answers from an extensive database collected by Dell technicians, service providers, and customers; click on online links to Dell's primary suppliers; and take three online courses on PC usage at no charge. The site enabled customers to select how they received online help, based on their comfort and experience with PC technology. The information available at this part of Dell's Web site was particularly helpful to the internal help-desk groups at large companies. In late 1999, customer visits to support.Dell.com were running at a rate of 19 million per year.

- *E-Support*—Dell had developed advanced technology called "E-Support—Direct from Dell" that helped Dell systems detect, diagnose, and resolve most of their own problems without the need for users to interact with Dell's support personnel. The goal of Dell's E-Support technology was to create computing environments where a PC would be able to maintain itself, thus moving support from a reactive process to a preventive one. Michael Dell saw E-Support as "the beginning of what we call self-healing systems that we think will be the future of online support."[20] Dell expected that by the end of 2000 more than 50 percent of the customers needing technical help would use E-Support—Direct from Dell. Management believed the service would shorten the time it took to fix glitches and problems, reduce the need for service calls, cut customer downtimes, and lower Dell's tech-support costs.

- *Dell Talk*—An online discussion group with 100,000 registered users, Dell Talk brought users and information technology (IT) professionals together to discuss common IT problems and issues.

- *Ask Dudley*—The Ask Dudley tool gave customers instant answers to technical service and support questions. Customers typed in the question in their native language and clicked on "ask."

In February 2000, 40 to 45 percent of Dell's technical support activities were being conducted via the Internet. Dell was aggressively pursuing initiatives to enhance its on-

---

[20]As quoted in *Austin American-Statesman*, August 26, 1999.

line technical support tools. Its top priority was the development of tools (as described in the above list) that could tap into a user's computer, make a diagnosis, and if the problem was software related, perform an online fix. Dell expected that such tools would not only make it easier and quicker for customers to resolve technical problems but would also help it reduce the costs of technical support calls (currently running at 8 million calls a year). The company estimated that its online technical support tools had resulted in 25 percent fewer support calls from users, generating savings of between $5 and $10 per call.

Management believed that the enhancements it was making to www.dell.com made it easier and faster for customers to do business with Dell by shrinking transaction and order fulfillment times, increasing accuracy, and providing more personalized content. According to management, a positive Web site experience was a bigger driver of "e-loyalty" than traditional attributes like price and product selection.

On-Site Service   Corporate customers paid Dell fees to provide support and on-site service. Dell generally contracted with third-party providers to make the necessary on-site service calls. Customers notified Dell when they had PC problems; such notices triggered two electronic dispatches—one to ship replacement parts from Dell's factory to the customer sites and one to notify the contract service provider to prepare to make the needed repairs as soon as the parts arrived.[21] Bad parts were returned to Dell for diagnosis of what went wrong and what could be done to see that the problems wouldn't happen again. Problems relating to faulty components or flawed components design were promptly passed along to the relevant supplier, who was expected to improve quality control procedures or redesign the component. Dell's strategy was to manage the flow of information gleaned from customer service activities to improve product quality and reliability.

On-Site Dell Support   A number of Dell's corporate accounts were large enough to justify dedicated on-site teams of Dell employees. Customers usually welcomed such teams, preferring to focus their time and energy on the core business rather than being distracted by PC purchasing and servicing issues. For example, Boeing, which had 100,000 Dell PCs, was served by a staff of 30 Dell employees who resided on-site at Boeing facilities and were intimately involved in planning Boeing's PC needs and configuring Boeing's network. While Boeing had its own people working on what the company's best answers for using PCs were, there was close collaboration between Dell and Boeing personnel to understand Boeing's needs in depth and to figure out the best solutions.

Migration to New Technology   Dell had opened facilities in both Europe and North America to assist its customers and independent software providers in migrating their systems and applications to Windows 2000, Intel's new 64-bit Itanium computer chip technology, and other next-generation computing and Internet technologies. Dell was partnering with Intel, Microsoft, Computer Associates, and other prominent PC technology providers to help customers make more effective use of the Internet and the latest computing technologies. Dell, which used Intel microprocessors exclusively in its computers, had been a consistent proponent of standardized Intel-based platforms because it believed those platforms provided customers with the best total value and performance. Dell management considered both Intel and Microsoft as long-term strategic partners in mapping out its future.

---

[21]Kevin Rollins, "Using Information to Speed Execution," *Harvard Business Review,* March–April, 1998, p. 81.

Customer Forums   In addition to using its sales and support mechanisms to stay close to customers, Dell held regional forums to stimulate the flow of information back and forth with customers. The company formed "Platinum Councils," composed of its largest customers in the United States, Europe, Japan, and the Asia-Pacific area; regional meetings were held every six to nine months.[22] In the larger regions, there were two meetings—one for chief information officers and one for technical personnel. As many as 100 customers and 100 Dell executives and representatives, including Michael Dell, attended the three-day meetings. At the meetings, Dell's senior technologists shared their views on the direction of the latest technological developments, what the flow of technology really meant for customers, and Dell's plans for introducing new and upgraded products over the next two years. There were also breakout sessions on such topics as how to manage the transition to Windows NT, how to manage the use of notebooks by people out in the field, and whether leasing was better than buying. Customers were provided opportunities to share information and learn from one another (many had similar problems) as well as exchange ideas with Dell personnel. Dell found that the information gleaned from customers at these meetings assisted in forecasting demand for the company's products.

Pioneering Leadership in Use of the Internet and E-Commerce Technology

Michael Dell believed that the Internet had revolutionary business potential, and he was instrumental in making Dell Computer a pioneering first-mover in using the Internet and e-commerce technologies. In a 1999 speech to 1,200 Dell customers, he said:

> The world will be changed forever by the Internet . . . The Internet will be your business. If your business isn't enabled by providing customers and suppliers with more information, you're probably already in trouble. The Internet provides a dramatic reduction in the cost of transactions and the cost of interaction among people and businesses, and it creates dramatic new opportunities and destroys old competitive advantages. The Internet is like a weapon sitting on a table ready to be picked up by either you or your competitors.[23]

Michael Dell believed that for a company to harness the power of the Internet and succeed in revolutionizing the way business was done, it had to observe three rules:

1. Give customers a better experience online than they could get offline.
2. Execute efficiently.
3. Recognize that compressing time and distance in business relationships with suppliers and customers to enhance the velocity of business transactions is the ultimate source of competitive advantage. (Dell was convinced that transacting business with suppliers and customers in real time drove big improvements in business efficiency—requiring fewer people, less inventory, and fewer physical assets and speeding new products to market.)

Dell Computer was rapidly gaining valuable experience and know-how in applying these rules to its business. For example, the company had created valuechain.dell.com, which provided suppliers with secure personalized access to Dell's operations through a single portal. This tool facilitated real-time collaboration on the quality of the items being supplied, helped assure continuity of supply and minimal components inventories,

---

[22]Magretta, "The Power of Virtual Integration," p. 80.

[23]Keynote speech given on August 25, 1999, in Austin, Texas, at Dell's "DirectConnect Conference."

and made it possible for engineers at Dell and its suppliers to jointly develop online designs of next-generation components and products. Dell had also created an online "scorecard" for suppliers showing their performance against the quality standards that had been agreed on and how well they were doing against other suppliers in the same class. Both tools helped the company achieve its strategic objectives of product quality and reliability, rapid inventory turnover, and low costs.

Dell was using the Internet to improve its execution efficiency in several ways. By greatly improving the company's capability to provide order status information quickly and conveniently over the Internet, the company had been able to eliminate tens of thousands of order status inquiries coming in by phone. Order status inquiries handled by phone typically cost the company between $3 and $10; however, the cost could be considerably more if a customer had 100 orders and the status of each one had to checked. Close to 80 percent of Dell's order status inquiries in 2000 were being handled via the Internet at a cost close to zero, saving Dell an estimated $21 million annually and freeing personnel to do higher-value-added activities.

Although Dell was doing a very good job in solving 80 percent of customer issues over the phone (compared to an industry average of 27 percent) and saving money by not having to dispatch an on-site service provider, the company was working to greatly improve its online diagnostic technical support tools—Support.Dell.com, Dell Talk, and Ask Dudley. Management believed that Web-enabled technical support would make it easier and quicker for users to get the technical support they needed, as well as reduce the costs of handling the current total of 8 million technical support calls a year.

In 1998 the company had used technology to tackle the challenge of reducing its infrastructure cost of handling messages from customers. Michael Dell explained:

> The needs for our e-mail structure had grown beyond the support we had internally. We faced a very serious challenge. We were receiving 2.7 million messages per week within Dell's system, 4.3 million per month over the Internet, and our user base was growing at the rate of 50 percent per year. To solve this, we consolidated 200 servers into about 25 PowerEdge servers running Microsoft Exchange. There was a 10 times reduction in the number of servers and the associated management costs. We migrated to Exchange and lowered our user cost by 29 percent.[24]

Other Elements of Dell's Business Strategy

Other element of Dell's strategy, in addition to those mentioned above, are discussed below.

Demand Forecasting Management believed that accurate sales forecasts were key to keeping costs down and minimizing inventories, given the complexity and diversity of the company's product line. Because Dell worked diligently at maintaining a close relationship with its large corporate and institutional customers and because it sold direct to small customers via telephone and the Internet, it was possible to keep a finger on the pulse of demand—what was selling and what was not. Moreover, the company's market segmentation strategy paved the way for in-depth understanding of customers' current needs, evolving requirements, and expectations. Having credible real-time information about what customers were actually buying and having firsthand knowledge of large customers' buying intentions gave Dell strong capability to forecast demand. Furthermore, Dell passed that information on to suppliers so they could

[24]Ibid.

plan their production accordingly. The company worked hard at managing the flow of information it got from the marketplace and quickly sending that information to both internal groups and vendors.

Forecasting was viewed as a critical sales skill. Sales-account managers were coached on how to lead large customers through a discussion of their future needs for PCs, workstations, servers, and peripheral equipment. Distinctions were made between purchases that were virtually certain and those that were contingent on some event. Salespeople made note of the contingent events so they could follow up at the appropriate time. With smaller customers, there was real-time information about sales, and direct telephone sales personnel often were able to steer customers toward configurations that were immediately available to help fine-tune the balance between demand and supply.

Research and Development Company management believed that it was Dell's job to sort out all the new technology coming into the marketplace and help steer customers to options and solutions most relevant to their needs. The company talked to its customers frequently about "relevant technology," listening carefully to customers' needs and problems and endeavoring to identify the most cost-effective solutions. Dell had about 1,600 engineers working on product development and spent about $250 million annually to improve users' experience with its products—including incorporating the latest and best technologies, making its products easy to use, and devising ways to keep costs down. The company's R&D unit also studied and implemented ways to control quality and to streamline the assembly process. Much time went into tracking all the new developments in components and software to ascertain how they would prove useful to computer users. For instance, it was critical to track vendor progress in making longer-lasting batteries because battery life was very important to the buyers of portable computers. Dell was the first company to put lithium ion batteries with a 5.5- to 6-hour life in all of its laptop models.

Advertising Michael Dell was a strong believer in the power of advertising and frequently espoused its importance in the company's strategy. His competitive zeal resulted in the company's being the first to use comparative ads, throwing barbs at Compaq's higher prices. Although Compaq won a lawsuit against Dell for making false comparisons, Michael Dell was unapologetic, arguing that the ads were "very effective" and that they allowed the company "to increase customer awareness about value."[25] Dell insisted that the company's ads be communicative and forceful, not soft and fuzzy.

The company regularly had prominent ads describing its products and prices in such leading computer publications as *PC Magazine* and *PC World*, as well as in *USA Today*, *The Wall Street Journal*, and other business publications. In the spring of 1998, the company debuted a major multiyear worldwide TV campaign to strengthen its brand image—the theme for the campaign was "Be Direct." A number of the ads featured Michael Dell talking about the importance of direct customer relationships, the company's attentive and responsive customer service, and the unique value created by the company's direct-sales and build-to-order approaches. One of Dell's tag lines was "Empower Your Business Through the Internet with Dell."

Dell's Increased Emphasis on Servers and Storage Devices Dell entered the market for low-end PC servers (under $25,000) in the second half of 1996. Its entry strategy included adding 23,000 square feet of production capacity suitable for cell manufacturing techniques and self-contained work teams, training 1,300 telemarketers

---

[25]"The Education of Michael Dell," p. 85.

to sell servers, assigning 160 sales reps with systems know-how to big customer accounts, and recruiting a staff of systems experts to help the sales reps. It also contracted with companies such as Electronic Data Systems, which had in-depth systems and networking expertise, to help provide service to large customers with extensive server networks.

There were several drivers behind Dell's entry into servers. The use of servers by corporate customers was growing rapidly. The margins on servers were large. Moreover, purchase price was not as significant a factor in selecting which brand of server to buy because servers required far more in the way of service, support, and software. Several of Dell's rivals, most notably Compaq Computer, were using their big margins on server sales to subsidize price cuts on desktops and notebooks in an attempt to win corporate PC accounts away from Dell. According to Michael Dell,

> We had to meet the challenge of extending the Dell brand beyond our strong desktop and notebook franchises. The next logical step was servers. Entering the server business was not only a huge opportunity but clearly a competitive necessity. An explosion of networked and internetworked systems was occurring throughout corporations, which meant that our present customers—the techno-savvy, second- or third-time buyers who were our core market—would be looking to make big purchases.
>
> At the same time, the emergence of industry standards for operating systems (Windows NT) and multiprocessor servers meant that Dell could develop its own server systems based on these standards and avoid massive investments in new proprietary technologies that would ultimately become very costly for our customers. It also meant that we did not have to acquire a competitor to enter the server business.
>
> We could profit by offering lower prices through the direct model. We could, in effect, shatter the price premiums customers were paying for proprietary server technologies.
>
> The alternative wasn't pretty. Servers were a force literally big enough to change the operating environment. If we ignored them, the market would consolidate around the top three providers—Compaq, IBM, and HP. We would be seen as a bit player, and would lose our standing with technology providers. And our operating margins would start to thin.
>
> Our large competitors also were using excessively high margins in servers to subsidize the less profitable parts of their business, like desktops and notebooks. If we didn't move into servers, we would be greatly exposed to attack in the desktop and notebook market.
>
> We had the opportunity to do with servers what we had originally done with desktops and then notebooks: rapidly build market share by offering higher performance at a lower price, simultaneously forcing our competitors to lower their server prices and collapse their margins to the point where they couldn't afford to subsidize their other product lines. We couldn't afford not to take such an opportunity.[26]

As Michael Dell predicted, Dell Computer's build-to-order, sell-direct strategy gave it a significant cost and pricing advantage over rival sellers of servers. When Dell launched its new PowerEdge server line, the servers from such competitors as Compaq, IBM, and Hewlett-Packard, all of which relied on networks of resellers, were priced 15 to 20 percent higher than comparable Dell models. To communicate to Dell employees the importance of achieving success in the server market, the company sent out companywide "Message from Michael" e-mails, put up posters in high-traffic areas, and talked through the strategy at numerous brown-bag lunches and company get-togethers.[27] It also staged an event called "The Great Dell Torch Event" for 7,000 employees in a downtown Austin auditorium, opened by Michael Dell running into the auditorium carrying an

---

[26]Dell, *Direct from Dell,* pp. 82–83.

[27]Ibid., p. 84.

Olympic-sized torch. In meetings with customers Michael Dell and Dell salespeople told customers to ask their server vendors to meet Dell's pricing so they could at least save money on server purchases if they did not opt to buy from Dell. In the first year that Dell competed in servers, rivals cut prices about 17 percent on their competing models.

Dell's objective was to achieve a double-digit share of the server market by year-end 1998; it achieved that goal in the middle of 1997. By year-end 1997, Dell had gone from 10th to 4th in market share worldwide. By the fall of 1998, Dell had passed IBM and Hewlett-Packard in the U.S. market, moving into second place with a 19 percent share; and Dell was the only server provider growing substantially faster than the rest of the market. During the 1997–99 period, Dell expanded its lineup of server products to include more powerful models, added modular features, and boosted its service capabilities for servers. By 2000, the company had captured a sizable share of the market for low-end servers and was a significant competitive force in the server segment.

More recently, Dell had expanded its product line to include storage devices designed to handle a variety of customers' needs for high-speed data storage and retrieval. Dell's PowerVault line of storage products had data protection and recovery features that made it easy for customers to add and manage storage and simplify consolidation. Dell management saw storage devices as a growth opportunity because the computing systems of corporate and institutional customers were making increasing use of storage devices.

Dell's Introduction of a WebPC   In December 1999, Dell unveiled a new line of PCs stripped of fancy features and equipped for easy, quick Internet access by novices. The new line included three models, ranging in price from $999 to $2,349. Each came with a monitor, printer, technical support options, and one-year subscription to Dell's Internet service, DellNet. Each of the new WebPCs could be plugged in and made Internet-ready in three steps. The main unit was 6 inches wide, 11 inches high, and 10 inches deep and weighed 10 pounds. Dell believed the new line would help broaden the market for its products and give it a growing presence in the consumer and small-business segments. According to Michael Dell, "If Dell executes in the consumer and small business market alone this could add an additional $10 billion in revenue over the next several years."[28] Two competitors were planning to launch comparable products. Compaq Computer had announced it would begin selling an iPaq PC in early 2000 for $499 without a monitor. Advanced Micro Devices planned to introduce its EasyNow model in late December at prices of $500 to $1,000.

Dell's Efforts to Promote Good Strategy Execution

Michael Dell was a strong believer that good planning and good strategy amounted to little without good strategy execution. To promote effective strategy execution, the company had adopted a number of policies and operating practices. The company stressed use of facts and data in daily decision making—"Facts are your friend" was a common phase at Dell and an integral part of the corporate culture. The company had developed detailed profit and loss statements for each part of the business, and managers were expected to make fact-based decisions according to their impact on the bottom line; those who resisted were forced out.

---

[28]As quoted in Connie Mabin, "Dell Focuses on Novice Users with Simple WebPC," The Associated Press State and Local Wire, December 1, 1999.

Because much of what had contributed to Dell's success went against the grain of conventional wisdom, Dell Computer made a conscious effort to hire employees who had open, questioning minds and were always ready to learn and try something new.[29] Job applicants were screened carefully; the company looked for people who not only were results-oriented, self-reliant, and intelligent but also expected change to be the norm and liked looking at things from a different angle and coming up with unprecedented, innovative solutions. People were hired not so much for their ability to come in and fill a job opening as for their capacity to grow and develop with the company over the long term. Once hired, Dell employees were encouraged to be innovative, to look for breakthrough ideas, to challenge the status quo, and to experiment with new or better ways of doing things. Self-criticism and acceptance of periodic "course corrections" were ingrained in the Dell culture; everyone could question how things were being done and offer suggestions for improvement. Michael Dell preached against complacency and satisfaction with the status quo:

> We try to avoid being too proud of our accomplishments . . . If we start to think we've made it, we're just setting ourselves up to be eclipsed by someone else . . . It's easy to fall in love with how far you've come and how much you've done. It's definitely harder to see the cracks in the structure you've built yourself, but that's all the more reason to look hard and look often. Even if something seems to be working, it can always be improved.[30]

A substantial part of the work process at Dell was organized around teams. Teams were given objectives and were held accountable for their performance. For example, on the factory floor people worked in teams of two to receive, manufacture, and pack an order for delivery to a customer. Profit-sharing incentives encouraged members to be productive as a team. Hourly metrics for team performance were posted on monitors on the factory floor so that each team could see how it was doing relative to other teams and to performance targets. Ratings of individual performance were based on a 360-degree performance appraisal that involved input from everyone with whom an employee worked rather than just supervisors.

The vast majority of Dell's employees were also stockholders as a result of the company's employee stock purchase plans, stock option grants, and a 401(K) plan in which Dell matched employee contributions with stock rather than cash. The compensation and incentives of Dell employees were tied to the health of Dell's business, measured chiefly by the company's return on invested capital (ROIC) and growth rate. Tying compensation increases and incentive awards to ROIC began in 1995 with a companywide push to educate all employees to the benefits of boosting ROIC that included e-mail "Messages from Michael," articles in the company newsletter, posters, and talks by managers. The company explained how employees could contribute to a higher ROIC by helping reduce cycle times, eliminating scrap and waste, increasing inventory turns, forecasting accurately, boosting sales volumes, controlling operating expenses, collecting accounts receivable more efficiently, and doing things right the first time.[31] Dell executives believed that focusing attention on ROIC mobilized employees around a single company goal. And they believed that treating employees as owners helped employees understand the drivers of the business, fostered a sense of pride, and got them much more involved in the process of questioning procedures, experimenting with new ideas, and learning better ways to do things.

To spur the process of looking for innovations and new opportunities, Dell management made a practice of setting stretch objectives. In 1997, the company set a target

---

[29]Dell, *Direct from Dell,* pp. 109–11.

[30]Ibid., pp. 128–29.

[31]Ibid., pp. 134–35.

of selling 50 percent of its systems at www.dell.com within the next few years. At the time, Web site sales were averaging $1 million per day and annual revenues were $12 billion. The 50 percent target was not picked out of the air but was based on the company's growth, the market potential of the company's products, and the perceived potential of online sales.

Dell management spent a lot of time communicating to employees—explaining what was going on, what the company's strategy was, where the company stood in the market, what its future plans were, and what the organization needed to do to achieve its objectives. Michael Dell conducted "town hall" meetings at various locations annually and spent a lot of time answering questions. Company successes were celebrated at get-togethers and via e-mail communications congratulating teams on big account wins or other special achievements. Best practices in one area were shared with other areas. Much communication took place in real time via extensive use of e-mail and the company intranet.

The company made a concerted effort to avoid hierarchical structure, believing that hierarchy stymied communication and resulted in slower response times. Michael Dell explained:

> We're allergic to hierarchy. Hierarchical structure to me fundamentally implies a loss of speed. It implies that there's congestion in the flow of information. It implies the need for layers of approval and command and control, and signoffs here, there, and everywhere. That's inconsistent with the speed with which we all need to make decisions, both as leaders and as a company, in this fast-paced marketplace . . . Time is everything—the sooner you deal with an issue, the sooner it's resolved.[32]

RECENT CHANGES IN THE STRATEGIES OF PC MAKERS

Rivalry among the world's makers of PCs was quite strong in 2000. As the CEO of Gateway put it in January, "The environment in which we are operating is tough and getting tougher." Competitive pressures, which had been mounting since 1997, had prompted a number of companies to alter their strategies for competing.

The Attempts of Several Manufacturers and Retailers to Clone Dell's PC Strategy

Dell's competitors—Compaq, IBM, Packard Bell NEC, and Hewlett-Packard—were shifting their business models to build-to-order manufacturing to reduce their inventories and speed new models to market. Compaq launched its build-to-order initiative in July 1997 and hoped to cut costs 10 to 12 percent. Compaq's revamped assembly plants were able to turn out a custom-built PC in three to four hours and could load the desired software in six minutes. Packard Bell NEC's program allowed customers to place orders by phone. But all three were finding that it was hard to duplicate Dell's approach because of the time it took to develop just-in-time delivery schedules with suppliers, to coordinate their mutual production schedules, and to shift smoothly to next-generation parts and components as they appeared on the market. It took extensive collaboration to plan smooth technology transitions. Compaq and Hewlett-Packard had spent 18 months planning their build-to-order strategies and expected it would take another 18 or more months to achieve their inventory- and cost-reduction goals.

---

[32]Ibid., pp. 133, 137.

At the same time, such computer retailers as Tandy Corporation's Computer City, CompUSA, OfficeMax, and Wal-Mart Stores had gotten into the build-to-order, sell-direct business. CompUSA was offering customers two lines of desktop computers that could be ordered at any of its 134 stores, by phone, at its Web site, or through its corporate sales force; its goal was to undercut Dell's price by $200 on each configuration. Wal-Mart was offering build-to-order PCs made by a contract manufacturer at its Web site.

Dell was seen as having the right strategy to appeal to customers well versed in PC technology who knew what options and features they wanted and who were aware of the price differences among brands. According to one industry analyst, "Dell is everybody's target. No matter who you talk to in the industry, Dell is the brand to beat."[33]

The Moves of PC Makers to Broaden Their Business

Several leading players in the PC industry made moves in late 1997 and early 1998 to expand into selling more than just PCs in an effort to improve profitability. The sharp declines in the prices of PCs had crimped gross profit margins and prompted such companies as Dell, Compaq, Gateway, Hewlett-Packard, and IBM to view selling PCs as an entrée to providing a bigger lineup of products.

To move beyond simple PC manufacturing, Compaq in late 1997 acquired Digital Equipment Company (DEC), which derived $6 billion in revenues from providing a range of PC services to corporate customers. Both Hewlett-Packard and IBM had always viewed the PC business as part of a larger portfolio of products and services they offered customers. A substantial portion of Hewlett-Packard's revenues and profits came from sales of servers and printers. IBM derived a big portion of its revenues from mainframe computers, software, and technical and support services.

Dell, Gateway, and several other makers of PCs for the home market had begun offering Internet access service to purchasers of their PCs. Gateway's chairman, Ted Waitt, explained, "We're about customer relations a lot more than we are about PCs. If we get a 5 percent margin on a $1,500 PC, we make $75. But if we can make $3 a month on Internet access, that's another $100 over three years. Three years from now, I don't think just selling PC hardware will allow anyone to have a great business."[34] PC makers were also selling printers, scanners, Zip drives, assorted software packages, and other computer-related devices at their Web sites to boost revenues and overall margins. Several PC makers had begun leasing PCs to individuals and households and to finance PCs on low monthly payment plans in hopes of getting the customer to trade in the old PC for a new PC later when the lease expired or the last payment was made.

PROFILES OF SELECTED COMPETITORS IN THE PC INDUSTRY

Below are brief profiles of Dell's principal competitors in the global PC market.

Compaq Computer

In 1999 Compaq Computer Corporation was the world's largest supplier of personal computer systems and the second largest global computing company (behind IBM),

---

[33]As quoted in *Business Week,* September 29, 1997, p. 38.

[34]David Kirkpatrick, "Old PC Dogs Try New Tricks," *Fortune,* July 6, 1998, pp. 186–88.

with annual sales of $38.5 billion and profits of $569 million. Compaq became the world's largest seller of PCs in 1995, displacing IBM as the world leader. Compaq acquired Tandem Computer in 1997 and Digital Equipment Corporation in 1998 to give it capabilities, products, and service offerings that allowed it to compete in every sector of the computer industry.[35] When Compaq purchased Digital, Digital was a troubled company with high operating costs, an inability to maintain technological leadership in high-end computing, and a nine-year string of having either lost money or barely broken even.[36] The acquisitions gave Compaq a product line that included PCs, servers, workstations, mainframes, peripherals, and such services as business and e-commerce solutions, hardware and software support, systems integration, and technology consulting. Compaq management believed that additional unit volume provided by the Digital acquisition permitted greater economies of scale in production and gave it more leverage in securing favorable pricing from component suppliers.[37] Digital's extensive service and support network allowed Compaq to offer a comprehensive portfolio of professional computing services and technical support through a global network of approximately 27,000 employees as well as 30,000 service delivery partners.[38] Compaq had very strong brand recognition because of its status as the global market share leader in the PC market.

Compaq's Strategy   Compaq's strategy was to sell almost exclusively through resellers—distributors and PC retailers, particularly large computer stores like CompUSA. In 1998 Compaq, responding to mounting competition in PCs, launched internal actions to emulate some of the key elements of Dell Computer's strategy. Compaq began efforts to switch from a build-to-stock to a build-to-order production model and intended to maintain Internet connections with its suppliers and customers to achieve a five-day or less cycle time between the receipt of an order and product shipment.[39] However, as of mid-1999 the company's order-to-delivery time was approximately 12 days (versus an order-to-delivery time of 3.1 days at Dell).[40] Compaq was also striving to improve inventory management and reduce transportation costs, but the results going into 2000 had been modest.[41] Because Compaq had bigger components inventories than Dell and because its resellers sometimes had sizable inventories of Compaq's models on hand, Compaq was slower than Dell in getting new generations of its PCs into the marketplace.

Compaq's extensive network of authorized reseller partners gave it strong distribution capability that covered more than 100 countries across the world. But Compaq's strategy of using reseller partners as its primary distribution channel was a weakness as well as a strength. Reliance on resellers put Compaq at a cost disadvantage relative to Dell, since Dell's direct sales approach entailed lower sales and marketing costs than

---

[35]"Can Compaq Catch Up?" *Business Week,* May 3, 1999, p. 163.

[36]Digital's competitive position is discussed in "Compaq-Digital: Let the Slimming Begin," *Business Week,* June 22, 1998.

[37]A discussion of the benefits of the Digital Equipment Corporation acquisition is presented in Compaq Computer Corporation's 1998 annual report; see www.compaq.com/corporate/1998ar/financials/MDA/purchased_nf.html.

[38]Compaq Computer Corporation 1998 10-K.

[39]Compaq Computer Corporation 1998 annual report; see www.compaq.com/corporate/1998ar/letter/english01_nf.html.

[40]"Can Compaq Catch Up?" p. 166.

[41]Compaq was said to have adopted a program that would reduce the number of destinations that the company shipped to by 70 percent by eliminating all but four distributors in North America in a May 10, 1999, *ComputerWorld* online news article; see www.computerworld.com/home/news.nsf/all/9905101compaq2.

Compaq's use of resellers. (Resellers had to mark up the factory price they paid Compaq to cover their own selling, general, and administrative costs and realize an adequate return on investment.) Compaq made a push in 1998 to promote direct sales over its Web site, an effort that irritated its 20 distributors and hundreds of reseller partners and may have prompted some resellers to push rival PC/server/workstation brands.[42] Nonetheless, there continued to be much debate among Compaq investors and Wall Street securities analysts about whether Compaq needed to put considerably more emphasis on direct sales and cut back its number of distributors in North America. Despite the pressures, Compaq management had so far refrained from further attempts to increase direct sales.

Compaq offered a full line of desktop PCs, from sub-$1,000 PCs to top-of-the-line models. It was an aggressive seller of PCs priced under $1,000. It also offered a broad line of laptop PCs. Compaq was also the market leader in PC servers priced under $25,000. Compaq's market strength was greatest among Fortune 1000 companies; it had weaker penetration in the small and medium business segments. To combat the volume discounts that Dell and other direct vendors typically used to help win the accounts of small and medium businesses, Compaq had recently begun working more closely with its resellers on special pricing to make the Compaq brand more competitive in the bidding process for these accounts. To boost its subpar 3 percent share of the Japanese market for PCs, in 1997 Compaq signed a deal that gave Canon Sales Company exclusive distribution and sales rights to Compaq's consumer-oriented Presario models.

Compaq's Acquisition of Digital Equipment Company   In early 1998, Compaq acquired the floundering Digital Equipment Company for $9.6 billion, a move intended to turn Compaq into more of a full-spectrum global supplier of computer hardware and services and put it into better position to challenge IBM as a "global enterprise computing company." Digital had 1997 revenues of $13 billion (versus $14.5 billion in 1996) and net earnings of $141 million (versus a loss of $112 million in 1996). The merged companies would have combined revenues of $37.6 billion, making Compaq the second largest computer company in the world. Following the merger, Compaq set a goal of $50 billion in revenues in 2000.

Digital considered itself a "network solutions company" with strengths in multivendor integration, Internet security, continuous computing, high-availability data, and high-performance networked platforms. Its chief products were large servers (those priced over $1 million), entry servers (those priced under $100,000), large computers and workstations, and personal computers (55 percent of revenues). Services accounted for 45 percent of revenues (about $6 billion); Digital had 25,000 engineers and support people in the field working with customers. (Compaq had 8,000 sales and support people in the field, many of whom spent much of their time servicing retailers of Compaq PCs.) Digital's gross margins on services averaged 34 percent compared to Compaq's 25 percent margins on PC sales. Compaq's corporate customers had been requesting the company to provide more service for years.

In May 1998, Compaq announced plans to cut about 15,000 jobs at Digital when the acquisition was completed; the layoffs were concentrated mainly in Digital's personal computer division, portions of its sales force, and corporate computer operations—where there were significant overlaps with Compaq's business. Digital had a total of 53,500 employees, down from a peak of 130,000 in the 1980s. But despite its recent

---

[42]"Can Compaq Catch Up?" p. 164. Many distributors and resellers carry more than one brand and can push sales of one brand over another if they are so inclined.

workforce downsizings, Digital in 1997 employed about 65 percent more people than Compaq to produce about half the volume of sales revenues. Compaq also moved aggressively to reduce Digital's high selling, general, and administrative (SG&A) costs (equal to 24 percent of total 1997 revenues) and bring them more in line with Compaq's SG&A expense ratio of 12 percent of revenues.

Compaq believed that Digital's expertise in networking and information systems integration, coupled with the combined product lines, would give it an advantage with large corporate customers over companies like Dell that offered mainly PC-related services. Compaq also believed that Digital's worldwide service and support capabilities would help it win corporate business for PCs, workstations, and servers away from IBM. (Prior to the Compaq-Digital merger, Dell had contracted with Digital's service organization to maintain its PowerEdge line of servers at a number of corporate accounts; following the merger announcement, Dell replaced Digital as a service provider.)

Problems at Compaq   Despite its status as the world's leading PC manufacturer and the new capabilities seemingly gained from the Tandem and Digital acquisitions, Compaq struggled throughout the 1997–99 period to maintain market share and profitability in the face of mounting price competition and declining PC prices. Furthermore, Compaq management got bogged down in trying to make a success of its acquisition of Digital. While Compaq was described as a company that was "consistently doing the right things and doing them well" at the time of the Digital acquisition, its efforts to get Digital's operations on track and integrated with those of Compaq were behind schedule and not going as well as had been anticipated.[43]

In April 1999, Compaq's board of directors removed CEO Eckhard Pfeiffer because of difficulty with the Digital acquisition and problems in executing the company's plans to copy Dell Computer's build-to-order, just-in-time-inventory, and direct-sales approaches.[44] After a three-month search to find a replacement for Pfeiffer from outside the company, the board chose an insider, Michael Capellas, the company's former chief information officer, to fill the vacant CEO position. Despite the leadership change and aggressive actions initiated by Capellas to return Compaq to profitable growth, Compaq's market share in PCs continued to erode in the United States, Europe, and Asia during the remainder of 1999. Compaq lost its claim to market share leadership to Dell in the U.S. market in the third quarter of 1999 and seemed in danger of losing its global market share leadership to Dell in 2000 if Capellas's turnaround efforts did not produce results. The financial performance of the company's three major business groups was as follows:

Business Group	1999 Revenues	1999 Operating Profit
Enterprise Solutions and Services	$20.1 billion	$2.3 billion
Products	13.5 billion	
Services	6.6 billion	
Commercial Personal Computing	12.2 billion	(448 million)
Consumer PCs	6.0 billion	262 million

---

[43]"Desktop and Mobile Weekly Update," *Dataquest*, February 12, 1998, p. 7.

[44]Compaq's difficulty in making a success of its Digital acquisition is discussed in "Compaq Chief Executive Pfeiffer Ousted," Associated Press Wire, April 19, 1999, and "Can Compaq Catch Up?" pp. 162–66.

Despite the weak 1999 performance, by early 2000 Compaq management believed that the aggressive actions taken in the last six months of 1999 were taking hold and laying the foundation for a comeback in 2000. Capellas said, "During the fourth quarter, we made great strides in defining a clear strategy, realigning for success, getting our cost structure in order, and re-energizing employees . . . We upped the pace in launching innovative new products, signing strategic partnership deals and alliances, and securing major customer wins."[45] Capellas went on to say that the performance of the Enterprise Solutions and Services group indicated "growing market acceptance of Compaq's high-end systems, solutions, and services, which customers are demanding to build nonstop 24×7 Internet computing environments." In January 2000, Compaq announced that it was spending $370 million to acquire certain assets of Inacom Corporation that would reduce inventories, speed cycle time, and enhance its capabilities to do business with customers via the Internet.

IBM

With 1999 sales of $87.5 billion and earnings of $7.7 billion, IBM was the world's largest seller of computer systems. IBM was considered a "computer solutions" company and operated in more segments of the overall computer industry than Dell. It had the broadest and deepest capabilities in customer service, technical support, and systems integration of any company in the world. The company's slow-growing computer hardware business had total 1999 revenues of over $37 billion from its internal and external sales of mainframe computers, PCs, servers, workstations, display devices, semiconductors, hard disk drives, printer systems, and storage and networking devices. IBM's global services business group, the company's fastest-growing group, was the world's largest information technology services provider, with 1999 sales of nearly $32.2 billion. The company's software business group had 1999 sales of over $12.7 billion and supported more than 29,000 independent software vendors (ISVs) to ensure that the company's software and hardware was included in ISV partner solutions.[46] In 2000, IBM had a lineup of over 40,000 hardware and software products.

IBM's Troubles in PCs   IBM's market share in PCs was in a death spiral—it had lost more market share in the 1990s than any other PC maker. Once the dominant global and U.S. market leader in the late 1980s and early 1990s, with a market share exceeding 50 percent, it was fast becoming an also-ran in PCs, with a global market share under 8 percent. Its last stronghold in PCs was in laptop computers, where its ThinkPad line was a consistent award winner on performance, features, and reliability. The vast majority of IBM's laptop and desktop sales were to corporate customers that had IBM mainframe computers and had been long-standing IBM customers.

Despite its eroding market share, IBM's position as the longtime global leader in mainframe computers and, more recently, as a broad line supplier of computer products and services gave it strong global distribution capability and potent brand-name credibility throughout the world. IBM distributed its PCs, workstations, and servers through reseller partners but relied on its own direct sales force for most corporate customers. IBM competed against its PC rivals by emphasizing confidence in the IBM brand and the company's long-standing strengths in software applications, service, and technical support. IBM had responded to the direct sales inroads Dell had made in the

---

[45]Compaq Press Release, January 25, 2000.
[46]IBM 1998 annual report, pp. 84–86.

corporate market by allowing some of its resellers to custom-assemble IBM PCs to buyer specifications; it was hoping this effort would cut costs up to 10 percent.

Going into 2000, IBM's personal systems (PCs and workstations) and server businesses accounted for just under 30 percent of corporate revenues, but both groups turned in weak performances in 1998 and 1999 and lost market share to rivals:

	Revenues		Pretax Profit	
	1998	1999	1998	1999
Personal Systems	$12.8 billion	$15.3 billion	($992 million)	($557 million)
Servers	$11.1 billion	$9.0 billion	$2.8 billion	$1.6 billion

IBM's PC group had higher costs than rivals, making it virtually impossible to match rivals on price and make a profit. In late 1999, IBM announced that it was discontinuing sales of its Aptiva Desktop PCs through retail channels in North America, although it would continue to sell Aptivas at its Web site. It also announced layoffs of up to 10 percent of its PC workforce and up to 6 percent of its server workforce. Like Dell, IBM was trying to cut technical support costs by getting its customers to use Internet-based support tools; for every service call handled through www.ibm.com, the company estimated it saved 70 to 90 percent of the cost of having a person take the call.[47] In 1999, IBM handled 35 million online service requests, saving an estimated $750 million in customer support costs.

To offset its declining share of PC and server sales, in 1998 and 1999 IBM moved to boost its R&D and manufacturing efforts to become a leading global supplier of computing components (hard drives and storage devices) and microelectronics products. During 1999, for example, it signed a long-term agreement with Dell to supply over $7 billion in components; it was increasing its sales of parts and components to other PC makers as well.

IBM's E-Business Strategy   Throughout the 1990s IBM had struggled to reinvent itself as the growing use of PCs continued to erode corporate dependence on mainframe computers and made mainframe sales and services a stagnating business. (Mainframe prices were falling faster than sales were rising.) While the company added new hardware and software products, revenue growth lagged and lower-cost rivals undercut many of IBM's strategic initiatives to grow. IBM's sales of computer hardware remained flat; revenue growth came chiefly from services and software. IBM's global dominance as a computer hardware systems provider faded. No cohesive new strategic theme really took root at IBM during the 1990s.

However, starting in 1998 and continuing on into 2000, the company's efforts to reinvent itself began to take on a distinct Internet and e-business theme. By early 2000 IBM was directing most of its strategic initiatives toward "e-business services" where it saw explosive growth opportunities. More than 50 percent of IBM's R&D budget was directed to Internet projects. Senior management believed that software and services were the soul of e-business and that the company had a full complement of resources to help corporate customers put integrated e-business capabilities in place. A growing majority of the company's 130,000 consultants were working to provide customers with integrated e-commerce and Internet technology solutions. The company

---

[47]Ira Sager, "Inside IBM: Internet Business Machines," *Business Week,* December 13, 1999, p. EB 34.

was opening e-business integration centers around the world where customers could meet with IBM specialists to develop next-generation e-business solutions. During the past three years, IBM had handled 18,000 Internet-related jobs for customers, ranging from Web page design to hosting entire online storefronts to hooking corporate databases into new online systems. IBM's revenues from pure e-business projects totaled $3 billion in 1999, but the company estimated that some $20 billion of its revenues was driven by customer demand for e-business solutions, an amount that was expected to grow significantly.

Most observers, as well as IBM executives, seemed to believe that IBM's future success depended far more on becoming the world's leading provider of e-business services than on strengthening its position as a provider of computer hardware. But it faced significant competition in e-business services and software from Intel (which was spending over $1 billion to set up rooms of servers to host Internet sites); Hewlett-Packard (which had a variety of initiatives aimed at do-it-yourself Internet technologies that required minimal consulting services and support); Microsoft (which was focusing increasing efforts on Internet-related software and serving e-business customers); Sun Microsystems; and numerous others.

Hewlett-Packard

Going into 2000, Hewlett-Packard (HP) was the world's leading seller of computer printers, the second-ranking seller of workstations, and a top-tier seller of PCs and servers. HP's product line also included scanners, digital cameras, storage devices, and networking software and equipment. The company recorded 1999 revenues and earnings of $42.4 billion and $3.1 billion, respectively.[48] Dell regarded Hewlett-Packard as a strong competitor because of the company's global leadership in printers (a 52 percent market share), HP's strong reputation with corporate customers in most all parts of the world, and its growing strategic emphasis on PCs, workstations, and servers. HP ranked fourth worldwide in desktop PC sales, first in worldwide sales of workstations, first in worldwide sale of handheld PCs, first in worldwide sales of both midrange and high-end servers running on UNIX operating systems, and among the top five worldwide vendors of servers running on Windows NT and Windows 2000. HP Pavillion PCs were the top-selling PC brand in U.S. retail stores. HP was a co-designer of Intel's new family of 64-bit Itanium microprocessors. HP's partnership with Intel on the Itanium was expected to put HP on the cutting edge of computer technology for the next several years and boost its brand image in PCs, workstations, and servers. The company spent $2.4 billion on R&D in 1998 and the same amount in 1999.

Hewlett-Packard marketed its PC line through resellers. HP's resellers could deliver orders to major corporate accounts within 12 to 24 hours. Hewlett-Packard had the capability to offer after-sale support to PC, workstation, and server purchasers around the world through 600 support offices, 35 response center locations in 110 countries, and a support staff of 17,500 people. The company had won numerous awards for the caliber of its services and technical support. It had 83,200 employees worldwide.

Over the past several years, HP had moved to improve operating efficiencies by outsourcing manufacturing assembly, reducing inventory and field-sales costs, and improving supply chain management. These efforts, combined with lowered component

---

[48]Hoover's, Inc., "Hoover's Company Profile Database for Hewlett-Packard," 1998, p. 1. HP's test and measurement business, which accounted for approximately 16 percent of 1998 sales, was spun off as a stand-alone company in March 1999; Hewlett-Packard Company 8-K (filed March 2, 1999), p. 1.

prices, had made HP aggressive in competing on price against its PC, workstation, and server rivals. Nonetheless, Hewlett-Packard's PC division, despite growing unit volume, was thought to be only marginally profitable. However, the company's sales of workstations and servers were major contributors to revenues and profits. In early 2000, the company reported that sales of home PCs and laptops were particularly strong.

Hewlett-Packard's board of directors chose Carly Fiorina, the head of Lucent Technology's Global Service Provider Business, as the company's new CEO in July 1999, to replace the company's retiring CEO. Fiorina had been designated by *Fortune* as the most powerful woman in business in 1998 and 1999. Believing that HP had grown sluggish and lacked entrepreneurial drive, Fiorina had immediately spearheaded initiatives to boost HP's revenue growth and profitability through increased attention to inventiveness and innovation. Fiorina's top priorities were to renew the company's energy and focus and to develop a stream of innovative products and new types of electronic services aimed at making the Internet "more warm, friendly, pervasive and personal." In late 1999, Fiorina announced a new global brand campaign and a new logo to reflect the reinvented, reenergized Hewlett-Packard.

Gateway

Gateway, formerly called Gateway 2000, was a San Diego–based company (recently relocated from South Dakota) with 1999 revenues of $8.6 billion and profits of $428 million. Founder and chairman Ted Waitt, 38, and his brother owned over 40 percent of the company. Waitt had dropped out of college in 1985 to go to work for a computer retailer in Des Moines, Iowa; after nine months, he quit to form his own company. The company, operating out of a barn on his father's cattle ranch, sold add-on parts by phone for Texas Instruments PCs. In 1987, the company, using its own PC design, started selling fully equipped PCs at a price near that of other PC makers. Sales took off, and in 1991 Gateway topped the list of *Inc.* magazine's list of the fastest-growing private companies. The company went public in 1993, achieving sales of $1.7 billion and earnings of $151 million. The company had differentiated itself from rivals with eye-catching ads; some featured cows with black-and-white spots, while others featured company employees (including one with Waitt dressed as Robin Hood). Gateway, like Dell, built to order and sold direct. It had entered the server segment in 1997. To promote the Gateway name in the retail marketplace, the company had opened 280 Gateway Country Stores—227 in the United States, 27 in Europe, and 26 in the Asia-Pacific region—that stocked Gateway PCs and peripheral products and that conducted classes for individuals and businesses on the use of PCs.

Going into 2000, Gateway was the number one seller of PCs to consumers. It was also a major contender in the small-business, educational, and government segments. Despite growing at a rate of nearly 38 percent annually in the 1994–97 period, Gateway saw its profit margins erode steadily from a high of 9.6 percent in 1992 to only 1.7 percent in 1997. Since then, however, company cost-cutting efforts and efficiency improvements had resulted in eight straight quarters of year-over-year margin improvement. Profits in 1999 were at record levels. Nonetheless, Gateway was feeling the pressures of falling PC prices and stiff price competition—although 1999 unit sales were up 32.3 percent over 1998 levels, revenues increased only 15.8 percent. The company's entry-level PC models, which started at $799, accounted for 20 percent of its sales to consumers.

To reduce its reliance on traditional PC sales, Gateway took aggressive steps in 1999 to diversify its revenue stream. In February, Gateway became the first PC maker to bundle its own Internet service with its PCs; at the same time, following Dell, Gateway launched an online software and peripheral Web store with more than 30,000 products. Meanwhile, Gateway increased its service and training offerings to consumers and small businesses at its 280 Country Store locations worldwide. In October, Gateway entered into a wide-ranging strategic alliance with America Online to accelerate distribution of each company's products and services. By the end of 1999, after adding 400,000 new subscribers in less than three months, Gateway's joint Internet service with AOL had more than 1 million subscribers. Gateway management believed its "beyond-the-box" strategy positioned the company extremely well for the future.

Gateway also took aggressive steps in 1999 to boost its sales to small businesses, government agencies, and educational institutions. It established a sales force operating out of its 280 Country Stores that called on area businesses and other organizations. An alliance with GE Capital was formed to promote technology solutions for large enterprises. In Europe, Gateway entered into a two-year partnership with ComputaCenter, Europe's leading information technology systems and services company, to sell and support Gateway PC products throughout Europe. During 1999, Gateway increased its sales over the Internet by 100 percent over 1998 levels.

To further enhance the Gateway brand with consumers, Gateway committed to sponsorship of the 2002 Winter Olympic Games in Salt Lake City, plus it entered into brand-enhancing alliances with Fidelity Investments and Nickelodeon. Gateway planned to open more than 100 new Country Store locations worldwide during 2000, including 75 in the United States. In early 2000, Gateway introduced a new line of home and small-business desktop PCs powered by Athlon microprocessors made by Advanced Micro Devices (AMD). The new Gateway Select PC line represented an effort to counter the difficulties the company was having in obtaining adequate supplies of Pentium microprocessors from Intel.

Toshiba Corporation

Toshiba was a $45 billion diversified Japanese electronics and electrical equipment manufacturer with 300 subsidiaries and affiliates worldwide; it ranked as the world's 26th largest corporation in terms of revenues and the world's seventh largest computer and electronics company. Toshiba produced and marketed portable and desktop computers, servers, voice-mail systems, digital business telephone systems, interactive voice-response systems, cable modems, networking systems, and digital, medical, and PC cameras. In the PC arena, Toshiba's biggest strength was in notebook PCs, where it had an 18 percent global share in 1999.

The company's Toshiba America Information System (TAIS) division, headquartered in Irvine, California, had annual sales of approximately $2.5 billion across the United States and Latin America. The TAIS division offered a wide array of portable PCs, selling both direct and through dealers—one of its largest U.S. dealers was Computer Discount Warehouse. In the mid-1990s, TAIS enjoyed a commanding lead over its U.S. laptop rivals in both channels, but its lead had been shrinking in recent years. During the 1996–99 period, TAIS's share of portable computer sales in the United States was in the 15 to 20 percent range. It had a negligible share of the desktop PC market.

Providers of House-Label Brands

There were about 30,000 resellers of generic, or "house-label," PCs in North America alone and countless thousands more worldwide. The generic segment constituted a $7 to $8 billion market in the United States and Canada, representing shipments of about 7 million units and 25 to 30 percent of sales through resellers. No single generic brand, however, accounted for more than 0.25 percent market share, and most had a lot smaller percentage share. Generic PCs assembled in" "screwdriver shops" had been a part of the PC business since its inception—Steve Wozniak and Steve Jobs launched Apple Computer from a garage using components they purchased. Rising technological savvy about how PCs worked and the widespread availability of individual components made it fairly easy for an enterprising operation to assemble a generic PC. Contract manufacturers of PCs, many of whom assembled name brands of PCs for several PC makers, were a major source of house-label PCs marketed by retailers. To keep costs and prices low, the makers of generic PCs typically incorporated components from low-end suppliers. Generic PCs appealed mainly to very price-conscious buyers. The quality and reliability of generic PCs varied from good to poor, depending on the caliber of their components. The makers of generic PCs generally took little responsibility for providing technical support; whatever technical support was available to users typically had to come from resellers.

MICHAEL DELL'S VIEW OF DELL COMPUTER'S BIGGEST CHALLENGES

Michael Dell believed Dell Computer's biggest challenge in the marketplace was to gain as much acceptance for the company's direct business model outside the United States as it had gained inside the United States. But an even bigger challenge, he believed, was gathering enough talented people to help the company pursue the opportunities in other countries. Dell was active in recruiting foreign nationals graduating from U.S. business schools. Those who hired on with Dell were sent to Austin, Texas, for a couple of years to learn about Dell and the Dell model and to work in various parts of the company's operations. Then they were given assignments to help in Dell's global expansion effort. Michael Dell believed the company needed the expertise of foreigners who knew Dell from the inside and who could help Dell Computer understand different cultures and respond in a sensitive manner to local customs and behaviors.

For the most part, Michael Dell was not particularly concerned about the efforts of competitors to copy many aspects of Dell's build-to-order, sell-direct strategy:

> The competition started copying us seven years ago. That's when we were a $1 billion business. Now we're $25 billion. And they haven't made much progress to be honest with you. The learning curve for them is difficult. It's like going from baseball to soccer . . . We're more challenged by new technologies on the market, some new computing model, something we haven't anticipated.[49]

Michael Dell's near-term vision was for the company to reach $50 billion in annual sales by growing more aggressively in the consumer and small-business segments in computer services, by increasing its market share in foreign countries, and by selling more powerful and more expensive servers to corporate customers.

---

[49]Comments made to students at the University of North Carolina and reported in the *Raleigh News & Observer,* November 16, 1999.

case 8 Peapod, Inc., and the Online Grocery Business

Alan B. Eisner
Pace University

Nicole Belmont
Pace University

Peapod, Inc., cofounded by brothers Andrew B. Parkinson and Thomas L. Parkinson in 1989, was a $68 million online grocery service that used both its own central warehouses and the retail stores of supermarket partners to fill customers' grocery orders. Peapod was a pioneer of the online grocery industry, getting its start on the Internet well before the Internet became a global phenomenon and well before such competitors as HomeGrocer.com, Webvan, and NetGrocer.com were even organized. However, the company had grown more slowly than first anticipated, revising its trial-and-error strategy several times to find a formula that would attract more customers and make the company profitable. In September 1999, Andrew Parkinson relinquished the position of CEO and turned the reins over to a new president and CEO, Bill Malloy, who had been recruited from AT&T Wireless to fine-tune and execute Peapod's latest order fulfillment strategy and capitalize on what the cofounders believed was a blossoming opportunity in online grocery sales. Andrew Parkinson stayed on as chairman of Peapod's board of directors.

Malloy faced three daunting challenges at Peapod. He had to prove that the company's newly revised business model was viable; that the company could be made profitable after six years of mounting losses; and that it could withstand competition from HomeGrocer.com, which had recently allied itself with Amazon.com, and from newly formed Webvan, which raised over $350 million in its initial public offering of common stock in the second half of 1999.

COMPANY BACKGROUND

As noted above, Peapod was an early pioneer in e-commerce, inventing an online home-shopping service for grocery items years ahead of the commercial emergence of the Internet. With its tagline "Smart Shopping for Busy People," the company began

Copyright © 2000 by Alan B. Eisner. All rights reserved.

C-174

providing home shopping in the early 1990s, going so far as to install modems in consumers' homes to provide an online connection. Until 1998, the company's business model involved filling customer orders by forming alliances with traditional grocery retailers. The company chose a retail partner in each geographic area where it operated and used the partner's local network of retail stores to pick and pack orders for delivery to customers. Peapod personnel would cruise the aisles of a partner's stores to select the items each customer ordered, pack and load them into Peapod vehicles, and then deliver them at times chosen by customers. Peapod charged customers a fee for its service and also collected fees from its retail supply partners for using their products in its online service. In its first years, Peapod built delivery capabilities in eight market areas:

Chicago, Illinois

Columbus, Ohio

Houston, Texas

Boston, Massachusetts

San Francisco/San Jose, California

Dallas, Texas

Austin, Texas

Long Island, New York

The company steadily built a base of about 90,000 to 100,000 customers across all eight markets; it filled over 700,000 orders in 1999. Peapod's revenues rose from $8.0 million in 1994 to $73.1 million in 1999 (see Exhibit 1). Meanwhile, the company made improvements in its Web site (www.peapod.com) and invested in proprietary software technologies to facilitate efficient order fulfillment and delivery routes, accumulate data on customer buying patterns, and better integrate pricing, merchandising, and product promotion. The company went public in June 1997, offering shares at $16. During 1999 and early 2000, Peapod's stock (listed on the NASDAQ National Market under the symbol "PPOD") traded mostly in the $8 to $12 range.

In 1997, faced with mounting losses despite growing revenues, Peapod management determined that its original, partner-based business model entailed too high a cost structure for the company to achieve profitable growth. The cofounders opted to shift to a new order fulfillment business model using a local company-owned, company-operated central distribution warehouse to store, pick, and pack customer orders for delivery. By mid-1999 the company had opened new distribution centers in three of the eight markets it served (Chicago, Long Island, and Boston); a fourth distribution center was under construction in San Francisco. Peapod stocked its distribution centers with products purchased at wholesale from a variety of food and household products companies, including Kellogg's, Kraft, Colgate-Palmolive, Frito-Lay, Coca-Cola, Clorox, Kimberly-Clark, Procter & Gamble, Nabisco, Ralston Purina, Nestlé, Walgreens, and in some cases, traditional retailers. Peapod management had announced plans to use the centralized distribution model in all eight markets over time and in all new areas it entered. The company was reportedly losing money in five of the markets it served in mid-1999.

PEAPOD IN EARLY 2000

Going into the new millennium, Peapod was the largest Internet supermarket, with over 90,000 customers (based on a count of customers who had placed an order within the past 12 months). It had a 30 percent share of the estimated $235 million market for

exhibit 1   Six-Year Summary of Peapod's Financial Performance, 1994–99 ($000s)

Date	Sales	Net Income	Earnings per Share
1999	$73,134	($28,450)	($1.62)
1998	69,265	(21,565)	(1.27)
1997	56,943	(12,979)	(0.87)
1996	27,642	(9,566)	(0.82)
1995	15,209	(6,592)	(0.79)
1994	8,005	(4,437)	(0.75)

grocery products sold online.[1] The eight market areas where the company presently operated had an estimated 6.6 million households, representing approximately 7 percent of total U.S. households. Delivery operations in these areas were conducted out of 22 order fulfillment locations. Exhibit 2 shows the company's eight metropolitan markets, the number of households represented in each market, and the company's local retail supermarket partners. Peapod processed an average of 2,000 orders daily; the average order size was $110–$115 but ran a bit lower in areas where the company used central distribution warehouses—Peapod stocked fewer items at its warehouses than its supermarket partners stocked at their stores. Management believed that Peapod's average order size was about five times the in-store average of supermarkets and convenience stores.

Management's vision for the company was expressed in three statements:

- *Our Dream*—To fundamentally improve people's lives by bringing interactive shopping to a broad consumer market.
- *Our Mission*—To be the world's leading and preferred provider of interactive grocery shopping services.
- *Our Passion*—To amaze and delight each one of our customers.

Peapod's recent income statements and balance sheets are shown in Exhibits 3 and 4.

Peapod's Customers

Peapod's target market was a middle- and upper-income household with PC-savvy adults who were stressed for time and didn't particularly enjoy grocery shopping. This was the basis for its tag line, "Smart Shopping for Busy People." The company's market research indicated that its typical customers were women between the ages of 30 and 54 who lived in dual-income households and had children. The incomes of customers covered a wide range, with a median annual income exceeding $60,000.

Peapod's Strategy

Peapod's strategy was to provide customers with a convenient, user-friendly, personalized way of shopping for grocery items online 24 hours a day, seven days a week. Its product offerings consisted of fresh meat, produce, deli and bakery goods, name-brand

---

[1]Peapod, Inc., Investor's Overview, www.peapod.com.

exhibit 2 Peapod's Metropolitan Markets, Household Exposure, and Retail Partners, February 2000

Metropolitan Market Area Served	Estimated Number of Area Households, 1998	Retail Partners	Peapod Distribution Center
Chicago, Illinois	1,732,000	Jewel Food Stores	Yes
Columbus, Ohio	398,000	Kroger	
Houston, Texas	939,000	Randalls Food and Drug	
Boston, Massachusetts	1,242,000	Stop and Shop	Yes
San Francisco and San Jose, California	840,000	Certified Grocers of California, Andronico's, and Walgreens	Yes
Dallas, Texas	995,000	Tom Thumb	
Austin, Texas	257,000	Randalls Food and Drug	
Long Island, New York	226,000	Giant/Edwards Super Foods Stores	Yes

exhibit 3 Peapod's Statements of Income, 1996–99 ($000, Except Per Share Data)

	1999	1998	1997	1996
Revenues				
Net product sales		$57,305	$43,487	$22,015
Member and retailer		9,650	11,234	4,558
Interactive marketing		1,460	2,222	1,069
Licensing		850		
Total revenues	$73,154	$69,265	$56,943	$27,642
Costs and expenses				
Cost of goods sold	$55,585	$53,903	$40,823	$20,485
Fulfillment operations	24,478	17,196	14,469	6,889
General and administrative	9,788	8,029	5,935	3,785
Marketing and selling	7,168	7,545	7,726	4,739
System development and maintenance	3,543	3,386	1,696	1,124
Depreciation and amortization	2,222	3,264	1,234	651
Total costs and expenses	$102,784	$93,323	$71,883	$37,673
Operating loss	($29,650)	($24,058)	($14,940)	($10,031)
Other income (expense)				
Interest income	$1,384	$2,683	$2,044	$537
Interest expense	(187)	(190)	(83)	(72)
Net loss	($28,453)	($21,565)	($12,979)	($9,566)
Net loss per share	($1.62)	($1.27)	($0.87)	($0.82)
Average shares outstanding	17,542,990	16,964,439	14,915,734	11,664,956

Source: Company 10-K and 10-Q filings.

exhibit 4   Peapod's Balance Sheets, 1997–99 ($000)

	1999	1998	1997
Assets			
Current assets			
Cash and cash equivalents	$ 3,343	$ 4,341	$54,079
Marketable securities	4,704	15,836	8,798
Receivables	1,498	2,516	1,195
Prepaid expenses	473	186	444
Other current assets	993	974	228
Total current assets	10,991	23,853	64,744
Property and equipment			
Computer equipment and software	6,737	4,010	4,499
Service equipment and leasehold improvements	4,189	2,147	1,053
Property and equipment, at cost	10,926	6,157	5,552
Accumulated depreciation	4,290	(2,252)	(2,301)
Net property and equipment	6,636	3,905	3,251
Noncurrent marketable securities and restricted cash	3,143	15,213	
Capitalized software development costs	—	—	998
Goodwill	—	—	117
Total assets	$20,780	$42,971	$69,110
Liabilities and stockholders' equity			
Current liabilities			
Accounts payable	$ 6,147	$ 3,442	$ 7,514
Accrued compensation	497	802	1,258
Other accrued liabilities	1,897	2,688	926
Deferred revenue	615	1,000	1,969
Current obligations under capital lease	690	590	727
Total current liabilities	9,846	8,522	12,394
Deferred revenue	95	448	1,212
Obligations under capital lease, less current portion	1,129	395	701
Total liabilities	11,070	9,365	14,307
Stockholders' equity			
Common stock ($.01 par value, 50 million shares authorized; 17,245,828 and 16,852,557 shares issued in 1998 and 1997)	$ 183	$ 172	$ 169
Additional paid-in capital	71,698	64,319	63,148
Note receivable from officer	(2,369)		
Unrealized gain on available-for-sale securities	(118)	83	—
Accumulated deficit	(58,513)	(30,060)	(8,495)
Treasury stock	(1,171)	(908)	(19)
Total stockholders' equity	9,710	33,606	54,803
Total liabilities and stockholders' equity	$20,780	$42,971	$69,110

Source: Company 10-K and 10-Q filings.

exhibit 5   Peapod's Welcome Page at www.peapod.com

Peapod.com

Your Personal Grocer & More.

Local Delivery | **Packages** | **About Peapod**

Welcome | How it works | Prices & Delivery Areas | Questions?

Check it out

New customer? Type your ZIP code below to enter the store and begin shopping. See list of current delivery areas below.

ZIP code _____

Already a Customer?

Please log in to the Local Grocery Delivery store using your username.

username _____

password _____

Peapod delivers to these metropolitan areas:
- Austin
- Boston
- Chicago
- Columbus
- Dallas/Fort Worth
- Fairfield County, Conn.
- Houston
- Long Island
- San Francisco/San Jose

Welcome to Peapod

America's #1 online grocer, delivering fresh food to your door.

Now delivering in Connecticut!

Top-quality products
- Fresh meat, deli, produce and bakery goods
- Name-brand packaged foods, household items, and health and beauty products

Saving money is easy
- Competitive prices and weekly specials
- No impulse shopping
- Manufacturers' coupons accepted

Convenience, pure and simple
- Shop anytime, night or day
- Choose your delivery time - any day of the week
- No more trips to the grocery store. No more checkout lanes. No more lugging groceries

First-rate customer service
- Trained shoppers hand-pick the freshest and best products - just like you would.
- Friendly drivers deliver your order right to your door.
- Customer Care handles your questions, comments and problems.

$20 in FREE groceries
click here

canned and packaged goods, household items, and health and beauty products—essentially the same perishable and nonperishable name-brand products typically found in local supermarkets or drugstores. Peapod's prices were competitive, and it had weekly specials; manufacturer's coupons were accepted. Delivery was available seven days a week and could be scheduled for the same day or next day at a time chosen by the customer. Peapod charged a fee for its online order and delivery service that varied by market area. In most markets customers had the option of paying a service charge per order (about $10 per delivery) or a flat rate for unlimited monthly deliveries.

The company's Welcome Page at its Web site is shown in Exhibit 5. The site was accessible to anyone using a Web browser, via personal computers, Web-enabled televisions, high-speed cable services, and wireless devices.

exhibit 6   Ordering Page at Peapod's Web Site

Peapod's Multifeatured, Highly Functional Web Site Technology

Peapod's easy-to-navigate Web site had variety of highly functional features that, management believed, helped encourage repeat purchases and differentiated Peapod from other e-tailers and direct competitors. Customers could shop for items in several ways. One was to browse aisles, moving logically from general product categories to individual items (see Exhibit 6). Another was to conduct product searches by brand name or category, which was particularly useful for redeeming coupons or purchasing recipe ingredients. Shoppers could also sort items in any product category alphabetically or by price, nutritional content (such as fat, calories, cholesterol, and sodium), sale items, and kosher status. Another feature stored a customer's last three grocery orders, eliminating the need to start a shopping list of frequently purchased items from scratch again. Other features included:

- An extensive library of product pictures, nutrition information, and product ingredients.
- An "Express Shop" that helped first-time shoppers build their order without having to browse through the aisles or search for items one at a time. For existing customers, Express Shop, in conjunction with the Previous Orders feature, allowed customers to easily add items to their order.
- A "SmartCart" that displayed a list of the items selected for purchase, as well as a running dollar total of the bill.
- The capability to generate Web pages based on a customer's shopping preferences, buying profile, and other variables so as to provide users with a customized shopping experience.
- A "Buddy E-Mail" function that delivered order confirmations to two different e-mail addresses—something that was useful in households where shopping duties were shared among members.

Gomez Advisors, a leading provider of Internet research and analysis, in September 1999 rated Peapod's Web site first in terms of ease of use among all online grocers.

The company's Web site technology was designed to capture behavioral information from users—mouse clicks, time spent viewing each page, coupon redemptions, and other factors. The tracking data allowed Peapod to generate dozens of metrics to evaluate the quality of its Web site and to identify opportunities to cross-sell additional goods and services.

Marketing and Advertising   Peapod's marketing objectives were to attract more users, to retain the business of current users, to increase the frequency with which users placed orders, to grow average order size, and to enhance awareness of the Peapod brand. To achieve these objectives, the company used radio and newspaper advertising, direct mail, ads on local mass transit systems, Internet advertising, and branding on delivery trucks and employee uniforms (see again Exhibit 5). Company personnel drove attention-getting green Volkswagen "Pod Bugs" with the Peapod insignia to help promote local awareness of the company. In 1999, the company's marketing and advertising budget was about $6 million, the majority of which was focused on growing the customer base and helping the company achieve the operating scale needed for profitability.

One Internet marketing effort the company had come up with to attract new customers was the Peapod Affiliate Program. Peapod started the program in April 1999 as a way of compensating other Web sites for promoting Peapod and providing links to Peapod from their site. Affiliates could earn a $15 commission for each referred visitor who placed an order with Peapod plus an additional $15 for a customer's third order.

To further promote consumer awareness of Peapod, the company had entered into an agreement with Hearst's HomeArts Network, a premier lifestyle site for women on the Web, whereby Peapod would be the exclusive Internet grocery service promoted on the HomeArts Network. The network provided online programming, as well as features from Hearst's 11 women's magazines, including *Redbook, Good Housekeeping, Cosmopolitan,* and *Country Living.* The HomeArts Network had a user base that strongly matched the target Peapod customer. Peapod had also formed a marketing alliance with Excite, Inc., that made Peapod the exclusive online grocer on Excite's Web site. The agreement with Excite gave Peapod exposure to an estimated 35 percent of all Internet users.[2]

Peapod Packages   To help build national presence and awareness of the Peapod brand, the company had begun promoting its "Peapod Packages" for shipment to any location (see Exhibit 7). The company had put together preselected themed product assortments targeting such niche occasions as the Super Bowl, Christmas, Thanksgiving, the arrival of a new baby, or a birthday. There were also care packages for college students and recipe/meal solutions in a box. Shoppers could create their own Peapod Package. Peapod planned to expand the Peapod Package line to include specialty and gourmet foods and gifts.

Distribution Center Operations and Order Fulfillment   Peapod's new $2 million distribution centers each stocked over 12,000 dry grocery, frozen, and dairy products, along with perishable products such as produce, meat, and prepared foods. Items were replenished on a just-in-time basis to optimize space utilization and ensure

---

[2]"Peapod Signs Multi-Year Internet Marketing Deal with Excite," www.peapod.com/v5/Html/Press/ press045.html.

exhibit 7   Examples of Peapod Packages

freshness.[3] While Peapod was opening distribution centers in each of its eight markets, it stated its intention to continue its partnerships with its present retail supermarket allies, albeit on a reduced basis. Until its new central warehousing model was perfected, Peapod was temporarily relying on these partners to stock its central warehouse with perishables, health and beauty aids, and other items it did not currently stock and to fill orders for delivery to those addresses not convenient to its warehouse. Moreover, such alliances gave Peapod an advertising channel for promoting its website at its partners' brick-and-mortar locations.

A major component of Peapod's strategy was to optimize its order fulfillment process from a cost standpoint. As the company began shifting from supermarket partnerships to centralized warehousing, it reengineered its product distribution and order fulfillment practices to reduce costs, minimize stockouts, improve the accuracy of order picking at warehouses, make it economical to accommodate higher order volumes, and ensure that orders were delivered within the scheduled time frame. New warehousing, order picking, and delivery routing software and systems had been designed and put in place.

Order fulfillment was managed by a handheld scanning device that contained pick data for a given metropolitan market area and controlled the order selection process in a manner calculated to minimize the labor time for picking and packing orders. The list of items for a particular order was sorted according to the location of each item in the warehouse, thereby requiring only one pass through the warehouse. The handheld unit displayed each item to be picked and provided a variety of features for assuring accuracy and allowing flexibility for handling exceptions. As individual items appeared on the screen, the picker confirmed the proper item by scanning the item's uniform product code, and was alerted if the wrong item had been scanned. If an item was out of stock, the device noted the out-of-stock status and, if requested by the customer, automatically directed the picker to the customer-designated substitution. A list of out-of-stock items was automatically transmitted to the manager to generate replacement orders.

---

[3]"Peapod Opens Centralized Operations Center in Chicago," Peapod Press Release January 25, 1999.

Delivery logistics were managed by a sophisticated computer program that provided time management information and point-to-point directions throughout the delivery route. The program accounted for traffic conditions, rush-hour volume, road construction, and other variables that could be predicted within the local area. Peapod drivers delivered the packages to each customer's doorstep or unloaded them in the kitchen (if requested) and obtained feedback from customers on the service. To build customer loyalty, Peapod tried to send the same delivery person to the homes of repeat customers. Peapod management was aggressively pursuing ways to fine-tune all of the new systems it had implemented.

So far, order volume had not reached levels that allowed Peapod's warehouse and order fulfillment operation to realize scale economies. The costs of fulfillment operations were 30 percent of sales revenues during the first nine months of 1999, partly because the company was using both central warehouses and the local stores of its retail supermarket partners to fill orders. However, management expected this percentage to decline as the company moved through the period of getting its warehouses up and operating, as experience with the new systems accumulated, and as order volume increased. For the company to become profitable, order fulfillment costs had to drop to a much smaller percentage of revenues.

Nonetheless, Peapod believed that its business model would give it a significant competitive advantage over traditional grocery retailers. By using the Internet to receive orders and central warehouse and distribution facilities to process them, Peapod eliminated the expenses associated with maintaining multiple retail locations in a metropolitan area. Moreover, its use of centralized inventory warehouses and just-in-time deliveries from suppliers led to high inventory turns and reduced stockouts, while at the same time lowering waste and spoilage of perishable goods and reducing the shrinkage associated with store personnel and customer handling of in-store products. Peapod management expected that the efficiencies of its business model would permit competitive pricing and, further, that its sophisticated Web technologies would result in being able to increase sales of high-margin products (private-label goods). Thus, the company expected that, over time, it ought to have higher gross margins and better bottom-line profitability than traditional grocery retailers.

Research and Data Partnerships with Suppliers

Peapod was leveraging the database it was accumulating from tracking user behavior and shopping patterns on its Web site. The company provided advertisers on its Web site with feedback on the effectiveness of marketing programs, and it provided a forum for consumer goods companies to conduct targeted advertising, test electronic couponing, and gather data on online purchasing behavior. The company had created research panels of users at costs that management believed were well below the costs of consumer panels used by Internet research firms. Peapod linked users from its eight markets to form a national online network of panelists and users, enabling the company to collect information on user attitudes, purchasing behavior, and demographics.

Peapod's database and membership profiles permitted it to deliver highly targeted ads and electronic coupons to users, as well as to count the number of Web-page exposures, click-throughs, coupon redemptions, and sales—the data were captured in a manner that allowed the company to measure the impact of a marketing program. Peapod had agreements to provide fee-based online marketing data and research services to a number of national consumer goods companies, resulting in annual revenues of

$1.0 to $1.5 million. Management believed that as Peapod's customer base grew, consumer goods companies would increasingly view Peapod as a powerful advertising venue as well as a valuable research tool, thereby generating additional revenues for Peapod. Participating subscribers included Kellogg's, Kraft, Colgate-Palmolive, Frito-Lay, Coca-Cola, Clorox, Kimberly-Clark, Ralston Purina, and Nestlé U.S.A.

Growth Strategies   Aside from its efforts to build order volume and add new customers in the eight markets where it already operated, Peapod's strategy to grow its business consisted of two major initiatives: (1) expanding into additional market areas and (2) moving beyond groceries and adding altogether new products and services to its lineup. Peapod management planned to use its central warehouse business model and new systems capabilities as the basis for expanding its service into a total of 40 metropolitan areas with 400,000-plus households. The company planned to keep its investment costs down by building economical $2 million distribution centers. Moreover, by establishing a local order fulfillment network with recurring grocery purchases as a foundation, Peapod management believed it would have a pipeline into customer households through which it could provide an increasingly wide range of goods and services at little incremental cost. Peapod management believed that its "last-mile" delivery network for groceries gave it an unparalleled opportunity to build the Peapod brand and to establish personal relationships with individual customers through regular deliveries. Management planned to transform Peapod into a one-stop online shopping site offering home delivery of a host of different products and services, thereby dramatically improving profitability.

As one of the first steps in expanding its product offerings, the company had recently formed a strategic product alliance with Walgreens. Under this agreement, Peapod would begin offering health and beauty products, household hardware and small appliances, electrical supplies, audio- and videotapes, stationery and art supplies, and seasonal items supplied by Walgreens.[4]

The major impediment to Peapod's growth strategies was a potential shortage of capital. The company had nearly $13 million in cash and marketable securities going into the fall of 1999, but the size of the company's losses was creating negative cash flows from operations. The company was depleting its cash reserves to cover the negative cash flow from current operations. Peapod management anticipated that its existing cash and marketable securities would be insufficient to fund the company's operations and capital requirements in 2000 and was therefore currently evaluating financing opportunities. Exhibit 7 shows recent trends in the company's stock price. Analysts following the company forecast that Peapod's losses would amount to $17–$20 million in 2000, equal to a negative $1.10 per share.

Management Changes

Peapod's top management team underwent significant change in 1999. Bill Malloy, brought in as president, chief executive officer, and a member of the board of directors, had established an impressive record of successfully launching new operations and new services while managing rapid growth at AT&T Wireless, and had been one of the key architects of AT&T's Digital One Rate strategy. Cofounder Andrew Parkinson, who stayed on as chairman of the board, began devoting his efforts full-time to Peapod's long-term strategy and business development. Malloy made several top-management

---

[4]"Peapod and Walgreen Co. Announce Product Alliance," Peapod Press Release, March 10, 1999.

changes in the months following his appointment. Michael Brennan was promoted to senior vice president of marketing and product management, George F. Douaire was made senior vice president of Peapod Interactive, and Robert P. Ziegler joined Peapod as director of Chicago operations. The top five officers under Malloy collectively had 36 years of experience in the online grocery business, and several officers had previous experience in packaged foods and consumer products at such companies as Kraft Foods and Procter & Gamble. Peapod employed approximately 475 full-time and 370 part-time employees in early 2000.

THE RETAIL GROCERY INDUSTRY

The U.S. retail grocery industry was a $430 billion business.[5] Sales of health and beauty aids amounted to an additional $200 to $225 billion. Forrester Research estimated that the total sales of grocery and household items, health and beauty items, and beverages in all types of retail outlets amounted to a $720 billion U.S. market.

The top five supermarket chains in 1999 were Kroger, with $43.2 billion in sales; Albertson's, with $35.9 billion; Wal-Mart, with $27 billion from its grocery operations; Safeway, with $26.5 billion; and Ahold, with $20 billion.[6] Slow growth and intense competition were driving supermarket industry consolidation. No supermarket chain had an industry market share much above 10 percent; the top five chains had a combined share under 30 percent. Supermarket sales had grown at an average of just 3.4 percent over the past 10 years, partly because more consumers were shifting some of their purchases to drug chain, wholesale club, and discount chain "supercenter" formats. Traditional grocers' share of total U.S. food sales had dropped from 42 to 40 percent over the last ten years.[7]

Typical supermarkets carried an average of 30,000 items, ranged in size from 20,000 to 40,000 square feet, and averaged $12 million in sales annually. Consumers tended to be price-conscious, and the industry was characterized by fierce price competition.

The supermarket business was a notoriously low-margin business with net profits of only 1 to 2 percent of revenues. Store profits depended heavily on creating a high volume of customer traffic and rapid inventory turnover, especially for perishables such as produce and fresh meat. Competitors had to operate efficiently to make money, and tight control of labor costs and product spoilage was essential. Because capital investment costs were modest, involving mainly the construction of distribution centers and stores, it was not unusual for supermarket chains to realize 15 to 20 percent returns on invested capital.

Supermarket Chains as Potential Competitors in the Online Grocery Segment Most supermarket chains were following developments in the online grocery industry carefully. While some observers believed that existing supermarket chains would be slow to enter into online sales for fear of cannibalizing their existing sales and undermining their brick-and-mortar investments, other industry observers expected supermarket chains to enter the online grocery segment, especially if

---

[5]Ronette King, "Grocery Mergers Are Part of the Growing U.S. Trend," *Times-Picayune,* October 13, 1999, p. A4.

[6]Joan Bergmann, "Food for Thought: Going into the Grocery Industry," *Discount Merchandiser,* May 1999, p. 36.

[7]Nora Aufretier and Tim McGuire, "Walking Down the Aisles," *Ivey Business Journal,* March–April 1999, p. 49.

online grocery sales took off. However, other supermarket industry analysts believed some existing supermarket chains would definitely not stand by idly and let online grocery companies steal market share without a fight. These analysts saw existing supermarket chains as potentially formidable competitors in the online segment because they had well-established supply chains, bought in volumes that gave them bargaining power with food and household product suppliers, had well-known brand names, knew local markets, and could use their distribution centers and neighborhood stores as bases from which to make home deliveries. As many as one-third of U.S. grocery chains were said to have experimented with some type of delivery service.[8]

Albertson's had recently begun testing the market by offering online shopping to customers in the Dallas/Fort Worth, Texas, area. Albertson's was well established in the Dallas/Fort Worth area, with numerous stores and a sizable share of the supermarket business. Management indicated that if its online venture in the Dallas/Fort Worth area was deemed successful, it would expand its online grocery service to other areas.

Clark's Supermarkets, a small, family-owned Colorado chain, announced plans in early 2000 to experiment with online grocery sales at its stores. Clark's intended to put the items stocked in its stores online, allowing customers to log on to its Web site and select the items they wanted. The company had designed a special cart that allowed store personnel to cruise store aisles and pick five orders simultaneously. Clark's strategy was to run the items through its checkout counters, pack them, and have them ready for customer pickup at a time chosen by customers. For the time being, Clark's did not plan to deliver orders to customers' homes. Clark's store in Steamboat Springs was selected to be the pilot for the online experiment; if the service proved popular and successful, Clark's intended to make it available at other Colorado store locations. Clark's saw online ordering as a time-saving service to customers; management did not expect the service to add substantially to the company's profitability.

THE ONLINE GROCERY SEGMENT

The online grocery shopping business was in its infancy in 2000. Analysts believed that online grocery sales amounted to about $235 million in 1999, less than 0.25 percent of total supermarket industry sales. There were 45 companies in the online market, and none were profitable yet.[9] So far, online grocery shopping had been slow to catch on, and industry newcomers had encountered high start-up and operating costs. Sales volumes were too small to permit profitability. The problem, according to industry analysts, was that consumers had been largely disappointed in the service, selection, and prices that they had so far gotten from industry members.

However, some analysts expected online grocery sales to grow at a rapid pace as companies improved their service and selection, PC penetration of households rose, and consumers became more accustomed to making purchases online.[10] Forrester Research forecast that online grocery sales could reach $3 billion by 2003 and as much as $85 billion by 2007. A two-year study by Consumer Direct Cooperative (CDC) concluded that online, consumer-direct grocery sales would account for between 8 and 12 percent of the total grocery market share by 2010.[11] CDC had also done a study of the types of online shoppers (see Exhibit 8). Most online grocery customers were believed to be either starved for time or averse to grocery store visits.

---

[8]Laurent Belise, "A Mouse in the Bakery Aisle," *Christian Science Monitor,* September 8, 1998, p. 11.

[9]Sharon Machlis, "Filling Up Grocery Carts Online," *Computerworld,* July 27, 1998, p. 4.

[10]Ibid.

[11]Terry Hennessy, "Sense of Sell," *Progressive Grocer,* August 1998, pp. 107–10.

exhibit 8   Types of Online Shoppers

Types of Online Shoppers	Comments
Shopping avoiders	Dislike going to the grocery; prime candidate for online grocery shopping
Necessity users	Have limited ability to go to the grocery store; strong candidate for using online grocery shopping as a substitute for in-store shopping
New technologists	Young and comfortable with technology; certain to experiment with buying products online; amenable to online grocery shopping if it is a pleasant and satisfying experience
Time-starved shoppers	Insensitive to price; don't mind paying extra to save time
Responsibles	Have available time; get an enhanced sense of self-worth from grocery shopping
Traditional shoppers	Older; may want to avoid technology and buying products online; very likely to prefer "touch and inspect" shopping in a grocery store

Source: A study by Consumer Direct Cooperative cited in Michael McGovern, "One Stop Shopping," *Transportation & Distribution* 39 (May 1998).

A MARC Group study concluded that "consumers who buy groceries online are likely to be more loyal to their electronic supermarkets, spend more per store 'visit,' and take greater advantage of coupons and premiums than traditional customers."[12] Another study found higher demand for produce online. Edward McLaughlin, head of the Food Industry Management Program at Cornell University, found that 12 to 16 percent of grocery expenditures through Peapod were for fresh produce, compared to the supermarket average of about 10 percent.[13] He reasoned that this outcome was because "decisions made through a computer are more rational, and choices are for healthier foods."

One of the problems with online grocery shopping was that consumers were extremely price-sensitive when it came to buying groceries. The prices of many online grocers were above those of supermarkets, and shoppers in many cases were unwilling to pay extra for the convenience of home delivery. Consumer price sensitivity meant that online grocers had to achieve a cost structure that would allow them to (1) price competitively, (2) cover the costs of picking and delivering individual grocery orders, and (3) have sufficient margins to earn attractive profits and returns on investment. Some analysts estimated that online grocers had to do 10 times the volume of a traditional grocer in order to be successful.[14] However, other analysts and several online grocers believed that the value chain of online grocers was more cost-effective than that of traditional supermarkets (see Exhibit 9).

Gomez Advisor's Ratings of Online Grocers

Gomez Advisors provided user-oriented ratings of numerous types of online companies, ranging from banks to auction sites to travel agents to sellers of sporting goods.

---

[12]Bob Woods, "America Online Goes Grocery Shopping for E-Commerce Bargains," *Computer News,* August 10, 1998, p. 42.

[13]"Net Profits: Making the Internet Work for You and Your Business," *Fortune,* Summer 1999, pp. 240–43.

[14]Lawrence M. Fisher, "On-Line Grocer Is Setting Up Delivery System for $1 Billion," *New York Times,* July 10, 1999, p. 1.

exhibit 9   Comparative Logistics for Traditional Supermarket versus Online Grocer

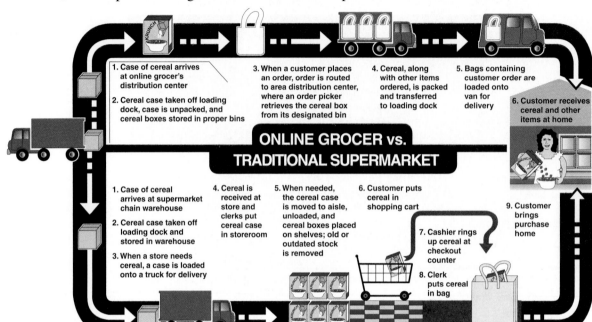

Source: Adopted and revised from E.81Z section of *Business Week,* July 26, 1999, p. EB46.

Many online shoppers were using the Gomez ratings to help them select which Internet providers to do business with. Gomez evaluated online grocers on five aspects:

- *Ease of use*—whether the Web site had well-integrated features that minimized order time and that gave shoppers product comparison capabilities.
- *Onsite resources*—the breadth of product selection and the quality of information resources provided to users.
- *Relationship services*—whether the grocer provided such "extras" as in-home visits with first-time customers, account representatives to answer questions, and willingness to fill unique orders.
- *Overall cost*—product costs (based on nonpromoted prices of a market basket of commonly purchased items), delivery charges, length and frequency of price promotions, and membership fees (including whether there were free trial periods for new members).
- *Customer confidence*—financial stability, reliability of customer service, and guarantees for what was sold.

Gomez also determined on the basis of its ratings which online grocers were most suitable for selective shoppers, bargain-hunting shoppers, time-constrained shoppers, and meal solution shoppers. Exhibit 10 reports the fall 1999 Gomez ratings of the top 10 online grocers.

PROFILES OF SELECTED PEAPOD COMPETITORS

Peapod management anticipated that the company would experience increasing competitive pressures in the online grocery segment. Competition was expected to come *exhibit 10* Gomez Ratings of the Top 10 Online Grocers, Fall 1999

Company	Ease of Use	Overall Cost	Customer Confidence	Onsite Resources	Relationship Services	Overall Score	Comments
Peapod	9.07	7.96	5.41	7.90	3.75	6.97	Rated third (score of 6.17) for time-short shoppers looking for the best deal with the least hassle
HomeGrocer.com	7.33	7.41	4.82	7.74	5.00	6.67	Rated second best (score of 7.02) for selective shoppers wanting *the* best products and delivery service; also rated second best (score of 6.80) for shoppers looking for specific meal solutions (recipes, seasonal foods, and prepared foods)
Webvan	8.22	7.16	2.63	7.32	5.00	6.36	Rated best (score of 7.23) for selective shoppers and best (score of 7.14) for shoppers looking for specific meal solutions
Streamline	4.62	5.93	5.16	7.47	7.50	6.31	Rated best (score of 6.92) for time-short shoppers
ShopLink	6.36	6.98	5.33	5.93	6.25	6.26	Rated second best for time-short shoppers (score of 6.70)
HomeRuns	5.56	8.75	4.97	3.41	2.50	5.18	Ranked best (score of 8.68) for bargain shoppers who love to browse and the thrill of shopping for the best deal
NetGrocer.com	8.22	3.33	2.97	5.49	3.75	4.70	
Albertson's	4.67	8.16	3.99	0.90	2.50	4.13	Ranked second (score of 7.54) for bargain shoppers
Grocer Online	5.42	3.46	6.64	0.36	2.50	3.73	
Your Grocer	4.53	3.84	5.91	2.70	5.00	3.68	

Source: www.gomez.com, February 6, 2000.

exhibit 11   Comparative Prices of Selected Online Grocers, February 2000

Grocery Item	Peapod's Price	Webvan's Price	HomeGrocer.com's Price	NetGrocer.com's Price
Lea & Perrin's Worcestershire sauce (10 oz.)	$2.19	$2.47	$2.25	$2.39
Campbell's Chunky Classic chicken noodle soup (19 oz.)	$2.45	$2.44	$2.19	$2.29
Bunch of green onions (scallions)	$0.50	$0.50	$0.49	Fresh produce not available
French's mustard squeeze (8 oz.)	$0.97	$0.97	$0.95	$0.99
Maxwell House Instant Crystals (8 oz.)	$4.89	$4.92	$5.49	$5.49
Kraft Macaroni and Cheese Deluxe (14 oz.)	$2.39	$2.47	$2.29	$2.49

Source: Company Web sites.

from (1) supermarket chains adopting "click-and-mortar" strategies and pursuing online sales as a new distribution channel to complement their traditional chain of retail outlets and (2) the aggressive market expansion efforts of the 45 companies already in the online segment. This section provides a brief look at three of Peapod's competitors in the online grocery business. Exhibit 11 provides a comparison of Peapod's prices for six selected items with those of Webvan, HomeGrocer.com, and NetGrocer.com.

Webvan Group, Inc.

Webvan's strategic intent was to become the market leader in the full-service online grocery and drugstore business. Louis H. Borders, a founder of the Borders Group who left the bookstore chain in 1992 to form his own investment firm, launched Webvan in Foster City, California, in June 1999 as one of the most ambitious e-commerce enterprises to date. Before going public, Webvan had attracted $122 million in investment capital from CBS, Yahoo!, Softbank, Sequoia Capital, Benchmark Capital, and Knight-Ridder and had recruited the head of Andersen Consulting, George Shaheen, to be its president and CEO.[15] Webvan completed an initial public offering of its stock in November 1999, raising $375 million in capital by selling 9 percent of its shares. The shares, initially priced by Goldman Sachs at $13 to $15 a share, rose to as high as $34 per share before ending the first day's trading at $24.875. The company's prospectus forecast that Webvan would post $11.9 million in revenues in 1999, $120 million in 2000, and $518.2 million in 2001. The prospectus also stated that company expectations were for a $73.8 million loss in 1999, a $154.3 million loss in 2000, and $302 million in losses in 2001.[16] The company shares traded in the $15 to $20 range in early 2000.

Webvan attracted about 10,000 customers in its first six weeks of operation in the San Francisco Bay area. The company had recruited several executives from Federal Express and was using FedEx's hub-and-spoke delivery system as a model for its own distribution system and delivery service. Webvan was using Wal-Mart as its example of

---

[15]Linda Himelstein, "Louis H. Borders," *Business Week,* September 27, 1999, p. 28.

[16]"Webvan Group Files Amended Prospectus for Initial Offering," *The Wall Street Journal,* October 13, 1999, p. A8.

breadth of product selection, Yahoo! as its model for speed, Amazon.com as its model for designing the kind of online shopping experience it wanted to provide, and eBay as its model for "warm-and-fuzzy" feel.[17] It had hired 80 software programmers to create proprietary systems that linked every aspect of its business processes and had recruited managers with expertise in logistics, grocery and drug retailing, and customer service.

Webvan's Strategy and Business Plan   To begin operations, Webvan had constructed a 330,000-square-foot prototype in Oakland, California, to service an area of 40 miles in any direction.[18] The $25 million facility included 4.5 miles of conveyor belts and temperature-controlled rooms to store wine, cigars, produce, meat, and frozen foods. It was designed to serve as many households as 20 to 25 supermarkets. The company planned to eventually stock 50,000 items, including an array of drug-store items, 300 varieties of fresh fruits and vegetables, 750 kinds of cheese, 500 types of cereal, 700 cuts of fresh meat and fish, 700 different wine labels, and chef-prepared meals that could be reheated in the microwave or oven. In the San Francisco market area, Webvan had formed alliances with leading local vendors to provide the freshest produce available; it planned to use such alliances in other markets as well. Webvan claimed that its prices were up to 5 percent less than those of local grocery stores. See Exhibit 12 for Webvan's home page.

Webvan had entered into an agreement with Bechtel Group, one of the world's largest engineering and construction firms, to build Webvan's distribution centers and delivery systems in 26 markets over the next two years. Webvan's projected investment costs for its distribution centers and delivery systems amounted to $1 billion. The company's second distribution center had recently been built in Atlanta.

Webvan's tracking systems monitored customer orders starting with the time they were placed on the company's Web site. Orders were directed from the Web site to the appropriate distribution center. Workers were located at order-picking stations scattered throughout each distribution center; their job was to pick items stocked in their area of the warehouse and put them in color-coded plastic tote bags that signaled whether the items were frozen, refrigerated, or dry. Pickers did not travel up and down aisles but instead moved no more than 20 feet in any direction to reach 8,000 bins of goods that were brought to the picker on rotating carousels. Once pickers completed their portion of a customer's order, the tote was transported on conveyors to other areas of the distribution center where pickers for the remaining items were located. After orders had made the necessary rounds through the warehouse, they were loaded onto trucks refrigerated at 35°F and taken to staging areas located throughout the metropolitan market area. From there, the totes were loaded onto one of the company's 60-plus vans for delivery to customers' homes. Staging areas were located so that Webvan's couriers did not have to travel more than 10 miles in any direction from the staging area to reach a customer's home. The couriers were trained to be courteous and friendly, and to act as customer service professionals and ambassadors for Webvan's service; they were not permitted to accept tips or gratuities. All of the logistics—how many items a tote bag should hold, how far pickers should travel to rotating carousels, how far trucks should travel from staging areas to make deliveries—had been carefully plotted to maximize efficiency.

Webvan management expected that each distribution center would be able to handle 8,000 orders a day (involving more than 225,000 items) and bring in $300 million

[17]Linda Himelstein, "Can You Sell Groceries like Books?" *Business Week,* July 26, 1999, p. EB-44.
[18]Ibid., p. EB-45.

exhibit 12 Webvan's Welcome Page at www.webvan.com

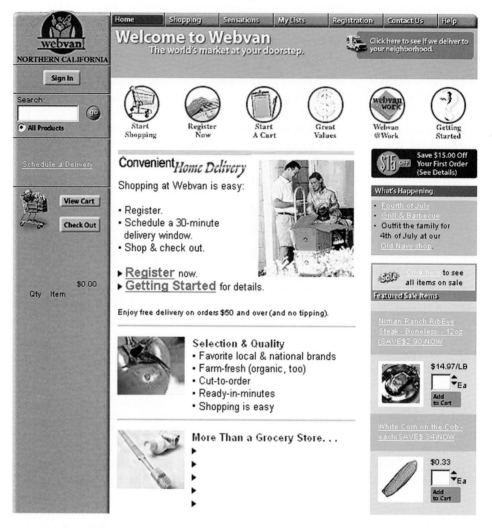

in annual revenues.[19] Louis Borders predicted that Webvan's business model would be so successful and efficient that the company would be able to charge lower prices than both traditional supermarkets and rival online grocers.

Webvan offered free delivery on orders over $50, whereas most other online grocers waived delivery fees only on orders over $75. And the company did not charge a membership fee. Orders were delivered within a 30-minute window selected by the customer. Webvan's Web site offered customers recipes and use of a weekly menu planner.

HomeGrocer.com

Founded in 1997, HomeGrocer.com provided online grocery ordering and delivery service to customers in Seattle, Washington; Portland, Oregon; Orange County, California; and portions of Los Angeles and San Bernardino County. HomeGrocer.com

---

[19]Ibid., p. EB-46.

exhibit 13   HomeGrocer.com's Welcome Page at www.homegrocer.com

offered a broad selection of items, including fresh produce, meats, seafood, dairy products, local specialty foods, health and beauty aids, household items, fresh flowers, pet supplies, best-selling books, video games, and movies. HomeGrocer.com used a distribution center model also; in early 2000, it had four distribution centers and was adding others in the newly entered Los Angeles area. HomeGrocer.com's signature peach-logo delivery trucks had multiple compartments that permitted products to be stored at their appropriate temperatures without affecting the temperatures of the other products.

Customers could order groceries via the Internet until 11 PM and select a 90-minute window for next-day delivery. HomeGrocer.com offered free delivery for all first orders and those $75 or more, in addition to toll-free customer support for its members. To underscore its commitment to quality, the company offered an unconditional 100 percent satisfaction guarantee. HomeGrocer.com had been recognized by Feedback Direct, a leading online customer service authority, as one of the top 50 North American companies to consistently demonstrate superior customer service. Exhibit 13 shows Homegrocer.com's home page.

Although HomeGrocer.com was a fairly small business, with fewer than 25,000 customers, it had ambitious plans to expand into 20 other markets in the near future, aided by a $42.5 million investment from Amazon.com.[20] Amazon's investment gave it a 35 percent stake in the company. Amazon had also recently invested in drugstore.com and Pets.com, and there had been speculation that Amazon might start to use HomeGrocer.com's vans to deliver CDs, books, and prescription drugs to customers' homes. Homegrocer.com had also received funding from the Barksdale Group, an investment firm run by James Barksdale, founder of Netscape, Martha Stewart Living

---

[20]Andrew Marlatt, "Amazon Diversifies Further with $42M Stake in Grocer," *Internet World,* May 24, 1999.

exhibit 14   NetGrocer.com's Welcome Page at www.netgrocer.com

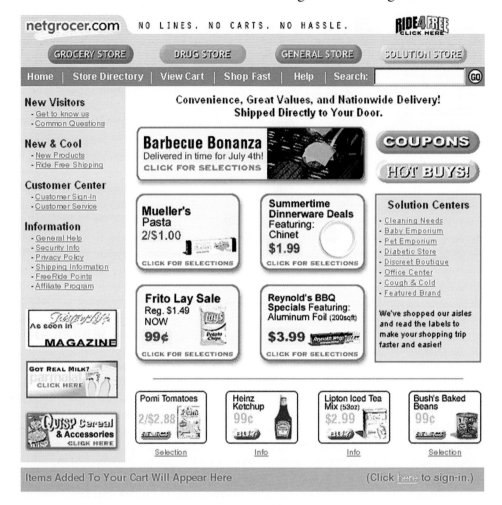

Omnimedia Inc., Hummer Winblad Venture Partners, and Kleiner Perkins Caufield & Byers.[21] The company had filed plans with the Securities and Exchange Commission to issue shares of its common stock to the public in the first half of 2000.

NetGrocer.com

NetGrocer.com began operations in 1995 and offered nationwide distribution through a large central warehouse located in New Jersey. NetGrocer.com's product line included canned and packaged grocery items, paper products, cleaning products, organic and natural foods, international food items, dog and cat foods, laundry items, health and beauty products, dietary supplements, pain relief products, fragrances, baby products, a variety of electronics items (cameras, film, calculators, data organizers, audio accessories, batteries, and video games), CDs, and gifts. It generally offered prices of 10 to 20 percent

---

[21]Rachel Beck, "Online Grocers Work to Build a Market," *Houston Chronicle,* May 30, 1999, p. 7.

less than supermarkets and free delivery for orders over $75. NetGrocer.com's orders were delivered by FedEx on the third business day after the order was received.

In 1999 NetGrocer.com relaunched its Web site following the removal of CEO Daniel Nissan and the firing of 80 percent of its staff. These changes, which occurred shortly after the company shelved its $38 million initial public offering, were attributed to market conditions and expense cuts. Since the launch of the new site, NetGrocer.com's average order size was up 40 percent and time spent on the site had increased dramatically.[22] Exhibit 14 shows NetGrocer.com's home page.

---

[22]Barry Janoff, "Point, Click, Shop," *Progressive Grocer,* June 1999, p. 31.

case 9 Cannondale Corporation

Romuald A. Stone
Keller Graduate School of Management

John E. Gamble
University of South Alabama

In early 2000 Cannondale Corporation was the world's leading manufacturer and marketer of high-performance aluminum bicycles. The company also marketed CODA bicycle components, HeadShok suspension forks, and a line of bicycle accessories including such items as clothing, packs, and bags. The company's bicycles, which carried its "Handmade in the USA" logo, were known for their innovative designs, light weight, exceptional performance, and durable construction and were sold in the United States and in more than 60 other countries. Since the company's founding in 1971, Cannondale's products had been recognized for their innovation by such publications as *USA Today, Sports Illustrated, Popular Science, Popular Mechanics,* and *Design News.* Cannondale's newest bicycle model, the Jekyll, had been named *Mountain Biking* magazine's "Bike of the Year" for 2000 and dubbed "a manufacturing masterpiece," "a masterful work of art," and "an outstanding achievement in lightweight, dual-suspension performance."[1]

Cannondale achieved success quickly after its founding, recording annual revenues of approximately $8 million by the late 1970s. However, the company's emergence as a major bicycle producer came about only in 1983, when it developed and produced the first affordable aluminum-frame bicycle. Cannondale's aluminum road bikes and its aluminum-frame mountain bike, introduced in 1984, were instant hits and allowed the company's revenues to grow at an annual rate of 30 percent between 1983 and 1985. The company's growth continued at a dramatic rate as the popularity of mountain biking grew exponentially during the late 1980s and early 1990s. In 1982, two years before Cannondale's introduction of its SM 500 mountain bike, there were approximately 200,000 mountain bikers in the United States. By 1992, the number of U.S. mountain bikers had grown to more than 8 million and mountain bikes accounted for 54 percent of U.S. bicycle sales. By 1996 Cannondale had become the leader of the high-performance mountain bike segment and its stock price had appreciated at an annual rate of 32 percent since its initial public offering in 1994.

In early 2000 the company's prospects for spectacular growth appeared to hinge not on the success of its mountain bikes but on its soon-to-be-introduced MX400 off-road motorcycle. The highly innovative aluminum-frame motorcycle was eagerly

[1]Cannondale press release, PR Newswire, January 31, 2000.

awaited by motocross enthusiasts and had been described by *Dirt Rider* magazine as "a monumental bike" that had forced "other manufacturers to rethink their current technology."[2] Cannondale remained a leader in the high-performance segment of the mountain bike industry with innovative products like the Jekyll, but its growth during the late 1990s had been severely restricted as the bicycle industry reached maturity during the mid-1990s and grew at an approximate annual rate of 2 percent during the late 1990s. Cannondale's revenue growth had slowed to an annual rate of 9.7 percent between 1995 and 1999 after growing at a compounded annual rate of 22.3 percent between 1991 and 1995. The company's decelerated growth rate was reflected in its stock price, which had steadily declined since its peak of $27 in 1997. As the company prepared to begin shipping the new MX400 in the spring of 2000, Cannondale's founder and CEO Joseph Montgomery hoped that the new motorcycle would be the strategic spark that the company needed to restart the share price growth it had experienced in earlier years. A summary of Cannondale Corporation's financial performance between 1991 and 1999 is shown in Exhibit 1. Exhibit 2 presents a graph of Cannondale's stock performance between 1995 and early 2000.

THE GLOBAL BICYCLE MARKET

With over 1 billion bicycles existing in the world, usage varied considerably, with about 70 percent of all bicycles used as a means of transportation, 29 percent used for recreational purposes, and about 1 percent used solely in racing events. In many countries bicycling was the primary means of land transportation for distances that made walking impractical. In China, for example, traffic controllers saw an average of 10,000 cyclists per hour pass the busiest urban intersections. In the city of Tianjin, with more than 4 million people, there were up to 50,000 cyclists per hour passing through high-traffic intersections. In countries with more developed economies, bicycling was more likely to be a secondary mode of transportation or restricted to recreational use.

Among the world's industrialized nations, Western Europeans were the biggest users of bicycles, with an estimated 115 million bicycle owners. Communities in the Netherlands, Denmark, and Germany were called bicycle-friendly because of their balanced use of bicycles for transport, recreation, and sport. Cycling facilities such as bike lanes and parking sites, along with traffic calming and intermodal transit links, encouraged people to use bicycles for as much as 20 to 50 percent of all urban trips.

In the United States, bicycles were employed mainly for recreation, with only about 5 percent of the country's 100 million bicycles used for transportation. Cycling was the fifth most popular recreational activity in the United States, behind exercise walking, swimming, exercising with equipment, and camping.

In some African and Latin American countries bicycle use was heavy, but governments in those geographic regions tended to stigmatize bicycles as "Third World" means of mobility. While many leaders in government enjoyed the prestige of cars and new highways, their people often relied on walking instead of cycling for essential transport. In countries with developing economies but well-established mass transit systems, such as Russia, bicycles were rare. However, in Eastern European nations such as Hungary, where mass transit was less available and economic conditions made automobile ownership difficult for most, bicycles were used widely and accounted for roughly half of all trips to work.

---

[2]Ibid.

exhibit 1   Consolidated Financial Data for Cannondale Corporation, 1991–99
(In Thousands of Dollars, Except Per Share Data)

	Twelve Months Ended		
	July 3, 1999	June 27, 1998	June 28, 1997
Statement of operations data			
Net sales	$176,819	$171,496	$162,496
Cost of sales	114,627	110,113	101,334
Gross profit	62,192	61,383	61,162
Expenses			
Selling, general and administrative	40,599	39,361	35,707
Research and development	10,222	6,750	3,576
Stock option compensation	—	—	—
Agent and distributor termination costs	—	—	—
Total operating expenses	50,821	46,111	39,283
Operating income (loss)	11,371	15,272	21,879
Other income (expense):			
Interest expense	(4,557)	(1,995)	(1,574)
Foreign exchange and other	1,160	653	843
Total other income (expense)	(3,397)	(1,342)	(731)
Income (loss) before income taxes, minority interest and extraordinary item	7,974	13,930	21,148
Income tax benefit (expense)	(2,051)	(4,578)	(7,642)
Minority interest in net loss (income) of consolidated subsidiary	—	—	—
Income (loss) before extraordinary item	5,923	9,352	13,506
Extraordinary item, net of income taxes[a]	—	—	—
Net income (loss)	5,923	9,352	13,506
Accumulated preferred stock dividends[b]	—	—	—
Income (loss) applicable to common shares and equivalents	$ 5,923	$ 9,352	$ 13,506
Per common share			
Income (loss) before extraordinary item[c]	$0.79	$1.11	$1.56
Income (loss)	$0.79	$1.11	$1.56
Weighted average common and common equivalent shares outstanding[d]	7,518	8,442	8,638
Balance sheet data			
Working capital	$ 74,894	$ 78,975	$ 77,196
Total assets	162,379	152,277	127,284
Total long-term debt, excluding current portion	55,997	40,352	20,319
Total stockholders' equity	75,010	78,238	81,621

[a]Extraordinary items consist of the costs relating to early extinguishment of debt, net of applicable tax benefit, if any.

[b]Reflects preferred stock dividends accumulated during the fiscal period. All cumulative preferred stock dividends were paid in 1995 at the time of the redemption of the preferred stock in connection with the company's initial public offering.

[c]No cash dividends were declared or paid on the common stock during any of these periods.

	Twelve Months Ended		Ten Months Ended		Twelve Months Ended	
	June 29, 1996	July 1, 1995	July 2, 1994	July 3, 1993	September 4, 1992	August 31, 1991
	$145,976	$122,081	$102,084	$80,835	$76,911	$54,544
	92,804	79,816	72,083	59,429	58,927	37,623
	53,172	42,265	30,001	21,406	17,984	16,921
	32,577	27,023	22,290	19,615	18,527	11,993
	2,837	1,751	1,317	1,105	1,314	907
	—		2,046	—	—	—
	—		—	271	1,196	—
	35,414	28,774	25,653	20,991	21,037	12,900
	17,758	13,491	4,348	415	(3,053)	4,021
	(2,224)	(3,929)	(4,460)	(4,177)	(2,990)	(1,976)
	414	24	324	828	(868)	419
	(1,810)	(3,905)	(4,136)	(3,349)	(3,858)	(1,557)
	15,948	9,586	212	(2,934)	(6,911)	2,464
	(5,802)	(1,353)	(791)	(179)	1,422	(959)
	—	—	—	—	850	(343)
	10,146	8,233	(579)	(3,113)	(4,639)	1,162
	—	(685)	—	(464)	—	—
	10,146	7,548	(579)	(3,577)	(4,639)	1,162
	—	(400)	(1,008)	—	—	—
	$ 10,146	$ 7,148	$ (1,587)	$ (3,577)	$(4,639)	$ 1,162
	$1.23	$1.18	$(.37)	$(.73)	$(1.08)	$0.28
	$1.23	$1.08	$(.37)	$(.83)	$(1.08)	$0.28
	8,216	6,606	4,246	4,291	4,296	4,179
	$ 62,032	$ 22,313	$ 6,366	$ 6,107	$ 3,615	$ 1,903
	109,945	84,008	67,870	65,245	57,877	35,617
	13,114	5,602	6,995	7,872	7,484	6,183
	68,294	36,088	9,640	8,220	4,525	6,893

[d]Shares underlying options granted during fiscal 1994 are treated as outstanding for fiscal 1994 and all prior periods, using the treasury stock method. Weighted average number of shares outstanding in 1995 reflects the issuance of 2,300,000 shares of common stock in connection with the company's initial public offering. Weighted average number of shares outstanding in 1996 reflects the issuance of 1,366,666 shares of common stock in connection with a public offering in fiscal 1996.

Source: Annual reports.

exhibit 2   Monthly Trading Range and Price-Earnings Ratio of
             Cannondale's Common Stock, 1995–January 2000

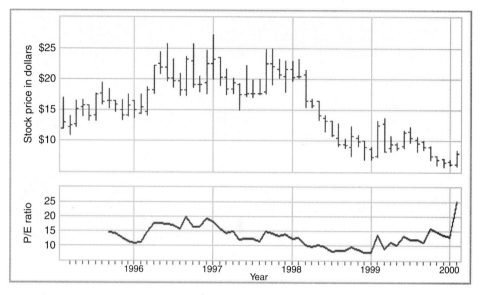

Most of the world's bicycles were made and used in Asia. Seventy-five percent of the world's bicycles were produced in China, India, Taiwan, Japan, and Thailand. With an average annual production of 30 million units, China produced more bicycles than any other nation in the world. In 1999 there were almost 1,000 bicycle parts makers and assembly plants in China, employing approximately 350,000 workers. About 20 million bicycles were produced each year for sale within China, while more than 10 million units were produced each year for export to other countries. The China Bicycle Company (CBC) of Guangzhou was one of the dominant Chinese bike manufacturers. The company was founded by Jerome Sze, a Hong Kong businessman, and began making bicycles for Western firms such as Schwinn in the 1970s. In 1992, CBC was rated as one of the top 10 foreign investment enterprises in China. Taiwan was the world's second largest producer and world's largest exporter of bicycles. During the late 1990s, over 70 percent of the bikes sold in the United States were made in Taiwan. The biggest Taiwanese bikemakers, Giant Manufacturing Company and Merida Industry Company, manufactured bicycles sold in the United States under brand names that included Trek, Schwinn, and Specialized.

THE U.S. BICYCLE INDUSTRY

In 1999 the U.S. bicycle industry was approximately a $5 billion per year industry, counting the retail value of bicycles, related parts, and accessories through all channels of distribution. There were over 100 brands of bicycles sold in the United States and an estimated 2,000 companies involved in either manufacturing or distributing cycling products. Bicycles were sold at nearly all full-line discount stores and sporting goods superstores, at many department stores, and at approximately 6,800 specialty bicycle stores. The annual U.S. sales of bicycles peaked in 1973 at 15.2 million units and averaged nearly 11.5 million units during the 1990s. Exhibit 3 presents annual U.S. bicycle sales between 1981 and 1998.

exhibit 3   U.S. Unit Sales of Bicycles (20-Inch and Larger Wheel
Sizes), 1981–98 (In Millions)

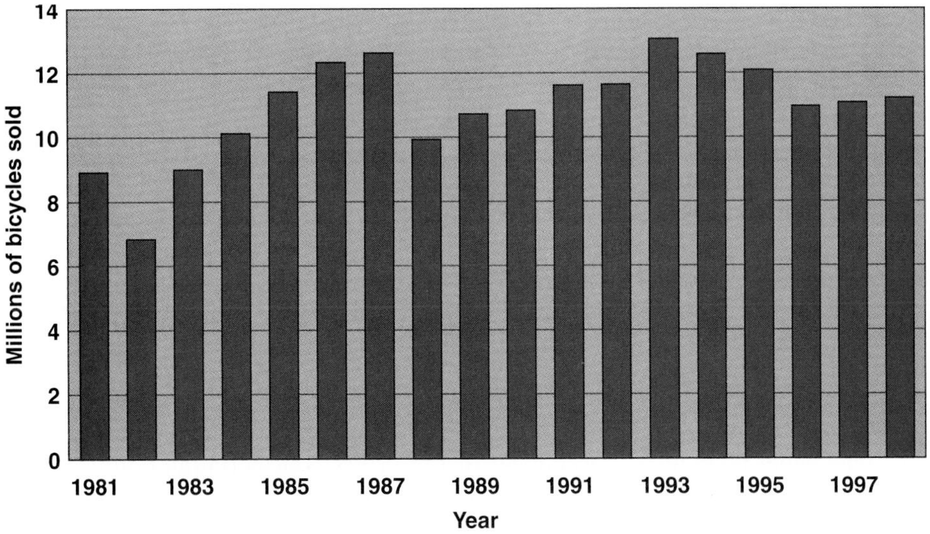

Source: Bicycle Manufacturers Association.

Market Segmentation by Bicycle Category

There were an estimated 54.5 million active adult cyclists in the United States in 1999
who used their bicycles at least once weekly. Adult bicycles fell into five broad categories: mountain, road-racing, multisport, recreational, and specialty. Mountain bikes
combined elements from classic balloon-tire bikes with the lightweight alloy components of quality road-racing bikes. These bikes also featured suspension systems, low
gears, beefed-up frames, and straight handlebars (allowing a more upright cycling position than road racing or recreational bikes) and were designed for reliable on-road
transportation and heavy-duty touring over rugged terrain. Mountain bikes, the largest
segment of the adult market, accounted for 63 percent of all bicycles sold in the United
States in 1997.

   Road-racing bikes were lightweight, with thin tires and drop (curved) handlebars.
Multisport bikes, designed for triathlons and other multisport races, were very aerodynamic and typically had smaller diameter wheels than traditional road racers. Recreational bikes, also known as comfort bikes, hybrids, or cross bikes, were typically more
comfortable versions of mountain bikes. The specialty bicycle market encompassed
various niche products, including tandem bikes, cruisers, and bicycle motocross (BMX)
bikes. Cruisers were styled similarly to the venerable Schwinn of the 1950s, with big
balloon tires, huge cushy saddles, and swept-back handlebars. BMX bikes, which featured 20-inch wheels, a relatively short but very strong and light frame, and no gears,
were originally designed for short races over dirt tracks but were more commonly used
by children and adolescents for everyday recreational use.

Factors Affecting Industry Demand

Federal Legislation   During the 1990s the U.S. government enacted legislation
that required communities to include cycling in local transit infrastructure planning.

For example, the 1990 Clean Air Act set standards for air quality and required some metropolitan areas to develop methods to reach compliance. One of the recommended approaches involved taking steps to make bicycling a more viable transportation alternative. In addition, the Intermodal Surface Transportation Efficiency Act (ISTEA) of 1991 recognized the transportation value of bicycling and walking and offered mechanisms to increase consideration of bicyclists' and pedestrians' needs within the nation's intermodal transportation system. Federal funding was available from a number of programs, and planning requirements for bicycling were established for states and metropolitan planning organizations. Other provisions of the act included the requirement that states establish and fund a bicycle and pedestrian coordinator in their departments of transportation, and that bicyclist and pedestrian safety continue to be priority areas for highway safety program funding.

However, the provisions of the 1990 Clean Air Act and the 1991 Intermodal Surface Transportation Efficiency Act had done little to create a boom in cycling. Most industry growth during the 1990s was attributable to a growing interest in physical fitness and the popularity of the mountain bike, rather than U.S. government mandates to make cycling an integral part of a balanced intermodal transportation system. There was some belief by industry participants that the 1998 Transportation Equity Act for the 21st Century (TEA-21) would better integrate cycling into mainstream transportation in the United States. TEA-21 would provide as much as $500 million between 1999 and 2003 to create walkable and bicycle-friendly communities that would make cycling and walking safe and practical alternatives to traveling by automobile.

The Appeal of Mountain Biking   The phenomenal growth in mountain biking had been a major factor in the overall growth of the domestic bicycle market during the mid-1980s and early 1990s. The number of mountain bikers in the United States grew from 200,000 in 1982 to approximately 8.5 million in 1997. Only in-line roller skating had grown faster than mountain biking among outdoor recreational and fitness activities between 1987 and 1998. However, by 1999 the mountain bike industry was mature; it remained among the most popular outdoor recreational activities, but its growth rate had slowed considerably (see Exhibit 4).

Three factors contributed to the popularity of mountain bikes: (1) They were more comfortable to ride than typical touring or racing models; (2) the bikes themselves greatly increased the terrain available to bicycles; and (3) more adults were turning toward outdoor activities in their leisure time. The introduction of mountain bike racing as an Olympic sport in 1996 reflected the growth of mountain bike racing as both a participant and spectator sport and created additional exposure for mountain biking. In addition, downhill racing proved to be increasingly popular with spectators, combining high speed and technically advanced equipment with the celebrity of professional athletes and emerging personalities in the sport. During the 1990s the ski resort industry increasingly promoted summer use of ski mountains for biking, with many ski resorts equipping ski lifts to carry bikes and riders uphill.

Factors Influencing Demand for Mountain Bikes in the Late 1990s

Environmental Regulation   The coverage of racing events in mountain bike magazines and the use of racing photos in mountain bike manufacturer advertisements had created a backlash against the industry by hikers and others wishing to preserve the environment. Opponents of mountain biking attempted to portray mountain bikers as

exhibit 4   U.S. Participation Rates of Selected Fitness and Sports
Activities, 1998

Activity	Number of U.S. Participation	Annual Change (1997–98)	11-Year Change (1987–98)
Aerobics	21,017,000	−7.9%	−1.0%
Fitness bicycling	13,556,000	n.a.	n.a.
Running/jogging	34,962,000	−4.2	−5.9
Stationary cycling	30,791,000	−3.9	0.1
Treadmill exercise	37,073,000	2.6	743.3
Stair-climbing machine exercise	18,609,000	3.9	777.5
Baseball	12,318,000	−7.2	−18.4
Basketball	42,417,000	−5.9	18.7
In-line roller skating	32,010,000	1.0	581.8
Recreational bicycling	54,575,000	n.a.	n.a.
Golf	29,961,000	−3.4	14.1
Mountain biking	8,612,000	2.1	469.5
Snowboarding	5,461,000	10.5	158.1
Scuba diving	3,448,000	27.7	41.7

n.a. = not available.

Source: Sporting Goods Manufacturers Association, "Sports Participation Trends Report, 1998."

crazed, out-of-control cyclists who destroyed trails and made it unsafe for hikers to enjoy national parks and other government lands. In response to the critics, the U.S. Forest Service had commissioned a survey in 1996 that looked at the impact of bicycles
on public lands. The survey found that 98 percent of National Forests reported mountain biking activity that ranged from 50 to 376,000 cyclists per year. Fifty percent of
national parks reported annual mountain bike usage by fewer than 4,500 visitors, while
25 percent of national parks reported more than 15,000 mountain bike riders per year.
Seventy percent of forest managers reported conflicts between cyclists and hikers, 59
percent were concerned that mountain bikes contributed to park safety problems, 58
percent believed that mountain bikes damaged park resources, and 48 percent wit-
nessed or knew of accidents in the park related to mountain bike usage.

The International Mountain Bike Association (IMBA) noted to its manufacturing
and retailing members that industry sales were directly tied to open biking trails. It developed a mantra of "No trails, no sales" and encouraged manufacturers to discontinue
ads that depicted racing photographs. The association also encouraged both manufacturers and retailers to take a proactive position in regard to safe and responsible cycling. The IMBA struck an agreement with the Sierra Club that called for wilderness
protection, socially responsible mountain biking, restricted trail access, trail user education, and open communication between local mountain biking groups and Sierra
Club entities. Additionally, the association maintained an active lobbying effort to ensure that lands regulated by the Bureau of Land Management and the U.S. Forest Service remained open to cycling.

Technological Innovation   Technological innovations became increasingly
important in the industry as rival mountain bike manufacturers attempted to outpace
the modest industry growth rate by introducing technological innovations in frames,

components, and suspension systems. Innovations diffused quickly throughout the industry as manufacturers kept adding features in attempts to maintain their historical growth rates. Cannondale was the first to offer affordable large-diameter aluminum-tube bicycles in the early 1980s, but by 1999 aluminum-frame bikes were produced by almost all bike manufacturers, including companies that manufactured inexpensive bicycles sold in discount stores. In 1999, aluminum frames were still found on high-end bikes, but other materials (such as carbon composites and titanium) were also used on more technologically advanced mountain bikes. The appeal of titanium frames was the material's light weight combined with strength. Like titanium frames, carbon composite frames were popular because they were light and strong but also because they could be molded into aerodynamic shapes. Steel- or aluminum-frame bicycle designs were typically bound to the traditional double-triangle shape. Other innovations that had become popular with cycling enthusiasts during the late 1990s included clipless pedals, disc brakes, automatic shifting, and suspension systems.

Front- and full-suspension systems were introduced during the early 1990s and quickly became a popular addition to high-end mountain bikes. The suspension systems provided greater comfort and control than what was available on nonsuspension bikes, and by 1999 suspension systems were found on most mountain bikes at midrange price points over $500. Suspension systems were also available on mountain bikes priced between $200 and $300 in discount stores. However, these lower-priced suspension bikes typically used poorer quality suspension systems and did not offer performance equal to that of higher-end suspension bikes. High-end mountain bike manufacturers sought out innovative features on a regular basis to maintain a comfortable level of differentiation over not only other high-end brands but also lower-priced bicycles that incorporated previous-generation mountain bike technology. K2's computer-chip-activated Smart Shock was an example of a technological innovation that could provide a bicycle manufacturer with the level of differentiation necessary to support premium pricing. The Smart Shock technology sampled the ground conditions and sent damping instructions to the shock 1,000 times per second to maximize tire-to-ground contact. K2 models equipped with the Smart Shock sold at prices between $900 and $2,200.

Market Segmentation by Channel of Distribution

Two primary distribution systems existed in the U.S. bicycle industry—large discount retailers and independent specialty bicycle shops. Department stores, discount stores, and toy stores accounted for about 70 percent of all units sold and about half of the total spent on bikes in 1997. Most of the bikes sold by mass merchandise retailers were offered at prices below $200 and tended to be heavy, without the precision machining or reliable components demanded by cycling enthusiasts. These low-end bikes were fine for cycling around the neighborhood but lacked the durability, reliability, and performance needed for serious biking. The discounters' advantages were price and convenience; their clientele consisted mainly of buyers looking for low-end, low-performance models.

Huffy Corporation, Murray Ohio Manufacturing, and Brunswick Corporation (producer of Roadmaster and Mongoose brands) were the three leading producers of bikes sold by large discounters, department stores, and discount sporting goods superstores. Other brands sold by large discounters were Magna, Pacific, Rand, and Kent. Discount store customers were not particularly brand-loyal and usually made their purchasing decisions based on price and some modest product preferences like bicycle type, color, and size. Competition among manufacturers of less-expensive bicycles, although always strong, had intensified during the 1990s as the discount retail industry had consolidated and low-priced imports from China and Taiwan had fueled a growing price war. Both domestic and Asian bicycle manufacturers were forced to add features and compete more aggressively on price to consistently win contracts with large retailers like Wal-Mart, Target, and Toys "R" Us. During the mid-1990s as little as 40 percent of the bicycles sold by discount retailers were produced outside the United States, but the growing price competition in the industry had compelled low-end manufacturers to abandon bicycle production in the United States. In 1999 both Huffy and Brunswick anticipated losses from their bicycle operations and closed their remaining U.S. production facilities. Both companies had announced that, following those closings, they would source 100 percent of their frames from Asian contract manufacturers.

About 30 percent of the 11 million bicycles sold in the United States during 1998 were sold by small specialty retailers with annual sales averaging about $500,000. These dealers, numbering about 6,800, typically had one location, were family owned, carried four to six brands of midrange to high-end bicycles, and sold about 500 to 600 bikes per year. The sales of parts, accessories, and service accounted for about 50 percent of specialty retailers' gross sales. About 80 percent of bicycles sold by specialty retailers were imported. High-performance bicycle manufacturers like Trek, Schwinn, Giant, Raleigh, Specialized, Cannondale, and Diamondback marketed their bikes exclusively through independent specialty dealers who could provide after-the-sale service for their products.

Specialty bicycle shops accounted for 30 percent of the industry's unit sales and about 50 percent of total dollar sales. Bicycle dealer brands generally started at prices above $200. The average price of a bicycle sold at a bicycle shop was about $350, though prices could range into the thousands. The independent bicycle dealer's ability to offer light, durable, properly assembled bicycles matched to the individual rider's needs worked to the dealer's advantage. In addition, specialty bike dealers commanded a vast majority of parts and accessories sales and virtually 100 percent of the service market. Dealers dominated the market for bicycles selling for $250 and higher. The growing interest in a total fitness lifestyle had also caught the attention of specialty bicycle dealers. Roughly 25 percent of the bicycle stores in the United States sold some kind of indoor exercise equipment (exercise bikes, weight machines, and all associated accessories).

Mountain bikes (26-inch wheel size) represented 55 percent of the bikes sold through the specialty channel in 1997. Mountain bikes had accounted for as much as 63 percent of independent dealer sales as recently as 1995. Children's bikes (20-inch wheels) were the fastest-growing bicycle category sold by specialty dealers, accounting for 33 percent of sales in 1997 versus 20 percent of specialty dealer unit sales in 1994. Recreational bikes were another rapidly growing category and accounted for 10 percent of dealer sales in 1997. It was expected that recreational comfort bikes would become a larger segment of the market as baby boomers aged and the over-40 age category grew. Most dealers had found that comfort bikes were gaining market share directly at the expense of low-end mountain bikes. Road racers accounted for only 2 percent of specialty retailer sales in 1997.

CANNONDALE'S RIVALS IN THE MOUNTAIN BIKE SEGMENT

Cannondale experienced little competition from the large manufacturers—such as Brunswick Corporation, Huffy Corporation, and Murray Ohio—that sold bicycles to discount retailers. For the most part, discount store brands were not sold by independent dealers and dealer brands were not carried in discount stores. The only exception was Mongoose, which had been a dealer brand until its acquisition by Brunswick in 1997. After the acquisition, Brunswick developed lower-priced Mongoose models for discounters as well as maintaining higher-priced models for its independent dealers. Once Mongoose became available at discount stores, many dealers chose to drop the Mongoose brand because of the difficulty in convincing consumers that the dealers' higher-priced Mongoose models, although similar in appearance, were of better quality than Mongoose models found in discount stores.

The high-performance segment of the bicycle industry was highly competitive in the United States and in many other countries. Competition was based primarily on perceived value, brand image, performance features, product innovation, and price. Competition in foreign markets was affected by duties, tariffs, foreign exchange fluctuations, taxes and the effect of various trade agreements and import restrictions. In 2000 there were several key competing brands in the industry.

In some instances competing brands were actually owned by the same parent corporation or holding company. As growth in the mountain bike segment had slowed during the 1990s and as bicycle manufacturers sought continued growth, a number of mergers and acquisitions involving key brands occurred. Owning more than one brand allowed manufacturers to gain greater coverage in specific geographic locations and communities even though dealers were frequently given some modest assurance of an exclusive territory. For example, Intrepid, Inc. (the parent of Trek bicycles), had acquired two high-end mountain bike manufacturers, Gary Fisher and Klein, which allowed the company to increase its network of retail dealers without alienating its Trek dealers. In addition, even though Trek, Klein, and Gary Fisher manufactured similarly equipped models, Intrepid's dealers were not exposed to the consumer price shopping that was seen by Mongoose dealers after Mongoose became available at discount stores. Other brands involved in mergers or acquisitions included Raleigh, Diamondback, Univega, Mishiski, GT, Dyno, Powerlite, and Robinson.

Cannondale's key competitors in 1999 are discussed in the following sections.

Schwinn Cycling & Fitness

Schwinn was founded in 1895 in Chicago by German bikemaker Ignaz Schwinn. At one time, Schwinn was the most prestigious bicycle company in the industry, with as much as 25 percent of the market and sales of 1.6 million units a year. During its first 100 years, Schwinn sold more than 40 million bicycles. Beginning in the 1970s changing consumer tastes and tough new competitors with lighter, more high-tech products began to slowly erode Schwinn's dominant position.

Rather than innovate, Schwinn became obsessed with cutting costs by moving production overseas. Initially, the company outsourced its bicycles from Japan. But by 1978 Taiwanese manufacturers were beating the Japanese on price. Schwinn shifted gears and began importing Taiwanese-made Giant bikes, on which Schwinn put its nameplate. When Giant became a competitor, Schwinn formed an alliance with the China Bicycle Company, but after a few years CBC also used the knowledge gained through collaborating with Schwinn to launch its own brand in the United States and compete against Schwinn.

To make matters worse, Schwinn made the strategic mistake of ignoring the mountain bike craze for most of the 1980s. By 1992, two-thirds of all bikes sold were mountain bikes. Schwinn managers were not alone in their complacency; many Schwinn retailers failed to notice key market trends or keep up with the technological changes sweeping the industry. The proverbial writing was on the wall, and Schwinn filed for Chapter 11 bankruptcy protection in 1992.

In 1993, what was left of Schwinn was purchased by an investor group for $43 million. Schwinn's new owners moved quickly to rebuild the Schwinn brand. The new owners immediately relocated the company to Boulder, home of the University of Colorado and thousands of outdoor enthusiasts. Historically, Schwinn was viewed as a maker of sturdy low-cost bikes, which was contrary to the 1990s consumer preference for the trendier high-performance mountain bikes. The Boulder culture helped Schwinn designers develop new models that included technological features and performance that better appealed to hardcore cyclists, who often influenced the purchases of less-avid cyclists. Even though Schwinn introduced better-styled and more technologically advanced bikes, its image was a major obstacle in turning around the company. As Greg Bagni, Schwinn's new vice president of marketing and product development, noted, the hardcore cyclists who were key to changing the public's perceptions of Schwinn's performance and quality "wouldn't be caught dead on a Schwinn."[3]

Schwinn's efforts to change its image required what Bagni said was a fundamental shift in strategy. "We've evolved from a marketing-driven company to a market-driven company. A marketing driven company will try to sell a warehouse full of yellow bikes . . . a market-driven company will determine what the consumer wants first."[4] In addition to determining what features consumers wanted, Schwinn also began showing up on the racing circuit, using cross-promotions with such well-known brands as Old Navy, Toyota, and MCI to promote Schwinn bikes and study what features appealed to hardcore cyclists.

Once Schwinn's turnaround was well under way, the company was sold again in 1997. The new owners retained Schwinn's management team and acquired GT Bicycles in 1998 to add complementary models to Schwinn's line and increase Schwinn's network of dealers. GT Bicycle was a leading designer, manufacturer, and marketer of mid- to premium-priced bicycles sold under the company's GT, Powerlite, Robinson, and Dyno brand names. GT Bicycles sold a full line of more than 40 bicycle models but was best known for its popular juvenile bikes. Like other manufacturers, GT promoted its brand through focused promotional efforts such as sponsorship of professional BMX racing teams and national, regional, and local bicycle races, as well as cooperative advertising programs with independent bicycle dealers.

Schwinn's turnaround and its addition of GT bikes put it into contention for a leadership position in the U.S. specialty retail channel. Schwinn and GT were strongest at low-end price points between $250 and $500 and together commanded an estimated market share of 18.8 percent at year-end 1999.

Intrepid, Inc.

Intrepid, Inc., was a privately held company that owned the Trek, Gary Fisher, and Klein mountain bike brands and LeMond road-racing bikes. The combined sales of the company's brands made it among the market share leaders in the specialty retailer channel. Trek was Intrepid's best-selling brand and was a pioneer in carbon-fiber frames. The Waterloo, Wisconsin, firm recorded revenues of about $400 million in 1997. Approximately 35 percent of its total revenue came from international sales. The

---

[3]Nancy Brumback, "Schwinn Cycles Fast to Finish First," *Brandmarketing*, December 1999, p. 6.

[4]L. Loro, "Schwinn Aims to Be a Big Wheel Again," *Advertising Age,* January 1995.

company employed 1,800 people worldwide to build and distribute its five bicycle lines, which included over 100 mountain bike, road-racing, touring, tandem, BMX, and children's models.

Trek began in 1976 by hand-building steel frames in a rented facility in Waterloo, Wisconsin. Pursuing high-quality workmanship, the firm expanded quickly, generating $750,000 in sales after just three years. It soon gained a reputation for quality American-made bicycles. By 1986, sales hit $16 million, but the company's rapid growth did not come without problems. The company sustained losses and accumulated unsold inventory, and employee morale was low. In stepped the founder of Trek, Dick Burke, who quickly took charge and articulated a back-to-basics philosophy that rallied employees and reenergized the company with a new mission statement: "Build a quality product; offer a competitive value; deliver it on time; and create a positive work environment."[5] In addition, Burke revised Trek's marketing strategy, developed new and innovative road bikes, and introduced a new line of mountain bikes. He emphasized quality and efficiency in his plant operations and pushed service excellence as the cornerstone of the sales department. As a result of these initiatives, Trek introduced a number of award-winning bicycles and steadily increased sales every year after 1987. Trek's Y-shaped carbon composite frame was one of the company's more innovative and popular products during the late 1990s and was available on many of its high-end bikes. In 1995, the designers working on Trek's Y-frame mountain bike project were named "Design Engineers of the Year" by *Popular Mechanics* and the Trek 970 Y-frame model was named *Mountain Bike* magazine's "Bike of the Year."

Trek's Y-frame was also available in an aluminum construction and could be outfitted with full suspension or in a hardtail configuration that included front suspension only. Trek's suspension could be adjusted to three positions that matched cross-country, downhill, or general riding or racing conditions. Trek also offered a women's frame with modified geometric proportions to better fit a female rider. Trek cosponsored racing teams with Volkswagen and the U.S. Postal Service and independently sponsored a triathlete team to race-test the company's upcoming generations of products. All three cycling teams won a number of prestigious events during 1999. Trek's most popular models sold at low-end and midrange price points between $250 and $1,200.

Intrepid's Gary Fisher and Klein lines of mountain bikes included a greater proportion of high-end models than its Trek line. The company acquired the Gary Fisher brand in 1993 to help it expand its dealer network further into communities that already carried Trek. Intrepid could offer a new dealer the ability to carry Gary Fisher models without offending its existing Trek dealers. Gary Fisher was a premier brand because of the line's award-winning design and performance and because of the notoriety of the company's founder and namesake. Gary Fisher was an accomplished road racer during the 1960s and 1970s who created the first mountain bike in 1974. In 1994 *Smithsonian Magazine* proclaimed Gary Fisher the "Founding Father of Mountain Bikes." Gary Fisher's mountain bike racing teams were co-sponsored with Saab and boasted a number of Olympic gold medal winners among its members. Gary Fisher models were priced comparably to Trek models although Gary Fisher had fewer low-end models between $250 and $500 than Trek.

While Fisher had fewer low-end models than Trek, Klein was Intrepid's high-end mountain bike brand, with prices beginning at over $1,200. Klein Bicycles began in

---

[5]Taken from "Reinventing the Wheel: A Brief History of the Trek Bicycle Corporation," company document.

1974 as an official MIT Innovation Center project when founder Gary Klein, a competition road racer, was enrolled in the university as an engineering graduate student. Gary Klein, along with three of his classmates and their MIT engineering professor, used a $20,000 grant from the university to develop one of the first aluminum-frame bicycles. The students and their professor built a number of prototypes in 1974 and displayed their refined bikes at an international cycle show in 1975. Upon graduation from MIT, Gary and one of the three classmates moved the operation from MIT to Gary's hometown of Chehalis, Washington, where the company's bicycles were still produced in 2000.

Klein Bicycles was known for its technological innovation and craftsmanship. The company was relatively weak in the midrange category but was among the leaders in high-end mountain bikes. Each Klein bicycle was built by hand, and every component was tested under a stringent quality control process. Klein used only certified aerospace-grade aluminum and custom-made, proprietary production equipment to assemble frames at alignment tolerances as exacting as ±.0002 inches. Klein also produced carbon composite frames that were used on some of its four basic road-racing and mountain bike series, which came in multiple configurations. All Klein mountain bike models were available with either hardtail frames or full-suspension systems. Klein Bicycles and Cadillac jointly sponsored the Team Catera racing team, which included such well-known cyclists as Golden Brainard, the fourth highest ranked American in world rankings.

Specialized Bicycles

Specialized Bicycles was a private firm founded by Mike Sinyard in 1974 in Morgan Hill, California, that got its start importing Italian-made bicycle components. In 1981 the company launched the first mass-produced mountain bike—the Stumpjumper (the original model is at the Smithsonian Institution in Washington, D.C.). Specialized also created the first professional mountain bike racing team in 1983, which Mountain Dew began sponsoring in 1996. The company also created and sponsored the Cactus Cup race series that allowed amateurs to race in events similar to professional races but at a level nonthreatening enough for first-time racers to have plenty of fun. During 1998 and 1999 Specialized Cactus Cup races were held in Canada, France, Japan, Brazil, and various locations throughout the United States.

Specialized's slogan was "Innovate or die," and it had been recognized for developing a number of technologically advanced bicycle materials and components used in the production of its mountain bikes. In 1988 Specialized's Stumpjumper Epic became the first mountain bike with a carbon-fiber frame, and in 1989 the company introduced the first composite-material bicycle wheel through a joint venture with DuPont. In 1990 Specialized began producing frames from its M2 metal matrix composite material of aluminum, silicon, copper, and magnesium. The company introduced advanced full-suspension bikes in 1993, and added an improved M4 metal matrix composite frame material in 1998. Specialized also produced a number of models that were equipped with aluminum frames. Other noteworthy innovations developed by Specialized included its S-works wheel sets, which a German university rated the industry's best in terms of rigidity and weight, and its Ground Control suspension systems, which helped keep the rear wheel on the ground even under bumpy surface conditions.

Specialized management believed that its culture was a key contributor to its success in designing innovative new mountain bikes. The company made a practice of hiring avid cyclists as engineers and managers and invited all of its employees along on its daily Specialized Lunch Rides. Each day Specialized employees at its Morgan Hill plant biked over off-road trails and winding roads with the latest Specialized equipment to relieve stress and test the company's newest products. After an hour or so of riding, the employees would take quick showers and head back to their desks to eat a sandwich and return to their work. The company also created a special S-Works R&D team that was allowed to build "dream bikes" without regard to a budget. Mike Sinyard said that the company had "never been satisfied with existing bicycle technology and S-Works allows us to push the edges of the design envelope. Once we perfect new designs for S-Works bikes we begin seeking ways to make those innovations trickle down to consumer price points, which allows us to offer elite design techniques at non-elite prices."[6]

Specialized also believed that its dealers should be knowledgeable about the latest technological innovations in the bicycle industry. The company's Specialized University offered the company's 5,000 dealers in 35 countries courses on the latest frame materials, frame design geometries, and other technological innovations. Specialized University also offered courses that educated dealers and their staffs on proper bicycle sizing and fitting and repair techniques. Specialized dealers carried a full line of 55 models of bicycles that each came in multiple configurations. Specialized's basic classes of bicycles included a BMX line; a juvenile line; two road bike models; and six low-end, midrange, and high-end mountain bike lines.

Giant Global Group

Giant, which began as a small Taiwanese exporter of bicycles in 1972, was the world's largest bicycle exporter in 1999, with 93 percent of its bicycles sold outside of Taiwan. In 1999 Giant bicycles were sold in 60 countries by more than 10,000 retail dealers across seven continents. The company's 1999 revenues were estimated at approximately $400 million. Giant's growth was made possible in large part by an early alliance with Schwinn, which gave Giant the market savvy and production know-how it needed to be a major competitive force in the industry.

Schwinn began importing a small quantity of bikes from Giant in 1978 when it began looking for a source of low-cost bicycles. Schwinn's sourcing from Giant increased in 1981 when Schwinn's Chicago plant went on strike. Deciding against negotiating a settlement with labor, Schwinn's management closed the plant and moved all its engineers and equipment to Giant's factory in Taiwan. As part of the deal with Giant, Schwinn management handed over everything—technology, engineering, volume—that Giant needed to become a dominant bikemaker. In return Schwinn imported the bikes and marketed them under the Schwinn name. By 1984, Giant was shipping 700,000 bicycles to Schwinn, representing 70 percent of the contract manufacturer's sales. By 1987, Giant was selling its own brand-name bikes in Europe and the United States. To gain market share, Giant told dealers its bikes were Schwinn clones and 10 to 15 percent cheaper. Giant also hired several Schwinn executives to help build up its U.S. distribution capabilities.

Giant's move to establish a brand name and move away from contract manufacturing continued throughout the 1990s, with the company dedicating 2 percent of its annual revenues to research and development and hiring 65 designers to develop features

---

[6]Specialized press release, www.specialized.com.

and performance that cycling enthusiasts demanded. Giant's R&D efforts paid off in the late 1990s as its image in the industry soared and it won numerous awards for design innovation. The company's MCR carbon composite bicycle was named the "Best New Product of 1998" by *Business Week,* and in 1999 its XtC SE1 mountain bike was named *Mountain Biking* magazine's "Bike of the Year." In praising Giant's race-ready mountain bike, the magazine's associate editor commented "I couldn't say enough great things about this bike. First and foremost, we were drawn to every aspect of the bike. A quick glance told us this bike was well thought out and was definitely going to be a contender."[7]

Giant began a racing program to promote the company's name among avid cyclists and signed top mountain bike racers to endorse the company's products. In 1998 the company's race teams were ranked numbers two and three worldwide in road racing, numbers three and four in cross-country mountain bike racing, and numbers two and three in downhill racing. Giant also entered into an agreement with outdoor retailer Eddie Bauer to build special edition bicycles that would be sold by Giant retailers. In 1999 Giant's reliance on contract manufacturing had been reduced to 30 percent of its production. Seventy percent of the bikes produced by the company were sold under the Giant brand at prices that typically ranged between $250 and $800 but went as high as $4,000. The company emphasized a "total best value" design and production approach that attempted to match rivals in terms of frame design, component quality, and finish while beating competing brands on price. Giant's 2000 model year product line included 43 models in the mountain bike, road-racing, BMX, hybrid, and juvenile classes.

The company added two plants in China during 1993 and built a plant in the Netherlands in 1997 to keep up with the increased demand for its bicycles. In 1999 the company produced about 2.5 million bicycles with about 1 million produced in Taiwan, 100,000 produced in the Netherlands, and about 1.4 million produced in China. Giant was expected to increase its production in the Netherlands to 400,000 units per year by 2001 and had discussed building production capacity in North America.

Derby Cycle Corporation

Nottingham, England–based Derby Cycle was among the world's largest designers, manufacturers, and marketers of bicycles, with 1997 sales exceeding $500 million. The company was established in 1986 with the acquisition of Raleigh, Gazelle, and Sturmey-Archer bicycles from Britain's TI Group. Throughout the late 1980s and 1990s Derby continued to add to its portfolio with acquisitions of popular brands like Nishiki, Univega, and Diamondback. The company sold more than 2.1 million bicycles in 1997 and was the largest seller of bicycles in the United Kingdom, the Netherlands, Germany, Canada, Ireland, and South Africa. Derby Bicycle operated manufacturing facilities in the United Kingdom, the Netherlands, Germany, Canada, and the United States. Derby was one of the top five producers of bicycles sold through the U.S. specialty retailer channel of distribution and targeted the low-end market with retail prices ranging from $250 to $500.

Diamondback, Derby Cycle's most popular brand of mountain bike sold in the United States, was among the leading brands in the low-end category and was known for incorporating innovative features at moderate prices. The company's 49 basic models of mountain bikes were equipped with either steel or aluminum frames and various

---

[7]Giant Manufacturing Company press release, www.giant-bicycle.com/aboutgiant/whatsnew.asp.

suspension options that ranged from a rigid frame to full suspension. Diamondback also offered bikes in the youth, BMX, hybrid, road-racer, cruiser, and fitness equipment segments. Diamondback and other Derby brands had lost some dealer orders in 1999 and 2000 because of consistently poor dealer service.

CANNONDALE'S HISTORY AND BACKGROUND

Joseph Montgomery, who grew up on an Ohio peach farm and later dropped out of college three times, began Cannondale Corporation in 1971 after having abandoned careers as a charter boat captain and a securities analyst. Joe Montgomery's first career change occurred after his charter boat sank under his command in shark-infested waters. Montgomery took a less life-threatening but more mundane position as a securities analyst in 1964, but after seven years on Wall Street changed careers again to start Cannondale. Joe Montgomery began Cannondale with the vision of making it the best cycling company in the world. His vision inspired 10 principles that made up the Cannondale philosophy:

1. We care about each other, our shareholders, our customers, and our vendors.
2. We produce a stream of innovative, quality products.
3. We devise flexible manufacturing processes that enable us to deliver those innovative, quality products to the market quickly and then back them with excellent customer service.
4. We limit our distribution to the best specialty retailers in the world.
5. We stay lean, remain competitive and entrepreneurial.
6. We put 90 percent of our profits back into the company to underwrite future growth; the balance we share with all of our employees.
7. We promote from within whenever possible.
8. We concentrate on detail, because the last 5 percent is often the difference between success and failure.
9. We continuously improve everything.
10. We govern our every deed by what is "just and right."

As of 2000 Joseph Montgomery had been Cannondale's only chairperson, president, and chief executive officer. The birth and early history of Cannondale was aptly captured in a 1986 article in *New England Business,* excerpted below.

> "I always wanted to start my own business," says the 46-year-old [Joe] Montgomery; he began the search for opportunities when he started working on Wall Street as an analyst in the 1960s for companies such as Prudential-Bache. His employers were looking for fast-track companies in leisure-time industries such as snowmobiles, but he was looking for less obvious opportunities.
>
> "The bike industry was a sleepy industry," Montgomery said. "The industry had old ideas and designs. Anyone who was really aggressive and designed a functional, quality product could make a go. It was a field ripe for new ideas." In 1972 he had one—a mini-trailer that bike campers could use to tow their gear. He quit his job and on the strength of a contract with a distributor, got a $60,000 loan to finance production.
>
> Sales for the trailer started soft and, working in improvised company offices above a pickle store in Cannondale, Conn., he developed bicycle accessories to expand the line. The timing was good. The 1973 Arab fuel embargo hit, sparking a two-year bike boom, and his sales leapt ahead to $2.3 million by 1974. Then, in 1975, recession hit and the boom

ended. The speed and degree of the drop in bike sales was terrifying. In 1974, 14.1 million units sold. In 1975, 7 million sold. Bike shops all over America closed.

"It was a big washout. A lot of people who were tired of some rat race and figured they'd open a bike shop went under. Our sales were cut in half, and we were stuck with $250,000 in bad debts." Having just gotten started, he wasn't about to file for bankruptcy protection.

"The worst thing you can do in this situation is put your head in the sand. You've got to call the guy and say, 'Look, I know what I owe. Here's my business plan, my cash flow analysis. Not only will I pay you what I owe you, I'll continue to buy from you.'"

His creditors liked his approach, and their cooperation helped the company out of trouble. But Montgomery acknowledges it was a sweat. "Very scary," he said. "Very scary."

Through the 1970s and early 80s, Cannondale quietly achieved steady annual sales at around $8 million and became known for an expanding line of quality bike camping equipment. Montgomery wanted to make a bicycle, though. In 1982, he got a letter from a 25-year-old engineer named David Graham, who felt he was stagnating in the Electric Boat facility in Groton, Conn.

"David wrote, 'I'm an engineer and I want to build an aluminum bike,'" Montgomery remembered. "We'd been working on bikes way back in the 70s, and I was pretty sure I wanted to make an aluminum one. Graham took a 50 percent pay cut to come here."

The first Cannondale aluminum bike came out in 1983. It hadn't been easy. There had been production problems: All the fabrication equipment for the aluminum frame had to be custom designed, and they had trouble getting components that would fit the unusually fat tubing. (Like almost all bike manufacturers, Cannondale makes practically nothing on their own bike except the frame. Gears, shifters, and other components are obtained from outside suppliers. Most of these are from the Far East, which somewhat dilutes current company efforts to position itself as an "American-made" bike.)

Finally, the bike hit dealers' floors. It was weird-looking, expensive at $600, and had a number of bugs still to be worked out. But the equipment nuts, the "spoke sniffers" who permeate the bicycling world and are ever on the lookout for something new, embraced it.

For them, the prime attractions were the technical advantages of aluminum. Aluminum, of course, is light, and in premium bikes, light weight is a vital sales point. Yet Cannondale bikes are not appreciably lighter than comparable steel frame bikes, because Graham took advantage of aluminum and used more of it, making the frame tubing thicker and making the bike structurally stiffer.

Ted Constantino, editor of Bicycle Guide, a Boston-based consumer specialty magazine, explains that a stiff frame without any "give" makes for a more efficient bike. "There's a feeling you get on a Cannondale that every kilowatt of energy you put into the pedal comes out the rear wheel."

As important to sales as what the frame does is its distinctive look. "It doesn't hurt," Montgomery ingenuously acknowledges. "If I'm a spoke sniffer, I am proud you can see that I ride something different."

. . . Cannondale as an American company is bucking prevailing trends in the bike industry. The majority of premium bikes sold in the United States are made in the Far East. European and American companies used to dominate until the mid-70s, when the now familiar one-two punch of high quality and low price from Japan hit the market. During the next ten years, old names such as Raleigh, Motobecane, and Puch ran into deep trouble.

But Cannondale saw sales explode right out to the gate; from 1983 to 1985 it grew at a 30 percent annual rate. They expanded their line from one model to 15. In 1984, Cannondale netted a lucrative contract making private-label bikes for L. L. Bean. Market demand and publicity within the industry helped it to expand its dealer network through North America, and then to Europe. It found itself continually expanding its headquarters in Georgetown, which now employs 80, and its production facility in Bedford, Penn., which now employs 175.

. . . If not the largest, it certainly may be the most talked about bike company. In that great consumer undercurrent of hearsay that can make or break a product, Cannondale has been designated as the "best" bike around. That means it's trendy. Trendy is transitory, and Montgomery knows he'll have to work hard to get beyond it. For now, though, trendy is OK. Trendy is something Joe Montgomery can take to the bank.[8]

CANNONDALE IN 2000

In 2000 Cannondale was a leading manufacturer and marketer of high-performance bicycles and high-performance bicycle components, with an estimated 20 percent share of the U.S. high-performance bicycle market. The company also provided its dealers with a full line of bicycle components, accessories, and men's and women's cycling apparel. The company had also set a spring 2000 launch date for its MX400 motocross motorcycle. Even though Cannondale management expected the MX400 to be an important contributor to its revenue growth in future years, the company's main business was high-performance bicycles. Cannondale was a leader in the use of lightweight aluminum as a material for bicycle frames and was the only bicycle manufacturer not to build bicycles from steel. With the exception of its carbon-fiber Raven model, all of Cannondale's bicycle models offered for the 2000 model year were constructed with hand-welded aluminum frames. The company's bicycles, marketed under the Cannondale brand name and carrying its "Handmade in the USA" logo, were sold through specialty bicycle retailers in the United States and in more than 60 other countries.

Cannondale's corporate headquarters was located in Georgetown, Connecticut, and its manufacturing facilities for bicycles, motorcycles, bicycle components, accessories, and clothing located in Bedford, Pennsylvania. At the end of July 1999, Cannondale employed a total of 779 full-time workers in the United States, 115 in its European subsidiary, 16 in its Japanese subsidiary, and 6 in its Cannondale Australia subsidiary.

Cannondale's Business Strategy

Cannondale's overall business strategy had a significant vertical integration component. The company manufactured its own frames in the United States, whereas most of its competitors imported their frames from Asia. Cannondale was one of the first companies to concentrate on aluminum frames and enjoyed the premier position in this category, as bicyclists continued to gravitate toward lighter, sturdier high-performance bicycles. In addition, Cannondale developed a proprietary component line under the Cannondale Original Design Application (CODA) brand that was used in a growing portion of its product mix and was becoming more important in the aftermarket. With components such as handlebars, brakes, cranks, and derailleurs comprising a significant portion of a bike's value, Cannondale hoped to gain a competitive advantage over manufacturers who relied on outside component suppliers such as Shimano, SunTour, and Campionolo.

Product Innovation   Cannondale's products were designed for cyclists who wanted high-performance, high-quality bicycles. It differentiated its bicycles through technological innovations that made its bicycles lighter, stronger, faster, and more comfortable than those of rivals. The company had an ongoing commitment to R&D and had continued to expand and develop its aluminum bicycle line with a series of innovations, focusing on proprietary frame designs, suspension systems, and components.

---

[8]R. E. Charm, "Like the Company's Sales, Aluminum Bike of Cannondale Stands Out from the Pack," *New England Business* 8, no. 3 (November 3, 1986), p. 41.

Each new frame or component innovation went through a two-month battery of tests in the company's $1 million-plus Q-Lab that included fatigue testing, impact testing, finite element analysis, computerized field testing, and brittle-coat testing. Cannondale's know-how and manufacturing skills enabled the company to be a first-mover and trendsetter. Its original product, the Bugger bicycle trailer, was an industry first that pioneered an entire product category. Cannondale produced the first-ever large-diameter, aluminum-tube bicycles in 1983. It introduced its first mountain bike in 1984. In 1990, the company led the industry in introducing suspension systems in bicycles and in 1996 created a lightweight thermoplastic carbon-skin frame that was bonded to a magnesium spine for its new Raven mountain bike. In 2000 the second-generation Raven frame was honored as one of the "Best of What's New" products by *Popular Science*. Joe Montgomery described his philosophy toward innovation: "We approach everything we do—and I mean everything—with an eye toward innovation. And to a large extent, it's the innovations we've developed on the design and manufacturing side that allow us to continually bring these exciting new products to market."[9] Exhibit 5 shows a time line of Cannondale's growth and key innovations since 1971.

Manufacturing   The centerpiece of Cannondale's manufacturing strategy was its flexible manufacturing system. The strengths of the system included reduced production time, simultaneous production of various models and small batch sizes without high tooling changeover costs. A patented process employed lasers and other devices to cut the uniquely configured joints of various bicycle models without individual setup or changeover. Patented self-fixturing joint designs and hold devices allowed the parts to interlock without special tools as they were readied for welding. The manufacturing system enabled the cost-effective production of a wide product line and a broad range of models in a single day in order to respond to consumer demands. Cannondale's proprietary manufacturing system had allowed the company to reduce the time to completed bike from 17 days to only 3. Further efficiencies in the development process for other parts were realized through a new prototyping and tooling center with computer-aided design and manufacturing (CAD/CAM) technology. The company was committed to maintaining its competitive position by supporting research into further improvements in its manufacturing process and drastically reducing the time required to design and produce new bike models.

Cannondale's CAD/CAM system, which automatically calculated specific tube lengths, and its computer-guided laser tube cutters allowed the company to offer custom-fitted bicycles. The company had built custom-fitted bikes since 1994 for its professional racing staff, and began to offer consumers in Japan, Europe, Australia, Canada, and the United States custom-fitted bikes in 1999. Cannondale was expected to introduce custom fitting in the remainder of the 60-plus international markets where its bicycles were sold in 2000. Cannondale charged a $400 custom fitting fee and could deliver the custom-made bike to the consumer within six weeks.

Cannondale considered its domestic manufacturing base a key competitive advantage. Whereas the majority of bike companies purchased most, if not all, of their models from huge Far Eastern manufacturers, Cannondale made its bike frames in Pennsylvania. As Montgomery explained, "When you go to Asia to get a new frame design manufactured, the manufacturer makes three bikes for each one you order; one for you, one to sell to another bike company, and one to sell under their own brand

---

[9]M. Sloane, "Cannondale: A Company Built on Innovation," *The Journal of Competitive Cycling* 1 (1995), pp. 7–10.

exhibit 5 25 Years of Cannondale Innovations

1971
Joe Montgomery starts Cannondale at the Cannondale train station in Wilton, Connecticut. Cannondale gets its name when employee Peter Meyers, ordering the company's first telephone from a pay phone at the station, is asked how the new company should be listed. Unsure of what to say, Peter notices the train station's sign and says, "Cannondale."

1972
The Bugger, the world's first bicycle-towed trailer, is introduced by Cannondale.

1974
The Toot seat bag, with a revolutionary flexible internal liner, helps Cannondale on its way to becoming the industry's leading bag manufacturer.

1977
Cannondale's Bedford, Pennsylvania, factory opens in a refurbished truck terminal. Total work force: 7.

1983
The ST500 — Cannondale's first bicycle, and the world's first affordable aluminum bike with large-diameter tubes — is introduced. Despite widespread industry skepticism, sales are strong.

1984
Cannondale produces its first mountain bike, the SM500, and its first road racing bike, the SR900.

1988
Cannondale bicycles make their Olympic debut at the Summer Games in Seoul, South Korea.

1989
Cannondale Europe is established in the Netherlands. European response to American-made Cannondales is enthusiastic, and sales quickly grow to 35% of total revenues.

1990
Patented Seat Cleat seat bag attachment system is introduced, immediately obsoleting all other mounting systems.

1991
Cannondale begins operations in Japan. The company ignores conventional wisdom by establishing a subsidiary and bypassing Japanese trading companies. Despite widespread industry skepticism, sales are strong.

2000
Cannondale's full-suspension Jekyll model named *Mountain Biking's* "Bike of the Year."

1999
Cannondale's first motorcycle named *Dirt Rider's* "Bike of the year."

1999
Cannondale named as one of the "Top 12 Road Bikes of All Time" by *Cycle Sport*.

1999
Cannondale introduces its "Custom Cannondale" fitting program that allows cyclists to order custom fitted bikes with more than 8 million possible combinations.

1999
Cannondale's Raven model equipped with a HeadShok Lefty forkset is chosen as one of *Popular Science's* "Best of What's New" awards.

1997
Cannondale introduces an aluminum full-suspension off-road wheel chair for disabled athletes.

1998
Cannondale is selected by Tommy Hilfinger to produce Hilfinger Sport special edition bicycle.

1996
Super V Active and Super V DH Active full-suspension models introduced.

1996
Cannondale introduces the light-as-titanium CAAD3 mountain bike and Slice monocuque carbon fiber road bike.

1994
C-Style apparel introduced, pioneering the move towards performance cycling garments made with natural fabrics and comfortable, relaxed fit.

1995
Silk Road suspension road bike — another industry first — debuts.

1994
Super V named one of the year's best products by *Business Week* magazine., and wins Design and Engineering Award from *Popular Mechanics* magazine.

1994
Volvo/Cannondale Mountain Bike Racing Team riders win seven World Championship medals (including four gold) and one National Championship

name. By the time your new bike finally makes it into bike shops, the market is flooded with similar designs." He went on to describe the advantage of operating his own factories:

> First off, our factories don't have other customers ahead of us in line. When we make an improvement, or add a model, the reaction is instantaneous. Also, our proprietary designs remain proprietary. And of course, our product doesn't spend an extra six months on the water or stuck in customs, before finally becoming available to customers.[10]

Even though Cannondale's U.S.-based manufacturing facilities were a valuable competitive resource, various equipment problems in its Bedford, Pennsylvania, plant had resulted in unfilled dealer orders during the fall of 1999 and had delayed the introduction of some 2000 models.

Purchasing   Aluminum tubing was the primary material used to manufacture bicycles. Cannondale entered into purchasing agreements with various aluminum suppliers to ensure favorable pricing and delivery terms and certain technical assistance, but believed that termination of its contracts would not have a significant impact on its costs because of aluminum's wide availability. Most of its bicycle components were purchased from Japanese, Taiwanese, and U.S. original equipment manufacturers (OEMs). Its largest component supplier was Shimano, which was the source of approximately 19 percent of total inventory purchases in 1999. Cannondale concentrated buying power among fewer suppliers, which allowed the company to secure higher-volume purchase discounts.

Marketing   The goal of Cannondale's sales and marketing program was to establish the company as the leading high-performance bicycle brand in the specialty bicycle retail channel. The marketing effort focused on promotion of the firm's product innovation, performance, and quality leadership; publicity generated from the Volvo/Cannondale mountain bike racing team; and a media campaign designed to attract consumers to specialty bicycle retailers. Cannondale also maintained an innovative Web site (www.cannondale.com) that averaged more than 25 million hits each month.

Promotion   In 1994, Cannondale formed the Volvo/Cannondale racing team. The team generated considerable publicity in both the cycling press and the general press and through television coverage. Cannondale leveraged the success of its racing team by using photo images of the athletes in print media, point-of-sale literature, banners, product packaging, and product catalogs. Since its inception in 1994, the Volvo/Cannondale team had won four World Championships, six World Cup titles, 28 top finishes in World Cup events, nine National Championships, two Pan Am Games gold medals, and a silver medal at the 1996 Summer Olympic Games in Atlanta, Georgia. In addition, Cannondale supported racing teams in other cycling areas, such as its road-racing team that was cosponsored with Saeco, an Italian firm that was the world's largest manufacturer of espresso machines and its SoBe/HeadShok grassroots squad that provided technical assistance to team riders and held instructional clinics for Cannondale retailers and their staff. SoBe, the leading maker of wellness beverages, also agreed to cosponsor Cannondale's planned MX400 motocross racing team.

Cannondale's print advertising focused on magazines for cycling enthusiasts and general lifestyle magazines to reach upscale adults with an interest in outdoor and leisure activities. In addition, Cannondale entered into a licensing agreement with Tommy Hilfiger in 1998 to produce a special Hilfiger Sport mountain bike that would

---

[10]Ibid.

be sold by Cannondale retailers. Cannondale management believed that the new Hilfiger bikes would draw customers who normally wouldn't shop in a bicycle store.

Sales and Distribution   Cannondale's distribution strategy was to sell its bicycles through specialty bicycle retailers who it believed could provide knowledgeable sales assistance regarding the technical and performance characteristics of its products and offer an ongoing commitment to service. Cannondale bicycles were not available through mass merchandisers, which generally carried lower-priced products and did not have the expertise to sell and support high-performance bikes. The company had not awarded exclusive rights to retailers in any territory. In 2000 the company sold its bicycles through 1,150 specialty retailer locations in the United States and Canada. Cannondale accessories were carried by an additional 500 retail locations in the United States and Canada. Before establishing a new dealer, the company considered such factors as market density in terms of competition, population, and demographics; ability of the retailer to optimize market penetration; commitment to service and the high-performance segment of the market; and dealer creditworthiness.

Research and Development   Cannondale's product development strategy was directed at continually making bicycles lighter, stronger, faster, and more comfortable. Its Volvo/Cannondale mountain bike racing team was closely tied to its R&D process, thus allowing regular testing of both prototypes and finished production models. Cannondale's vice president of R&D explained the company's view of the R&D function and team sponsorships as follows: "Most bike companies view racing as a marketing tool, and while we enjoy the exposure the team provides, for us it's primarily a research and development tool. That's why we continue to support racing so aggressively. We make high-end, high-performance bicycles and we use the athletes' feedback to bring fresh innovations to our bikes. That's why we partially fund the team from our R&D budget, and why you'll always find more Cannondale engineers than marketing people at the races."[11] This collaboration, combined with the racing experience of its engineering staff, produced revisions, new designs, and new product ideas. The company had spent more than $20 million on research and development between 1997 and 1999 and held 35 U.S. patents related to various products, processes, and designs.

Cannondale had developed several proprietary suspension systems and enhancements. Its HeadShok incorporated the suspension and steering mechanisms into one unit built into the head tube of the bicycle. This design provided more accurate steering control than other front-suspension models and also allowed easy adjustability while riding. Cannondale's HeadShok line included 14 models in 2000 and was highlighted by its new Lefty fork, which featured a telescoping blade that reduced weight while delivering 100 millimeters of travel. The Lefty had a distinctive look because of its single fork, which extended down the left side of the bicycle's front wheel.

To ensure structural integrity of its designs, an experimental stress and analysis laboratory was used to collect data on stresses placed on products during actual riding conditions. This information was analyzed and incorporated into the design of new products through its computer-aided design system. In addition, stress analysis testing was conducted during production to verify conformance to design specifications.

International Operations   Cannondale entered the international market in 1989 when it established a European subsidiary, Cannondale Europe, in the Netherlands. Although Cannondale Europe assembled bikes, using imported parts and frames from Cannondale's U.S. facility, it was primarily a selling and distribution organization

---

[11]Cannondale press release, www.cannondale.com/bikepres/19981204.html.

exhibit 6   Selected Financial Data for Cannondale Corporation, by Geographic Area, 1997–99 (In Millions)

	1999	1998	1997
Net sales			
United States	$ 72,413	$ 75,193	$ 80,542
Germany	26,639	25,382	23,569
Other European countries	59,008	52,603	43,478
All other countries	18,759	18,318	14,907
	$176,819	$171,496	$162,496
Identifiable assets			
United States	$ 54,798	$ 37,937	$ 21,905
Netherlands	2,886	3,141	2,949
All other countries	449	380	522
	$ 58,133	$ 41,458	$ 25,376

Source: Cannondale Corporation 1999 10-K.

that reached all of Western Europe directly and served Eastern Europe through distributors. The company sold its bicycles and accessories directly to approximately 1,400 dealers in Austria, Belgium, Denmark, Finland, Germany, Italy, Ireland, Luxembourg, the Netherlands, Norway, Spain, Sweden, Switzerland, and the United Kingdom. Sales growth in Europe, where cycling was second only to soccer in popularity among sports, had averaged a compound growth rate of 12.4 percent between 1993 and 1999.

Cannondale Japan was established in 1992. This subsidiary imported fully assembled bikes and was primarily a selling organization. The company sold bicycles and accessories directly to 300 retailers in Japan and sold accessories only to an additional 27 Japanese retailers. Cannondale's penetration of the Japanese market was estimated to be below 1 percent.

Cannondale Australia was established in 1996 when Cannondale purchased the assets of Beaushan Trading Party Limited. Cannondale's Australian subsidiary imported fully assembled bicycles and a full line of accessories and sold them in Australia and New Zealand to approximately 200 retailers. Exhibit 6 presents Cannondale's net sales contribution and value of identifiable assets by geographic area.

Cannondale's Product Line

Bicycles   In 2000, Cannondale offered 71 models of bicycles, all of which except its carbon-fiber Raven model featured aluminum frames. Cannondale's full-suspension mountain bikes (Super V Raven, Super V, Freeride, and Jekyll) featured front and rear suspension to allow for greater control and comfort at high speeds without sacrificing light frame weight. Cannondale's new Jekyll models included a distinctly different frame design that allowed the geometry of the bike to be customized to the rider's preference by dialing in the head angle and the bottom bracket height. The Jekyll also used the company's new HeadShok Lefty fork that had three times the torsional stiffness of other top forks and weighed just 3.7 pounds. The Jekyll was chosen as *Mountain Biking* magazine's 2000 "Bike of the Year" in its March 2000 issue.

Cannondale's Raven mountain bike was equally innovative. The Raven's frame was made from a carbon composite skin that was stretched over a magnesium spine. The bare frame weighed only 4.7 pounds yet was as rigid as Cannondale's aluminum-frame bicycles. The bike was equipped with Cannondale's HeadShok Lefty fork set and CODA hubs, crank, pedals, saddle, and brakes. The Raven was listed among the four most innovative products, discoveries, or technologies of 1999 by *Popular Science.* The company also offered a variety of front-suspension and rigid-frame mountain bikes among its product line. Cannondale's Smooth Riding Bicycle (SRB) line of mountain bikes was introduced in 1998 and used a mountain bike frame but was outfitted with a wider saddle and tires that were suitable for on-road or off-road use. The SRB also had a more upright riding position that made casual riding more comfortable than a typical mountain bike position. In describing the SRB's place in Cannondale's product line, the company's bicycle product manager said, "Not everyone wants to thrash singletrack or dice it up in the pelotron. But just because a customer wants a more recreational-style bike doesn't mean they want it to be heavy or of poor quality."[12]

Cannondale offered a number of hybrid and comfort bikes to appeal to the cyclist who wanted to cruise around town, get aerobic exercise, commute to work, or occasionally ride off-road trails. Cannondale's comfort bikes were available in full-suspension, front-suspension, or rigid-frame models. Hybrid models were equipped with either front-suspension or rigid frames. Cannondale offered cyclocross bikes for competition in mixed off-road and obstacle races and multisport bikes designed for triathlon and duathlon events.

Cannondale's high-performance road-racing bikes had steep frame angles and a short wheelbase for nimble handling and were equipped with either a front-suspension or rigid frame. In 1999 Cannondale was selected as one of the "Top 12 Road Bikes of All Time" by *Cycle Sport,* a magazine devoted to European road racing. The company's touring bikes included many of the performance features of its other models, but with a longer wheelbase that provided stability when riders were carrying additional gear for camping and touring. Cannondale's flexible manufacturing techniques allowed for small production runs of specialty bicycles such as tandem bikes, which were produced in both mountain bike and road-racing models. Cannondale's product line by category for 2000 is shown in Exhibit 7.

Bicycle Accessories   The accessory line helped the company to capitalize more fully on its distribution channels' capability and, at the same time, build brand-name recognition. As with bicycles, Cannondale sought to differentiate its accessories through innovation.

- *Packs and bags*—Cannondale offered a variety of bags and panniers (bags mounted on the sides of the wheels for touring): mountain bike bags, lightweight, moderate-capacity road bike bags; and large capacity touring bags. The company also made fanny packs, duffels, and a backpack designed specifically for cyclists. The patented Seat Cleat bag attachment was honored by *Industrial Design* magazine for its design innovation.

- *Apparel and footwear*—Cannondale offered a complete line of men's and women's cycling apparel, including such garments as shorts, jerseys, jackets, and skinsuits. The company's line consisted of four lines: Vertex, a high-performance,

---

[12]Ibid.

exhibit 7   Cannondale's Number of Models in Each Bicycle Category for 2000

Bicycle Category	Number of Models
Mountain bikes	
Full suspension	11
Front suspension	13
Nonsuspended	3
Road bikes	
Front suspension	3
Nonsuspended	15
Multisport recreational	2
Hybrid	7
Comfort	7
Specialty	
Tandem	5
Touring	3
Cyclocross	2
Total	71

Source: Cannondale Corporation 1999 10-K.

competition-level line; HpX, a versatile line of performance-oriented apparel for riders of all abilities; Terra, a more loosely cut line for off-road riding; and a women's Sport line of tailored, form-fitting garments. Some Cannondale apparel was made from its proprietary Micro-C fabric that forced moisture away from the body. Cannondale's Arago clipless compatible mountain biking shoe was very lightweight and contoured to the foot yet stiff enough to efficiently transfer leg energy to the pedal and crank.

- *Components*—Cannondale's proprietary HeadShok front-suspension forks were an important point of differentiation from other bicycle manufacturers, which virtually all used the same brand of forks produced by one of two independent suppliers. Most of the company's HeadShok forks functioned with the bicycle's frame as part of an integrated system, but the 2000 model HeadShok Lefty was a single-legged suspension system that could be mounted on Cannondale frames or other brands of frames. The Lefty had been recognized for its innovative design by such publications as *Design News, Popular Mechanics,* and the *New York Times.*

  In 1994 Cannondale began sales of CODA components—featuring brakes, handlebars, bar-ends, seat binders, grips, cranksets, and hubs—and began using these components on certain models of its bikes. The company focused its R&D efforts on developing products superior to or more cost-effective than those available from other parts manufacturers. Cannondale's proprietary components like its CODA Competition suspension seatpost not only helped differentiate the company's bikes from brands that used similar components but also provided an additional source of revenue from aftermarket retail sales.

- *Other accessories*—Cannondale's other accessories included tools, pumps, water bottles, and bicycle trailers manufactured by third parties and sold under the Cannondale brand name.

Cannondale's Diversification into Motorcycles

In February 1998 Cannondale founder and CEO Joe Montgomery announced that the company would transfer its bicycle frame design and production skills to the off-road motorcycle industry. Cannondale said that it would bring at least three design innovations to the $700 million market for dirt bikes. Cannondale's new motorcycle would have a radical new engine design, include a unique single-pivot swingarm rear suspension, and be constructed of large-diameter aluminum tubing that would provide greater frame stiffness and lighter weight than a steel frame. Many motorcycle industry observers believed that Cannondale could deliver on its promise to bring new innovations to the industry. The publisher of *Motocross Action Magazine* cautioned skeptics, "Don't discount the bicycle manufacturer's ability to compete in the motorcycle world. Today's mountain bikes far exceed motorcycles in the use of creative metallurgy, CAD-CAM frame design, innovative suspension systems, in the case of Cannondale, an American production facility that can easily produce a high-end product."[13]

MX400 engine innovations included a liquid-cooled, reversed cylinder head, and innovative air intake design, an electric starter, and fuel injection. Cannondale designers said that the reverse cylinder head allowed the engine to have a more upright placement and a lower center of gravity that would aid in the motorcycle's off-road handling. Also, the reverse head allowed the air intake to face the front of the bike and the exhaust to face the rear, away from the water-cooled engine's radiator. The MX400's forward air intake was built into the steering head of the motorcycle's frame and helped supply a flow of debris-free cool air needed for greater power output and a wider powerband. The long air intake also improved low-speed throttle response. The electric starter feature was already available on almost all street bikes but was not usually found on dirt bikes. Cannondale management believed that the electric starter would be a convenience feature that motocrossers would appreciate—starting a dirt bike often took a considerable amount of strenuous kicking because of the very high compression single-cylinder engine designs. The MX400's fuel injection system that provided better throttle response and less maintenance than a carburetor was expected to take much of the engine-failure-related frustration out of motocross.

The MX400's use of fuel injection also allowed Cannondale's design team to create a rear suspension where the shock absorber was positioned at the optimal angle because there was no carburetor blocking the way. The rear suspension was a unique single-pivot linkless design that required less maintenance and provided greater rigidity than traditional motorcycle rear-suspension systems. The entire MX400 frame was built from Cannondale's trademark large-diameter stiff aluminum tubing and was designed to keep the motorcycle's center of gravity low. Commenting on the company's use of large-diameter aluminum tubing and a single-pivot swingarm, Cannondale's director of marketing said, "Flex resistance is every bit as critical to the performance of a motorcycle frame as it is to the performance of a bicycle frame. Whether it's a bicycle or a motorcycle, you want to minimize side-to-side flex in order to preserve steering precision and stability. Wimpy frames and rear suspensions with long, flexible, linkages can't deliver the kind of handling you need in a high-performance vehicle."[14]

By summer 1998 Cannondale began testing 11 different prototypes of the MX400's new engine and frame. The MX400's final test came in November 1999 when the

---

[13]"Bicycle-Maker Cannondale to Unveil New Motorcycle at Indianapolis Trade Show," PR Newswire, February 12, 1999.

[14]Cannondale press release, www.cannondalemotorcycle.com/press/19980501.html.

motorcycle took first place in its racing debut. The MX400 won two 5-lap races on a small 1.25-mile track located near Cannondale's Beford, Pennsylvania, production facility. The MX400 won both races by more than a minute. The MX400 was named *Dirt Rider* magazine's "Bike of the Year" in late 1999. In reviewing the bike's design innovations, the magazine's editor said, "The MX400 looks more like a high-dollar project from a secret division of a major automobile manufacturer than a first attempt from a leader in the pedal power industry."[15] A *Dirt Action* writer concurred with *Dirt Rider*'s assessment of the new Cannondale motorcycle: "The MX400 contains enough innovation to make everything else with knobbies appear quaintly antique. The other manufacturers are going to hate this bike, because it forces them to move motocross machines into a new technological era."[16] The motorcycle was scheduled for a summer 1999 launch, but unforeseen production problems had delayed the MX400's shipment to Cannondale's network of 159 independent motorcycle dealers in 38 states to the spring of 2000. In January 2000 Cannondale's orders for its new MX400 had exceeded its projected sales forecast by more than 80 percent. Cannondale management planned to capitalize on the initial success of the MX400 with the unveiling of several additional motorcycles at the motorcycle industry's 2000 trade show held in Indianapolis, Indiana.

---

[15]As quoted in Cannondale's 1999 annual report.
[16]Ibid.

case 10 Competition in the Retail Brokerage Industry in 2000

Arthur A. Thompson
The University of Alabama

John E. Gamble
University of South Alabama

The competitive structure of the $14 billion U.S. retail brokerage industry was undergoing significant change in early 2000. Prior to the emergence of the online brokerage segment in 1995–96, investors who wanted to buy or sell shares of common stock had to place an order with one of the nearly 600,000 registered brokers who worked at such traditional full-service brokerages as Merrill Lynch, Paine Webber, and Prudential Securities or limited-service discount brokerage firms like Charles Schwab, Quick & Reilly, and Siebert Securities. During the 1996–98 period, the emergence of online trading via the Internet created a three-tier industry structure—full-service brokers, limited-service discount brokers, and new-breed online brokers.

But mushrooming growth in online trading and the competitive effects of investors moving their accounts to online brokerages to take advantage of low-cost commissions and convenient point-and-click investing quickly put full-service brokers and, to a lesser extent, discount brokers in a strategic bind. If full-service brokers began offering online trading options to their customers to counter the market inroads of online brokerages, they undermined the big stream of commission revenues they had historically earned and risked alienating their thousands of professional brokers who delivered services to clients and whose incomes were tied to the size of the commission fees they generated. However, when longtime industry leader Merrill Lynch announced in June 1999 that it would overhaul its full-price/full-service business model and begin offering its customers online trading at $29.95 per trade, the resistance of full-service and discount brokers to online trading crumbled.

By early 2000 virtually all the leading retail brokerage firms in the United States had either added online trading to the list of services they provided to customers or were planning to do so in a matter of months. Full-service brokerages were scrambling behind the scenes to revise their strategies and business models and trying to reassure their brokers that online trading would not wipe out their jobs. The distinction between traditional brokers and online brokers was fading as the Internet came to be seen as a required distribution channel. Competition among retail brokerages of all types, which

exhibit 1   Estimated Market Shares of the Leading Online Brokerage
Firms, First Quarter 1998–2000 (Based on Daily
Trade Volume)

	Estimated Share of Daily Trades		
Brokerage Firm	**Fourth Quarter, 1999**	**First Quarter, 1999**	**First Quarter, 1998**
Charles Schwab & Co.	22.0%	27.9%	32%
E*Trade	15.3	13.3	12
Waterhouse Securities	13.3	11.7	9
Fidelity (a unit of Fidelity Investments—the leading provider of mutual funds in the United States)	11.4	10.1	8
Datek Online	10.0	10.1	7
Ameritrade	8.8	8.3	6
DLJdirect (a unit of Donaldson Lufkin & Jennrette—a prominent investment banking firm)	3.8	3.8	4
Suretrade/Quick & Reilly (a subsidiary of Fleet Financial—a leading New England bank)	2.0	2.2	4
Morgan Stanley Dean Witter Online (formerly Discover Brokerage Direct)	1.5	2.8	4
All others	11.9	12.6	14
			100%

Source: U.S. Bancorp Piper Jaffray, Inc.

historically had centered on price and breadth of service, was starting to include other areas. And several online brokerage competitors, led by Charles Schwab and E*Trade, were launching a variety of new strategic initiatives to stake out far broader market positions than ever before. Schwab was rapidly transforming itself into a full-service online financial services firm; it could no longer be looked on as a limited-service discount broker with a big stake in online trading. Other brokerages that had pioneered the online trading segment were also branching out to leverage the business potential of the Internet and try to become the financial and investing enterprises of the future.

In addition to adjusting their strategies and business models, many brokerages were rapidly expanding their involvement in electronic communications networks (ECNs), which allowed stock trades to be conducted by computers using software that matched sell orders and buy orders. ECN technology was fast emerging to permit worldwide trading of stocks 24 hours a day, seven days a week. In the past 24 months, eight ECN companies offering automated trading without human intervention had sprung into existence.

The industry landscape was changing fast, and it was unclear how things would play out. Exhibit 1 shows the market shares of the leading online brokerage firms.

INDUSTRY BACKGROUND

"Traditional" Full-Service Brokerages

Historically, full-service brokerage firms had dominated the retail brokerage business, accounting for over 75 percent of investor accounts and assets at retail brokerages. Full-service firms provided an array of financial services to clients—checking accounts;

credit cards; individual retirement accounts (IRAs) and Keogh accounts; retirement planning; mortgages; all kinds of investment advice; and, most recently, online trading services. They functioned as a principal gateway for clients in buying and selling stocks, bonds, mutual funds, options, futures, and other securities. Services were delivered through a network of local offices and highly compensated professional brokers/financial consultants whose job was to woo clients, learn their investment likes and dislikes, provide sound investment advice, execute buy-sell trades, and serve as the principal point of client contact and the marketing of services. Brokers who were good at attracting well-to-do clients, giving attentive personal service, actively helping their clients make a good return on their investments (which generally meant steering them into high-performing stocks, mutual funds, and bonds), and generating a big volume of commission income and fees for the firm typically commanded six-figure compensation packages.

The commissions charged by full-service firms for executing buy-sell orders through a broker varied with the number of shares and with the price of the stock but could exceed $1 per share. For instance, Merrill Lynch's commission schedule resulted in the following charges:

Number of Shares	Price per Share	Commission	Cost as a % of Total Dollar Value of Trade	Cost per Share Traded
100	$ 50	$ 105.00	2.10%	1.05
300	65	236.25	1.21	0.79
500	4	96.74	4.84	0.19
500	10	161.78	3.23	0.32
1,000	114	968.82	0.85	0.97
1,000	20	373.80	1.87	0.37
1,000	30	472.76	1.58	0.47
3,000	114	2,234.96	0.65	0.74
3,000	20	761.25	1.27	0.25

See Exhibit 2 for a comparison of the commissions charged by various types of brokers.

Full-service firms maintained sizable research staffs that generated a stream of ongoing reports on companies, industries, and particular types of investments—all intended to serve as a resource for brokers in furnishing clients with valuable investment information. Full-service firms relied on the proprietary investment information they generated for their clients as a differentiating factor. They believed this information, the full range of services offered, and the personal service rendered by their staffs of professional brokers justified the premium commissions they charged on stock trades.

Starting in the late 1980s and continuing into the late 1990s, the full-service brokerage segment had consolidated through mergers and acquisitions. Going into 2000, the principal full-service brokerage firms were Merrill Lynch, Paine Webber, Morgan Stanley Dean Witter, Salomon Smith Barney, and Prudential Securities, but the segment also included 10 to 15 prominent full-service regional firms such as A. G. Edwards, Robinson-Humphrey, J. C. Bradford, and Edward D. Jones.

Discount Brokerage Firms: The New Breed of Competitors in the 1985–95 Period

In the mid-1980s, Charles Schwab & Co., Quick & Reilly, and several other start-up brokerage enterprises mounted a price-based competitive challenge to the full-service

exhibit 2   Comparative Commissions Charged by Major Types of
Brokerage Firms, Spring 2000

	200 shares at $20	3,000 shares at $10
Full-service brokers		
Average commission	$116.90[a]	$672.59[a]
Discount brokers		
Average commission	66.09[a]	145.05[a]
Online/Internet brokers		
Charles Schwab	29.95	30.00[b]
Morgan Stanley Dean Witter Online	29.95	30.00[c]
DLJdirect	20.00	60.00[d]
E*Trade		74.95
For NYSE-listed stocks	14.95	
For NASDAQ stocks	19.95	
Fidelity	14.95	14.95
Web Street Securities	14.95	Free for stocks listed on the NASDAQ
Waterhouse Securities	12.00	12.00
Datek Online	9.99	9.99
Ameritrade	8.00	8.00
Suretrade	7.95	7.95
Brown & Co.	5.00[e]	5.00[e]

Note: These commission fees are for trades placed at the market price prevailing at the time of execution; orders that specified a limit price often entailed an added fee—equal to $5 at Fidelity, Ameritrade, and Brown & Co.

[a]As of spring 1998.

[b]Schwab's fee structure was a flat $29.95 on all trades up to 1,000 shares or a flat 3 cents per share on all trades of more than 1,000 shares. Active traders were eligible for a special rate of $14.95.

[c]Morgan Stanley Dean Witter Online's fee structure was a flat $29.95 on all trades up to 1,000 shares (telephone orders were $39.95); trades in excess of 1,000 shares were charged at a rate of 3 cents per share for the entire order (telephone orders were 4 cents per share for the entire order).

[d]DLJdirect's fee structure was a flat $20.00 on all trades up to 1,000 shares with a surcharge of 2 cents per share on all shares over 1,000 per trade. Clients with $1 million in DLJdirect accounts paid a fee of $20.00 per trade up to 5,000 shares, with a 2-cent surcharge per share thereafter.

[e]Brown & Co. charged $5.00 on trades up to 5,000 shares; trades greater than 5,000 shares were $5.00 plus a retroactive 1-cent surcharge per share thereafter—hence a trade of 6,000 shares carried a $65 commission; broker-assisted orders were an additional $7.

Source: Credit Suisse First Boston Co. and company advertising and Web sites.

brokers with a limited-service strategy that featured discount commissions. Schwab quickly emerged as the largest and best-known of the discount brokers, using a strategy that stressed heavy media advertising and a comparatively extensive menu of services and product offerings. Because of its reputation and service, Schwab could charge commissions that were only about 30 percent below full-service firms—its fees were the highest of the so-called discount brokers. "Second tier" discount brokers offered much deeper discounts and were content to build their business around serving active traders and bargain hunters and offering minimal services beyond trade execution.

Growing numbers of investors opened accounts with discount brokers during the 1985–95 period. The cut-rate commissions of discount brokers appealed to knowledgeable investors who took very active roles in managing their portfolios, traded stocks frequently (perhaps making a number of trades each business day), and wanted to keep the costs of moving in and out of particular stocks to a bare minimum. Because commissions were a major cost item, active traders were quite interested in locating their accounts at a brokerage that would execute their buy-sell orders at an economical price. Such investors typically used a wide variety of sources to obtain their investment information and were quite willing to forgo the professional advice and proprietary investment research information that were the trademarks of the full-service brokers. The lower fee structure of discount brokers also appealed to economy-minded investors with modest account balances, since lower transactions costs meant they could put a bigger fraction of their limited funds in the investments of their choice.

Discount brokers were able to undercut the commissions of full-service brokers by eliminating the expensive staffs of investment researchers and professional brokers. Trades were executed by salaried customer service representatives who manned phone lines to provide quotes and handle buy-sell orders but who were precluded from giving investment advice. These representatives were hired for their skills in giving courteous, friendly service over the phone and were paid salaries of $28,000 to $40,000 annually; some firms had modest incentive bonuses for representatives based on the number of phone calls they handled daily and the volume of trades they executed. Discount brokers typically provided customers with little, if any, investment information or news updates on companies. A few had a network of local offices to serve walk-in customers in large metropolitan areas, but the majority did business primarily by phone and operated mainly out of a central office with perhaps a few branch offices.

Meanwhile, large national and regional banks, wanting to move a step closer to becoming one-stop financial centers, formed discount brokerage units as an added convenience and service to customers and as a way to attract self-managed IRAs and other retirement plan accounts. Banks with discount brokerage units usually staffed their various banking offices and branches with personnel who were able to answer questions, open brokerage accounts, and in some cases sell mutual funds. However, all stock transactions were normally initiated over the phone with customers speaking directly to brokerage representatives located in a central office. Several mutual fund firms, like Fidelity Investments, also started discount brokerage units, chiefly as a service for the investors who owned some of their mutual funds and to attract new investors. Fidelity already had a number of offices nationwide and toll-free phone lines to serve its mutual fund clients as well as the internal infrastructure to accommodate securities trading; hence, it was simple and inexpensive for Fidelity to piggyback a discount brokerage on top of its existing resource capabilities.

The Emergence of Online Brokerage Firms, 1995–99

Online brokerages began making their appearance in 1995 as use of the Internet exploded and problems of data security were reduced to tolerable levels. By 1998, the online segment had over 60 competitors, versus just 15 in mid-1996. A number of the new entrants were start-up ventures launched by young Internet entrepreneurs—two of the most notable were E*Trade and Web Street Securities. Other online brokerages were established by discount brokerages like Schwab and Quick & Reilly, mutual fund firms like Fidelity, and other financial institutions to provide an additional service for their existing customers and bring in new revenues. The owners and managers of the online trading firms were for the most part convinced that "the Internet was it" and that the future of retail brokerage was in online trading.

The Rapid Growth in Online Trading   While traditional full-service and discount brokerages initially saw online trading as an attraction mainly for computer enthusiasts interested in playing with technology, it didn't take long for online trading to become mainstream. Internet-savvy investors, intrigued with handling their own trades, tracking their portfolios automatically, and saving on commissions, evidenced immediate interest in opening online accounts. Thus, online trading volume climbed swiftly:

Period	Average Number of Trades per Day*
March 1997	95,500
June 1998	228,000
December 1999	807,000

*Estimates provided to case researchers by U.S. Bancorp Piper Jaffray.

A *Fortune* reporter described the appeal of the online trading experience as follows:

> Buying and selling stocks online just feels different, exhilarating even . . . First, it's convenient and private. You can get quotes and research without a broker's assistance, and you don't have a salesman . . . second-guessing your investment decisions. Second, it's fun. The colors, the graphics, the thrill of being connected to the beating heart of capitalism. Place an order for 100 shares of GM, click, and seconds later it's yours . . . Third, your online account comes loaded with useful information: Most online brokers throw in free access to news stories and press releases, stock charts, earnings projections, even analysts' reports.
>
> And of course, it costs just a fraction of the $125 that a mainline discounter would charge . . . And the price keeps getting lower.[1]

A Florida retiree said, "I can take a position in a stock for, say, $30. At other places, the commission could be $300 to $400. I can sell a stock, then buy it back, and I don't feel like it is costing me an arm and a leg."[2] A 45-year-old female software consultant observed, "The costs have gone way down and it's so easy now."[3] An investor who had switched to an online brokerage from a full-service firm commented, "My broker was so nice, but boy, they were robbing me. All he ever did was place my trades. I can do that for myself."[4]

There were approximately 412,000 online accounts in early 1995; a year later there were over 800,000, and going into 2000 the number was over 13 million—1.8 million new online accounts were added in the fourth quarter of 1999, the largest quarterly jump in the history of the online brokerage business. Assets in online accounts rose 35 percent in 1999, to $900 billion. The percentage of all retail brokerage trades placed online jumped from less than 8 percent in 1996 to 17 percent in 1997 to 25 percent in mid-1998, to 37 percent in the first half of 1999, and to an estimated 48 percent in the second half of 1999.

---

[1]David Whitford, "Trade Fast, Trade Cheap," *Fortune,* February 2, 1998, p. 112.

[2]"The New Stock Traders," *Business Week,* May 4, 1998, p. 134.

[3]Ibid., p. 126.

[4]As quoted in "With the World Wide Web, Who Needs Wall Street?" *Business Week*, April 29, 1996, p. 120.

The Value Chain of Online Brokers   Compared to traditional brokers, Internet brokers used a radically different value chain to deliver services to investors. They kept overhead low by having few offices and no commission-based brokers. While they had small staffs of salaried "financial consultants," registered representatives, and trained customer service personnel answering phones for customers who needed to talk to a "live broker," they relied mainly on the Internet for communicating with customers. Typically, online brokers set up a Web site that interested investors could explore—some parts of the site were free and open to everyone; other parts required that the user have an account and were accessible only by entering the account number and password. It was possible to open up an account by filling out a form online (or else request that new account information and forms be sent through the mail). The Web sites of online brokers allowed customers to obtain delayed and real-time stock quotes, place buy-sell orders, get order confirmations, check account balances, track portfolio performance, view historical charts, check mutual fund data and ratings, peruse industry and company news, and gain access to research reports from a variety of investment research specialists. Customers could access their account information at night and on weekends, and place orders for execution at the next market opening. Some online brokerages developed their own proprietary software for operating their Web sites and maintaining customer account information; others relied on outside vendors for all or most of their requirements and paid a royalty per trade.

Competition among Online Brokers   During the latter half of 1997, aggressive online newcomers led by Ameritrade and Suretrade cut their commission fees and launched multimillion-dollar advertising campaigns to attract new accounts and gain market share. A brief but lively price war ensued, driving average commission fees for leading online brokerages down from just over $50 per trade in early 1996 to about $15 in late 1997. However, since then, prices had stabilized:

Period	Average Commission Charged by Top 10 Online Brokerages
Q1 1996	$52.89
Q1 1997	32.19
Q1 1998	15.53
Q4 1998	15.75
Q4 1999	15.50

Source: Based on data compiled by Credit Suisse First Boston and U.S. Bancorp Piper Jaffray and reported in Theresa W. Carey, "Better, Not Just Bigger," *Barron's Online,* March 13, 2000.

In early 2000, online commission fees per trade ranged from a high of $29.95 at well-known online brokers like Charles Schwab to $14.95 at E*Trade and Fidelity to $8 at Ameritrade and $7.95 at Suretrade to $5 at Brown & Co. and to $1.50 per trade at CyBerCorp (whose customers were hyperactive day traders that often made hundreds or even thousands of trades a day).

Throughout 1996–99, as Web technology progressed, data transfers via modems and servers became faster, and software capabilities were upgraded, competitors in the online segment made their Web pages livelier, easier to navigate, and more informational. Exhibit 3 shows the variety of features and services being offered by online brokerages during the 1997–99 period. To differentiate themselves and attract customers, *exhibit 3*   Features and Services Offered by Online Brokerages, 1998–99

- Ability to open an account online or via mail-in forms; account demos; tutorials for using account software.
- Technical support via e-mail or a toll-free line during business hours Monday through Friday. A few firms had tech-support hot lines open 24 hours a day, seven days a week. Response times varied from firm to firm, running from under a minute on average to as much as 15 minutes on average.
- Account information—ability to log on to the account and get price updates on each holding in the portfolio. Most brokerages updated the prices at the close of each trading day; several updated prices and account balances every 15 to 20 minutes; and a few brokerages had invested in the capability to provide updates instantly as stock prices changed.
- Account security.
- Free, unlimited delayed quotes (usually 15 or 20 minutes behind the latest executed trade).
- A limited number (usually 100) of free real-time quotes per transaction. A fee was charged for real-time quotes in excess of the specified number. To deliver real-time quotes, the broker had to have software capability to update stock prices directly on the screen each time they changed and then have a source from which to obtain the real-time quotes (often an outside vendor such as Thomson Financial—a primary provider of real-time quotes to many brokerages).
- Full customer control over placing buy-sell orders.
- Confirmations of trades, usually within a few seconds of placing the order.
- A variety of investment products available online—stocks, bonds, options, and mutual funds.
- Access to historical information—charts showing price and trading volume histories, 52-week high-low trading range, dividend histories, price-earnings ratios, charts showing how the stock price has performed versus various market indexes such as the S&P 500 and the Dow-Jones Industrial Average.
- Business news from such sources such as Dow-Jones, CNN, Bloomberg, Reuters, Business Wire, Standard & Poor's, *Fortune,* and *Business Week.*
- Mutual fund ratings from Morningstar and others.
- Daily market news summaries from CBS Market Watch, Briefing.com, and others.
- Press releases from companies.
- A selection of research links to 10-K reports, annual reports, earnings forecasts by First Call or Zack's Research, the latest analysis of various technical indicators, company histories and background, securities analyst recommendations, and investment advice from various sources.
- The ability to talk to a financial consultant or registered representative if the need arose.
- Electronic fund transfer services.
- IRAs and 401(K) retirement accounts.
- Checking accounts.
- Electronic bill payment.
- Credit and debit cards.
- Full disclosure of commission schedules and a list of fees for IRAs, bounced checks, margin loans, and other services (posted on the Web site for convenient review by customers).
- Investment tools to screen stocks based on criteria chosen by the customer.
- Financial planning and portfolio optimization tools.
- Online educational tools to teach do-it-yourself investors about the basics of investing, managing a retirement plan, and the fundamentals of stock analysis.
- Alerts issued to customers if the outlook for one of their stocks changed suddenly or if the price of a stock in their portfolio swung up or down by a sizable amount in the course of daily trading sessions.

Note: This listing is a representative compilation of features and services offered by the various online brokerages. However, the actual mix of features and services offered by any one particular brokerage firm varied from brokerage to brokerage. Features were in a constant state of flux during 1997–98 as brokerages upgraded or redesigned their Web sites; but by late 1999 the fast and furious pace of features changes and new additions had moderated.

online firms competed on the basis of commission fees, the variety of services offered, Web site features, the amount and caliber of information available at their Web sites, and the tools made available to track portfolios and research companies. Rivals were in a continual race to upgrade and add features, improve their services, expand the amount of information available at their websites, and add valuable research links.

To attract investor attention and build market share, the new online brokerage firms in mid-1997 launched multimillion-dollar advertising campaigns, using screen ads on high-traffic Internet sites, TV and radio spots, and print ads in *USA Today, The Wall Street Journal, Business Week, Fortune, Smart Money,* and other business-oriented magazines. The rush of new entrants made it virtually imperative for competitors to use the mass media to establish visibility and quickly build brand-name awareness. Most of the leaders in the online segment continued to advertise heavily through 1998 and 1999, both to attract new customers and to strengthen name recognition. Industry participants had geared up to spend a combined $1.5 billion on ads to attract new customers during 2000.

Alliances between Online Brokers and Information Providers

Most online brokers did not develop their own information content, but rather formed alliances and strategic partnerships with firms in the business of providing investor information via the Internet. Online brokers needed the content of information providers to make their research and data offerings at their Web sites more appealing to customers and competitive with rival brokerages. Information providers were interested in making their services available to online brokers and their customers in order to broaden their user base—information providers made their money either by providing their information for a fee (paid either by the online broker or their customers) and/or by selling advertising space on their Web sites where their information products were delivered. Once an online broker and an information provider agreed on an alliance or contractual fee arrangement, it was a simple, inexpensive task for broker Webmasters to incorporate direct links on their Web pages to the chosen providers of investor information.

The Responses of Full-Service and Discount Brokers to Online Trading, 1996–99

Full-service and discount brokers initially responded to the growing interest in online trading by creating Web sites for their own customers. No online trading was offered, but clients were offered tidbits of current information (daily market commentaries, recent market indexes updated daily or weekly, and perhaps a sample research report) and their attention called to the range of benefits the brokerage offered. Salomon Smith Barney went a step further; in exchange for registering, browsers at the Internet site could get the firm's current top 10 stock picks and click on links to other Web sites with pertinent information. In early 1996, Prudential Securities became the first full-service broker to offer customers Internet access to account balances and to provide delayed stock quotes. Other full-service and discount brokers soon followed Prudential's lead in providing customers an alternative to tracking their stocks from newspaper listings or calling their broker for quotes. But to access their account information online, the customers of full-service brokers first had to sign up with the broker to obtain the needed software (sometimes paying a one-time fee of $25), install the software on their computers, and use a secure browser (either Netscape Navigator or Internet Explorer). In contrast, the software employed by over three-fourths of the online brokers allowed customers to use the Internet to access their accounts without having to install special proprietary software on their computers.

However, with the exception of Morgan Stanley Dean Witter—which set up a separate unit, Discover Brokerage, to pursue the online brokerage business—none of the leading full-service brokerage firms gave clients an online trading option prior to late 1999. Until then, they had taken the position that the new online brokers did not have the financial strength and brand-name credibility to pose a serious competitive challenge. And they expressed confidence that few of their customers would see the Internet as an appealing substitute for the personalized counsel of a flesh-and-blood broker.

As the marketing executive of one full-service brokerage put it in 1996, "It's really not a concern. We find investors want ongoing advice and counsel."[5] Another industry expert predicted, "You'll see more people shifting back to a full-service house because they want hand-holding in a crisis."[6]

On the other hand, several prominent discount brokerages—namely, Charles Schwab, Quick & Reilly, and Fidelity Discount Brokerage—wasted no time in pursuing the opportunities in online trading. Schwab management, believing that the Internet held tremendous potential, moved early and aggressively to make online trading an integral component of its strategy. Having the best-known reputation of the online competitors, Schwab quickly became the market leader in the online segment. Several of the smaller deep-discount brokerages whose clientele consisted of active traders looking to trade at the lowest possible price also set up online units as a way to retain their current customers and attract additional bargain-hunting traders—a prominent example was Ameritrade. But the majority of discount brokers, like their full-service counterparts, were reluctant to embrace online trading and adopted a wait-and-see posture until competitive pressures in 1999 forced them to accept the handwriting on the wall.

COMPETITIVE CONDITIONS IN 2000

Of the approximately 65 million brokerage accounts in the United States in early 2000, roughly 45 million accounts were at traditional full-service brokers like Merrill Lynch, Morgan Stanley Dean Witter, Salomon Smith Barney, PaineWebber, Prudential Securities, and lesser-known regional firms. Discount brokers had an estimated 8 million accounts and online brokerages had an estimated 12 million accounts. Close to 35 million U.S. households had one or more brokerage accounts (often at both full-service or discount brokers and at online brokers), and household participation was rising, due to growing interest in participating in the booming stock market that had characterized the 1996–99 period. A 1999 government survey indicated that 49 percent of U.S. households had investments in the stock market in 1998 compared to 32 percent in 1989. Moreover, at least 6 million U.S. households had a net worth of over $1 million each. More than 3 million households in the United States had investable assets in excess of $1 million, and the number of these households was expected to grow 13 to 14 percent per year during the 2000–2003 period. A number of analysts predicted that over the next three to five years nearly all investors would be using the Internet to access their accounts. A mid-1999 survey by two research firms found that over 16 million people were interested in beginning online trading.

Industry analysts estimated that 55 to 60 percent of all retail brokerage trades would be placed online during 2000, with the percentage continuing to edge upward. Given the recent surge in online trading activity, it seemed likely that online brokers would be executing an average of 900,000 to 1 million trades per day by year-end 2000 and perhaps as many as 1.5 million daily by 2003. In early 2000, daily trading volume on the New York Stock Exchange (NYSE) averaged around 900 million shares, but a daily volume in excess of 1 billion shares was not uncommon; trading volumes on the National Association of Securities Dealers Automated Quotations (NASDAQ) averaged around 1.2 billion shares and on heavy trading days sometimes ranged as high as 1.8 billion shares. On the AMEX the daily trading volume was only about 50 million shares. Currently, an estimated 30 to 40 percent of the total daily trading volume was being handled by online

---

[5]Ibid., p. 121.
[6]"Schwab Is Fighting on Three Fronts," *Business Week,* March 10, 1997, p. 95.

brokers—traditionally, much of the daily trading volume was accounted for by institutions and mutual funds, which often traded large blocks of shares (5,000 to 20,000 shares or more). But recently the activities of day traders buying and selling small blocks of 100 to 500 shares several hundred times a day had driven up trading volumes and the share of total trading volume handled by online traders.

Industry analysts at Forrester Research were predicting that the $900 billion in assets in online accounts at year-end 1999 would exceed $3 trillion by 2003 and that the number of online accounts would grow from 12 million to 40 or 45 million as investors at full-service firms opted to use the online trading options these firms were putting in place and as online brokerages attracted more accounts. Commission revenues at online brokerages only were expected to reach $2.5 billion in 2000, up from $600 million in 1997. Revenues of online brokerage firms from all sources (commissions on stock trades, fees from mutual fund sales, interest earned from customers' margin accounts, underwriting fees, and other sources) were projected to jump from just over $4 billion in 1999 to around $10 billion in 2002.

Among the 280 firms offering retail brokerage services to investors in 2000, over 160 provided online trading to customers (the actual number varied almost weekly due to new entrants and merger/acquisitions among existing participants). Banks with discount brokerage operations were among those who had moved slowest in instituting online trading; however, in the years to come they were expected to begin providing an online trading option as part of their online banking offering. Goldman Sachs and J. P. Morgan were among the well-known financial services firms to announce they would offer online trading beginning in 2000.

With full-service firms being only in the beginning stages of offering online trading to customers, it was too early to gauge how many of their customers would begin to do part or all of their trading online and what this might do to their revenue streams from commissions. But it was perfectly clear that the livelihoods of professional brokers, whose incomes depended on the stream of commission fees they generated, were going to be increasingly at risk and that there might be a diminishing need for full-service brokers to maintain an extensive network of branch offices. And most observers believed that full-service brokerage firms would need a new business model and new revenue-generating strategies to continue to be profitable.

A survey commissioned by Fidelity Investments revealed that online investors were, for the most part, pleased with their experience. The main regret of 10 percent of the respondents was that they had not begun online trading earlier. The study showed that investors with online accounts increased their trading from 2.7 to 5.5 trades per month during the first 90 days of going online, but then slowed to an average of 4.5 trades per month.

The Dilemma of Full-Service Brokers in Entering the Online Segment

For full-service firms, entering the online brokerage business posed several internal and competitive dilemmas. The biggest was the "channel conflict" between competing in two segments that offered customers different prices and service levels. At the very least, it was awkward for a full-service brokerage firm, on the one hand, to ask customers to pay a $1,000 commission for buying 1,250 shares of Microsoft if the trade was placed through their longtime broker and, on the other hand, give them the option of making the same purchase online for a fee of only $29.95. Furthermore, giving customers a high-commission/low-commission option put a heavy burden on professional

exhibit 4   The Case for Online Investing versus the Case for Using a Full-Service Broker

The Case for Online Investing	The Case for Using a Full-Service Broker
• Cheaper commissions	• Receive professional advice
• No pressure and no cold calls from a broker	• Better execution
• Faster execution	• Trade less, invest more
• Volumes of information and investment tools are available online to provide stock-picking ideas; one does not need a broker to get stock-picking ideas	• Hand-holding in a bear market
• Online investing is more fun	• Have somebody to call and talk to
• A personal relationship with a broker is not particularly valuable—it's mostly chitchat and, if that is what a person wants, it is available for free in a chat room	• Get stock-picking ideas
• The record of brokers in picking stocks for clients is not very inspiring	• It is easier to get orders through by telephone than by computer
• While most brokers are professional, some are slick-talking salespeople who prod clients to trade too much and push high-fee products so they can earn more commissions	• It is good to have a professional broker looking out for your interests

Source: Adapted from Jonathan Clements, "Yes You Should, No You Shouldn't," *The Wall Street Journal,* June 14, 1999, p. R21.

brokers to figure out how they could continue to deliver value-added services that would generate a sustainable stream of commission fees if many of their clients shifted to online trading. As one broker expressed it, "It's much more difficult if I'm a broker and I'm providing this value-added service, and I turn around and my client can get a trade for $16 a share" from the same company.[7] Another dilemma concerned advertising and promotion. Most online brokers touted their low commissions in their ads, the range of services offered, and the "no pressure" freedom that online trading gave individual investors. Such ads conflicted with the persona of a full-service brokerage delivering custom-tailored services and trustworthy advice from professional brokers whose prices were justified by the value being provided. Exhibit 4 provides a comparison of the reasons given to use an online broker versus the reasons given to use a full-service broker.

Morgan Stanley Dean Witter, which had 11,500 professional brokers, had tried to detour the dilemma by setting up a wholly separate subsidiary, Discover Brokerage Direct, believing that a separate brand name, separate offices and operations, and separate strategies and appeals would help contain the channel conflict between the two businesses. The separation was seen as a way to avoid antagonizing the company's professional brokers who prized the names Morgan Stanley and Dean Witter and hated the notion of their own firm offering a low-price trading option under the same brand names. However, in late 1999, as most full-service brokers were making plans to incorporate an online trading option, Morgan Stanley Dean Witter decided to bring Discover's operations under the

[7]As quoted in "Channel Conflict," *The Wall Street Journal,* June 14, 1999, p. R9.

umbrella of its full-service brokerage business and renamed the subsidiary Morgan Stanley Dean Witter Online.

THE ECONOMICS OF ONLINE TRADING

Online trading was considered by analysts to be a potentially lucrative business despite the lower commissions per trade. The revenues of online brokerage firms came from four main sources:

- The commission income from executing customer trades.
- The interest earnings on loans to customers who purchased stocks on margin.
- The interest earned on the cash balances in customer accounts.
- The payments for order flow received from the market makers in each NASDAQ-listed stock.

Revenues from Commissions

Online brokers derived between 40 and 70 percent of their revenues from commission fees, depending on their commission structure. While the fee per trade varied anywhere from $5 to $29.95 (see Exhibit 2), a majority of online brokers charged a flat fee per trade on trades up to 1,000 shares, abandoning the practice used by full-service brokerages of basing the commission on the number of shares and the price per share. Fees were frequently higher on trades of more than 1,000 shares. The fees of online brokers were higher for buying or selling options and for orders that specified a limit price than for buying or selling stocks at the market price. The fees for handling mutual funds purchases or sales varied from broker to broker; many charged nothing (partly as a promotion to help attract new accounts and partly because mutual funds companies had waived their charges on sales made through online brokers as a way to attract investors to their mutual fund families). Exhibit 5 shows the fee schedule for Web Street Securities.

Revenues from Margin Loans and Account Balances

A number of active traders financed a portion of their stock purchases with funds borrowed from their broker. Such purchases were called margin purchases and the loans were referred to as margin loans. The interest rate that brokers charged on margin loans depended partly on the going short-term prime rate and partly on the size of the loan. The broker's base interest rate (referred to as the broker's call rate) typically was pegged 1 to 1.25 percent below the prime. The loans to customers were then made at the broker's call rate plus as little as 0.5 percent or as much as 2 percent depending on the size of the loan. (See Exhibit 5 for an example of one online broker's schedule of interest charges on margin loans.) Brokers used the cash balances in customers' accounts as a source of funds for making margin loans. Money market conditions in 1998 allowed brokers to earn a spread of 4 to 5 percent on margin loans, paying roughly 3 to 4 percent on customer cash balances and realizing an average of 8 to 9 percent on margin loans. Margin loans were a major revenue source; according to Ameritrade's CEO, "That's where we really make our money."[8] In early 2000, margin loans made by retail brokerage firms were at an all-time record high of $240 billion; the total value of all stocks traded on U.S. stock exchanges was $17 trillion.

---

[8]Whitford, "Trade Fast, Trade Cheap," p. 112.

exhibit 5   Commission Schedule for Web Street Securities, April 2000

Trades Executed via the Internet
- Any listed stock trade; any size $14.95
- NASDAQ stock trade under 1,000 shares $14.95
- NASDAQ stock trade 1,000 shares or more*   Free
- Equity and index options $14.95 plus $1.75 per contract
- Mutual funds transaction $25.00

Trades Executed via a Live Representative
- Any listed stock trade, any size $24.95
- NASDAQ stock trade under 1,000 shares[†] $24.95
- NASDAQ stock trade 1,000 shares or more[†] $24.95
- Equity and index options $24.95 plus $1.75 per contract
- Mutual funds transaction $25.00
- Bonds—government, municipals, corporate   Contact a Web Street account executive for pricing.

Margin Rates
- $0–$4,999   2% above broker call[‡]
- $5,000–$9,999   1¾% above broker call
- $10,000–$14,999   1½% above broker call
- $15,000–$19,999   1¼% above broker call
- $20,000–$24,999   1% above broker call
- $25,000+   ¾% above broker call

*On stocks trading over $2.00 per share. For stocks trading $2.00 and under per share, $14.95
[†]On stocks trading over $2.00 per share. For stocks trading $2.00 and under per share, $24.95 plus one cent per share.
[‡]Broker call as quoted in *The Wall Street Journal* (7.75% as of April 2000).
Source: www.webstreetsecurities.com, April 14, 2000.

Brokers earned additional interest income by investing any cash balances in customer accounts not used to make margin loans in Treasury bills or other short-term securities. Such short-term investments tended to yield brokers a net margin of 1 to 2 percentage points between the yield on short-term securities and the rate brokers paid customers on account cash balances.

Net interest income from both margin loans and short-term investments was said to average between $8 and $10 per trade.[9] Brokers could also obtain a small amount of revenue from fees earned in lending the shares in customer accounts to traders wishing to sell a stock short.

Order Flow Payments from Market Makers

Payments for order flow originated with firms that specialized in "making a market" for over-the-counter stocks (such as those listed on the NASDAQ, which were not traded on a central trading floor, giving brokers flexibility on where to send investors' incoming orders for execution). A market maker had responsibility for actually executing trades and, in accord with NASDAQ rules, posting the price within 90 seconds

---

[9]Suzanne Wooley, "Do I Hear Two Bits a Trade?" *Business Week,* December 8, 1997, p. 113.

of the trade. Market makers bought a stock at the bid price and sold a stock at the asking price; they executed trades for both investors and their own accounts. The spread between the bid and asking prices on over-the-counter stocks was typically one-eighth of a point or $0.125 per share. Market makers made their money on the spread, buying at the bid price and selling at the asking price and also on trading shares for their own account. The market maker adjusted the bid-ask range up or down in response to the changing balance of incoming orders to buy or sell and in response to changing bid-ask prices.[10] To keep the number of shares being bought or sold in close balance, market makers adjusted the asking price upward when buy orders exceeded sell orders at the prevailing price or when eager buyers were upping their bid prices. Similarly, market makers lowered the asking price when sell orders exceeded buy orders and when bid prices were weakening. Thus the trades being executed by market makers always reflected demand-supply conditions at that point in time.

When the stock markets were closed (normal business hours were 9 AM to 4 PM Eastern time, Monday through Friday), brokers could execute trades for investors on electronic communications networks (ECNs) such as Reuter's Instinet. Also, NASDAQ allowed firms to execute trades on its electronic system, called SelectNet, during regular business hours.

Because there were several market makers or specialists for each stock listed on the NASDAQ, specialists competed against each other for business in executing the trades for those stocks in which they were market makers. To give brokers an incentive and a reward for sending trades their way, market makers typically paid brokers a piece of the spread between the bid price and the asking price of the shares traded.[11] The "kickbacks" from market makers were said to account for about 20 percent of an online broker's overall revenues.[12] Such payments could range from $1 to $2 on a 100-share trade of a $10 stock to perhaps $20 on a 1,000-share trade of a $50 stock or even $100 on a 5,000-share trade of a $75 stock. It was the payments on order flow from market makers that allowed Web Street Securities to execute large trades on the NASDAQ for "free."

Both margin loans and payments from market makers for order flow were a bigger percentage of overall revenues for online brokers than for discount and full-service brokers. One top Ameritrade official said, "I can see a time when, for a customer with a certain size margin account, we won't charge commissions. We might even pay a customer, on a per trade basis, to bring the account to us."

Recently, order flow payments had come under criticism because of the potential they had for ethics problems. Arthur Levitt, chairman of the Securities and Exchange Commission, argued that order flow payments induced brokerages to direct trades to those market makers offering the best order flow payments, a practice that conflicted with a broker's responsibility to get the best price execution for its customers. SEC commissioner Laura Unger had taken the position that online brokers should be required to give out information on their order-routing practices, revealing to customers

---

[10]Investors wanting to sell shares could either indicate a lower limit price they would accept or could place an order to sell at the market price. Likewise, buyers could either specify a maximum or limit price they were willing to pay or could agree to pay the market price at the time the trade was executed. Most buyers and sellers placed their orders "at the market" since they could get the price at which the last few trades were made and since their order would be executed within less than a minute—the orders of Internet traders were usually confirmed within 30 seconds.

[11]The size of the spread between the bid and asking prices came under scrutiny by the National Association of Securities Dealers and federal government officials in 1997–98. Pressure to lower the spread to one-sixteenth of a point resulted.

[12]Cited in Whitford, "Trade Fast, Trade Cheap," p. 112.

the amount of the payments they got by routing orders to market makers. Harsher critics maintained that order flow payments were nothing other than bribes.

The Cost Structure of Online Trading

The current overall cost per trade at an online brokerage was said to average about $5 once a firm's trading volume reached levels that allowed it to fully utilize technology and front-end investments to put the necessary systems in place. The key operating-cost items were the software and the network of servers to allow customers to log on to the trading system, place and confirm orders, execute trades, and track account balances. Once a firm had the required software package and internal support systems to track account balances and clear trades, it could simply add server capacity and customer service personnel as trading volumes grew. As a result, online brokerages could achieve profitability at much lower trading volumes than traditional full-service and discount brokerages whose operations and processes were more labor intensive and who had to spread the fixed costs of their employees and branch office networks over many trades to achieve low unit costs.

Some online brokers had in-house capability to develop and upgrade their own proprietary software and self-clear the transactions of customers; others paid external software developers and related data processing providers fees amounting to $1 to $3 per trade. The reliance on computers and the Internet for interfacing with customers greatly reduced labor costs and the need for walk-in offices. Having customers log on to their accounts and place their own orders also eliminated most order-entry errors, which were often quite expensive for traditional full-service and discount brokerage firms to untangle. Customer trades were usually executed and confirmed within 15 to 30 seconds of placing the order; many customers stayed at the site long enough to get confirmation. Traditional brokers printed and mailed order confirmations to customers. Use of the Internet to provide customers with information further meant much lower costs for telephones, postage, brochures, and other printed materials (research reports, copies of company news releases, and other information of interest).

Extensive advertising and marketing campaigns were deemed necessary at many online brokerages to establish the company's name firmly in the minds of investors who were thinking of opening an online account, to build the size of their account base to more economic levels and spread out fixed costs, and to convey to mainstream investors that online trading was simple, economical, convenient, and fun. Whereas discount brokers spent about 4 to 7 percent of revenues on advertising, the advertising budgets of online brokers were currently running 15 to 20 percent of revenues. Ameritrade spent $40 to $50 million on a 1998 media campaign promoting its low $8 fee on most trades. Suretrade reportedly spent $30 million on its 1997–98 campaign to advertise its $7.95 commission and trading services. E*Trade in 2000 was in the midst of a $350 million, 18-month marketing campaign.

In addition to data processing software, Web page construction, and marketing, online brokers had to maintain ample capacity to handle trading volume. On a number of occasions in 1997 and 1998, customers of several online brokerages experienced delays in logging on to their accounts to make trades because brokers did not have the server capacity to handle the volume of traffic on their Web sites. By mid-1998 most online brokers had added sufficient capacity to handle peak demands on their systems; logjams were a rare occurrence in 2000. However, from time to time, online brokers' systems went down due to equipment or software failures, causing temporary annoyances to customers and generating embarrassing publicity in the media.

Cost-Sharing Synergies with Sister Businesses   Although industry analysts believed that online brokerage firms could, in time, realize profit margins of 15 to 20 percent of revenues, heavy expenditures for advertising and front-end technology costs had crimped profitability. *The Wall Street Journal* reported in March 1998 that only 30 percent of the 50 online brokerages interviewed were profitable and just 20 percent were breaking even.[13] Analysts estimated that an online brokerage operation could make money at commissions as low as $5 a trade if (1) they were a subsidiary of a discount or full-service brokerage and already had their own clearing operations and other supporting infrastructure in place or (2) they were part of an investment firm affiliated with a stock exchange that also had the back-office capability to handle the settlement of securities transactions and take care of other essential customer accounting and data processing operations.[14] The economies of an online brokerage being able to share the costs of such back-office operations with a sister discount or full-service brokerage (or another investment firm with back-office infrastructure) were said to be substantial. Likewise, an online brokerage unit could realize cost savings if it could draw on the offices, customer service personnel, or registered representatives of a sister full-service or discount brokerage to help service the needs of its online customers.

THE RISE OF ELECTRONIC COMMUNICATION NETWORKS

One of the most profound brokerage-related developments of 1999 was the astonishing growth of electronic communication networks (ECNs), which used computers to match buy and sell orders and execute trades without going through traditional market makers. An investor could place an order through an online broker, and if the broker's computer could find a seller at a matching price in an ECN, the order could be executed with no human intervention, at a fraction of the cost of using brokers and market makers. At year-end 1999, ECNs accounted for 33 percent of NASDAQ volume; Rule 390 of the New York Stock Exchange prohibited many NYSE-listed blue-chip stocks from being traded outside the NYSE and regional exchanges. However, bowing to pressure from the Securities and Exchange Commission to open up the trading of NYSE-listed stocks to competition, the NYSE indicated that it planned to withdraw Rule 390 sometime in 2000.

There were 10 ECNs operating in early 2000, several of which were owned wholly or partly by online brokers—E*Trade was an 18 percent owner of Archipelago; Datek Online was the owner of Island ECN, and Schwab, Fidelity, and DLJdirect were involved in REDIbook. Instinet, owned by Reuters, was by far the largest of the ECNs, with revenues of around $850 million in 1999 and a pretax profit margin of around 31 percent. Island was said to execute trades involving as many as 100 million shares per day but had generated revenues of just $14 million in the first nine months of 1999 based on its typical net fee of $1.50 per 1,000 shares (a fee far below what Instinet charged). REDIbook executed orders averaging about 70 million shares daily. Most of the ECNs were losing money due to expanding payroll and marketing costs associated

---

[13]Daisy Maxey, "Analyst Sees On-Line Brokers Expanding Range of Services," *The Wall Street Journal Interactive Edition,* March 9, 1998.

[14]Wooley, "Do I Hear Two Bits a Trade?" p. 112.

with gearing up for higher trading volumes; to be profitable, the network companies needed large-scale volumes.

Moreover, the competing ECNs were not connected as of early 2000, resulting in fragmentation of buy-sell orders and occasional failure to execute a customer's order promptly due to lack of a buy-sell match in a particular ECN. To rectify this situation and respond to pressures from the Securities Exchange Commission (SEC) to create maximum liquidity for all NASDAQ-listed stocks, officials at NASDAQ had initiated efforts to connect the ECNs and, further, to link them to NASDAQ trading to create a single comprehensive electronic central order book accessible to all market makers and ECNs. The central NASDAQ Order Display or "window" would collect and display all quotes and orders to buy the 5,000-plus NASDAQ stocks. To win the cooperation of market makers and ECNs, NASDAQ proposed allowing market makers and ECNs to retain ownership of their orders displayed in the aggregated NASDAQ system. Moreover, investors everywhere could tap into the system to view trades as they were executed and to see the number of shares available at various bid and ask prices. SEC chairman Arthur Levitt saw a single electronic trading system linking all buyers and sellers as a means of boosting competition among market makers and ECNs, executing trades faster, improving service, and lowering trading fees. Levitt believed that Rule 390 blocked competition in stock trading, and he had pushed the NYSE into agreeing to modify Rule 390 as part of his push to establish a central trading system.

ECNs had the potential for saving investors money on each NASDAQ trade by bypassing market makers, who made money off each trade by maintaining a spread between bid (buy) and asked (sell) prices. Most analysts and SEC officials expected that the ECNs would consolidate or be acquired by the major exchanges. According to one analyst, "It is inconceivable . . . that the current environment of nine or ten ECNs is tenable"; he predicted that the total would soon fall to one or two. Some analysts believed that two or three ECNs might attract enough volume to emerge as exchanges in competition with the NYSE and NASDAQ. REDIbook ECN in March 2000 had completed linkage of its system to those of Archipelago, Island Trading, and MarketXT for distribution of after-hours prices and orders.

ECNs also paved the way to trade stocks 24 hours a day, seven days a week on a global scale. According to an Archipelago executive:

> The end game here is, off a platform in America, Europe, and Asia, having a 7x24 electronic stock exchange. In terms of how we get there, I can give you all kinds of scenarios—it changes by the half-hour . . . Step one is to create one book [of quotes]. But in terms of the big picture, anyone who claims to know where this is going is lying to you.

As an initial response to recent developments, both the NYSE and NASDAQ were readying plans to become public companies and to begin offering after-hours trading. The NYSE was also moving on plans to set up an electronic trading network and abandon its long-standing practice of having trades handled by people on the floor of the exchange.

GOMEZ RATINGS OF THE ONLINE BROKERAGE FIRMS

One independent industry authority, Gomez Advisors, ranked over 50 of the estimated 160-plus online brokerage services on a variety of factors to determine who was "best." Gomez had created a scorecard rating each brokerage service on a scale of 1 to 10 on five criteria:

- *Ease of use*—such factors as availability of tutorials, well-integrated features, and ability to customize use.
- *Customer confidence*—including size of capital base, phone response times, tracking of Web site availability, and disclosure of fees and key information about trading rules.
- *On-site resources*—including real-time quotes, charts, news updates, editorial content, and screening tools for stocks and mutual funds.
- *Relationship services*—such factors as real-time updating of stock holdings and account balances, educational content, site security, sophisticated alerts for stock price changes or special news.
- *Overall cost*—commissions, fees, and margin rates.

There were subcategories for each of the five criteria, resulting in consideration of as many as 100 factors to determine a company's rating. Gomez arrived at its ratings by means of direct examination, trial sampling e-mail and telephone support services, a broker's Web site and customer support, a questionnaire, and a telephone interview. Gomez then used a proprietary process to weight the scores to determine which firms were best suited for (1) life-goal planners managing their own individual retirement portfolio of mutual funds, (2) hyperactive traders looking for low commissions and fast execution, (3) serious investors looking for high-quality information, investment tools, and research, and (4) one-stop shoppers interested in a comprehensive package of financial services. Exhibit 6 shows the Gomez rating for the 15 highest rated firms as of late 1999—the latest Gomez ratings of online brokerages can be seen at www.gomez.com.

Numerous publications, including *Barron's, Money, PC World,* and *SmartMoney,* also published ratings of online brokers using their own particular methodology and criteria; while the ratings of who was best and why varied from publication to publication, many of the same brokerages tended to appear on all of the top 10 lists. *Barron's* 1998 survey revealed that during the past 12 months the entire group of online brokers studied had made tremendous strides in upgrading the quality of their Web sites, citing the availability of more research information and more online help. *Barron's* March 2000 survey found even bigger strides in the quality of online brokerages; *Barron's* gave its highest rating (four stars) to DLJdirect, Merrill Lynch Direct, and National Discount Brokers based on trade execution, ease of use, reliability, amenities, and commissions. The high ratings for Merrill Lynch and DLJdirect were primarily due to the research and reports they made available to customers.

Exhibit 7 provides comparative fourth-quarter 1999 statistics for the leading online brokers. Profiles of selected online, discount, and full-service brokers are presented below.

Charles Schwab & Co., Inc. (www.schwab.com)

Charles Schwab & Co. was the fourth largest U.S. financial services company, with 6.7 million active accounts, $765 billion in customer assets (as of February 2000), and 1999 revenues of $3.9 billion and net profits of $589 million. It had an estimated 35 percent market share in the discount brokerage segment and a 22 percent share in the online brokerage segment. Schwab opened 1.5 million new accounts in 1999, helping boost its commission revenues from $1.31 billion in 1998 to $1.86 billion in 1999. Schwab's earnings had grown at a compound rate of nearly 35 percent since 1992 and its stock price had outperformed other major brokerage stocks. About 30 percent of Schwab's customer assets and 10 percent of its customer accounts were managed by 5,800 independent, fee-based investment advisers; these advisers opened Schwab ac-

exhibit 6 Gomez Advisors' Ratings of 15 Leading Online Brokers, Winter 1999

Online Brokerage	Ease of Use	Customer Confidence	On-Site Resources	Relationship Services	Overall Cost	Overall Score	Comments
1. Charles Schwab	7.39	6.91	8.54	8.84	4.35	7.64	Rated first for life-goal planners and one-stop shoppers and second for serious investors; has a comparatively high commission structure
2. E*Trade	8.10	6.15	8.90	7.67	6.62	7.63	Rated first for hyperactive traders and serious investors; rated second for life-goal planners
3. DLJdirect	7.46	8.35	8.35	5.62	6.21	7.28	One of the more expensive online brokers; only clients with over $100,000 in assets have access to DLJ research and IPO stocks
4. Fidelity Investments	5.63	5.71	8.94	8.23	4.61	7.06	Rated third for one-stop shoppers
5. National Discount Brokers	7.18	6.40	7.72	5.82	6.49	6.73	
6. A. B. Watley	5.44	8.10	6.49	4.90	8.48	6.45	Rated second for active traders; excellent site performance and excellent telephone and e-mail customer service
7. My Discount Broker	6.14	6.55	6.41	4.91	8.18	6.19	Excellent 24x7 telephone and e-mail customer service
8. American Express Brokerage	5.04	6.15	6.06	6.62	7.02	6.15	
9. Suretrade	4.92	6.84	6.59	4.44	9.89	6.14	Rated third for active traders; has knowledgeable and timely telephone and e-mail customer service
10. Morgan Stanley Dean Witter Online	7.56	5.63	6.46	5.35	3.95	5.93	An expensive commission schedule
11. Waterhouse Securities	1.60	7.16	7.26	5.43	8.44	5.92	Does not provide real-time account balances and holdings
12. Datek Online	6.49	7.32	4.32	4.18	9.41	5.82	
13. Ameritrade	3.35	7.69	5.65	4.30	8.90	5.68	
14. Quick & Reilly	5.10	7.42	6.40	3.40	6.88	5.67	
15. Web Street Securities	4.47	6.80	5.76	4.33	8.37	5.66	

Source: Web site for Gomez Advisors (www.gomez.com), February 14, 2000.

***exhibit* 7**   Comparative Statistics for the Leading Online Brokers, Fourth Quarter 1999*

Online Broker	Average Number of Trades per Day	Number of Customer Accounts	Assets in Customer Accounts	Assets per Customer Account
Charles Schwab	177,400	3,300,000	$348,000,000	$105,500
E*Trade	123,250	1,881,000	44,000,000	23,400
Waterhouse Securities	107,146	1,300,000	88,000,000	67,700
Fidelity	92,354	3,466,000	269,000,000	77,600
Datek Online	81,040	340,000	10,600,000	31,200
Ameritrade	71,269	686,000	31,600,000	46,100
DLJdirect	30,500	347,000	21,700,000	62,500
Scottrade	22,050	201,000	5,252,000	26,100
CyBerCorp	14,213	3,000	202,000	67,300
Suretrade	13,200	158,000	2,400,000	15,200
Morgan Stanley Dean Witter Online	12,500	193,000	9,500,000	49,200
National Discount Brokers	11,703	196,000	10,830,000	55,300
Dreyfus	10,125	44,000	7,225,000	164,200
Web Street Securities	4,535	88,000	800,000	9,100
Quick & Reilly	3,300	86,000	3,962,000	46,100
All others	32,375	700,000	46,200,000	66,000
Total/Average	806,961	12,987,000	$899,970,000	$69,300

*Data represent domestic online trading activity and do not include broker-assisted trades.
Source: U.S. Bancorp Piper Jaffray and company documents.

counts for their clients and used Schwab's Institutional division to execute buy and sell orders for their clients at the online rate of $29.95 per trade.[15]

According to co-CEO Charles Schwab, the company's mission was "to coach people on investing."[16] Schwab's strategy was geared to service and product variety, innovation, value pricing, and its own unique style of "full-service investing" in which information flowed freely and investors made their own decisions with objective help and advice when they needed it.

Service and Product Variety   Schwab made its services available to customers via a multichannel delivery system that included the Internet, branch offices, a voice recognition quote and trading service, a Touch-Tone telephone quote and trading service, e-mail and wireless technologies, multilingual and international services, and direct access to Schwab professionals day or night. Schwab had been especially successful in catering to small investors. The company had recently retooled its customer service program after studying the practices of such companies as McDonald's and FedEx; a top official explained, "Our current push is to make sure that our customers who need help get it and that our customers who don't, don't get it—and don't have to pay for it."[17]

---

[15]By utilizing Schwab's customer account and trading services, these outside investment advisers avoided the costs of having to design and operate systems to handle transactions and account tracking functions for their clients. Schwab also acted as the custodial agent for the assets in these accounts.
[16]As quoted in *Business Week,* May 25, 1998, p. 123.
[17]"Schwab Is Fighting on Three Fronts," p. 95.

Schwab offered customers a very broad lineup of products that included stock trading, the usual variety of checking account and credit card services, IRA and Keogh retirement plans, and the ability to invest in a broad selection of mutual funds.

Innovation   Schwab was regarded as an industry innovator and the company that had pioneered the marriage of technology and investment advice. In 1974, Schwab became the first brokerage firm to discount its commissions, thus triggering the advent of the discount brokerage segment. In 1984, the firm started a new trend in how mutual funds were sold, launching its innovative OneSource and Mutual Fund Marketplace programs, which by 1998 provided customers with the ability to purchase 1,400 mutual funds through their Schwab account without having to open an account directly with mutual fund providers. Schwab's supermarket approach, which let customers choose among many mutual funds and consolidate their holdings in one account, proved extremely popular among small investors building a retirement nest egg and managing their own IRAs and Keogh plans. Schwab's fees from mutual fund sales accounted for 20 percent of revenues.

The company had built a reputation as an aggressive user of new technology to cut costs and pass the savings on to customers. The company spent about 13 percent of its revenues for new technology. When online trading first made its appearance in 1995, Schwab quickly set its sights on being a leader in electronic brokerage—by year-end 1995 its electronic brokerage unit had 336,000 accounts with $23 billion in assets utilizing the firm's proprietary e.Schwab electronic trading software. Schwab launched trading on the Internet at its Web site in May 1996.

Schwab had made the Internet a centerpiece of its strategy for delivering research, information, and services to account holders. In January 1998, Schwab began offering online trading seminars and providing walk-in customers access to the Internet at its branch offices. It also launched an Analyst Center on its Web site that gave all online customers access to research information from Dow Jones, Standard & Poor's, First Call, and Big Charts at no cost. Customers could receive security analyst reports and consensus opinions on stocks and industries. Customers who had $50,000 or more in their accounts and averaged four trades monthly had access to their own Web pages, a software tool for identifying stocks meeting whatever criteria the investor specified, online interviews with top executives, a one-page report card on 7,000 mutual funds, and a customized one-page comparison of the investor's mutual funds against the performance of major stock indexes.

Because the online brokerage business had become so competitive, with the relatively similar offerings among most of the firms, many analysts believed that Schwab might pursue another reinvention of the business model for brokerage firms. In late 1999, Schwab had partnered with Ameritrade and TD Waterhouse to invest in an online investment bank that would give their customers big allocations of hot initial public offerings of stock of new dot-com companies. The company had recently purchased CyBerCorp, the leading online firm catering to active traders and day traders, and U.S. Trust, a wealth management firm serving affluent individuals and families through 24 offices in nine states. Schwab co-CEO David Pottruck explained the reason for the acquisition of U.S. Trust as follows:

> The baby boomers are emerging as a dominant wealth segment in the United States. They bring with them a desire for a high degree of control, a willingness to embrace technology for their investing needs and an unwillingness to compromise. Many of these investors will demand wealth management services—supported by the unique strengths of the Internet— that offer them more control and information than has ever been available before. At the same time, we believe that these investors are underserved—no one has garnered a truly

significant share of this expanding market; no one has developed a comprehensive wealth management service especially for the needs of the emerging affluent investor.

Through U.S. Trust, we will be able to provide the trust, financial and estate planning, and private banking services that are so crucial to wealth management. Our investment manager clients have told us repeatedly that trust and private banking services are absolutely essential in order to serve affluent clients well.

Value Pricing   Because of its strong reputation among middle-income and value-conscious investors and its comparatively wide range of products and services, Schwab had been successful in maintaining a higher commission structure than other discount and online firms. Schwab management was opposed to attracting business solely on the basis of low price, believing that the range and quality of its services and products justified a price premium over the fees of deep discounters. One executive was quoted as saying, "We have no intention of doing $7 trades."[18] However, in February 2000, Schwab moved to become more price-competitive by cutting its online commissions from $29.95 per trade to a low of $14.95 for customers making 60 or more trades in a quarter.

Online Trading   As the leading electronic brokerage, Schwab had 3.3 million online accounts as of March 2000, up from 1.5 million accounts in May 1998, and 638,000 in early 1997. Online customer assets were nearly $350 billion, compared to $103 billion in April 1998 and $80 billion in December 1997. In February 2000 Schwab handled an average of 280,000 online trades daily. The company's Web site averaged 40 million hits a day in January 1999 versus 20 million in October 1998. Schwab had invested heavily to make its Web site user-friendly and multifeatured. The site, anchored around Schwab's Analyst Center, reflected the firm's strategic direction for its online service—offering retail investors access to "full-service" online investing. Top management believed Schwab offered online investors a combination of multiple service options, technology, access to information and guidance, and value pricing that was unequaled in the brokerage industry. Schwab's latest Web site feature, introduced in early 2000, was Stock Analyzer, a proprietary, step-by-step guide designed to help Schwab customers evaluate individual stocks and make better-informed, more intelligent investing decisions. Designed as both an education and research tool, Schwab's Stock Analyzer walked investors through the stock research process and provided access to current securities analyst recommendations and earnings projections on over 10,000 stocks. Schwab management saw Stock Analyzer as a one-stop destination for both stock research and interpretation and a tool "to make 'smart investing' easier than ever before." Schwab also offered its customers research reports on individual companies from analysts at Credit Suisse First Boston.

In the late 1970s about 95 percent of Schwab's business was done through branch walk-ins or telephone calls to branch office personnel; in 1998, only 5 percent of the firm's business was done in branch offices. In early 2000, close to 75 percent of the trades executed for the company's 6.7 million accounts were done via the firm's online trading service, compared to 48 percent in 1998 and 28 percent in 1997. The balance was done by customers telephoning their orders to personnel in the company's central call centers.

The growth in Schwab's online trading volume had cut its average commission per trade from $68.50 in 1996 to $49 in early 1998 and $40 in early 2000. This had resulted in the duties of its salaried customer representatives shifting from taking orders for trades to talking with clients about financial planning, estate planning, mutual fund

---

[18]Ibid.

selection, the pros and cons of variable annuities, retirement planning, fixed-income investing, and insurance.

Recent Developments at Schwab   Schwab president and co-CEO David S. Pottruck described the company's strategy and recent accomplishments as follows:

Competitive responses during 1999 highlighted both the power of our vision for redefining full-service investing and the importance of our relentless focus on finding better ways of serving our customers. Our leadership in providing Clicks and Mortar access—combining people and technology—was very much in evidence throughout the year, starting with the introduction of our Schwab Signature Services program. This program provides enhanced personal and online services for customers with higher asset balances or trading volumes with Schwab. We increased our full-time equivalent employees by 4,800 in 1999, including an increase of 2,200, or 47 percent, in customer contact staff. We also opened 49 branches, bringing our year-end total to 340.

Our advances in leveraging technology to improve customer service during 1999 included the launch of SchwabAlerts, which delivers investment and market activity news to customers via both wireless and e-mail. We also started providing our customers with eConfirms, a service that delivers trade confirms electronically. In addition, we have moved many administrative services, including new account openings, contact information updates and check requests, to fully automated Web-based processes. We worked with Excite, Inc., to introduce MySchwab, which enables users to customize a personal home page with their choice of news and information. Other achievements during the year included the introduction of two research tools for mutual funds—Advanced Mutual Fund Screener and Fund Details, which enable customers to access detailed information on all Morningstar, Inc., rated funds. Additionally, for our more active customers we launched and then enhanced Velocity, our desktop trading system.

We made more than a thousand changes to our Web site during the course of 1999 to improve its content and functionality, including enhancements to the Analyst Center research function and the introduction of MyResearch report, which enables customers to design research reports with the information they find most useful. We believe that our leadership in online financial services is reflected in the continued growth in customer use of this channel at Schwab—during the fourth quarter of 1999, online trades made up 73 percent of all trades at Schwab, up from 61 percent during the fourth quarter of 1998. At year-end 1999, we had 3.3 million online accounts with $349 billion in assets, up 50 percent and 100 percent, respectively, from year-end 1998. Our online industry leadership is also reflected in the awards we earned during the year. We swept many of the number one online broker rankings, being recognized as the world's leader by Gomez Advisors, Inc.; Forrester Research, Inc.; Money, SmartMoney, and PC World magazines; and J. D. Power and Associates. Our investment in systems capacity, which totaled $126 million for the year, doubled our trade processing capabilities over the past 12 months, and enabled us to accommodate single-day records of 78 million Web site hits, 62,000 simultaneous customer Web sessions, and 228,000 online trades during December.

Securities market access is another area where we have continued to harness technology to improve customer service. In September 1999, we announced our participation in the REDIbook ECN LLC electronic communications network, which has subsequently enabled Schwab to launch an extended-hours trading session for certain NASDAQ and selected exchange-listed stocks. In order to enhance customer access to initial public offerings we worked with TD Waterhouse Group, Inc., Ameritrade, Inc., and three leading venture capital firms to form a new online investment bank that will focus on information technology and Internet companies. In addition, a precedent-setting no-action letter from the Securities and Exchange Commission will enable us to be the first brokerage firm to provide customers with access to Internet-based presentations by companies in the process of going public. We've also teamed up with OffRoad Capital to provide improved access to private equity investment opportunities.

We moved to expand our international presence through several transactions during the year, including the acquisition of Priority Brokerage Inc. and Porthmeor Securities Inc. of Toronto to form Charles Schwab Canada, Co. We also initiated a joint venture with the Tokio Marine and Fire Insurance Co., Ltd., to develop a full-service brokerage operation for Japanese investors. We extended online and telephonic brokerage services to Swiss investors through our UK operation, and we also formed a joint venture with ecorp Limited to bring Schwab-style service to Australia. Revenues from our international operations rose 68 percent to over $250 million in 1999.

We built our mutual fund offering during 1999 by adding 5 new proprietary Schwab-Funds and 412 new third-party funds to our Mutual Fund Marketplace. Our customers now have access to almost 2,000 funds from 316 families, including 1,143 Mutual Fund One-Source funds. Customer assets in OneSource funds topped $100 billion during December 1999, ending the year at $102 billion, while customer assets in SchwabFunds passed $100 billion earlier in the year and ended 1999 at $108 billion. Overall, customer asset balances in mutual funds totaled $285 billion at month-end December, up 35 percent from December 1998.

Charles Schwab was ranked eighth on *Fortune*'s list of the 100 best companies to work for in America and was rated number two in *Working Woman* magazine's list of the top 25 companies for executive women. Schwab was also named a 1999 Catalyst Award winner as one of the three firms that had done the most to advance women in business.

E*Trade Group (www.etrade.com)

E*Trade had grown rapidly into one of the best-known online personal financial services firms. It operated the world's most visited online investing site (with 300 million page views per month) and served customers at sites in the United States, Japan, Great Britain, Sweden, France, Australia, New Zealand, Korea, and Canada. E*Trade was building the first global cross-border trading network for online investors in an effort to make trading in foreign securities accessible to retail, corporate, and institutional investors alike. E*Trade had been ranked the number one online brokerage by Gomez Advisors in four of the past five quarters and been rated the top online brokerage by Lafferty Information and Research Group, *PC Magazine,* and *Smart Computing Magazine.* According to an August 1999 poll by Opinion Research Corp., E*Trade was one of the top four most recognized e-commerce brands among U.S. adults.

Company Background E*Trade was formed in 1982 to develop automated trading services for Charles Schwab & Co. and Fidelity Investments. E*Trade began its online trading service in 1992, surviving as a fledgling pioneer until the industry began to take off in 1995. In the first five months of 1996, E*Trade's active accounts grew from 38,000 to 65,000 and its monthly trading volume jumped from 50 million to 170 million shares. Led by 51-year-old Christos Cotsakos, who became CEO in March 1996 after career stints at FedEx and Dun & Bradstreet, E*Trade went public in August 1996, raising $46 million from its initial public offering of stock to fund expansion and build a leadership position in the online trading industry. By early 1997, E*Trade was opening 500 accounts and bringing in $8 to $10 million in assets a day; its customers were placing about 6,000 online trades daily. In late 1997, E*Trade opened a Mutual Fund Center that allowed customers to select from among 4,600 mutual funds at a flat sales commission of $24.95 and, with its acquisition of OptionsLink from Hambrecht & Quist, it began providing stock-option management services for 94,000 employees at 79 companies. The company had $7.8 billion in customer assets in 325,000 accounts and 600 employees as of January 1998; it handled an average of 23,200 trades a day in the first quarter of 1998.[19]

In the summer of 1998, Cotsakos got approval from the company's board of directors to quadruple E*Trade's advertising budget to $175 million a year for each of the next two years (spending a total of $350 million through mid-2000), a move that would wipe out the company's small profits and make it unprofitable until the number of customer accounts and the firm's trading volume grew substantially. In addition, E*Trade allocated around $100 million (about 12 percent of revenues) to upgrade its technology, its Web site capacity, and its operating systems over the next 18 months. To make the company more price-competitive, E*Trade cut its commission rates seven times before arriving at its present $14.95 fee for stocks listed on the NYSE and $19.95 for stocks listed on the NASDAQ. Lower commissions and heavy marketing boosted the number of customer accounts to over 1 million in early 1999.

Recent Developments   While the company had reported a small profit in 1996, 1997, and 1998, E*Trade lost $54.4 million on revenues of $621 million in the fiscal year ending September 30, 1999. In the first quarter of fiscal year 2000 ending December 31, 1999, E*Trade reported after-tax losses from ongoing operations of $38 million on revenues of $246 million. The company's stock price had performed well for shareholders until recent months. It split two-for-one twice in early 1999, rising to an all-time split-adjusted high of $72 in April 1999 before falling back to trade in the mid-30s in early 2000, when the company's losses mounted and traditional full-service brokers moved to institute online trading options for their customers.

E*Trade acquired 330,000 net new accounts during the last three months of 1999, bringing its total active accounts to nearly 1.9 million and customer assets to $44 billion (an average of just over $22,000 per account, but far below the average of $115,000 per account at Schwab and the more than $400,000 per account at Merrill Lynch). The company spent nearly $80 million on marketing in the third quarter of 1999 to add 310,000 new accounts—$238 per new account, reportedly one of the lowest acquisition costs per net new account in the industry. Average transactions per day were in the 130,000 to 140,000 range in the first quarter of 2000, up from 43,000 in the last quarter of 1998. Starting in August 1999, E*Trade cut its commissions on active traders' transactions to $4.95 per trade from $14.95 per trade.

In late 1999, E*trade moved to further expand its customer base and diversify its revenue stream by acquiring Telebanc Financial, the largest online-only bank in the United States, for $1.8 billion; through Telebanc, E*Trade provided customers with online checking accounts, ATM cards, printed checks, and bill-paying services. Also during 1999, E*Trade acquired a 28 percent ownership of E*Offering, an online investment bank; 2 percent of E-Loan, an online loan service that matched borrowers with willing bank lenders; 18 percent of Archipelago ECN; and 100 percent of ClearStation, a Web site with original financial news and 250,000 users. The company had started an E*Trade family of mutual funds, added bond trading to its site, and developed plans to launch Web sites in over a dozen additional countries. E*Trade had entered into strategic alliances with Bond Exchange (to provide bond trading services), First USA (to provide credit cards), InsWeb (an online insurance provider), TheStreet.com and Bridge Information (financial news providers), and Briefing.com and Banc Boston Robertson Stephens (to provide investment research).

---

[19]*The Wall Street Journal,* June 2, 1998, p. C20.

E*Trade management saw these acquisitions and alliances as providing substantial cross-selling opportunities. The day after the Telebanc deal was announced, for example, E*Trade and Telebanc put together a package deal where Telebanc offered a one-year 6.5 percent certificate of deposit—a hefty 208 basis-point premium over the national average—exclusively to E*Trade customers. The promotion attracted 6,000 responses within three weeks.

E*Trade's Strategic Vision   Chris Cotsakos was regarded as an energetic evangelist for online trading who had innovative ideas for making E*Trade a market leader. Cotsakos said, "When the business was just getting started, we went after the early adopters, people who were techno-savvy. Now we're after the mainstream."[20] He believed the handwriting was on the wall for the army of brokers employed at full-service firms: "The days of the $100,000 broker are coming to an end."[21] In an interview published in *Leaders* in 1997, Cotsakos said, "I believe the brokers will have to migrate to a different type of position, like an advisor or consultant to the individual investor. I believe the days of the huge commissions and huge salaries are numbered . . . Brokerage is not a field I would recommend my daughter go into." He foresaw online brokerages outcompeting full-service firms and evolving into one-stop financial services enterprises:

> What we really see ourselves migrating to is a financial services gateway, where people can have access to our proprietary information as well as other content we can aggregate. That way, they can have one-stop shopping with a customized, personalized screen that meets all their financial needs, whether it's banking, buying flowers, viewing their stock portfolio, downloading information to their tax advisors, or doing a transaction.[22]

By early 2000, Cotsakos's vision of having E*Trade's Web site function as a financial online hub where consumers went for self-service investing, banking, insurance, loans, and financial planning was taking on some new twists. Cotsakos's latest idea was to add an array of multimedia features to the E*Trade Web site that would position E*Trade as a "digital financial media" provider. In early 2000, E*Trade launched the first phase of a $100 million initiative that would:

- Permit customers to have personalized Web pages.
- Give E*Trade the capability to broadcast live TV-quality video feeds of news and interviews with company CEOs.
- Permit online chats with financial advisers, loan agents, and investment analysts who had researched particular companies and industries.
- Enable E*Trade to run ads and promotions on personalized Web pages that were tailored to individual interests (such as the latest airline discounts for frequent travelers).
- Provide customers with an electronic calendar that alerted them by e-mail or notices on the Web site of upcoming news and earnings release dates of companies in their portfolio.
- Provide E*Trade's services over handheld devices, cable-TV boxes, and satellite-TV systems as well as PCs.

---

[20]As quoted in Whitford, "Trade Fast, Trade Cheap," p. 112.

[21]As quoted in *Institutional Investor,* January 1997, p. 23.

[22]As quoted in "Declaring War On Brokerage Fees," *Leaders,* April–May–June 1997.

As one E*Trade executive put it, "E*Trade is all about empowering individuals with the right tools and information to take control of their financial lives."

Cotsakos believed that E*Trade needed a remarkable and distinctive corporate culture to propel the company to success. He spent considerable time on culture-building activities, seeking to build a company with wildly creative, hypercompetitive people who were closely knit into a family. To emphasize the need for speed, he organized a day where employees raced Formula One racing cars at speeds of up to 150 miles an hour; to create a loose atmosphere, he encouraged employees to carry around rubber chickens and wear propeller beanies; to promote employee bonding and a team spirit, he had managers attend a cooking school where they had to work closely with one another to prepare a gourmet dinner. To help develop the capabilities to beat out other dot-com rivals, he stressed inventiveness, moving at Internet speed, and bold, aggressive action. The following two quotes represent Cotsakos's ideas:

> We pay big money for intellectual capital and speed. One of the things I learned from my experiences in Vietnam is that if you go in half-way, you can't win. You've got to have not only ground cover but air cover. You've got to bring in the heavy artillery. You've got to go out and say, "I'm here, I've arrived, and I'm not going to be messed with."[23]

> At E*Trade, we're predatory. We believe we have a God-given right to market share.[24]

In a feature article on Chris Cotsakos and E*Trade a *Business Week* reporter observed:

> E*Trade has to be on the offensive, given Cotsakos's ambitions. His dream is to assemble a financial services empire that not only overtakes online rival Charles Schwab but also matches the breadth of brick-and-mortar giants such as Merrill Lynch & Co. and Citigroup. The competition is intense. Schwab is in the lead—and a handful of feisty, barebones Net brokers are doing trades at $8 a pop, compared with $14.95 for E*Trade. Cotsakos has to beat back the Net players and grow fast before Merrill Lynch and others bring all their marketing muscle to bear on the Web.[25]

Ameritrade (www.ameritrade.com)

Ameritrade Holding Corp. was an Omaha-based firm with four subsidiaries: Ameritrade and Accutrade—both deep-discount brokerages with online trading units; AmeriTrade Clearing, which provided securities clearing services for its two sister brokerages, banks, and other brokers and securities dealers; and AmeriVest, which provided discount brokerage services to banks, savings and loan associations, and credit unions. The company successfully completed an initial public offering of common stock in March 1997 and its shares were traded on the NASDAQ. Over the past four years, Ameritrade had transformed itself from a small midwestern discount brokerage into a well-known national brand with 560,000 accounts, over $20 billion in customer assets, 1999 revenues of $268 million and net earnings of $11.5 million. It was the fifth largest online broker in terms of accounts. Its extensive advertising campaigns had given it one of the best-known brand names in the online brokerage segment.

Ameritrade Holding Corp. launched its Ameritrade deep-discount brokerage and no-frills online service in the fall of 1997. The Ameritrade brokerage subsidiary was formed by consolidating three small company-owned brokerages—Ceres Securities (a deep-discount brokerage the company started in 1994); K. Aufhauser (a New York firm acquired in 1995 that had launched the first Internet trading site in August 1994); and

---

[23]As quoted in Daniel Roth, "E*Trade's Plan for World Domination," *Fortune,* August 2, 1999, p. 96.

[24]As quoted in Louise Lee, "Tricks of E*Trade," *Business Week,* February 7, 2000, p. EB-21.

[25]Ibid.

eBroker (a deep-discount online brokerage formed in 1996 to target the most price-sensitive online traders). Ameritrade immediately attracted the attention of online investors with its fees of $8 for Internet trades and a $25 million ad campaign consisting of TV spots, print ads in *USA Today* and *The Wall Street Journal,* radio ads, and direct mail. Ameritrade's primary market target was investors who were comfortable with computers, knowledgeable about how to find investment-related information on the Internet on their own, didn't like going through a broker, and were looking to execute their trades at a very low cost. To help build its customer base and increase brand awareness, Ameritrade had entered into strategic marketing agreements for services and content with America Online, CompuServe, Excite, Intuit, Infoseek, the Microsoft Network, Yahoo!, The Motley Fool, and the *USA Today* Information Network. These agreements gave Ameritrade valuable exposure and gave Ameritrade customers access to a wider range of information and resources and improved trading experiences. By year-end 1997 Ameritrade had added 51,000 new accounts, bringing its account total to 147,000.

In 1998 Ameritrade introduced a new computer game called Darwin, distributed free on CD-ROM, as an educational tool for novice investors who wanted to learn about the Black/Scholes model, butterfly spreads, and other tricks of options trading in a setting with the excitement and features of the popular video game Doom.[26] Ameritrade executives, having spent time in investor chat rooms on the Internet, could tell from the comments and complaints that investor losses on options trading were often the result of the trader's own lack of understanding and know-how.

Ameritrade had been a consistent leader in innovation and was the first brokerage to see the value of aggressive advertising. Ameritrade spent 100 percent of its revenues on advertising and marketing in the fourth quarter of 1997, producing 50 percent account growth in 90 days and a tripling of accounts over the next year. The company spent $44 million on advertising in 1998 and $60 million in 1999, boosting its account total to 560,000 and helping grow revenues by 250 percent. Until mid-1999 Ameritrade had turned its growth into premarketing operating income of roughly $10 per transaction, a 40 percent margin. (See the analysis in Exhibit 8 for a breakdown of Ameritrade's revenues, costs and profits per transaction by quarter and by year.) However, in the second and third quarters of 1999 the company's nonmarketing expenses increased dramatically, from $38 million in the first quarter to $62 million in the third quarter, pushing premarketing operating income down to $4 per transaction (Exhibit 8). Ameritrade had ambitious plans to spend close to $200 million on marketing and advertising starting in the fourth quarter of 1999 and continuing through the first quarter of 2001 to build its accounts and trading volume to levels that would cover the increased expenses and restore its margins. As shown in Exhibit 8, analysts at Credit Suisse First Boston expected that the increase in marketing expenditures would result in Ameritrade incurring a loss in 2000.

The Quick & Reilly Group/Suretrade

The Quick & Reilly Group was a subsidiary of FleetBoston Financial Inc., the largest bank in New England. It consisted of Quick & Reilly, Inc., the third largest discount brokerage in the United States, with 1 million accounts and 120 branch offices; U.S. Clearing, a clearing and trade execution service for more than 350 brokerage and banking firms; JJC Specialist, the second largest specialist on the floor of the NYSE, which made a market in the stocks and securities for 229 NYSE-listed companies; Nash Weiss, which made a market in 3,500 over-the-counter stocks; and Suretrade, a deep

---

[26]Whitford, "Trade Fast, Trade Cheap," p. 114.

exhibit 8 Ameritrade's Revenue-Cost-Profit Economics per Transaction, by Quarter and by Year, 1998–99, with Estimates for Fiscal Year 2000

	1998 Fiscal Year				1999 Fiscal Year				2000 Fiscal Year Estimates						Est.
	Dec-97	Mar-98	Jun-98	Sep-98	Dec-98	Mar-99	Jun-99	Sep-99	Dec-99	Mar-00	Jun-00	Sep-00	1998	1999	2000
Commissions	$ 22.51	$ 18.73	$ 17.82	$ 17.22	$ 16.36	$ 15.47	$ 14.92	$ 14.72	$ 14.65	$ 14.50	$ 14.40	$ 14.25	$ 18.54	$ 15.26	$ 14.43
Interest income	$ 18.71	$ 14.26	$ 13.97	$ 13.02	$ 10.27	$ 8.15	$ 8.30	$ 11.13	$ 10.00	$ 10.83	$ 10.83	$ 10.83	$ 14.44	$ 9.39	$ 10.66
Less interest expense	$ 8.12	$ 6.44	$ 6.17	$ 5.60	$ 4.39	$ 3.39	$ 3.21	$ 4.40	$ 3.69	$ 4.83	$ 4.17	$ 4.50	$ 6.34	$ 3.79	$ 4.32
Net interest income	$ 10.59	$ 7.82	$ 7.81	$ 7.42	$ 5.87	$ 4.76	$ 5.10	$ 6.73	$ 6.31	$ 6.00	$ 6.67	$ 6.33	$ 8.10	$ 5.60	$ 6.34
Equity income from investments	$ 1.89	$ 1.16	$ 1.84	$ 0.05	$ —	$ —	$ —	$ —	$ —	$ —	$ —	$ —	$ 1.10	$ —	$ —
Other income	$ 1.65	$ 1.28	$ 1.31	$ 1.12	$ 0.99	$ 0.79	$ 0.76	$ 0.82	$ 0.72	$ 0.65	$ 0.61	$ 0.57	$ 1.29	$ 0.83	$ 0.63
Net revenues	$ 36.63	$ 28.98	$ 28.77	$ 25.81	$ 23.23	$ 21.02	$ 20.78	$ 22.26	$ 21.68	$ 21.15	$ 21.68	$ 21.15	$ 29.03	$ 21.68	$ 21.40
Compensation and benefits	$ 9.65	$ 7.64	$ 7.92	$ 6.99	$ 5.99	$ 4.93	$ 5.58	$ 7.48	$ 6.75	$ 6.25	$ 6.00	$ 5.50	$ 7.81	$ 6.01	$ 6.06
Commissions and clearing	$ 1.39	$ 1.25	$ 1.29	$ 1.14	$ 0.83	$ 0.72	$ 0.52	$ 0.61	$ 0.56	$ 0.55	$ 0.54	$ 0.53	$ 1.25	$ 0.65	$ 0.54
Communications	$ 4.46	$ 3.21	$ 2.61	$ 1.93	$ 1.54	$ 1.49	$ 1.37	$ 1.63	$ 1.52	$ 1.44	$ 1.43	$ 1.35	$ 2.80	$ 1.50	$ 1.43
Occupancy and equipment	$ 2.77	$ 2.19	$ 2.03	$ 2.39	$ 1.84	$ 1.52	$ 1.54	$ 2.05	$ 1.80	$ 1.67	$ 1.60	$ 1.52	$ 2.30	$ 1.73	$ 1.64
Other expense	$ 7.61	$ 5.69	$ 4.69	$ 3.95	$ 3.80	$ 3.85	$ 4.85	$ 6.73	$ 6.64	$ 6.84	$ 6.41	$ 6.13	$ 5.11	$ 4.92	$ 6.47
Operating expense	$ 25.88	$ 19.98	$ 18.54	$ 16.39	$ 13.99	$ 12.51	$ 13.86	$ 18.49	$ 17.27	$ 16.75	$ 15.99	$ 15.04	$ 19.26	$ 14.81	$ 16.14
Pre-marketing operating income	$ 10.75	$ 9.01	$ 10.23	$ 9.42	$ 9.24	$ 8.51	$ 6.92	$ 3.77	$ 4.41	$ 4.40	$ 5.69	$ 6.11	$ 9.76	$ 6.88	$ 5.26
Advertising and promotion	$ 35.59	$ 9.22	$ 3.89	$ 2.52	$ 4.30	$ 4.34	$ 3.21	$ 7.42	$ 9.72	$ 8.24	$ 7.51	$ 3.71	$ 9.44	$ 4.82	$ 6.99
Pre-tax operating income	$(24.83)	$ (0.22)	$ 6.34	$ 6.90	$ 4.94	$ 4.17	$ 3.71	$ (3.65)	$ (5.31)	$ (3.84)	$ (1.81)	$ 2.40	$ 0.32	$ 2.06	$(1.73)
Amortization	$ 0.13	$ 0.09	$ 0.07	$ 0.06	$ 0.04	$ 0.03	$ 0.02	$ 0.03	$ 0.02	$ 0.02	$ 0.02	$ 0.02	$ 0.08	$ 0.03	$ 0.02
Nonrecurring items	$ —	$ —	$ 0.59	$ (0.91)	$ (2.27)	$ —	$ —	$ (0.63)	$ —	$ —	$ —	$ —	$(0.13)	$(0.58)	$ —
Net income before taxes	$(24.70)	$ (0.13)	$ 7.00	$ 6.05	$ 2.71	$ 4.20	$ 3.74	$ (4.25)	$ (5.29)	$(3.82)	$ (1.79)	$ 2.42	$ 0.27	$ 1.50	$(1.71)
Taxes	$(8.91)	$ (0.04)	$ 2.46	$ 2.15	$ 0.96	$ 1.50	$ 1.32	$ (1.53)	$ (1.90)	$(1.37)	$ (0.64)	$ 0.87	$ 0.07	$ 0.53	$(0.61)
Extraordinary items	$ —	$ —	$ —	$ —	$ —	$ —	$ —	$ —	$ —	$ —	$ —	$ —	$ —	$ —	$ —
Net income	$(15.79)	$ (0.09)	$ 4.54	$ 3.90	$ 1.75	$ 2.70	$ 2.41	$ (2.72)	$ (3.39)	$ (2.45)	$ (1.15)	$ 1.55	$ 0.20	$ 0.97	$ (1.09)

Source: Equity Research, Credit Suisse First Boston Corp., November 5, 1999. Used with permission.

discount Internet brokerage that began doing business in November 1997. When Quick & Reilly was acquired by FleetBoston in early 1998, FleetBoston immediately moved to make Quick & Reilly products available to Fleet's customers and to market Fleet's products to Quick & Reilly customers; the cross-selling was immediately apparent at Quick & Reilly's Web site (www.quick-reilly.com).

Quick & Reilly was the first NYSE member firm to offer discount commissions to individuals in 1975. It launched its Internet trading system in November 1996 and gained a reputation as one of the fastest, easiest-to-use, and most comprehensive trading systems on the Internet. The company's Web site had been continuously enhanced since its introduction.

Suretrade (www.suretrade.com)   Since its launch in 1997 Suretrade has grown to over 360,000 customer accounts and nearly $2 billion in customer assets. It was considered the Wal-Mart of the online brokerage industry. Suretrade's $7.95 commission fee for market orders was among the lowest in the online brokerage segment (limit orders carried a $9.95 fee). It had one of the lowest margin rate schedules and offered a wealth of free research, real-time quotes, news, charting, portfolio and life planners, stock and mutual fund screeners, and 24-hour online broker-assisted help. Customers could choose to invest in over 3,000 mutual funds. Suretrade had a reputation for fast, accurate trade execution and its Web site was considered easy to navigate. It was recognized as one of the leading online brokerages, earning strong rankings in *Smart Money, Time, Business Week, Money,* and *Kiplinger's.*

At its Web site Suretrade was up front with customers about what they could expect:

> How can we bring you such an extraordinary value, combining excellent Internet trading functionality, content and security, along with a fantastic low commission structure? Our relationship will be an electronic one. It costs us less to answer e-mails than it costs us to answer phone calls. Remember, our great prices aren't for everyone. They are for brokerage clients ready to conduct their affairs electronically. Our low commissions are the reward for clients who are committed to electronic brokerage.[27]

Morgan Stanley Dean Witter Online (www.msdw.com)

Morgan Stanley Dean Witter Online (formerly Discover Brokerage Direct) got its start in electronic brokerage as Lombard Institutional Brokerage, a small discount firm in San Francisco that began offering online trading in September 1995. Lombard was acquired by Dean Witter Discover in January 1997 to serve as its online entry, which changed Lombard's name to Discover Brokerage Direct to create a stronger association with the 40 million holders of the Discover Card. Dean Witter Discover then acquired the Morgan Stanley Group (a leading Wall Street investment banking firm) in May 1997. The new company, Morgan Stanley Dean Witter, had 1999 revenues of $34 billion and earnings of $4.7 billion. The company had three core businesses—securities, asset management, and its Discover Card credit services—creating a company with great financial strength, global scope, and market leadership in a variety of financial service businesses. Dean Witter was the third largest full-service brokerage, with over 450 U.S. branch offices, over 12,600 brokers, 4 million customer accounts, and $425 billion in customer assets.

---

[27]Company Web site, April 17, 1998.

The company's strategy during the Discover Brokerage era was to compete on value and service. Top management saw price cutting as "a dangerous strategy."[28] Discover Brokerage began an extensive marketing campaign in January 1998 to build a bigger customer base; its campaign included a direct mail appeal to the more than 40 million holders of the Discover card. The company's ads in 1998–99 featured its number one ratings by *Barron's* and *Smart Money*. Discover Brokerage featured commissions as low as $14.95 a trade, 24-hour customer support, and access to over 3,500 mutual funds (many with no loads or transaction fees); customers could also place trades with a registered professional or by Touch-Tone phone. Discover's Web site provided customers with numerous data and research options and featured up-to-the-minute account information—customers could watch the prices change for their holdings as trades were executed. Discover also offered extensive customizing ability so clients could design their own investment-information centers according to their own interests. Discover Brokerage was the only online brokerage to win *a Barron's* four-star rating four years in a row; it also earned a top five-star rating in *Kiplinger's* 1999 survey of online brokerages and a 1998 top rating from *Smart Money*. However, Discover Brokerage achieved only modest success in the marketplace, having attracted about 180,000 accounts and generating an average of 11,000 trades per day when it was renamed Morgan Stanley Dean Witter Online in October 1999.

Morgan Stanley Dean Witter Online charged customers $29.95 for online trades and $39.95 for broker-assisted trades for orders of 1,000 shares or less. For orders over 1,000, online trades were 3 cents per share and broker-assisted trades were 4 cents per share. Customers had access to Morgan Stanley Dean Witter analyst research, electronic funds transfer, check writing, money market funds, extended hours trading, wireless trading (through TradeRunner, a wireless investing service), and a product where they could purchase a "blue-chip" basket of 10 selected stocks for a flat $49.95 commission price. Customers could also choose a plan in which they got unlimited free trades for a single asset-based fee that decreased from 2.25 percent for accounts under $100,000 to 0.30 percent for accounts over $10 million.

Web Street Securities (*www.webstreet.com*)

Web Street Securities was small, privately held brokerage formed by two entrepreneurs, Joe and Avi Fox, both in their 30s, whose prior venture was a failed international investment banking firm they had founded. After a month and a half of research into online trading during the summer of 1996, the two brothers decided to cast their future with online brokerage. Web Street opened its doors for business in August 1997. It launched its bid for investor attention and market share in early 1998 with a $20 million national advertising campaign featuring attention-getting TV spots (that intoned "You're a player now" when the head of the household portrayed in the ad opened an account online), and full-page media ads in *USA Today* and other publications

Web Street had pioneered several innovations—streaming real-time quotes, pop-up order confirmation messages, and an exclusive one-page "Trading Pit" screen that displayed all the needed information to place a trade and provided customers with access to their positions, real-time account balances, order status, and links to research and news all on one page (see Exhibit 9). Customers could customize their Trading Pit screen to display streaming real-time quotes for designated stocks on their watch lists.

---

[28]"Wooley, Do I Hear Two Bits a Trade?" p. 96.

exhibit 9   Web Street Securities' Innovative Trading Pit Screen

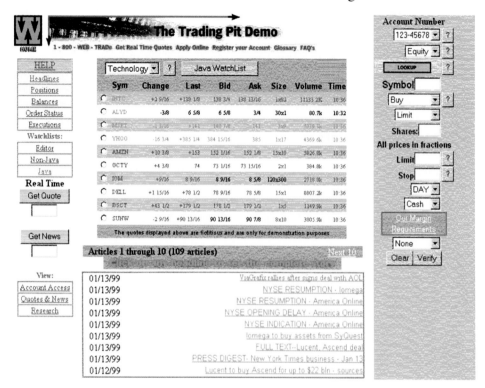

The one-page Trading Pit screen permitted customers to buy and sell with just one click, keep an eye on the streaming quotes of watch-listed stocks, and watch their holdings being updated on the screen as trades occurred. At the Trading Pit customers could, in addition, get real-time updates of account information (customers could watch their holdings being updated on the screen as trades occurred) and click on news updates and research sources. Customers could place broker-assisted trades at $24.95. They could also purchase bonds (corporate, municipal, state, or federal) and any of 4,000 mutual funds from 250 mutual fund families; no commissions were charged on mutual fund purchases. Registered brokers and customer service representatives were on duty 24 hours a day, seven days a week.

However, Web Street had grown more slowly than anticipated during the 1998–99 period and was not believed to be profitable given its present scale of operation.

DLJdirect (www.dljdirect.com)

DLJdirect was the online trading service of Donaldson Lufkin & Jenrette, a premier investment research house and one of the 10 largest investment banking firms, with 1999 revenues of $7.1 billion and more than 10,000 employees in 17 cities in the United States and 15 cities in Europe, Latin America, and Asia. The firm's businesses included securities underwriting, sales and trading, investment banking, financial advisory services, investment research, online brokerage services, and asset management. It was the fifth largest lead manager of initial public offerings and the largest underwriter of high-yield bonds. DLJ and its affiliates handled about 10 percent of the trading volume of the New York Stock Exchange. DLJ's research operation had been ranked among the five best investment research firms for 25 straight years by *Institutional Investor,* whose research covered 1,100 companies in 80 industries.

Originally launched as PC Financial Network, DLJdirect pioneered online investing in the late 1980s. DLJdirect had 1999 revenues of $238 million and earnings of $6.9 million versus 1998 revenues of $118 million and earnings of $1.5 million. However, in the third quarter of 1999, DLJdirect reported a loss of $3.3 million on revenues of $54.9 million followed by a net loss of $2.0 million on record revenues of $76.3 million in the fourth quarter of 1999. At year-end 1999, DLJdirect had 347,000 active online accounts, with assets of $22 billion, equal to $63,400 per account; it added 40,000 net new accounts in the fourth quarter, with assets of $7.4 billion. DLJdirect executed 5.8 million trades in 1999; average daily trades reached 38,000 in December 1999.

DLJdirect provided access to its service both through the Internet and through the major online services (America Online, Prodigy, and CompuServe); customers could also place trades with brokers or through Touch-Tone phones. Clients could trade stocks, options, bonds, and Treasuries and could select from about 7,000 mutual funds (out of the 9,500 currently available funds). Online clients with account balances of $100,000 or more were provided access to DLJ's proprietary research information on 1,100 companies as well as opportunities to buy initial public offerings of stock in which DLJ was a lead manager or participant. In addition, DLJdirect offered real-time quotes, stock and portfolio alerts, a personal stock ticker, and screening tools.

DLJdirect promoted itself as "a serious company for the serious investor." The company received *Barron's* highest rating (four stars) in a March 13, 2000, article reviewing the top 27 online brokers; *Barron's* evaluation criteria included trade execution process, ease of use, reliability and range of offerings, amenities, and commissions. The Lafferty Group, which rated about 500 Web sites in all sectors of the global financial services industry, gave DLJdirect a five-star rating (46 points out of a possible 50 points) during the fourth quarter of 1999. During 1999, DLJdirect had also been rated the top online brokerage by *Forbes, Time Digital, Worth,* Keynote Web Brokerage Index, and Gomez Advisors.

Datek Online Holdings, Inc. (www.datek.com)

Until September 1999, Datek Online was headed by Jeffrey A. Citron, a 29-year-old who had started working at 17 as an office clerk in a small Brooklyn, New York, brokerage called Datek Securities. By age 20, Citron had earned $1 million trading securities and was driving a Mercedes. A few years later, Citron and co-worker Joshua Levine used their computer skills to automate much of Datek's brokerage operations and started to explore ways to computerize stock trades. When in 1988 NASDAQ ordered securities dealers who were market makers in over-the-counter stocks to execute small orders via a computerized electronic system, Citron and Levine came up with a software trading system that allowed Datek Securities to become the biggest brokerage that executed small trades and to make millions of dollars in trading profits—the company had trading profits of about $95 million in 1996, up from $3.8 million in 1992.[29] Citron and Levine became multimillionaires. Jeffrey Citron was labeled a "technology wizard" by *Forbes* and as "one of the 20 most important players on the financial Web" by *Institutional Investor.* But during the 1991–96 period, various officials at Datek Securities were censured, fined, and suspended by the National Association of Securities Dealers on several occasions for violating trading rules in executing small trading orders on the

---

[29]*New York Times,* May 10, 1998, section 3, p. 4.

NASDAQ. Datek Securities was also on the losing end of numerous customer arbitrations alleging violations such as unauthorized trading or failure to execute customer orders.

In 1992, Citron and Levine founded a company (what is now Island ECN) to function as a computerized stock exchange, utilizing software they had created—the company was quite successful and, by 1998, was handling 4 percent of all NASDAQ trading volume.[30] In 1993, Jeffrey Citron formed his own brokerage firm, which he sold a few months later to Joshua Levine. In 1995, Citron established a company to sell electronic trading software, while Levine formed two companies—Big Think (to supply Datek Securities with new computer technology) and Big J Software, a software consulting company whose principal clients were securities firms. In early 1996, Citron, Levine, and Sheldon Maschler, former chief trader at Datek Securities who was the central figure in many of the firm's trading violations and was later suspended from securities trading for one year beginning in February 1997, formed a company to develop and license trading software to Datek Securities and other online brokerage operations; the new company achieved revenues of nearly $100 million in 1996. In 1997, Datek Securities established Datek Online as an Internet brokerage and Jeffrey Citron became CEO. In early 1998, Datek Securities and Levine's Big Think were merged as Datek Online Holdings; Citron, Levine, Erik Maschler (son of Sheldon Maschler), and several others emerged as the principal owners. In 1998 the old Datek Securities unit was sold in an effort to help disassociate Datek Online from its troubled past, but in 2000 the trading and lending practices at the old Datek Securities were still under investigation by the SEC and the U.S. Attorney's Office in Manhattan.

In early 1997, Datek had 10,000 online accounts; in April 1998, it reportedly had 80,000 accounts, containing $1.5 billion in assets. In mid-1999, Datek had 253,000 online trading accounts containing $6 billion in customer assets. A principal reason for Datek's success was its innovative software programs—it had the fastest execution of electronic stock trades, and it offered customers both streaming quotes and free real-time quotes. The firm's systems were based on superfast trading software technology that it was marketing to day-trading firms. Datek Online's low commissions also appealed to active traders. Aside from having spurred trading innovations with its Island ECN, Datek Online was recognized for setting standards for speed and service in the online brokerage business. In 2000, Datek was the fifth largest online brokerage firm.

Jeffrey Citron and the other investors in Datek Online were forced to scrap plans for taking the company public in mid-1998 amid publicity over the continuing investigations of Datek Securities. A lengthy feature article in the *New York Times* in May 1998 detailed the numerous entanglements of Datek Online's owners with Datek Securities and the many sanctions imposed on Datek Securities. However, the article indicated that Jeffrey Citron had recently tightened management controls at Datek Online Holdings, outlawed certain questionable trading practices, hired a major accounting firm as auditor, and completed the sale of the company's Datek Securities trading unit, the center of most of the questioned practices and the target of several ongoing investigations of securities fraud. The purchasers of the securities trading unit, renamed Heartland Securities, were two of the current owners of Datek Online Holdings, Erik Maschler and Aaron Elbogen; in 1970, Elbogen had been one of the original cofounders of Datek Securities.

In early 1999, Edward Nicoll, a 46-year-old Wall Street executive who had earned a law degree from Yale in 1998 without ever having attended college, was brought in to head Datek Online's operations and work with Citron to turn Datek into a quality

---

[30]Ibid.

firm. Nicoll assumed a significant ownership stake in the firm as part of his agreement to join Datek Online. In July 2000, Groupe Arnault of Paris and TA Associates of Boston contracted to invest $195 million in new capital into Datek, but a third investor, Vulcan Ventures (owned by Microsoft cofounder Paul Allen) backed out of a $50 million commitment at the last minute, citing "due diligence" problems. Vulcan also dropped plans to invest $25 million in Island ECN in return for a 12 percent ownership stake. In an article reporting on the Vulcan withdrawal, the *New York Times,* citing people close to the ongoing investigations into Datek Securities, said that during the period when Jeffrey Citron and Sheldon Maschler were the principal traders at Datek Securities the company was involved in a number of money-laundering operations. In October 1999, TD Waterhouse also stepped back from a $25 million investment in Datek, even though TD Waterhouse was a company that Edward Nicoll had cofounded and helped run for 16 years. Both Vulcan and Waterhouse, while attracted by the company's technological innovativeness and rapid growth, were believed to have had second thoughts about partnering with Datek because of its scandal-plagued background. Datek was expected to use the nearly $300 million in planned capital infusions to upgrade its technology at Datek Online and to help prepare Island ECN to become a full-fledged stock exchange (a petition had been filed with the SEC).

To help polish the firm's tarnished reputation and attract investment capital to upgrade its technology, Jeffrey Citron had resigned as chairman and CEO of Datek in September 1999 and relinquished his seats on the board of directors of both Datek and Island. Edward Nicoll replaced Jeffrey Citron as CEO. While Citron still owned about a third of Datek Online Holding's outstanding shares, he had put his shares into a trust for two years so that they could not be used to influence the board during that time. However, Citron's departure and the appointment of Nicoll as his replacement, which occurred while TD Waterhouse was still considering investing in Datek, were insufficient to keep Waterhouse from backing away from its deal with Datek.

Nicoll hoped that Datek Online's prior history and ties to Datek Securities would fade into the background, allowing the company to go public sometime in 2000.

Merrill Lynch (www.ml.com)

Merrill Lynch was a diversified financial services firm whose principal businesses were in investment banking, full-service brokerage, and asset management. It was the world leader in full-service brokerage, with 950 branch offices in 40 countries, approximately 19,000 brokers and account executives worldwide, 8 million retail customer accounts (covering about 5 million households), and $1.34 trillion in its retail brokerage accounts. The firm had an exceptionally broad range of investment products and services, and the name Merrill Lynch was known to virtually all investors worldwide. Merrill Lynch consistently ranked among the leading research providers in the industry, covering some 3,700 companies in 55 countries with its staff of roughly 680 analysts. Current information on all these companies was available to all retail clients through their brokers and could also be accessed online. In the securities-dealer side of its brokerage business, Merrill Lynch was a market maker for the stocks of 550 U.S. companies and 4,800 foreign companies traded in over-the-counter markets. In 1999, Merrill Lynch had total revenues of $21.9 billion and net income of $2.6 billion. Retail brokerage commissions from stock trading accounted for $3.6 billion of Merrill Lynch's revenues, up from $3.2 billion in 1998 and $1.8 billion in 1995.[31] The company had a total of 67,200 employees.

_____

[31] 1999 Merrill Lynch Factbook, p. 16.

Top management's vision was for Merrill Lynch to be a world-class company that delivered global products, services, and intelligence of the highest caliber through trusted local relationships and to build leadership positions in securities markets throughout the world. Management was committed to serving clients through personalized advice and guidance, helping to create customized solutions to individualized client problems and expertly implement and execute financial plans for clients.

Because of its strong strategic emphasis on using brokers to deliver personalized client services, Merrill Lynch had held back in pursuing online trading. Prior to its June 1999 announcement that it would give its clients an online trading option, Merrill Lynch's only concession in using online capabilities was to create a software package for clients to install on their own computers that allowed them to access their accounts and review account balances; customers were charged $25 for the software. A Merrill Lynch executive indicated that the reason the firm hadn't rushed to offer online trading was "this is not one of the highest-rated things that our clients are asking for."[32]

In December 1999, Merrill Lynch launched its online trading program, called Merrill Lynch Direct. According to a Merrill Lynch executive:

> Merrill Lynch Direct offers far more than just online trading execution. With features such as real-time account positions, tax-management information, the Global Investor Network for research, banking services and online shopping with an exceptional Visa Signature Rewards program, self-directed investors will be able to use this site to help manage all aspects of their financial lives.

Users of ML Direct could obtain help to make informed investment decisions using such information sources as Merrill Lynch's industry-leading research, S&P stock reports, real-time Dow Jones news stories and headlines; S&P stock, bonds and earnings guides and dividend records; as well as daily news feeds from PR Newswire and Business Wire. Merrill Lynch's Global Investor Network (GIN) provided investment research in streaming video; GIN was updated daily with audio and video reports from Merrill Lynch analysts, economists, mutual fund managers, and financial planning experts who covered markets around the world. Merrill Lynch's online clients also had unlimited access to:

- Real-time stock quotes.
- Stock, mutual fund, and fixed-income scanners.
- Retirement, education, and savings goal calculators.
- Comprehensive investor education information.
- Asset allocation and other extensive charting capabilities.

Clients who used Merrill Lynch Direct did not have access to one-on-one advice from the firm's professional financial consultants; broker-assisted trades were not a part of the Merrill Lynch Direct service. Those who wanted one-on-one professional advice could opt for Merrill Lynch's Unlimited Advantage program, a service that combined unlimited online trading and trading through a personal broker for an annual fee ranging from 0.2 percent to 1.0 percent of the assets under management, subject to an annual minimum of $1,500.

Merrill Lynch had invested in Archipelago ECN and several other electronic trading and marketing systems in order to participate in what management saw as a rapidly changing brokerage and trading environment.

---

[32]As quoted in *The Wall Street Journal,* June 2, 1998, p. C20.

American Express Brokerage (www.americanexpress.com)

One of the newest industry participants was American Express Brokerage, which launched a new online trading service in the fall of 1999; the new service replaced American Express's Financial Direct, an online brokerage site, introduced in 1996, that never caught on. American Express offered its new brokerage service through its American Express Financial Advisors unit, which had a force of 9,300 advisers. Clients of these advisers were charged an annual fee based on a percentage of the assets in their accounts. American Express Brokerage's commission schedule varied according to how the trade was placed and the size of a customer's account:

Online trades with an account balance of:	
Less than $25,000	$14.95 (for all stock trades up to 3,000 shares/trade)
$25,000 to $99,999	Free unlimited buys, $14.95 sells
$100,000 and above	Free unlimited buys and sells
Voice response/Touch-Tone trading	$19.95 (for all stock trades up to 3,000 shares/trade)
Trades placed with an adviser	$44.95 (for all stock trades up to 3,000 shares/trade)

American Express Brokerage was able to provide free trading on large accounts because of the annual fees charged on the assets in each account and because it was able to defer some of the costs with the order flow fees it received from market makers.

American Express Brokerage offered nearly 2,000 mutual funds from such recognized fund families as Janus, American Century, Scudder, and T. Rowe Price. Customers could also purchase certificates of deposit and buy insurance. All account holders had access to unlimited check writing, ATM privileges, and bill-paying options. In August 1999, American Express had launched an online bank, and in September 1999 it had introduced a credit card, aimed at active Internet shoppers, that used a chip embedded in the card to provide added security features.

case 11 eBay: King of the Online Auction Industry

Louis Marino
The University of Alabama

Patrick Kreiser
The University of Alabama

As Pierre Omidyar (pronounced oh-*mid*-ee-ar), chairman and founder of eBay, set his morning copy of *The Wall Street Journal* down on the desk, he nervously wondered how long eBay's amazing run of success would continue. He had just read an article detailing the explosion in sales of Amazon.com to $650 million during the fourth quarter of 1999, a number that exceeded the company's entire sales for the year of 1998. Even more disconcerting to Pierre was that online auctions were the fastest-growing part of Amazon's business in 1999. Competition from Amazon.com, Yahoo!, and several other enterprising dot-com companies that had started holding auctions at their Web sites had reduced eBay's dominant market share from 80 percent to 60 percent during 1999. Other outsiders, including Microsoft and Dell, had announced plans to fund new ventures to enter the online auction business.

When Pierre formed eBay in 1995, he had never imagined the company would become so successful. He had continued to work at his old job even after forming eBay. Soon, however, he realized that the online auction industry represented a tremendous market opportunity—eBay gave hobbyists and collectors a convenient way to locate items of interest, a way for sellers to generate income, and a means for bargain hunters to pick up a wanted item at less than they might have paid in a retail store. Still, the rapid growth of eBay had surprised almost everyone (see Exhibit 1).

By 1999, when people thought about online auctions, the first name that popped into their heads was eBay. Going into 2000, eBay had created the world's largest Web-based community of consumer-to-consumer auctions using an entertaining format that allowed people to buy and sell collectibles, automobiles, jewelry, high-end and premium art items, antiques, coins and stamps, dolls and figures, pottery and glass, sports memorabilia, toys, consumer electronics products, and a host of other practical and miscellaneous items. At year-end 1999, eBay had listed over 3 million items in over 3,000 categories; browsers and buyers could search listings by item, category, key word, seller name, or auction dates. The company Web site had approximately 10 million registered users and, *exhibit 1*   Selected Indicators of eBay's Growth, 1996–99

	1996	1997	1998	1999
Number of registered users	41,000	341,000	2,181,000	10,006,000
Gross merchandise sales	$7 million	$95 million	$745 million	$2.8 billion
Number of auctions listed	289,000	4,394,000	33,668,000	129,560,000

on average, attracted 1.8 million unique visitors daily. EBay members listed more than 375,000 items on the site every day.

However, Pierre Omidyar, Margaret Whitman (eBay's president and CEO), and other eBay executives were well aware that eBay needed to address a myriad of emerging market challenges. The complexion of the online auction industry was changing almost daily. While eBay's management team had met past challenges successfully, it wasn't going to be easy to hurdle the competitive and market challenges ahead.

THE GROWTH OF E-COMMERCE AND ONLINE AUCTIONS

Although the ideas behind the Internet were first conceived in the 1960s, it wasn't until the 1990s that the Internet garnered widespread use and became a part of everyday life. The real beginning of the Internet economy took place in 1991, when the National Science Foundation (NSF) lifted a restriction on commercial use of the Internet, making electronic commerce, or business conducted over the Internet, a possibility for the first time. By 1996, there were Internet users in almost 150 countries worldwide, and the number of computer hosts was close to 10 million. International Data Corporation (IDC) estimated there would be 320 million Internet users worldwide by 2002 and 500 million by year-end 2003.

The GartnerGroup forecast that business-to-business e-commerce would grow from $145 billion in 1999 to $7.29 trillion in 2004, while business-to-consumer revenues would climb from $31.2 billion in 1999 to over $380 billion in 2003. Within the business-to-consumer segment, where eBay operated, U.S. e-commerce accounted for over 65 percent of all Internet transactions in 1999 but was expected to account for only about 38 percent in 2003, due to rapid expansion in other parts of the world.

Business-to-consumer e-commerce in Europe was projected to grow from $5.4 billion in 1999 (17.3 percent of the world total) to over $115 billion (more than 30 percent of the world total) by 2003. As can be seen from Exhibit 2, online auction sales of collectibles and personal merchandise was expected to represent an $18.7 billion market in 2002.

Key Success Factors in Online Retailing

While it was relatively easy to create a Web site that functioned like a retail store, the big challenge was for an online retailer to generate traffic to the site in the form of both new and returning customers. Most online retailers strived to provide extensive product information, include pictures of the merchandise, make the site easily navigable, and have enough new things happening at the site to keep customers coming back. (A site's ability to generate repeat visitors was known as "stickiness.") Retailers also had

exhibit 2 Estimated Growth in Global E-Commerce and Online Auction Sales, 1999–2004

	1999	2000	2001	2002	2003	2004
Estimated business-to-business sales	$145 billion	$403 billion	$953 billion	$2.18 trillion	$3.95 trillion	$7.29 trillion

Source: GartnerGroup.

Estimated Growth in Global Business-to-Business E-Commerce

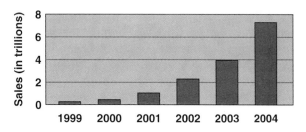

Online Auction Sales of Collectibles and Personal Merchandise
(Sales in billions of dollars)

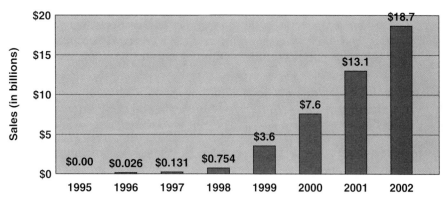

Source: Keenan Vision Inc. Mercury News.

to overcome users' nervousness about using the Internet itself to shop for items they generally bought at stores and their wariness about entering their credit card numbers over the Internet. Online retailing had severe limitations in the case of those goods and services people wanted to see in person to verify their quality. From the retailer's perspective, there was the issue of collecting payment from buyers who wanted to use checks or money orders instead of a credit card.

HISTORY OF AUCTIONS

An auction is a method of buying and selling goods to the highest bidder. A seller offers a particular product or service for sale, and the buyer who makes the highest offer for it is considered the auction winner. As the demand for a particular good rises among the buyers (typically due to its scarcity or desirability), the price also rises. Competition among bidders for a desirable good drives up the price. Sometimes the highest bid will exceed the generally accepted market value of the good, a phenomenon known as the "winner's curse." In this situation, the buyer becomes so emotionally attached to the good or to placing the highest bid that he or she ends up bidding more than the good would cost in a nonauction setting.

The first known auctions were held in Babylon around 500 BC. In these auctions, women were sold to the highest bidder on the condition that they marry the auction winner. In ancient Rome, soldiers would auction the spoils of their victories and wealthy citizens would auction their expensive belongings and prized possessions. In 193 AD, the entire Roman Empire was put up for auction after the emperor Pertinax was executed. Didius Julianus bid 6,250 drachmas per royal guard and was immediately named emperor of Rome. However, Julianus was executed only two months later, indicating that he may have been the first-ever victim of the winner's curse.

Since that time, auctions have been conducted in every corner of the globe. The possessions of deceased Buddhist monks were auctioned off as early as the seventh century. In the late 16th century, auctions began to be held in taverns and alehouses in Great Britain. Sotheby's was founded in 1744, and Christie's was established in 1766; both have now become world-renowned auction houses for rare and valuable items. Auctions for tobacco, horses, and other domestic animals were commonplace in colonial America.

Auctions have endured throughout history for several reasons. First, they give sellers a convenient way to find a buyer for something they would like to dispose of. Second, auctions are an excellent way for people to collect difficult-to-find items, such as Beanie Babies or historical memorabilia, that have a high value to them personally. Finally, auctions are one of the "purest" markets that exist for goods, in that they bring buyers and sellers into contact to arrive at a mutually agreeable price. Experts estimated that the national market for auctions, garage sales, flea markets, and classified purchases was greater than $100 billion in 1999.

ONLINE AUCTIONS

Online auctions worked in essentially the same way as traditional auctions, the difference being that the auction process occurred over the Internet rather than at a specific geographic location with buyers and sellers physically present. In 2000, there were three categories of online auctions:

1. Business-to-business auctions, which accounted for $2.5 billion in sales in 1998 and involved such items as computers, used equipment, and surplus merchandise.
2. Business-to-consumer auctions, in which businesses sold goods and services to consumers via the Internet. Many such auctions involved companies interested in selling used or discontinued goods, or liquidating unwanted inventory.
3. Person-to-person auctions, which gave interested sellers and buyers the opportunity to engage in competitive bidding.

Since eBay's pioneering of the person-to-person online auction process in 1995, the number of online auction sites on the Internet had grown to well over 1,600 by the end of 1999. Forrester Research predicted that 6.5 million customers would use online auctions in 2002. In 1999 an estimated 8.2 percent of Internet users registered at an auction site; the percentage was expected to be 14.5 percent by 2002.

Online auction operators could generate revenue in four principal ways:

1. Charging sellers for listing their good or service.
2. Charging a commission on all sales.

3. Selling advertising on their Web sites.
4. Selling their own new or used merchandise via the online auction format.

Most sites charged sellers either a fee or a commission and sold advertising to companies interested in promoting their goods or services to users of the auction site.

Auction Software Packages

In 1996, OpenSite Technologies began to offer packaged software applications to firms interested in creating their own online auction Web sites. Moai Technologies and Ariba, Inc., were other sources for auction software. The ready availability of commercial software packages made it easy for firms to create and operate online auction sites. OpenSite had marketed over 600 auction packages to such companies as The Sharper Image, CNET, and John Deere. OpenSite claimed that its purpose was to bring together "buyers and sellers, helping businesses dynamically manage inventory, create sales channels, attract customers, and test market new products, to create efficient markets for goods and services."

Providers of Site Hosting and Online Auction Services

Auction firms could, if they wished, outsource all the hosting functions associated with online auctions to independent site-hosting enterprises and could even turn the entire auction process over to an independent online auction specialist. FairMarket, the leader in auction outsourcing in 1999, provided companies such as ZDNet, MicroWarehouse, and CollegeBytes.com with a means of selling their goods at online auction at FairMarket's Web site. The use of site hosts and independent online auction services was a particularly appealing option for companies that wanted to use online auctions as a distribution channel but preferred to devote only minimal time and energy to site construction and upkeep. By paying FairMarket an annual hosting fee between $2,000 and $10,000, as well as a percentage fee on all transactions, firms were able to have an auction site without having to worry about the hassle of site upkeep.

Online Auction Users

Participants in online auctions could be grouped into three categories: (1) bargain hunters, (2) hobbyists/collectors, and (3) sellers.

Bargain Hunters   Bargain hunters viewed online auctions primarily as a form of entertainment; their objective usually was to find a great deal. One bargain hunter described the eBay experience as follows:

> A friend and I would spend one day a week going flea marketing and auctioning. Since school has started again, time has become a hot commodity. We've found that we can use eBay to fill that flea marketing, auctioning need. We'll call each other, then get on eBay and hunt and find things together even though we can't be together. EBay has definitely been a great way to spend quality time together!

Bargain hunters were thought to make up only 8 percent of active online users but 52 percent of eBay visitors. To attract repeat visits from bargain hunters, industry observers said, sites must appeal to them on both rational and emotional levels, satisfying their need for competitive pricing, the excitement of the search, and the desire for community.[1]

Hobbyists and Collectors   Hobbyists and collectors used auctions to search for specific goods that had a high value to them personally. They were very concerned with both price and quality. Collectors prized eBay for its wide variety of product offerings. One user commented:

> My sister collects Princess House hand-blown ornaments. She needed the first three to complete her series. I posted to the Wanted Board several times, and also put a note on my About Me page. Well, we have now successfully completed her series. We could never have done this without eBay because the first one is so hard to find. Thanks eBay!

Sellers   Those in the sellers category could be further differentiated into at least three types: casual sellers, hobbyists/collectors, and power sellers. Casual sellers included individuals who used eBay as a substitute for a classified ad listing or a garage sale to dispose of items they no longer wanted. While many casual sellers listed only a few items, some used eBay to raise money for some new project. One such seller stated:

> Thank you! After just starting to use your site less than a month ago, I have increased my earnings by over $1,000. I have not yet received all the cash, but so far the response has been fantastic. This all started with a Kool-Aid container and four cups I had that were collecting dust in a box in the attic. I was "browsing for bargains" and saw someone else had made $29.00 from those plastic things! I was AMAZED! Needless to say, I listed them. I only made $8.00, but I received my first positive feedback. Since then I am listing daily.
>
> My wife and I are scrimping to save for an adoption of a baby. The fees are much more than our modest income can afford, and this extra cash will come in handy. My wife and I sincerely thank you and your company for the opportunity to be a part of eBay.

Sellers who were hobbyists or collectors typically dealt in a limited category of goods and looked to eBay as a way to sell selected items in their collections to others who might want them. Power sellers were typically small to medium-sized businesses that favored eBay as a primary distribution channel for their goods and often sold tens of thousands of dollars' worth of goods every month on the site. One estimate suggested that while these power sellers accounted for only 4 percent of eBay's population, they were responsible for 80 percent of eBay's total business.[2]

Concerns about Buyer Addiction to Online Auctions

Some members of the online auction community reportedly found the experience so intriguing that they became addicted. According to the Center for Online Addiction, symptoms of online auction addiction ranged from "using online auctions as a way of escaping from problems or relieving feelings of helplessness, guilt, anxiety, or depression" to "needing to bid with increasing amounts of money in order to achieve the desired excitement."[3] The center predicted that "online auction houses will be the next frenzy leading to shopping addiction" and had treated online auction addicts who had to take out a second mortgage or file bankruptcy as a result of their excessive online purchases.[4] One online auction addict told of his experience as follows:

---

[1]"Internet Consumer Segments Identified for First Time," PR Newswire, April 17, 2000.

[2]Claire Tristram, "'Amazoning' Amazon," www.contextmag.com, November 1999.

[3]www.netaddiction.com, April 16, 2000.

[4]Ibid.

It became critical when my boss confronted me. [My employer] had monitored my Internet use, and it was even more than I was aware of. My boss told me he had no choice but to terminate me. I've been at this job almost five years, have achieved recognition at the national level for the program, and have previously been a very capable employee. How can I [justify] throwing all that away? There is no doubt, though, that my productivity had really begun to suffer.

I was truthful with my boss about how this had become a compulsion I just could not control. I attributed it to some real stresses in my personal life, and kept telling myself that when things settled down, I would get a handle on it. He has put me on [administrative] leave while he thinks things over.[5]

PIERRE OMIDYAR AND THE FOUNDING OF EBAY

Pierre Omidyar was born in Paris, France, to parents who had left Iran decades earlier. The family emigrated to the United States when Pierre's father began a residency at Johns Hopkins University Medical Center. Pierre grew up in modest circumstances; his parents divorced when he was two but remained near each other so he could be with both of them. Pierre's passion for computers began at an early age; he would sneak out of gym class in high school to play with computers. While still in high school, at age 14 he took his first computer-related job in the school's library, where he was hired for $6.00 an hour to write a program to print catalog cards.[6] After high school Pierre attended Tufts University, where he met his future wife, Pamela Wesley, who came to Tufts from Hawaii to get a degree in biology. Upon graduating in 1988, the couple moved to California, where Pierre, who had earned a BS in computer science, joined Claris, an Apple Computer subsidiary in Silicon Valley, and wrote a widely used graphics application, MacDraw. In 1991, Omidyar left Claris and cofounded Ink Development (later renamed eShop), which became a pioneer in online shopping and was eventually sold to Microsoft in 1996. In 1994 Omidyar joined General Magic as a developer services engineer and remained there until mid-1996, when he left to pursue full-time development of eBay.

Internet folklore has it that eBay was founded solely to allow Pamela to trade Pez dispensers with other collectors. While Pamela was certainly a driving force in launching the initial Web site, Pierre had long been interested in how one could establish a marketplace to bring together a fragmented market. Pierre saw eBay as a way to create a person-to-person trading community based on a democratized, efficient market where everyone could have equal access through the same medium, the Internet. Pierre set out to develop his marketplace and to meet both his and Pamela's goals. In 1995 he launched the first online auction under the name of Auctionwatch at the domain name of www.eBay.com. The name eBay stood for "electronic Bay area," coined because Pierre's initial concept was to attract neighbors and other interested San Francisco Bay area residents to the site to buy and sell items of mutual interest. The first auctions charged no fees to either buyers or sellers and contained mostly computer equipment (and no Pez dispensers). Pierre's fledgling venture generated $1,000 in revenue the first month and an additional $2,000 the second. Traffic grew rapidly, however, as word about the site spread in the Bay area; a community of collectors emerged, using the site to trade and chat—some marriages resulted from exchanges in eBay chat rooms.[7]

---

[5]www.auctionwatch.com, April 16, 2000.

[6]tbwt.com/interaction/1pomid/1pomid.htm.

[7]Quentin Hardy, "The Radical Philanthropist," *Forbes,* May 1, 2000, p. 118.

exhibit 3   eBay's Income Statements, 1996–99 ($000, Except Per Share Figures)

	1996	1997	1998	1999
Net revenues	$32,051	$41,370	$86,129	$224,724
Cost of net revenues	6,803	8,404	16,094	57,588
Gross profit	25,248	32,966	70,035	167,136
Operating expenses				
Sales and marketing	13,139	15,618	35,976	95,956
Product development	28	831	4,640	23,785
General and administrative	5,661	6,534	15,849	43,055
Amortization of acquired intangibles	—	—	805	1,145
Merger related costs		—	—	4,359
Total operating expenses	18,828	22,983	57,270	168,300
Income (loss) from operations	6,420	9,983	12,765	(1,164)
Interest and other income (expense), net	(2,607)	(1,951)	(703)	21,377
Income before income taxes	3,813	8,032	12,062	20,213
Provision for income taxes	(475)	(971)	(4,789)	(9,385)
Net income	$ 3,338	$ 7,061	$ 7,273	$ 10,828
Net income per share				
Basic	$0.39	$0.29	$0.14	$0.10
Diluted	.07	0.08	0.06	0.08
Weighted average shares				
Basic	8,490	24,428	52,064	108,235
Diluted	45,060	84,775	116,759	135,910

Source: Company financial documents.

By February 1996, the traffic at Pierre Omidyar's site had grown so much that his Internet service provider informed him that he would have to upgrade his service. When Pierre compensated for this by charging a listing fee for the auction, and saw no decrease in the number of items listed, he knew he was on to something. Although he was still working out of his home, Pierre began looking for a partner and in May asked his friend Jeffrey Skoll to join him in the venture. While Jeff had never cared much about money, his Stanford MBA degree provided the firm with the business background that Pierre lacked.[8] With Pierre as the visionary and Jeff as the strategist, the company embarked on a mission to "help people trade practically anything on earth." Their concept for eBay was to "create a place where people could do business just like in the old days—when everyone got to know each other personally, and we all felt we were dealing on a one-to-one basis with individuals we could trust."

In eBay's early days, Pierre and Jeff ran the operation alone, using a single computer to serve all of the pages. Pierre served as CEO, chief financial officer, and president, while Jeff functioned as co-president and director. It was not long until Pierre and Jeff grew the company to a size that forced them to move out of Pierre's living room, due to the objections of Pamela, and into Jeff's living room. Shortly thereafter, the operations moved into the facilities of a Silicon Valley business incubator for a time until the company settled in its current facilities in San Jose, California.

Exhibits 3 and 4 present eBay's recent financial statements.

---

[8]Adam Cohen, "The eBay Revolution," www.time.com.

exhibit 4   eBay's Consolidated Balance Sheets, 1997–99 ($000)

	December 31, 1997	December 31, 1998	December 31, 1999
Assets			
Current assets			
Cash and cash equivalents	$3,723	$ 37,285	$219,679
Short-term investments	—	40,401	181,086
Accounts receivable, net	1,024	12,425	36,538
Other current assets	220	7,479	22,531
Total current assets	4,967	97,590	459,834
Property and equipment, net	652	44,062	111,806
Investments	—	—	373,988
Deferred tax asset	—	—	5,639
Intangible and other assets, net	—	7,884	12,675
Total assets	$5,619	$149,536	$963,942
Liabilities and Stockholders' Equity			
Current liabilities			
Accounts payable	$ 252	$ 9,997	$ 31,538
Accrued expenses and other current liabilities	—	6,577	32,550
Deferred revenue and customer advances	128	973	5,997
Debt and leases, current portion	258	4,047	12,285
Income taxes payable	169	1,380	6,455
Deferred tax liabilities	—	1,682	—
Other current liabilities	128	5,981	7,632
Total current liabilities	1,124	24,656	88,825
Debt and leases, long-term portion	305	18,361	15,018
Other liabilities	157		
Total liabilities	1,586	48,998	111,475
Series B mandatorily redeemable convertible preferred stock and Series B warrants	3,018	—	—
Total stockholders' equity	1,015	100,538	852,467
Total liabilities and stockholders' equity	$5,619	$149,536	$963,942

Source: Company financial documents.

EBAY'S TRANSITION TO PROFESSIONAL MANAGEMENT

From the beginning Pierre Omidyar intended to hire a professional manager to serve as the president of eBay: "[I would] let him or her run the company so . . . [I could] go play."[9] In 1997 both Omidyar and Skoll agreed that it was time to locate an experienced professional to function as CEO and president. In late 1997 eBay's headhunters came up with a candidate for the job: Margaret Whitman, then general manager for Hasbro Inc.'s preschool division. Whitman had received her BA in economics from Princeton and her MBA from the Harvard Business School; her first job was in brand

[9]*Business 2.0,* "Billionaires of the Web," The Candyman, June 1999.

management at Procter & Gamble. Her experience also included serving as the president and CEO of FTD, the president of Stride Rite Corporation's Stride Rite Division, and as the senior vice president of marketing for the Walt Disney Company's consumer product division.[10]

When first approached by eBay, Whitman was not especially interested in joining a company that had fewer than 40 employees and less than $6 million in revenues the previous year. It was only after repeated pleas that Whitman agreed to meet with Omidyar in Silicon Valley. After a second meeting, Whitman realized the company's enormous growth potential and agreed to give eBay a try. According to Omidyar, Meg Whitman's experience in global marketing with Hasbro's Teletubbies, Playskool, and Mr. Potato Head brands made her "the ideal choice to build upon eBay's leadership position in the one-to-one online trading market without sacrificing the quality and personal touch our users have grown to expect."[11] In addition to convincing Margaret Whitman to head eBay's operations, Omidyar had been instrumental in helping bring in other talented senior executives and in assembling a capable board of directors. Notable members of eBay's board of directors included Scott Cook, the founder of Intuit, a highly successful financial software company, and Howard Schultz, the founder and CEO of Starbucks. (For a profile of eBay's senior management team, check out the Company Overview section at www.ebay.com.)

Whitman ran the operation from the time she came on board. Omidyar, who owned 27.9 percent of eBay's stock (worth approximately $6 billion as of March 2000), spent considerable time in Paris. He and Pamela, still in their mid-30s and concerned about the vast wealth they had accumulated in such a short period of time, were devoting a substantial amount of their energy to exploring philanthropic causes.[12] They had decided to give most of their fortune to charity and were scrutinizing alternative ways to maximize the impact of their philanthropic contributions on the overall well-being of society. Jeffrey Skoll owned 16.7 percent of eBay's shares (worth about $3.6 billion), and Margaret Whitman owned 5.2 percent (worth about $1 billion).

HOW AN EBAY AUCTION WORKED

EBay endeavored to make it very simple to buy and sell goods (see Exhibits 5 and 6). In order to sell or bid on goods, users first had to register at the site. Once they registered, users selected both a user name and a password. Nonregistered users were able to browse the Web site but were not permitted to bid on any goods or list any items for auction. On the Web site, search engines helped customers determine what goods were currently available. When registered users found an item they desired, they could choose to enter a single bid or to use automatic bidding. In automatic bidding the customer entered an initial bid sufficient to make him or her the high bidder and then the bid would be automatically increased as others bid for the same object until the auction ended and either the bidder won or another bidder surpassed the original customer's maximum specified bid. Regardless of which bidding method they chose, users could check bids at any time and either bid again, if they had been outbid, or increase their maximum amount in the automatic bid. Users could choose to receive e-mail notification if they were outbid. Once the auction had ended, the buyer and seller were each notified of the winning bid

---

[10]www.ebay.com, Company Overview page.
[11]eBay press release, May 7, 1998.
[12]Hardy, "The Radical Philanthropist."

exhibit 5   eBay's Instructions for Becoming a New Bidder

Source: pages.eBay.com/help/basics/n-bidding.html.

and were given each other's e-mail address. The parties to the auction would then privately arrange for payment and delivery of the good.

Fees and Procedures for Sellers   EBayers were not charged a fee for bidding on items on the site, but sellers were charged an insertion fee and a "final value" fee; they could also elect to pay additional fees to promote their listing. Listing, or insertion, fees ranged from 25 cents for auctions with opening bids between $0.01 and $9.99, to $2.00 for auctions with opening bids of $50.00 and up. Final value fees ranged from 1.25 to 5 percent of the final sale price and were computed based on a graduated fee schedule in which the percentage fell as the final sales price rose. As an example, in a basic auction with no promotion, if the item had brought an opening bid of $100 and eventually sold for $1,500, the total fee paid by the seller, would be $33.88—the $2.00 insertion fee plus $31.88. The $31.88 is based on a fee structure of 5 percent of the first $25.00 (or $1.25), 2.5 percent of the additional amount between $25.01 and $1,000.00 (or $24.38), and 1.25 percent of the additional amount between $1,000.01 and $1,500.00 (or $6.25).

A seller who wished to promote an item could choose a bold heading for an additional fee of $2.00. A seller with a favorable feedback rating (discussed below) could have his or her auction listed either as a "Featured Auction" for $99.95, which allowed the seller's item to be rotated on the eBay home page, or as a "Category Featured Auction" for $14.95, which allowed the item to be featured within a particular eBay category.

exhibit 6   eBay's Instructions for Becoming a New Seller

eBay

| Browse | Sell | Services | Search | Help | Community |

basics | buyer guide | seller guide | my info | billing | rules & safety

Billpoint, the best way to send and receive payment on eBay!
Business Exchange—eBay's small business marketplace.
Local Trading—buy or sell in a region near you!

Search
☐ Search titles **and** descriptions

Smart Search

New to Selling?

It's so easy—you'll love it! Here's what to do...

1. First, you'll need to register, if you haven't done so already.

2. **Set up your selling account.** Place your credit card on file with eBay and you're ready to sell! If you'd like to accept credit card payments from winning bidders, sign up for Billpoint online payments.

3. **Gather the info** you'll need before you prepare your listing:
   - your item description
   - the URL (web site address) for any photos (see the photo tutorial)
   - the category you'll list under

4. Go to the Sell Your Item form, **fill in the info**, and review your listing. Be sure to check the information carefully, then click on Submit My Listing.

5. You'll see a confirmation page; **jot down the info**, such as your item number. This will be helpful if you want to update your listing, and to keep track of your item's status as your very own auction progresses!

6. When your auction closes, **contact your winning bidder** or bidders within three business days. You'll want to confirm the final cost, including any shipping charges, and tell them where to send payment. When the bidder meets your payment terms, you fulfill your end of the agreement by sending them your item. Your auction forms a binding contract between you and the winning bidder or bidders.

And then that's it—your item is sold!

Source: pages.eBay.com/help/basics/n-selling.html.

For $1.00, a seller could choose to place a seasonal icon (such as a shamrock in connection with St. Patrick's Day) next to his or her listing. A seller could also include a description of the product with links to the seller's Web site. In addition, a seller could indicate a photograph in the item's description if the seller posted the photograph on a Web site and provided eBay with the appropriate Web address. Items could be showcased in the Gallery section with a catalog of pictures rather than text. A seller who used a photograph in his or her listing could have this photograph included in the Gallery section for 25 cents or featured there for $19.95. A Gallery section was available in all categories of eBay. Certain categories of items—such as real estate, automobiles, and "Great Collections"—had special promotion rates.

New sellers were required to file a credit card number with eBay for automatic monthly billing, while sellers who had opened accounts prior to October 22, 1999, could alternatively choose a pay-as-you-go method. The latter option, however, was relatively unattractive since it allowed eBay to block any account whose balance due reached $25.00. The block was removed once the fee was paid, or once the seller had registered a credit card with eBay.

How Transactions Are Completed   When an auction ended, the eBay system validated that the bid fell within the acceptable price range. If the sale was successful, eBay automatically notified the buyer and seller via e-mail; the buyer and seller could then work out the transaction details independent of eBay. At no point during the process did eBay take possession of either the item being sold or the buyer's payment. Rather, the buyer and seller had to independently arrange for the shipment of and payment for the item; buyers typically paid for shipping. A seller could view a buyer's feedback rating (discussed below) and then determine the manner of payment, such as personal check, cashier's check, or credit card, and also whether to ship the item before or after receiving payment. Under the terms of eBay's user agreement, if a seller received one or more bids above the stated minimum, or reserve, price, the seller was obligated to complete the transaction, although eBay had no enforcement power beyond suspending a noncompliant buyer or seller from using eBay's service. In the event the buyer and seller were unable to complete the transaction, the seller notified eBay, which then credited the seller the amount of the final value fee. When items carrying a reserve price sold, sellers were credited the $1.00 reserve fee. Invoices for placement fees, additional listing fees, and final value fees were sent via e-mail to sellers on a monthly basis.

Feedback Forum   In early 1996 eBay pioneered a feature called Feedback Forum to build trust among buyers and sellers and to facilitate the establishment of reputations within its community. Feedback Forum encouraged individuals to record comments about their trading partners. At the completion of each auction, both the buyer and seller were allowed to leave positive, negative, or neutral comments about each other. Individuals could dispute feedback left about them by annotating comment in question. By assigning values of $+1$ for a positive comment, 0 for a neutral comment, and -1 for a negative comment, each trader earned a ranking that was attached to their user name. A user who had developed a positive reputation over time had a color-coded star symbol displayed next to his or her user name to indicate the amount of positive feedback. The highest ranking a trader could receive was "over 10,000," indicated by a shooting star. Well-respected high-volume traders could have rankings well into the thousands. Users who received a sufficiently negative net feedback rating (typically a -4) had their registrations suspended and were thus unable to bid on or list items for sale. EBay users could review a person's feedback profile before deciding to bid on an item listed by that person or before choosing payment and delivery methods. A sample user profile is shown in Exhibit 7.

The terms of eBay's user agreement prohibited actions that would undermine the integrity of the Feedback Forum, such as leaving positive feedback about oneself through other accounts or leaving multiple negative comments about someone else through other accounts. EBay's Feedback Forum system had several automated features designed to detect and prevent some forms of abuse. For example, feedback posted from the same account, positive or negative, could not affect a user's net feedback rating by more than one point, no matter how many comments an individual made. Furthermore, a user could only make comments about his or her trading partners in completed transactions.

exhibit 7   A Sample Feedback Forum Profile

Source: www.ebay.com, April 14, 2000.

The company believed its Feedback Forum was extremely useful in overcoming users' initial hesitancy about trading over the Internet, since it reduced the uncertainty of dealing with an unknown trading partner.

EBAY'S STRATEGY TO SUSTAIN ITS MARKET DOMINANCE

Meg Whitman assumed the helm of eBay in February 1998 and began acting as the public face of the company. Pierre Omidyar stepped back to become chairman of eBay's board of directors and focused his time and energy on overseeing eBay's strategic direction and growth, business model and site development, and community advocacy. Jeff Skoll, who became the vice president of strategic planning and analysis, concentrated on competitive analysis, new business planning and incubation, the development of the organization's overall strategic direction, and supervision of customer support operations.

The Move to Go Public

Within months of assuming the presidency of eBay, Whitman took on the challenge of preparing the company to raise capital for expansion through an initial public offering (IPO) of common stock. Through a series of road shows designed to convince investors of the potential of eBay's business model, Whitman and her team generated significant interest in eBay's IPO. When the shares opened for trading on September 24, 1998, eBay's executives had high hopes for the offering, but none of them dreamed that it would close the day at $47, or 160 percent over the initial offering of $18 per share. The IPO generated $66 million in new capital for the company and was so successful that *Bloomberg Personal* magazine designated eBay as the "Hot IPO of 1998"; *Euromoney* magazine named eBay as the best IPO in the U.S. market in January 1999. The success of the September 1998 offering led eBay to issue a follow-up offering in April 1999 that raised an additional $600 million. As a qualification to the IPOs, eBay's board of directors retained the right to issue as many as 5 million additional shares of preferred stock with no further input from the current shareholders in case of a hostile takeover attempt.

With the funds received from the IPOs, eBay launched strategic initiatives aimed at six specific objectives:[13]

1. Growing the eBay community and strengthening our brand, both to attract new members and to maintain the vitality of the eBay community;
2. Broadening the company's trading platform by growing existing product categories, promoting new product categories, and offering services for specific regions;
3. Fostering eBay community affinity and increasing community trust and safety through services such as user verification and insurance;
4. Enhancing Web site features and functionality through the introduction of personalization features such as About Me, which permits users to create their own home page free of charge, and the Gallery, an opportunity for sellers to showcase their items as pictures in a photo catalog;
5. Expanding pre- and post-trade value-added services, such as assistance with scanning and uploading photographs of listed items, third-party escrow services and arrangements to make shipping of purchased items easier;
6. Developing international markets by actively marketing and promoting our Web site in selected countries.

To pursue these objectives, eBay employed three main competitive tactics. First, it sought to build strategic partnerships in all stages of its value chain, creating an impressive portfolio of over 250 strategic alliances with companies such as America Online (AOL), Yahoo!, Lycos, Compaq, and Warner Brothers. Second, it actively sought customer feedback and made improvements based on this information. Third, it actively monitored the external environment for developing opportunities.

eBay's Business Model

EBay's business model was based on creating and maintaining a person-to-person trading community where buyers and sellers could readily and conveniently exchange information and goods. EBay's role was to function as a value-added facilitator of online buyer-seller transactions by providing a supportive infrastructure that enabled buyers and sellers to come together in an efficient and effective manner. Success depended not only on the quality of eBay's infrastructure but also on the quality and quantity of buyers and

---

[13]Company S-1 filing with the Securities and Exchange Commission, March 25, 1999, p. 4.

sellers attracted to the site; in management's view, this entailed maintaining a compelling trading environment, a number of trust and safety programs, a cost-effective and convenient trading experience, and strong community affinity. By developing the eBay brand name and increasing the customer base, eBay endeavored to attract a sufficient number of high-quality buyers and sellers necessary to meet the organization's goals. The online auction format meant that eBay carried zero inventory and could operate a marketplace without the need for a traditional sales force.

Growing the eBay Community and Strengthening the Brand

In developing the eBay brand name and attracting new users, the company initially relied largely on word-of-mouth advertising, supplemented by public relations initiatives such as executive interviews and speaking engagements, special online events, and astute management of the public press. Then, with funds from the public offerings of common stock, eBay expanded its marketing activities to include advertising online as well as in traditional media, such as national magazines like *Parade, People, Entertainment Weekly, Newsweek,* and *Sports Illustrated.* A cornerstone of the strategy to increase eBay's exposure was the formation of alliances with a variety of partners, including Kinko's, First Auction, and Z Auction as well as Internet portals AOL, Netscape, and GO.com.

The Alliance with First Auction   In January 1998, eBay entered into a marketing agreement with First Auction, the auction division of the Internet Shopping Network. The terms of this agreement allowed both companies to advertise their services on each other's sites. While both organizations offered online auctions, eBay featured person-to-person trading, and First Auction engaged in business-to-consumer transactions, which eBay did not consider direct competition. A similar agreement was formed in February 1998 with Z Auction, another vendor-based auction site.

Alliance with America Online   EBay's initial alliance with AOL, announced in February 1998, was limited to eBay's providing a person-to-person online auction service in AOL's classifieds section. However, in September 1998 this agreement was expanded. In return for $12 million in payments over three years, AOL made eBay the preferred provider of personal trading services to AOL's 13 million members and the 2 million members of AOL's affiliate CompuServe. In 1998 eBay also became a "distinguished partner" of Netscape's Netcenter. In February 1999 eBay's relationship with Netscape was broadened to include banner ads and bookmarks. In March 1999 eBay's arrangement with AOL was expanded to feature eBay as the preferred provider of personal trading services on all of AOL's proprietary services, including Digital Cities, ICQ, CompuServe (both international and domestic), Netscape, and AOL.com. In return for this four-year arrangement, eBay agreed to pay CompuServe $75 million and to develop a co-branded version of its services for each of AOL's properties involved in the agreement, with AOL receiving all of the advertising revenues from these co-branded sites.[14]

The Alliance with Kinko's   In February 2000, eBay formed strategic marketing agreements with Kinko's, a global retail provider of document copying and business services, and GO.com, the Internet arm of Walt Disney Company. EBay's alliance

---

[14]eBay's 1999 10-K report.

with Kinko's allowed eBay to place signage in Kinko's stores across the country, and to offer its users 15 minutes of free computing rental at Kinko's locations. In return, eBay featured Web links to Kinko's Web pages in eBay's Computer, Business/Office, and Big Ticket categories, and encouraged users to go to Kinko's for photo scanning, e-mail, document faxing, and teleconferencing services.

The Alliance with GO.com   The long-term intention for the cooperative agreement with GO.com was for eBay to eventually become the exclusive online trading service across all of Disney's Internet properties. In the initial stages of the agreement, however, eBay was only to market and develop co-branded person-to-person and merchant-to-person sites on behalf of the Walt Disney company.[15]

Broadening the Trading Platform

Efforts intended to broaden the eBay trading platform concentrated on growing the content within current categories, on broadening the range of products offered according to user preferences, and on developing regionally targeted offerings. Growth in existing product categories was facilitated by deepening the content within the categories through the use of content-specific chat rooms and bulletin boards as well as targeted advertising at trade shows and in industry-specific publications. Further, in April 1998, custom home pages were created for each category so collectors could search for their next treasured acquisition without having to sort through the entirety of eBay's offerings.

In June 1999 eBay formed a collaborative relationship with the Collecting Channel, a portal owned by ChannelSpace Entertainment, Inc. The Collecting Channel was a premier Internet information source for virtually every conceivable category of collectibles. It delivered content in ways ranging from original audio/video programming to live chats to live video conferencing. EBay's agreement called for The Collecting Channel to provide in-depth content to eBay collectors and for eBay, in return, to provide links to The Collecting Channel's Web site.

Part of eBay's strategy to broaden its user base was to establish regional auctions. In 1999 eBay launched 53 regional auction sites focused on the 50 largest metropolitan areas in the United States. Management believed that having regional auction sites would encourage the sale of items that were prohibitively expensive to ship, items that tended to have only a local appeal, and items that people preferred to view before purchasing. EBay had also done several promotional or feature auctions, partnering with Guernsey to sell home-run balls hit by baseball stars Mark McGwire and Sammy Sosa in their 1998 home-run race and partnering with BMW in 1999 to auction the first BMW X5 sports activity vehicle to be delivered, with the proceeds going to the Susan G. Komen Breast Cancer Foundation.

Additional efforts to broaden the trading platform involved the development of new product categories. Over 2,000 new categories were added between 1998 and 2000, bringing the total to 3,000 categories (greatly expanded from the original 10 categories in 1995). One of the most significant new categories was eBay Great Collections, a showcasing of rare collectibles such as coins, stamps, jewelry, and timepieces as well as fine art and antiques from leading auction houses around the world. This category came from eBay's April 1999 acquisition of Butterfield and Butterfield, one of the world's largest and most prestigious auction houses.

---

[15]eBay press release, www.ebay.com, February 8, 2000.

The growing popularity of automobile trading on the eBay Web site prompted the creation of a special automotive category supported by Kruse International, one of the world's most respected organizations for automobile collectors. The automotive category was further expanded in March 2000 through a partnership with AutoTrader.com, the world's largest used-car marketplace, that established a co-branded auction site for consumers and dealers to buy and sell used cars.

Fostering eBay Community Affinity and Building Trust

Since its founding in 1995, eBay had considered developing a loyal, vivacious trading community to be a cornerstone of its business model. To foster a sense of community among eBay users, the company employed tools and tactics designed to promote both business and personal interactions between consumers, to foster trust between bidders and sellers, and to instill a sense of security among traders.

Interactions between community members were facilitated through the creation of chat rooms based on personal interests. These chat rooms allowed individuals to learn about their chosen collectibles and to exchange information about items they collected. To manage the flow of information in the chat rooms, eBay employees went to trade shows and conventions to seek out individuals who had both knowledge about and a passion for either a specific collectible or a category of goods. These enthusiasts would act as community leaders or ambassadors; they were never referred to as employees but were compensated $1,000 a month to host online discussions with experts.

Although personal communication between members fostered a sense of community, as eBay's community grew from "the size of a small village to a large city"[16] additional measures were necessary to ensure a continued sense of trust and honesty among users. One of eBay's earliest trust-building efforts was the 1996 creation of the Feedback Forum, described earlier.

Unfortunately, the Feedback Forum was not always sufficient to ensure honesty and integrity among traders. While eBay estimated that far less than 1 percent of the millions of auctions completed on the site involved some sort of fraud or illegal activity, some users would agree with Clay Monroe, a Seattle-area trader of computer equipment, who estimated that while "ninety percent of the time everybody is on the up and up . . . ten percent of the time you get some jerk who wants to cheat you."[17] Fraudulent or illegal acts perpetrated by sellers included misrepresentation of goods; trading in counterfeit goods or pirated goods that infringed on others' intellectual property rights; failure to deliver goods paid for by buyers; and shill bidding, whereby sellers would use a false bidder to artificially drive up the price of a good. Buyers could manipulate bids by placing an unrealistically high bid on a good to discourage other bidders and then withdraw their bid at the last moment to allow an ally to win the auction at a bargain price. Buyers could also fail to deliver payment on a completed auction.

Recognizing that fraudulent activities represented a significant danger to eBay's future, management took the Feedback Forum a step further in 1998 by launching the SafeHarbor program to provide guidelines for trade, provide information to help resolve user disputes, and respond to reports of misuse of the eBay service.[18] The SafeHarbor

---

[16]Tristram, "'Amazoning' Amazon."

[17]Stephen Buel, "eBay Inc. Feeling Growing Pains," *San Jose Mercury News,* December 26, 1998.

[18]eBay 10-K, filed July 15, 1998.

initiative was expanded in 1999 to provide additional safeguards and to actively work with law enforcement agencies and members of the trading community to make eBay more secure. New elements of SafeHarbor included free insurance, with a $25.00 deductible, through Lloyd's of London for transactions under $200.00; enhancements to the Feedback Forum; a new class of verified eBay users with an accompanying icon; easy access to escrow services; tougher policies relating to nonpaying bidders and shill bidders; clarification of which items were not permissible to list for sale; and a strengthened anti-piracy and anti-infringement program. The use of verified buyer and seller accounts was viewed as especially significant because it allowed eBay to ensure that suspended users did not open new eBay accounts under different names. User information was verified through Atlanta-based Equifax Inc.

To implement these new initiatives between 1999 and 2000, eBay increased the number of positions in its SafeHarbor department from 24 to 182, including full-time employees and independent contractors. It also organized the department around the functions of investigations, community watch, and fraud prevention. The investigations group was responsible for examining reported trading violations and possible misuses of eBay. The fraud prevention group mediated customer disputes over such things as the quality of the goods sold. If a written complaint of fraud was filed against a user, eBay generally suspended the alleged offender's account, pending an investigation. The community watch group worked with over 100 industry-leading companies, ranging from software publishers to toy manufactures to apparel makers, to protect intellectual property rights. To ensure that illegal items were not being sold and sale items listed did not violate intellectual property rights, this SafeHarbor group automated daily keyword searches on auction content. Offending auctions were closed and the seller was notified of the violation. Repeated violations resulted in suspension of the seller's account.

As eBay expanded its categories to include Great Collections and the new automobile categories, new safeguards were introduced to meet the unique needs of these areas. In the eBay Great Collections category, the company partnered with Collector's Universe to offer authentication and grading services for specific products such as trading cards, coins, and autographs. In the automobile area, eBay partnered with carclub.com to provide users with access to carclub.com's inspection and warranty service.

Enhancing Web Site Features and Functionality

In designing its Web site, eBay went to great lengths to make it intuitive, easy to use by both buyers and sellers, and reliable. Efforts to ensure ease of use ranged from narrowly defining categories (to allow users to quickly locate desired products) to introducing services designed to personalize a user's eBay experience. Two specific services developed by eBay to increase personalization were "My eBay" and "About Me."

My eBay was launched in May 1998 to give users centralized access to confidential, current information regarding their trading activities. From his or her My eBay page a user could view information pertaining to his or her current account balances with eBay; feedback rating; the status of any auctions in which he or she was participating, as either a buyer or a seller; and auctions in favorite categories. In October of the same year, eBay introduced the About Me service, which allowed users to create customized home pages that could be viewed by all other eBay members. These pages could include elements from the My eBay page such as user ratings or items the user had listed for auction, as well as personal information and pictures. This service not only increased customer ease of use but also contributed to the sense of community among the traders; one seller stated that the About Me service "made it easier and more rewarding for me to do business with others."[19]

When eBay first initiated service, the only computer resource it had was a single Sun Microsystems setup with no backup capabilities. By 1999 eBay's explosive growth required 200 Windows NT servers and a Sun Microsystems server to manage the flow of users on the site, process new members, accept bids, and manage the huge database containing the list of all items sold on the site. On June 10, 1999, the strain of managing these processes while attempting to integrate new product and service offerings proved too much for the system and the eBay site crashed. It stayed down for 22 hours. The outage not only seriously shook user confidence in eBay's reliability but also cost the company some $4 million in fees; the company's stock price reacted to the outage by falling from $180 to $136.[20]

Unfortunately, the June 10 site crash proved to be the first in a string of outages. While none of them was as significant as the first (most lasted only one to four hours), confidence in eBay continued to decline in both the online community and on Wall Street as eBay's stock fell to $87\frac{11}{16}$ in August 1999. To counter these problems, eBay sought out Maynard Webb, a premier software engineer and troubleshooter who was working at Gateway Computer.

Webb put a moratorium on new features until system stability was restored. Webb believed that it was virtually impossible to completely eliminate outages, so he set a goal of reducing system downtime and limiting outages to one hour.[21] To achieve this goal Webb believed he would need a backup for the 200 Windows NT servers, another for the Sun Microsystems unit, and a better system for managing communications between the Windows NT and Sun systems. In attacking these challenges, eBay acquired seven new Sun servers, each valued at $1 million, and outsourced its technology and Web site operations to Exodus Communications and Abovenet. These outsourcing agreements were intended to allow Exodus and Abovenet to "manage network capacity and provide a more robust backbone" while eBay focused on its core business.[22] While eBay still experienced minor outages when it changed or expanded services (for example, a system crash coincided with the introduction of the 22 regional Web sites), system downtime decreased. However, the stability of the system under eBay's explosive growth and continuous introduction of new features and services was a major and continuing management concern.

Expanding Value-Added Services

To make it easier for eBay's sellers and buyers to transact business, in 1998 the company announced that it would offer an "'end-to-end' person-to-person trading service . . . [by providing] a variety of pre- and post-trade services to enhance the user experience."[23] Pretrade services that eBay planned to offer included authentication and appraisal services, while planned post-trade services included third-party escrow services as well as shipping and payment services.

---

[19]Ann Pearson, in an eBay press release dated October 15, 1998.

[20]Julie Pita, "Webb Master," *Forbes*, December 13, 1999.

[21]Ibid.

[22]eBay press release, October 8, 1999.

[23]eBay S-1 filed July 15, 1998, p. 46.

In preparation for Christmas 1998, eBay formed alliances with Parcel Plus, a leading shipping service, and with Tradesafe, and I-Escrow, both of which guaranteed that buyers would get what they paid for. According to eBay's agreement with I-Escrow, monies paid to the seller were held in an escrow account until the buyer received and approved the merchandise. EBay's arrangement with Tradesafe called for the seller to register a credit card with Tradesafe to guarantee funds up to $1,200; proceeds of a sale were deposited directly into the seller's bank account. If the buyer was not satisfied with the transaction, all or part of the money was refunded. Both I-Escrow and Tradesafe charged a small percentage of the purchase price for their services.

In April 1999, eBay entered into a five-year partnership with Mail Boxes, Etc. (the world's largest franchiser of retail business, communications, and postal service centers), and iShip.com (the leader in multicarrier Web-based shipping services for e-commerce) to offer person-to-person e-commerce shipping solutions.[24] EBay's agreement with iShip gave eBay users access to accurate zip-code-to-zip-code shipping rates with various shipping services and allowed users to track packages. The agreement with Mail Boxes, Etc. (MBE), required eBay to promote MBE's retail locations as a place where sellers could pack and ship their goods; eBay and MBE were contemplating expanding their agreement to allow buyers to open and inspect their newly purchased goods at MBE retail stores prior to accepting the shipment.

To facilitate person-to-person credit card payments, eBay acquired Billpoint, a company that specialized in transferring money from one cardholder to another. Using the newly acquired capabilities of Billpoint, eBay was able to offer sellers the option of accepting credit card payments from other eBay users; for this service, eBay charged sellers a small percentage of the transaction. EBay's objective was to make credit card payment a "seamless and integrated part of the trading experience."[25] In March 2000, eBay and Wells Fargo, the owner-operator of the largest Internet bank, entered into an arrangement whereby Wells Fargo would purchase a minority stake in Billpoint and Billpoint would use Wells Fargo's extensive customer care and payment processing infrastructure to process credit card payments from eBay buyers to eBay sellers.

In January 2000, eBay entered into an exclusive agreement with E-Stamp that allowed E-Stamp to become the exclusive provider of Internet postage from the U.S. Postal Service on eBay's Web site. In return for being prominently featured on eBay's website, E-Stamp gave eBay users easy access to its Web site, offered them reduced fees for its service, and gave them a significant discount on the E-Stamp Internet postage starter kit. According to sources close to the deal, E-Stamp paid eBay close to $10 million a year for gaining such access to eBay's customers.[26]

Developing International Markets

As competition increased in the online auction industry, eBay began to seek growth opportunities in international markets in an effort to create a global trading community. While international buyers and sellers had been trading on eBay for some time, there were no facilities designed especially for the needs of these community members. In entering international markets, eBay considered three options. It could build a new

---

[24]eBay press release, April 8, 1999.

[25]eBay press release, May 18, 1999.

[26]Jane Weaver, "eBay: Can It Keep Customers Loyal?" www.zdnet.com, May 13, 2000.

user community from the ground up, acquire a local organization, or form a partnership with a strong local company. In realizing its goals of international growth, eBay employed all three strategies.

In late 1998, eBay's initial efforts at international expansion into Canada and the United Kingdom relied on building new user communities. The first step in establishing these communities was creating customized home pages for users in those countries. These home pages were designed to provide content and categories locally customized to the needs of users in specific countries, while providing them with access to a global trading community. Local customization in the United Kingdom was facilitated through the use of local management, grassroots and online marketing, and participation in local events.[27]

In February 1999, eBay partnered with PBL Online, a leading Internet company in Australia, to offer a customized Australian and New Zealand eBay home page. When the site went live in October 1999, transactions were denominated in Australian dollars and, while buyers could bid on auctions anywhere in the world, they could also search for items located exclusively in Australia. Further, local chat boards were designed to facilitate interaction between Australian users, and country-specific categories, such as Australian coins and stamps as well as cricket and rugby memorabilia, were offered.

To further expand its global reach, eBay acquired Germany's largest online person-to-person trading site, alando.de AG, in June 1999. EBay's management handled the transition of service in a manner calculated to be smooth and painless for alando.de AG's users. While users would have to comply with eBay rules and regulations, the only significant change for alando.de AG's 50,000 registered users was that they would have to go to a new URL to transact their business.

To establish an Asian presence, in February 2000 eBay formed a joint venture with NEC to launch eBay Japan. According to the new CEO of eBay Japan, Merle Okawara, an internationally renowned executive, NEC was pleased to help eBay in leveraging the tried-and-trusted eBay business model to provide Japanese consumers with access to a global community of active online buyers and sellers. In customizing the site to the needs of Japanese users, eBay wrote the content exclusively in Japanese and allowed users to bid in yen. The site had over 800 categories ranging from internationally popular categories (such as computers, electronics, and Asian antiques) to categories with a local flavor (such as Hello Kitty, Pokémon and pottery). The eBay Japan site also debuted a new merchant-to-person concept known as Supershops, which allowed consumers to bid on items listed by companies.

Honors and Awards

As a result of the relentless implementation of its business model, eBay had met with significant success. Not only was the company financially profitable from its first days (see again Exhibits 3 and 4), but it had won many prestigious honors and awards in 1998 and 1999. Among the most significant were Best Internet Auction Site (*San Francisco Bay Guardian,* July 1998); Electronic Commerce Excellence (CommerceNet, October 1998); Top E-Commerce Program/Service (Computer Currents Readers' Choice Awards, February 1999); Editor's Choice Award (*PC* magazine, March 1999), and Top 50 CEOs (*Worth* magazine, May 1999).

---

[27]eBay 10K filed March 30, 2000.

HOW EBAY'S AUCTION SITE COMPARED WITH THAT OF RIVALS

Auction sites varied in a number of respects: site design and ease of use, the range of items up for auction, number of simultaneous auctions, duration of the bidding process, and fees. Gomez Advisors, a company designed to help Internet users select which online enterprises to do business with, had developed rankings for the leading online auction sites as a basis for recommending which sites were best for bargain hunters, hobbyists/collectors, and sellers. To be considered in the Gomez ratings, an auction site had to (1) have more than 500 lots of original content; (2) conduct auctions for items in at least three of the following six categories: collectibles, computers/electronics, jewelry, sports, stamps/coins, and toys; (3) have more than five lots in each qualifying category; and (4) have sustained bidding activity in each category. Exhibit 8 shows the winter 1999 Gomez ratings of online auction competitors—the latest ratings can be viewed at www.gomez.com.

EBAY'S MAIN COMPETITORS

In the broadest sense, eBay competed with classified advertisements in newspapers, garage sales, flea markets, collectibles shows, and other venues such as local auction houses and liquidators. As eBay's product mix broadened beyond collectibles to include practical household items, office equipment, toys, and so on, the company's competitors broadened to include brick-and-mortar retailers, import/export companies, and catalog and mail order companies. Management saw these traditional competitors as inefficient because their fragmented local and regional nature made it expensive and time-consuming for buyers and sellers to meet, exchange information, and complete transactions. Moreover, they suffered from three other deficiencies: (1) they tended to offer limited variety and breadth of selection as compared to the millions of items available on eBay, (2) they often had high transactions costs, and (3) they were "information inefficient" in the sense that buyers and sellers lacked a reliable and convenient means of setting prices for sales or purchases. Thus, eBay's management saw its online auction format as competitively superior to these rivals because it (1) facilitated buyers and sellers meeting, exchanging information, and conducting transactions; (2) allowed buyers and sellers to bypass traditional intermediaries and trade directly, thus lowering costs; (3) provided global reach, greater selection, and a broader base of participants; (4) permitted trading at all hours and provided continuously updated information; and (5) fostered a sense of community among individuals with mutual interests.

From an e-commerce perspective, Amazon.com and Yahoo! Auctions had emerged as eBay's main competitors going into 2000, but FairMarket, AuctionWatch, GO Network Auctions, and Auctions.com were beginning to make market inroads and contribute to erosion of eBay's share of the online auction business. Moreover, the prospects of attractive profitability and low barriers to entry were stimulating more firms to enter the online auction industry and imitate eBay's business model. EBay management saw competition in the online auction industry as revolving around 10 factors: the volume and selection of goods, the population of buyers and sellers, community interaction, customer service, reliability of delivery and payment by users, brand image, Web site construction, fees and prices, and quality of search tools.

exhibit 8   Comparative Gomez Advisors' Ratings of Leading Online Auction Sites

A. Ratings Based on Site Characteristics (Rating scale: 0 = lowest; 10 = highest)					
Auction Site	Ease of Use[a]	Customer Confidence[b]	On-Site Resources[c]	Relationship Services[d]	Overall Score
1. eBay	9.07	6.99	8.40	8.40	7.97
2. Amazon.com	9.05	8.49	7.03	6.17	7.67
3. Yahoo! Auctions	8.69	6.91	4.18	8.62	7.11
4. GO Network Auctions	9.14	7.44	6.49	5.89	7.00
5. FairMarket Network	7.97	6.89	6.73	5.17	6.42
6. Auctions.com	8.22	6.78	5.50	5.10	6.41
7. utrade	8.87	4.60	2.43	6.57	5.65
8. Boxlot	7.20	7.83	3.19	4.09	5.63
9. Haggle Online	7.62	4.65	4.80	4.72	5.29
10. edeal	8.05	4.04	2.35	5.83	5.17
11. ehammer	7.59	5.35	4.21	3.15	5.09

[a]Based on such factors as screen layout, tightly integrated content, functionality, useful demos, and the extensiveness of online help.
[b]Includes the reliability and security of the online auction site, knowledgeable and accessible customer service, and quality guarantees.
[c]Based on the range of products, services, and information offered, information look-up tools, and transactions data.
[d]Based on personalization options, programs and perks that build a sense of community and customer loyalty to the site.

B. Ratings Based on Type of Auction Site User (Rating scale: 0 = lowest; 10 = highest)*			
Auction Site	Bargain Hunters	Hobbyists/Collectors	Sellers
1. eBay	8.43	7.98	7.94
2. Amazon.com	7.46	7.71	6.87
3. Yahoo! Auctions	7.37	6.67	6.96
4. GO Network Auctions	6.84	6.72	6.54
5. FairMarket Network	6.16	6.44	6.10
6. Auctions.com	5.94	6.31	5.47
7. utrade	5.65	5.01	5.34
8. edeal	5.61	4.83	4.89
9. ehammer	5.05	5.27	4.60
10. Haggle Online	5.00	4.88	5.07
11. Boxlot	4.79	5.57	4.57

*Each of the four criteria in part A above were weighted according to their perceived importance to bargain hunters, hobbyists/collectors, and sellers. These criteria were then averaged together to develop a score for each of the three types of online auction site users.
Source: Gomez Advisors, www.gomez.com, March 2, 2000.

Exhibit 9 provides selected statistics for the leading competitors in the online auction market. Exhibit 10 provides comparative financial data, and Exhibit 11 provides comparative Web site traffic.

Amazon.com

At the end of 1999, Gomez.com ranked Amazon.com as the second best online auction Web site. Amazon.com, created in July 1995 as an online bookseller, had rapidly

exhibit 9   Selected Auction Statistics for eBay, Amazon, and Yahoo!, December 1999

	eBay	Yahoo! Auctions	Amazon.com
Number of items listed for auction	3.8 million	1.3 million	415,000
Percentage of listed auctions closing with a sale	65%	14%	11%
Average number of bids per item	3.03	0.59	0.33
Average selling price for completed auctions	$65.19	$31.09	$25.77

Source: Taken from "Internet: eBay: Crushing the Competition," *Individual Investor,* January 21, 2000.

exhibit 10   Comparative 1999 Financial Statistics for eBay, Amazon, and Yahoo!*

	eBay	Amazon.com	Yahoo.com
Net revenues	$224,724,000	$1,639,839,000	$588,608,000
Cost of goods sold	57,588,000	1,349,194,000	92,334,000
Net income	10,828,000	(719,968,000)	61,133,000
Net income per share	0.04	(2.20)	0.20

*Includes all business areas for Amazon.com and Yahoo!, not just online auctions.
Source: 1999 Company financial statements.

exhibit 11   Number of Unique Visitors during December 1999

Web Site	Total Number of Unique Visitors
Yahoo! sites	42,361,000
GO Network	21,348,000
Amazon.com	16,631,000
eBay.com	10,388,000

Source: www.mediametrix.com.

turned into a full-line, one-stop-shopping retailer with a product offering that included books, music, toys, electronics, tools and hardware, lawn and patio products, video games, software, and a mall of boutiques (called z-shops)—some 18 million items at last count. Amazon.com was the Internet's number one music, video, and book retailer. The company's 1999 revenues of $1.64 billion were up 169 percent over 1998, but despite the company's rapid revenue growth it was incurring huge losses due to the expenses of (1) establishing an infrastructure to support its sales (the company expanded its worldwide distribution capacity from 300,000 square feet to over 5 million square feet in 1999) and (2) attracting customers via advertising and online:

Year	Net Loss
1996	$ 6.2 million
1997	31.0 million
1998	124.5 million
1999	720.0 million

While Amazon's management was under mounting pressure to control expenses and prove to investors that its business model and strategy were capable of generating good bottom-line profitability, it was clear that management's decisions and strategy were focused on the long term and on solidifying Amazon's current position as a market leader. Management believed that its business model was inherently capital efficient, citing the fact that going into 2000 the company had achieved annualized sales of $2 billion with just $220 million in inventory and $318 million in fixed assets. The company's customer base rose from 6.2 million to 16.9 million during 1999. The company invested more than $300 million in infrastructure in 1999 and opened two international sites, Amazon.co.uk and Amazon.de. These two sites, along with Amazon.com, were the three most popular online retail domains in Europe. Amazon also entered into a number of strategic alliances. During the fourth quarter of 1999 and the first month of 2000, the company announced partnerships with NextCard, Ashford.com, Greenlight.com, Audible, and living.com, as well as an expanded partnership with drugstore.com. It already had e-commerce partnerships with Gear.com; Homegrocer.com; Della.com (an online service for gift registry, gift advice, and personalized gift suggestions); Pets.com; and Sotheby's (a leading auction house for art, artiques, and collectibles).

With its customer base of almost 17 million users in over 150 countries and a very well-known brand name, Amazon.com was considered an imposing competitive threat to eBay. Amazon.com launched its online auction site in March 1999. The site charged sellers for listing their products and also charged a commission on sales. Although Amazon's selection of auctions did not match the one offered by eBay, the company reported that online auctions were the fastest-growing part of its business. The number of auctions on Amazon grew from 140,000 to 415,000 during the second half of 1999. Amazon.com offered three major marketplaces for its users: Auctions, zShops, and sothebys.amazon.com. Its auction site formed partnerships with DreamWorks to promote that company's films *Stuart Little* and *American Beauty* (72 auctions, averaging 27 bids per auction, total gross merchandise sales of over $25,000, yielding an average of over $400 per item) and with television celebrity Oprah Winfrey (25 auctions, averaging 38 bids per auction, total gross merchandise sales of over $130,000, yielding an average of over $6,000 per item).[28] An example of an auction from the Amazon.com Web site is shown in Exhibit 12.

Yahoo! Auctions

Yahoo.com, the first online navigational guide to the Web, launched Yahoo! Auctions in 1997. Yahoo.com offered services to nearly 120 million users every month and the Yahoo! Network operated in North America, Europe, Asia, and Latin America. Yahoo! reported net revenues of $588 million in 1999 (up 140 percent from 1998) and net income

---

[28]Amazon.com press release, February 2, 2000.

exhibit 12   Representative Screen from an Amazon.com Auction

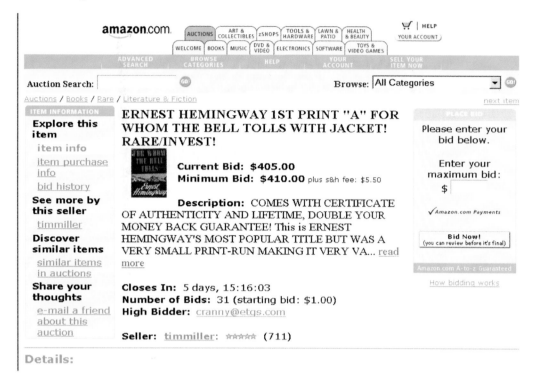

Details:

of $142 million. Yahoo's user base grew from 60 million to 120 million during 1999, and 40 million of these users were outside the United States. In December 1999, Yahoo's traffic increased to an average of 465 million page views per day. Yahoo! had entered into numerous alliances and marketing agreements to generate additional site traffic and was investing in new technology to improve the site's performance and attractiveness.

Its auction services were provided to users free of charge, and the number of auctions listed on Yahoo! increased from 670,000 to 1.3 million during the second half of 1999. Yahoo! Auctions was expanded to include Hong Kong, Taiwan, Korea, Mexico, Brazil, and Denmark at the end of 1999. Localized Yahoo! auctions outside the United States were being conducted in 16 countries in 11 different languages. Yahoo! Japan Auctions was the largest localized online auction service in Japan. At the end of 1999, Yahoo! launched Yahoo! Merchant Auctions and Featured Auctions in order to allow retailers and sellers to promote their auctions. Yahoo! Auctions also offered many extra services to its users. Gomez.com rated Yahoo! Auctions as the number one online auction site in the Relationship Services category. An example of a screen from Yahoo! Auctions is shown in Exhibit 13.

FairMarket

FairMarket, a new online auction provider that went online in September 1999, had quickly emerged as one of the leading providers of private-label, outsourced, networked auction services for business clients. It offered a number of formats: hosted auctions, fixed-price auctions, declining-price or markdown auctions for merchants wishing to dispose of overstocked merchandise, and shopping-by-request services. The company was

exhibit 13   Example of a Screen from a Yahoo! Auction

formed through an alliance of Microsoft, Dell Computer, Lycos, Excite, CBS Sportsline, CompUSA, and several others. The FairMarket network of auctions included Alta Vista Auctions, CityAuction, Excite Auctions, GO Auction, Lycos Auctions, and MSN Auctions. The company went public in early 2000, raising approximately $75 million to support expansion.

FairMarket managed and maintained online auctions for such customers as JCPenney (which had auctions that allowed customers to purchase new, quality merchandise and auctions that incorporated an automatic markdown format for overstocked merchandise from JCPenney retail store and catalog operations); the Times Digital Company (which conducted local auctions in New York City and other locations); Dell Computer (which held auctions for customers wishing to sell their used computers and for equipment coming off lease); Ritz Camera (which used auctions to sell end-of-life camera equipment); Outpost.com (which auctioned a mix of new and refurbished computer and computer accessory items); and SportingAuction (which used FairMarket's network systems to auction an extensive selection of high-quality sporting goods).

FairMarket received a percentage fee of all the items sold on auctions it conducted for its customer-sellers.

AuctionWatch

AuctionWatch.com was formed in July 1998 and incorporated in January 1999 as a privately held company backed by several venture capital firms and private investors. The company, a very small online auction site originally, had raised $10 million in capital in August 1999 to expand both its site and its available features. The AuctionWatch site was designed to model eBay, and had many of the same types of offerings. By the end of 1999, AuctionWatch.com was conducting over 25,000 auctions daily, had served over 2 million auction images per day, and received over 20,000 posts each month in its visitor center. AuctionWatch catered to businesses looking to use online auctions as a new distribution channel and to attract new customers. One of the unique features at Auction-Watch was a content service that allowed users to compare and contrast the fee structures of the top consumer-to-consumer, business-to-consumer, and business-to-business auction sites; the information was updated monthly.

As of April 2000, AuctionWatch had over 250,000 registered users and was conducting about 1 million auctions monthly. AuctionWatch attracted 1.7 million unique visitors in March 2000, an increase of over 100 percent from February and over 500 percent from December 1999. In the first quarter of 2000, businesses and auction enthusiasts used AuctionWatch to sell over $120 million worth of merchandise.

GO Network Auctions

GO.com was the result of a November 1999 merger between Walt Disney's online unit, the Buena Vista Internet Group (BVIG), and Infoseek Corporation. The company oversaw ABC.com, ESPN.com, and Disney.com, as well as several other popular Web sites; its chief activity was serving as the Internet business arm of the Walt Disney Company. The GO.com portal focused on entertainment, leisure, and recreation activities. The online auction section of the GO Network, auction.go.com, was experiencing rapid growth. GO Network Auctions offered over 100 product categories and provided users with a guarantee against fraudulent listings; one of its main features was auctioning Disney products, including movie sets, props, and memorabilia from movies from Walt Disney Studios and from ABC-produced shows. The Web site was also considered extremely easy to navigate. Gomez.com ranked GO Network Auctions number one in the Ease of Use category among online auctions.

In February 2000, GO.com and eBay announced a four-year agreement to develop and market online trading and auction experiences in a co-branded person-to-person site and new merchant-to-person sites. According to terms of the agreement, eBay would ultimately become the online trading and auction service for all of Disney's Internet properties, including the GO Network portal, and would collaborate on merchant-to-person auctions for authenticated products, props, and memorabilia from throughout the Walt Disney Company.

Auctions.com

Auctions.com was originally launched as Auction Universe in November 1997. After being acquired by Classified Ventures in 1998, the site was relaunched as Auctions.com on December 13, 1999. The company claimed to be "the world's fastest growing online auction network" at the beginning of 2000.[29] Auctions.com had hundreds of categories and several thousand product listings available for users. Not only did the company's Web site offer 24-hour customer service support, but it also had the premier online transaction security program (Bid$afe). The Federal Trade Commission claimed that Bid$afe was one of the "best fraud protection programs on the Web."[30]

Formed in 1997 and headquartered in London, QXL.com was moving rapidly to try to dominate the online auction market in Europe. Rather than create one Web site for Europe, QXL's strategy was to methodically enter one European country after another, launching its own new sites in some countries and acquiring already established players in others. While QXL was thinking globally, it was acting locally, operating in 12 different languages, accommodating 12 different currencies (until use of the euro), and tailoring its merchandise features to the preferences of users in each country, QXL's market reach included Great Britain, Germany, France, Italy, Spain, the Netherlands, Denmark, Finland, Poland, Norway, and Sweden. QXL was developing technology so that it could quickly and economically customize its sites for each country. Currently, however, its sites were slow and antiquated compared to eBay.

In 2000, the online aution market in Europe was much less developed than in the U.S.; there were not as many Internet users and many European Web surfers were leery of entering bids to purchase an item online. To combat the wariness of online auctions exhibited by actual and prospective visitors to its online auction site, QXL was conducting a number of auctions for goods put up for sale by retail merchants. QXL management reasoned that site visitors who were reluctant to buy items from a stranger would feel comfortable enough to enter bids to buy merchandise from an established retailer.

NICHE AUCTIONS

Many new competitors had also begun offering auctions targeted at smaller segments of the online auction industry. These auctions primarily specialized in one product or service type, such as computers/electronics, fine art, industrial products, music-related goods, international auctions, and just about any other product or service imaginable. There were sites offering laptop computers (AuctionLaptops.com), guitars (Guitarauction.com), German wines (Koppe and Partner Wine Auctions), and even a site that auctioned nothing but racing pigeons (ipigeon.com). There were several significant companies conducting niche auctions:

- *Outpost.com*—Outpost.com was founded in 1995 to service primarily the small-office/home-office market. By the end of 1999, the company offered over 170,000 products online, primarily in the computer/electronics area. Bizrate.com rated Outpost.com the number one consumer shopping experience on the Web, and Forrester Research awarded the company the 1999 number one PowerRanking for Computing. The company had half a million customers and 4 million monthly visitors. In 2000, the company announced separate partnerships with Golf Galaxy and Computer.com. Outpost claimed to differentiate itself from other online auction sites "by focusing on the needs of the customer and delivering its services with reliability,

---

[29]www.auctions.com/backgrounder.asp, April 20, 2000.
[30]Ibid.

fully encrypted secure servers, depth of product selection and building a team of dedicated and knowledgeable professionals that support all efforts of the business."[31]

- *eWanted.com*—eWanted.com pioneered the idea of the "backward auction" in October 1998. A backward auction was the exact opposite of a traditional online auction. Buyers would place ads specifying the item they wanted, as well as the product's primary characteristics. Then sellers would browse these ads and submit offers to the buyers. The theory was that sellers would compete with each other for a particular buyer, thus driving the auction price down. In return, sellers entered a marketplace where they knew that buyers existed for their particular product or service.

- *eRock.com*—eRock.com specialized in offering rock-and-roll memorabilia to "serious die-hard fans, collectors, and dealers."[32] The site had 12 different categories of music auctions available, and also offered a chat room for users to talk about their musical interests and links to the Web pages of several popular rock groups.

THE FUTURE

As eBay headed into the second quarter of 2000, it was looking for new avenues to expand its services. According to Brian Swette, eBay's chief operating officer, the company was "at the five yard line with its core business."[33] The next driver of the company's growth was expected to be international expansion, followed by business-to-business and automobile and regional sites.[34] Swette predicted that each of these areas could wind up "as large as the core eBay."[35]

In response to the increasing opportunities in the business-to-business auction segment, and the number of small companies trading on eBay, the company developed the eBay Business Exchange in March 2000. To avoid head-on competition with other auction sites in this market segment, eBay was focusing on businesses with fewer than 100 employees. Swette saw Business Exchange as a natural evolution of eBay's business model and expected that larger companies would eventually participate. Specific categories offered in the new eBay Business Exchange included computer hardware, software, electronics, industrial equipment, office equipment, and professional tools.

EBay had recently announced plans to enter France, Europe's third largest online commerce market. EBay management viewed France as critical in capturing the European market. However, well-established competition existed in the French market in the form of QXL.com, the leading British online auctioneer, and the I-Bazar Group, a France-based corporation that had anticipated eBay's arrival in 1998 and purchased the domain name eBay.fr.

While the number of concurrently active eBay auctions soared from approximately 1 million to 4.5 million between 1998 and year-end 1999, from January 2000 to March 2000 the number of auctions was holding at a relatively constant 4.2 to 4.4 million. EBay spokesperson Kevin Pursglove dismissed the flat trend, stating, "Listings are an

[31] www.outpost.com, Investor Relations, April 20, 2000.

[32] www.erock.com, April 20, 2000.

[33] "The One Thing Not for Sale on eBay," www.thestandard.com, April 20, 2000.

[34] Ibid.

[35] Ibid.

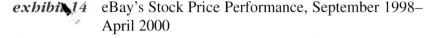

exhibit 14   eBay's Stock Price Performance, September 1998–April 2000

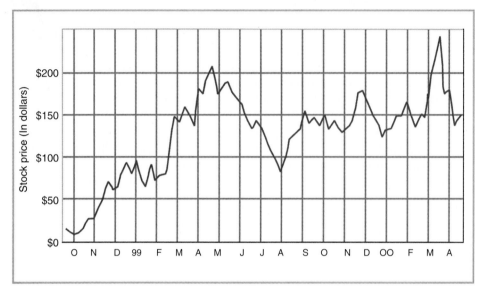

interesting thing to look at, but sellers are more interested in selling their merchandise."[36] Wall Street analysts, however, saw the lack of growth in the number of auctions as signaling a coming slowdown in eBay's revenue and profit growth and an indication of market share erosion.

Pierre Omidyar folded his newspaper to prepare for a meeting with Meg Whitman and Jeff Skoll to discuss two developing situations. The first topic on the list was to review the possibility of a cross-marketing strategic alliance with competitor Yahoo! to gain broader exposure to Yahoo's broad customer base. Partnering with a competitor that also offered auction services seemed to have pluses and minuses. The second item on the agenda involved the potential of launching storefront operations where eBayers could purchase goods at a fixed price, much like Amazon. As he headed down the hall to the meeting, Pierre recalled a statement that Meg Whitman had made in a recent interview: "I have this philosophy that you really need to do things 100 percent. Better to do 5 things at 100 percent than 10 things at 80 percent. Because the devil in so much of this is in the detail and while we have to move very, very fast, I think you are not well served by moving incredibly rapidly and not doing things that well."[37] Given recent developments, Pierre was forced to wonder if they were operating at 100 percent. Also, if Forrester Research was correct in their recent prediction that the majority of online retailers would be out of business by the end of 2000, would 100 percent be enough?[38] The recent drop in the company's stock price had been troubling (see Exhibit 14), and the company needed to launch strategic initiatives that would sustain rapid growth and get it back on the road to market dominance.

---

[36]"Auction Growth Slows at eBay, Can Earnings' Growth be Far Behind?" *Barron's Online,* April 17, 2000.

[37]"What's behind the Boom at eBay?" *Business Week Online,* May 21, 1999.

[38]Forrester.com press release, April 11, 2000.

case 12 | CDnow in the Online Music Business

Alan B. Eisner
Pace University

Nicole Belmont
Pace University

CDnow was one of the world's largest e-commerce retailers of music products, with 1999 sales of $147 million, up from $56 million in 1998. Visitors to its Web site (www.cdnow.com) could choose from a lineup of more than 500,000 items that included music CDs and DVDs, videotapes, cassettes, traditional vinyl albums, custom CDs, 650,000 sample sound clips, and music downloads. CDnow was one of the first sites to offer the sale of music downloads and currently offered both free and purchasable music downloads. The site also featured daily news about developments in the music industry, feature stories, exclusive interviews with artists, and a list of bestsellers. In addition, site users could obtain a list of selections and recommendations tailored to their individual music preferences.

CDnow's Web site was one of the best-known and most-visited online music destinations, with an average daily audience of over 800,000 people. Over 3.2 million customers had made purchases since the inception of CDnow in August 1994; 1.6 million of these made their first purchase in 1999. The company's vision was to create an online music destination with unprecedented access to and coverage of the world of music. Part of the CDnow vision was "to make every visit to the site, whether for browsing or buying, a valuable and rewarding experience." CDnow catered to Internet users in the United States, Europe, and the Middle East; visitors could browse the contents of CDnow's site in any of eight languages—English, French, Spanish, Portuguese, Dutch, German, Italian, and Japanese.

COMPANY BACKGROUND

CDnow, based in suburban Philadelphia, was founded by twin brothers Jason and Matthew Olim in 1994. Their goal was to "build a better music store through intelligent album recommendations, custom CDs, music samples, a vast library of reviews and fea-

exhibit 1   Six-Year Financial Summary for CDnow, 1994–99

Year	Revenues	Net Income	Earnings per Share
1999	$147,189,000	($121,527,000)	($4.32)
1998	56,395,000	(43,769,000)	(2.79)
1997	17,373,000	(10,747,000)	(1.42)
1996	6,300,000	(1,810,000)	(0.29)
1995	2,176,000	(201,000)	(0.03)
1994	103,000	(58,000)	(0.01)

Sources: CDnow Corporate Web site, SEC filings, and disclosure.

tures from top music writers and exclusive editorial content."[1] The Olim brothers formed a company that prided itself on broad selection, informative content, easy-to-use Web site navigation and search capabilities, a high level of customer service, competitive pricing, and personalized merchandising and recommendations.

The concept for CDnow came to Jason Olim while he was looking through a stack of albums in a record store. Jason had stopped asking clerks for advice because of their lack of knowledge and instead brought music encyclopedias with him on music-buying trips. Jason Olim said, "It suddenly occurred to me one day that I could take the information in guide books . . . put it in a database, and with that database I could take the products that were also available for sale . . . and I could merge it together and make it available on the Internet."[2]

Within 24 hours, Jason had formulated a business plan, which he quickly showed to his brother Matthew, who was studying astrophysics at Columbia University. CDnow was born through the combination of Matthew's expert computer-programming skills and Jason's business skills. The company began in their parents' basement with a $20,000 initial investment. Sales were $14 their first month.

The company went public in February 1998 at a price of $16 per share, raising $88.5 million in equity capital. The shares had traded as high as $39 in 1998, but since then had lost favor with investors. During 1999, the stock traded in the range of $10 to $25. Jason Olim was president and CEO of the company; his brother Matthew was principal software engineer and a member of the company's board of directors. The two brothers each owned 9 percent (or 2,960,000 shares) of the company's outstanding stock. In February 2000, Michael Krupit, formerly the company's vice president of technology, was named chief operating officer and assigned responsibility for day-to-day operations and the company's organizational structure. The company had just over 500 employees.

Since the launch of the company's Web site, CDnow's revenues had expanded rapidly, growing at an average annual compound rate of 187 percent during the 1995–99 period (see Exhibit 1). But the company had yet to earn a profit; in fact, losses were mounting, as shown in Exhibit 2. The company was financing its expansion and covering negative cash flows with capital raised from its public sale of stock in February 1998, but cash reserves were dwindling. The company had cash and cash equivalents of

---

[1]"CDnow Breaks New Ground for Online Shopping with Personalization Technology," PR Newswire, September 16, 1998, p. 916.

[2]John Wilen, "Going for Miles Inspires CDnow," *Philadelphia Business Journal,* October 17, 1997, p. 16.

exhibit 2   Consolidated Statements of Income for CDnow, 1995–99

	1999	1998	1997	1996	1995
Net sales	$147,189,405	$56,394,606	$17,372,795	$6,300,294	$2,176,474
Cost of sales	118,037,621	45,250,328	13,847,773	5,074,087	1,815,672
Gross profit	29,151,784	11,144,278	3,525,022	1,226,207	360,672
Operating expenses					
Operating and development	23,421,062	8,000,023	2,541,434	669,280	149,982
Sales and marketing	89,734,790	44,572,304	9,607,603	765,156	229,912
General and administrative	11,736,503	4,244,194	1,953,078	563,593	180,573
Amortization of goodwill	25,786,261	202,801			
Other operating charges				1,024,030	
Total operating expenses	150,678,616	57,019,322	14,102,115	3,022,059	560,467
Operating loss	(121,526,832)	(45,875,044)	(10,577,093)	(1,795,852)	(199,665)
Interest and other income	2,688,882	2,742,581	201,650		
Interest expense	(391,075)	(636,458)	(371,962)	(14,556)	(1,248)
Net loss	($119,229,025)	($43,768,921)	($10,747,405)	($1,810,408)	($200,913)
Net loss per share	($4.32)	($2.79)	($1.42)	($0.29)	($0.03)
Weighted average number of shares outstanding	27,618,917	15,712,857	7,845,684	6,139,072	6,000,000

Source: CDnow's 1999 10-K report to the SEC.

$20.6 million as of December 31, 1999, compared to $49.0 million as of December 31, 1998 (see Exhibit 3). However, at year-end 1999, CDnow had a working capital deficit of $37.2 million, owing to a sharp climb in accounts payable and the company's eroding cash position.[3]

THE ONLINE MUSIC INDUSTRY

Exhibit 4 shows the structure of the overall music industry. Exhibit 5 presents the sales of prerecorded music by category. In 1998, U.S. online music sales were an estimated $152 million, equal to about 1 percent of recorded music sales (see Exhibit 6).[4] Preliminary estimates were that sales in 1999 reached $375 million.[5] Internet sales of music, however, were predicted to grow to $2.6 billion annually by 2003 and account for close to 14 percent of all U.S. retail music sales (Exhibit 7).[6] According to a survey conducted by Strategic Record Research, 38.4 percent of consumers were expected to spend more on music in 1999 than in 1998 (see Exhibit 8).[7] This online spending was predicted to come from an increasingly Internet-enabled generation of consumers.

---

[3]A company's working capital is defined as current assets minus current liabilities.

[4]"Recorded Music Market Healthy as Current Releases and CD Albums Gain," *Research Alert,* August 6, 1999, p. 1.

[5]Patrick M. Reilly, "Barnesandnoble.com to Join a Crowd of Firms Offering 'Online Music Stores,'" *The Wall Street Journal,* July 7, 1999, p. B2.

[6]"Record Stores Face New Era Personal Touch Called Key to Staying in Sync as Online Sales Pick Up," *Bloomberg News,* July 22, 1999, p. C3.

[7]"Clothes and Home Goods Give Music a Run for the Money," *Billboard,* May 16, 1998, p. 110.

exhibit 3   Condensed Balance Sheet Data for CDnow, 1998–99

	1999	1998
Assets		
Current assets		
Cash and cash equivalents	$ 20,612,706	$49,041,370
Accounts receivable, net	4,068,700	839,672
Prepaid expenses and other	5,580,241	8,322,889
Total current assets	30,261,647	58,203,931
Property and equipment	17,216,980	6,643,995
Goodwill and other intangibles	70,121,321	833,735
Other assets	1,201,809	3,361,982
Total assets	$118,801,757	$69,043,643
Liabilities and Stockholders' Equity		
Current liabilities		
Current portion of long-term debt	$ 1,670,838	$ 822,043
Accounts payable	46,431,122	10,306,323
Accrued merger costs	1,384,679	—
Accrued expenses	17,927,779	4,667,395
Total current liabilities	67,414,418	15,795,761
Long-term debt	2,629,359	1,750,892
Common stock subject to put rights	2,999,995	—
Deferred rent liabilities	992,696	358,053
Common stock	204,573,908	102,137,536
Additional paid-in capital	14,589,814	4,325,817
Deferred compensation	(61,905)	(216,913)
Accumulated deficit	(174,336,528)	(55,107,503)
Total stockholders' equity	44,765,289	51,138,937
Total liabilities and stockholders' equity	$118,801,757	$69,043,643

Source: CDnow 1999 10-K report.

The Attractiveness of Online Music Retailing

Several factors made the online music retailing business attractive relative to traditional retail stores. Online technology featured many multimedia options that enabled consumers to listen to sound samples; search for music by genre, title, or artist; and access a wealth of information and events, including reviews, related articles, music history, news, and recommendations. Online retailers could more easily obtain extensive demographic and behavioral data about their customers, providing them with greater direct marketing opportunities and the ability to offer a more personalized shopping experience. In addition, online retailers could offer consumers significantly broader product selection, the convenience of home shopping, and 24-hour-a-day, seven-day-a-week operations available to any foreign or domestic location with access to the Internet. Typical retail music stores stocked around 12,000 items, but the total could range as high as 50,000 items for megastores. According to Jupiter Communications, a marketing research firm, approximately 80 percent of unit sales at traditional retail stores came from roughly 20 percent of the available titles.

exhibit 4   Music Industry Market Structure

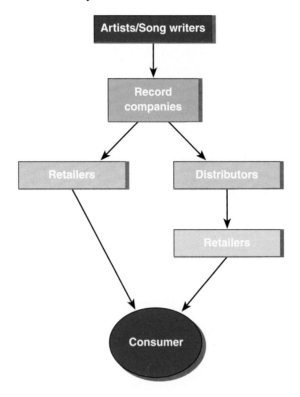

exhibit 5   Percentage of Music Sales by Category

Music Category	1998 Recording Sales by Genre
Rock	25.7%
Country	14.1
R&B	12.8
Pop	10.0
Rap/Hip Hop	9.7
Gospel	6.3
Classical	3.3
Jazz	1.9
Other	11.3
	100.1%

Source: *Research Alert,* August 6, 1999.

Physical-store-based retailers had to make significant investments in real estate, inventory, and personnel for each store location. Online retailers generally incurred a fraction of these costs due to centralized distribution and virtually unlimited merchandising space. It was cost-effective for online retailers to offer a broader range of titles and information than brick-and-mortar music retailers, especially titles issued by independent

exhibit 6   Percentage of 1998 Music Sales by Type of Retailer

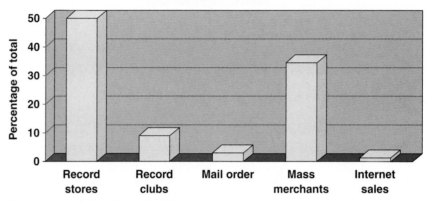

1998 Music Sales

Source: Research Alert, August 6, 1999.

exhibit 7   Online Music Sales Estimates

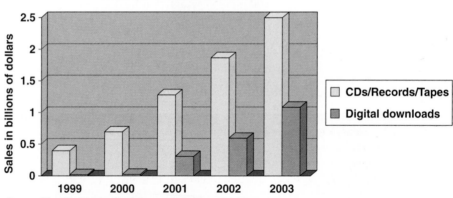

Predicted Online Music Sales

Source: The Washington Post, August 3, 1999.

exhibit 8   Population Groups Most Likely to Increase Music Spending

Population Groups Most Likely to Spend More	Percentage Indicating a Desire to Increase Music Spending
Males 18–25	11.6%
Males 12–17	11.5
Females 12–17	11.6
Females 35–44	11.6

Source: Billboard Magazine survey, May 16, 1998.

labels, which accounted for a growing percentage of new titles. Independent labels accounted for 21 percent of the total music market in 1996 versus only 12 percent in 1992, and they released 66 percent of the titles in 1996. It was burdensome for brick-and-mortar music retailers to stock and promote more than a few of the independent labels, creating a gap that online retailers could economically fill. Online retailers, however, faced significant technology costs associated with operating a cutting-edge online store and sizable marketing and promotion costs to build site traffic, which offset many of their cost advantages over brick-and-mortar retailers.

From a demographic standpoint, persons over 30 years old were accounting for a growing percentage of music sales—48 percent of total sales in 1997 versus 34 percent in 1996. Online retailers saw the Internet as a particularly attractive medium for marketing music titles to middle- and upper-income customers in the over-30 age group because their purchases were less likely to be "hits-driven." A bigger fraction of this population group had diverse music interests, which made them more likely to shop online, where they could select from hundreds or thousands of titles. Moreover, they could afford to buy more titles at one time, were likely to have access to computers, and had credit cards with which to make electronic payments.

Competitive Threats to Online Music Retailing

Online music retailers saw record clubs as a potentially serious competitive threat. After experiencing declining sales and buyer interest during the 1995–97 period, record clubs had rejuvenated their business by relaxing their membership policies. "Hassle-free memberships" gave customers up to two years to purchase a minimum of six titles, and clubs had abandoned the annoying practice of automatically shipping a club-designated CD if subscribers did not reply in time.[8] Record clubs had also improved their customer service and were putting substantially more resources into advertising and marketing.

Another potential threat to online music retailers (and music retailers in general) was the rapidly rising popularity of direct digital distribution, which allowed consumers to download individual songs from the Internet and copy them directly onto CDs, a practice that many observers saw as having the potential to revolutionize the whole music industry.[9] Recording studios saw digital downloads as a major threat to their role because artists could make their own recordings, distribute them directly over the Internet, and thus earn well above what they received in royalties from the record companies. (See Illustration Capsule 16 in Chapter 4 of the text for a breakdown of the recording industry value chain.) Such a move—said to be under consideration by some artists, especially those who were unsigned by the major recording studios—held the potential for cutting the record producers and brick-and-mortar retailers out of the industry value chain entirely. Sales of digital music downloads, estimated at a meager $1 million in 1999, were predicted to reach $1.1 billion by 2003.[10] To capitalize on growing buyer

---

[8]Michael Christman, "Record Clubs Utilize New Strategies," *Billboard,* January 30, 1999.

[9]"On-line Retailing Expands but Has Yet to Come of Age," *Music Business International,* August 1998.

[10]Stephanie Stoughton, "The Score on Downloads: Analysts Sing Praises of Online Music Trend," *Washington Post,* August 3, 1999, p. E1.

exhibit 9   Market Reach of the Most Popular Internet Portals

	Percent of the Online Population Reached
America Online	48.3%
Yahoo!	44.4
Microsoft Network	35.4
Netscape	27.7
Excite	26.2

Source: Newsbytes News Network, April 21, 1998.

interest in digital downloads and counter the competitive threat to their business, Sony, Universal Music, and BMG Entertainment had announced plans to begin selling downloadable CDs directly to online shoppers.

Price discounting was becoming a bigger factor in the online music segment's competitive environment. Online retailers were more aggressive in discounting their prices and running special promotions than were traditional store retailers, record clubs, and record companies with online stores. For example, most record companies had established online sites to sell directly to the consumer, but their prices were generally higher than those of online music retailers like CDnow and Amazon.com; this was partly to avoid creating channel conflict and angering the traditional brick-and-mortar music retailers on whom the record companies depended for most of their sales. Online retailers could offset the revenue loss from price discounting with the fees they earned from selling advertising space on their Web sites.

Profit Margins of Online Music Retailers

Online music retailers were struggling to make a success of their business model. Most were plagued with losses, owing to capital expenditures for state-of-the-art Web site technology and very large marketing and advertising expenditures to build site traffic. To turn losses into profits, online retailers had to achieve a large volume of sales and, at the same time, keep a tight rein on marketing costs. According to one observer, "Everyone is losing money because the margins are so low. What people are shooting for is an established market share by 2002. It is important that you be No. 1, No. 2, or maybe No. 3." An official with the Association of Internet Professionals said, "You build the name, you build the brand, then you make the money."[11] Jason Olim, CDnow's CEO, believed that "given time, the market will support only three or four brands."

To build sales and market share, online retailers had to build strong brand awareness and generate heavy site traffic. One way of doing this was by allying with Yahoo!, America Online, and the other portals that Web surfers used as gateways for sessions on the Internet and paying them substantial sums for advertising space. Getting lots of exposure on the major portals (see Exhibit 9) was deemed critical to building traffic, since it was difficult for online music retailers to differentiate on the basis of product selection (most of the major online music retailers had extensive selections to choose

---

[11]Associated Press, "Music Retailer Is Attempting to Build a Noteworthy Company," *Buffalo News,* June 9, 1998, p. 7D.

from). The big Internet retailers were willing to pay to lock up advertising space and Web links on the leading portals for as long as two to four years. To counter the exclusive promotional arrangements that several of the online music retailers had negotiated with prominent portals, rivals were shifting more money to traditional media advertising. CDnow had run advertisements on the Howard Stern show, placed print advertisements in such music publications as *Spin* and *Variety,* and negotiated promotional deals with MTV and the Rolling Stone Network.

CDNOW IN 2000

CDnow was a major player in the online music industry, with a 33 percent market share in 1999. CDnow faced competition from many different kinds of competitors entering the online music industry. Competitors included online music retailers, in-line music retailers, book retailers, movie retailers, book and music clubs, and record companies. Notable competitors included such online retailers as Amazon.com, Borders.com, Barnesandnoble.com, MuZic.com, Rock.com, Buy.com, and CD Universe; brick-and-mortar retailers like Tower Records, Musicland, and Sam Goody's; Columbia House and other record clubs; and record companies Sony and BMG (which were launching online sites). In the online segment, rivalry revolved around brand recognition, selection, price, the effectiveness of advertising and customer acquisition efforts, the variety of value-added services provided on company Web sites, ease of site use, site content, quality of customer service, and technical expertise. Several of CDnow's online rivals had longer operating histories, a larger customer base, greater brand recognition, and significantly greater financial, marketing, and technological resources. CDnow's executives viewed entry barriers as minimal because an online retailer could launch a new site at relatively low cost. They saw competition in the overall retail music business as being intense and evolving rapidly because of spreading consumer interest in digital downloading of music recordings (as opposed to purchasing CDs and cassettes).

Management believed that, as digital downloading of music grew in popularity, CDnow's broad base of music buyers, its relationships with record labels, and use of the most advanced Web technology would position the company as a leader in offering music fans secure, speedy, high-quality downloads. The company's interactive media division developed content for the Web site that included news about music artists, artist interviews and reviews, and a community where unsigned bands could promote their recordings.

CDnow strived to make its online store appealing, informative, and authoritative. Exhibit 10 shows CDnow's home page. CDnow had designed its Web site to be intuitive and easy to use, endeavoring to allow customers to learn about, find, and order CDs and other music-related products with a minimum of effort. Customers could focus their searches with a "fast-find" search engine, browse among top sellers and other featured titles, read reviews, listen to music samples, participate in promotions, and check the status of their orders. New users could access an information page designed to give shoppers a quick understanding of the site and its many features. To encourage purchases, CDnow rotated promotions among items throughout the store; it frequently discounted recent releases and popular titles. To encourage the purchase of multiple titles, CDnow lowered shipping costs for larger orders. Customers could pay for orders with a credit card, check, or money order.

As the result of the acquisition of superSonic Boom, Inc., CDnow had the technology to allow customers to build customized CDs from a collection of 60,000 individual

exhibit 10   CDnow's Home Page, April 2000

songs by various artists. Buyers selected their favorite songs to create a full-length CD, added a personalized title, and wrote their own liner notes. Custom CDs were an especially popular item for Valentine's Day gifts and for Christmas and other holidays. In addition, CDnow sold branded custom CDs to other companies for corporate promotions, in volume as well as on demand. CDnow manufactured and shipped each custom CD from its Fort Washington facility and, on occasion, used third parties to provide manufacturing and shipping.

exhibit 11   CDnow's Order Fulfillment Process

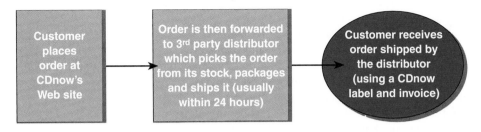

Recent Traffic at CDnow's Web Site

In February 2000, CDnow attracted a record 5.7 million unique visitors to its Web site, making it the 33rd most visited domain according to data compiled by Media Metrix. The company's February audience was larger than either MP3.com's or MTV.com's. CDnow was the fifth largest Internet shopping site, with an 8.1 percent reach among all Web users; it was the only music destination among Media Metrix's list of the top 10 shopping sites. CDnow's unique customer count increased to 3.5 million in February 2000, up from 3.2 million in December 1999. Average page views per visit reached a high of 9.9 pages, and visitors spent an average of 1 minute 48 seconds viewing each page, well above CDnow's typical average of 1 minute 20 seconds per page. According to PCData's February list of Internet buyers, CDnow ranked first by completing over 1 million transactions, ahead of Amazon.com. However, CDnow's February 2000 transactions were boosted by redemption of coupons for free custom CDs in a promotional campaign cosponsored by Pizza Hut. CDnow included the amount of coupons redeemed to purchase merchandise in its reported revenues (coupons redeemed accounted for 4.9 percent of CDnow's reported revenues in 1999 and 3.2 percent in 1998). Site-tracking data revealed that 63 percent of CDnow's retail sales revenues were generated by repeat customers, a statistic that management believed confirmed the attractiveness of the content of CDnow's Web site.

These traffic statistics were instrumental in helping CDnow sell advertising on its Web site and gain sponsors for product promotions. Part of CDnow's revenue-generating strategy was to leverage its site traffic and paying customer base by selling advertising and sponsorships to companies interested in promoting their own goods and services to CDnow's customer base and daily Web site audience. Recent advertisers included Oracle, Oldsmobile, and United Airlines. Advertising revenues totaled $8.8 million in 1999, up 626 percent over 1998.

CDnow's Order Fulfillment Process

CDnow's inventory was owned and held by outside vendors who shipped directly to CDnow's customers. The breadth of inventory maintained by these vendors provided CDnow with the ability to maintain high order-fill rates. CDnow updated the items available on its site daily, using inventory information supplied by its vendors; this feature enabled customers to check availability before placing an order. Orders were transmitted to the appropriate vendor at least once daily (usually more often); vendors shipped orders using a CDnow label and invoice normally within one business day after the order was placed with CDnow (see Exhibit 11). Shipping fees were $2.99 for the first CD and 99 cents for each additional CD up to a maximum of $4.97.

For an added fee, customers could request next-day delivery. Vendors billed CDnow for the cost of merchandise as well as shipping and handling. CDnow processed customer billing through a third-party credit card processor.

CDnow's primary order fulfillment vendor was Valley Media, the second largest U.S. wholesaler of records, cassettes, and compact discs and a specialist in handling order fulfillment activities for most online music retailers.[12] Although Valley Media handled about 85 percent of CDnow's orders, the music seller also used the order fulfillment services of Alliance OneStop Group to provide greater breadth of selection to customers and deeper inventories of fast-selling items. Orders for videos and DVDs were filled through the services of Baker & Taylor, and MSI of Miami was used to fill orders produced by foreign record companies, including 60,000 international titles from an order fulfillment center in the Netherlands that serviced European markets. Valley Media offered customers (online music companies and retailers) the widest selection of music titles and had a state-of-the-art inventory, order-filling, and shipping system that allowed it to provide customers with next-day delivery service.[13]

In order to preserve their relationships with the traditional brick-and-mortar music retailers, most record companies were very reluctant to do business directly with online retailers. Thus, Amazon.com was the only major online music retailer that bought products directly from record companies, stocked them in company-owned warehouses, and had internal systems for filling, packing, and shipping customer orders.[14] However, Amazon, still working to develop its own next-day delivery capabilities, used the services of Valley Media for customers who requested next-day delivery.

CDnow's Strategic Marketing Alliances

CDnow's biggest promotional and marketing alliance was with America Online. Under the marketing agreement with AOL, CDnow and AOL shared revenues generated from the sale of advertising, sponsorships, CDs, and related merchandise derived from CDnow's being featured as the exclusive online music retailer within AOL's Music Space Channel and its featured position on AOL's Shopping Channel. CDnow could take advantage of banner advertising opportunities on AOL and was assigned specific keywords on AOL's search engine. Its agreement with AOL continued through August 31, 2000. CDnow had also entered into promotional alliances with Yahoo!, Excite, Lycos, Webcrawler, Tripod, and Geocities in an effort to extend its reach and gain a presence on the sites of the major portals and search engines. The company's agreement to be the exclusive retailer of CDs and other music-related products on the Lycos and Tripod Web sites, however, became the subject of litigation in July 1999, when CDnow filed a lawsuit alleging breach of contract with regard to the Web site linking arrangements.

Most recently, CDnow had entered into a multiyear integrated marketing agreement with MTV Networks whereby CDnow, MTV, and VH1 instituted cross-promotions through online retailing and content, event sponsorships, and on-air advertising.[15] MTV and VH1's online sites provided links to CDnow, and CDnow offered music news

[12]Don Jeffery, "Cyber Selling," *Billboard,* July 18, 1998, p. 29.

[13]"California-based Music, Video Distributor Enjoying Good Growth," *Tribune Business News,* November 10, 1997, p. 1110.

[14]Ed Christman, "Amazon.com Buys Directly from a Major," *Billboard,* October 17, 1998, p. 10.

[15]Carla Hay, "MTV Networks, CDnow Make Marketing Deal," *Billboard,* June 6, 1998, p. 71.

provided by MTV and VH1, as well as a "Now Playing" ticker highlighting each channel's programming schedule. CDnow also was the exclusive online retailer for the MTV Music Awards. Both CDnow and MTV had very high expectations for the marketing alliance. Jason Olim said, "This alliance with MTV and VH1 affords CDnow the opportunity to take its integrated marketing strategy to the next level. They are the only brands that have the true horsepower to move consumers from their televisions to their computers, and that's what marketing convergence is all about." Matt Farber, MTV/VH1's senior vice president of programming enterprises, was equally enthusiastic, saying, "We chose CDnow because their sole business is the music transaction business online, and they've created a leading brand name in their field, just as MTV and VH1 have. CDnow's marketing strategies also mutually complement MTV and VH1's strategies."

Another multiyear marketing alliance had been negotiated with the Rolling Stone Network. Visitors to the CDnow site were provided access to over 30 years of Rolling Stone music coverage, and visitors to the Rolling Stone Network were provided a link to CDnow's music products. The Rolling Stone's content available through CDnow included landmark covers, cover story excerpts, reviews, award-winning features, and the magazine's "Random Notes," "Grapevine," and "The Industry" columns.

The payments made by CDnow to its marketing alliance partners were much of the reason the company's sales and marketing expenses had risen from $44.6 million in 1998 to $89.7 million in 1999 and were a principal contributor to the company's reported 1999 losses of $119 million.

CDnow's Efforts to Employ New Technologies at Its Web Site

CDnow was making an effort to keep its Web site on the cutting edge of technology. The company's operating and development expenses of $23.4 million in 1999 (versus $8.0 million in 1998) reflected increased spending for the systems and telecommunications infrastructure necessary to support increased traffic and transactions volume. Management saw site and systems improvements as necessary to avoid losing out to other online competitors, but in early 2000 several competitors—Amazon.com in particular—were devoting substantially more resources to site and systems development than CDnow. CDnow had deployed systems for online content dissemination, online transactions processing, customer service, market analysis, and electronic data interchange. Much of its software was proprietary and had been developed both to minimize the engineering required to maintain a growing array of merchandise items and content and to reduce the effort it took to make changes and updates to CDnow's site. The company used redundant data storage systems, multiple servers, and multiple dedicated Internet connections to maintain round-the-clock operations.

In years past, CDnow's pioneering use of technology had proved a key element in its climb into the ranks of leading online music retailers. CDnow's Web site employed such popular online shopping features as shopping cart software, buy-Web links, intelligent album recommendations, and RealAudio samples.[16] Picking up on the popularity of personalized services among Internet users, CDnow had developed My CDnow and Album Advisor as service features to help visitors find the music selections they liked. CDnow's Jason Olim said, "My CDnow is the most important innovation since

---

[16]Brett Atwood, "Music Site Masters Get Cosmic Credit," *Billboard,* April 19, 1997, p. 81.

my brother and I launched the store four years ago. This ground-breaking tool enables each of our customers to create their own music store."[17] My CDnow features included a Wish List, which allowed customers to keep a list of music products for future visits, a Gift Registry and a personal music consultant through Recommends and Favorite Artists. This service kept customers in touch with their favorite artists and provided features such as a music rating system and a personal order history.

Album Advisor asked customers to name three artists they liked or were interested in; it then made recommendations based on which albums by these artists had been bought the most frequently by other CDnow customers. Customers could then listen to RealAudio clips of selections from the recommended albums. Research indicated that people were 82 percent more likely to purchase music online if they were first able to hear a selection or two from an album.[18] According to CDnow's vice president of technology and creative services, "Intelligent recommendations are critical for operating a virtual store that combines content and commerce. Customers are getting better judgment from artificial intelligence than they would from the human intelligence of most clerks at a retail store."[19]

CDnow's Affiliate Program

To encourage grassroots Web sites to sell CDnow merchandise and provide a link to CDnow, management had come up with an incentive program it called Cosmic Credit. Through this plan, CDnow reached out to those Web sites that were developed by independent artists and musicians and fan sites devoted to particular music artists. Since inception of the program, 230,000 Web sites had agreed to participate and were provided with embedded hyperlinks through which potential customers could be immediately connected to the CDnow site; 85,000 new Web sites had been added as participants during 1999. CDnow's goal for this program was to build a community among fan sites. Member sites received commissions in store credit or cash based on the dollar purchases made by people using the link. The credit incentives ranged from 7 to 15 percent, and member sites could opt for quarterly cash payments when they accumulated credits of $100 or more; there were also monthly bonuses for sites that generated the highest volumes of sales. The 230,000 affiliate sites were a significant source of traffic and new customers for CDnow.

Sales and Marketing Strategies

In addition to the strategic alliances and marketing agreements described earlier, CDnow used "co-marketing advertising" to help build brand awareness and drive traffic to its Web site. In January 2000, for example, CDnow joined with Pizza Hut in an integrated promotion whereby Pizza Hut customers who purchased a Big New Yorker Pizza received an access code to make their own custom CD at www.cdnow.com. The promotion was advertised via signs and placards in participating Pizza Huts, radio spots, and network TV commercials that aired in January and February (including one Super Bowl spot in January). The success of this promotion was a big factor in the record high traffic at CDnow's site in February 2000. Management planned to continue its use of such promotions.

---

[17]"CDnow Breaks New Ground for Online Shopping with Personalization Technology."

[18]"Internet Audio Clips Bolster Online Sales," *Music Week,* September 19, 1998, p. 10.

[19]Lynda Radosevich, "Al Wises Up," *InfoWorld,* August 3, 1998, p. 60.

Another marketing strategy was the use of personalized e-mails to target prospective and existing customers with messages and special promotions. The e-mails contained such information as purchase recommendations based on the customer's indicated interests and prior purchases, information concerning new releases, and announcements of special merchandise promotions. Directed e-mails were sent to visitors who had registered at CDnow's site but had not yet made a purchase and to previous buyers who had not made a recent purchase.

Customer Service

CDnow management believed that attentive customer service was critical to retaining and expanding its customer base. Customer service representatives were available 24 hours a day, seven days a week to provide assistance via e-mail, phone, or fax. Customer service representatives handled questions about orders, took credit card information over the phone, and helped customers find music titles. The company strived to answer all e-mails within 24 hours. It had 140 customer service representatives. CDnow offered seven foreign language versions of its Web site (in addition to English) that contained translations of account registration and ordering instructions. It supported its international sales efforts with customer service representatives fluent in nine languages.

Growth and Expansion Strategies

CDnow was aggressively attempting to grow sales and strengthen its competitive presence by expanding into foreign markets, diversifying its product line, and making new acquisitions.

CDnow Europe   CDnow was boosting its presence in the European market as fast as resources permitted. A European warehouse was being opened to handle order fulfillment for consumers in Europe and the Middle East. CDnow expected this move to lower shipping costs and reduce delivery delays to buyers in 37 countries in Europe and the Middle East. To broaden its appeal to foreign buyers, CDnow had added 100,000 international selections to its product offerings and opened a multilingual customer service center. Jason Olim explained, "CDnow is building a better music store for our European and Middle Eastern customers, who can now enjoy one-stop shopping for local and U.S. product which is shipped from a centralized location."[20] International sales accounted for 20 percent of CDnow's total revenue in 1999.

To give it better exposure to European users of the Internet, in 1998 CDnow entered into a promotional arrangement with search engine Lycos Bertelsmann in what was claimed to be Europe's biggest e-commerce deal to date. Jason Olim saw the agreement as key to CDnow's European strategy: "This deal initiates CDnow's international marketing efforts. In Europe, we needed a company that would enable us to target each country."[21] The agreement called for CDnow to become the exclusive music retailer for Lycos Bertelsmann in 11 European countries including Britain, France, Germany, Italy, Spain, Switzerland, and the Benelux countries. (The fees CDnow paid Lycos Bertelsmann for the exclusive promotional arrangement were not fully disclosed.) The Internet exposure that CDnow received in Europe as a result of its agreement with Bertelsmann paved the way for CDnow to sell CDs in Britain at U.S. prices, providing customers a saving of up to 50 percent on recommended retail prices for

[20]"CDnow Announces Launch of CDnow Europe," CDnow press release, August 17, 1998.

[21]"U.S. CD Firm Nets Online Deal for European Outlet," *Marketing*, April 16, 1998, p. 8.

CDs in Britain. CDnow was featured on all Lycos sites in Europe and potential customers were delivered to CDnow's Web site through banner ads, links, and Keyword Interactive Text Insertion software.

To further strengthen its ability to attract foreign customers, CDnow contracted with Yahoo! to be the premier music retailer of many of Yahoo's World Sites. CDnow was featured on Yahoo UK, New Zealand, Korea, Singapore, Yahoo Chinese, Yahoo en Español, and Yahoo's Chinese- and Spanish-language Web guides. The agreement expanded CDnow's previous agreement with Yahoo! that made CDnow the exclusive music retailer on Yahoo's main directory in the United States.

Product Line Expansion   To broaden its appeal to site visitors, CDnow began selling movies and music videos in both VHS and DVD formats in December 1999. It also began merchandising T-shirts and music accessories. From time to time, the company ran special promotions of audio and video equipment, such as DVD players and CD recorders. Management expected to continue to widen the range of the company's product offerings.

Acquisition of SuperSonic Boom   In early 1999, CDnow acquired superSonic Boom, the first company to offer custom CDs on the Internet. SuperSonic Boom offered 12,000 titles in its catalog and had over 60,000 titles licensed. Customers could make selections from the company's collection of recordings, choose the playing sequence, create an album title, and build custom CDs. CDnow management believed superSonic's technological capabilities in custom CDs represented a valuable way to enhance and differentiate the company's product lineup. Jason Olim explained, "SuperSonic Boom provides us with a talented management team and custom digital capabilities that will significantly expand the level of personalization in the CDnow shopping experience. We believe this technology empowers our customers to create unique products for gifts, as well as their own listening pleasure."[22]

Merger with N2K, Inc.   In 1998, CDnow merged with its largest competitor, N2K, which operated an online music store called Music Boulevard. At the time, this move created the industry's largest e-commerce site devoted to music and music-related products and the third largest online retailer in terms of sales revenues.[23] Jon Diamond, cofounder and vice chairman of N2K, commented:

> The merger of CDnow and N2K unites the two leading brands in online music, creating the most powerful franchise in our marketplace, and one of the clear leaders among Internet companies. Our respective companies are coming together at a uniquely opportune time, having already made the necessary investments to develop solid technology platforms, key alliances, and organizations of talented executives and relationships of trust with music consumers. This is a "win/win" providing customers with a truly superior music experience online and enhancing the value of the companies.

As part of the merger arrangement, a new publicly traded company, also called CDnow, Inc., was formed. Existing CDnow shareholders received 1.0 shares of common stock in the new company for each share they owned, and N2K existing shareholders received 0.83 shares in the new company. Jon Diamond, N2K's CEO, became chairman of CDnow's board of directors.

The merger gave the new CDnow the largest selection of music items available anywhere, combined the two original companies' musical expertise, and gave the new company a broader Internet presence. N2K had specialized in classical, jazz, and country

---

[22]"CDnow Acquires superSonic Boom," CDnow press release.

[23]"N2K Inc. and CDnow, Inc., Announce Merger Plans," CDnow press release, October 23, 1998.

exhibit 12 Amazon.com Music Store Features Added in 1999

Free digital downloads that enable customers to try before they buy
Amazon.com's Music Store dedicated an area of its store to free, full-length song downloads from established artists, major-label performers, and independent artists.

Expanded selection of music from independent artists unavailable in most stores
Customers could find thousands of noteworthy CDs by independent artists and labels. With these features, customers could easily explore and discover great new music from independent artists in any genre.

Classical music center
No other music store—physical or online—offered classical music experts and novices a greater selection of classical music or more ways to discover excellent classical recordings.

Information on new titles—before they are released
At Amazon.com, customers could order CDs before they were released and receive them on the day of release.

Source: Adapted from "No. 1 Online Music Retailer Amazon.com," Amazon.com press release, February 2, 2000.

music, while CDnow had previously specialized in rock and pop music. In the years leading up to the merger, the two companies had been battling for market share. Additionally, it created opportunities for cost reductions and new efficiencies. A major benefit of the merger, from CDnow's perspective, was the $27.8 million in cash that N2K had at the time of the merger. Without this cash, CDnow would have had a negative cash balance at the end of 1999 (see again exhibit 3).

However, a major driver of the merger was the need to counter Amazon.com's entry into the online music segment. Amazon became a major player in the online music industry overnight. Although it began selling music only in June 1998, Amazon's revenues from music product sales in the fourth quarter of 1998 totaled $50 million (CDnow's revenues totaled $56 million for all of 1998).[24] Amazon.com's instant success was attributed to its strong brand-name recognition among Internet users, the size and makeup of its customer base, and the fact that many buyers of books were also buyers of music—at Amazon, they could now purchase both.

AMAZON.COM

Amazon began operations on the Web in July 1995 as a bookstore. However, by the beginning of 2000, Amazon had diversified its product offerings to include more than 18 million unique items in such categories as books, CDs, toys, electronics, videos, DVDs, home improvement products, software, and video games. Amazon's strategy was to become a dominant online retailer by continually adding new product categories. Amazon.com, considered the "number one place to save money on the Internet," had more than 1 million registered users. Amazon's strategic vision was to be the premier "customer-centric company, where customers could find and discover anything they may want to buy online."[25] Amazon offered basically the same customer service and ease-of-use features as CDnow and was willing to match any new features that CDnow developed (see Exhibit 12). Amazon also invested heavily in a network of

[24]Richard Tedesco, "Amazon Gets More Tuneful," *Broadcasting & Cable,* June 14, 1999, p. 108.

[25]"Amazon.com Announces Profitability in U.S.-based Book Sales," Amazon.com press release, February 2, 2000.

company-owned warehousing and distribution centers to reduce its dependence on fulfillment houses.

CDNOW'S MERGER WITH COLUMBIA HOUSE

On July 13, 1999, CDnow reached an agreement with Time Warner and Sony Corporation to merge their jointly owned Columbia House with CDnow to form a new company by the first quarter of 2000. Scott Flanders, formerly CEO of wireless products vendor Telestreet.com, was designated to serve as CEO of the new company.[26] According to terms of the merger agreement, Sony and Time Warner would each own 37 percent of the new company and CDnow shareholders would own the remaining 26 percent.

The plan was for CDnow to continue as an online music retailer with a wider product selection and for Columbia House to continue to operate as a membership-based club. The merger offered significant advantages for all parties involved. CDnow would receive financial backing and cheaper access to prerecorded music products marketed by Sony and Time Warner, plus it would gain access to Columbia House's database of 16 million active music customers and 45 years of direct marketing experience. Sony and Time Warner would gain a solid foothold in online music sales and an online vehicle for selling music via digital downloading. Also, the new company would be able to negotiate promotion and marketing arrangements with Time Warner's Warner Music Group and other media holdings.

An Unexpected Turn of Events

On March 13, 2000, CDnow, Time Warner Inc., and Sony Corporation abruptly announced cancellation of their merger plans, raising questions about the immediate future of both CDnow and Columbia House. The merger died because of a sharper-than-expected decline in Columbia House's performance since early fall 1999. According to Jason Olim, the merger fell apart because Columbia House's projections for 2000 were lower than expected; a major motivation for the merger from CDnow's perspective was that Columbia House's cash flows would support CDnow's growth and expansion until it reached profitability. Olim indicated that the latest Columbia House projections showed its cash flows would be insufficient to support CDnow, plus it had a higher debt load than CDnow executives had anticipated. While Time Warner officials admitted that Columbia House's 1999 results were below expectations and thus a major factor in the merger abandonment, they noted that CDnow's results were also weaker than expected and that a main reason for calling the merger off was the difficulty of gaining Federal Trade Commission approval for the merger. Another complicating factor was said to be the pending merger of America Online and Time Warner.

As part of the merger termination agreement, Time Warner and Sony agreed to invest $21 million in CDnow through the purchase of 2.4 million additional shares of CDnow's common stock and to convert an existing $30 million loan commitment to CDnow into long-term convertible debt. Jason Olim indicated that only half of the loan had been used, giving the company a net infusion of $36 million in new capital in addition to the company's existing cash balance.

---

[26]Ed Christman, "CDnow/Col. House Co. Takes Shape," *Billboard,* October 2, 1999, p. 12.

As part of its announcement of the merger termination, CDnow said that it had retained Allen & Company, an investment bank, to explore its strategic options. Nancy Peretsman, an Allen & Company executive, said, "Based on CDnow's position in the marketplace, Allen & Company is very optimistic about finding interest in attractive strategic transactions."[27] CDnow also announced that the company's operating goals for 2000 included significant reduction of operating expenses by lowering marketing expenses. However, the company said it did not plan any layoffs of personnel.

During the next several days, CDnow's stock price dropped from around $9 per share to trade in the $3 to $4 range. In the company's 1999 annual report, released March 29, 2000, Arthur Andersen, the company's auditor, expressed "substantial doubt" about the company's ability to stay in business due to a shortage of working capital, losses from operations, and significant payments due in 2000 for its marketing agreements with Internet portals and other allies. However, company officials stated that CDnow had cash and other sources of liquidity totaling $40 million and that it had sufficient cash flows to meet its obligations through September 2000. Jason Olim said,

> Our business is one that is fundable. We are confident we will be able to close a strategic transaction with a strategic investor in the next few months that will give the company the liquidity to get through to profitability.

There was considerable speculation as to who might be interested in partnering with, acquiring, or merging with CDnow. One potential was to find a music retailer that did not have significant online retailing operations, such as Musicland or Trans World Entertainment Corp., whose chains included Camelot Music and The Wall. Another possibility was Viacom, the owner of MTV and VH1, which already had a relationship with CDnow.

---

[27]"CDnow Retains Allen & Company to Explore Strategic Options," CDnow press release, March 13, 2000.

case 13 Callaway Golf Company

John E. Gamble
University of South Alabama

As Ely Callaway walked through the sea of drivers, irons, putters, golf apparel, golf bags, and training devices displayed at the 2000 PGA Merchandise Show in Orlando, Florida, and toward Callaway Golf Company's booth, he noted that the eyes cast toward him seemed to express a greater sense of anticipation and curiosity than usual. As one of the most recognizable figures in the golf equipment industry, he had grown accustomed to his celebrity status among the golfing world and was aware that both rivals and retailers alike anxiously awaited the new products his company typically launched at the industry's premier annual trade show. However, the drama and suspense surrounding Callaway's new products at the February 2000 show were very different from usual. Callaway had gone ahead and introduced its innovative Big Bertha X-14 irons and Big Bertha Steelhead Plus metal woods in January. The PGA Merchandise Show had been saved for the introduction of the company's highly touted and much-anticipated Callaway golf ball.

Callaway Golf Company had become the leader in the golf equipment industry by developing technologically advanced golf clubs that compensated for the poor swing characteristics of most amateur golfers. During a golf swing, the clubhead travels in an arc around the golfer's body, making contact with the ball for 300 to 500 milliseconds. During this very brief period of contact, inertia is transferred from the clubhead to the ball, and the ball is propelled forward at a speed of up to 150 miles per hour. There are an infinite number of variations in a golfer's swing that can alter the swing path, causing the clubhead to strike the ball not squarely but somewhat off-center, at an angle. The more that a golfer's swing path deviates from square contact with the ball, the greater the loss of accuracy and distance. A golfer loses approximately 12.5 yards of distance for every millimeter that the ball is struck off the clubhead's center.

Ely Callaway, the founder of Callaway Golf Company, understood the importance of the physics of golf, so much so that he made the phrase, "You can't argue with physics," an early company slogan. Callaway Golf revolutionized the golf industry in 1990 by introducing an oversized clubhead called the Big Bertha that was more forgiving of golfers' swing imperfections. A Callaway executive stated in a 1995 *Fortune* interview that the company's objective was to design a club that would allow golfers to "miss [the center of the clubhead] by an inch" and still achieve distance and accuracy.

The company's high-tech golf clubs became so popular with golfers in the 1990s that Callaway Golf's revenues and profits grew by 1,239 percent and 1,907 percent, respectively, between 1991 and year-end 1996. With the company's competitive position securely rooted and a line of innovative new clubs ready for a 1997 launch, Ely Callaway retired as CEO in mid-1996 and turned to Callaway Golf Company president Donald Dye to become the new CEO. Soon after Ely Callaway's retirement, Callaway Golf Company's fortunes reversed due to a variety of factors, including the Asian financial crisis, poor global weather conditions, strategic miscues on the part of Callaway's executives, and the introduction of innovative clubs by rivals. The reversal led to nearly an 18 percent sales decline in 1998. Callaway Golf also broke its string of 24 consecutive quarters of growth in net income in early 1998 and went on to record a net loss of $26.5 million for the entire 1998 fiscal year.

Ely Callaway returned as CEO in November 1998 to launch a vast turnaround effort that included the development of new models of golf clubs and a $54.2 million restructuring program, which brought a number of operational improvements and cost-reduction initiatives. Callaway Golf Company returned to profitability and recaptured a great deal of its lost market share in 1999, but on February 4, 2000, the entire golf industry watched intently as Ely Callaway launched the company's new Rule 35 golf ball. Callaway's entry into the golf ball market had been vigilantly anticipated since mid-1996 when Ely Callaway announced the formation of the Callaway Golf Ball Company, and was considered by many industry participants to be the biggest event in the golf equipment industry since the debut of the Big Bertha. Callaway's managers and investors expected the entry to become a catalyst for the company's future growth. Exhibit 1 presents a summary of Callaway Golf Company's financial performance between 1989 and 1999.

COMPANY HISTORY

When Ely (rhymes with *feely*) Reeves Callaway Jr. graduated from Emory University in Atlanta, his father said, "Don't go to work for the family."[1] Ely Callaway Sr. and almost everyone else in La Grange, Georgia, worked for the younger Callaway's uncle, Fuller Callaway. Fuller Callaway owned a number of farms, 23 cotton mills, the local bank, and the local department store. Heeding his father's advice, Ely Callaway Jr. decided to join the army just prior to World War II. By the age of 24, he had achieved the rank of major and had become one of the army's top five procurement officers responsible for purchasing cotton clothing for the U.S. armed forces. At the peak of World War II, Callaway's apparel procurement division of the U.S. Army purchased 70 percent of all cotton clothing manufactured by the U.S. apparel industry.

After the war, Callaway was hired as a sales representative with textile manufacturer Deering, Millikin & Company. He rose quickly through the company's ranks by selling textiles to the manufacturers from which he had purchased apparel while in the Army. Callaway was later hired away from Deering, Millikin by Textron, which subsequently sold its textile business to Burlington Industries—at that time the largest textile manufacturer in the world. Ely Callaway was promoted to president and director of Burlington Industries, but he left the company in 1973 after losing a bid to become its chief executive officer.

Callaway had long believed that Burlington Industries' success was a result of its ability to provide customers with unique, superior-quality products. When Callaway left Burlington and the textile industry, he decided to launch his own business founded on that same philosophy. In 1974 he established Callaway Vineyard and Winery outside of

---

[1]*Inc.*, December 1994, p. 62.

exhibit 1 Callaway Golf Company, Financial Summary, 1989–96 (In thousands, except per share amounts)

	1999	1998	1997	1996	1995	1994	1993	1992	1991	1990	1989
Net sales	$714,471	$697,621	$842,927	$678,512	$553,287	$448,729	$254,645	$132,058	$54,753	$21,518	$10,380
Pretax income	$85,497	($38,899)	$213,765	$195,595	$158,401	$129,405	$69,600	$33,175	$10,771	$2,185	$329
Estimated ranking within industry—sales	1st	1st	1st	1st	1st	1st	1st	2nd	6th	14th	23rd
Pretax income as a percent of sales	12%	–6%	25%	29%	29%	29%	27%	25%	20%	10%	3%
Net income	$55,322	($25,564)	$132,704	$122,337	$97,736	$78,022	$42,862[a]	$19,280	$6,416	$1,842	$329
Net income as a percent of sales	8%	–4%	16%	18%	18%	17%	17%[a]	15%	12%	9%	3%
Fully diluted earnings per share[c]	$0.78	($0.38)	$1.85	$1.73	$1.40	$1.07	$0.62	$0.32	$0.11	$0.04	$0.01
Shareholders' equity	$499,934	$453,096	$481,425	$362,267	$224,934	$186,414	$116,577	$49,750	$15,227	$8,718	$6,424
Market capitalization at Dec. 31	$1,349,595	$769,725	$2,120,813	$2,094,588	$1,604,741	$1,127,823	$901,910	$245,254	—[b]	—[b]	—[b]

[a]Includes cumulative effect of an accounting change of $1,658,000.

[b]The company's stock was not publicly traded until February 1992.

[c]Adjusted for all stock splits through February 10, 1995, not adjusted for February 10, 1995, stock split.

Source: Callaway Golf Company annual reports.

San Diego. The well-known northern California vineyards scoffed at Callaway's entry into the industry and predicted a rapid failure of the venture. Not only did Callaway have no experience running a winery but, additionally, no vineyard had ever been successful in the San Diego area. Ely Callaway understood the risks involved and was much better prepared to run a start-up vineyard than skeptics believed. He began by transplanting the very best grape vines from Italy to California and hired winemaking experts to manage the day-to-day operations of the vineyard. Callaway's strategy was to focus on a narrow segment of the wine market where competition with the established wineries was not as strong and barriers to entry were relatively low. Callaway Vineyard and Winery limited distribution of its products to exclusive restaurants that chose to stock only the highest-quality wines. The company made no attempt to distribute its high-quality wines through traditional retail channels. In 1981, Ely Callaway sold the company to Hiram Walker & Sons, Inc., for a $14 million profit.

In late 1982, Ely Callaway decided to enter the golf club industry and, once again, apply his concept of "providing a product that is demonstrably superior to what's available in significant ways and, most importantly, pleasingly different."[2] Callaway purchased Hickory Stick USA, a manufacturer and marketer of replicas of old-fashioned hickory-shafted clubs, for $400,000. From the outset, Callaway grasped the limitations of the company's hickory-shafted product line and realized that the company would have to extend its offerings beyond replicas of antique golf clubs to provide an acceptable return on his investment.

Callaway noticed that most golf equipment had changed very little since the 1920s and believed that many golfers would purchase technologically advanced golf equipment if it would improve their game. Ely Callaway and Richard C. Helmstetter—Callaway Golf's senior executive vice president and chief club designer—put together a team of five aerospace and metallurgical engineers to develop the S2H2 (short, straight, hollow hosel) line of irons. The S2H2 line was introduced in 1988 and was well received by golfers. The following year the company introduced S2H2 traditional-sized metal woods, and in 1990 it introduced the Big Bertha driver—named after the World War I German long-distance cannon. The Big Bertha was revolutionary in that it was much larger than conventional woods and lacked a hosel so that the weight could be better distributed throughout the clubhead. This innovative design gave the clubhead a larger sweet spot, which allowed a player to mis-hit or strike the golf ball off-center of the clubhead and not suffer much loss of distance or accuracy. By 1992 Big Bertha drivers were number one on the Senior PGA, the LPGA, and Hogan Tours. Callaway Golf Company became a public company on February 28, 1992. By year-end 1992 its annual revenues had doubled to $132 million, and by 1996 Callaway Golf had become the world's largest manufacturer and marketer of golf clubs, with annual sales of more than $678 million.

Ely Callaway's 1996 Retirement and the Formation of the Callaway Golf Ball Company

Callaway Golf continued to lead the golf equipment industry through the mid-1990s with innovative new lines of clubs. The company also introduced a line of golf apparel in 1996 that was available to golfers through an exclusive licensing agreement with Nordstrom. In May 1996, Ely Callaway announced that even though he would remain

---

[2]*Business Week,* September 16, 1991, p. 71.

involved in the promotion of the Callaway Golf products, he was transferring his position as chief executive officer to the company's president, Donald Dye. Dye had been a business associate of Ely Callaway since 1974, when Callaway was in the wine business. Ely Callaway simultaneously announced that he and Charles Yash, Taylor Made Golf Company's CEO and president, would launch Callaway Golf Ball Company as a subsidiary of Callaway Golf. "We believe that there is a good and reasonable opportunity for Callaway Golf Ball Company, in due time, to create, produce and merchandise a golf ball that will be demonstrably superior to, and pleasingly different from, any other golf ball we know of," said Callaway.[3] Yash, who had been the general manager of Spalding's golf ball business and who turned around Taylor Made with the introduction of the Burner Bubble driver, resigned his post at Taylor Made to become president and CEO of the new venture. Upon announcing his decision to work with Callaway, Yash commented, "This is an exciting and most unusual opportunity to develop a new and important golf ball franchise with Ely Callaway for Callaway Golf Company. As a competitor, I have been in awe of Callaway's accomplishments. As his partner, I look forward to the exciting opportunities and challenges Ely and I are sure to find in this new venture."[4]

Callaway Golf Company's 1998 Performance and the Return of Ely Callaway as CEO

A variety of events occurred shortly after Ely Callaway's retirement that resulted in Callaway Golf's loss of market share in fairway woods and its poor financial and market performance in 1998. The U.S. and international markets for golf clubs moved from rapid growth to maturity during 1997 and 1998 after a large percentage of avid golfers purchased titanium drivers and saw little reason to upgrade again until dramatic innovations were available. Global market maturity was compounded by the Asian financial crisis that began in late 1997 and made the export of U.S.-made products, especially expensive luxury goods like Callaway golf clubs, unaffordable for many Asians. Also, heavy global rainfall caused by El Niño contributed to an overall decline in the number of rounds played around the world in 1998. In addition, many club manufacturers believed that the United States Golf Association's (USGA) discussions during 1998 to limit innovations in golf club design caused many golfers to postpone club purchases. The USGA had considered a number of limitations on club design, but ultimately decided to bar only a "spring-like effect" in golf clubs. The USGA advised Callaway Golf that none of its products violated the new regulation.

The emergence of shallow-faced fairway woods had as much to do with Callaway's downturn as any other single event. Callaway had dominated the market for fairway woods since the early 1990s, when the Big Bertha line gained in popularity. By 1996 no other manufacturer came close to Callaway in building a loyal following among fairway woods customers. Even when Callaway users experimented with a rival's new driver, they frequently stayed with Callaway for their fairway woods. However, Callaway's dominance in fairway woods was severely challenged in 1997 when relatively unknown golf manufacturers Adams Golf and Orlimar Golf each heavily

---

[3]"Donald H. Dye Given CEO Duties at Callaway Golf Company." *Two-Ten Communications, Ltd.,* 1996. www.twoten.press.net:80/stories/96/05/13/headlines/appointments_callaway.html, February 6, 1997.

[4]"Keeping His Eye On the Ball," *ParValu Stock Update,* 1996. www.golfweb.com:80/gi/parvalu/updates/03.html, February 6, 1997.

promoted a line of shallow-faced fairway woods that they claimed made it easier for golfers to hit a ball off the fairway or from a poor lie. The two challengers each ran a series of highly successful infomercials that demonstrated the clubs' performance and led to phenomenal sales growth for both companies. Adams' and Orlimar's success came more or less directly at the expense of Callaway. No other golf club manufacturer sold large volumes of fairway woods, so when golfers purchased the new clubs offered by Adams and Orlimar, it was typically Callaway that lost sales and market share.

Callaway CEO Donald Dye took much of the blame for Callaway's failure to predict the popularity of shallow-faced woods and was also ultimately responsible for initiatives that took management's focus off of golf clubs. Under Dye, Callaway Golf began new ventures in golf course and driving range management, opened interactive golf sites, created a new player development project, and launched a golf publishing business with Nicholas Callaway, the youngest son of Ely Callaway and a successful publisher of tabletop books. After a record year in 1997, the company's financial and market performance suffered immensely during 1998. In October 1998, Donald Dye resigned as Callaway's CEO and Ely Callaway returned to rebuild the company.

Ely Callaway's first efforts on his return to active management at Callaway Golf were to "direct [the company's] resources—talent, energy, and money—in an ever-increasing degree toward the creation, design, production, sale and service of new and better products."[5] As part of his turnaround strategy, Ely Callaway also initiated a $54.2 million restructuring program that involved a number of cost-reduction actions and operational improvements. During 1997 and 1998 the company had built up a large inventory of older model clubs that were not sold before the latest clubs were shipped to retailers. Callaway management liquidated the inventory of older generation clubs to generate cash flow and improve the company's financial position. In addition, the company divested its interest in noncore businesses began under Dye and combined the administrative and manufacturing functions of Odyssey Golf and Callaway Golf. Callaway's business restructuring eliminated a variety of job responsibilities and thus resulted in the loss of 750 positions from all functional areas of the company. Callaway Golf Company's income statements for 1993 through 1999 are presented in Exhibit 2. Exhibit 3 presents the company's balance sheets for 1993–99. The company's market performance is graphed in Exhibit 4.

THE GOLF EQUIPMENT INDUSTRY

In 1999, more than 26 million Americans played golf. Of these, 5.4 million were considered avid golfers, playing more than 25 rounds of golf annually. The number of U.S. golfers was expected to grow 1 to 2 percent annually through 2010 as the baby boom generation aged and had more free time and disposable income. In 1999 the typical golfer was a 39-year-old male with a household income of $66,000 who played golf about twice a month. Many women, juniors, and senior citizens also enjoyed the sport. In 1999 there were 5.7 million women and 2.1 million junior golfers aged 12 to 17 in the United States. Seniors accounted for 25 percent of all U.S. golfers in 1999. The average golf score was 97 for men and 114 for women. Only 6 percent of men and 1 percent of women golfers regularly broke a score of 80. Exhibit 5 provides the number of U.S. golfers during various years between 1986 and 1999.

---

[5]Callaway Golf Company 1998 annual report.

exhibit 2   Callaway Golf Company, Income Statements, 1993–99 ($000, except per share amounts)

	1999	1998	1997	1996	1995	1994	1993
Net sales	$714,471	$697,621	$842,927	$678,512	$553,287	$448,729	$254,645
Cost of goods sold	376,405	401,607	400,127	317,353	270,125	208,906	115,458
Gross profit	338,086	296,014	442,800	361,159	283,162	239,823	139,187
Selling, general, and administrative expenses	224,336	245,070	191,313	155,177	120,201	106,913	—
Research and development costs	34,002	36,848	30,298	16,154	8,577	6,380	3,653
Restructuring and transition costs	(181)	54,235	—	—	—	—	—
Litigation settlement	—	—	12,000	—	—	—	—
Income (loss) from operations	79,909	(40,139)	209,189	189,828	154,384	126,530	68,416
Interest & other income, net	9,182	3,911	4,586	5,804	4,038	2,879	1,184
Interest expense	(3,594)	(2,671)	(10)	(37)	(21)	(4)	—
Income before income taxes and cumulative effect of accounting change	85,497	(38,899)	213,765	195,595	158,401	129,405	69,600
Provision for income taxes (benefit)	30,175	(12,335)	81,061	73,258	60,665	51,383	28,396
Cumulative effect of accounting change	n/a	n/a	n/a	n/a	n/a	n/a	(1,658)
Net income	$55,322	($26,564)	$132,704	$122,337	$97,736	$78,022	$42,862
Primary earnings per share	$0.79	($0.38)	$1.94	$1.83	$1.47	$1.14	$0.62
Fully diluted earnings per share	$0.78	($0.38)	$1.85	$1.73	$1.40	$1.07	$0.60
Common equivalent shares	71,214	69,463	71,698	70,661	69,855	73,104	68,964

Source: Callaway Golf Company annual reports.

Golf was popular in developed countries worldwide—especially so in Asia, where there were over 3,500 courses and 16 million golfers. Most of Europe's 2 million-plus golfers resided in England, France, Germany, Scotland, Ireland, and Sweden. The sport was becoming popular in former Soviet-bloc countries—such as Croatia, Slovenia, the Czech Republic, Poland, and Russia—but was not expected to grow dramatically until the economies of those countries stabilized. Russia's first country club opened in Moscow in 1993; by 2000, it had 550 members, who had each paid a $28,000 membership fee for the privilege to play the Robert Trent Jones–designed course. However, only 70 of the club's members were Russian. Some teaching professionals working in Russia projected that there could be 100,000 golfers in Russia by 2025, but in 2000 there were fewer than 500 Russians who could be called avid golfers.

The wholesale value of golf equipment sales in the United States had increased from $740 million in 1986 to over $2.7 billion in 1999. In 1999 the U.S. market for golf balls accounted for about 25 percent of the industry's wholesale sales. The wholesale

exhibit 3 Callaway Golf Company, Balance Sheets, 1993–99 ($000)

	1999	1998	1997	1996	1995	1994	1993
Assets							
Current assets							
Cash and cash equivalents	$112,602	$ 45,618	$ 26,204	$108,457	$ 59,157	$ 54,356	$ 48,996
Accounts receivable, net	54,525	73,466	124,470	74,477	73,906	30,052	17,546
Inventories, net	97,938	149,192	97,094	98,333	51,584	74,151	29,029
Deferred taxes	32,558	51,029	23,810	25,948	22,688	25,596	13,859
Other current assets	13,122	4,310	10,208	4,298	2,370	3,235	2,036
Total current assets	310,472	323,606	281,786	311,513	209,705	187,390	111,466
Property, plant, and equipment, net	142,214	172,794	142,503	91,346	69,034	50,619	30,661
Other assets	120,143	127,779	112,141	25,569	11,236	5,613	2,233
Total assets	$616,783	$665,827	$561,714	$428,428	$289,975	$243,622	$144,360
Liabilities and shareholders' equity							
Current liabilities							
Accounts payable and accrued expenses	$ 46,664	$ 35,928	$ 30,063	$ 14,996	$ 26,894	$ 17,678	$ 11,949
Accrued employee compensation and benefits	21,126	11,083	14,262	16,195	10,680	9,364	6,104
Accrued warranty expense	36,105	35,815	28,059	27,303	23,769	18,182	9,730
Accrued restructuring cost	1,379	7,389	—	—	—	—	—
Income taxes payable	—	9,903	—	2,558	1,491	11,374	n/a
Total current liabilities	105,274	184,008	72,384	61,052	62,834	56,598	27,783
Long-term liabilities	11,575	18,823	7,905	5,109	2,207	610	n/a
Shareholders' equity							
Common stock	763	751	743	729	709	680	676
Paid-in-capital	307,329	258,015	337,403	278,669	214,846	75,022	60,398
Unearned compensation	(2,784)	(5,653)	(3,575)	(3,105)	(2,420)	(3,670)	(2,591)
Retained earnings	288,090	252,528	298,728	238,349	131,712	114,402	58,094
Less grantor stock trust*	(93,744)	(54,325)	(151,315)	(152,375)	(119,913)	—	—
Total shareholders' equity	499,934	453,096	481,425	362,267	224,934	186,414	116,577
Total liabilities and shareholders' equity	$616,783	$655,827	$561,714	$428,428	$289,975	$243,622	$144,360

*The sale of 5,300,000 shares to the grantor stock trust had no net impact to shareholders' equity. The shares in the GST may be used to fund the company's obligations with respect to one or more of the company's nonqualified employee benefit plans.
Source: Callaway Golf Company annual reports.

value of the international golf ball market was estimated at $1.5 billion. Exhibit 6 provides wholesale sporting goods equipment sales for selected years during the 1986–99 period. The growth in golf equipment sales during the early 1990s was attributable not so much to an increase in the number of golfers as to the introduction of technologically advanced equipment offered by Callaway Golf and other manufacturers like Ping and Taylor Made. Many of these technological advances made the game much easier for be-

***exhibit* 4**   Monthly Performance of Callaway Golf Company's Stock
Price, 1992–March 2000

(a) Trend in Callaway Golf Company's Common Stock Price

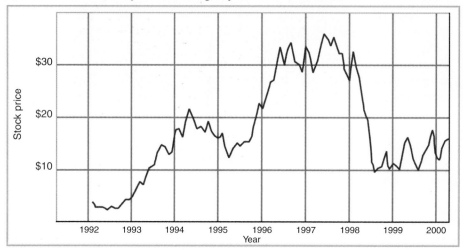

(b) Performance of Callaway Golf Company's Stock Price versus the
S&P 500 Index

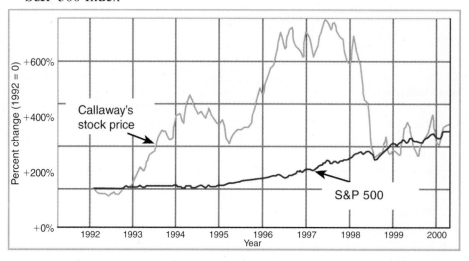

ginners to learn than was possible with older equipment. Additionally, experienced
players frequently looked for equipment that could help them improve their game.
However, it was expected that in the early 2000s the sales of golf equipment would
grow only modestly since most avid golfers had already upgraded their equipment and
were unlikely to do so again unless major new innovations came about.

Key Technological Innovations

The golfing industry had come up with four major innovations that made it easier for
golfers to hit better shots and improve their scores: (1) perimeter weighting in the late

exhibit 5   Number of U.S. Golfers, 1986, 1991, 1993, 1995, 1997, 1999

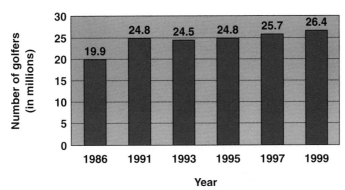

Source: National Golf Foundation.

exhibit 6   Wholesale Sales of Sporting Goods Equipment, 1986, 1993–99 (In Millions of Dollars)

Type of Equipment	1999*	1998	1997	1996	1995	1994	1993	1986
Exercise	$ 3,635	$ 3,400	$ 3,180	$ 2,890	$ 2,510	$ 1,825	$ 1,755	$ 680
Golf	2,770	2,800	2,749	2,463	2,130	1,793	1,490	740
Camping	1,700	1,620	1,590	1,500	1,508	1,275	1,225	580
Baseball/softball	340	340	338	350	349	348	328	240
Soccer	230	220	208	200	185	175	155	90
Tennis	220	215	235	240	235	259	380	255
Total sports equipment	$17,805	$17,350	$17,064	$16,395	$15,379	$13,877	$12,433	$8,250

*Estimated

Source: Sporting Goods Manufacturers Association, *1997–1999 State of the Industry Reports*.

1960s, (2) metal woods in the early 1980s, (3) graphite shafts in the late 1980s, and (4) oversized clubheads in the early 1990s. Perimeter weighting came about due to the poor putting of Karsten Solheim, a General Electric mechanical engineer, who took up golf at the age of 47 in 1954. Solheim designed a putter for himself that he found provided more "feel" when he struck the ball. Solheim moved much of the clubhead weight to the heel and toe, leaving a cavity at the rear and center of the club. Perimeter-weighted or cavity-back clubs had a larger "sweet spot" because of a higher moment of inertia or resistance to twisting. The resistance to twisting reduced the gear effect of the clubhead and resulted in straighter, longer shots with irons. In addition to perimeter weighting, Karsten Solheim also developed the investment-casting manufacturing process. This process allowed clubheads to be formed from molds, rather than forged from steel—the traditional manufacturing process.

Solheim made his putters by hand from 1959 until 1967, when he left GE and founded Karsten Manufacturing. By the 1970s, Karsten was manufacturing a full line of perimeter-weighted putters and irons that carried the Ping brand name. Solheim chose this name because of the sound the cavity-back clubhead made when it struck the ball. Karsten Manufacturing's line of Ping putters and irons was thought to be among the most technologically advanced throughout the 1980s and reigned as the market leader. Karsten Manufacturing was renamed Ping, Inc., in 1999. In 2000, over 95 percent of all irons and putters sold worldwide were perimeter-weighted.

Ping's investment-casting manufacturing process also made the manufacture of perimeter-weighted "metal woods" possible. Taylor Made designed the first metal wood which, like the perimeter-weighted irons, had the advantage of a larger sweet spot than traditional clubs. Although they actually had no wood components, metal woods were so named because it had been traditional to use wooden clubs for driving from the tee and for long fairway shots. The hollow metal head made it possible to move the weight to the heel and toe of the clubhead, as was done with perimeter-weighted irons. Conventional wood heads were made of solid persimmon and had a uniform weight distribution.

The characteristics of the golf club shaft affected a club's performance almost as much as the clubhead did. Distance and accuracy were largely a function of shaft characteristics. Weak or overly flexible shafts could torque as a result of the swinging action and the weight of the clubhead. The torquing of the shaft created a gear effect that resulted in a mis-hit golf ball. Additionally, the flex of the shaft had the ability to increase clubhead speed and improve accuracy. Shafts with greater flex at the tip or clubhead end were advantageous to high handicappers because they helped produce greater clubhead speed at the point of contact with the golf ball, caused the ball to have a higher trajectory, and promoted greater distance. Professional and low-handicap golfers preferred shafts that flexed a few inches higher or nearer the grip because a higher flex point produced added control of the shot.

Graphite shafts were introduced in 1969 by Shakespeare, but were not accepted by golfers because they flexed too much and overly dampened the feel of the club striking the ball. By the early 1990s, technological advances in graphite materials, shaft design, and production had eliminated the previous torsion problems, and graphite shafts quickly gained acceptance by both amateur and professional golfers. Shaft manufacturers were using aerospace technology to improve graphite shafts that had as many as 14 to 16 layers of composite materials (carbon fibers, Kevlar, boron, glass-fiber-reinforced epoxy resins, and synthetic fibers). In 1998, graphite shafts were used in 86 percent of drivers, 77 percent of fairway woods, and 46 percent of irons. Because of the higher prices commanded by graphite, the dollar volume of graphite shaft sales exceeded that of steel alloy shafts by a greater margin than the unit volume differential.

Callaway Golf was the first golf club manufacturer to actually increase the size of the hollow metal wood and make the size of the sweet spot bigger. The larger the clubhead, the bigger the sweet spot, but weight was the primary constraint in increasing clubhead size. If oversized clubheads were too heavy, golfers could not achieve as much speed as they could with lighter clubheads. Slower clubhead speeds resulted in shorter flight distances. The vice president of research and development for a golf club manufacturer described the challenge of trying to increase the size of metal wood clubheads as follows:

> The problem with a big driver is that you have to keep the total weight about the same as a normal-sized driver in order to give the same feel to the golfer. You can't build an overweight club or one that you can't swing at the same speed. A slightly bigger head pulls a little more drag through the air, but it's negligible. Making a bigger head is like blowing

bubble gum. You have the same amount of gum but you've got to make a bigger bubble, so the metal walls will be thinner.[6]

Companies experimented with a number of materials, including stainless steel, titanium, silicon aluminum carbide, and thermoplastics, to find a way of increasing clubhead size without adding weight to the clubhead or diminishing its structural integrity. By 1992, most manufacturers had discovered that titanium was the best material for oversized drivers because the material was 20 percent lighter and 40 percent stronger than stainless steel. By using titanium, club manufacturers were able to increase the size of oversized drivers by about 30 percent. A golf club design engineer explained why material selection was vital to the structural integrity of the clubhead:

> Keeping weight to a minimum is the single biggest aggravation. Once you have a shape you're comfortable with, the challenge is to design a driver that will meet your weight standards. Everybody wants to go bigger, bigger, and bigger in drivers, but as you go bigger, your wall gets thinner. You could make a driver three times the normal size, but it would be like tinfoil. It would fold up and crush on impact.[7]

During the late 1990s, innovators like Callaway Golf and Taylor Made began to use combinations of metals in the design of oversized metal woods and irons. In 1997 Callaway introduced a line of irons that were 85 percent titanium and 15 percent tungsten. A tungsten insert was placed directly at the center of the enlarged sweet spot of the titanium clubface to add weight to the portion of the clubhead that should actually strike the ball. The addition of tungsten to the clubhead concentrated 40 percent of the clubhead weight directly at the sweet spot and made it possible to create an oversized clubhead with a weight concentration designed to maximize the energy transfer from the clubhead to the ball. Taylor Made introduced tungsten-titanium oversized clubs shortly after Callaway's introduction of its tungsten-titanium Great Big Bertha irons. In 1998 Callaway and Taylor Made introduced tungsten-titanium woods and Orlimar boasted clubheads that were made from three different metals. Cleveland Golf introduced a four-metal oversized clubhead design in 1999. In 2000 all major golf club manufacturers had at least one oversized exotic metal driver with a graphite shaft in its product line.

Competitive Rivalry in the Golf Equipment Industry

For decades, the golf equipment industry had been dominated by Wilson Sporting Goods, MacGregor Golf, Inc., and Spalding Sporting Goods. All three companies were very conservative in their approach to new product development, sticking to lines of the standard steel-shafted, forged-steel clubs that had been popular since the 1920s. They were caught completely off guard by the success of companies like Ping, Taylor Made, and Callaway Golf. Amateur golfers readily accepted the technological advances offered by the new golf companies and the market shares of the established brands of the three traditional industry leaders quickly eroded. An executive for one of the new manufacturers stated that Wilson's inability to introduce innovative products of its own had resulted in the company's market share diminishing to a "rounding error."[8]

---

[6]*Machine Design,* April 23, 1992, p. 32.
[7]Ibid.
[8]*Fortune,* June 12, 1995, p. 110.

In the late 1980s as many as 20 manufacturers accounted for about 80 percent of all golf equipment sales, but by 1997 the industry had already consolidated to the point where 6 companies commanded over 80 percent of the market for golf equipment. It was estimated that, of the more than 350 manufacturers in existence, only those 6 were profitable. During the late 1990s industry consolidation stimulated attrition as many smaller club manufacturers exited the industry. Even though longtime industry participants like Wilson, MacGregor, and Spalding were still in business and had attempted to introduce technologically advanced lines of clubs, they had all largely failed in regaining lost market share.

Manufacturing   Most club makers' manufacturing activities were restricted to club assembly, since clubhead production was contracted out to investment casting houses and shafts and grips were usually purchased from third-party suppliers. Most golf club companies offered two to four general models of irons and woods built around proprietary heads that were internally developed. Each clubhead model line was equipped with shafts of varying flex that were either proprietary designs or standard models purchased from shaft manufacturers. Grip manufacturers such as Eaton/Golf Pride and Lamkin offered a number of models, but club manufacturers usually chose to purchase a limited variety of grips from a single source, since most golfers did not have strong preferences for one brand of grip over another. Some club manufacturers used custom grips bearing the company name and logo, while others used standard grips.

The brand and type of shaft had a relatively important influence over golfers' perceptions of club quality and performance. Most golfers had a strong preference for either steel or graphite and some preference for certain manufacturers. True Temper had one of the best reputations in steel shafts and had dominated that segment of the industry ever since it introduced the steel shaft in 1924. Most club manufacturers purchased standard steel shafts from a sole supplier rather than developing proprietary steel shafts or using a multiple sourcing strategy.

As the 1990s progressed, a larger and larger percentage of golfers' preferences shifted to graphite shafts for both drivers and irons. Graphite shaft manufacturers could easily produce a broad line of shafts with varying degrees of flex at a number of flexpoints. Many golfers were persuaded that the unique characteristics of graphite contributed to game improvement. Companies such as Aldila, United Sports Technologies, HST, Unifiber, and Graman USA were competent manufacturers of high-quality graphite shafts and had made it difficult for True Temper to build a dominant market share in the graphite segment as it had done in steel.

Some companies such as Callaway Golf independently designed their shafts, while others collaborated with shaft manufacturers to develop proprietary graphite shafts. Taylor Made's innovative "bubble shaft" was co-designed and manufactured by respected graphite shaft producer HST. Cobra Golf was the only golf manufacturer to vertically integrate into shaft production and produce 100 percent of its shafts inhouse. Cobra Golf was acquired by American Brands (renamed Fortune Brands in 1998 when its cigarette business was divested), which also owned Foot-Joy (a leading maker of golf shoes) and Titleist (the maker of the most popular brand of golf balls and also a producer of golf clubs and other golf equipment). Cobra's golf club shaft facilities were used to produce a portion of the shafts needed for Fortune's Titleist golf clubs.

Marketing   As television networks aired increasing numbers of professional golf tournaments, endorsements by professional golfers started to play a major role in the marketing of golf equipment. The dollar volume of player endorsements was estimated to be three times greater than the projected total Professional Golfers Association (PGA) year 2000 prize money payout of $132 million.

Professional golfer endorsements had been instrumental in the success of some fledgling companies. In 1990, Cobra Golf offered Greg Norman shares of stock and Australian distribution rights to the new company's products in return for the golfer's use and endorsement of Cobra equipment. Norman accepted the offer and, after the company went public, sold 450,000 Cobra shares for $12 million. Norman received an additional $30 million from the sale of his remaining Cobra Golf shares when American Brands acquired Cobra in 1996. Norman's endorsement of Cobra golf clubs helped make Cobra Golf an almost immediately identifiable brand in the golf equipment industry and an attractive acquisition target. Fortune Brand's belief in endorsements led the company to offer Tiger Woods a $20 million five-year contract upon his professional debut in 1996 to endorse Titleist drivers, irons, and balls. Woods's endorsement of the company's newly designed lines of clubs resurrected the brand's presence in clubs, particularly so in woods, where its new 975D driver became one of the top-selling clubs of 1999. Prior to Woods's endorsement of Titleist clubs, the company was primarily thought of as a golf ball company.

Tiger Woods's entry into the PGA set a new standard for endorsement contracts— the $20 million Woods received in 1996 for endorsing Titleist golf clubs and balls was surpassed by the $40 million he received for endorsing Nike apparel and footwear for a five-year period. In 1999 Woods signed a five-year renewal with Nike for $90 million. Tiger Woods also signed a two-year, $10 to 15 million deal with Buick to appear in Buick ads and carry the Buick logo on his golf bag. Woods's five-year renewal with Titleist provided a $2 million annual fee to use Titleist balls and clubs in PGA tournaments; this contract was primarily a defensive measure for Fortune Brands since Woods's Nike and Buick contracts prevented him from appearing in Titleist advertisements or displaying the Titleist logo on his golf bag. Tiger Woods's success in landing large endorsement contracts had spilled over to other professional golfers to some degree, but in 2000 no other golfer had been able to garner contracts in the same range as those signed by Woods.

Most pro-line or high-quality golf equipment manufacturers distributed their products through on-course pro shops and a select number of off-course pro shops, such as Edwin Watts and Nevada Bob's. The off-course pro shops were quickly accounting for the largest portion of retail golf club sales because they carried a wider variety of brands and marketed more aggressively than on-course shops. Most on-course pro shops sold only to members and carried few clubs since their members purchased golf clubs less frequently than apparel and footwear. In 1997 on-course pro shops carried, on average, 4 brands of drivers, 4 brands of irons, and 6 brands of putters, while off-course pro shops carried, on average, 12 brands of drivers, 18 brands of irons, and 17 brands of putters.

Pro-line manufacturers chose to limit their channels of distribution to on-course and off-course pro shops because they believed that PGA professionals had the training necessary to properly match equipment to the customer. Manufacturers such as Taylor Made, Callaway, and Ping all provided the pro shops with inexpensive devices that gave an estimate of the golfer's swing characteristics. The pro could take the readings from these devices and then custom-fit the golfer with the proper clubs. Custom fitting could be done more precisely with more expensive, specialized computer equipment, but most pro shops had not invested in the new technology. The Sportech Swing Analyzer aided in custom fitting by recording 12 swing variables, such as clubhead speed and path, club face angle at impact, ball position, the golfer's weight distribution, ball flight pattern, and ball flight distance. The pro could use the fit data provided by the Swing Analyzer to select the appropriate club for the customer. Golf equipment manufacturers expected a larger percentage of golfers to demand more precise custom fitting from retailers in the future.

Pro shops generally chose to stock only pro-line equipment and did not carry less expensive, less technologically advanced equipment. Low-end manufacturers such as Spalding, MacGregor, and Dunlop sold their products mainly through discounters, mass merchandisers, and large sporting goods stores. These retailers had no custom-fitting capabilities and rarely had sales personnel who were knowledgeable about the performance features of the different brands and models of golf equipment carried in the store. The appeal of such retail outlets was low price, and they mainly attracted beginning golfers and occasional golfers who were unwilling to invest in more expensive equipment.

CALLAWAY GOLF COMPANY

Callaway Golf Company's competitive strategy was rooted in Ely Callaway's philosophy that true long-term success comes from innovative products that are "demonstrably superior to, and pleasingly different from" the products offered by industry rivals. Ely Callaway believed that due to the difficulty of the game of golf (there was tremendous room for variation in *each* swing of the club and for off-center contact with the ball), serious golfers would be willing to invest in high-quality, premium-priced equipment, like the Big Bertha driver and the titanium Great Big Bertha driver, if such clubs could improve their game by being more forgiving of a less-than-optimum swing. Since the introduction of Callaway's S2H2 line of irons in 1988, the company had sought to develop, manufacture, and market the most technologically advanced golf clubs available. In addition, Richard Helmstetter and his team of engineers sought quantum leaps in club performance, rather than incremental improvements, with each new line of clubs introduced by the company.

Callaway's "Demonstrably Superior and Pleasingly Different" Value Chain

Callaway Golf Company's ability to develop "demonstrably superior and pleasingly different" golf clubs was a result of activities performed by the company throughout its value chain. Callaway's differentiation was achieved through both its unique value chain and through its ability to out-execute its rivals where value chain similarities existed.

Product Development and the Helmstetter Test Center   When Ely Callaway purchased Hickory Stick USA he believed strongly that developing "demonstrably superior and pleasingly different" golf clubs would be more closely related to the company's physics-oriented R&D than would a focus on cosmetics. Richard Helmstetter and his engineering team were critical to the execution of Callaway's competitive strategy. As of 2000 Callaway Golf had consistently outspent its rivals on R&D. In 1999 alone, the company spent $27 million on research and development related to its golf club business—more than most of its key rivals' combined R&D budgets. The company's R&D efforts allowed it to continually beat its competitors to the market with new innovations. Callaway's engineers developed the first oversize driver in

1990, were the first to make clubheads even larger by using titanium, and were the first to use a combination of materials (titanium and tungsten) in clubhead design.

Callaway Golf opened the Richard C. Helmstetter Test Center in 1994 to support its research and product development efforts. The test center was located about a mile from Callaway's main campus and included a laboratory and a golfing area. The test center laboratory was home to Helmstetter's engineers, who worked both on teams and individually to develop new models of clubheads and shafts. Callaway's products were designed on powerful workstations running computer-aided design (CAD) software similar to that used in the aerospace industry. The CAD software allowed engineers not only to design new clubheads and shafts but also to conduct aerodynamic and strength testing in a simulated environment. Actual physical models could be created from the computer-generated images through the use of numerically controlled systems. The center's "destruction and durability" laboratory used robots and air cannons to establish minimum thresholds of strength and durability for prototypes of new models of clubheads and shafts.

The club-fitting and specifications area of the test center used the company's Callaway Performance Analysis System to match equipment to a golfer's swing characteristics. The internally developed proprietary video and computer system used stereo imaging techniques to capture a sequence of eight multiple exposures of the clubhead and ball at various time intervals immediately before and after a golfer hit the ball into a net approximately 10 feet from where it was struck. Callaway's proprietary computer software analyzed the video images of the clubhead's approach to the ball and the ball's rotational patterns over its first few feet of flight to make a variety of calculations needed to project the ball's ultimate path. The projected path was displayed on a six-foot video screen that showed the ball's flight along the 18th fairway at Pebble Beach. The computer system also recorded the clubhead speed, ball velocity, side spin, back spin, attack angle, and launch angle to calculate the efficiency rating, carry, roll, total distance, and dispersion (deviation from a straight path). All of these statistics were projected on the screen, along with the image of ball's flight down the fairway. The equipment allowed the company to build a set of clubs for the touring professional that had the perfect swing weight, frequency, loft, lie, and length to maximize distance and accuracy.

The Helmstetter Test Center's golfing area was an 8.1-acre outdoor testing facility that included three putting and chipping greens, a deep pot bunker, a shallow fairway bunker, and a 310-yard fairway that was 80 yards wide at its narrowest point. Sensors located along the fairway recorded the distance and dispersion of any ball landing in the test area. Atmospheric conditions, such as wind speed, direction, temperature, barometric pressure, humidity, and dew point were recorded by three weather stations located around the test site. The facility also included an artificial tee box and green that accurately simulated a real green. Ball reaction on the simulated green was almost identical to that on the other three greens and allowed the company to continue testing while the natural test site was being irrigated or mowed.

The Helmstetter Test Center had two primary uses: It provided an ideal place to custom-fit clubs for the touring pros who used Callaway equipment, and it allowed Callaway R&D staff to test new products during their developmental stage. Once a professional's new clubs were fitted using the video and computer capabilities of the Callaway Performance Analysis System, the touring pro could then use the golfing area to hit balls and fine-tune his or her clubs by requesting minor modifications to the clubhead or shaft. Callaway included nontouring professionals in addition to engineers among its R&D staff. The golfing staff was critical to the product development process

since engineers were able to refine new prototypes based on the feedback and recommendations of Callaway's R&D staff golfers. Callaway's engineers also tested prototypes with robots to evaluate the distance and accuracy of the club, but only a human
could evaluate the feel of a golf club striking a ball.

Callaway's Purchasing and Production Processes   Once its clubheads
were designed on a CAD system and tested in the Helmstetter Center, stainless-steel
master plates were cut by Callaway to the exact specifications called for by the system.
Each clubhead mold was made by pouring liquid wax between the stainless-steel master plates. The wax clubheads were removed from the master plates and sprayed with
a mixture of highly heat resistant material. The wax was melted out of these heat-
resistant molds, leaving a hollow core. The hollow molds were then sent to an investment casting house, where either stainless steel or titanium was poured into the molds.
The casting house then broke away the mold and welded, sanded, and painted the clubheads before sending them to Callaway for further assembly.

Callaway Golf used five investment casting houses, all of which underwent extensive screening and were closely monitored during the casting process. Callaway management believed that it was particularly important to supervise the casting process
since poor casting could produce clubhead inconsistencies that could lead to poor performance or product failures. Callaway had entered into a joint venture with Sturm,
Ruger & Company in 1995 to produce its clubheads but had since recognized that quality clubheads could be obtained through outsourcing. Even though Callaway Golf was
certain it would obtain high-quality clubheads through its sourcing agreements, it made
daily inspections of incoming clubhead shipments using the materials analysis and
durability-testing capabilities of the Helmstetter Center.

Like Callaway's clubheads, all of its shafts were designed and tested at the Helmstetter Center. Callaway manufactured all prototype shafts by hand at the testing center but contracted shaft production out to independent shaft manufacturers once
specifications were established for the various graphite shafts used in its product line.
As with clubheads, shafts were drawn from incoming shipments and tested at the company's R&D facility. Steel shafts were contracted out and inspected in a similar fashion. Callaway had produced as much as 50 percent of its graphite shafts internally
during the late 1990s but outsourced 100 percent of its shaft requirements in 2000.

Callaway Golf's cell manufacturing process allowed the company to include quality control inspections throughout each club's assembly. In addition, the assembly plant
was highly automated, with all processes requiring very tight tolerances performed by
computer-controlled machinery. For example, the drilling necessary to produce Callaway's tapered bore-thru hosels was done by a series of precision drill presses that ensured that each hosel was drilled at the correct angle. Once the hosel had been drilled
through, the clubhead moved to a production station that checked the lie and loft angles
of the club and made any necessary corrections by slightly bending the clubhead to the
proper angle.

Each shaft was inspected for fractures prior to insertion into the clubhead, and then
the entire assembled club was weighed to assess the swing weight. Callaway production workers could choose between medallions of four different weights to bring a finished iron to the exact specified swing weight. The chosen medallion was permanently
affixed to the back of the clubhead with a press. Swing weights for assembled woods
were brought to their specifications by inserting epoxy through a small hole in the rear
of the clubhead.

After undergoing a baking process that dried the glue used to attach the shaft to the
clubhead, each club was fitted with a grip using a laser alignment device, airbrushed

with details like the club number and Callaway trademarks, and then visually inspected for blemishes or other imperfections. Each finished club was wrapped by hand to protect its finish during shipping.

Sales and Customer Service   New product development at Callaway Golf Company was a cross-functional effort that included not only the R&D staff but also the company's sales and advertising staffs. Callaway sales and advertising personnel would evaluate new designs created by the company's aerospace engineers and recommend design changes based on their knowledge of the market. Once a new design was settled on, Callaway's sales force and internal advertising staff would create a name for the new product line, an advertising campaign, and promotional materials that would accompany the product launch in parallel with the R&D staff's developmental and testing processes.

Callaway's customer service department was viewed as a critical component of the company's overall level of differentiation. The customer service staff was made up of experienced employees who were offered a generous compensation package that included commissions for superior performance in meeting the needs of Callaway's retailers and consumers. Many of Callaway's rivals viewed customer service as a low-value-adding activity and typically made customer service a place for entry-level employees to become acquainted with the business. Each of Callaway Golf's customer service representatives received eight weeks of training before being allowed to handle a customer service inquiry. No other company in the industry provided more than three weeks of training to its customer service personnel. In addition to providing extensive training, Callaway promoted a team-oriented atmosphere that allowed the company's knowledge base to expand through the mentoring of newer employees by longtime customer service employees.

The entire customer service staff was empowered to make a final decision regarding a consumer or retailer complaint or warranty claim. Callaway customer service personnel were allowed to make decisions that might be pushed to the CEO at some other golf equipment companies. For example, if a golfer was vacationing and had a problem with a club, a customer service staff member could instruct the consumer to visit a local retailer to pick up a replacement club. If the consumer was out of the country and was not near a Callaway retailer, the Callaway employee was allowed to send a new club to the customer via Federal Express. Callaway customer service staff members were also known to send a gift to club owners who had experienced problems with Callaway equipment. Callaway's two-year warranty on all of its products entitled the owner to replace any defective product with a new product rather than return the product for a repair. In addition, Callaway generally chose to replace defective or broken clubs for the life of the club rather than stick to its two-year warranty period. A Callaway sales executive remarked, "A bad experience with a Callaway product usually winds up making someone a Callaway customer for life."

Callaway Golf's Product Line

Metal Woods   Callaway Golf's Big Bertha driver was the most innovative club in the industry when it was introduced in 1990. Its key features were a bigger clubhead, a bigger sweet spot, and a longer shaft, all of which helped to improve the consistency with which a golfer could drive the ball off the tee. Callaway wasted no time in capitalizing on the explosive popularity of its new driver; company managers understood that once a driver developed a following among golfers, these golfers usually wanted other woods to match it. The company subsequently introduced a series of fairway woods—a 2 wood, a

3 wood, a 5 wood, two styles of 7 woods, a 9 wood, and an 11 wood—to complement the Big Bertha driver. Many golfers rushed to buy not only the Big Bertha driver but also the company's other Big Bertha metal woods; it was common for Big Bertha enthusiasts to have three or four of the Big Bertha fairway woods in their bag.

Four years later, the company again moved to set itself apart from rival equipment makers (most of whom had by then come out with imitative versions of the Big Bertha line) by introducing the Great Big Bertha driver, made out of strong, lightweight titanium. The driver had a clubhead 30 percent larger than the original Big Bertha driver but was still just as light because of the substitution of titanium for stainless steel in the clubhead and the use of a graphite shaft; the Great Big Bertha (GBB) was the industry's most technologically advanced golf club and retailed for $500 (a heretofore unheard-of price for a single golf club).

Callaway's introduction of its titanium Biggest Big Bertha in 1997 again caught industry rivals off guard as they moved to match the size of the GBB. The Biggest Big Bertha (BBB) was 15 percent larger than the titanium Great Big Bertha (and the titanium clubs produced by Callaway's rivals) and was equipped with a 46-inch lightweight shaft. The total weight of the BBB was less than the total weight of the titanium GBB and the stainless steel Big Bertha drivers, which had 45- and 44-inch shafts, respectively.

The size of Callaway woods began to decrease with the introduction of its Big Bertha (BB) Steelhead metal woods in 1998 and Hawk Eye titanium metal woods in 1999. The BB Steelhead line was created in response to the popularity of the shallow-faced woods introduced by Orlimar and Adams in 1998. BB Steelhead drivers and fairway woods had a lower center of gravity than GBB and BBB woods, but had a higher profile than Adams and Orlimar woods. The BB Steelhead line incorporated the best features of both competing club designs by maintaining a very low center of gravity but having a larger clubface, which prevented the golfer from hitting below the ball, as was frequently done by amateur golfers using shallow-faced woods.

The BB Steelhead Plus was introduced in January 2000 as an improvement to the BB Steelhead line of drivers and fairway woods. Like the BB Steelhead line, the BB Steelhead Plus included a precision-cast steel chip to lower the club's center of gravity but featured variable clubface thickness that optimized energy transfer between the clubhead and the ball. Callaway's Variable Face Thickness Technology, developed through computer modeling and player testing, allowed the company to vary the clubface thickness to maximize perimeter weighting while keeping an elliptical area near the center of the clubface relatively thick. This thickness directly at the sweet spot of the clubface provided more energy transfer when a ball was well struck, while the perimeter weighting and thin walls near the outside edges of the clubface provided more forgiveness if a ball was mis-hit. Callaway's BB Steelhead Plus metal woods and its Variable Face Thickness Technology are described in the Callaway print ad shown in Exhibit 7. Callaway's Great Big Bertha Hawk Eye titanium drivers and fairway woods featured a titanium body and crown plate and Callaway's exclusive tungsten gravity screw, which accounted for only 2 percent of the clubhead volume but 25 percent of its overall weight. The lightweight titanium clubhead body and crown plate allowed Callaway to increase the overall size of the driver and the sweet spot, while the tungsten screw performed a number of functions. First, the use of tungsten low in the club created a low center of gravity, which helped the golfer produce a high trajectory. The tungsten screw also was strategically positioned in the sole of the clubhead to create Callaway's Draw Bias Technology, which drew the clubhead square at impact and reduced the likelihood of a slice. The tungsten screw also increased backspin, which helped produce greater distance. Exhibit 8 presents a print ad for Callaway's line of GBB Hawk Eye metal woods.

exhibit 7   Sample Ad for Callaway Golf's New Big Bertha Steelhead Plus Metal Woods

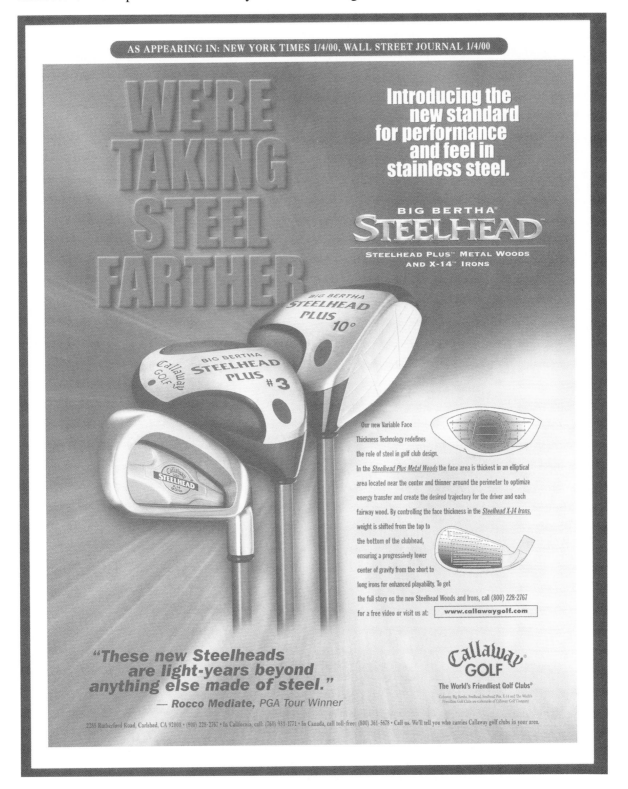

exhibit 8   Sample Ad for Callaway Golf's New Hawk Eye Metal Woods

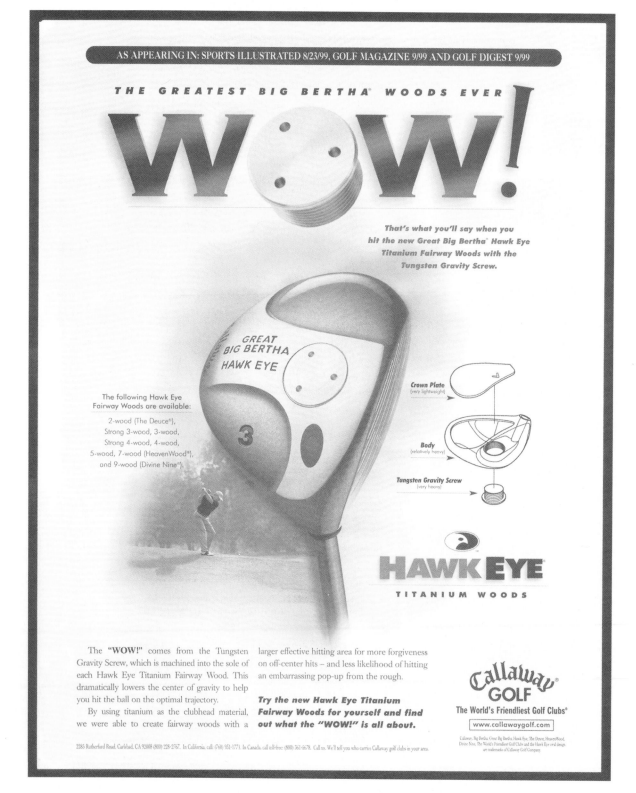

Irons To capitalize on the initial popularity of the Big Bertha metal woods, Callaway Golf introduced lines of stainless-steel and graphite-shafted Big Bertha irons in 1994. In 1997 the company introduced Great Big Bertha tungsten-titanium irons, which included a tungsten insert located in the sole of the club that lowered the clubhead's center of gravity. The use of titanium allowed Callaway to increase the overall size of the clubface, creating a larger sweet spot, while the tungsten insert allowed Callaway to keep the center of gravity low and add weight to the sweet spot. This low center of gravity and concentration of weight in the sweet spot allowed the irons to hit higher, straighter shots.

Callaway's Hawk Eye tungsten-injected titanium irons, introduced in 1999, included innovative design improvements over the original GBB tungsten-titanium irons. The Hawk Eye titanium irons included a hidden cavity that ran the length of the clubhead and extended upward behind the hitting area. Small, uniform tungsten spheres were added by a computer weigh station to the cavity through a port and then covered with a dense molten metal to permanently lock them into place. Each iron contained a different number of spheres depending on the optimal center of gravity for the loft of the club. Once the appropriate number of tungsten spheres and the molten metal were added to the clubhead, the weight port was hidden by a Hawk Eye medallion. The Tungsten Weight Matrix that resulted from the addition of the spheres occupied only 27 percent of the volume of a Callaway Hawk Eye 5-iron yet accounted for 45 percent of the clubhead's weight. The weight matrix created a low center of gravity that acted much like the gravity screw used in Hawk Eye metal woods and allowed golfers to create a high shot likely to maintain a straight path.

Callaway Golf replaced its stainless-steel Big Bertha irons in 1998 with its Big Bertha X-12 irons. The X-12 line of irons included a number of improvements over the Big Bertha irons and became the best-selling iron in the company's history. The X-12 line featured a narrower sole than Big Bertha irons, which made it easier to hit shots out of the rough. Big Bertha X-12 irons also had a multilayer design effect on the back of the clubface that allowed Callaway designers to locate the center of gravity at the ideal location for each length iron. The introduction of a variable 360-degree undercut channel also aided Callaway engineers in placing the center of gravity at the best possible location on the clubhead.

Callaway replaced the X-12 line of irons in 2000 with the Big Bertha X-14 Steelhead line. The X-14 featured Callaway's Variable Face Thickness Technology, which tapered the clubface from top to bottom and from heel to toe to create better perimeter weighting than previous generations of Callaway irons. The technology also allowed Callaway engineers to move the center of gravity to the ideal location on each iron. For example, the X-14 short irons had a higher center of gravity to provide extra control on approach shots, while the midlength irons and long irons had a lower center of gravity to produce a higher ball flight. Exhibit 9 shows a sample ad for Callaway Golf's X-14 irons.

Putters Callaway Golf Company manufactured and marketed Bobby Jones, Carlsbad, and Tuttle lines of putters and the Odyssey brand of putters. Callaway had moderate success with its own Callaway putter lines, but its acquisition of Odyssey in 1997 made it the leading producer of putters in 2000. The 12 Bobby Jones putters and four Carlsbad putters were all made from stainless steel and came in blade and mallet styles. The Tuttle putter came in one model, which was unique in that it actually resembled a Big Bertha driver but was the size of a putter. Odyssey became known as an innovator in putters when it became one of the first companies to introduce polymer clubface inserts. Many golfers preferred putters with an insert since the soft material

exhibit 9   Sample Ad for Callaway Golf's New Big Bertha Steelhead X-14 Irons

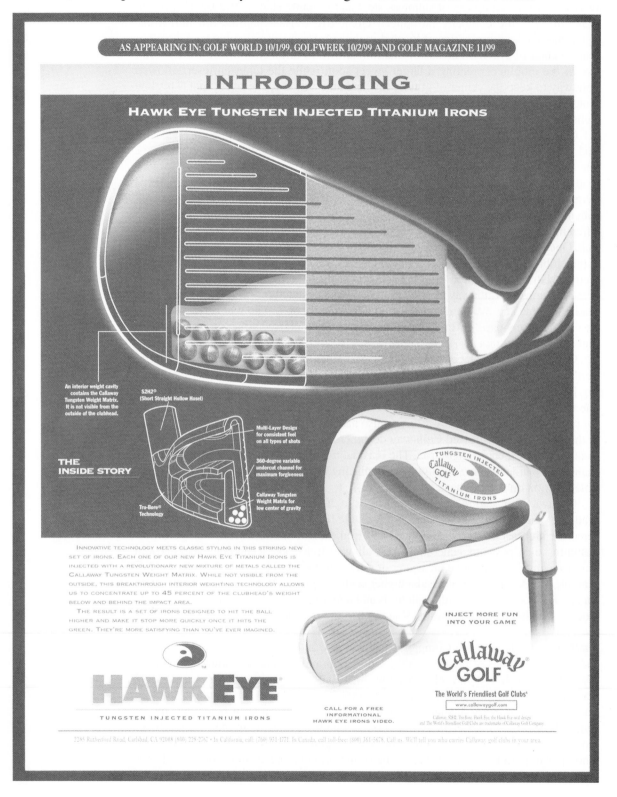

created a softer noise and provided more feel when putting a ball. Callaway's Odyssey putter was one of the two leading brands of putter in 2000 (Ping and Odyssey regularly exchanged the number one title) and was available in 26 different blade and mallet designs. Each of Odyssey's 26 models of putters featured its Stronomic polymer insert, available in three degrees of softness. In early 2000, Odyssey introduced its White Hot line of putters, which used Callaway's golf ball material as a clubface insert.

Callaway's Battle against Patent and Trademark Infringement

Ever since the Big Bertha driver had gained mass acceptance by professional and amateur golfers, Callaway Golf had been attacked by small golf companies offering clubs that were so similar in design and appearance that they infringed on Callaway's patents and trademarks. Although they looked like the branded clubs, the knockoff clubs were of inferior quality and typically sold for as much as 75 percent less than name-brand clubs. Some knockoff brands outsold the brands offered by such well-known makers as Hogan, Cleveland, and MacGregor. Callaway Golf was extremely committed to battling the makers of knockoff and counterfeit clubs. The company hired a retired U.S. Army counterintelligence expert to investigate trademark infringement cases and also worked in this area with private investigators, U.S. Customs, and U.S. marshals. In early 2000, Callaway Golf carried out a four-state sweep against illegal club makers that netted $65,000 worth of Callaway golf clubs that had been stolen and were being sold over the Internet; officials seized 5,800 golf clubs, including Canterbury Big Bursar V-17 irons and Connection Golf Big Bernard Steelclad metal woods. However, even when patent infringers and counterfeiters were caught and convicted, it was difficult to collect damages because such companies usually had minimal assets to seize.

Callaway Golf also aggressively protected its legal rights when it believed that a branded rival infringed on its patents or made false claims about either its own products or Callaway's products. In 1998 Callaway brought a suit against Spalding Sports Worldwide for trademark violation after Spalding created a line of System C golf balls and claimed they were specifically designed for Callaway clubs. The two parties settled in 1999, with Spalding agreeing to pull the line of golf balls. In addition, after a legal challenge from Callaway, Orlimar Golf was ordered by the court to retract advertisements falsely claiming that it was the number one metal wood used on the PGA tour. In 1999 Callaway Golf saw that the vice president of Callaway Golf Ball Company could in no way be involved with Taylor Made's golf ball operations after the Callaway employee left with company trade secrets to become Taylor Made's president and CEO. Callaway Golf also forced an apology from the CEO of La Jolla Golf after Callaway found that La Jolla's chief executive had used a fictitious name to make untrue and disparaging remarks about Callaway golf clubs on the Internet.

Endorsements and Use of Callaway Products by Golf Professionals

Callaway golf clubs were popular with both professionals and amateurs alike. Callaway drivers were endorsed by the professional golfers listed in Exhibit 10. However, many professional golfers used Callaway equipment even though they were not paid to endorse the company's products. In 1999 Callaway drivers were used in 61 wins, *exhibit 10*   Callaway Golf Company Staff Professionals, 2000

Tour	Staff Players
Professional Golfers Association	Stephen Ames Paul Azinger Oline Browne Carlos Franco Brian Henninger Rocco Mediate Jesper Parnevik Paul Stankowski
Senior Professional Golfers Association	Bob Charles Jim Colbert Jim Dent Dave Eichelberger Bruce Fleisher David Graham Orville Moody Walter Morgan Bob Murphy
Ladies Professional Golfers Association	Jane Geddes Rachel Hetherington Rosie Jones Emilee Klein Leta Lindley Cindy McCurdy Liselotte Neumann Alison Nicholas Annika Sorenstam
European Professional Golfers Association	Mark McNulty Colin Montgomerie Eduardo Romero

Source: Callaway Golf 2000 catalog.

Callaway irons were used in 37 wins, and Odyssey putters produced 36 wins in a total of 186 PGA, LPGA, Senior PGA, Nike, and European PGA professional tournaments. A comparison of clubs used by professionals in all five tournaments is presented in Exhibit 11.

CALLAWAY GOLF'S MAJOR COMPETITORS

Callaway management considered its strongest competitive rivals to be Ping and Taylor Made because of those companies' track records in product innovation and their strong brand-name recognition: Ping irons had dominated the industry during much of the 1980s and 1990s (the perimeter-weighting feature pioneered by Karsten was a major technological breakthrough and had since become the industry standard in designing irons), while Taylor Made's distinctive bubble shaft was also considered to be a high-tech innovation. Other key rivals of Callaway Golf Company were Titleist, Adams Golf, and Orlimar Golf. Exhibit 12 presents a price comparison of golf equipment produced by Callaway Golf Company and its key rivals.

exhibit 11   Golf Club Use Comparison among Professional Golfers
(All tours combined), 1998–99

	1999	1998
Drivers		
Callaway	38.5%	55.2%
Titleist	24.2	16.9
Ping	13.4	n.a.
Taylor Made	5.3	8.0
Orlimar	3.0	0.1
All others	15.6	17.5
Total drivers	100.0%	100.0%
Fairway woods		
Callaway	52.1%	48.3%
Orlimar	17.9	10.5
Taylor Made	8.8	13.3
Titleist	4.5	5.1
Cleveland	3.1	n.a.
All others	13.6	20.3
Total fairway woods	100.0%	100.0%
Irons		
Callaway	18.3%	19.4%
Ping	15.0	15.3
Mizuno	15.0	14.1
Titleist	14.5	12.6
Taylor Made	4.4	4.7
All others	32.8	33.9
Total irons	100.0%	100.0%
Putters		
Odyssey	28.9%	31.0%
Ping	21.8	24.8
Titleist	19.8	18.7
Never Compromise	11.2	3.7
Tear Drop	4.0	n.a.
All others	14.3	16.0
Total putters	100.0%	100.0%

n.a. = Not available.
Source: Callaway Golf Company annual reports and Darrell Survey.

Ping

Ping had not been well known for its drivers but had been one of the industry's premier manufacturers of irons since its Ping Eye 2-irons were introduced in the mid-1980s. The company's Ping Eye 3-irons that were introduced in 1999 were among the most popular irons with both professionals and amateurs. Ping Eye 3-irons were one of the two leading brands of irons sold in the United States and were frequently the most-used iron in various professional tournaments. Ping Eye 3s were available with a compact

exhibit 12   Retail Price Comparison of Equipment Produced by
Leading Golf Equipment Companies, March 2000

Brand	Titanium Drivers	Graphite-Shafted Stainless-Steel Irons (Set of 8)	Putters (Price Range of Most Popular Models)	Golf Balls (Price per Ball—Based on Single Sleeve)
Callaway Golf/Odyssey	$400	$900	$90–$200	$3.60
Ping	$400	$850	$80–$140	n.a.
Taylor Made	$300	$750	$100	$3.33
Titleist	$400	$870	$270	$3.33
Adams Golf	$300	Not carried	n.a.	n.a.
Orlimar Golf	$300	$800	n.a.	n.a.

n.a. = Not applicable.

Source: Edwin Watts Golf Shops and International Golf Discount, March 11, 2000.

blade-style clubhead designed for low-handicap golfers and with an oversized clubhead that had greater perimeter weighting for more forgiveness. All Ping Eye 3-irons featured a custom tuning port that was very similar in appearance to Callaway's tungsten weight matrix port, but functioned differently. Rather than acting as a port to add tungsten weights, Ping's custom tuning port allowed the company to make minor adjustments to the loft and lie of the club during custom fitting.

Ping had elected not to introduce a titanium driver until 1998, because the company's engineers believed that the material provided no advantage over stainless steel. However, in 2000 its 323-cc displacement TiSI titanium driver was actually the largest custom-fit driver available. Ping also offered Ti3 titanium fairway woods that featured a zirconium soleplate and a tungsten bottom weight that were both intended to lower the club's center of gravity. Ping also offered an i3 line of stainless-steel fairway woods in five different lofts.

Ping's greatest strength was in putters, where it alternated every quarter or so with Odyssey as the number one brand of putters in the U.S. and international markets. Depending on the tournament, Ping putters were often used by professional golfers more than any other brand. Ping had 46 models of putters that were made from either antiqued manganese bronze, stainless steel, or laminated maple. Certain Ping putters featured inserts made from an elastomer compound, aluminum pixels, or copper pixels. Ping began offering custom-fit clubs in the 1960s, and in 2000 all Ping metal woods, irons, and putters could be custom-fitted to golfers who desired that service.

Taylor Made–Adidas Golf

Taylor Made was founded in 1979 by Gary Adams, who mortgaged his home and began production of his metal woods in an abandoned car dealership building in McHenry, Illinois. Both touring pros and golf retailers were skeptical of the new club design until they found that the metal woods actually hit the ball higher and farther than persimmon woods. By 1984, Taylor Made metal woods were the number one wood on the PGA tour and the company had grown to be the third largest golf equipment company in the

United States. In 1984 the company was acquired by France-based Salomon SA, which provided the capital necessary for the company to continue to develop innovative new lines of clubs. The company's sales had stalled during the late 1980s and early 1990s until it introduced its Burner Bubble drivers in 1994. The bubble shaft design allowed some of the shaft weight to be moved from underneath the grip to just below the grip. Taylor Made management claimed that this weight relocation decreased the club's inertia, which resulted in faster clubhead acceleration. The bubble shaft also featured a reinforced midsection, said to minimize any twisting of the clubhead during the swing.

Many of the company's innovations in drivers and fairway woods mirrored those of Callaway Golf. In 1996, shortly after Callaway's introduction of the Great Big Bertha, Taylor Made had come out with an oversized titanium driver that had its differentiating bubble shaft and copper-colored clubhead. Taylor Made also produced and marketed a line of irons with its patented bubble shafts and introduced a line of bubble-shafted tungsten-titanium irons and a new titanium bubble-shafted T2 driver in 1997. The T2 and Taylor Made's tungsten-titanium irons appeared in retail locations at approximately the same time that the Biggest Big Bertha and the Big Bertha tungsten-titanium irons made their debut. Also in 1997, Taylor Made and its parent were both acquired by the Germany-based sports conglomerate Adidas.

In 2000 Taylor Made offered titanium FireSole metal woods and irons that featured a tungsten sole plug and SuperSteel stainless-steel metal woods and irons. The FireSole was Taylor Made's answer to Callaway's Hawk Eye lines of metal woods and irons, while its promotion of its SuperSteel line touted many of the same benefits as Callaway's BB SteelHead Plus metal woods and X-14 irons. Taylor Made also offered FireSole Rescue clubs, which had a large tungsten sole attached to a reduced-size titanium clubhead that placed 75 percent of the clubhead's weight below the equator of the ball. The rescue woods had an ultralow center of gravity and could be used on either the fairway or the rough. In early 2000 Taylor Made's Rescue fairway woods were unique; no products of similar appearance were offered by other major club manufacturers. Taylor Made also had a line of putters that featured a polymer clubface. Taylor Made introduced its InterGel line of golf balls in 1999.

Fortune Brands/Acushnet (Titleist and Cobra Golf)

The Acushnet Company was a rubber deresinating company founded in 1910 in Acushnet, Massachusetts. The company opened a golf ball division in 1932 when founder Phil Young believed that a bad putt during a round of golf he was playing was a result of a faulty ball rather than his poor putting. Young took the ball to a dentist's office to have it X-rayed and found that the core of the ball was indeed off-center. Young believed that Acushnet could develop and manufacture high-quality golf balls and teamed with a fellow MIT graduate, Fred Bommer, to create the Titleist line of balls. Young and Bommer introduced their first Titleist golf ball in 1935, and by 1949 Titleist had become the most-played ball on the PGA. In 2000, Titleist was still the number one golf ball on the PGA, being used by more than 75 percent of all professional golfers in tournament play. Acushnet also manufactured and marketed a Pinnacle line of golf balls, developed in 1980 as a lower-priced alternative to Titleist branded golf balls.

Acushnet's acquisition of John Reuter, Jr., Inc., in 1958 and Golfcraft, Inc., in 1969 put Titleist into the golf club business. Titleist's Reuter Bull's Eye putter became a favorite on the PGA tour during the 1960s, and its AC-108 heel-toe weighted irons were among the most popular brands of irons during the early 1970s. In 1996 the Acushnet Company was acquired by American Brands, which had increased its presence in the golf equipment industry in 1985 when it acquired Foot-Joy, the number one seller of golf gloves and shoes. Also in 1996 American Brands acquired Cobra Golf for $715 million. The company's golf and leisure products division had an operating profit of $147 million on sales of $965 million in 1999.

Acushnet's two golf club brands maintained separate sales forces, but every other value chain activity was combined for overall cost savings whenever possible. The Titleist brand of clubs had achieved only moderate success after Ping's perimeter-weighted clubs became popular in the 1980s, but Titleist had become much more successful during the late 1990s due to Tiger Woods's endorsement of the company's irons and metal woods. In 2000 Titleist's 975D driver, used by Tiger Woods, was among the more popular drivers with both professionals and amateurs. The 975D was an oversized titanium driver designed for a flatter ball flight to help a golfer achieve greater roll once the ball hit the ground. The Titleist titanium 975R was a variation of the 975D, which had a more shallow face and a slightly smaller clubhead. Titleist also offered a line of 975F stainless-steel fairway woods in 2000.

Titleist had two lines of stainless steel irons: the DCI 990 and DCI 981. The DCI 990 was intended for low-handicap golfers and had a reduced clubface offset and more weight toward the lower portion of the heel, where better golfers were more prone to mis-hit a golf ball. The DCI 981 line, designed for higher-handicap golfers, had an offset clubface, a low center of gravity, and more weight toward the toe of the clubface of short irons. The overall design objectives of the 981 line were to produce higher trajectories and more forgiveness. The DCI 981 also was available in an SL series intended for seniors or other golfers with less clubhead speed. All Titleist irons and metal woods were available with either steel or graphite shafts. Titleist also marketed a line of 17 different Scotty Cameron putters in stainless steel, teryllium, or platinum finishes. Some Scotty Cameron putters included an elastomer membrane covering the clubface.

In 1996, Cobra Golf held the industry's number two spot in irons and was number three in drivers and fairway woods (behind Callaway and Taylor Made). Cobra's popularity was a result of Greg Norman's endorsement of the clubs and the company's strategy of reducing the loft of its irons. The reduced loft added considerable distance to each club. For example, a golfer switching to King Cobra irons might pick up 20 yards or more on each club. Cobra Golf's King Cobra drivers were also considered a long-distance club.

After its acquisition by Acushnet, Cobra began to rapidly lose market share in both irons and metal woods. The company was forced to change its marketing approach since its high-profile, aggressive marketing practices clashed with the wishes of Acushnet's managers, who preferred a conservative approach to marketing. In addition, Acushnet management believed that Cobra should redesign its clubs to promote forgiveness at the expense of distance. Loyal Cobra customers were disappointed when they found that Cobra new models of clubs did not offer any greater distance than other brands. The decline in demand forced Cobra into a practice of deep discounting, which encouraged golfers to wait for the company to cut prices before they purchased the latest Cobra products. Cobra Golf also lost a considerable number of retailers during the later 1990s. The combination of missteps by Acushnet and Cobra Golf managers had all but made Cobra an afterthought by 1999.

Cobra struggled to rebuild its image and market presence after its strategic gaffes of the late 1990s. In 1999 the company launched a Web site and print ads that promoted its products as hip, nonconformist alternatives to the more technology-based golf clubs on the market. In early 2000 Cobra had abandoned this new image and recast itself as a more mainstream golf company.

Cobra's new products for 2000 included its Gravity Back drivers and fairway metal woods, which featured a titanium clubhead with a bronze alloy backweight placed at the rear of the clubhead. The bronze alloy backweight was designed to give the club a lower center of gravity. The Gravity Back fairway woods also featured a copper-tungsten sole weight to further lower the center of gravity. Cobra's CXI stainless-steel irons featured an *X*-like design on the backside of the clubface to more evenly disperse weight throughout the rear of the cavity back club. In 1999 Cobra Golf introduced Cobra Dista golf balls, which came in four models.

Adams Golf

Barney Adams founded Adams Golf in 1987 in Plano, Texas, as a golf club components supplier and contract manufacturer. In 1995 the company introduced its Tight Lies line of fairway woods, which featured an innovative low-profile clubface with a very low center of gravity. The shallow clubface and low center of gravity enlarged the effective hitting area of the clubface and created shots with a higher trajectory than shots with traditional-sized metal woods of the same loft. Tight Lies fairway woods were named the "Breakthrough Product of the Year" in 1997 by the Golf Market Research Institute and were rated the "Best of the Best" fairway woods in an independent real-golfer comparison in 1998. Adams Golf went public in July 1998 at an initial offering price of $16.00. The company recorded 1998 sales and earnings of $85 million and $13 million, respectively. In 1997 Adams had revenues of $37 million and a net loss of $5 million.

Adams's success became more difficult to maintain after other leading golf club manufacturers offered new lines of fairway woods with a shallower face than their previous models. In 1999 Adams Golf's revenues had declined to $54 million and the company recorded a net loss of $11 million. The company's stock traded below $2.00 during the first three months of 2000. Adams Golf's product line for 2000 included its Tight Lies^2 fairway woods, which had a deeper clubface than the original Tight Lies fairway woods. The new Tight Lies^2 retained the key features of the original Tight Lies line, but its deeper clubface made it easier to hit from the rough. In 1999 Adams introduced a line of SC series drivers, which were available in four different clubface curvatures designed to correct either a slice, a fade, or a hook. One SC driver featured a neutral clubface curvature for golfers without swing path problems. Adams also offered Assault VMI (variable moment of inertia) irons, which were heavier than most other brands of irons and used a patented mathematical formula to determine the ideal weight of the club based on the overall club length, shaft length, grip weight, and shaft weight.

Orlimar Golf Company

Orlimar Golf Company was founded in 1960 by Lou Ortiz in the basement of a converted stable in San Francisco. The company was a little-known maker of custom clubs primarily used by professionals and had annual sales of under $1 million in 1996. The company exploded onto the broad market for golf clubs in 1998 when it introduced its Tri-Metal fairway woods. Orlimar's Tri-Metal woods were made of stainless steel, copper, and tungsten and featured a low center of gravity and a shallower clubface than Callaway's GBB fairway woods. The combination of three metals and the low profile made the Tri-Metal instantly popular with professionals and amateurs alike. By year-end 1998 the company's sales had grown to more than $50 million and it was named as the fastest-growing private company in the San Francisco Bay area.

The company added drivers and irons to its product line in 1999 as its sales of fairway woods began to decline after Callaway's fairway woods began to recapture market share lost in 1997 and 1998. Orlimar's 2000 lineup of new products included its Tri-Metal Plus fairway woods and drivers and Tri-Metal irons. Like Orlimar's original Tri-Metal woods, Tri-Metal Plus fairway woods and drivers were made from stainless steel and included a copper tungsten sole plate to lower their center of gravity, but the Plus line had a deeper clubface than the original Tri-Metals. The clubface of the Tri-Metal Plus metal woods was coated with an Alpha Maraging Face material that the company claimed was harder than titanium. Orlimar's Tri-Metal irons were made from the same materials as the company's metal woods and were designed to produce high trajectories and longer distance than competing clubs.

Callaway's Prospects for Growth and the February 2000 Launch of the Callaway Golf Ball

Callaway's introduction of its new Rule 35 golf ball had been eagerly awaited since mid-1996, when Ely Callaway announced the formation of Callaway Golf Ball Company and the move of Charles Yash from Taylor Made to the new company. Whereas Nike had entered the golf ball industry in 1999 by outsourcing its production to Bridgestone and Taylor Made chose its mode of entry by purchasing an existing plant from a competitor, Ely Callaway had chosen a more time-consuming route to enter market for golf balls by electing to construct a new golf ball facility and internally develop an all-new ball. He noted: "This is the first time in the modern history of the industry, to our knowledge, that anyone has built a major-production golf ball business from scratch. After analyzing all of our other options, which included buying an existing company, buying an existing plant or buying a golf ball from another manufacturer and merely stamping our name on it, we decided this was the best way to go in order to create a superior product now and for the future."[9]

Callaway Golf spent three years developing in parallel its new golf ball and its state-of-the-art production facility. The company's entry into the market represented a $170 million investment in the research and development of the ball, construction of the 225,000-square-foot production facility, and development and purchase of special manufacturing equipment. Callaway's manufacturing facility and its equipment were designed specifically for the unique production requirements for the new ball.

Ely Callaway believed that the company's custom-designed manufacturing equipment and facility would contribute to the company's competitive strength and the ball's success: "No one else has the collection of late 90s equipment that we have, everything you need to make a better ball. No one has put it together and purchased it all the way we have. Some of the companies, because of the age of some of their equipment, just can't utilize the latest equipment without going outside."[10] Callaway's competitors were so interested in the company's new golf ball facility that they took aerial photographs of the plant's foundation as it was under construction.

Callaway Golf Ball Company engineers, recruited from Du Pont and Boeing, used aerodynamic computer programs (first used by Boeing and General Electric) to evaluate more than 300 dimple patterns and more than 1,000 variations of ball cores, boundary layers, and cover materials to create the new Rule 35 ball. Callaway engineers

[9]"Play Ball: Callaway Introduces the Rule 35," www.pgatour.com.
[10]"Long on Promises, Short on Explanation," *Golfweek,* February 5, 2000.

designed only two models of the Rule 35 ball—choosing to develop a "complete-performance" ball rather than separate balls developed for spin, control, distance, and durability. Ely Callaway explained the company's product development objectives as follows: "We have combined all of the performance benefits into one ball so players no longer need to sacrifice control for distance, or feel, or durability. Each Rule 35 ball contains a unique synergy of distance, control, spin, feel and durability characteristics. This eliminates confusion and guesswork in trying to identify the golf ball that is right for each individual golfer."[11]

Callaway's production process used computers to mill the rubber core, control injection molding of a boundary layer, and deposit a proprietary urethane coating to golf balls as they were assembled. The golf balls then moved through a transparent tube to a battery of diagnostic machines that ensured that each ball was exactly the same. A laser was then used to twice measure the depth of each of the ball's 382 dimples, and an electrical process was used to bond paint to the ball securely and evenly. Each ball was then X-rayed and machine-inspected before being packed or rejected. Callaway's production process included 16,000 quality assurance checkpoints, and Callaway employees were allowed to stop the flow of balls at the first sign of defects.

Callaway's Rule 35 balls were differentiated from competing brands in a large number of ways. The name Rule 35 was a play on the 34 long-standing rules of golf published by the USGA and the Royal & Ancient Golf Club of St. Andrews. Ely Callaway suggested that there should be a 35th rule of golf—"Enjoy the game."[12] The complete-performance balls came in only two variations, whereas the golf balls offered by competitors came in as many as 10 models. The blue-logo Callaway ball was called the Softfeel and had all of the same characteristics as its red-logo Firmfeel ball but had a slightly softer feel. Ely Callaway believed the availability of only two complete-performance balls and the avoidance of a discussion of the technical aspects of the balls' design and construction would make it easier for golfers to purchase golf balls: "We know there is a lot of complex science that goes into making a golf ball, but we don't think there should be a lot of complexity to buying one."[13] Callaway later commented, "We've come up with two balls. That's it. We're not gonna tell you much about them. We have only two, you make the choice. If you like a soft feel, you try this one (blue). If you like a firm feel, you try this one (red). We don't say a damn thing about how far they go. We don't say a word about compression or the construction or the details of the cover. We just say, 'Try them.' We believe that either one of them will give you more of what you've been looking for in one ball than anything else."[14]

Callaway Golf Ball Company's CEO, Chuck Yash, discussed the company's philosophy behind offering only two models of the Rule 35 and why the company refused to comment on the ball's technology: "Our basic aim in this process was to make a ball that reflects the parent company's philosophy and vision of creating a 'demonstrably superior and pleasingly different' product. We also set out to cut through the noise regarding the performance claims by most of the competitors' products, and all of the techno-babble about various polymers and compressions and dimple patterns and claims regarding the longest distance balls. What we have in Rule 35 is a very clear

---

[11]"Callaway Enters the Ball Game," *Show News,* February 5, 2000.

[12]"Play Ball: Callaway Introduces the Rule 35."

[13]"Callaway Enters the Ball Game."

[14]"Long on Promises, Short on Explanation."

exhibit 13   Estimated Manufacturing Shares of the Leading Producers of Golf Balls, 12 Months Ending September 30, 1999

	Dollars	Units
Titleist	36%	29%
Top-Flite/Spalding	23	27
Pinnacle	11	14
Maxfli	8	7
Wilson	7	8
Slazenger	5	3
Precept	3	2
Dunlop	2	3
Taylor Made	1	1
All others	4	6
Total	100%	100%

Source: Callaway Golf Company

message. If you prefer a firm feel, our Firmfeel ball has everything you need in performance. If you prefer a softer feel, our Softfeel ball is the choice. It's that easy."[15]

Callaway golf balls were further differentiated by their logo and packaging. The Callaway name used a stylized script rather than the Old English script used on Callaway golf clubs, and the company's logo was comprised of a letter *C* created from a rendering of the bottom of a golf cup. The balls were also packaged in sleeves of 5 and packs of 10 rather than sleeves of 3 or packs of 12 like other brands. Callaway Golf Ball Company's national sales manager explained why Callaway chose unique packaging for its golf balls: "When we were doing our research, we couldn't find a single person who could tell us why golf balls were packaged in sleeves of three or in dozens. When we discovered that the average golfer uses 4.5 balls per round, we decided the five-ball sleeve was the right way to go with packaging."[16] In addition, unlike the packaging of other brands of balls, Callaway's packaging included only the name and logo printed on a translucent plastic box rather than the name and product performance characteristics printed on a cardboard box. Callaway's use of a five-ball sleeve also allowed its golf balls to be placed away from other brands of balls since most retailers' display cases were designed for three-ball sleeves.

Even though the industry had long been dominated by Titleist and Spalding (see Exhibit 13), many analysts believed that Callaway's ability to develop technologically advanced products, its marketing expertise, and its established retailer network would allow the company to quickly gain a 2 to 3 percent share of the market and achieve $60 to $70 million in sales during 2000. Analysts also speculated that Callaway Golf Ball Company could hit sales of over $200 million within two years of the ball's launch. It was expected that Callaway's golf ball operations would considerably impact the company's net profit since profit margins in the premium segment of the golf ball market ranged between 60 and 75 percent. In addition, golf ball sales were less seasonal since

---

[15]Callaway press release, February 4, 2000.
[16]"Callaway Enters the Ball Game."

they were consumable items that were purchased throughout the year. Also, unlike a $500 driver, golfers could not delay the purchase of golf balls until they felt financially ready to make a large purchase. The company's objective was for the Rule 35 to capture a 10 percent share of the market within two years and ultimately become one of the two top brands of golf balls. "We have 7 million people out their playing our products, and 80 percent of them think they're the best clubs in the world," said Ely Callaway. "We have almost a guaranteed 'try' on our new products."[17] Callaway further commented, "We're going to sell a lot of balls."[18] An advertisement for the Rule 35 golf ball is shown in Exhibit 14 on the following page.

In February 2000 a survey of golf equipment company executives voted Callaway's Big Bertha driver the best golf product of the century by a 2-to-1 margin. The same group of executives called Ely Callaway the most influential golf trade person of the 1990s. As he approached his 81st birthday, Ely Callaway had vowed to retire by December 31, 2000, and make Chuck Yash the new CEO and president of Callaway Golf Company as well as Callaway Golf Ball Company. Just prior to the PGA Merchandise Show, Chuck Yash commented on his growing responsibility at Callaway Golf Company and the importance of its golf ball operations to the company's future growth: "The trust and faith Ely and the board of directors and the shareholders have shown in us is extraordinary. It has allowed me to use my 20 years of golf experience to build an organization and a team that, we believe, can have a significant impact. That is the way we are looking at things now, as a long-term commitment. It will take years before we feel we can compete with the leading companies in the golf ball market. But that is our objective. If we do that right, we have the potential to continue to grow."[19]

---

[17]"Rule 35 Tees Off," *San Deigo Union-Tribune,* February 4, 2000.

[18]"Play Ball: Callaway Introduces the Rule 35."

[19]"On the Spot: Chuck Yash," *Golf Product News,* January/February 2000.

exhibit 14   Sample Ad for Callaway Golf's Rule 35 Golf Ball

case 14 drkoop.com

Nicole Herskowitz
University of Michigan

Michael Iverson
University of Michigan

Fred Howard
University of Michigan

Janet Mehlhop
University of Michigan

Pilar Speer
University of Michigan

As Dennis Upah, cofounder of drkoop.com, sat in his small, dimly lit office sipping a glass of water, he thought back to an earlier conversation with his partner, C. Everett Koop, former surgeon general of the United States. He kept coming back to the comment that Dr. Koop had made: "I am excited about how the Web has greatly enhanced consumers' abilities to access health care information. I firmly believe that empowered consumers make better, more informed decisions with their physicians. Our new Web site gives Americans one premier location on the Net to find trusted, quality health care information."[1]

Since the drkoop.com launch in late 1998, the company had quickly grown to be the largest Web-based health information service, but revenues were far short of what was needed to make the new company profitable. Although the new company was focused on providing health care information, Dennis knew the site had to make a profit to keep shareholders happy and to ensure that the business would survive. He thought idly, "This tap water is terrible. I hope we soon turn a profit so we can afford a water cooler!" But he quickly jumped back to the issue that was troubling him: What strategy did drkoop.com need to pursue to sustain its early success? Sites offering medical advice were proliferating, and several competitors were mounting offensives to challenge drkoop.com.

THE HISTORY OF MEDICAL ADVICE

People have sought knowledge about their ailments as far back as ancient times, when medicine men performed spells and advised people on their spiritual and mental health. In modern times, people have come to rely on their personal physicians for medical advice. For sicknesses like the flu or the common cold, there is a lot of information available from local pharmacists, the media, and friends, not to mention each individual's own personal experience with various remedies. For those who want detailed information or want to doctor themselves with assorted natural herbs, vitamin supplements, and

---

[1] "Dr. Koop's Community," 1998 Business Wire, Inc., July 20, 1998.

This case was prepared under the supervision of Professor Alan Afuah, University of Michigan, for purposes of class discussion © 1999 by the case authors. All rights reserved.

other remedies available without a prescription, there are also numerous books, magazines, and health foods advisories. Numerous support organizations have sprung up in recent years to help people afflicted with cancer, diabetes, and other serious illnesses.

In addition to conducting its own R&D efforts to discover new prescription drugs to cure or prevent ailments of all types, the pharmaceutical industry contributes to health research organizations. Bristol-Myers Squibb, for example, donated $23 million through the Bristol-Myers Squibb foundation in 1997. A large portion of this money went to organizations such as the National Cancer Foundation and the National Diabetes Foundation. Pharmaceutical firms also help inform patients of new treatment options through media advertising, Web sites, other forms of publications, and extensive collaboration with patient support and prevention groups.

In late 1999, all pharmaceutical companies had extensive Web sites with numerous links and information options that addressed their primary treatment areas. Companies like Medtronic and Guidant had Web sites with specific areas dedicated to various types of cardiovascular problems. On Medtronic's site, for example, there were pages dedicated to ventricular fibrillation that not only featured medical advice but also contained many links to associated sites such as that of the American Heart Association.

MEDICAL ADVICE ON THE INTERNET

The first Web sites pertaining to health care were created by pharmaceutical firms as part of their efforts to begin conducting business-to-business e-commerce with pharmaceutical distributors, drugstore chains, and physicians who wrote prescriptions. In the beginning, most pharmaceutical firms used their Web sites to advertise their products and services. However, they soon discovered that the aspect of the Internet that attracted the most users was information. Sites providing a wealth of free, informative, interesting, and valuable content began seeing thousands and then millions of unique hits each quarter. The appeal of good information quickly caught the attention of entrepreneurs who seized on the potential for providing medical information via the Internet.

Medical information Web sites were launched to provide the public with readily accessible and accurate information on a broad variety of health-related topics, curtailing the need for people to rely totally on a physician or medical specialist for answers to their questions or concerns. Site founders, recognizing "the value of the Internet as a viable tool for educating the public," saw themselves as performing a valuable public service by creating open access to tens of thousands of pages of reliable and trustworthy health care information.[2] The information on their sites was compiled from books and articles by well-known physicians, journals reporting medical research and the latest studies, information-providing partners, a medical advisory board, and various other medical experts.

Medical information Web sites began popping up left and right in the 1997–99 period. With competition on the rise, medical information providers were forced to add services to their sites in order to maintain growth in number of hits and unique viewers. Following the business models from other content provider Internet companies, the idea of "chat rooms" quickly found its way into the online health care scene. But to combat the potential for misleading or inaccurate information to be dispensed in chat rooms, most medical sites developed an "Ask the Expert" feature to help site users get accurate, timely answers to their questions. Several medical information providers had recruited experts, including physicians and specialists, to give advice to site users and respond to specific questions. Additionally, most medical sites, concerned with maintaining the

---

[2] www.drkoop.com/aboutus/koop.

integrity and objectivity of the information being provided, set up "stringent rules governing the ethics of the sites, including how advertising and editorial content should be addressed."[3]

WHO IS DR. KOOP?

Dr. C. Everett Koop became a well-known public figure while serving as surgeon general in the Reagan administration. He played a prominent role in building public awareness of the acquired immune deficiency syndrome (AIDS) and was often in the public limelight crusading against the destructive effects of tobacco. As surgeon general, he was a strong proponent of tough antismoking regulations. Following his tenure as surgeon general, Dr. Koop continued his mission of encouraging good health. His latest effort was to help found and launch drkoop.com as a provider of medical information.

Dr. Koop was born in Brooklyn, New York, in 1916. After earning his M.D. from Cornell University in 1941, he worked at Children's Hospital at the University of Pennsylvania for 35 years. During his tenure there, he built a reputation as one of the nation's best pediatric surgeons. From 1981 to 1989, Dr. Koop served as surgeon general of the U.S. Public Health Service and director of international health. In 1999, Dr. Koop continued to lead an active role in the health community and health education through writings, electronic media, public appearances, and personal contacts. He taught medical students at Dartmouth College, where the Koop Institute was based. He was chairman of the National Safe Kids Campaign, Washington, D.C., and produced 75 point-of-diagnosis videos during 1999–2001 for Time-Life Medical, of which he was chairman of the board.

The Web site was named after its 83-year-old cofounder to provide credibility and to give the site a competitive edge over rival medical information providers. Cofounder Dennis Upah believed Dr. Koop's name was an incredible asset. Upah said, "He's the most trusted man in health care. He's an icon. With that comes a tremendous responsibility and scrutiny."[4] In a recent survey by Bruskin-Goldring, almost 60 percent of consumers recognized Dr. Koop, and of that percentage, nearly half believed him to be a top authority on health care issues.[5] In return for use of his name, Dr. Koop agreed to receive a royalty equal to 2 percent of revenues from sales of the company's current products and up to 4 percent of revenues derived from sales of new products. However, this agreement was later modified; the royalty payments were eliminated and in their place Dr. Koop was granted rights to purchase 214,000 shares of drkoop.com's stock at an exercise price of $17.84. The rights vested at the rate of 8,900 shares per month.

DRKOOP.COM IS BORN

After incorporating in July 1997, Empower Health Corporation launched the drkoop.com Web site on July 20, 1998, as a comprehensive consumer health care portal providing information on acute ailments, chronic illnesses, nutrition, and fitness and wellness, as well as access to medical databases, publications, and real-time medical news. The company said its mission was to "empower consumers with the information and resources they need to become active participants in the management of their own

---

[3]Ibid.

[4]"i:20 drkoop.com's Dennis Upah," *Crain Communications,* November 1999.

[5]PR Newswire Association, Inc., March 29, 1999.

health." At the time, Dr. C. Everett Koop, the chairman of Empower, said, "I am excited about how the Web has greatly enhanced consumers' abilities to access health care information. I firmly believe that empowered consumers make better, more informed decisions with their physicians. Our new website gives Americans one premier location on the Net to find trusted, quality health care information."[6] The company went public in June 1999 at a price of $9; the stock price jumped to as high as $40 in July 1999 but then declined and traded in the $11–20 range during the last quarter of 1999 and in early 2000. The company's initial public offering raised about $85 million in new capital.

To build drkoop.com brand awareness, Empower Health partnered with USWeb Corporation, a specialist in Web audience development. Together, they devised a strategy built around innovative banner advertising and media placement of ads, search engine optimization, and online public relations and promotions.[7] In its first 90 days, the site attracted more than 1 million visitors. By June 1, 1999, the company had attracted 6 million unique users and signed up 280,000 registered members.

The initial success continued on into the second half of 1999, drawing over 15 million page views in October 1999.[8] In November 1999, Media Metrix ranked the site as the number one health Web site, and PC Data noted that it was the number one health Web site from March 1999 through November 1999. Media Metrix ranked drkoop.com as 25th in its News/Information/Entertainment category. During the fourth quarter of 1999, drkoop.com attracted 11.8 million unique visitors, who viewed 49.4 million pages. By January 2000, the company had 1 million registered users.

THE MARKET OPPORTUNITY FOR DRKOOP.COM

Health care was the largest segment of the U.S. economy in the late 1990s, accounting for annual expenditures of roughly $1 trillion.[9] Health and medical information was one of the fastest-growing areas of interest on the Internet. According to Cyber Dialogue, an industry research firm, during the 12-month period ended July 1998, approximately 17 million adults in the United States searched online for health and medical information, and approximately 50 percent of these individuals made offline purchases after seeking information on the Internet. Cyber Dialogue estimated that approximately 70 percent of the persons searching for health and medical information online believed the Internet empowered them by providing them with information before and after they went to a doctor's office. Cyber Dialogue also estimated that the number of adults in the United States searching for online health and medical information would grow to approximately 30 million in the year 2000, and they would spend approximately $150 billion for all types of health-related products and services offline.[10] Exhibit 1 shows the size of the various U.S. health care market segments. Medical information providers hoped to tap into a piece of this business.[11]

[6]"Dr. Koop's Community."

[7]"USWeb Audience Development Practice Helps Establish Success of Leading Consumer Healthcare Site," 1998 Business Wire, Inc., November 19, 1998.

[8]"drkoop.com Breaks 15 Million Page Views for October," PR Newswire, November 22, 1999.

[9]See Hoover's online database (www.hoovers.com/industry/snapshot/0,2204,23,00.html). See also Thomas E. Miller and Scott Reents, "The Health Care Industry in Transition," *Cyber Dialogue,* 1998.

[10]Miller and Reents, "The Health Care Industry in Transition."

[11]Ibid.

exhibit 1   Size of the U.S. Health Care Market, 1997

1997 Annual Market Size (in $ billions)

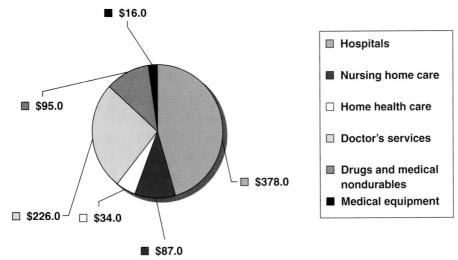

■ $16.0

■ $95.0

□ $226.0   □ $34.0

■ $87.0

□ $378.0

- □ Hospitals
- ■ Nursing home care
- □ Home health care
- □ Doctor's services
- ■ Drugs and medical nondurables
- ■ Medical equipment

Source: Hoover's online database.

DRKOOP.COM'S BUSINESS MODEL AND STRATEGY

In the company's prospectus for its common stock offering in mid-1999, management described the objective and business model for drkoop.com:

> Our objective is to establish the drkoop.com network as the most trusted and comprehensive source of consumer health care information and services on the Internet. Our business model is to earn advertising and subscription revenues from advertisers, merchants, manufacturers, and health care organizations who desire to reach a highly targeted community of health care consumers on the Internet. We also earn revenues by facilitating e-commerce transactions, such as sales of prescription refills, vitamins and nutritional supplements, and insurance services offered by outside parties.

Drkoop.com's strategy incorporated the following key elements:

- Establish the drkoop.com brand so that consumers associate the trustworthiness and credibility of Dr. C. Everett Koop with the company.
- Provide consumers with high-quality health care content to attract users to www.drkoop.com and promote their loyalty to the company's Web site.
- Distribute drkoop.com content to affiliated portals and other Web sites that (1) have established themselves as pathways for a broad variety of information and (2) have the potential to drive traffic to drkoop.com and provide broad exposure to the drkoop.com brand.
- Develop and expand online health care communities to allow users with similar health-related experiences to exchange information and gather news and knowledge in a secure, anonymous environment.

- Provide consumers with unique tools, such as one that educates consumers on the interaction among various drugs and other substances.
- Deploy a comprehensive personal medical record that will allow users to establish and maintain a lifelong record of their health and medical information in a secure portion of the company's database.
- Provide an attractive Web site that can deliver advertising in a highly targeted manner, thereby commanding higher advertising rates.
- Facilitate e-commerce transactions offered by merchants, manufacturers, and service providers to a highly targeted community of health-conscious consumers.

Strategic Partnerships

A chief component of drkoop.com's strategy was to partner with organizations that would add to its content and service offerings, further expand its business model into traditional areas of the health care industry, and grow its viewing base. To develop content for its Web site, drkoop.com had partnered with the following eight organizations:

- *The American Council on Science and Health*—The ACSH was an independent, nonprofit, tax-exempt organization that conducted studies and did research in such areas as food, nutrition, chemicals, pharmaceuticals, lifestyles, the environment, and health. A board of 300 physicians, scientists, and policy advisers peer-reviewed all reports and published papers.
- *Cleveland Clinic Foundation*—The Cleveland Clinic integrated hospital patient care, research, and medical education in a private, nonprofit group practice with 1,000 salaried physicians. In 1999, *U.S. News and World Report* ranked the Cleveland Clinic best in the country for cardiac care and the fourth best hospital overall.
- Dartmouth Medical School—The Dartmouth Medical School provided consumer health and medical information on more than 60 medical topics along with analysis on leading medical research and trends written by staff and experts.
- *Lifescape.com*—Lifescape provided timely news articles, clinical information, and state-of-the-art assessment tools in areas relating to family, relationships, emotional health, and mental well-being.
- *Multum Information Services*—Multum provided drkoop.com with a comprehensive and up-to-date database of drug information that was the basis for drkoop.com's trademarked DrugChecker tool.
- *Screaming Media*—Screaming Media provided drkoop.com with late-breaking, real-time news and editorials on health and health care issues from over 50 wire services.
- *World Book*—World Book contributed use of its trusted and thorough World Book Rush–Presbyterian–St. Luke's Medical Center Medical Encyclopedia.
- *Shared Medical Systems*—SMS was a provider of software that enabled secure online data exchanges between patients, their physicians, and local health care organizations.

Going into 2000, drkoop.com had over one dozen agreements to be the exclusive or preferred provider of health care information for particular Web sites. The major ones were as follows:

- *Infoseek and Buena Vista Internet*—To enhance brand awareness and increase traffic on its Web site, drkoop.com entered into agreements with Infoseek Corporation and the Buena Vista Internet Group, a unit of the Walt Disney Company, to be the exclusive provider of health and related content on three Web sites of the Go Network: Go.com Health Center, ESPN.com Training Room, and the Family.com Health Channel. In addition, drkoop.com became the exclusive pharmacy and drugstore, health insurance, and clinical trials partner in the Go.com Health Center. Under the Infoseek agreement, drkoop.com was also the premier health content provider for ABCnews.com. The agreement was for the period April 1999 to April 2002 and called for drkoop.com to pay Infoseek and Buena Vista approximately $58 million in total consideration.

- *Adventist Health System*—In January 1999, drkoop.com exchanged 2,615,677 shares of preferred stock for $3.5 million in cash plus a 10 percent share of HealthMagic. HealthMagic was a subsidiary of Adventist Health Systems and a developer of a personal medical record application.[12] This partnership gave the company access to and use of a personal medical record application and secured Adventist as a customer in the Community Partner program.

- *FHC Internet*—FHC purchased 1.1 shares of drkoop.com common stock at the offering price of $9 as part of an agreement for FHC to sponsor drkoop.com's mental health center.[13] FHC Internet was a subsidiary of Foundation Health Systems that specialized in the outsourcing of disease management programs for local health care organizations.

- *Quintiles International*—Quintiles entered into an agreement with drkoop.com to jointly develop a clinical trials information center. Quintiles was the world's largest provider of clinical research services to pharmaceutical companies and, as part of the agreement, purchased $5 million worth of shares of drkoop.com at the IPO price of $9. The clinical trials center provided visitors to the drkoop.com site with information about clinical trials that were currently going on across the country. Visitors could fill out an online prescreen form for various clinical trials, which was then forwarded to study sites. Drkoop.com received approximately $100 for each referral. Quintiles expected the agreement to help it speed recruit of candidates for clinical trials, lower prescreening costs, and create a larger pool of potential candidates for participation in clinical trials.[14]

- *America Online*—Drkoop.com's agreement called for it to provide medical information services to America Online and CompuServe members as well as to AOL's Internet portals—AOL.com, Netscape.com, and DigitalCity.com. To gain exposure to the 70-plus million users from the five entities combined and the benefits of AOL's sales force, drkoop.com agreed to pay AOL $89 million over the next four years and also to give AOL warrants to purchase 1.6 million shares of drkoop.com's stock at an exercise price of $15.94. Drkoop.com received an $8 million license fee for the use of a co-developed personal medical record.

- *Phar-Mor*—Drkoop.com's partnership with Phar-Mor, an online drugstore, involved Phar-Mor's sponsoring a monthly drkoop.com pharmacy newsletter. Users of Phar-Mor's Web site were directed to drkoop.com to gain necessary medical information, while visitors to drkoop.com could click on links to Phar-Mor's Web site.

- *DrugEmporium*—DrugEmporium and drkoop.com signed an agreement in October 1999 whereby drkoop.com visitors could purchase over 20,000 discounted products sold by DrugEmporium. Shoppers at DrugEmporium could go directly to

---

[12]Bear Stearns Equity Research, Health Care Industry, July 27, 1999.

[13]Ibid.

[14]Ibid.

drkoop.com for further information on products they were considering. Further, drkoop.com's DrugChecker was integrated into the purchase of all prescription drugs at DrugEmporium, automatically checking for any potential problems.

- *Other Alliances and Comarketing Partnerships*—drkoop.com had partnered with such health care providers and HMOs as Highmark (one of the 10 largest insurers in the United States); MemorialCare (a large health care system serving more than 14 million residents in Los Angeles and Orange County); Scott and White Hospital and Clinic (one of the largest multispecialty hospitals in the United States); Promina Health Systems (a nonprofit health care organization serving 4.3 million residents in the Atlanta area); the Cleveland Clinic (with a staff of over 850 physicians); and the Baptist Health System (serving 3.5 million residents in the Miami, Florida, area). In addition to these agreements, drkoop.com had agreements to provide content, establish direct links to each other Web sites, or otherwise gain market exposure with The Weather Channel, Physicians' Online, Salon.com Health & Body, SeniorNet, @Home, Roadrunner (the cable-based Internet service provider of Time Warner and Media One cable systems), Tallahassee Memorial HealthCare, and Yahoo Health.

Community Partners and Television Partners   Through the Community Partner Program, drkoop.com enrolled hospitals and health systems as local affiliates, allowing them to integrate the drkoop.com brand and content into their online initiatives. Participating health care organizations could draw on the content and resources at the drkoop.com Web site to supply their patients with online health care information and interactive capabilities, thus helping patients to educate themselves and make more informed decisions. In February 2000, there were more than 300 local health care facilities participating in the Community Partner Program. In recent months, drkoop.com had also begun a Television Partner Program and was supplying content to 18 local television stations.

Using the Partnerships to Build a "Network"   The company saw all these content and affiliate partnerships as a central part of its strategy to create

> an Internet-based consumer health care network that . . . provides individuals with trusted health care content, services, and tools to empower them to better manage their health. Our network affiliates include other Internet portals, Web sites, health care organizations, and traditional sources of health and medical news. Establishing affiliations with traditional media outlets allows us to deliver quality health care content to a targeted audience. Affiliates provide local, relevant information directly to a local audience. Through this unique means of distribution, drkoop.com is building a leading network of health content and editorial-based, breaking health news on the Internet.[15]

drkoop.com's Recent Marketing and Promotion Efforts

To build brand awareness and traffic, drkoop.com advertised on high-frequency Web sites such as Yahoo! Competitors were pursuing much the same approach. WebMD.com advertised on NetZero, a free Internet service provider for consumers, and Onhealth.com also advertised on Yahoo! Also, drkoop.com had entered into arrangements with local TV stations to give the stations content for health-related news stories in exchange for a drkoop.com "plug" at the end of a news story on a health issue.

[15]Company documents.

In late 1999, drkoop.com launched a $10–$15 million advertising campaign to build brand recognition.[16] Management believed that growing competition among medical information providers on the Internet made higher levels of advertising necessary. The company had also employed Creative Artists Agency (CAA) to help build awareness and use of its Web site.[17]

drkoop.com's Revenue Sources

The company generated revenue from selling advertising on its site, licensing its content to others, and partnerships with others. The big revenue generator was selling Web site ads. DrugEmporium was the only sponsor of the Web site. The site was covered with DrugEmporium advertisements and direct links to facilitate over-the-counter medication purchases. Advertising was also being sold to the company's Community Partners (local hospitals) and health insurance companies. Actual and projected financial statements for drkoop.com are shown in Exhibits 2, 3, and 4.

INFORMATION AND CONTENT AT THE DRKOOP.COM WEB SITE

The drkoop.com Web site contained over 70,000 pages of health information and tools for users. The tag line for the site mirrored Dr. Koop's belief that "the best prescription is knowledge." Going into 2000, the site served as a content and community portal with links to other information sources. Information at the site was organized around six categories:

- News
- Family
- Resources
- Wellness
- Community
- Conditions

Users could sign up to become drkoop.com members; membership enabled them to access interactive tools, community bulletin boards, and chat rooms. The site allowed members to customize their own drkoop.com homepage to cover whatever topics, health issues, and diseases that interested them.

News

The drkoop.com News section provided the latest and most critical information about health. Users could review recent and late-breaking information about product recalls, health-related editorials, health events, polls, special reports, and sports medicine. The site included reports and press releases from such sources as the American Council on Science and Health (ACSH) and the Occupational Safety and Health Administration (OSHA). Using drkoop.com's HealthSearch feature, members could readily locate

---

[16]"i:20 drkoop.com's Dennis Upah."

[17]CAA provides strategic consulting services in marketing and technology areas and holds alliances with Internet incubator, idealab! and communications consulting and advertising company, Shepardson, Stern and Kaminsky.

exhibit 2 Actual and Projected Income Statements for drkoop.com, 1997–2001
(In Millions of $, Except for Per Share Data)

	Income Statement Data					Revenue-Cost-Margin Analysis				
	1997	1998	1999	2000*	2001*	1997	1998	1999	2000*	2001*
Revenues										
Advertising	—	—	$ 7.7	$ 23.3	$42.3	N/A	N/A	81.1%	72.7%	63.4%
Content licensing	—	—	1.7	6.7	17.1	N/A	N/A	17.9	20.8	25.6
Other	—	—	0.1	2.1	7.4	N/A	N/A	1.1	6.5	11.0
Total revenues	—	$0.04	$ 9.5	$ 32.1	$66.7	N/A	N/A	100.0%	100.0%	100.0%
Cost of operations										
Production, content, and product development	$ 0.5	$ 4.4	$ 9.4	$ 20.8	$23.5	N/A	N/A	98.9%	64.9%	35.2%
Sales and marketing	—	2.0	45.6	34.6	35.8	N/A	N/A	480.0	107.7	53.6
Total cost of sales	$ 0.5	$ 6.4	$55.0	$ 55.4	$59.3	N/A	N/A	578.9%	172.6%	88.8%
Gross income	($ 0.5)	($ 6.4)	($47.9)	($ 23.3)	$ 7.4					
Gross margin %	NM	NM	NM	(72.6%)	11.1%					
General and administrative expense	$ 0.2	$ 2.6	$ 9.5	$ 10.6	$12.2	N/A	N/A	100.0%	33.0%	18.3%
Operating income	($ 0.6)	($ 9.0)	($57.4)	($ 33.9)	($ 4.8)					
Operating margin	NM	NM	NM	(105.6%)	(7.2%)					
Nonoperating income and expenses										
Interest (net)	—	—	$ 1.3	$ 1.7	$ 1.7	N/A	N/A	13.7%	5.3%	2.5%
Other	—	—	—	—	—	N/A	N/A	0.0	0.0	0.0
Pretax income	($ 0.6)	($ 9.0)	($56.1)	($ 32.2)	($ 3.1)	N/A	N/A	(590.5%)	(100.3%)	(4.6%)
Pretax margin	NM	NM	NM	(100.3%)	(4.6%)					
Provision for income taxes	—	—	—	—	$ 0.6					
Tax rate	0%	0%	0%	0%	(18%)					
Income before nonrecurring items	($ 0.6)	($ 9.0)	($56.1)	($ 32.2)	($ 3.6)	N/A	N/A	(590.5%)	(100.3%)	(5.4%)
Nonrecurring items	—	—	—	—	—					
Net income	($ 0.6)	($ 9.0)	($56.1)	($ 32.2)	($ 3.6)	N/A	N/A	(590.5%)	(100.3%)	(5.4%)

*Estimated.

NM = Not meaningful. N/A = Not applicable.

Source: Company reports; Bear, Stearns & Co. Inc. estimates.

exhibit 3   drkoop.com's Balance Sheet Data, 1998–1999, with Estimates for 2000–2001*
 ($ In Millions, Except for Share Data)

	December 1998	December 1999	December 2000*	December 2001*
Assets				
Current assets				
Cash and equivalents	—	$ 35.7	$ 19.9	$ 11.1
Accounts receivable	—	10.5	9.6	14.5
Other	—	22.6	5.9	5.9
Total current assets	$ 0.1	$ 68.9	$ 35.4	$ 31.5
Property, plant, and equipment	$ 0.3	$ 10.4	$ 1.0	$ 2.2
Investment	—	$ 5.0	$ 5.0	$ 5.0
Licenses	—	2.8	2.1	1.2
Other	—	12.4	—	—
Total assets	$ 0.4	$ 99.5	$ 43.6	$ 39.9
Liabilities and stockholders' equity				
Current liabilities				
Accounts payable	$ 0.8	$ 8.2	$ 5.0	$ 5.0
Accrued liabilities	0.5	9.6	2.7	2.7
Deferred revenue	—	3.4	0.7	0.7
Notes payable	0.5	—	0.3	0.3
Total current liabilities	$ 3.0	$ 23.2	$ 8.7	$ 8.7
Other	—	—	—	—
Redeemable preferred stock	$18.4	—	—	—
Preferred stock	—	—	—	—
Common stock	—	—	—	—
Capital in excess of par	—	$149.4	$133.5	$129.9
Retained earnings (deficit)	(19.6)	(75.7)	(94.9)	(94.9)
Other	(1.4)	(2.4)	(3.9)	(3.9)
Total stockholders' equity	($21.0)	$ 71.3	$ 34.8	$ 31.2
Total liabilities and stockholders' equity	$ 0.4	$ 99.5	$ 43.6	$ 39.9
Selected financial statistics				
Current ratio	0	7.7	4.1	3.6
Days sales outstanding	N/A	94	80.4	65.2
Book value/share	N/A	$ 2.23	$ 1.14	$ 0.99
Return on equity	N/A	N/A	N/A	N/A
Cash flow per share	($0.32)	($ 0.41)	($1.00)	($ 0.06)
Free cash flow per share	($0.33)	($ 0.41)	($1.04)	($ 0.12)
Long-term debt/total capital	0%	0%	0%	0%

*Estimated.

Source: Company reports; Bear, Stearns & Co. Inc. estimates.

archived articles relating to all types of health concerns. The search function not only scanned the drkoop.com site but also searched the MedLine database of medical journals and the National Cancer Institute's bibliographic database for relevant articles or abstracts.

exhibit 4   drkoop.com's Statement of Cash Flows, 1998–1999, with Projections for 2000–2001 ($ in Millions, Except for Share Data)

	1998	1999	2000*	2001*
Cash flows from operating activities				
Net income	($9.0)	($ 68.2)	($32.2)	($ 3.6)
Depreciation and amortization	0.1	1.4	1.8	1.8
Other	0.1	26.5	—	—
Change in current account				
Accounts receivable	—	(4.7)	(4.9)	(4.9)
Increase in other assets	—	—	—	—
Accounts payable	2.1	(0.1)	—	—
Accrued liabilities and other assets	—	(0.2)	—	—
Deferred revenue	—	(0.5)	—	—
Other	—	(6.0)	—	—
Cash provided by operating activities	($6.8)	($ 50.7)	($35.4)	($ 6.7)
Cash flows from investing activities				
Capital expenditures	($0.3)	($ 0.6)	($ 1.3)	($ 2.1)
Net cash used in investing activities	($0.3)	($ 0.6)	($ 1.3)	($ 2.1)
Cash flows from financing activities				
Net long-term financing	$0.5	—	—	—
Preferred stock issuances	6.6	$ 5.8	—	—
Common stock issuances	—	90.0	—	—
Other	—	12.0	—	—
Net cash provided in financing activities	$7.1	$107.8	—	—
Net increase (decrease) in cash	—	$ 56.6	($36.7)	($ 8.8)
Cash beginning of year	—	—	56.6	19.9
End of year	—	$ 56.6	$19.9	$11.1
Cash flow/share	($0.3)	($ 2.25)	($1.00)	($0.06)
Free cash flow (FCF) per share	($0.3)	($ 2.27)	($1.04)	($0.12)

	1998	1999	2000*	2001*
Cash flow from operations minus net loss (income)	$2.2	$ 17.5	($ 3.1)	($ 3.1)
EBITDA*	(9.0)	(41.6)	(32.1)	(3.0)
Free cash flow (FCF)	(6.5)	(50.1)	(34.1)	(4.6)

*Estimated.

* Earnings before interest, taxes, depreciation, and amortization.

Source: Company reports; Bear, Stearns & Co. Inc. estimates.

Family

The Family section of the drkoop.com Web site was divided into subcategories, including Children, Men, Women, and Elderly. The Web site had received accolades as a superior health care destination for women and children. On November 8, 1999, eHealthCare World awarded drkoop.com a gold medal in the category "Best Site for Women" based on meeting women's needs for its health and medical news, information, education, advice, support, and community events.[18]

---

[18]"drkoop.com Web Site Dominates Awards at eHealthcare World," PR Newswire, November 8, 1999.

Resources

Drkoop.com provided users with a variety of content and tools for users to personalize their experience at the Web site. Drkoop.com's Personal Drugstore was a central location where consumers could find information about prescription drugs and check drug interactions. DrugChecker, a proprietary drkoop.com technology, enabled consumers to ensure that their medications did not interact with each other or with food to cause adverse reactions. Such information was considered vital information, considering that the American Medical Association reported adverse drug interactions were the fourth leading cause of death in the United States. Over 100,000 deaths in 1997 were attributed to the adverse affects of prescription drugs.[19] Drkoop.com's DrugChecker technology received a gold medal as the "Best Interactive Assessment Tool" in the eHealthcare World awards.[20] Members could download the DrugChecker tool and add it to their personal Web site, free of charge. In late 1999, over 9,500 Web sites were making DrugChecker available.[21]

Drkoop.com's Personal Insurance Center helped consumers evaluate insurance plans through access to an insurance library, a glossary of terms, and expert advice. Users could review frequently asked questions, search archived questions, and send their questions to insurance expert Jim Perry, the director of state affairs for the Council for Affordable Health Insurance. The Personal Insurance Center pages contained advertisements with direct links to several health insurance sites, including eHealthInsurance.com and Quotesmith.com, that provided online policy information and premium quotes. This section of the site was recognized for its extensive library of insurance articles, information on insurance programs by state, Medicare and Medicaid information, and tools for choosing an insurance policy.[22] Drkoop.com won a silver medal at the eHealthcare World Awards as the "Best Managed Care Site."

Prior to proliferating use of the Internet, information about clinical trial results and registration was limited for patients. Drkoop.com had recently begun disseminating information about clinical studies; this included such things as patient information, trial procedures, how research was conducted, and how consumers could participate in a Quintiles clinical study. Drkoop.com had formed a partnership with Quintiles, the world's leading provider of health care services to the pharmaceutical industry and largest clinical trials management organization, whereby drkoop.com was compensated for successfully recruiting qualified participants into clinical trials.

Drkoop.com had a database and directory of health resources in local communities. A regional directory helped consumers locate hospitals; however, the directory listings were limited to hospitals that participated in the drkoop.com Community Partner Program.[23] A Physician Locator tool, provided by the American Board of Medical Specialties (ABMS), allowed members to search and verify the location and specialty of any physician certified by the member boards of the ABMS. When members clicked on the Physician Locator service, they were automatically transferred to the ABMS site. The Resources section also provided links to pharmacy sites where consumers could order and reorder their prescriptions with doctor approval. When asked if prescriptions

---

[19]"Dr. Koop's Community."

[20]"drkoop.com Web Site Dominates Awards at eHealthcareWorld."

[21]Ibid.

[22]Ibid.

[23]Hospitals that participate in the Community Partner Program pay $50,000 to $100,000 per year to license drkoop.com health care information to use on their Web sites. In addition, direct links are provided from the drkoop.com site to their individual Web sites.

will be given almost exclusively online, Donald Hackett, president and CEO of drkoop.com, did not expect the Internet to become the chief vehicle for providing prescriptions to patients. He said:

> Although I'm a technologist at heart, there's a tremendous amount of human interaction that needs to take place. But even when the consumer needs to schedule the appointment, you can eliminate waste from the system with new technology. This technology is about streamlining the screening process.[24]

Other resources included drkoop.com's rankings of other health sites (not including major competitors such as WebMD and onhealth.com) and a list of books recommended by drkoop.com experts and community leaders. Through an alliance with Amazon.com, users wishing to purchase any of the recommended books were automatically sent the Amazon.com site.

Wellness

The primary topics in the Wellness section were fitness and prevention. There was advice on weight loss, along with diet-oriented chat rooms and recipes for diet foods. Consumers could use this section to plan a workout routine that matched diet and time constraints. The section's theme was that by staying healthy and fit, people could prevent many illnesses.

In further support of the wellness theme, there were pages devoted to one of Dr. C. Everett Koop's favorite subjects: the evils of smoking. In addition to extensive information on the effects of smoking on the body, there was information on quitting programs and support groups. Much of the information concerning smoking reflected Dr. Koop's strong personal views.

Community

Drkoop.com's underlying philosophy of getting people together and giving them the tools and information to improve their health was much in evidence in the Community section of the Web site, which had more than 130 interactive chat rooms and message boards devoted to specific afflictions and health problems. Users could click on any of the 130-plus topics and join in on chat room discussions, read message board postings, and post messages sharing their own experiences and views. In addition, there were daily topics of discussion where participants could "listen in" on discussions not only with other patients, but also with doctors.

The Community section had a constant stream of banner ads and large sidebar ads from sites such as DrugEmporium.com; links to these sites made it convenient for site users to purchase health care products and services online. The ads often focused on the particular disease that the user was currently examining.

Conditions

The Conditions section was an online encyclopedia of medical advice. Visitors could research almost any disease or mental health issue they had questions about. It also offered shortcuts to advice pages for first aid and for common symptoms such as back

---

[24]"Posts," *The Standard,* June 28, 1999.

pain or insomnia. The first-aid pages provided advice on a wide variety of topics, from animal bites to sunburn.

Site Disclaimer/Liability

The drkoop.com site had a disclaimer on every Web page that stated, "This information is not intended to be a substitute for professional medical advice. You should not use this information to diagnose or treat a health problem or disease without consulting with a qualified health care provider. Please consult your health care provider with any questions or concerns you may have regarding your condition."[25]

Site Awards

On November 4, 1999, drkoop.com won more awards than any other health care Web site at eHealthcare World Awards in New York. The site received two Gold and two Silver awards, in recognition of its trusted content and health care information for consumers. However, the drkoop.com Web site had been criticized by the American Medical Association for not providing sufficient information related to sponsorship and commerce relationships.

DRKOOP.COM'S MEDICAL ADVISORY BOARD

To help develop the content of the medical information and resources available at its website, drkoop.com had created a Medical Advisory Board consisting of Dr. C. Everett Koop and five others:

- Dr. Nancy Snyderman—a member of the company's board of directors, the medical correspondent for ABC (who made frequent appearances on *Good Morning America, 20/20,* and the *ABC Evening News*), a monthly columnist for *Good Housekeeping,* the author of a book on health care for women over 40, the author of several published papers and an associate clinical professor at the California Pacific Medical Center and the University of California–San Francisco.
- Dr. James F. Dickson III—a former deputy assistant secretary of health and assistant surgeon general, the author of over 50 published papers on surgery and biomedical research, the editor of six books, and a fellow of the American College of Surgeons.
- Dr. Bruce Hensel—an Emmy Award–winning medical, health, and science editor/reporter for NBC4's *Channel 4 News;* the host of *4 Your Health!;* a local Emmy Award–winning series of half-hour specials featuring the latest in medical breakthroughs, information, and technology; an associate professor of medicine at UCLA; and the winner of several other awards for medical education.
- Dr. Stanley Joel Reiser—a professor of humanities and technology in health care at the University of Texas–Houston Health Care Center, the author of over 120 articles and books, a noted speaker on medical topics, and recognized authority on medical ethics, the assessment of medical technologies, the role of values in governing health care organizations, and public health care policy.
- Dr. Michael Seth Shaw—president of Health Science Media (a health care education, communications, and media company in Atlanta, Georgia) since 1979; a

---

[25]Disclaimer present on every page of the drkoop.com Web site.

graduate of Emory University School of Medicine; and a member of several medical organizations.

COMPETITION AND PROFILES OF SELECTED RIVALS

Competition in the online medical information provider industry was strong and getting stronger. Hundreds of sites providing various kinds of medical information had emerged over the past two years. All of the most popular sites provided extensive consumer health information, chat rooms, expert advice, links to products and comprehensive and fully tailored health care publications for professionals of all specialties.

In addition to the companies that specialized primarily in online health and medical information, large medical and health care companies were establishing an Internet presence. Some provided medical information, but the primary focus of most such companies was on marketing health insurance and/or over-the-counter drug products. Most pharmaceutical companies had portions of their corporate Web sites dedicated to consumer health information. One big player in this area was Merck, which published an online "medical bible." The pharmaceutical companies were not direct competitors of medical information providers like drkoop.com because their main focus was to sell pharmaceutical products, but they were still players in the online medical information market.

Drkoop.com's management expected that competition among these sites to obtain content would likely increase the fees charged by high-quality content providers, perhaps driving up costs significantly. In addition, competition was forcing all medical information providers to try to set themselves apart on the basis of differentiating Web site features. The addition of new features required rivals to continue to improve the technology underlying their Web sites, also driving up costs significantly.

In October 1999, PC Data ranked drkoop.com as the number one dedicated health care site, based on Web site traffic, for the seventh consecutive month (see Exhibit 5).[26] According to PC Data, the site was the 43rd most popular site on the Internet overall.

Brief profiles of selected leading online medical information providers are presented below.

Healtheon/WebMD.com

Drkoop.com's strongest competitor was Healtheon/WebMD Corporation, which claimed to be the first comprehensive online health care portal.[27] The company was formed by a merger of Healtheon and WebMD in May 1999. Following the merger, the companies combined their consumer Web sites, MyHealtheon.com and MyWebMD.com, into one site (www.webmd.com). Healtheon/WebMD was building a system of software and services to automate such tasks as HMO enrollment, referrals, data retrieval, and claims processing for use by insurers, doctors, pharmacies, and consumers. The site also offered physician communications services, physician references, medical information and news, and personalized content to its users. Healtheon/WebMD had revenues of $28.7 million in the quarter ending September 1999.

In early December 1999, Rupert Murdoch's News Corp. formed a $1 billion partnership with Healtheon/WebMD in one of the largest media and Internet deals to date.[28]

---

[26]PR Newswire Association, October 7, 1999, Financial News section.

[27]www.ixl.com/success/webmd/index.html.

[28]www.thestandard.com/article/display/0,1151,6224,00.html.

exhibit 5   Traffic Statistics on Medical Information Provider Web Sites, September 1999

Company	Number of Unique Hits, September 1999
drkoop.com	5,539,000
onhealth.com	2,262,000
discoveryhealth.com	1,077,000
webmd.com	765,000
thriveonline.com	753,000
healthyideas.com	714,000
intelihealth.com	675,000
allhealth.com	596,000
AOLhealth.com	568,000
Healthcentral.com	532,000
medscape.com	415,000
ama-assn.org	404,000
mediconsult.com	225,000

News Corp. became a 10.8 percent owner of Healtheon/WebMD, providing $700 million in "branding services" over 10 years, purchasing $100 million of Healtheon/WebMD's stock, investing $100 million cash in the Internet company, and signing a $62.5 million five-year licensing deal to syndicate WebMD's daily broadcast content. In describing the partnership, News Corp. president and COO Peter Chernin said, "Companies traditionally re-purpose print or broadcast content for the Web. With this deal, we're using the Web as a source for original, unique programming which will be leveraged across all media owned by News Corp."[29] The goal of this partnership was to drive television viewers to medical Web sites and vice versa, creating single health care information brands across all media. Industry observers speculated that the News Corp. partnership could give Healtheon/WebMD an advantage in internationalizing online health care.

Mediconsult.com

Mediconsult's mission was to provide timely, comprehensive, and accessible information on chronic medical conditions, using the latest available technology to deliver information efficiently. Its Web site featured a fee-based service, *MediXpert,* which let visitors present a case to a medical specialist who responded with a confidential report. Mediconsult had no affiliation with any HMO, hospital, or other health care organization in order to ensure unbiased, objective, credible information. Management insisted that all information on its site "pass a rigorous clinical review process before we deem it worthy" of the consumer.[30] The site also had a powerful search engine, Medisearch, which allowed quick keyword inquiries. Mediconsult reported revenues of $3.1 million for the quarter ending September 1999.

[29]thestandard.com.

[30]www.mediconsult.com.

In September 1999, Mediconsult.com acquired Physicians Online in a stock deal valued at $180 million. The acquisition was expected to help Mediconsult.com take advantage of the recent introduction of online medical records and other services designed to connect doctors and patients and deliver health care.[31]

The Health Network.com

The Health Network was a 50/50 partnership between FOX Entertainment Group and AHN Partners, LP, that combined the leading health cable television channel (The Health Network) with one of the most visited health information sites on the Internet (ahn.com, recently renamed TheHealthNetwork.com). The partnership promoted itself as a one-stop television and Internet site where consumers could find information, support, and the motivation needed to make decisions about leading a healthy life. The Health Network reached more than 17 million households in all 50 states through cable and satellite and could be seen via the Internet with live streaming video. Its Web site was the premier source of live medical events, such as the first live Internet birth and the first live Internet triplet birth.

Viewers, whether online or watching on television, were provided information by doctors and other experts in a clear, interesting, and easy-to-understand manner. In addition, the online site provided original programming, breaking news, exercise and nutrition guides, expert medical advice, and in-depth information. Online users could connect directly with both credible medical professionals and people who had similar interests in specific health categories such as women's health, parenting, and heart health.

Medscape

Medscape's home page was comprehensive, well organized, and user-friendly. It featured the Medscape Network (for student, nurses, physicians), Medscape Resources, My Medscape (records personalized info from previous visits) and an Editorial Board. In addition, Medscape published *Medscape General Medicine,* an online, peer-reviewed medical journal, and it offered a database of continuing medical education programs, an online bookstore, and physician Web sites for its members.

Medscape produced the consumer-oriented CBS *HealthWatch.* In July 1999, CBS acquired a 35 percent stake in Medscape in exchange for $157 million in advertising and branding services. The company had recently announced a content agreement with America Online. The three-year arrangement called for Medscape to develop co-branded health sites for AOL's 18 million subscribers. In exchange, Medscape will pay AOL $33 million for two years.

Medscape reported revenues of $3.1 million for the quarter ending September 1999.

The American Medical Association Web Site (www.ama-assn.org)

The American Medical Association (AMA) represented about 35 percent of U.S. doctors (down from 50 percent in 1975). A core objective of the AMA was to be the world leader in obtaining, synthesizing, integrating, and disseminating information on health and

---

[31]www.thestandard.com/article/display/0,1151,6224,00.html.

medical practice. The AMA published numerous journals, and its corporate Web site, a portion of which was accessible to members only, provided valuable online information. The general public could use the site to look for medical group and physician locators; to get medical advice about injuries, illnesses, and specific conditions; and to read about general health information. Consumers could also learn about the association's advocacy and legislative initiatives and read about topics on medical ethics and education.

Revenue erosion from declining membership was expected to cause the AMA to devote time and resources to enhancing and promoting the public part of its Web site as a way of rejuvenating its revenue stream.

OnHealth.com

OnHealth Network Company was a consumer health information company based in Seattle. Its Web site was not tied to a particular doctor group, health system, or insurance company. OnHealth.com offered both proprietary and syndicated content. Most information came from the *New England Journal of Medicine,* Cleveland Clinic, Beth Israel Deaconess Medical Center, and physicians who taught at Harvard, Columbia, and Stanford. A unique feature on the site's home page was the Herbal Index, which contained 140 descriptions of alternative health remedies. About 80 percent of OnHealth's audience was female.

The company had negotiated agreements to provide content to several Web sites, including America Online and WebTV. In December 1999, OnHealth.com signed an agreement with Ask Jeeves, Inc., a leading provider of natural-language question-answering services on the Web for consumers and businesses. This deal will provide OnHealth with prominent brand positioning.[32]

The site was supported by advertising. Advertisers included Johnson & Johnson and Pfizer. Site operators claimed that the information about a topic was not influenced by the advertisements displayed on that page, indicating, "If it ever appears otherwise to you, please let us know."[33]

Affiliates of Van Wagoner Capital Management owned about 39 percent of the company. OnHealth reported revenues of $1 million for the quarter ending September 1999.

iVillage's www.allHealth.com

iVillage's Web site targeted women aged 25 to 49 through more than 15 "channels" focusing on topics such as health, food, parenting, relationships, and shopping. The health sections of the site were at betterhealth.com or allhealth.com. The sites used the tag lines "Take Charge of Your Health!" and "Information you need from a Community you can trust."[34] Site features included extensive chat rooms, weekly polls, and shopping. iVillage members could "ask the experts" for medical advice. iVillage generated more than 80 percent of its revenue from advertising, but the company was looking to enlarge its online product offerings; its first step in this direction was a line of baby products offered at iBaby.com. In the quarter ending September 1999, iVillage reported revenues of $10.7 million.

---

[32]www.askjeeves.com. Investor Relations.

[33]onhealth.com/chl/info/item.asp.

[34]www.allhealth.com.

Candice Carpenter, iVillage's CEO, commenting on the recent merger between Healtheon and WebMD, said, "I think it's pretty obvious there needs to be some (more) consolidation. We've got to clean this up a little. I don't know who's going to do it, but somebody should step up to the plate to do that job."[35]

CONFLICTS OF INTEREST AND ETHICS CONCERNS

There vas a growing concern among many medical information providers about the potential for conflicts of interests and potential liability in providing inaccurate information, diagnosis, and prescribing drugs online. In a proactive attempt to address such issues, Dr. C. Everett Koop initiated a meeting of interested parties. The meeting resulted in the formation of a coalition of 16 companies, including Healtheon/WebMD, Medscape Inc., America Online Inc., and drkoop.com, to develop an ethical code of conduct for Internet-based medical information providers. Alliance members accounted for 27 percent of total Internet audience traffic.[36] The group was working to create a set of recommended policies and practices for advertising, privacy, and content that would ensure the reliability of health information that consumers accessed through e-health providers. Donald Kemper, the chairperson of Hi-Ethics, stated that "our ultimate goal is to guide a future of consumer confidence in health care information."[37]

FUTURE OUTLOOK FOR DRKOOP.COM

Donald W. Hackett, president and CEO of drkoop.com, believed the company had a promising future:

> The successful execution of our business strategy has firmly positioned the company for growth. Our registered users are growing at a healthy pace, we are rapidly extending our reach, our advertising and sponsorship pipeline is strong, and the drkoop.com brand name continues to be recognized as an industry leader. Looking ahead, we intend to leverage the strength of our domestic business to accelerate expansion into international markets. We recently announced our first alliance with Australia's Medweb and anticipate continued international expansion in the first half of 2000.

Nonetheless, Hackett and company cofounder Dennis Upah knew the challenges ahead were formidable. Medical sites on the Internet were proliferating. Competition was becoming stronger. WebMD and Rupert Murdoch's News Corp. had announced plans to put more than $1 billion into developing their medical information site. Companies like Healtheon/WebMD were partnering with hospitals to provide services other than medical information. While there were many opportunities for medical information providers, it was far from clear which business model and strategy made the most sense for drkoop.com. And even more important, drkoop.com was "burning" through its cash reserves and looking at negative cash flows for some time to come. A number of investors were becoming increasingly concerned about the company's financial position and the viability of its business model.

---

[35]www.thestandard.com/article/display/0,1151,4839,00.html.

[36]"Leading E-Healthware Companies Form Alliance to Benefit Internet Consumers," Business Wire, November 4, 1999.

[37]Ibid.

case 15 WingspanBank.com

Laura Cooke
University of Michigan

Hyung Kim
University of Michigan

Liza Hovey
University of Michigan

Paul Rakowski
University of Michigan

> [WingspanBank] cannibalize[s] existing business to build new business.[1]
> —John B. McCoy, President and CEO, Bank One Corporation

It was Monday, November 15, 1999, and John B. McCoy already felt like it had been a long week. *The Wall Street Journal* had announced the impending departure of James Stewart,[2] chief executive of Wingspan, and investors and media hounds alike were clamoring for more details.

McCoy remembered Wingspan's first days, when he worried about the many Internet start-ups beginning to offer a wide array of financial services. Reasoning that bankone.com was insufficient to stem the tide, he launched WingspanBank.com as a freestanding Internet bank.[3] After all, he thought, if customers were going to abandon brick-and-mortar banks in favor of Internet banks, Bank One should offer the best choice: WingspanBank.com.

Thus, WingspanBank.com was launched on June 24, 1999, under the auspices of the First USA division of Bank One. Unfortunately, the First USA division had performed poorly since then, and analysts had been questioning whether the excitement of launching WingspanBank.com had distracted management from its core business—credit cards.[4]

As McCoy considered the situation, several questions came to mind: Had he been right about permitting cannibalization? What is the role of Wingspan at Bank One? What is the future of Bank One in the era of e-commerce?

BACKGROUND

There was a lot for McCoy to consider. The final decades of the 20th century had brought changes to every possible dimension of banking. From changes in government

---

Prepared under the supervision of Professor Allan Afuah. University of Michigan. Some data, names and situations have been disguised to maintain confidentiality.

[1]"Internet Defense Strategy: Cannibalize Yourself," *Fortune,* September 6, 1999, p. 122.

[2]"Bank One Says CEO of Internet Venture, Wingspan, Will Resign at Year's End," *The Wall Street Journal,* November 15, 1999, p. B11.

[3]"Internet Defense Strategy: Cannibalize Yourself," pp. 121–34.

[4]"WingspanBank: Losing Its Wings?" *The Industry Standard* (www.thestandard.com/article/display/0,1151,7658,00.html?05).

exhibit 1   Bank One Milestones

1868	F. C. Session founds Commercial National Bank in Columbus, Ohio.
1929	Commercial National and National Bank of Commerce combine to form City National Bank and Trust.
1935	First John (H.) McCoy becomes bank president.
1958	Second John (G.) McCoy becomes bank president.
1966	City National Bank introduces first Visa (then Bank.Americard) credit card outside California.
1967	First Banc Group of Ohio formed as holding company for City National Bank; First Banc buys Farmers Savings and Trust of Mansfield, Ohio.
1977	First Bank introduces first cash management account in partnership with Merrill Lynch.
1979	Company changes name to Banc One; all affiliated banks renamed Bank One.
1984	Third (and present) John (B.) McCoy becomes bank president; federal government relaxes restrictions on interstate banking; and Banc One expands into Indiana, Kentucky, Michigan, and Wisconsin.
1989	Banc One enters Texas market with acquisition of 20 failed Mcorp and other banks.
1991	Banc One enters Illinois.
1992	Banc One enters Arizona and Utah.
1994	Banc One begins major consolidation effort.
1996	Banc One buys Premier Bancorp., Louisiana's number three bank.
1997	Banc One acquires number four card issuer, First USA, and buys Liberty Bancorp of Oklahoma.
1998	Banc One acquires First Chicago NBD in $30 billion stock swap and changes name to Bank One Corporation, based in Chicago, Illinois; Bank One is number four banking company in United States. The company launches bankone.com, which offers traditional banking services to current customers (and general information about Bank One Corporation).
1999	Bank One becomes world's largest issuer of Visa credit cards; it also launches WingspanBank.com (as unit of First USA division), which offers wide array of financial services—including insurance, mortgage, and mutual fund services.

Sources: Bank One Corporation 1998 annual report; Hoover's Company Capsules; and WingspanBank Marketing.

regulations to the emergence of the Internet, the ever-changing landscape for financial service companies brought difficult challenges and uncertain opportunities.

History of Bank One

Just as its official all-capital-letter name BANK ONE CORPORATION (hereinafter Bank One) proclaims, this financial institution thinks big, and its recent history (see Exhibit 1) shows that it embraces innovations. Among them are the first Visa (then called BankAmericard) credit card service outside California in 1966, and the first cash management account in 1977, which combined the higher interest rates of a brokerage account with the flexibility of checking services.

The bank—founded in 1868 and called City National Bank after the merger of two Columbus, Ohio, banks in 1929—also has a strong history of acquisitions. In 1967, its management created a holding company to enable expansion and named it First Banc Group of Ohio to skirt legal restrictions on the use of the word *bank*. Its acquisition of a bank in neighboring Mansfield, Ohio, initiated a string of intrastate acquisitions.

exhibit 2   Summary Balance Sheet for Bank One, 1997–1998
(In Millions of $)

	Year Ended December 31st	
	1998	1997
Assets		
Cash and due from banks	$ 19,878	$ 15,380
Interest-bearing due from banks	4,642	6,910
Funds and securities under resale agreements	9,862	9,168
Trading and derivative products	12,299	9,869
Investment securities	44,852	26,039
Loans, net	153,127	156,762
Bank premises and equipment, net	3,340	3,426
Other assets	13,496	11,818
Total assets	$261,496	$239,372
Liabilities and stockholders' equity		
Deposits, total	$161,542	$153,726
Short-term borrowings, total	40,101	33,152
Long-term debt	21,295	20,543
Other liabilities	17,998	12,901
Total liabilities	$240,936	$220,322
Stockholders' equity		
Preferred stock	$ 190	$ 326
Common stock, $0.01 par value	12	12
Surplus	10,769	12,584
Retained earnings	9,528	8,063
Other	61	(1,935)
Total stockholders' equity	$ 20,560	$ 19,050
Total liabilities and stockholders' equity	$261,496	$239,372

Source: Bank One Corporation 1998 annual report.

When restrictions on interstate banking were removed in 1984, Banc One (changed from First Banc in 1979) expanded into Arizona, Illinois, Indiana, Kentucky, Michigan, Texas, Utah and Wisconsin—primarily through stock swaps.

Following its "merger of equals" (under Banc One leadership) with First Chicago NBD in 1998, Bank One (so renamed after the merger) was the fourth largest banking company in the United States (see Exhibits 2 and 3). In addition, the recent acquisition of credit card issuer First USA made Bank One, already the number three issuer, the largest issuer of Visa credit cards in the world.

First USA featured a more entrepreneurial culture than Bank One and also brought significant e-commerce expertise in the form of its Internet Marketing Group. In its efforts to develop an e-commerce strategy for First USA and implement firstusa.com, this group had learned important lessons and forged useful relationships. The Internet Marketing Group made it possible for Bank One to take fuller advantage of the mounting Internet explosion than its current presence. BankOne.com (see Exhibit 4) was

exhibit 3   Summary Income Statement for Bank One, 1997–1998
             (In Millions, except for Per Share Data)

	Year Ended December 31st	
	1998	1997
Interest income		
Interest income, total	$17,524	$17,545
Interest expense, total	8,177	8,084
Less provision for credit losses	1,408	1,988
Net interest income after credit losses	$ 7,939	$ 7,374
Noninterest revenue		
Market-driven revenue	$ 546	$ 552
Fee-based revenue	6,728	5,645
Other	797	497
Total noninterest revenue	$ 8,071	$ 6,694
Noninterest expense		
Salaries and benefits	$ 4,477	$ 4,224
Net occupancy and equipment	845	739
Depreciation and amortization	680	693
Outside service fees and processing	1,349	1,145
Marketing and development	1,024	837
Communication and transportation	781	711
Merger-related and restructuring charges	1,062	337
Other	1,327	1,054
Total	$11,545	$ 9,740
Earnings before income taxes	$ 4,465	$ 4,427
Applicable income taxes	1,357	1,467
Net income	$ 3,108	$ 2,960
Earnings per share, basic	$ 2.65	$ 2.48
Earnings per share, diluted	$ 2.61	$ 2.43

Source: Bank One Corporation 1998 annual report.

meant simply to offer online services to current customers of Bank One and to serve as the corporation's online information presence.

Explosion of the Internet

By the late 1990s, the Internet had already transformed itself from a convenience for academics and curiosity for intellectuals to a viable commercial force and powerful business tool. Three primary phenomena converged to spur this emergence:

- *More people had access to the Internet.* Personal computers (PCs) and Internet access became increasingly affordable and reliable. Frenetic competition, learning effects, and scale economies in the PC and Internet industries even made it possible

exhibit 4   BankOne.com Start Page

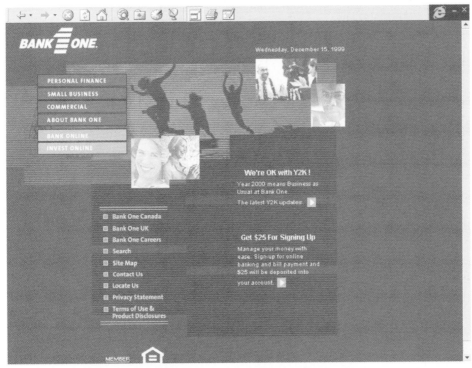

Source: www.bankone.com.

for some companies to offer free PCs to consumers willing to purchase Internet access (and vice versa). In addition, the network software offered security and ease of use. By 1998, over 50 percent of U.S. households had personal computers (PCs), and over 30 percent had Internet access (see Exhibit 5).

● *The Internet offered something for everyone.* Internet companies were enjoying extraordinary market valuations, and no one wanted to be left out. For instance, the market value of online toy merchant eToys surpassed the market value of Toys "R" Us within its first day of trading. As a result, seemingly every business looked for ways to offer its products and services on the Internet, and consumers invested what they could. With this infusion of capital and labor, the Internet grew, and the number of online destinations grew sixfold between 1996 and 1999.[5]

● *People became comfortable with e-commerce.* Consumers were doing more and more business on the Internet. Advances in Internet security assuaged fears, and as the Internet became more familiar and affordable, people could and would spend more time "surfing" and buying. As a result, the $7.8 billion online retail market of 1998 is projected to reach $108 billion by 2003 (see Exhibit 6).

With the longest economic expansion in the history of the United States as a backdrop, the Internet was real, and e-commerce an undeniable force.

---

[5]Forrester.com, October 15, 1999.

exhibit 5   Number of U.S. Consumers with PCs and Internet Access

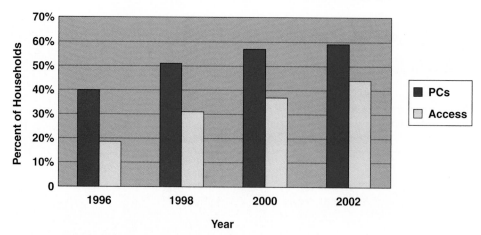

Source: Forrester Research.

exhibit 6   U.S. Online Retail Spending

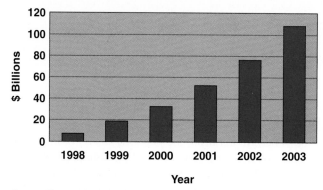

Source: Forrester Research.

Internet Banking

As the Internet achieved greater prominence, online banking emerged. Early Internet-only entrants included Telebank, Net.B@nk (see Exhibits 7 and 8) and Security First Network Bank. Offering cost savings to suppliers and convenience to consumers, Internet banking appeared poised for tremendous growth. Not only did Internet-only banks avoid the overhead expenses incurred by brick-and-mortar locations, but an online transaction cost only 1 cent, compared to $1.07 for a traditional face-to-face transaction (see Exhibit 9). Internet banks could pass these cost savings on to customers in the form of higher interest rates and lower service fees (see Exhibits 10 and 11).

In the mid-1990s the industry began its climb, despite federal banking regulations that limited its growth. For instance, unlike other Internet ventures, online banks had to generate sufficient revenue to cover such expenses as marketing and administration. Nevertheless, pure Internet banks continued to appear, and in October 1998, Compu-Bank became the first national virtual bank to receive a charter from the Office of the

***exhibit* 7**   Net.B@nk.com Start Page

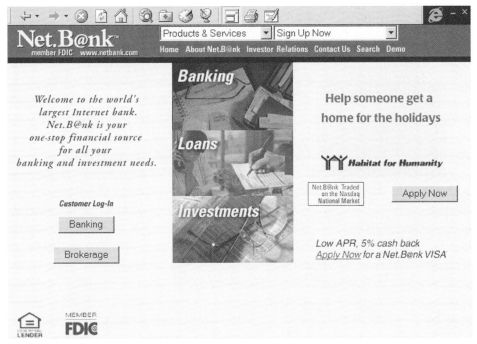

Source: www.netbank.com.

Comptroller of the Currency and approval from the Federal Deposit Insurance Corporation (FDIC).

With interest rates rising and fees falling at online banks, Internet banking burgeoned in the late 1990s. In 1998 alone, the number of households using online banking nearly doubled, to 7 million, and estimates suggest that this number will reach 24 million by 2002.[6] Ominously, this growth, while rapid, pales in comparison to that of other financial services like online brokerage.

Witnessing this growth, traditional brick-and-mortar banks began to acknowledge the importance of this new channel and worked to develop Internet strategies. Among the first were large national banks like Bank of America, Citibank, and Wells Fargo. Their initial Internet attempts meant limited services such as the ability to check balances and transfer funds. The primary purpose of their Internet sites was to retain existing customers and provide information about retail products at brick-and-mortar locations. Soon, however, such other banking giants as Citibank, American Express, and Bank One would work to create separate entities under which to develop true online offerings (see Exhibit 12).

Traditional banks had many assets to leverage in developing Internet products. Customers could use pre-existing ATM networks without per-use transaction fees. In addition, individuals could make deposits at bank locations, electronically or by "snail

---

[6]"Take Your Banking Online" (cnnfn.com/1999/05/21/banking/q_online_banks/), May 21, 1999.

exhibit 8   Net.B@nk Summary Income Statement, 1998–1999
(In Thousands of $)

	Six Months Ended June 30th	
	1999	**1998**
Interest income		
Interest income, total	$17,979	$6,459
Interest expense, total	10,290	4,017
Net interest income	$ 7,689	$2,442
Noninterest income		
Noninterest income, total	$ 477	$ 226
Noninterest expense, total	5,851	2,570
Net noninterest income	($ 5,374)	($2,344)
Provision for loan loss	$ 105	$ 10
Earnings before income taxes	$ 2,210	$ 88
Income tax (expense) benefit	(751)	(30)
Tax benefit of loss	—	3,059
Net income	$ 1,459	$3,117

Source: NetBank Investor Relations.

exhibit 9   Estimated Banking Transaction Costs

Transaction Type	Per Unit Cost
Face-to-face (with teller)	$1.07
Mail-in	0.73
Telephone*	0.54
Automated teller machine	0.27
Internet	0.01

*Balance inquiry or money transfer.

Source: "Cyber-Banking Breaks New Ground, Expands towards Mainstream," *Bank Rate Monitor,* January 12, 1999.

mail." Finally, traditional banks' strong brand recognition meant virtually instant trust with potential online clientele.

Established banks faced special challenges, too. General concerns about online privacy and security took on heightened importance when considering individuals' finances. In addition, the considerable investments were unlikely to bring short-term returns. Indeed, this new channel could cannibalize existing business. Furthermore, their conservative outlook coaxed most traditional banks to view the Internet as a revenue source—not as another branch location—and many actually charged customers for online transactions.

Quickly, however, online banks began to recognize that banking services—not venue—would continue to provide most of the revenue. Pete Kight, CEO of CheckFree

exhibit 10   Comparative Interest Rates of Selected Banks,
                December 1999

Bank	Checking*	Savings*
AmEx Membership Bank	2.00%	2.00%
Bank One	1.49%	1.49%
Bank of America	0%	1.00%
Chase.com	0.75%	2.13%
Citif/i	0%	2.47%
CompuBank	3.00%	3.50%
NetB@nk	Up to 3.93%	N/A
Telebank	Up to 3.68%	Up to 4.88%
WingspanBank.com	Up to 4.5%	N/A
Mean	0.84%	2.13%

*For balances of $0–$15,000.
Source: Company Web sites as of December 13, 1999.

exhibit 11   Comparative Fees of Online Banks, December 1999

	Savings Account	Bill Payment Services	Out-network ATM	Monthly Service Fee	Minimum Account Balance	Online Brokerage Link	Instant Credit Access
AmEx Membership B@nking	Free	Free	Free[1]	None	Yes	Yes	
bankofamerica.com	Free				Yes		
bankone.com	Free						Yes
citif/i	Free	Free	Free	None		Yes	
chase.com	Free						Yes
CompuBank	Free	Free	Free[1]	None	Yes		
NetB@nk		Free		None		Yes	
Telebank	Free	Free		None	Yes[2]	Yes	
wellsfargo.com	Free	Free[3]			Yes	Yes	
WingspanBank.com		Free	Free[4]	None		Yes	Yes

All offer free interest checking and in-network ATM use.
[1]Maximum 4 surcharges per month reimbursed.
[2]Interest not paid on balance below $1,000.
[3]With minimum balance.
[4]Up to $5 per month.
Source: Company Web sites as of December 6, 1999.

Corporation, the premier bill payment and presentment service for online banks, summed it up: "You don't open a new branch and ask your customers to pay to bank there. You need to open a branch online because that's where your customers are."

By November 1999, the landscape looked fragmented, and the competition fierce. Already there were more than 500 online banks,[7] and another 1,000 were predicted

---

[7]"True U.S. Internet Banks," *Online Banking Report,* November 29, 1999.

exhibit 12   Internet-only Divisions of Established Banks

	Internet-only Division	Launch Date
Bank One	Wingspan.com	June 1999
Citibank	Citif/i	August 1999
American Express	Membership B@nking	July 1999
Central Bank USA	USAccess Bank	Pending
Texas Capital Bank	BankDirect	Pending

Source: Team Research.

to launch in the next year. The Federal government further spurred competition in November with the repeal of the Glass-Steagall Act, removing barriers among banks, brokerages and insurance companies (see Exhibit 13). E*Trade quickly announced its intention to purchase Telebank, an early Internet-only bank. Bill Wallace, CIO of Wingspan, describes an even more chaotic scenario: "The other potential competitors that keep me up at night are the Yahoos and AOLs of the world. They have the customer base, but currently face a barrier to entry in being unable to secure charters. If this [barrier] opens up . . ."

To finish Wallace's thought: new entrants vying for space would simply overrun the online banking industry.

WINGSPANBANK.COM

Completing 119 acquisitions in the past 15 years had helped make Bank One the fourth largest bank in the United States. For the 21st century, however, CEO John McCoy looked to another avenue for growth—the Internet.[8]

The Decision to Launch

This fundamental shift in strategy came during a trip in the fall of 1998 that McCoy took with Dick Vague, then head of the First USA Division and a Bank One executive vice president. McCoy and Vague visited Internet companies like Yahoo!, Excite, and America Online. The ostensible purpose was for Vague to negotiate marketing deals for First USA's credit cards.[9] Significantly, however, McCoy began to see the power of the Internet in general and of online banking in particular.

This exposure served as the foundation for a new type of bank within Bank One and a new growth strategy. McCoy quipped that Bank One might never buy another bank because of the tremendous growth potential he saw in the Internet.

In February 1999 McCoy gathered key Bank One executives to discuss what type of online bank to create. The result was WingspanBank.com—a broad-based, Internet-only bank that met all of a customer's financial service needs through one integrated user ID.

---

[8]"Taking Flight with Wingspan," *Crain's Chicago Business,* August 2, 1999.
[9]"Bank One: Nothing but Net," *Business Week,* August 2, 1999.

exhibit 13   Glass-Steagall Act

On November 12, 1999, United States President Bill Clinton signed a new financial modernization bill into law, the Gramm-Leach Act, thus repealing the significant restrictions that had been placed on financial institutions in the United States by the Depression-era legislation, the Glass-Steagall Act. That bill had regulated the industry by preventing banks, insurance companies and brokerage firms from entering into each other's lines of business.

The essence of the Glass-Steagall Act had been to separate commercial and investment banking. Its intention was to protect the commercial customers since it was born out of the concept that the investing activities of bankers in the 1920s had led to the stock market crash and resulting Great Depression of the 1930s. As financial markets have become more accessible to the consumer through such means as the Internet and the Securities and Exchange Commission has been diligent in keeping the markets transparent, such protection no longer was relevant.

While for the most part individual consumers were unaware of the restrictions caused by Glass-Steagall, much infighting had resulted over the years between various financial institutions desiring to offer a wider variety of services to their customers. It is anticipated that with the Act's repeal, many mergers will take place in the financial services industry and that competition will increase significantly. The lines between banks, brokerage firms and insurance companies has certainly been blurred.

Source: Dee DePass, The Minneapolis Star Tribune, November 13, 1999.

The Vision

> *If your bank could start over, this is what it would be.*
> —WingspanBank.com slogan

To herald this new Internet-only bank, senior management wanted to create a new brand. James Stewart, the original CEO of Wingspan, explained:

> We wanted something that was unique to online and financial services. We wanted a name that was not necessarily a literal name like Internet bank.com but something that could ultimately come to mean something. Like Amazon didn't mean "books online" and Excite didn't mean "search engine"—but now they do.[10]

The team looked to the market for this new name. After a series of focus groups, potential customers and senior management agreed upon Wingspan. Wingspan symbolized the breadth of new products and emphasized the fresh start. With their early entry into the market, the team hoped that WingspanBank would soon become synonymous with "Internet banking."

WingspanBank should be more than simply Bank One online—indeed, bankone.com already existed. WingspanBank should be a "one-stop shop" for financial services: checking, savings, direct deposit, credit cards, installment and other loans, investments, bill payment, financial planning, CDs, mortgages, insurance, and more. Multiple "best-in-class" vendors would provide these services, permitting Wingspan-Bank customers to use a variety of financial institutions through one channel.

Michael Cleary, president of Wingspan commented:

> Bank One has a multibrand strategy on the Internet. Our goal is to create different products for different customers with different needs. Bank One is for the brick-and-mortar customer

---

[10]*Crain's Chicago Business,* August 2, 1999.

with a regional focus. Wingspan is for an Internet customer with a national focus. To make a consumer products analogy, you may not know whether a customer wants Tide or Wisk, but either way, P&G will make sure to provide it.

The essence of WingspanBank, however, would be convenient, comprehensive, and objective solutions to customers' problems at competitive prices—not merely products. Wingspan committed to becoming a "trusted adviser" to its customers. Cleary noted:

> Offline banks have promised for years to be the trusted adviser for customers. The Internet provides us with the tools to do that. [But] only time will tell whether people will provide the information we need to deliver that value.

The scope was national—extending beyond the 14 states where Bank One operated. The primary target market for WingspanBank.com was a segment that bankone.com could not reach—the growing core group of Internet users who disdain traditional banks. Wingspan wanted both present and future users of Internet banks, especially those who currently bank with Bank One competitors. Even taking Bank One's own customers was deemed acceptable.

Implementation

Jim Stewart was selected to be CEO of Wingspan and an "iBoard of Directors" of technology leaders was created. Together, they set a time frame of 90 days to launch, but where should WingspanBank be born in order to foster creativity, innovation, and speed to market?

The answer was First USA. According to Cleary:

> Bank One bought First USA for its speed and marketing savvy. First USA has the entrepreneurial spirit and acts quickly. I never thought it could move so fast, but indeed it is a fast company.

First USA understood direct marketing and lived to "test and learn." In addition, its Internet Marketing Group had recent experience in the Internet world, and its culture appeared to align well with the goals of Wingspan.

Around 30 external vendors were selected to speed launch and expand product offerings in keeping with the Wingspan vision. These partners comprised the best service providers for each product area. Though invisible in most cases to WingspanBank customers, they directly represented the brand and were thus crucial to the success of the venture. All partners began work based on verbal agreements—time constraints prevented legal negotiations. The work required to implement so much functionality in so little time meant 18-hour days for Wingspan employees and partner staff alike.

Meanwhile Carol Knight, a former First USA consultant, had been selected to head up the marketing and PR efforts. Within the first month, her group conducted over 60 focus groups! These groups clarified what consumers wanted from an Internet bank and helped refine Wingspan's goals.

For instance, consumers' main concern was trustworthiness of the site, followed closely by price. Ease of use and customer service became paramount, increasing the importance of site design and seamless integration of the multiple vendors. Thorough testing before launch was essential—any technical difficulty with the site could sabotage the new brand. A customer's first impression of WingspanBank.com was critical.

Customers also believed putting all of their assets in one place was risky, but using multiple vendors made them feel more secure. This sentiment reassured Wingspan management that partnerships and offerings of non–Bank One products on the site were keys to success. Customers also desired personal financial management (PFM). Although these checking and bill-payment services offered no profit margin, customized PFM could ultimately generate revenue by permitting targeted products such as loans to be "pushed" to consumers.

The marketing team of 30—including Wingspan's advertising and public relations agencies, First USA staff and external consultants—was also developing a plan in keeping with the Wingspan vision. The perceived importance of marketing shows in the nearly $100 million allocated from a total annual operating budget for Wingspan of approximately $150 million.[11] The plan included network TV spots, radio ads, celebrity personalities, press releases, and news features. Each of these activities was critical to the establishment of a stand-alone brand.

Unlike traditional Bank One advertising, which was regional, this campaign demanded national exposure, especially in markets where Bank One did not have a presence (to minimize cannibalization). Cities such as Boston, Seattle, and Philadelphia were ideal. However, the campaign also had a presence in California and Texas, which were existing Bank One markets.

The timeliness was critical to the plan:

> The ad agency had eight weeks to design a campaign and shoot a commercial. The actors practiced a script with no bank name because it was not yet determined. The day of the commercial shoot when the name was revealed, the biggest concern was whether the actors would be able to make this change.[12]

WingspanBank.com was launched on June 24, 1999 (see Exhibit 14)—just 123 days from kickoff. McCoy was very visible during this time, including an interview for *The Wall Street Journal* during which he announced the financial impact to Bank One. In the first year, WingspanBank was expected to dilute the value of Bank One's stock by 5 cents per share; in the second year, to add 5 cents per share; and in the third year, to add 20 cents per share.

Current State

By most measures, Wingspan succeeded in meeting its goals.

Culture   Being an Internet start-up within a larger organization offers both opportunities and challenges. Kevin Watters, Wingspan's senior vice president of marketing, summarized the advantages:

> Compared to other Internet banks Wingspan has the cash resources of Bank One and First USA, which means enormous marketing dollars. In addition, we are able to mine data from First USA to provide better offers via direct mail and email than competitors. That's a 70-million-cardholder database to pull from. There is also shared learning across the three organizations (Bank One, First USA and Wingspan).

Cleary noted the challenges:

> It's sometimes hard to act like an Internet company. There is no currency like an e-trade—currency for marketing deals, advertising, and talent. Businesses are about people and if we don't have what Internet-savvy people want, we're handcuffed. We're also responsible for

---

[11]"Bank One Says CEO of Internet Venture, Wingspan, Will Resign at Year's End."

[12]Telephone interview with Michael Cleary, President, Wingspan, December 6, 1999.

exhibit 14   WingspanBank.com Start Page

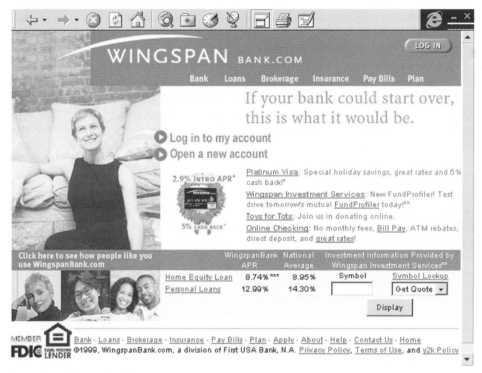

Source: www.wingspanbank.com.

part of an earnings stream at Bank One, and we all know that at Internet start-ups, earnings don't drive success. We're forced to look at profitability [earlier].

Customer Base   Within its first 90 days of operations, Wingspan had signed up 50,000 customer accounts. By comparison, Net.B@nk, which had been operating for over three years, had only 35,000 customers. On the other hand, bankone.com had 350,000 customers, nearly 8 million people were online, and 200,000 of them used Internet-only banks.

Wingspan wants to know whether their customers will switch among banks or remain loyal. Wingspan's "stickiest" products so far include online bill payment and direct deposit. With these products, customers spend a great deal of time and provide specific information to the bank, thus increasing their switching costs. In fact, Wells Fargo research indicates that online customers using bill payment services are 16 times more likely than brick-and-mortar customers to stay with the bank and be profitable.[13]

In terms of "mindshare" and general awareness, Wingspan has hit its goals but still hopes to target better the core Internet banking consumer through both traditional and Internet advertising. In addition, a recent alliance with Lycos through which Lycos customers can bank through a co-branded Wingspan-and-Lycos site may represent future direction.

Services   Customers can use Bank One's ATMs for free—but not the tellers and other face-to-face branch services. Customers can complete applications online, get

---

[13]Telephone interview with Peter Kight, Chief Executive Officer, CheckFree Corporation, December 1, 1999.

approved, and start banking in the same online session, which is unusual—most online banks make customers wait for passwords received via e-mail. Customers can also receive virtually instant decisions on products ranging from credit cards to installment loans—the response to an online home equity loan application takes only 50 seconds! Many WingspanBank services and rates are not available to Bank One customers. For example, Bank One customers pay $4.95 per month for the same bill-payment services Wingspan customers get for free.

Since the launch, Wingspan had continued to demonstrate its commitment to its vision through continual spending and maintenance of product quality. For example, in its commitment to maintain the best portfolio of products and services, management added CheckFree Corporation, the leading supplier of bill payment services, to the list of vendors. According to CIO Wallace, "Wingspan will continue to look at all vendors in the marketplace and select the best ones."

The original plan added novel, meaningful functionality to the site every four to six weeks. Wingspan currently was making site changes over a six-to-eight-week time frame, but it continued to innovate. According to Cleary, there was still much to do:

> We launched quickly to beat Citibank and American Express, to test and to learn. There are many things not done at launch that we must complete in order to reach our goals. For example, we have not yet implemented many of our cross-selling techniques. Wingspan needs to recognize customers when they come to the site using CRM [customer relationship management] tools to deepen the relationship.

Wallace reflected on the future as well:

> The model for Wingspan must change from product- to relationship-focused. In the past 25 years, banks created complicated views of banking and took away customers' control over their finances. Wingspan can erase the complexity and give customers back this control. For example, if there is $10,000 in a checking account, we can automatically issue a CD for the unused portion so that customer earns an extra $25. This adds value to the relationship.

Wingspan was expected to continue its furious growth and use its flexibility and size to its advantage. Relative to other Internet banks, Wingspan had higher brand awareness, better prices, and leaner operations, allowing it to provide customer enhancements that other companies could not readily match.

THE DILEMMA

John McCoy liked what Wingspan had achieved, but he was concerned. Shares of Bank One had fallen more than 40 percent since May. The First USA division suffered $70 billion in outstanding receivables, and expensive advertising campaigns had yet to deliver predicted returns.[14] Furthermore, the press unrelentingly included Wingspan in its criticism of Bank One even though Wingspan revenues meant little to a banking behemoth with $260 billion in assets. Was it because several executives at Wingspan—including Dick Vague and now James Stewart—had departed?

It was ironic, McCoy thought, that Wingspan had met virtually all of it goals and led the industry, yet remained underappreciated outside—and maybe even inside—Bank One. Given all this, he had to ask himself: Now what?

---

[14]Ibid.

case 16 | Ben & Jerry's—Japan

James M. Hagen

Cornell University

On an autumn evening in Tokyo in 1997, Perry Odak, Angelo Pezzani, Bruce Bowman, and Riv Hight gratefully accepted the steaming hot oshibori towels that their kimono-bedecked waitress quietly offered. After a full day of meetings with Masahiko Iida and his lieutenants at the Seven-Eleven Japan headquarters, the men from Ben & Jerry's welcomed the chance to refresh their hands and faces before turning to the business at hand. It had been just over nine months since Odak had committed to resolving the conundrum of whether to introduce Ben & Jerry's ice cream to the Japan market and, if so, how. The next morning would be their last chance to hammer out the details for a market entry through Seven-Eleven's 7,000 stores in Japan or to give the go-ahead to Ken Yamada, a prospective licensee who would manage the Japan market for Ben & Jerry's. Any delay in reaching a decision would mean missing the summer 1998 ice cream season, but with Japan's economy continuing to contract, perhaps passing on the Japanese market would not be a bad idea.

Perry Odak was just entering his 11th month as CEO of the famous ice cream company, named for its offbeat founders. He knew that the Seven-Eleven deal could represent a sudden boost in the company's flagging sales of the past several years. He also knew that a company with the tremendous brand recognition Ben & Jerry's enjoyed needed to approach new market opportunities from a strategic, not an opportunistic, perspective. Since meeting Masahiko Iida, the president of Seven-Eleven Japan, just 10 months earlier, Odak had been anxious to resolve the question of whether entering the huge Japanese market via Seven-Eleven was the right move or not.

BEN & JERRY'S BACKGROUND: 1978 TO 1997

1978 to 1994: Growth from Renovated Gas Station to $160 Million in Sales[1]

Brooklyn, New York, schoolmates Ben Cohen and Jerry Greenfield started their ice cream company in a defunct gas station in Burlington, Vermont, in 1978, when both were in their mid-20s. The combination of their anticorporate style, the high fat content of their ice cream, the addition of chunky ingredients, and catchy flavor names like Cherry Garcia found a following. In addition to selling by the scoop, they began selling

[1]Monetary values are in U.S. dollars unless otherwise noted.

pints over the counter, and the business grew. With the help of less visible team members Jeff Furman and Fred (Chico) Lager, the founders took the company public to Vermont stockholders in 1984, later registering with the Securities and Exchange Commission (SEC) for nationwide sale of stock. The company name was Ben & Jerry's Homemade, Inc., and it began trading over the counter with the symbol BJICA.

Stockholder meetings were outdoor festivals where standard attire included cutoffs and tie-dyed T-shirts and where Cohen was liable to call the meeting to order in song. Cohen and Greenfield determined that in addition to being fun to work for, the company would be socially responsible, known for its "caring capitalism." Highlighting its community roots, Ben & Jerry's would buy its cream only from Vermont dairies. In the case of one of its early nut flavors, Rain Forest Crunch, the nuts would be sourced from tribal cooperatives in South American rain forests where nut harvesting would offer a renewable alternative to strip-cutting the land for wood products, and where the co-op members would, hopefully, get an uncommonly large share of the proceeds. As another part of its objective of caring capitalism, Ben & Jerry's gave 7.5 percent of pretax profits to social causes like Healing Our Mother Earth, which protected community members from local health risks, and the Center for Better Living, which assisted the homeless.

The product Cohen and Greenfield were selling was exceptionally rich (at least 12 percent butterfat, compared with about 6 to 10 percent for most ice creams). It was also very dense, due to a low overrun (low ratio of air to ice cream in the finished product). This richness and density qualified it as a superpremium ice cream. Häagen-Dazs (founded in New Jersey in 1961) was the only major competitor in the superpremium market. While Häagen-Dazs promoted a sophisticated image, Ben & Jerry's promoted a funky, caring image.

As Ben & Jerry's began to expand distribution throughout the Northeast, it found it increasing difficult to obtain shelf space in supermarkets. Charging Häagen-Dazs with unfairly pressuring distributors to keep Ben & Jerry's off their trucks, Greenfield drove to Minneapolis and gained national press coverage by picketing in front of the headquarters building of food giant Pillsbury, which had earlier acquired Häagen-Dazs. His homemade sign read, "What is the Doughboy afraid of?"—a reference to Pillsbury's mascot and to the company's apparent efforts against the underdog ice cream makers from Vermont. This David versus Goliath campaign earned Ben & Jerry's national publicity and, when combined with some high-powered legal action, gave the company freer access to grocery store freezer compartments.

A policy at Ben & Jerry's was that the highest-paid employee would not be paid more than seven times what the lowest-paid worker earned. Part of the anticorporate culture of the company was a policy that allowed each employee to make up his or her own job title. The person who might otherwise have been called the public relations manager took the title "Info Queen." Cohen and Greenfield took turns running the company. Whether despite or because of these and other unusual policies, the company continued to grow (see Exhibit 1). In 1985 the company bought a second production plant, this one in nearby Springfield, Vermont. A third plant was later built in St. Albans, Vermont. By the late 1980s, Ben & Jerry's ice cream had become available in every state of the union.

1994 to 1997: Responding to Fallen Profits

By 1994, sales exceeded $150 million, distribution had extended beyond the U.S. borders, and the company had over 600 employees. The future was not encouraging, though, with 1994 actually bringing in a loss. While Ben & Jerry's unquestionably held the second largest market share (at 34 percent compared to Häagen-Dazs's 44 percent) *exhibit 1*　　Ben & Jerry's Annual Sales, 1983–97 (In Millions)

Sales	
1983	$ 1.6
1984	4
1985	9
1986	20
1987	32
1988	47
1989	58
1990	77
1991	97
1992	131
1993	140
1994	149
1995	155
1996	167
1997	174

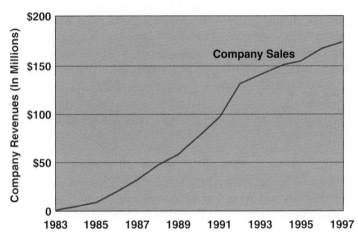

Source: Ben & Jerry's annual reports.

of the American superpremium market, the company had started to lose its place. Net income had also suffered badly since reaching a high in of $7.2 million in 1993 (see Exhibit 2). While Cohen was most often the company's CEO, much of the company's growth occurred while Chico Lager was either general manager or CEO between 1982 and 1990. Cohen was particularly engaged in efforts to further the cause of social justice by such activities as attending meetings of similarly minded CEOs from around the world. Board member Chuck Lacy had taken a turn at the helm, but he lacked aspirations for a career as a CEO, just as the company's namesakes did. The slowdown in growth and retreat in market share comprised a threat to the company's survival and to the continuation of its actions and contributions for social responsibility.

The company had never had a professional CEO and had avoided commercial advertising, relying for publicity on press coverage of its founders' antics and social interest causes. This approach was apparently losing its effectiveness, and the company could no longer feature an underdog image in its appeals for customer support. Relaxing the rule on executive compensation, the company launched a highly publicized search for a CEO, inviting would-be CEOs to submit a 100-word essay explaining why they would like the job. In 1996, Bob Holland, a former consultant with McKenzie Corporation, took the presidency, bringing a small cadre of fellow consultants with him. All of Holland's highly schooled management sensibilities were put to the test as he took over a company that had lacked effective management in recent years, commencing employment for a board of directors that was suspicious of traditional corporate culture. By this time, Cohen, Greenfield, and Furman still had considerable influence over the company, controlling about 45 percent of the shares. This permitted them, as a practical matter, to elect all members of the board of directors and thereby effectively control the policies and management of the firm. Holland's relationship with the board didn't work, and 18 months later he was out, the company's decline had not been reversed, and morale among the employees was at a low.

While the board was willing to pay a corporate-scale salary to its CEO, it was unwilling to let go of the company's tradition of donating 7.5 percent of before-tax profits to not-for-profit social causes. A spirit of socially responsible business management

exhibit 2   Ben & Jerry's Net Income, 1990–97 (In Millions)

	Net Income ($ Millions)
1990	$2.60
1991	3.73
1992	6.67
1993	7.20
1994	−1.86
1995	5.94
1996	3.92
1997	3.89

Source: Ben & Jerry's annual reports.

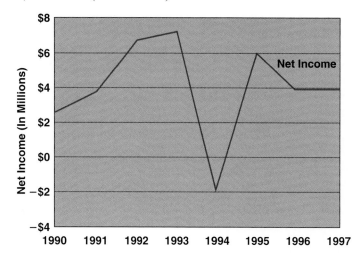

would need to continue, as that was still the company's stock in trade as much as the ice cream was. With this, as well as the need to survive, in mind, the board hired Perry Odak at the recommendation of one of its members. Odak was offered a base salary of $300,000, with a start date in January 1997.

While Odak had grown up on a dairy farm in upstate New York, it was not his dairy background that landed him the job as CEO of Ben & Jerry's. His experience at turning around troubled companies was far more important. Odak was recruited away from a consultancy assignment at U.S. Repeating Arms Company, which he had been instrumental in turning around from its decline into red ink. That position had followed a diverse series of others ranging from senior vice president of worldwide operations of Armour-Dial, Inc., to president of Atari Consumer Products, along with numerous consultancies and entrepreneurial activities that included the start-up team and management of Jovan, a fragrance and cosmetic company. A professional manager who thrived on challenges and abhorred mere maintenance of a company, Odak had entered the business world with a degree in agricultural economics from Cornell University, topped with graduate coursework in business.

THE MARKET FOR SUPERPREMIUM ICE CREAM

Ice cream is noted as far back as the days of Alexander the Great, though it was first commercially manufactured in the United States in 1851. By 1997, almost 10 percent of U.S. milk production went into ice cream, a $3.34 billion market. The ice cream brands that dominated American supermarket freezer cases are listed in Exhibit 3 and Exhibit 4. National (as opposed to regional) branding of dairy products, including ice cream, was a recent phenomenon. Dreyer's (owned in part by the Swiss food giant Nestlé and branded Edy's on the East Coast) was the biggest brand, at 13.9 percent of the U.S. market, in terms of value. The next biggest was Breyer's, a unit of the Dutch-English firm Unilever, at 12 percent. Blue Bell (from Texas) was fourth biggest at 5.2 percent, and Häagen-Dazs (owned by the UK beverage and food company then known as Grand Metropolitan) was at 4.6 percent. Ben & Jerry's came in at about 3.6 percent of the market. Healthy Choice Premium ice cream (owned by the agribusiness and consumer food firm ConAgra) was close behind, with 3.2 percent. Starbucks (one of Dreyer's brands) had 1.0 percent. The

exhibit 3   Top U.S. Ice Cream Brands, 1996–97

	Sales ($ Millions)
All brands	$3.34
Store brands	1.00
Dreyer's/Edy's premium	0.46
Breyer's premium	0.40
Blue Bell premium	0.17
Häagen-Dazs	0.15
Ben & Jerry's	**0.12**
Healthy Choice premium	0.10
Starbucks premium	0.03
Homemade premium	0.02
Breyer's Free premium	0.02

Source: Ben & Jerry's.

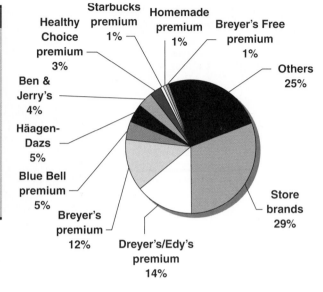

biggest share of the market (some 30.2 percent) came from retailers' private-label products, and a number of economy brands (with which Ben & Jerry's did not regard itself to be competing) made up the balance.

There are considerable economies of scale in ice cream production, so despite the advantages of having dispersed production in order to reduce costs of transporting the frozen finished product or the highly perishable cream, milk, and egg yolks that are principal raw ingredients, each major manufacturer generally had only a few plants to serve vast markets. Market leader Häagen-Dazs had just two plants in the United States, while Ben & Jerry's had three. Even with relatively few plants, Ben & Jerry's was operating at only about half of plant capacity in 1997.

While the Ben & Jerry's brand had the country's fifth highest share of the ice cream market (in terms of value), it still accounted for only a small 3.6 percent of the market. Ben & Jerry's, though, measured its competitive strength not in general ice cream sales (including many store brands and economy ice creams), but rather in sales of superpremium (high-fat-content) ice cream. The market for this product was much less fragmented, with Häagen-Dazs getting 44 percent and Ben & Jerry's getting 34 percent of the $361 million of supermarket (excluding convenience store and food service) sales measured and monitored by scanner data. If the two companies' frozen yogurts and sorbets were included, their market shares would be 36 percent for Ben & Jerry's and 42 percent for Häagen-Dazs. Both companies specialized in superpremium products, with additional sales being derived from sorbets, frozen yogurts, and novelties. Häagen-Dazs had really pioneered the category back in 1961 when Reuben Mattus founded the company in New Jersey. The company was later acquired by the giant food company Pillsbury, which in turn was bought in 1989 by the UK liquor and food giant Grand Metropolitan.

Both Ben & Jerry's and Häagen-Dazs had achieved national distribution, primarily selling their product in supermarkets and convenience stores. Ben & Jerry's had 163 scoop shops, compared to 230 Häagen-Dazs shops. Dairy Queen (with 5,790 shops worldwide) and Baskin Robbins dominated the scoop-shop business, though their products were not superpremium. Prices for Ben & Jerry's and Häagen-Dazs would range from $2.89 to $3.15 per pint, often more than twice as expensive as conventional (high-overrun/lower-butterfat) ice cream and premium brands. Starbucks and

exhibit 4   U.S. Market Share of Superpremium Brands, 1997

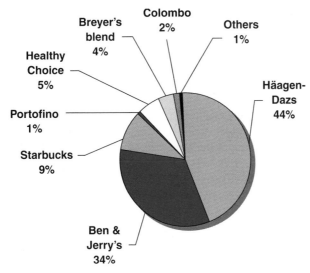

Source: Ben & Jerry's.

Portofino ice creams were other, much smaller contenders in the United States, with their "premium plus" products characterized by a butterfat content slightly under that of the superpremium category.

Statistical evidence indicated that ice cream consumption increased with income and education. Starting in the mid-1990s, though, sales growth started to fall off and Ben & Jerry's experienced a decline in profits, even suffering a loss in 1994. Häagen-Dazs and Ben & Jerry's product sales were very widely available across the entire U.S. market, and it was clear that future growth would have to come from new products or from new (non-U.S.) markets. More troubling was that Ben & Jerry's was beginning to lose market share in both the total ice cream market and, more important, the superpremium market.

BEN & JERRY'S INTERNATIONAL SALES

Ben & Jerry's was intentionally slow to embrace foreign markets. Cohen was opposed to growth for growth's sake, so the company's few adventures overseas were limited to opportunistic arrangements that came along, primarily with friends of the founders. Meanwhile Häagen-Dazs had no such hesitation. By 1997, it was in 28 countries with 850 dipping shops around the world. Its non-U.S. sales were about $700 million, compared to about $400 million of domestic sales. Ben & Jerry's, on the other hand, had foreign sales of just $6 million, with total sales of $174 million. In terms of non-U.S. superpremium ice cream sales, Häagen-Dazs and Ben & Jerry's were still the leading brands, but Häagen-Dazs was trouncing Ben & Jerry's.

Canada

Ben & Jerry's first foreign entry was in Canada in 1986, when the company gave a Canadian firm all Canadian rights for the manufacture and sale of ice cream through a licensing agreement. While about one-third of the product was exported from the United States, high Canadian tariffs (15.5 percent) and particularly quotas (only 347 tons annually) made export impractical. In 1992 Ben & Jerry's repurchased the Canadian license and as of 1997 there were just four scoop shops in Quebec. The Canadian dairy industry remained highly protective even after enactment of the North American Free Trade Agreement.

Israel

Avi Zinger, a friend of Ben Cohen's, was given a license, including manufacturing rights, for the Israel market in 1988. His 1997 sales totaled about $5 million, but the only revenue accruing to Ben & Jerry's Homemade, Inc., would be licensing income, and this amount was negligible. To ensure quality coming from the plant in Yavne, Israel, Zinger and his staff received training at the Waterbury factory. As of fall 1997, there were 14 Ben & Jerry's scoop shops in Israel, with the shops selling such items as gifts, baked goods, and beverages in addition to the ice cream. Zinger also sold Ben & Jerry's products through supermarkets, hotels, delis, and restaurants.

Russia

The company entered into its first foreign joint venture in 1990 by establishing the firm Iceverk in the Russian republic of Karelia, which is Vermont's sister state. This grew out of Cohen's travel to Karelia as part of a sister-state delegation in 1988. A goal of the joint venture was to promote understanding and communication between the peoples of these two countries. The joint venture agreement specified the following division of ownership shares: Ben & Jerry's, 50 percent; the Intercentre cooperative, 27 percent; Petro Bank, 20 percent; and Pioneer Palace (a facility similar to a YMCA that provided the location), 3 percent. Half of any profits would stay with Iceverk, and the balance would be divided among the partners. Ben & Jerry's contributed equipment and know-how to the venture, while the local partners provided the facilities for the factory and for two scoop shops. After considerable, mostly bureaucratic, delays, the shops opened in July 1992. By 1993, there were three scoop shops and about 100 employees. Iceverk opened several more scoop shops, and the venture began to sell pints in supermarkets locally, as well as in Moscow. Ben & Jerry's hired James Flynn to put his University of New Hampshire marketing degree to good use by serving as marketing rep in Moscow. Sales improved as food-service customers increasingly bought the product. In 1996, Ben & Jerry's terminated the joint venture, giving its equity and equipment at no cost to its joint venture partners. A retrospective view of that decision is that the company felt that the management time needed to keep the partnership going was too demanding, given the perceived potential. Iceverk no longer uses the Ben & Jerry's name, though it does continue to make ice cream in Petrozavodsk, Karelia's capital.

United Kingdom

In 1994 there was much discussion at Ben & Jerry's headquarters in Burlington about whether the company was ready to strategically (rather than just opportunistically) move into international markets. Susan Renaud recalled the consensus being that no, they were not, but just three months later the company shipped a container of product to Sainsbury, an upscale supermarket chain in the United Kingdom. Cohen had met a Sainsbury executive at a meeting of the Social Venture Network, and the executive had encouraged him to ship over some product. This launch was made with no idea of what the pricing would be and no knowledge of what kind of packaging and ingredients were acceptable in that market. The company was shipping a 473-milliliter package, while the standard was 500 milliliters. With its foot in the door, the company thought it best to try other outlets in England, as well. It tried out one distributor, which had agreed to donate 1 percent of its Ben & Jerry's turnover to charity. Sales did not materialize, and another distributor was tried, this time without the charity constraint. The product had a distinctive market position, with one radio commentator alleged to have said, "If Häagen-Dazs is the ice cream you have after sex, Ben & Jerry's is the ice cream you have instead of sex." By 1997, UK sales totaled $4 million.

France

In 1995, the company entered France with great ambivalence. CEO Bob Holland was all for entering the French market, and the company sent off a container of product to Auchan, a major retailer to which Cohen was introduced through Social Venture Network ties. As global protests grew over French nuclear testing, though, there were discussions in the company about withdrawing from the French market or vocally protesting against the French government. With this internal disagreement concerning the French market, there was no marketing plan, no promotional support, and no attempt to address French labeling laws. The company hired a French public relations firm, noted for its alternative media and social mission work, and separately contracted with a sales and distribution company. But there was no plan and nobody from Ben & Jerry's to coordinate the French effort. In 1997, sales in France were just over $1 million.

Benelux

Ben & Jerry's entry into the Benelux market was also without strategic planning. In this case, a wealthy individual who had admired the company's social mission asked to open scoop shops, with partial ownership by the Human Rights Watch. By 1997, there were three scoop shops in Holland. Sales totaled a mere $287,000, but there was the prospect of using the product reputation from the scoop shops to launch supermarket and convenience store sales.

Summary of International Sales

In short, Ben & Jerry's fell into several foreign markets opportunistically, but without the consensus of the board and without the necessary headquarters staff to put together any kind of comprehensive plan. As the company had never developed a conventional marketing plan in the United States, it lacked the managerial skill to put together a marketing campaign for entering the foreign markets.

As a result, by 1997, Ben & Jerry's international sales totaled just 3 percent of total sales. While the company had nearly caught up with Häagen-Dazs in U.S. market share, Häagen-Dazs was light years ahead in the non-U.S. markets. With declining profits and domestic market share at Ben & Jerry's, it was beginning to seem time to give serious attention to international market opportunities.

FOCUS ON MARKET OPPORTUNITIES IN JAPAN

Background on the Market for Superpremium Ice Cream in Japan

In the 1994–96 period, when Ben & Jerry's was having its first taste of a hired professional CEO (Bob Holland), the company struggled with the prospects of strategically targeting a foreign market and developing a marketing plan for its fledgling overseas operations. In particular, the company made inquiries about opportunities in Japan, the

exhibit 5   Size of Japan's Ice Cream Market

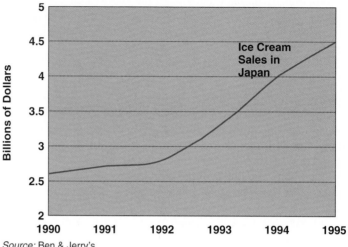

Source: Ben & Jerry's.

second largest ice cream market in the world, with annual sales of approximately $4.5 billion (see Exhibit 5). While the market was big, it was also daunting. Japan was known to have a highly complex distribution system driven by manufacturers, its barriers to foreign products were high, and the distance for shipping a frozen product was immense. Ben & Jerry's would be a late entrant, more than 10 years behind Häagen-Dazs in gaining a foothold in the market. In addition, there were at least six Japanese ice cream manufacturers selling a superpremium product. A major Japanese frozen desserts company, Morinaga Seika, had made proposals to Ben & Jerry's on two different occasions in 1995. In both cases the proposals were rejected. In January 1996, Morinaga actually conducted focus groups to evaluate Ben & Jerry's products. It was beginning to seem appropriate to take a closer look at the Morinaga proposals and other options.

Despite the challenges of entering Japan, that market had several compelling features. Japan was arguably the most affluent country in the world, Japanese consumers were known for demanding high-quality products with great varieties of styles and flavors (which practically defined Ben & Jerry's) and it seemed that the dietary shift toward more animal products was still under way. By 1994, Japan's 42-kilogram annual per capita consumption of milk was less than half that (103 kilograms) of the United States, and cheese consumption was about one-tenth that of the United States. Commercial dairy sales had really only taken off after World War II, when school lunch programs were initiated with milk as a regular component. Incomes in Japan increased dramatically from the 1950s to the 1980s so that animal-based food products and home refrigerators were affordable to a large number of people.

Though Häagen-Dazs's financial figures were not published by its parent, Grand Metropolitan, market intelligence suggested that the ice cream maker had Japanese sales of about $300 million, with Japan providing the highest margins of any of its markets. Häagen-Dazs had managed to capture nearly half the superpremium market in Japan. It entered the market as an imported product and later began production in Japan at a plant owned jointly by Häagen-Dazs, Sentry, and Takanashi Milk Products. About 25 percent of Häagen-Dazs's sales there appeared to be from scoop shops. In addition to gaining visibility through scoop shops, Häagen-Dazs operated a fleet of ice cream parlor buses (with upper-deck café tables) at exhibitions and other public gatherings. On the one hand, Häagen-Dazs would be a formidable competitor that would likely guard its market share. On the other hand, there would be no apparent need for Ben & Jerry's to teach the local

exhibit 6   Japanese Superpremium and Premium Sales by Package

	Brand	Size (ml)	Price (Yen)
Home cup	Bleuge	950	950
Pint	Häagen-Dazs	474	850
	Lotte	470	850
	Meiji	470	950
Personal cup	Häagen-Dazs	120	250
	Meiji	145	250

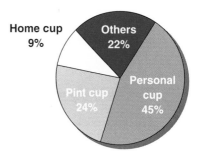

Source: Fuji Keizai Co.

market about superpremium ice cream. The market seemed to welcome imported ice cream, and expectations of falling tariffs on dairy products suggested new opportunities for ice cream imports from abroad. Häagen-Dazs's flavors in Japan were generally the same as those in the United States, with some modifications, such as reduced sweetness. While prices were attractive in Japan, about $6 per pint, it was unclear how much of that would go into the pockets of the manufacturer versus various distributors.

In contemplating an entry into the Japanese market, it was hard to avoid thinking about the case of Borden Japan. Borden introduced a premium ice cream to the market in 1971 through a joint venture with Meiji Milk. The product was highly successful, and Borden was leader of the category. In 1991, the Borden-Meiji alliance came to an end and Borden had extreme difficulty gaining effective distribution. Borden did not follow industry trends toward single-serving cups of ice cream, and it suffered greatly when distributors started lowering the price of the product, sending the signal to consumers that Borden was an inferior product. After sales had fallen by more than two-thirds in just two years, Borden withdrew from the Japanese market. Desserts were uncommon in Japan, leaving ice cream primarily for the snack market. Thus, single-serving cups (about 120 milliliters) became popular, accounting for about 45 percent of sales (see Exhibit 6), and ice cream came to be sold increasingly in convenience stores. By 1993, about a quarter of all ice cream sales were in convenience stores, compared to 29 percent in supermarkets (see Exhibit 7).

One concern at Ben & Jerry's was its size. With total worldwide sales of just over $150 million, it was very small in comparison to Häagen-Dazs, which had estimated sales of $300 million in Japan alone. At least five Japanese companies already in the superpremium market were larger than Ben & Jerry's, with leaders Glico, Morinaga, Meiji, and Snow Brand all having total ice cream sales three to four times that of Ben & Jerry's, and in each case ice cream was just part of the company's product line.

Cohen was not very enthusiastic about the sort of financial or managerial commitment that was apparently required to enter the Japanese market, and he couldn't see how entering that market fit in with the company's social mission. Others on the board shared his attitude. Two immediate problems were that entering Japan would not be the result of any social mission (the concepts of social mission and corporate charity being very foreign in Japan), and the company's lack of international success suggested that it may already have been spread too thin in too many countries. Jerry Greenfield, however, was interested enough to visit Japan on a market research tour in early 1996. The purpose was to see just how Ben & Jerry's might gain distribution if the company were to enter the Japanese market. Valerie Brown of Ben & Jerry's fledgling marketing department accompanied Greenfield. Contacts for the visit came primarily from Valerie's classmates at Harvard Business School, from a consulting company, and from the Japan External Trade Organization.

***exhibit* 7**   Japanese Ice Cream Market by Channel

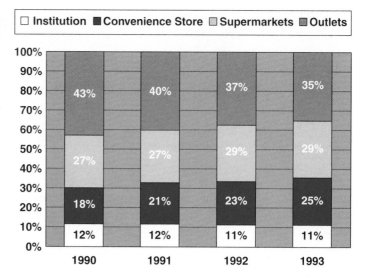

	Cumulative Annual Growth, 1990–93
Institution	−1.7%
Convenience stores	8.3
Supermarkets	1.8
Outlets	−4.4

Source: Ice Cream Data Book (Morinaga).

Alternative Strategies for a Ben & Jerry's Entry into Japan

In his visit to Japan, Greenfield was willing to consider entry into Japan through such diverse distribution channels as Amway Japan, Domino's Pizza, and department stores. One of his meetings was with the Japanese distributor of Dreyer's, the American company with partial ownership by the Swiss food giant Nestlé. Dreyer's, not being perceived as a direct competitor, was Ben & Jerry's largest distributor in the United States. Dreyer's had licensed its trademark with a joint venture operation in Japan in 1990. Sales had since fallen, and the joint venture seemed to have had difficulty with its biggest customer, Seven-Eleven Japan. The retailer's demands for just-in-time delivery required Dreyer's to maintain large inventories, and the retailer demanded the right to rapidly drop flavors that did not meet sales expectations.

Another meeting was with a high-level team of Seven-Eleven executives, including Masahiko Iida, the senior managing director, and Yasayuki Nakanishi, the merchandiser of the foods division. Iida expressed interest in selling Ben & Jerry's ice cream, suggesting that Ben & Jerry's could sell directly to Seven-Eleven, avoiding some of the distribution costs that are typical of the usual multilayer distribution system in Japan. On the other hand, a major American beverage distributor in Japan warned that it would be the kiss of death to enter the market through some kind of exclusive arrangement with a huge convenience store chain like Seven-Eleven. The balance of power would be overwhelmingly in the retailer's favor.

Meiji Milk Products (with $447 million of ice cream sales), in combination with its importer, the giant Mitsubishi Trading Company, expressed interest in distributing Ben & Jerry's products. This team clearly had very strong distribution resources, including an exclusive supply contract for Tokyo Disneyland. One concern was that Meiji already had a superpremium brand called Aya. Despite Meiji's strong interest, though, this option had probably become a long shot on account of earlier protests by Ben & Jerry's leadership of deforestation practices by another division of Mitsubishi.

Other marketing possibilities that had surfaced in 1996 included an arrangement with the advertising agency that had charge of Japan Airlines' in-flight entertainment, as well as a chance to open a scoop shop at a highly visible new retail development about to be built at Tokyo Disneyland. If anything, the many options, focus groups, and proposals made the decision about what to do with Japan even more difficult. The fact that the Ben & Jerry's board was divided on whether the company even had any business in a Japanese launch discouraged further action. By late 1996, Holland was following up discussions with a well-recommended Japanese American who was available to oversee marketing and distribution of Ben & Jerry's products in Japan. Ken Yamada, a third-generation Japanese American from Hawaii, had obtained the Domino's Pizza franchise for Japan. His compensation would be a margin on all sales in Japan. When Bob Holland's employment with Ben & Jerry's ended later in the year, Holland was still in discussion with Yamada, but he was still lacking the enthusiastic support of the board of directors for a possible entry into Japan.

A Fresh Look at the Options in Japan

Perry Odak assumed leadership of Ben & Jerry's in January 1997, inheriting the file of reports on possible strategies for entering the Japanese market. Neither the file nor institutional memory indicated much momentum leading toward any one of the Japanese strategies. In being hired, however, Odak had the board's agreement that the company's sales (and especially profits) must grow and that non-U.S. markets were the most likely key to that growth.

In February 1997, Odak added a business-related detour to a scheduled trip to Thailand with his wife. He stopped by Tokyo for a courtesy call to Mr. Iida, the president of Seven-Eleven Japan, a controlling parent company of Seven-Eleven U.S.[2] This was to more or less make up for Ben & Jerry's inability to send a CEO to a January "summit" meeting in Dallas at which Mr. Iida and the head of the U.S. Seven-Eleven operations had wished to meet face to face with the leaders of its major suppliers. Seven-Eleven U.S. was, in fact, Ben & Jerry's biggest retail outlet and Ben & Jerry's was a major supplier to Seven-Eleven.

After about 10 minutes of pleasantries at this introductory meeting at the Seven-Eleven headquarters in Tokyo, Iida asked Odak point blank: "Is there anyone at Ben & Jerry's who can make a marketing decision? We'd like to sell your product, but don't know how to proceed or with whom." Rather taken aback at this surprisingly direct inquiry, Odak replied that he could indeed make a decision and he resolved to sort through the options and get back to Iida in short order.

Back in Burlington, Odak installed Angelo Pezzani as the new international director for Ben & Jerry's Homemade. Odak had known Pezzani since 1982 when they both started work at Atari on the same day. Pezzani's position was then general consul of Atari Consumer Products Worldwide. Going over the options with Pezzani, it appeared that partnering with Yamada was still the strongest option for entering Japan, but the Seven-Eleven option had not yet been well developed for consideration. Yamada represented considerable strength with his Domino's success and with the fact that Domino's

---

[2]A brief explanation of the relationship between the Japan Seven-Eleven organization and the U.S. 7-Eleven organization is in order. 7-Eleven convenience stores originated in Texas in 1927 as a retail concept of Southland Corporation, which had been in the ice business. Southland began using the 7-Eleven banner in the 1950s because the stores would be open from 7 AM to 11 PM. The business grew through company-owned and franchised stores. Southland gave a master franchise for Japan to the Ito Yokado Company, a large supermarket operator there, which in turn established Seven-Eleven Japan to conduct the 7-Eleven business in Japan through company-owned and franchised stores. In the 1980s, Southland was in financial distress and Ito Yokado, along with its subsidiary, Seven-Eleven Japan, bailed out Southland, acquiring a controlling interest in the company. In this light, Odak's dinner with Iida in Japan constituted a sort of executive summit between Ben & Jerry's and its largest customer.

already offered ice cream cups as part of its delivery service in Japan. Possible draw-backs were his insistence on having exclusive rights to the entire Japanese market, with full control of all branding and marketing efforts there.

Pezzani and Odak decided to continue negotiations with Yamada, keeping that op-tion alive, and to simultaneously let Iida know that they wanted to explore options with Seven-Eleven. They requested an April meeting with Iida in Japan to move things along. The April meeting would include Mr. Nakanishi, the head of frozen ice desserts for Seven-Eleven Japan, and Bruce Bowman, Ben & Jerry's head of operations. To work out ground arrangements for the meeting, Odak and Pezzani needed someone on the ground in Japan. They called on Rivington Hight, an American who had learned Japanese in the U.S. intelligence service, married a Japanese woman, and lived in Japan for much of the past 30 years. No stranger to Odak or Pezzani, Hight had also worked for Atari in 1982 as president of Atari Japan. Like Odak and Pezzani, he had held a va-riety of management positions and consultancies in the years since.

The April meeting in Japan was basically intended to lay the framework to begin hashing out the many details that would be involved if Ben & Jerry's were to enter the Japan market through Seven-Eleven. It was a chance for the critical players in each com-pany to get together. Perry brought Pezzani, Bowman, and Hight. Arriving at the Ito-Yokado/Seven-Eleven headquarters building at the foot of Tokyo Tower, the Ben & Jerry's team walked into a lobby full of sample-laden salespeople and manufacturers nervously awaiting their chance to put their products on the shelves of some 7,000 stores. The receptionist quickly identified Odak and company and immediately put VIP pins on their dark lapels, directing them to the VIP elevator that went straight to the ex-ecutive suite on the 12th floor. A hostess there immediately guided the group across the plush white carpeting to a spacious meeting room, where they were served tea while awaiting Iida and Nakanishi. Odak arrived with more questions than answers, but he was determined that any product Ben & Jerry's might sell in Japan would be manufactured in Vermont, where the company had considerable excess capacity. Also, the costs of la-bor and raw dairy products were higher in Japan than the United States, so the 23.3 per-cent tariff and cost of shipping seemed not to be prohibitive. As a result of the Uruguay Round of the General Agreement on Tariffs and Trade (the former name of the World Trade Organization), the tariff would be reduced to 21 percent in the year 2000. The in-troductory meeting went well, but they had not yet addressed any of the difficult issues except to establish that it would be possible to export the product from Vermont to Japan.

Wrestling with the Details of the Seven-Eleven Option

Odak, Pezzani, and Bowman had a full plate of issues to resolve. The first question was market. Iida had said he was interested in Ben & Jerry's product because it was some-thing new to Japan and particularly unique with its chunks. Seven-Eleven had even tried to get a Japanese company to co-pack a chunky superpremium ice cream, but the Japanese packer was unsuccessful with its production processes. Research supporting a clear market for this novel product in Japan was scant, though it seemed unlikely that Seven-Eleven would commit shelf space to a product it had any doubt about and both Iida and Nakanishi certainly knew their market. A skeptical view of Seven-Eleven's in-terest in bringing Ben & Jerry's to Japan was that Seven-Eleven's combined U.S. and Japanese operations would become so important to Ben & Jerry's (potentially account-ing for a substantial portion of its sales) that Seven-Eleven could, in some fashion, control the ice cream maker. Even if that were not part of Seven-Eleven's motivation, it could be a concern.

While Ben & Jerry's management was leaning toward an entry into Japan, it was not a foregone conclusion. The entry would require a commitment of capital and managerial attention. As the product would be exported from the United States, there would be the risk of negative exchange rate movements that could make exports to Japan no longer feasible, thus making Ben & Jerry's financial picture less predictable. Commodity risk was also a serious concern in that the price of milk could rise in the United States, hurting Ben & Jerry's relative to competitors producing ice cream in Japan.

Assuming that an entry into the Japanese market was desirable, there were a number of apparent options for gaining distribution there, making it necessary to seriously consider the pros and cons of entering by way of Seven-Eleven. The most obvious pro was immediate placement in the freezer compartments of over 7,000 convenience stores in that country. In the early 1990s, the convenience store share of the ice cream market had increased and it appeared that these stores were now accounting for at least 40 percent of superpremium ice cream sales in Japan. Equally positive was the fact that Seven-Eleven had taken advantage of its size and its state-of-the art logistics systems by buying product directly from suppliers, avoiding the several layers of middlemen that stood between most suppliers and Japanese retailers. These cost savings could make the product more affordable and/or allow a wider margin to protect against such risks as currency fluctuation.

On the negative side, if the product was introduced to the market through a convenience store and it was just one of many brands there, would it be able to build its own brand capital in Japan as Häagen-Dazs had? Would the product essentially become a store brand? Without brand capital it could be difficult to distribute the product beyond the Seven-Eleven chain. An alternative approach of setting up well-located scoop shops, along with an effective marketing or publicity campaign, could give the product cachet, resulting in consumer pull that could give Ben & Jerry's a price premium as well as a range of marketing channels. Would committing to one huge retail chain be a case of putting too many eggs in one basket? A falling out between Ben & Jerry's and Seven-Eleven Japan could leave the ice cream maker with nothing in Japan. Even during discussions with Ben & Jerry's, the retailer was known to be terminating its supply agreement with the French ice cream manufacturer Rolland due to allegedly inadequate sales. Presumably Seven-Eleven could similarly cut off Ben & Jerry's at some future date.

While weighing the pros and cons of the business arrangement, there were also production issues Ben & Jerry's had to consider. Nakanishi insisted the ice cream be packaged only in personal cups (120 milliliters) and not the 473 milliliter (pint) size that Ben & Jerry's currently packed. The main argument for the small cups was that ice cream is seldom consumed as a family dessert in Japan, but rather is consumed as a snack item. A secondary argument was that, for sanitation purposes, customers liked their own individual servings. Cake, for example, was generally served in restaurants with each slice individually wrapped. Nakanishi's insistence was despite the fact that Seven-Eleven stocked Häagen-Dazs and some of its local competitors in both sizes.

Bruce Bowman embraced the challenge of designing a production system that would accommodate small cups that the company had never packed before. It seemed that about $2 million of new equipment would be needed, though it could be installed in the existing buildings. The sizes of some of the chunks would have to be reduced in order for them to not overwhelm the small cups. Besides requiring these known adjustments to production operations, Seven-Eleven might be expected to request other product changes. Japanese buyers were known for being particularly demanding in their specifications.

Ben & Jerry's had long been shipping ice cream to the West Coast and to Europe in freezer containers. Shipments to Japan were feasible, though the Seven-Eleven approach to just-in-time inventory procedures would make delivery reliability especially key and, of course, costs would have to be minimized. Logistics research indicated it would likely take at least three weeks' shipping time from the plant in Vermont (the St. Albans plant would be used if the Japanese plan was implemented) to the warehouse in Japan. Because of the Japanese label needed in Japan, production would have to carefully meet the orders from Seven-Eleven. The product could not be shifted to another customer, nor could another customer's product be shifted to Japan.

A number of sticky points needed to be resolved. In addition to changing the package size, Seven-Eleven wanted to provide its own design for the package art, and the design would definitely not include a photo of Ben and Jerry. Packaging had always been an important part of the Ben & Jerry's product. Funky lettering and the images of Ben and Jerry are part of what made the product unique. If Seven-Eleven were given control over the package art, what would that do to the benefits of developing a global branded product? Would consumers be confused about the placement of the product as they traveled? On the other hand, the carton designs had already been evolving somewhat and maybe a bit more evolution would satisfy Seven-Eleven. In fact, the earlier focus groups by Morinaga brought out the concern that it was too bad the "strange Ben & Jerry's packaging" had to detract from the good ice cream.

Ben & Jerry's sent a number of samples to consider and Nakanishi developed a short list that would be tested (if the deal went forward) in a couple dozen Seven-Eleven stores so that the top five flavors could be identified for the market entry. Chunky Monkey was near the top of Nakanishi's list, though the name absolutely had to change, he said. It turned out that only minor ingredient modifications would be needed to reduce the sweetness and to replace "vegetable gum" with "protein solids."

Through numerous communications and several meetings during the summer of 1997, a number of issues were discussed and resolved. For example, Seven-Eleven would acquire only a six-month exclusive right to Ben & Jerry's, and even that would be only for the specific flavors being sold to Seven-Eleven. Because of its relatively small size and inability to cover a loss, Ben & Jerry's was asking for sale terms that would transfer title (and all risk) for the product at the plant gate. It also was asking for 12 weeks' lead time on any order to allow for sourcing of ingredients, as well as efficient production scheduling. It appeared that these requests would not be too burdensome for Seven-Eleven. The sensitive issue of price was intentionally left until late in the discussions. Häagen-Dazs was being sold for 250 yen per 120 milliliter cup, and Seven-Eleven wanted to position Ben & Jerry's at a slightly lower price point. This would be problematic for Odak, who had recently increased the domestic price for Ben & Jerry's ice cream in part to support the product's position as equal or superior in quality to Häagen-Dazs.

A concern yet lurking in the boardroom in Burlington, Vermont, was what the company's social mission in Japan would be. Since the early 1990s, the company had moved beyond using its profit to fund philanthropy. The new imperative was to better the workplace, community, and world through regular day-to-day operations. On the other hand, profits were still needed in order to even have day-to-day operations, and a new market (such as that in Japan) could be the ticket to those profits. In the meantime, no particular social mission had emerged from the summer discussions of entering the Japanese market.

The Approaching Deadline for a Summer 1998 Launch in Japan

Odak and his staff had made steady progress narrowing and developing their Japanese options during the summer of 1997. If they were to enter the Japanese market for the summer 1998 season, though, they would have to commit to one plan or another no later than autumn 1997. Two distinct entry options had emerged.

The Yamada option was largely the same as it had been at the beginning of the year. His proposal was to have full control of marketing and sales for Ben & Jerry's in Japan. He would position the brand, devise and orchestrate the initial launch, and take care of marketing and distribution well into the future. He would earn a royalty on all sales in the market. By giving Yamada full control of the Japan market, Ben & Jerry's would have instant expertise in an otherwise unfamiliar market, as well as relief from having to address the many issues involved in putting together an entry strategy and in ongoing market management. Yamada knew frozen foods and had an entrepreneurial spirit and marketing savvy, evidenced by his success in launching and building up the Domino's Pizza chain in Japan. Giving up control of a potentially major market, though, could not be taken lightly. Because Yamada would invest his time in fleshing out and executing a marketing plan only after reaching agreement with Ben & Jerry's, there was no specific plan available for consideration. Even if there were, Yamada would retain the rights to change it. For the near term, however, Yamada would expect to add selected flavors of Ben & Jerry's ice cream cups to the Domino's delivery menu, providing an opportunity to collect market data based on customer response.

The Seven-Eleven option would leave Ben & Jerry's in control of whatever market development it might want to pursue beyond supplying Seven-Eleven in Japan. While Seven-Eleven would provide an instant entry to the market, the company would not be in a position to help Ben & Jerry's develop other distribution channels in Japan. The retailer thought it could sell at least six cups per day at each store, which would be the minimum to justify continuing to stock Ben & Jerry's. Looking at the size of Seven-Eleven's ice cream freezer cases suggested that this would require approximately 10 percent of Seven-Eleven's cup ice cream sales to be Ben & Jerry's products. Ben & Jerry's was as yet unknown in Japan, and it did not have the budget for a marketing campaign there. Sales would have to rely primarily on promotional efforts by Seven-Eleven, but the company was making no specific commitment for such efforts.

Another option was increasingly compelling—that of holding off on the market entry. Japan's economy was continuing to languish, with increasing talk that it could be years before recovery. A financial crisis that had commenced with a devaluation of Thailand's currency in July 1997 seemed to be spreading across Asia. If the pending Asian crisis hit an already weakened Japanese economy, the economics of exporting ice cream from Vermont to Japan could become infeasible.

Though the value of the yen had recently fallen to 125 yen to the dollar, Ben & Jerry's could still sell the product at the plant gate at an acceptable profit with room for both shipping expense and satisfactory margins for Seven-Eleven and its franchisees. If the rate went as high as 160 yen to the dollar, then the price in Japan would have to be raised to a level that might seriously cut into demand, especially relative to Häagen-Dazs, which had manufacturing facilities in Japan.

It would be a long evening meal as Odak, Pezzani, Bowman, and Hight gave their final thoughts to the decision before them. Not only had Odak promised Iida that he could make a decision, but Yamada needed an answer to his proposal as well. In any event, Ben & Jerry's had to proceed with one plan or another if it was going to have any Japanese sales in its 1998 income statement.

case 17 Viña San Pedro

David Wylie
Babson College

Viña San Pedro (VSP) was the third largest winery in Chile, with 1998 sales of 37 billion Chilean pesos (CP). Bonifacio Correa had planted the original vines with French stock in 1865 on the farm in Molina that the family had owned since 1701. For years, VSP wines enjoyed a reputation of being one of the finest in the country, and the vineyard remained in the Correa family until 1941. New owners expanded the vineyard so that by 1994, 1,150 hectares[1] were in production, making it the largest single-site vineyard in the country. It was, however, barely profitable and survived primarily by producing inexpensive wines for the domestic market.

COMPAÑA CERVECERIAS UNIDAS

In 1994, Compaña Cervecerias Unidas S.A. (CCU), a diversified beverage company that operated primarily in Chile and Argentina, purchased a 48.4 percent share of VSP stock for CP 7.8 billion. In 1992, CCU issued 4,520,582 American depository shares (ADSs) in an international American depository receipt (ADR) listed on the NASDAQ.[2] In 1996, it completed another ADR, thereby raising U.S. $155 million in additional capital. CCU shares also traded on the Chilean stock exchange. In 1998, CCU had sales of CP 280 billion and was the dominant player in the domestic beer market with a 91 percent market share. (See Exhibit 1 for CCU financial statements, Exhibit 2 for exchange rate information, and Exhibit 3 for inflation rates.) It was also the second largest beer seller in the Argentine beer market; the second largest Chilean soft-drink producer; the largest Chilean mineral water producer; and, with the acquisition of VSP, the third largest producer of wine in Chile. The management of CCU recognized VSP as a diamond in the rough.

CCU had been established in 1902 following the merger of two existing brewers. By 1916, it owned and operated the largest brewing facilities in Chile. It had also expanded its operations to include the production and marketing of soft drinks in 1907 and began bottling and selling mineral water products in 1960.

In 1986, following an economic crisis in Chile, Inversiones y Rentas was formed as a closed corporation to purchase the company out of receivership, and it still held 63 percent of the company. Inversiones y Rentas was owned 50 percent by Quiñenco S.A., a holding company beneficially owned by the Luksic family, and 50 percent by

Prepared under the supervision of Professors U. Srinivasa Rangan and Steve Allen of Babson College. The authors would like to thank the Institute for Latin American Studies at Babson College for its contribution to this effort.

[1]A hectare is 100 meters square, or about 2.5 acres.
[2]CCU traded on the NASDAQ under the symbol CCUUY.

exhibit 1   CCU Financial Statements (In Millions of Chilean Pesos as of
December 31, 1998)

	Consolidated Income Statement		
	1996	1997	1998
Revenues	252,019	272,477	280,111
Cost of goods sold	(122,694)	(126,200)	(127,643)
Selling, general, and administrative expenses	(98,366)	(103,076)	(107,849)
Operating income	30,959	43,202	44,618
Operating margin	*72.3%*	*15.9%*	*15.9%*
Nonoperating result	(4,823)	5,777	4,777
Taxes	(2,570)	(4,303)	(4,644)
Minority interest and others	(3,417)	(5,678)	(5,437)
Net income	20,149	38,998	39,315

	Consolidated Balance Sheet		
	1996	1997	1998
Current assets	152,487	208,932	217,493
Fixed assets	263,931	276,000	287,164
Other assets	44,404	50,656	62,726
Total assets	460,822	535,588	567,384
Current liabilities	79,136	89,830	82,334
Long-term liabilities	113,097	98,827	102,282
Minority interest	38,072	42,086	49,164
Shareholder equity	230,517	304,845	333,604
Total liabilities and shareholders' equity	460,822	535,588	567,384

	Segment Performance		
Consolidated Results	1996	1997	1998
Net revenues			
Beer Chile	113,794	117,972	117,081
Beer Argentina	24,868	35,213	37,746
Soft drinks & mineral water	92,718	90,699	88,063
Wine	20,024	28,237	36,825
Others	10,911	8,641	10,780
Intercompany transactions	(10,296)	(8,284)	(10,383)
Total	252,019	272,477	280,111

(*continued*)

Paulaner-Salvator Betwiligungs AG, a holding company for the Schörghuber Group.
All of the common stock was owned by private parties but was listed on the Chilean
Stock Exchange.

Quiñenco S.A. was engaged in a wide variety of businesses in Chile and Argentina.
It controlled more than 50 companies engaged in telecommunications, manufacturing,

exhibit 1   (*continued*)

Consolidated Results	Segment Performance		
	1996	1997	1998
Cost of goods sold			
Beer Chile	47,309	45,750	42,387
Beer Argentina	13,814	19,760	19,927
Soft drinks & mineral water	49,271	43,504	42,954
Wine	12,699	17,502	24,180
Others	9,898	7,968	8,577
Intercompany transactions	(10,296)	(8,284)	(10,383)
Total	122,694	126,200	127,643
Selling, general, and administrative expenses			
Beer Chile	42,307	42,345	40,931
Beer Argentina	11,510	15,033	20,218
Soft drinks & mineral water	36,327	36,323	36,056
Wine	6,884	8,168	9,400
Others	1,338	1,207	1,245
Total	98,366	103,076	107,849
Operating income			
Beer Chile	24,179	29,878	33,763
Beer Argentina	(457)	420	(2,399)
Soft drinks & mineral water	7,120	10,872	9,053
Wine	442	2,566	3,244
Others	(324)	(534)	958
Total	30,959	43,202	44,618
Operating margin	*12.3%*	*15.9%*	*15.9%*
Nonoperating results			
Financial income	3,185	8,302	11,577
Income from investments in related companies	2,132	2,142	880
Other nonoperating income	2,313	7,669	7,954
Amortization	(2,583)	(2,590)	(1,143)
Interest expenses	(7,995)	(7,039)	(7,429)
Other nonoperating expenses	(1,443)	(2,315)	(7,054)
Price-level restatement	(432)	(392)	(9)
Total	(4,823)	5,777	4,777
Income tax	(2,570)	(4,303)	(4,644)
Minority interest	(3,417)	(5,704)	(5,464)
Amortization of negative goodwill		26	27
Net income	20,149	38,998	39,315
Other relevant information			
Sales volumes (thousands of hectoliters)	8,681	9,312	9,471
EBITDA (Operating income + Depreciation + Amortization)	57,226	71,674	74,619
EBITDA Margin	*22.7%*	*26.3%*	*26.6%*

Source: CCU annual report, 1998.

exhibit 2　Historical Exchange Rates (Average Annual)

Year	CP$/U.S.$	U.S.$/CP$
1991	326	.00306
1992	346	.00289
1993	375	.00267
1994	418	.00239
1995	410	.00244
1996	412	.00243
1997	420	.00238
1998	455	.00220

Note: Official exchange rates of the Chilean peso were pegged to the U.S. dollar from 1975 to July 3, 1992, at a rate adjusted daily determined by monthly rates of national and world inflation. On January 26, 1992, the Central Bank revalued the peso, reducing the official dollar exchange rate by 5 percent, which meant that it dropped from 395 to 375 pesos. On July 3, 1992, in a move designed to halt currency speculation, Chile announced that the peso would no longer be measured exclusively against the dollar but rather would use a blend of the dollar, the German mark, and the Japanese yen in a 50-30-20 ratio.

exhibit 3　Consumer Price Index (Period Averages, Annual Percentage Rate)

	All Items	Food	Housing	Clothing
1992	15.5	18.0	14.4	15.4
1993	12.7	10.9	13.8	10.5
1994	11.4	9.8	12.2	3.0
1995	8.2	8.3	7.6	(1.2)
1996	7.4	6.1	7.7	(7.1)
1997	6.1	7.1	5.9	(4.7)

food processing and distribution, financial services, cable television, hotels, and commercial printing, altogether controlling approximately 6 percent of the Chilean gross national product. The Schörghuber Group's interests were more concentrated in Europe, with holdings primarily in other beverage companies, real estate, hotels, and aircraft leasing.

In 1994, CCU diversified its operations both in the international and domestic markets. In October, it purchased a 48.4 percent interest in Viña San Pedro. In November, it created the ECUSA joint venture with Argentinean bottler BAESA for the production, bottling, and marketing of soft drinks and mineral water products in Chile. It also acquired a 27 percent interest in a Croatian brewer, an interest that was increased to 43 percent by 1997.

THE EARLY YEARS OF CCU CONTROL

During the first few years of CCU control, management focused on reducing costs, increasing distribution, and increasing the quality of VSP wines. By 1995, debt had been reduced by CP 7.8 billion, CP 864 million had been invested in expanded capacity for aging wines, and CP 178 million had been invested in planting new vineyards for producing premium red wines. As a result of these added investments, CCU's total ownership position increased to 51.2 percent. Since new plantations took several years to become productive and higher quality wine required time to age, delivery of finished wine from its own vineyards remained level at about 11 million liters and was almost exclusively devoted to exports. The balance of 24 million liters was sold domestically and was created from grapes purchased from independent growers.

CCU had also assumed responsibility for the distribution of VSP wines in all but the most remote areas of Chile and quintupled the number of customers to 30,000. Domestic sales increased by 29 percent between 1995 and 1996, although a 5.5 percent rise in the average price for a case of wine sold had contributed to this increase. In 1996, after three years of losses, VSP finally boasted a profit of CP 305 million. (See Exhibit 4 for VSP financial statements.)

In 1997, Matias Elton joined VSP as president. A graduate of Georgetown University and experienced in the U.S. fruit importing industry, he was charged with the task of growing domestic market share, increasing quality to capture higher margin sales, expanding export sales, and achieving further economies of scale.

During Elton's first year, another CP 17.7 billion was invested to further increase capacity. New hectares of vineyards were acquired and planted, storage capacity increased to 36.3 million liters, and bottling capacity expanded from 22,600 to 25,100 bottles per hour. During the year, VSP's total production grew to over 44 million liters of wine, 45 percent of which was from its own vineyards. CP 8.2 billion was invested in vineyard (planting represented CP 4.5 million per hectare), CP 3.0 billion in vinification capacity, CP 819 million in aging capacity, and CP 5.6 billion in bottling capacity. Elton also reorganized the company so that each function had clear reporting responsibilities and to make Wilfred Leigh, the export manager, directly report to him rather than to the individual responsible for domestic sales. (See Exhibit 5 for an organization chart.)

In July of 1998, Patricio Jottar joined CCU as its new president. Armed with a clear vision for the company's future, he saw that while there might be some product cannibalization, further synergies could be gained among the CCU companies. Existing distribution capabilities of CCU could be further leveraged. Administrative expenses (human resources, legal, engineering, accounting, auditing) could be reduced with the use of common resources. Influence on regulatory bodies and lobbying efforts could be enhanced. Finally, knowledge about trends, prices, global markets, and retailers could be shared among all the CCU companies. Meanwhile, Jottar had implemented a new set of objectives for the company based on return on capital employed (ROCE) rather than just on profitability.[3]

THE WINE COUNTRY OF CHILE

Just south of Santiago, Chile, the central plateau opened between the mountains, boasting the perfect soil, drainage, and climate for grapes to flourish.[4] Traveling south along

---

[3]Jottar estimated the weighted average cost of capital to be 12 percent. Capital employed was defined as operating assets less operating liabilities.

[4]Thomas P. McDermott, Michael Amorose, and Gerwin Neuman, *A Catalog of Chilean Wines,* July 1997.

exhibit 4   VSP Financial Statements (Thousands of Chilean Pesos)

Balance Sheet		
	Fiscal Year Ending	
	December 31, 1998	**December 31, 1997**
Assets		
Cash and equivalents	378,388	1,004,285
Net receivables	9,015,694	5,241,443
Inventory	13,710,656	10,853,815
Prepaid expenses	52,484	75,530
Prepaid taxes	1,922,132	345,218
Other current assets	150,078	2,666,036
Total current assets	25,229,432	19,354,101
Land	5,585,210	3,407,403
Plant and equipment	13,959,211	11,262,972
Accumulated depreciation	5,744,390	4,945,413
Net property, plant, and equipment	13,800,031	9,724,962
Other long-term assets	15,371,155	6,244,174
Revaluation of long-term assets	3,202,659	3,291,692
Intangible assets	3,232,837	3,215,013
Total assets	60,674,472	42,662,168
Liabilities and shareholders' equity		
Accounts payable	4,141,784	3,850,157
Short-term debt and current long-term debt	13,560,048	6,163,769
Allowances and escrow	871,881	877,465
Income taxes payable	55,974	—
Payable to related businesses	3,945,518	8,605
Dividends payable	—	120
Other current liabilities	1,007,160	1,923,078
Total current liabilities	23,582,365	12,823,194
Long-term debt	9,920,870	5,055,874
Provision for risk and other charges	75,562	101,607
Minority interests	510	204
Total liabilities	33,579,307	17,980,879
Common stock	26,006,880	26,006,880
Capital surplus	1,089,436	1,089,436
Retained earnings	(1,151)	(2,415,027)
Common shareholders' equity	27,095,165	24,681,289
Total liabilities and shareholders' equity	60,674,472	42,662,168
		(continued)

the Pan American Highway, orchards gave way to vineyards that spread as far as the eye could see until they were interrupted by the snow-capped Andes Mountains on the east and the Cordillera Mountains, which parallel the Pacific ocean, on the west. (See Exhibit 6 for map of South America.) This region, only about 75 miles wide and 200 miles long, was considered to be the source of the choicest wines in Chile. Runoff from

exhibit 4   (*continued*)

Income Statement		
	Fiscal Year Ending	
	December 31, 1998	December 31, 1997
Net revenue	34,902,924	25,651,657
Cost of goods sold	24,087,037	16,957,841
Gross margin	10,815,887	8,693,816
Selling and general expenses	6,886,678	5,982,628
Operating income	3,929,209	2,711,188
Interest income	108,112	193,204
Other income and expenses—net	264,980	143,822
Interest expense	1,503,635	1,094,036
Monetary correction	(320,586)	244,392
Pretax income	2,478,080	2,198,570
Income taxes	63,899	5,560
Minority interest	305	43
Net income	2,413,876	2,192,967

Cash Flow Statement		
	Fiscal Year Ending	
	December 31, 1998	December 31, 1997
Beginning cash balance	3,670,321	1,673,022
Cash flow from operations	(5,005,034)	(660,308)
Increase in debt—net of payments	9,557,545	6,752,528
Increase in debt to related companies	3,585,581	—
Total cash flow from financing activities	13,143,126	6,752,528
Cash flow from capital expenditures	(11,261,154)	(3,940,222)
Total cash flow	(3,123,062)	2,151,998
Effect of inflation	(18,793)	(154,699)
Net cash flow after inflation	(3,141,855)	1,997,299
Ending cash balance	528,466	3,670,321

Note: The Chilean Cash Flow statement differs from that of the United States.

the snowfields of the Andes provided abundant irrigation, while the mountains along the coast protected the valley from too much direct rainfall. Toward the north, the hills were covered in sagebrush and cactus, and toward the south the climate became too cool and moist to nurture the best grapes. Small vineyards dotted the valley, nestled among dominant giants: Concha y Toro, Santa Rita, and Viña San Pedro.

Wine production in Chile dated back more than 400 years, but quality wines only began to appear in the first half of the 19th century after European vines were introduced. Beginning in 1860, European vineyards were ravaged for almost 30 years by the destructive phylloxera plague. Chile was left unaffected and, indeed, in 1998 was the only country in the world that continued to produce from original rootstock.

exhibit 5 The New VSP Organization

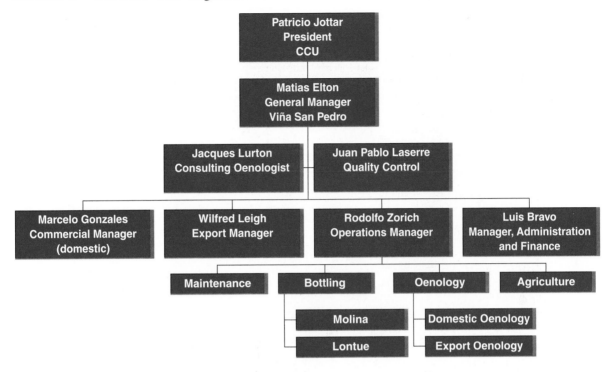

In 1938, new plantings were prohibited in an effort to curb alcoholism in the country, although by 1973, per capita consumption was still high, at 59 liters. The new Augusto Pinochet government, recognizing that wine could become an important export, lifted the ban in 1973, and both the quality and quantity of wine production grew. Better segmentation of grapes and selection practices by producers to create high-end labels allowed the creation of some very top-quality, higher priced labels in addition to the more popularly priced table wines and varietals. By 1997, total Chilean production had risen to 418 million liters, mainly from the introduction of better agricultural practices to enhance productivity and from the introduction of better processing technologies. There were about 61,000 hectares planted in vineyards in Chile by the end of 1997. Concha y Toro had 3,843 hectares, Santa Rita 2,057, and VSP 1,700. They had winemaking capacity of 107 million, 56 million, and 53 million liters, respectively.

While Pinochet had encouraged production in 1973, he also imposed a curfew that contributed to a drop in domestic consumption. By 1985, consumption had declined to 400 million liters, or 36.9 liters per capita, and by 1997 Chile's 15 million inhabitants consumed only 211 million liters of wine each year, or about 14.4 liters per capita. Industry analysts, however, expected consumption to increase by 4 percent per year, to 239 million liters by 2001. The domestic market had thus not offered great opportunities for growth among wineries. This market was extremely price-sensitive, and production became consolidated among the largest wineries that had the greatest economies of scale. Some smaller vineyards focused on producing premium wines. Others sold cheap wines within the very local "informal market," while still others were content to sell their grape production as raw material to the larger producers.

exhibit 6   Map of South America

Chilean wines proved to be a hit in the international market, particularly for lower cost wines. The ideal climate and isolation from those pests that often forced wine-makers to be aggressive with the application of pesticides contributed to quality. High yields and low labor costs provided a lower cost of production than in other countries. Chilean vineyards yielded more than twice the harvest of grapes from each hectare than European vineyards. Since winemaking was so labor-intensive, Chile's indus-try-friendly labor laws, low wages, and a labor union presence that was the lowest in the entire Western Hemisphere reduced the cost of labor. In addition, a strong national health care system allowed temporary labor to be readily available. Also, the seasonal difference from wine regions in the Northern Hemisphere gave Chile a unique advantage in marketing seasonal wines. The result of all this was a lower price for high quality—hence, good value.

By 1987, Chilean wines began attaining a level of quality acceptable by international oenophiles.[5] Exports of wine from Chile had grown from 11 million liters in 1987 to 43 million liters in 1990 to 207 million liters in 1997 as the average price per liter sold rose from $.62 to $1.86.

THE WINES OF VIÑA SAN PEDRO

VSP made a full range of wines, from the Gato brand at the low end to the award-winning Cabo de Hornos at the top end (see Exhibit 7 for a complete list of San Pedro wines). Generally, wines were classified as popular, varietal, and reserve. Like the other large wineries, VSP purchased grapes from local growers to be made into Gato and other popular wines destined for the domestic market. For the export market, however, it used only high-quality grapes from its own vineyards. In addition, it exported some wine in bulk to countries such as France where the cost of production was higher and bulk wine could be mixed with wine of domestic origin to add volume. Most countries allowed up to 10 percent of a wine to be of foreign origin while still being labeled as domestically produced.

The following table shows the VSP product sales mix in 1997 (in millions of liters):

	Popular	Varietal	Reserve	Bulk	Total
Export	.6	15.6	.3	2.0	18.5
Domestic	24.5	.8	.1	0.0	25.4
Total	25.1	16.4	.4	2.0	43.9

Gato

Gato wine was a popularly priced wine that was sold both in the domestic and export markets. For the domestic market, it was produced primarily from purchased "country" grapes and packaged in five-liter jugs, plastic/cardboard containers, and cardboard one-liter Tetra-Packs. Approximately 70 percent of VSP domestic sales were in Gato Tetra-Packs, 15 percent in jugs, and 9 percent in bottles. The remaining 6 percent of domestic sales were bottled varietal and reserve wines.

Gato wine was not aged but rather was packaged and sold as soon as fermentation was complete. For the export market, it was made from high-yield grapes from the company vineyards and packaged in bottles. The red wine was blended from cabernet-sauvignon and Merlot grapes, while the white wine was a combination of sauvignon and chardonnay grapes. An average hectare for the production of Gato wines produced about 17.9 tons of grapes per year, and the company estimated that it required about $1.56 million in working capital for every million liters of Gato wine.

---

[5]Lovers or connoisseurs of wines.

exhibit 7   Viña San Pedro Wines

Name	Category	Brand	Packaging	Size (cc)	Retail Price ($U.S.)
Cabo de Hornos	Premium	San Pedro	Bottle	750	39.10
Castillo de Molina	Reserve		Bottle	750	10.90
Seleccion del Directorio	Reserve	Santa Helena	Bottle	750	7.60
35 Sur	Varietals		Bottle	750	6.50
Siglo de Oro	Varietals	Santa Helena	Bottle	750	4.30
Gato	Year Wine		Bottle	750	3.30
Urmeneta	Year Wine		Bottle	750	3.50
Gran Vino	Year Wine	Santa Helena	Bottle	750	2.20
Gato	Year Wine	San Pedro	Carton	1,000	2.10
Santa Helena	Year Wine	Santa Helena	Carton	1,000	1.60
Etiqueta Dorada	Year Wine	San Pedro	Carton	1,000	1.30
Gato	Year Wine	San Pedro	Jug	5,000	9.80
Santa Helena	Year Wine	Santa Helena	Jug	5,000	7.60
Etiqueta Dorada	Year Wine	San Pedro	Jug	5,000	5.40

Other lines of San Pedro popular wines included Etiqueta Dorada and Santa Helena Gran Vino.

Varietal

Varietal wines were each made from a single variety of grape and aged for up to a year in stainless-steel tanks before being bottled and sold. The grapes used were from VSP's own vineyards that yielded about 12.7 tons per hectare.

VSP varietal wines included Castillo de Molina, 35 Sur, a higher-priced Gato, Siglo de Oro, and a Santa Helena Gran Vino.

Reserve

Reserve wines were often a blend of several different varieties of grapes, and again made only from grapes from VSP's own vineyards. These vineyards received special treatment in order to raise the proportion of grape skins to pulp, since the skins imparted a richness to the flavor of the wine. These grapes, therefore, were stressed at certain intervals to impede growth. Consequently, these vineyards only produced about eight tons per hectare. Reserve grapes were all hand-picked, and those destined for white wine were all picked at night to reduce the added oxidation that occurred with exposure to the sun. To add flavor, the wine was fermented in large oak casks rather than stainless-steel tanks. Reserve wines required a longer aging period, usually in either French or American oak barrels, depending on the flavor desired. The wine was further aged in bottles to allow the tannins to blend into the wine. The wine was not sold for two years after harvest.

Reserve wines in the VSP portfolio included a Castillo de Molina; Las Encinas (a special dry white reserve wine); and the top of the Santa Helena line, Seleccion del Directorio.

Premium Reserve

At the top of the scale was the premium reserve wine, Cabo de Hornos. While very little of this wine was produced, it allowed the winery to boast of its winemaking capabilities, a stature that was frequently confirmed in international wine competitions. The small vineyard dedicated to the premium reserves produced only about 10.7 tons per hectare. Again, these wines were aged in oak barrels and again in bottles, taking three years before being sold.

VINICULTURE

The prevailing sentiment was that while quality was not everything, it remained "number one, two, and three" in importance. Jacques Lonton was the oenologist from France who was brought in to consult in developing broad product definition strategies and to fine-tune final mixing formulas. He told the VSP managers that he thought that the quality of wines was derived 80 percent in the fields in growing the grapes, 15 percent in vintification, and the rest in "art."

Not all vines were treated equally. Growing techniques varied according to subtle variations in soil and irrigation conditions and climatic differences between fields depending on where they lay in the valley floor. Even more important were the kind of grapes being grown and the quality of grapes desired. Certain grapes needed more sunlight than others and might be planted in rows at different angles to the sun, pruned so that the leaves created different shade patterns, or irrigated at varying intervals or intensity according to the amount of water content for the grapes which the oenologist had specified. Some vines might be irrigated frequently and during periods of maximum grape growth in order to maximize volume. Others required more irrigation at peak growth periods for the vines in order to encourage more foliage to protect the grapes from the sun.

Picking grapes was a science unto itself. As the grapes matured, the sugar content of grapes was monitored by Bernard Fresius, the head agriculturist, to help decide exactly when the harvest should occur according to the type of wine desired and the type of grapes. Grapes for the lower grade wines could be harvested mechanically. In contrast, some varieties of grapes and those for the higher grades of wine needed to be picked by hand and indeed might require harvesting in several waves to make sure that only clusters that were at the ideal level of ripeness were harvested.

Fresius was the only employee to actually live at the vineyard. He occupied a renovated farmhouse overlooking the vineyards and mountains with his wife and two young children. While his formal role was to translate the specifications for grapes required for the following season into growing strategies, he constantly monitored the condition of the vines. Usually he patrolled the vineyards in his car, but it was not unusual to find him on horseback, riding down the rows while stopping frequently to examine a shoot, new leaf, or ripening cluster of grapes. He had graduated from agricultural school and, while he only had to take the exam to become a licensed oenologist, he preferred to stay in the vineyards and leave the oenology to the five full-time oenologists who designed the wines and monitored their fermentation, mixing, and aging to assure the required taste, quality, and complexity.

Fresius developed the annual plans for the vineyards, which were then interpreted into monthly plans by the two agronomists who reported to him. Each had responsibility for 600 hectares. Three agrarian technicians reported to each agronomist. They prepared weekly plans for the 200 hectares under their control. Four full-time laborers and four tractor drivers reported to each agrarian technician. These individuals prepared and managed the daily vineyard plans for the 44, on average, seasonal laborers. Seasonal labor worked about 37,000 man days each year, peaking during the three two-month periods devoted to pruning, canopy management, and harvesting. They were paid an average of about $11.25 per day. The total cost to the company was a little more than $17.25 per day after health insurance contributions and administrative costs.

Machines were available and could be used for some of the operations like canopy management and harvesting, but they were expensive: about $130,000 each. They could each handle about 150 hectares, doing the work otherwise done by about 80 laborers, but since the work came in distinct waves, usually it was more cost-effective to rent the machines and pay, on average, $300 per hectare per year in rental fees. Hiring laborers to do the same work, in contrast, cost $650 per hectare per year. The following table shows the growing costs per hectare in 1997 (in thousands of Chilean pesos):

	Reserve Wines	Varietal Wines	Gato Wines
Manual labor	398	379	423
Consumables	121	164	175
Machine	94	163	142
Total	613	706	741
Liters/Hectare	10,684	12,716	17,948

VINIFICATION

After the grapes were harvested in March, they were loaded into bins at the end of each row of vines and trailered in to the winemaking facility. There, a machine de-stemmed and gently crushed the grapes to release the juice, or "must."

For red wines, the must and skins were transferred into fermentation vats made either of stainless steel or wood. For white wines, sulfur dioxide was first added to the must to prevent oxidization that would result in a less fruity wine. Sediment was removed from the must before it was transferred into the fermentation vat.

There, grape sugar was converted into alcohol through the action of natural yeast found in grape skins (or sometimes by the addition of special yeast strains).

Alcoholic fermentation for red wines took place over a period of 5 to 10 days. Most red wines were fermented to complete dryness, with little or no residual sugar remaining. Alcoholic fermentation for white wine lasted longer than for red (12 to 15 days) and at cooler temperatures so that more of the juices' natural aromas were retained. Letting all of the grape sugar turn into alcohol made dry white wines.

Some wines were then "macerated," or left to soak with the skins, pulp, and dead yeast cells (together called "marc") for up to 18 days, during which time the alcohol extracted pigment, tannins, and flavors from the marc.

After fermentation and maceration, if specified, the fermented grape juice (called free-run wine) was separated from the marc. Then the marc was pressed to extract any remaining wine. This wine, called "vin de presse," had highly concentrated flavors, tannins, and colors and could be blended back into the wine to achieve the desired style and flavor.

Sometimes, red wine went through an additional fermentation process known as secondary fermentation, which converted naturally occurring malic acid to lactic acid.

exhibit 8   Sales History of VSP (Volume in Millions of Liters)

Year	Domestic	Export	Total
1995	18.0	9.4	27.4
1996	23.8	11.6	35.4
1997	25.4	18.6	44.0
1998	28.7	23.1	51.8

This lowered a wine's acidity and made it softer and more pleasant to drink. In white wine production, malolactic fermentation risked lowering the wine's acidity too much, so it had to be accomplished with great skill and subtlety.

The next stage was clarification. The wine was filtered and run through a centrifuge to separate the clear wine from any remaining particles.

The final stage of the vinification process was blending, where the winemaker combined wines made from different grape varieties and vats to create the desired bouquet, style, and flavor of wine. This stage was completed in August.

Popularly priced wines were ready to be bottled and sold immediately. The varietal wines were bottled and aged for several months before being sold. Reserve wines, however, required further aging. Red wine could be aged for up to two years in oak barrels to impart structure, additional tannin, and flavor. Finally, it was bottled and stored in cellars for further aging or shipped to distributors. Aging was much shorter for white wines than for reds. Some was aged for up to one year in oak barrels to give it additional structure and flavor; however, most white wines were bottled within a year after harvest.

More complex white wines such as Viña San Pedro "Encinas" required a special treatment. It, like its red counterpart, was aged for up to two years in oak barrels to increase richness before bottling and distribution.

THE MARKET FOR VSP WINES

Historically, VSP's sales had been almost exclusively domestic, but as export sales grew it was becoming very clear that the future for VSP profitability was in that market. In 1998, it had leap-frogged from being the number five exporter to being number two with sales of 23.1 million liters, second only to Concha y Toro (see Exhibit 8). VSP had proven that it could produce wine at a level of quality that was acceptable to the international community. While its Cabo de Hornos wine was the clear leader in terms of quality and price, very little was produced. Its primary purpose was to prove VSP's capabilities. Most of the wine exported was in the lower price range.

The economics of the export market was very different from that of the Chilean market. The greater need for marketing and the higher cost of buying grapes from independent producers drove domestic profitability into negative territory, while the less marketing intensive wines produced from VSP's own grapes were very profitable (see Exhibit 9). For the larger vineyards that purchased much of their grape requirements from independent growers, the inflation-adjusted cost in pesos to purchase grapes for wine production had risen almost 400 percent between 1992 and 1998 from $.50 per liter to $1.25 in just the last two years. In contrast, the actual production cost of grapes

exhibit 9   Cost-profit Economics of VSP Wine Production, as a Percent of Total Sales Revenues

	Domestic	Export
Sales	100%	100%
Production costs		
Wine	56	25
Packaging	20	20
Labor	4	4
Total production cost	80	49
Gross margin	20	51
Marketing	10	2
Overhead	20	20
Profit (loss)	(10%)	29%

exhibit 10   Grapes Purchased*

	1996	1997	1998	1999	2000	2001	2002	2003
Own grapes used for exported wines	100%	60%	50%	60%	65%	70%	70%	70%
Grapes purchased as % of total production		41%	52%	52%	49%	47%	46%	38%

*Actual 1996–1998, forecast for 1999–2003.

remained at only $.34 per liter. Meanwhile, domestic wine prices did not increase at the same pace, placing a strong squeeze on margins.

Elton planned to tackle the situation on two fronts. First, the vineyards that were being planted would come into production in the next several years, driving the cost down and quality up (see Exhibit 10). More aggressive marketing and a more flexible packaging technology would drive domestic promotions to gain market share. This market, however, did not promise the growth of the export market. In the fast-growing export market, sales of those wines that could be sold in the same year as the harvest would be promoted to drive cash flow. Then slowly, higher quality, higher priced, and higher margin wines would be introduced into markets where VSP wines had become accepted.

DOMESTIC MARKET

Domestic sales of wine were dominated by three vineyards with 52.1 percent of the market: Concha y Toro, Santa Rita, and VSP (see Exhibit 11). The rest of the market was highly fragmented among a number of smaller wineries. While the so-called formal market paid an 18 percent value-added tax and a 15 percent alcohol excise tax, an informal market of small vineyards that avoided these tax burdens was about a quarter the size of the formal market.

The domestic market was less quality-conscious than the export market and was more sensitive to price. Of all domestically sold wine, 70 percent was sold in cardboard *exhibit 11* Domestic Market Share

Winery	1997	1998
Concha y Toro	23.5%	24.0%
Santa Rita	17.0	21.1
Viña San Pedro	11.6	10.7
Total	52.1%	55.8%

exhibit 12 Prices and Market Share of Major Brands of One-Liter Cardboard Containers of Wine

Brand	Winery	Retail Price (CP)	Market Share*
Santa Rita 120	Santa Rita	1,062	8.3%
Clos Pirque	Concha y Toro	1,012	6.4
Santa Carolina	Santa Carolina	992	0.2
Ochagavia	Santa Carolina	970	0.6
Gato	San Pedro	996	4.7
Fressco	Concha y Toro	819	1.3
Santa Helena	San Pedro	787	4.1
Bodega 1	Santa Rita	783	3.3
Etiqueta Dorada	San Pedro	762	1.5
Planella	Santa Carolina	761	2.6
Santa Rita Carrera	Santa Rita	733	1.3
Fray Leon	C. Vieja	732	1.1
San Jose	Tocornal	711	1.4
Tocornal	Concha y Toro	797	3.9
Grosso	FCO de Aguirrre	669	1.6
Total			42.3%

*Share of total Chilean wine market, September 1998.

containers, 20 percent in five-liter jugs or plastic/cardboard containers, and 10 percent in bottles. The average price for wine in cardboard containers was only $1.75, while only 14 percent of bottled wine sold for less than $2.20. Of bottled wine, 73 percent was sold at prices ranging from $2.20 to $4.40 (see Exhibit 12).

VSP domestic sales were concentrated in cardboard containers with 87.7 percent of sales, with only 4.5 percent in bottles, 5.5 percent in jugs, and 2.3 percent in plastic/cardboard containers. Its average price for wine sold in cardboard containers was CP 952 per liter, about 5 percent lower than the other market leaders. Consumer research revealed, however, that consumers perceived the wines of VSP competitors to be of somewhat better quality than those of VSP, even though VSP was the only winery in the group which produced a full range of wines.

Marketing practices varied among the leaders, with Santa Rita spending about 46 percent of total Chilean wine marketing expense, Concha y Toro 29 percent, and VSP only 3 percent. Marketing expenditures were concentrated in newspaper and magazine advertising, point of purchase, and billboards.

VSP distributed its wine in Chile exclusively through the CCU distribution network except in the most remote regions. CCU maintained a sales force of 500 people, had 20 warehouses around the country, and kept a delivery fleet of 450 trucks. Of its sales, 74 percent were beer, 21 percent soft drinks, and 5 percent wine. Eighty-one percent of the wine sold was on a cash basis, while the remaining 19 percent was sold on a 30-days-payable basis.

The base of VSP customers had grown from about 6,000 to over 30,000 through the efforts of the CCU distribution system. Of its sales, 37 percent were directly to retailers, 23 percent to wholesalers who sold to smaller retailers, 23 percent to supermarkets, and 12 percent to bars and restaurants.

VSP's objective for the domestic market within four years was to capture a 20 percent market share in the cardboard-carton market and an 8 percent share in the bottled-wine market. The net result would be attaining a total domestic market share of 15 percent. This meant an increase of 11 million liters over the next five years.

Clearly this was an aggressive set of goals, but marketing executives were confident that they could pull it off. While one key element of the strategy was to increase the marketing budget to 12 percent of sales with a message promoting the quality of its wines, the primary tool was to differentiate VSP wines with the use of a new cardboard packaging system.

All of the major wineries used a system called Tetra-Pack, which fed rolls of printed cardboard into a machine which created the box, filled it with wine, and sealed it. While the system was inexpensive to operate on a per unit basis, it was quite inflexible. Each machine had to be devoted to a single-size box. VSP had been approached by SIG Combibloc, a German competitor of Tetra-Pack. VSP had negotiated an exclusive agreement for use of the Combibloc system in Chile until 2001. This system allowed a single machine easily to bottle different package sizes. The company would provide the machines at no cost to VSP as long as VSP purchased the collapsed boxes from them. (See Exhibit 13 for description of Combibloc system.)

VSP marketing executives saw the use of the Combibloc system as an innovative approach to differentiating their wines in the marketplace. They hoped that a promotion aimed at increasing the perception of quality and a new program to sell 1.1-liter boxes for the same price as competitors were selling 1.0-liter boxes would net a significant gain in market share.

EXPORT MARKET

In 1998, over 90 Chilean vineyards exported wine, but the 4 largest vineyards accounted for 65 percent of that amount. Most of these vineyards competed on the basis of good value since they had a cost/quality advantage over other producing countries. The smaller vineyards tended to target the higher end of the market, while the larger vineyards targeted the larger part of the market that demanded better quality at lower prices.

Indeed, exports accounted for much of the growth of VSP in recent years. VSP managers were quick to admit that the character of the individual markets were the most important component of exporting, but that finding and maintaining good relationships with importers was crucial. VSP did virtually no advertising in other countries, leaving *exhibit 13*   The Combibloc System

---

The new combibloc filling machine generation: Efficient—compact—easy handling

The new machine generation from SIG Combibloc International GmbH is setting new standards in the aseptic filling sector: With an output of 10,000 to 12,000 beverage cartons per hour—depending on the format—the combibloc system is currently the fastest aseptic filler worldwide.

Four-track operating mode

Speed alone is not everything: The machines also offer high efficiency. Since this is combined with simple operation and maintenance, the new filling machine generation can really help to lower customers' filling costs. The high filling rates are primarily achieved by the four-track operating mode.

The new machine generation, like the old, is suitable for filling a wide variety of products, ranging from juice and milk to water and wine.

Optimized production

A reduction in operating costs is guaranteed, for instance, by shorter preparation and cleaning times and longer production times. For example, the time needed to prepare for production is cut by 30 minutes as a result of simultaneous sterilization of the filling machine (with H_2O_2) and the filling station (with steam) as well as a reduction in the number of parts that have to be installed. Optimization of the cleaning process reduces personnel time by a further 30 minutes. This is due to:

● Easy access for cleaning and operating staff
● Automatic coupling device for CIP and sterilization
● Simultaneous cleaning of filling system and filling machine
● Hygienic design of the aseptic zone

In addition, the new filling technology offers low-foam filling. Consequently there is no need for a defoamer. Depending on the product, continuous production times of more than 44 hours can be achieved in this way.

The lower service costs also make an important contribution towards reducing costs. In spite of its high performance, the new machine generation is less susceptible to wear—because fewer moving parts are used and, of course, on account of the four-track operating mode. Exchangeable modules also lead to shorter maintenance times.

Other advantages of the new filling machine generation from SIG Combibloc are ease of handling, computer-aided control (by touch screen) and, last but not least, the low space requirement of the machines. Carton off-take to one side—in the case of four-track operation—also saves space and simplifies installation of downstream systems such as the tray packer.

Size flexibility

Like all other combibloc machines, the new filling machine generation offers all the well-known advantages of the combibloc system, for instance, size flexibility: This means that each machine can be converted for up to five different carton sizes within just a few minutes.

With the new filling machine generation, SIG Combibloc offers attractive arguments for marketing aseptic products. This is because the new filling machines can optimize production conditions for filling companies and, consequently, improve competitiveness.

Source: www.combibloc.com.

the responsibility for selling to the importers and to the wholesalers who were their customers. In 1998, VSP exported through 64 agents to 49 countries. Typically, importers took a 20 percent markup as did wholesalers. The retailer added a 26 percent markup, on average, to wines (see Exhibit 14 for the economics of export sales). One of the

exhibit 14   Value Chain Economics of Wine Exporting (In U.S. Dollars)

Retail price	**$10.00**	
Retail markup	2.06	26.0% of wholesaler price
Wholesaler price	7.93	
Wholesaler markup	1.32	20.0% of importer price
Importer price	6.61	
Importer markup	1.10	20.0% of vineyard price (revenue)
Gross revenue to vineyard	5.51	
Export cost		
Commissions, freight, duty	0.22	4.0% of vineyard revenue
Foreign marketing	0.11	2.0
Administrative costs—exports	0.11	2.0
Total export cost	0.44	8.0
Net revenue to vineyard	5.07	92.0
Allocated export costs	0.55	10.0
Financial costs and monetary correction	0.22	4.0
Contribution from sales	4.30	78.0
Cost of sales		
Raw material	1.54	28.0
Direct materials	1.65	30.0
Direct labor	0.11	2.0
Depreciation	0.11	2.0
Total cost of sales	3.42	62.0
Net profit from exports	$ 0.88	16.0%

advantages of selling wines in the popular price range was, VSP marketers thought, that there was less need for promotional activity, particularly in a market that was largely driven by price. (See Exhibit 15.)

On the negative side, export sales were subject to the volatility of exchange rates, often making planning more difficult. This was especially critical at VSP since expenses were almost entirely denominated in Chilean Pesos, while export revenues were denominated in a number of different currencies. (See Exhibit 16).

Exports to Japan represented a major opportunity, but was somewhat muted by a recent downturn in economic conditions there. Japanese consumers had begun to appreciate higher quality imported wines and consumption had risen to .5 liters per person per year in 1995. By 1998, it had risen to 1.4 liters, but much of this increase was in lower priced wines. This was the demand that had driven VSP's success in Japan as exports to the Pacific Rim had risen from 4 percent of its total exports in 1996 to 15 percent in 1998. Per capita consumption was expected to increase further by 2001 to 2.2 liters, still below the three-liter world average.

The United States and Canada appeared to be particularly ripe markets for expansion. There, VSP sales had grown to 2.6 million liters in 1998, primarily driven by sales on the West coast of the United States. The strategy was to continue to build *exhibit 15*   History of VSP Exports (Number of Nine-liter Cases)

	1994	1995	1996	1997	1998	1999 (4 months)	1998 Price/Liter*	Market Share†
England	61	159	194	393	546	121	$2.00	16.9%
United States	92	79	116	166	284	146	1.89	5.8
Japan	4	4	13	67	253	25	2.49	7.8
Sweden	61	84	90	111	145	53	1.93	27.2
Paraguay	176	215	180	208	139	23	1.58	54.3
Finland	39	70	120	162	131	39	2.24	56.4
Brazil	82	70	71	129	118	6	2.00	38.2
Holland	14	63	62	78	118	8	2.02	21.3
Canada	74	94	89	88	97	37	1.85	10.7
Venezuela	19	52	59	69	85	13	1.92	28.4
Other countries	151	157	296	599	648	212	1.98	
Total	773	1,047	1,290	2,070	2,564	683	$2.01	

*Price per liter expressed in U.S. $ at average exchange rates for 1998 (CP 455 per U.S. $).

†To be read: 1998 market share by volume of Viña San Pedro wines as percentage of Chilean bottled wine sold in the country. For example, Viña San Pedro wines held a 16.9% market share of Chilean wines exported to England in 1998.

exhibit 16   Exchange Rates in Major Export Countries

Country	Currency	1994	1995	1996	1997	1998	1999
England	Pound	632.9	628.9	628.9	719.4	724.6	781.3
United States	Dollar	429.2	403.2	404.9	423.7	440.5	469.5
Japan	Yen	3.8	4.0	3.9	3.7	3.3	4.2
Sweden	Krona	10.5	53.9	61.2	61.7	55.2	58.7
Paraguay	Guarani	0.2	0.2	0.2	0.2	0.2	0.2
Finland	Markka	73.7	84.7	93.1	91.8	80.6	93.6
Brazil*	Real		476.2	416.7	416.7	393.7	389.1
Holland	Guilder	237.0	226.8	228.3	238.7	247.5	264.6
Canada	Dollar	326.8	287.4	299.4	307.7	308.6	307.7
Venezuela	Bolivar	4.0	2.4	1.4	0.9	0.9	0.8

Note: Exchange rates expressed in Chilean pesos per foreign currency on the first day on each year.

*On July 1, 1994, the "real" replaced the "cruzeiro real" at a rate of 1:2,750.

strong distributor relationships and market share in new areas with sales of Gato wine. The resultant brand recognition and cash flow would smooth the way towards maintaining market share in popularly priced wines while introducing higher priced varietal and reserve wines. (See Exhibits 17 and 18.) Specifically, the goal was to increase their percentage of export sales into the United States from 11 percent in 1998 to 20 percent by 2001. This meant an increase from 3.4 million 750cc bottles to 7.2 million bottles. (See Exhibit 19 for wine sales in various international markets and Exhibit 20 for summary of major importers and exporters of wine).

exhibit 17   1997–2001 Export Strategy*

	1997	1998	1999	2000	2001
Volume (millions of liters)	18.6	23.1	27.7	37.4	46.7
Market share					
Volume	8.6%	9.0%	11.0%	13.0%	15.0%
Value	8.1	8.7	9.3	10.5	11.2
Mix by segment					
Popular	93.2	84.0	82.0	78.5	75.0
Varietal	4.9	12.0	13.0	14.5	15.0
Reserve	1.9	4.0	5.0	7.0	10.0
Mix by container					
Bottles	87.6	93.0	93.0	94.0	95.0
Others	12.4	7.0	7.0	6.0	5.0
Mix by region					
United Kingdom, United States, Canada	33.0	32.2	35.4	43.0	50.0
Latin America	22.0	20.4	16.9	14.0	12.0
Europe and Asia	45.0	47.4	47.7	43.0	38.0
Marketing as % of sales	2.2	2.1	4.0	5.0	5.0

*Actual for 1997–1998, planned for 1999–2001.

exhibit 18   Export Objectives for VSP

Variety	1997	2001
Reserve	1.9%	7.0%
Varietal	4.9	14.5
Popular	93.2	78.5

Competing in the United States was a challenging proposition. There was heavy competition in the popularly priced segment from wineries such as fellow Chilean winery Concha y Toro, which sold about 50 percent of its exports to the United States, and the California based giant, Gallo, which had over 30 percent share of the U.S. market and spent over half of the total amount spent on advertising wine in the country.

LOOKING TO THE FUTURE

By early 1999, the new vines were just beginning to bear fruit as the expanded winery was being completed. As Elton prepared his objectives for the next few years, several unresolved issues still remained. How fast should he push the growth of the company? Should he wait for the success of the recent investments in capacity to be proven or forge ahead? If he pushed into foreign markets, where should that effort be focused and *exhibit 19*   Still Wine Sales in Major Markets by Value (U.S. $ Billion)

	1992	1993	1994	1995	1996	CAGR[†] 1992–1996	1997	1998	1999	2000	2001	CAGR[†] 1997–2001
France	7.81	8.46	8.80	9.01	9.30	4.5%	9.60	9.85	10.08	10.29	10.55	2.4%
United States	5.94	6.51	6.88	7.19	7.40	5.7	7.55	7.70	7.84	7.98	7.61	1.8
United Kingdom	4.06	4.61	5.24	5.54	6.05	10.5	6.42	6.80	7.20	7.61	8.02	5.7
Italy	4.30	4.42	4.50	4.60	4.69	2.2	4.81	4.97	5.13	5.29	5.44	3.1
Germany	3.93	3.65	3.73	3.79	4.26	2.3	4.28	4.34	4.40	4.48	4.55	1.5
Argentina	1.10	1.15	1.35	1.49	1.58	9.6	1.67	1.77	1.89	2.02	2.17	6.8
Austria	1.21	1.29	1.38	1.43	1.48	5.2	1.52	1.57	1.64	1.70	1.78	4.0
Greece	0.71	0.82	0.87	1.11	1.33	17.2	1.45	1.58	1.73	1.88	2.04	8.9
Canada	1.05	1.09	1.20	1.26	1.30	5.5	1.36	1.43	1.50	1.58	1.65	5.0
Australia	0.81	1.01	0.96	1.03	1.16	9.9	1.25	1.34	1.45	1.55	1.66	7.4
Russia*	0.00	0.17	0.35	0.83	0.98	1184.4	1.21	1.46	1.72	1.98	2.24	16.7
Belgium	0.76	0.78	0.78	0.81	0.82	1.9	0.78	0.75	0.72	0.69	0.66	−4.1
Switzerland	0.73	0.73	0.75	0.76	0.77	1.3	0.74	0.73	0.71	0.69	0.67	−2.5
Sweden	0.68	0.68	0.76	0.76	0.74	2.3	0.79	0.84	0.89	0.95	1.01	6.3
Poland	0.29	0.34	0.44	0.50	0.61	20.6	0.69	0.79	0.89	1.00	1.12	12.9
Portugal	0.62	0.56	0.56	0.55	0.55	−2.9	0.54	0.52	0.51	0.50	0.49	−2.4
Spain	0.43	0.48	0.51	0.55	0.55	6.4	0.55	0.56	0.57	0.58	0.59	1.8
Japan	0.46	0.42	0.38	0.36	0.45	0.4	0.47	0.50	0.53	0.55	0.58	5.4
South Africa	0.39	0.40	0.43	0.44	0.45	3.7	0.45	0.46	0.46	0.47	0.48	1.6
Chile	0.37	0.37	0.36	0.33	0.36	−0.5	0.38	0.40	0.42	0.45	0.47	5.5

*Value distorted by currency instability.
[†]CAGR = Compound average growth rate.
Source: Euromonitor.

exhibit 20   Major Importers and Exporters of Wine, 1995
(In Millions of Liters)

	Imports	Exports
Germany	877	230
United Kingdom	639	0
France	600	1,140
Russia	300	0
United States	275	133
Spain	236	626
Belgium	230	0
Netherlands	188	0
Switzerland	187	0
Canada	148	0
Denmark	130	0
Japan	108	0
Italy	0	1,583
Argentina	0	215
Bulgaria	0	190
Moldova	0	166
Portugal	0	155
Chile	0	129
Hungary	0	127
Australia	0	115

with what products? The big concern was what might happen if the market continued to grow beyond expectations. If supply were low, VSP might be forced to allocate production among importers and jeopardize carefully nurtured relationships. In addition, he now had to meet the new ROCE objectives.

case | 18 Campbell Soup Company in 2000

John E. Gamble
University of South Alabama

Arthur A. Thompson, Jr.
University of Alabama

As the new millennium began, Campbell Soup's CEO, Dale Morrison, was wrestling with how to get the company's underperforming business portfolio back on track and satisfy shareholder expectations of a steadily rising stock price. Morrison was the third CEO in recent years to struggle to develop a diversification strategy for Campbell that could produce attractive growth in revenues and profits. Under two prior CEOs, George McGovern and David Johnson, Campbell's business portfolio had been re-vamped, but the gains in performance had proved temporary and the overall results somewhat disappointing. Now the challenge to restore luster to Campbell's business lineup and build shareholder wealth rested with Dale Morrison.

Going into 2000 Campbell Soup Company was one of the world's leading manu-facturers and marketers of branded consumer food products, with approximately 24,500 employees, 1999 revenues of $6.4 billion, 30 manufacturing plants in six nations, and over 2,000 products on the market. Its major brands in the United States were Campbell's flagship red-and-white label canned soups, Prego spaghetti sauces, Godiva chocolates, Pepperidge Farm baked goods, V8 vegetable juices, Swanson broths, Franco-American canned pastas, and Pace Mexican salsas. Arnott's baked goods and Home Pride sauces were the best-selling Campbell brands in various international markets.

COMPANY BACKGROUND

The company was founded in 1869 by Joseph Campbell, a fruit merchant, and Abram Anderson, an icebox maker, and was originally known for its jams and jellies. In 1891 it was incorporated as the Joseph Campbell Preserve Co. in Camden, New Jersey. John T. Dorrance, a brilliant 24-year-old chemist with a PhD from the Massachusetts Insti-tute of Technology, was hired by the company in 1894 and three years later developed a process for canning soup in condensed form. The new process took water out of the soup during the canning process and thus dramatically reduced production and distrib-ution costs. Soups made with the new production process were awarded the gold medal at the 1900 Paris Exhibition and by 1905 were selling at the rate of 40,000 cases per week. John T. Dorrance purchased the company in 1900, and it was entirely owned by his family until 1954. It was reincorporated as the Campbell Soup Company in 1922.

When John Dorrance died in 1930, he left an estate of over $115 million—the nation's third largest at that time. He also left a company devoted to engineering, committed to providing good products (in recessions it would rather shave margins than cut back product quality or raise price), and obsessed with secrecy. His successor, John T. Dorrance Jr., headed the company for the next 24 years (1930–54) and few, if any, important decisions were made at Campbell without his approval. In 1954, the company went public, with the Dorrance family retaining majority control. In 1999, the Dorrance family still owned about 50 percent of Campbell's stock and, despite having relinquished direct management control, still exerted considerable shareholder influence. Four of Campbell Soup's 16 board members were grandchildren of John T. Dorrance Sr.

Over the years Campbell had diversified into a number of businesses—Swanson frozen dinners, Pepperidge Farm bakery products, Vlasic pickles, Franco-American spaghetti products, Recipe pet food, various fast-food restaurant chains, Godiva chocolates, and even retail garden centers. However, canned soup had always remained Campbell's core business. The company had had three chief executive officers over the last 20 years, and its corporate strategy had evolved with each change in leadership. The company's diversification strategy and new investment priorities had shifted as each new CEO pursued a course to build value for Campbell Soup Company's shareholders.

THE GORDON McGOVERN ERA: 1980–89

Gordon McGovern was in business school when Margaret Rudkin, founder of Pepperidge Farm, spoke to his class. She told how she had built her bread company from scratch in an industry dominated by giants. McGovern was impressed. He wrote to Rudkin for a job, received it in 1956, and began his climb through Pepperidge Farm's ranks. When Campbell acquired Pepperidge Farm in 1961, it had sales of $40 million and had only reached $60 million when McGovern became Pepperidge Farm's president in 1968. When McGovern was named president of Campbell in 1980, Pepperidge Farm's annual sales had grown to $300 million under his leadership. McGovern implemented several key elements of Pepperidge Farm's strategy when he took over at Campbell: creativity and a willingness to experiment, emphasis on new product development, and building strong competencies in marketing.

McGovern's Corporate Strategy as Campbell's CEO

During the McGovern years, Campbell's strategic focus was on the consumer. The consumer's "hot buttons" were identified as nutrition, convenience, low sodium, attractive price, good quality, and unique products—and managers were urged to press those buttons. Business unit managers were expected to be responsive to consumer perceptions, needs, and demands regarding nutrition, safety, flavor, and convenience. Key business unit strategies included (1) improving operating efficiency, (2) developing new products to capitalize on consumer trends, (3) updating advertising for new and established products, and (4) continuing Campbell's long-standing emphasis on high production standards and premium-quality products.

Early in his tenure, McGovern developed a five-year plan that featured four financial performance objectives: a 15 percent annual increase in earnings, a 5 percent increase in volume, a 5 percent increase in sales (plus inflation), and an 18 percent return on equity by 1986. The two cornerstones of McGovern's growth strategy were (1) developing and introducing new products and (2) making acquisitions every two years that would bring in $200 million in annual sales. Campbell's acquisition strategy was to look for small, fast-growing food companies strong in product areas where Campbell had no presence and companies on the fast track that were in rapidly growing product categories or industries. Under McGovern, Campbell made a number of acquisitions:

1982

- Mrs. Paul's Kitchens, Inc., a processor and marketer of frozen prepared seafood and vegetable products, with annual sales of approximately $125 million (acquired at a cost of $55 million).
- Snow King Frozen Foods, Inc., engaged in the production and marketing of a line of uncooked frozen specialty meat products, with annual sales of $32 million.
- Juice Bowl Products, Inc., a Florida producer of fruit juices.
- Win Schuler Foods, Inc., a Michigan-based producer and distributor of specialty cheese spreads, flavored melba rounds, food service salad dressings, party dips, and sauces, with annual sales of $6.5 million.
- Costa Apple Products, Inc., a producer of apple juice retailed primarily in the eastern United States, with annual sales of $6 million.

1983

- Several small domestic operations, at a cost of $26 million, including:
  —Annabelle's restaurant chain of 12 units in the southeastern United States.
  —Triangle Manufacturing Corp., a manufacturer of physical fitness and sports medicine products.

1984

- Mendelson-Zeller Co., Inc., a California distributor of fresh produce.

1985

- Continental Foods Company SA and affiliated companies, which produced sauces, confectioneries, and other food products in Belgium and France; the cost of the acquisition was $17 million.
- A 20 percent ownership interest in Arnott's Ltd., an Australian producer of cookies and crackers.

1988

- Freshbake Foods Group, a British producer of baked goods.

Campbell's Business Portfolio under McGovern

During the McGovern era, Campbell Soup Company was organized into six business units—Campbell U.S., Pepperidge Farm, Vlasic Foods, Mrs. Paul's Kitchens, Other United States, and International. Sales and profit performance by division are shown in Exhibit 1.

The Campbell U.S. Business Unit   In 1989 the Campbell U.S. division was the company's largest operating unit, accounting for just over 50 percent of corporate revenues. The Campbell U.S. division was divided into eight profit centers: soup, frozen foods, grocery, beverage, food service, poultry, fresh produce, and pet foods.

exhibit 1 Performance of Campbell's Divisions under Gordon McGovern, 1980–89 ($ Millions)

	1989	1988	1987	1986	1985	1984	1983	1982	1981	1980
Campbell U.S.										
Sales	$2,776	$2,584	$2,445	$2,507	$2,500	$2,282	$1,987	$1,773	$1,678	$1,608
Operating earnings	175	272	284	302	292	278	250	211	190	205
Pepperidge Farm										
Sales	548	495	459	420	426	435	433	392	329	283
Operating earnings	54	58	54	46	39	35	43	41	35	29
Vlasic Foods										
Sales	441	353	283	263	199	193	168	149	137	130
Operating earnings	39	30	22	24	16	14	13	12	10	8
Mrs. Paul's Kitchens										
Sales	140	150	153	141	138	126	108	—	—	—
Operating earnings	0.4	(4)	10	8	11	14	10	—	—	—
Other United States*										
Sales	—	—	59	76	81	84	64	56	27	35
Operating earnings	—	—	(2)	(7)	(3)	(2)	(1)	(1)	(1)	1
International										
Sales	1,527	1,037	898	766	716	624	599	643	694	512
Operating earnings	($ 81)	$ 58	$ 69	($ 61)	$ 35	$ 34	$ 33	$ 46	$ 46	$ 33

*Division eliminated in 1988 and replaced with a new division named Campbell Enterprises.

Source: Campbell's annual reports.

[Handwritten notes:] Not performing well.

[Handwritten note at bottom:] Get rid of fresh bake foods (U.K.) and Italian businesses.

Exhibit 2 shows the brands Campbell had in this division and the major competitors each brand faced during most of the 1980s.

The soup business group alone accounted for more than 25 percent of the company's consolidated sales (as compared to around 50 percent in the 1970s). Campbell's flagship brands of soup accounted for 80 percent of the $1 billion–plus annual canned soup market; in 1989, Campbell offered grocery shoppers over 50 varieties of canned soups. Heinz was the second largest soup producer, with 10 percent of the market. Heinz had earlier withdrawn from producing Heinz-label soups and shifted its production over to making soups for sale under the private labels of grocery chains; Heinz was the leading private-label producer of canned soup, holding almost an 80 percent share of the private-label segment.

Although the soup business was relatively mature (McGovern preferred to call it underworked), Campbell's most ambitious consumer research took place in this unit. McGovern opted to grow Campbell's soup sales by turning out a steady flow of new varieties in convenient packages: "Ethnic, dried, refrigerated, frozen, microwave—you name it, we're going to try it."[1] In 1985, Campbell entered the $290 million dry-soup-mix market dominated by Thomas J. Lipton Inc., a business unit of Unilever. Dry-soup sales in the United States were growing faster than sales of canned soup. Lipton's aggressive response to test marketing of an early Campbell dry-soup product resulted in Campbell's rushing a six-flavor line into national distribution ahead of schedule.

In 1982 McGovern caused a stir when he announced publicly that Campbell's Swanson TV-dinner line was "junk food": "It was great in 1950, but in today's world it didn't go into the microwave; it didn't represent any variety or a good eating experience to my palate."[2] Over the past five years, Swanson's sales volume had slipped 16 percent. He maintained that consumers had discovered better-quality options to the TV-dinner concept. Campbell's frozen foods group answered the challenge by creating a new frozen gourmet line, LeMenu. Campbell committed about $50 million in manufacturing, marketing, and trade promotion costs when initial market tests of the LeMenu line proved encouraging.

LeMenu products—packaged on round heatable plates and featuring such selections as chicken cordon bleu, al dente vegetables, and sophisticated wine sauces—produced 21 percent growth in the frozen meal unit, with sales of $150 million during its first year of national distribution (1984), double Campbell's sales projection. In addition, the Swanson line of TV dinners was overhauled to put in less salt and more meat stock in gravies, add new desserts and sauces, and create new packaging and a redesigned logo.

The grocery business unit's star was Prego spaghetti sauce. By 1984 the Prego brand had captured 25 percent of the still-growing spaghetti sauce market, becoming the number two sauce, behind Ragu. A Prego Plus spaghetti sauce line was introduced in 1985.

Pepperidge Farm   Pepperidge Farm was Campbell's third largest division in 1989, with 10 percent of the company's consolidated sales. Although the division was one of Campbell's best performers during the late 1970s (with sales rising at an average compound rate of 14 percent), by the mid-1980s growth had slowed and a number of newly introduced products had produced disappointing results (Star Wars cookies, Vegetables in Pastry). To remedy the division's weak performance, a number of steps were taken:

---

[1]As quoted in *Business Week,* December 24, 1984, p. 67.

[2]Ibid.

exhibit 2   The Campbell U.S. Division: Products, Rival Brands, and Competitors as of 1985

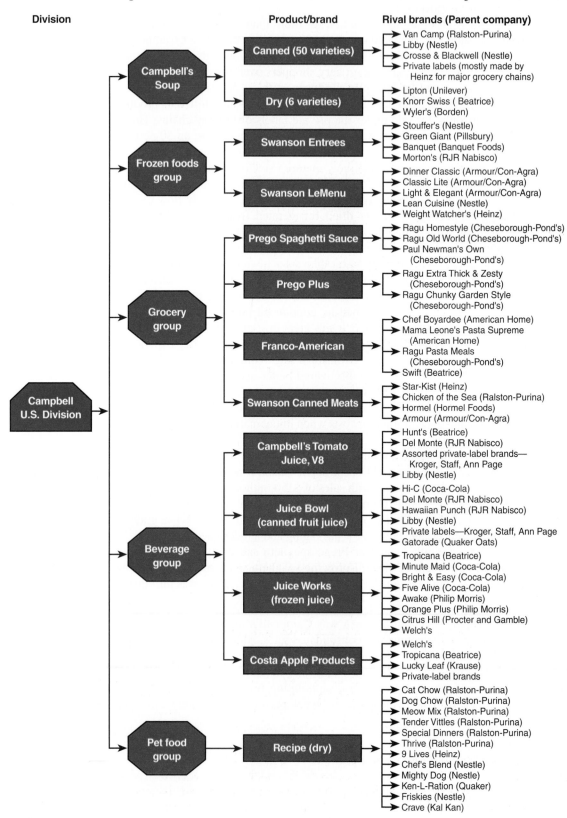

exhibit 3   The Pepperidge Farm Division: Products, Rival Brands, and Competitors in 1985

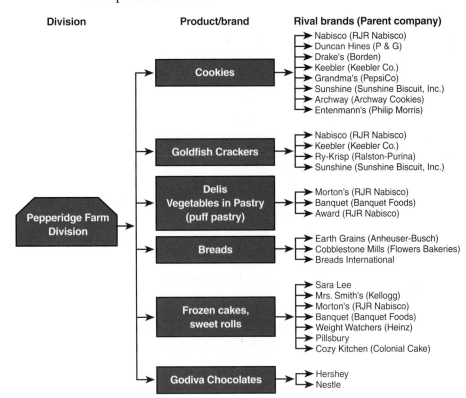

Division	Product/brand	Rival brands (Parent company)

Pepperidge Farm Division

Cookies
- Nabisco (RJR Nabisco)
- Duncan Hines (P & G)
- Drake's (Borden)
- Keebler (Keebler Co.)
- Grandma's (PepsiCo)
- Sunshine (Sunshine Biscuit, Inc.)
- Archway (Archway Cookies)
- Entenmann's (Philip Morris)

Goldfish Crackers
- Nabisco (RJR Nabisco)
- Keebler (Keebler Co.)
- Ry-Krisp (Ralston-Purina)
- Sunshine (Sunshine Biscuit, Inc.)

Delis Vegetables in Pastry (puff pastry)
- Morton's (RJR Nabisco)
- Banquet (Banquet Foods)
- Award (RJR Nabisco)

Breads
- Earth Grains (Anheuser-Busch)
- Cobblestone Mills (Flowers Bakeries)
- Breads International

Frozen cakes, sweet rolls
- Sara Lee
- Mrs. Smith's (Kellogg)
- Morton's (RJR Nabisco)
- Banquet (Banquet Foods)
- Weight Watchers (Heinz)
- Pillsbury
- Cozy Kitchen (Colonial Cake)

Godiva Chocolates
- Hershey
- Nestle

- The Costa Apple Products unit, acquired in 1982, was transferred to the Campbell U.S. beverage group.
- Pepperidge Farm divested itself of operations that no longer fit into its strategic plan, including Lexington Gardens, Inc., a garden center chain.
- Deli's Vegetables in Pastry went back into research and development to improve quality.
- A new management team was put in place and a comprehensive review of each product was initiated.

Exhibit 3 shows Pepperidge Farm's product portfolio during the 1980s.

Vlasic Foods   Vlasic, Campbell's fourth largest division, was the leading producer and marketer of pickles and relishes in the United States, with a 31 percent market share. During the 1982–84 period, Vlasic also had responsibility for Win Schuler Foods, a Michigan-based maker of cheese spreads, melba rounds, party dips, sauces, and salad dressings. Win Schuler was purchased in 1982, and its products were marketed in several states in the upper Midwest. When sales of the Win Schuler unit flattened in 1984, partly due to a sagging Midwest economy, McGovern transferred the unit to the refrigerated foods group in the Campbell U.S. business division.

In 1985 Vlasic implemented new labels that used color bands and a new flavor scale to help consumers find their favorite tastes quickly on the supermarket shelf. Following up on marketing research indicating consumer desires for new and interesting flavors, Vlasic had introduced Zesty Dills and Bread and Butter Whole Pickle lines in

1985. Heinz was Campbell's leading national competitor in this area, but there were a number of important regional and private-label brands that competed with Heinz and Vlasic for shelf space.

Mrs. Paul's Kitchens   The Mrs. Paul's business unit produced frozen fish entrees, frozen breaded vegetables, and frozen chicken nuggets. When Campbell acquired Mrs. Paul's in 1982, it was rumored that Heinz and Pillsbury, among others, were considering the same acquisition. In 1983, the Mrs. Paul's division responded to consumer preferences for convenience seafood products that were nutritious, low in calories, microwavable, and lightly coated by introducing Light & Natural Fish Fillets. Quality improvements were also made in existing products, and a promising new product line, Light Seafood Entrees, was introduced in 1984. Market share increased about 25 percent over 1983, and Light Seafood Entrees went national in 1985. This line, which featured seven varieties of low-calorie microwavable seafood dishes, accounted for 11 percent of 1985's volume. However, sales of the company's established product lines of breaded seafood items eroded in the years following acquisition because these items had to be fried in cooking oil prior to serving. Revenues had dropped in both 1988 and 1989, and the division was barely profitable in 1989 (see again Exhibit 1).

Campbell's Other United States Business Unit   Grouped into the Other United States business division were Triangle Manufacturing Corporation, a health-and-fitness products manufacturer; Campbell Hospitality, a restaurant unit that operated 59 Pietro's restaurants, 15 Annabelle's restaurants, and 6 H. T. McDoogal's restaurants; and Snow King Frozen Foods, Inc., a manufacturer of frozen specialty meat products. Triangle's best-known product line was The Band wrist and ankle weights, which had the number two position in its market category, with a market share of 14 percent. Triangle was trying to build on its strength by entering the exercise equipment market and by selling its products internationally. The Campbell Hospitality division struggled through most of the 1980s to sustain sales and earnings growth. Snow King was also a weak performer. In 1988, this division was reorganized and renamed Campbell Enterprises; it included Triangle Manufacturing; Godiva International; V8 and Campbell Juices; Campbell Food Services; Snow King Frozen Foods; and Pietro's, Annabelle's, and H. T. McDoogal's restaurant chains. All three restaurant chains were divested in 1989.

Campbell's International Business Unit   The International business unit was Campbell's second largest division throughout the 1980s and accounted for about one-fifth of corporate revenues in 1989. Campbell International had subsidiaries in about 12 foreign countries as of 1989 and had plans to expand further. The division was reorganized in 1985 to build a more solid base for sales and earnings growth. McGovern's goal was for the International division to contribute 25 percent of Campbell's corporate sales and earnings. His strategy was to develop and strengthen Campbell's presence in international markets and to make Campbell a premier international company.

A number of acquisitions were completed in 1989 to strengthen Campbell's international competitive position. The Habitant soup and pickle brands, the Laura Secord brand of jams, and a refrigerated distribution company were all acquired by Campbell's Canadian subsidiary. In Europe, Campbell acquired a German specialty food importer and an Italian producer of institutional foods. Also during 1989, the company increased its ownership in Australia's leading cookie company, Arnott's Ltd., to 32 percent; acquired 50 percent ownership in an Australian juice manufacturer; and obtained complete ownership of Melbourne Mushrooms. The International division's three biggest profit contributors in 1989 were Campbell Soup Canada, the European food and confectionery group, and the operations in Australia.

Even though the company had a number of successes internationally, Campbell management had encountered some difficulties. Campbell's Italian business suffered losses during 1989 as a result of excessive costs brought on by an aggressive and poorly controlled attempt to build market share. Campbell was also having difficulty with making its recently acquired Freshbake Foods unit profitable. The UK food processing company was struggling to absorb a number of acquisitions it had made prior to its acquisition by Campbell in 1988. Campbell management found it necessary to institute an extensive restructuring process at Freshbake, including closing a number of plants.

McGovern's Approach to Managing Campbell's Business Portfolio

Every Saturday morning McGovern did his family's grocery shopping, stopping to straighten Campbell's displays and inspect those of competitors, studying packages and reading labels, and trying to learn all he could about how and what people were eating. He encouraged his managers to do the same. Several board meetings were held in the backrooms of supermarkets so that afterward directors could roam the store aisles interviewing customers about Campbell products.

McGovern decentralized Campbell management to facilitate entrepreneurial risk taking and new product development, devising a new compensation program to reward these traits. He restructured the company into some 50 autonomous units, each with the leeway to develop new products even if the new product ideas were closely related to another business unit's products. Thus, the Prego spaghetti sauce unit—not the frozen food group—initiated frozen Mexican dinners. And although it wasn't his job, the director of market research created Today's Taste, a line of refrigerated entrees and side dishes. "It's like things are in constant motion," the director said. "We are overloaded but it's fun."[3]

McGovern believed the new structure encouraged managers of business units, who had to compete for corporate funding, to be more creative and venturesome in developing promising products:

> These business divisions allow the company to really get its arms around chunks of the business. The managers are answerable to the bottom line—to their investments, their hiring, their products—and it's a great motivation for performance.[4]

As part of this motivation, Campbell began annually allotting around $30 to $40 million to support new ventures and the creation of new product families; it often took $10 million to develop and test new products. In addition, it took $10 to $15 million in advertising and couponing to launch a new brand. McGovern believed a special new product venture fund was needed to encourage managers to think big in terms of new product development. He emphasized that it was no disgrace to fail if the effort was a good one. High failure rates were common in the industry—only about 20 percent of new products lasted more than one year on the market—but Campbell's failure rate on

---

[3]As quoted in *The Wall Street Journal,* September 17, 1984, p. A10.

[4]*Advertising Age,* January 3, 1983, p. 38.

new product introductions was running even higher. In fact, during the 1980s, only about one out of eight new Campbell products reaching the market was successful.

Every Friday morning McGovern held meetings to discuss new products. The fact-finding sessions were attended by financial, marketing, engineering, and sales personnel. Typical McGovern questions included: "Would you eat something like that?" "Why not?" "Have you tried the competition's product?" "Is there a consumer niche?"[5]

McGovern's New Product Development and Marketing Strategies

McGovern instituted a number of internal changes to make Campbell's product development strategy produce the desired results. Much revolved around efforts to enhance the sophistication of Campbell's corporate marketing strategies and approach to marketing research. Under McGovern, Campbell's market research unearthed several findings and projections that drove the company's product development effort:

- Women comprised 43 percent of the workforce (with a level of 50 percent projected by 1990).
- Two-income marriages represented 60 percent of all U.S. families and accounted for 60 percent of total family income.
- Upper-income households would grow 3.5 times faster than the total household formations.
- More than half of all households consisted of only one or two members; 23 percent of all households contained only one person.
- More and more consumers were exhibiting a growing preference for refrigerated and fresh produce over canned and frozen products.
- The percentage of meals eaten at home was declining.
- Nearly half of the adult meal planners in the United States were watching their weight.
- Poultry consumption had increased 26 percent since 1973.
- Ethnic food preparation at home was increasing, with 40 percent, 21 percent, and 14 percent of households preparing Italian, Mexican, and Oriental foods, respectively, at home from scratch.
- There was a growing consumer concern with food avoidance: sugar, salt, calories, chemicals, cholesterol, and additives.
- The "I am what I eat" philosophy had tied food into lifestyles that embraced exercise machines, hot tubs, jogging, racquetball, backpacking, cross-country skiing, and aerobic dancing.

In response to growing ethnic food demand, Campbell began marketing ethnic selections in regions where consumer interests for particular food types were strong. For instance, it marketed spicy Ranchero Beans only in the South and Southwest, and its newly acquired Puerto Rican foods only in New York City and Florida (which had sizable Puerto Rican populations).

---

[5]*The Wall Street Journal,* September 17, 1984, p. A10.

Campbell's product-development guidelines emphasized convenience, taste, flavor, and texture. The strategic themes McGovern stressed were these:

- Concentrate on products that represent superior value to consumers and constantly strive to improve those values.
- Develop products that help build markets.
- Develop products that yield a fair profit to Campbell.

In pursuing these guidelines, Campbell adopted several operating practices:

- Using ongoing consumer research to determine eating habits; this included checking home menus, recipes, and food preparation techniques to learn which food items were served together.
- Studying meal and snack occasions to learn which household members participated so that preliminary estimates of volume potential could be made for possible new products and product improvement ideas.
- Testing new or improved products in a large enough number of households across the United States that reliable national sales projections could be made. Once a product met pretest standards, testing in a sample of supermarkets and sales outlets was conducted.
- Rolling out the new products on a regional or national plan and using test-market data to establish the sequence in which area markets should be entered.

By 1983 McGovern's strategy had turned Campbell into the biggest generator of new products in the combined food and health-and-beauty aids categories, with a total of 42 new products. Prego spaghetti sauce, LeMenu frozen dinners, Great Starts breakfasts, and Chunky New England Clam Chowder were among the leading products introduced by Campbell Soup during the early 1980s. Meanwhile Campbell's marketing budget grew from $275 million in 1982, to $488 million in 1985, and to $552 million in 1989. Ad expenditures jumped from $67 million in 1980 to $197 million in 1989. Prior to McGovern, Campbell often trimmed ad spending at the end of a quarter to boost earnings.

In 1982 McGovern was named *Advertising Age*'s Adman of the Year for his efforts in transforming Campbell into "one of the most aggressive market-driven companies in the food industry today."[6] *Advertising Age* cited the company's emphasis on nutrition and fitness as opposed to the former "mmm, mmm, good" emphasis on taste. Print ads featured government studies concerning soup's nutritional values and a new slogan, "Soup is good food."

Production, Quality, and Cost Considerations during the McGovern Era

Gordon McGovern also stressed the importance of high production quality; a 1984 article in *Savvy* quoted him as saying, "I want zero defects. If we can't produce quality, we'll get out of the business." That same year, Campbell held its first Worldwide Corporate conference dedicated to quality. Hundreds of Campbell managers from all levels and most company locations spent three days at this conference. Management believed that the ultimate test of quality was consumer satisfaction, and the company's

---

[6]*Advertising Age,* January 3, 1983, p. 38.

goal was to instill a strong quality consciousness among employees in every single operation throughout the company.

Before McGovern took over, Campbell used to adjust the design of new products so that they could be produced with existing equipment and plant facilities. For example, a square omelet was specified for Swanson's breakfasts because it was what the installed machine would make. After McGovern's appointment, although low-cost production was still a strategic factor, market considerations and consumer trends—not existing machinery and production capabilities—were deciding factors in production, packaging, and labeling. Still, the company spent between $150 million and $300 million annually throughout the 1980s for improved equipment, new plants and plant expansions, better packaging technology, and distribution facilities.

Campbell executives believed the company's key strengths during the 1985–89 period were (1) a worldwide system for obtaining ingredients; (2) a broad range of food products that could be used as a launching pad for formulating, producing, and marketing new products; and (3) an emphasis on low-cost production.

Campbell's Performance under Gordon McGovern

McGovern's campaign for renewed growth via new product introduction and acquisition produced good results early on. By year-end 1984 sales were up 31 percent—to $3.7 billion—and earnings had risen by 47 percent—to $191 million. During McGovern's 10-year reign as CEO, Campbell introduced 922 new items—more than any other food-processing company. By the late 1980s however, there were signs that Campbell's brand managers had become so involved in new product development that they had neglected the old stand-by products as well as slighting cost-control and profit margin targets. According to one Campbell executive:

> We became fat cats. We said, "We can't fail." We began to throw things against the marketplace that had long paybacks and were in processes, packaging, and distribution that we didn't understand.[7]

Campbell's growth in operating earnings for fiscal years 1985–89 fell short of McGovern's 15 percent target rate, and McGovern in 1989 initiated several internal restructuring moves to eliminate many of the inefficiencies and cost excesses that had crept into the company's operations and new product development efforts. A summary of Campbell Soup's financial performance between 1989 and 1999 is presented in Exhibit 4.

McGOVERN'S RESIGNATION AND THE RECRUITMENT OF A REPLACEMENT

Beginning in the late 1980s, the heirs of John T. Dorrance began to show frustration with Campbell Soup's industry-lagging performance and began to openly criticize McGovern's approach to running the company. Quaker Oats management believed that the Dorrance family might be interested in a merger between the two companies and approached Campbell's chairman of the board, Robert Vlasic, in March 1989 to explore the issue. The Dorrance heirs were split on the prospect of a merger, with one faction publicly announcing its intent to sell its shares and another vying to block a

---

[7]As quoted in *Financial World*, June 11, 1991, p. 53.

exhibit 4 Financial Summary, Campbell Soup Company, 1989–99 (In Millions, Except Per Share Amounts)

	1999	1998	1997	1996	1995	1994	1993	1992	1991	1990	1989
Net sales	$6,424	$6,696	$7,964	$7,678	$7,250	$6,664	$6,577	$6,263	$6,204	$6,205	$5,672
Earnings before taxes	1,097	1,073	1,107	1,179	1,042	963	520	779	667	179	107
Earnings before cumulative effect of accounting change	1,097	1,062	713	802	698	630	257	491	402	4	13
Net earnings	724	660	713	802	698	630	8	491	402	4	13
Taxes on earnings	373	384	394	395	344	333	263	309	266	175	93
Interest—net	173	175	165	126	115	64	74	87	90	94	56
Earnings per share	1.63	1.46	1.51	1.61	1.40	1.26	0.02	0.97	0.79	0.01	0.03
Dividends per share	0.89	0.82	0.75	0.67	0.61	0.55	0.46	0.36	0.28	0.25	0.23
Wgt. avg. shares outstanding	445	460	472	498	498	501	504	504	508	518	518
Capital expenditures	297	256	331	416	391	421	371	362	371	397	302
Depreciation and amortization	255	261	328	326	294	255	242	216	209	201	192
Assets	5,522	5,633	6,459	6,632	6,315	4,992	4,897	4,353	4,149	4,115	3,932
Stockholders' equity	$ 235	$ 874	$1,420	$2,742	$2,468	$1,989	$1,704	$2,027	$1,793	$1,691	$1,778

Source: Campbell annual reports.

merger at all costs. The heirs supporting Campbell Soup's independence successfully prevented a merger but were unable to bring prompt reconciliation among the family.

Disenchanted with the family squabble and stung by outspoken criticism of his performance by family members, Gordon McGovern resigned as CEO and took early retirement in November 1989. Campbell's search for a replacement, spearheaded by Ippy Dorrance and Robert Vlasic, quickly focused on Gerber's CEO, David Johnson, as best candidate to replace McGovern. A native of Australia, David Johnson had a bachelor's degree in economics from the University of Sydney and an MBA from the University of Chicago. Starting out as a management trainee with the international division of Colgate-Palmolive in Australia, he moved up through the ranks to become managing director of Colgate's South African operations in 1967. In 1973, he moved to Hong Kong as president of Warner-Lambert/Parke Davis Asia; there, exposed to the Orient's fundamentally different customs and approaches, he came to appreciate that if managers were creative enough to look beyond accepted solutions to business problems, it was easy to find innovative answers. Looking back on his Hong Kong experiences, Johnson observed that he gained "an elasticized mind, opened to a greater run of possibilities than I'd ever known before."[8] Warner-Lambert brought Johnson to the United States in 1976 as president of its personal products division; a year later, he was promoted to president of the company's American Chicle division. When Warner-Lambert acquired Entenmann's in 1979, Johnson took over as head; he then moved to General Foods when GF acquired Entenmann's from Warner-Lambert in 1982. As Entenmann's chief executive from 1979 to 1987, he engineered the company's drive from a regional to a national provider of bakery products, more than quadrupling sales and profits. In 1987, Johnson left Entenmann's to become CEO of Gerber Products, a company whose performance had been lackluster for several years. He proceeded to craft a turnaround strategy for Gerber that involved divesting seven business divisions (toys, furniture, trucking) and refocusing Gerber's attention on its core baby-foods business. By 1990, 27 months after Johnson became CEO, Gerber's sales were up 30 percent, profits were up 50 percent, and the stock price had tripled. With the Dorrance family's blessing, Campbell lured Johnson away from Gerber as McGovern's successor.

THE DAVID JOHNSON ERA: 1990–97

When David Johnson became chairman and CEO of Campbell Soup Company in January 1990, he saw his first priority as crafting a strategy for Campbell that would grow earnings and win the confidence of the Dorrance heirs. While at Gerber, Johnson viewed Campbell, a competitor of Gerber's in some product categories, as an underperforming company that was a likely target for corporate raiders, once even commenting, "Boy, that's a troubled company. I could really run that one."[9] In interviewing for the job at Campbell, Johnson determined that the arguments and differences between the Dorrance family and Campbell's prior management were more a function of "poor results" than of activist family members wanting to meddle in company affairs or the desire of some to sell out their stake and invest their inheritance elsewhere. Johnson deemed the challenge worthy for several reasons:

---

[8]Jeffrey Zygmont, "In Command at Campbell," *Sky Magazine,* March 1993, p. 60.
[9]As quoted in *Fortune,* September 9, 1991, p. 143.

It was a company that was founded on incredible strength on which you could build. I knew that it had excellent R&D. I knew it had terrific brands. It had lost its direction, lost its focus, was underperforming, and I knew that it could be refocused and reorganized within six months, and that we could really get it going very quickly.[10]

Johnson immediately embarked on a course of boosting Campbell's performance quickly, not only to pacify disgruntled shareholders but also to get the company's stock price high enough to discourage would-be acquirers from launching a takeover attempt:

Under those circumstances, when you come in, it's not the pretties of "Here is my vision. Let me explain the principles from the book." When you move in, you've got to do it in an exciting fashion, lay down the challenge—Boom! Strike! Crash! It's short-term focus. You know that dirty word we're all accused of? "Short term." Isn't it terrible? Under those circumstances, if you don't win the first year, if you don't win in the short term, you're dead.[11]

Johnson's Turnaround Strategy

To spur Campbell's managers and give them something to shoot for in rejuvenating the company's performance, Johnson set financial objectives of 20 percent earnings growth, 20 percent return on equity, and 20 percent cash return on assets: "I used to say, if perfect human vision is 20-20, then perfect business vision is 20-20-20, which was shorthand for earnings, return and cash."[12] This was followed by the establishment of four corporate-level strategic principles to guide the creation of business and functional strategies in each divisional unit:

- The primary purpose of the corporation is to *build shareholder wealth*. It is imperative to provide dividend growth and long-term stock appreciation to reward the stockholders of the corporation.

- Campbell must exploit its *brand power.* Campbell's strong brands have been the basis of the company's strength's over the past 90 years and should be the focal point for the future.

- Campbell's ability to sustain its brand power and build on its powerful brands is only possible through *people power.* The company's employees have to be responsible for maintaining the existing brands, for building on these brands, and for finding new markets for these brands. Campbell should encourage individual risk-bearing and teamwork with rewards linked to results.

- It is important to *preserve the company's independence.* Management needs to preserve the heritage of Campbell Soup Company and resist any outside thrust for control through delivery of superior performance on building long-term shareholder wealth.

Johnson disagreed with McGovern's view that Campbell's growth should come primarily from the acquisition of small, fast-growing food companies and from the introduction of new products that served some niche of the food industry. Instead, Johnson believed that Campbell Soup should concentrate on growing sales of its best-known brands—the red-and-white soup line, Prego, Pepperidge Farm, Vlasic, and Swanson—and to increase its U.S. market share in these product categories. During the 1980s, for

---

[10]As quoted *in Sky Magazine,* March 1993, p. 54.

[11]As quoted in *Fortune,* December 14, 1992, p. 112.

[12]Ibid.

example, Campbell's tonnage in canned soups had risen a paltry 1 percent annually and Campbell's market share of the U.S. soup market, according to Wall Street estimates, had slipped from a lofty 80 percent in the 1950s and 1960s to 70 percent in the mid-1980s to around 65 percent in 1990. Johnson also decided to press harder and faster than McGovern had to gain increased penetration of foreign markets.

While McGovern had pursued ways to reduce costs and eliminate inefficiencies during his 1989 restructuring, Johnson saw opportunities to achieve further economies and better profit margins, principally by eliminating unprofitable and slow-selling items from Campbell's product lineup and by divesting peripheral lines of businesses that did not complement the company's strengths or bolster the market power of its flagship brands. Consequently, the strategy Johnson crafted to boost Campbell's performance incorporated six major initiatives:

- Divesting poorly performing and nonstrategic business units and reorganizing Campbell's six divisions.
- Eliminating weak items from the company's product lineup.
- Requiring that new product introductions exploit Campbell Soup's strengths, core competencies, and organizational capabilities as well as have the potential to achieve the three 20-20-20 financial performance targets.
- Focusing on the global marketing of the company's competencies and capabilities.
- Installing and expanding low-cost business systems at the corporate level to support the operations of the business divisions.
- Improving utilization of assets to maximize the return to stockholders.

Exhibit 5 shows the business lines that were divested—Johnson saw all of them as either nonstrategic and unrelated to Campbell's core competencies or as chronic money losers or low-return businesses. This pruning of Campbell's portfolio resulted in the sale of 8 plants and the shutdown of 12 plants worldwide plus a workforce reduction of 8,000 people during Johnson's first 18 months as CEO. As the remaining plants bid to absorb the production of the closed plants, overall capacity utilization rose from 60 to 80 percent; Campbell's Maxton, North Carolina, plant was able to increase its output 50 percent and become Campbell's first canned-soup plant to drive manufacturing costs below 50 percent of the retail price of its products. Included among the initial plant closings was the company's 131-year-old Camden, New Jersey, plant with its distinctive water towers painted to look like giant Campbell Soup cans.

Johnson's restructuring continued throughout his tenure, with major initiatives approved by the board in 1993 and 1996. The 1993 restructuring program identified six plants and 14 businesses that were to be sold. In 1996 the board approved an additional restructuring that eliminated not only additional plants and businesses but also 2,100 administrative and operational positions at various Campbell Soup facilities. Both restructuring programs were intended to shift production from underutilized or inefficient production facilities to more cost-effective locations and eliminate nonstrategic poor-performing businesses from the portfolio. Under Johnson, Campbell Soup went on to divest a total of 26 businesses that had an average net profit margin of 1 percent. Campbell Soup also closed a total of 10 older and inefficient plants between 1990 and 1997 to boost capacity utilization.

Once Johnson assessed that the turnaround was well under way, he complemented the divestitures with 20 acquisitions of higher-margin business with ample growth potential to complete the portfolio restructuring initiative. In 1996 David Johnson commented on the strategy of moving Campbell from a position of "best in class" to "best

exhibit 5 Divested Campbell Soup Company Businesses, 1990–96

- Fried chicken plant in Sumpter, South Carolina
- Salmon Farms
- Snow King Frozen Foods—frozen meat products
- Triangle Manufacturing Corporation—a health-and-fitness products manufacturer
- Mushroom farms
- Menderson-Zeller, Inc.
- Recipe Pet Food
- D. Lazzaroni Cookie Company (Italy)
- Win Schuler Foods, Inc.
- Juice Bowl
- Juice Works
- The fresh produce and frozen vegetable portions of the UK Freshbake Foods Group— the frozen entree portion of Freshbake was retained.
- Campbell Chilled Foods, Ltd. (United Kingdom)
- Mrs. Paul's frozen seafood
- Poultry processing operations
- Marie's salad dressings
- Beeck-Feinkost GmbH chilled foods (Germany)
- Beef farms in Argentina
- Durkee and Early California olives
- Groko BV frozen vegetable processing (Holland)

Source: Campbell annual reports and 10-Ks.

in show," the contribution of the newly acquired businesses, and the company's prospects for growth:

> We begin this new attack from a position of great strength. Our balance sheet and cash flow are strong. Since 1990, we have divested non-strategic and low-margin businesses with approximately $800 million in sales and acquired strategic, higher-margin businesses with more than $1.2 billion in sales, including Mexican sauce leader Pace Foods. Our management team has transformed Campbell into a place where results count and where the bar is constantly raised . . . We are poised for breaking away from our competitors in the food industry. This strategic growth plan is designed to vault our company into the ranks of the world's renowned consumer goods companies, in terms of financial profile and market multiple.[13]

Exhibit 6 presents a listing and description of business acquisitions initiated by David Johnson. By year-end 1996 the new businesses Johnson had added to Campbell's portfolio achieved an average net profit margin of 12 percent.

Many of Johnson's acquisitions were intended to add brands and infrastructure that were necessary for the growth of Campbell's international business. The acquisition of Pace Foods was one of the few acquisitions not specifically aimed at growing international food sales. Pace Foods, the leading U.S. producer and marketer of Mexican salsa, was Campbell's biggest acquisition ever. The $1.12 billion purchase price represented five times Pace's sales and 20 times its earnings. A number of companies, including Heinz and Lea & Perrin, had been attempting to buy Pace for a number of

---

[13]As quoted in PR Newswire, September 5, 1996.

exhibit 6   Businesses Acquired by Campbell Soup, 1994–97

1994 (Acquisitions totaled $14 million)
- Dandy mushrooms (Australia)
- Fray Bentos canned meats (Australia)

1995 (Acquisitions totaled $1.26 billion)
- Pace Foods—the leading salsa brand in the United States, with annual sales of $700 million. The company was purchased for $1.12 billion.
- Increase in share ownership of Arnott's Ltd. to 65 percent.
- Fresh Start Bakeries—maker of buns and English muffins for quick-service restaurants in the United States, Europe, and South America. At the time of the acquisition, the company had approximate annual sales of $75 million, 480 employees, and had been a supplier to McDonald's for more than 30 years. The business was integrated into Campbell's Food Service unit.
- Stratford-upon-Avon Foods—a food-service company operating in the United Kingdom with annual sales of $60 million. The business manufactured, marketed, and distributed canned baked beans, vegetable and fruit products, and branded and private-label pickles.
- Greenfield Healthy Foods—U.S. manufacturer of all-natural, low-fat cakes and cookies. The company provided Pepperidge Farm with new resources to enter the $800 million healthy-snack category.
- Homepride sauces—the best-selling cooking sauce in the United Kingdom. The business, purchased for an estimated $93 million, allowed Campbell to build gravy and sauce sales in the United Kingdom.

1996 (Acquisitions totaled $186 million)
- Joint venture began between Arnott's Ltd. and Helios Foods, one of Indonesia's most prominent food companies—thereby providing Arnott's with biscuit manufacturing capability in Asia.
- Joint venture began in Malaysia with Cheong Chan that provided manufacturing facilities for canned soups, ketchup, and soy sauces in Southeast Asia. Campbell Soup also acquired a minority interest in Cheong Chan.
- Joint venture between Godiva and J. Osawa Ltd. to immediately open 33 retail stores and outlets for Godiva chocolates. An additional 20 stores were planned to open by the year 2000.
- Increase in share ownership of Arnott's Ltd. to 70 percent.

1997 (Acquisitions totaled $228 million)
- Erasco Group—the leading wet-soup brand in Germany, with annual sales of $223 million and 900 employees. The business was purchased for approximately $210 million. Campbell management believed that the acquisition would accelerate the company's growth throughout Germany and the European Union.
- Kettle Chip Company—salty-snack company operating in Australia and acquired for $18 million.

years, but owner Kit Goldsbury was not interested. The chief operating officer of Pace Foods stated that Goldsbury agreed to the sale to Campbell because Goldsbury could identify with and liked Campbell's management team.[14]

As a product category, salsa (a spicy blend of jalapeños, tomatoes, onion, and garlic) surpassed ketchup in 1991 as the nation's best-selling condiment. The salsa category grew at just under a 13 percent compound annual growth rate from 1988 to 1993

---

[14]*The Wall Street Journal,* November 29, 1994, p. A3.

as sales increased from $325 million to $700 million. The rapid growth in sales of salsa products was attributed to its spicy flavor and low fat content (a jar of Pace salsa contained no fat and only 70 calories), to the excellent way it complemented such snack foods as tortilla chips, to growing consumer popularity of Mexican dishes, and to a fast-increasing Hispanic population.

Johnson's Revised New Product Development and Marketing Strategies

David Johnson instituted a more cautious approach to new product development and challenged Campbell marketers to become more aggressive in marketing the company's products. Johnson was quick to comment, "There's no such thing as mature markets, only tired marketers,"[15] when told that low industry growth rates were obstacles to growth. New product ideas were more heavily researched and tested before they were put on the market. Moreover, new products were expected to provide quicker paybacks on investment; potential products that held little promise for near-term profitability and for meeting the 20-20-20 financial performance standards were tabled.

The search for new product ideas was limited to areas where Campbell had production and marketing expertise; as one executive put it, "We want to be in areas we know we are good at and in processes we are good at."[16] Despite the more conservative approach to new product development, Campbell introduced nearly 300 new products during Johnson's first three years as the company's chief executive. Johnson committed between $77 million and $88 million annually to R&D during his last three years as CEO to improve existing products and to develop new products that would be successful in U.S. and international markets. New items included cream of broccoli soup (which became the first new soup since 1935 to rank in the top five best-selling soups), Joseph A. Campbell premium-quality ready-to-serve soups, cheese tortellini soup, Light 'n Tangy V8, Swanson Kids Fun Feast frozen dinners, Vlasic Sandwich Stackers, Prego pizza sauce, and more varieties of Pepperidge Farm products. Johnson suggested that the company's new approach to product development had been successful in developing products that consumers desired and had allowed the company to achieve sales growth in traditionally mature markets: "Innovations and breakthroughs are so simple, but they come only if you're immersed in your field and determined to make the necessary connections. For instance, take our Stackers, which are pickles sliced to lay flat on a sandwich. A simple idea, but it took off: The overall Stackers market grew 55% last year. In addition, we're tapping into growing consumer segments, such as the healthy food category. For example, our new line of cream soups is 98% fat free."[17]

Johnson's Corporate Reorganization

Johnson's reorganization effort aimed at capturing strategic-fit benefits among related products and product families Johnson concluded that McGovern's 50 autonomous units had resulted in lack of communication and cooperation between the different business units. For example, the U.S. soup division once ran a promotion with Nabisco

---

[15]As quoted in *Chief Executive,* November 1996.

[16]As quoted in *Financial World,* June 11, 1991, p. 53.

[17]As quoted in *Chief Executive,* November 1996.

crackers even though Pepperidge Farm produced a competing product. Also, U.S. tomato paste plants did not share technology with Mexican tomato paste plants since the Mexican plants were in a different division. A three-division structure was established during Johnson's first year as Campbell CEO to improve communication and technology sharing between businesses in similar product categories and geographies (see Exhibit 7). This initial structure was modified three times over the next five years. Each shuffling of businesses within the three-division structure was directed at improving the strategic fit within the portfolio of businesses. The series of new alignments also helped Campbell Soup put more emphasis on the company's international businesses.

Johnson's International Push

Johnson was convinced that a sizable fraction of Campbell Soup's growth should come from international expansion because the world market for processed food products was projected to grow over twice as fast as the 1 percent growth rate projected for the $200 billion U.S. food-processing industry. By 2000, Johnson wanted at least one-third of Campbell's revenues to come from outside of the United States. Johnson saw such companies as Coca-Cola and Gillette, whose international operations contributed 70 to 80 percent of total sales, as prototypes for Campbell Soup's future:

> Clearly, we're not going to be a Coca-Cola or Gillette in two years, but we're inching toward that aim as we go into the next century . . . We're expanding in the United Kingdom, Canada, and Australia, and trying to establish more beachheads in Asia Pacific. Our acquisition of Germany's Erasco increases our total international soup sales to 21 percent of total soup sales. We bought an operation in Malaysia called Cheong Chan, where we're now making the investments that will enable us to produce soup instead of importing it. We're looking for ventures in China and growing in Taiwan.

Campbell marketed its soups in Mexico, Canada, Argentina, Poland, Hong Kong, and China, and its baked goods in Europe and Asia Pacific. In 1993 Campbell increased its 33 percent share of Australia's Arnott's Ltd. to 58 percent to gain an organizational base for increasing its long-term presence in baked goods in the Pacific Rim and Asia. Johnson increased Campbell's ownership of Arnott's further to 65 percent in 1995 and to 70 percent in 1996. To help familiarize himself with Campbell's international operations and to better gauge the company's potential for foreign expansion, Johnson had all of Campbell's top international executives report directly to him for the first 12 months he was at Campbell.

International marketing of prepared foods was not easy. Taste preferences varied significantly from country to country (and sometimes within countries), prompting international producers to employ multicountry strategies to gear product characteristics to local preferences and eating habits. Campbell's 1988 acquisition of Britain's Freshbake Foods Group never performed up to expectations partly because Campbell management didn't cater adequately to the taste preferences of British consumers. Also, Campbell's penetration of the European soup market had proved more difficult than originally expected because the predominant forms of store-bought soups on the continent were dry soups and ready-to-serve soups; demand for Campbell's mainstay condensed soups was virtually nonexistent in Europe, and consumers had to be persuaded of the merits of switching to a different preparation technique.

Campbell management opened a Hong Kong taste kitchen as part of the company's effort to ensure that the products it introduced would appeal to Asia's 2 billion consumers, whose average per capita soup consumption averaged six bowls per week. The Hong Kong kitchen proved to be a success, having a role in creating such popular *exhibit* 7   Comparison of Campbell's Business Unit Structure under Gordon McGovern and David Johnson

Campbell's Structure under Gordon McGovern		Campbell's Structure under David Johnson		Campbell's Structure under Dale Morrison	
Division	**Example Brands/Services**	**Division**	**Example Brands/Services**	**Division**	**Example Brands/Services**
Campbell U.S.		**U.S.A.**			
● Soup Group	Red-and-white, Healthy Request, Chunky	● U.S. Soup Group	Dry and canned soup, Franco-American	**Soups and Sauces**	All worldwide dry and canned soups, Franco American pastas, V8, Campbell's tomato juice
● Frozen Food Group	Swanson, LeMenu	● Beverage Group	V8, Campbell's tomato juice		
● Grocery Group	Prego, Franco-American, Swanson canned meats	● Meal Enhancement Group	Open Pit barbecue sauce, Pace salsas, Vlasic, Prego, food service		Prego spaghetti sauces, Pace salsas, Swanson broths,
● Beverage Group	Campbell's tomato juice, V8, Juice Bowl, Juice Works	● Frozen Foods Group	Swanson		Erasco, Cheong Chan, Home Pride, Leibig, Stockpot
● Pet Food Group	Recipe				
Pepperidge Farm	Pepperidge Farm breads, cookies, Godiva chocolates, Costa apple juice, Deli's frozen entrees	**Bakery and Confectionery**	Arnott's Ltd., Pepperidge Farm, Delacre, Godiva Chocolatier, Lami Lutti confections, Kettle Chips	**Biscuit and Confectionery**	Arnott's Ltd., Pepperidge Farm, Godiva Chocolatier, Kettle Chips
Vlasic	Pickles and relishes				
Mrs. Paul's	Frozen fish, frozen chicken, frozen vegetables				
Other U.S.	Triangle Manufacturing Corp.—fitness products Campbell Hospitality—restaurants Snow King Frozen Foods—frozen meats				
Campbell International	Soup—Canada and Mexico Fresh Bake Foods Group (Britain)—baked goods	**International Grocery** ● International Soup Group	Red-and-white canned soup, Erasco, Cheong Chan, Home Pride	**Away from Home**	Distribution and Campbell soups, Pace salsas, and specialty kitchen entrees to food-service markets
		● International Specialty Foods	Stratford-upon-Avon, Fray Bentos, Swift		

Source: Campbell annual reports.

exhibit 8   Sales and Earnings of Campbell Soup Company, by Geographic Region, 1991–99 ($ Millions)

	1999	1998	1997	1996	1995	1994	1993	1992	1991
United States									
Net sales	$4,808	$4,850	$5,495	$5,332	$5,012	$4,639	$4,744	$4,649	$4,496
Earnings before taxes	1,196	1,124	1,155	1,123	957	854	715	809	695
Europe									
Net sales	630	859	1,201	1,122	1,143	1,041	1,050	1,043	1,149
Earnings before taxes	32*	36*	50	71	74	64	(170)	45	49
Other countries									
Net sales	1,054	1,044	1,408	1,347	1,179	1,011	917	652	656
Earnings before taxes	$ 121	$ 123	$ 122	$ 172	$ 171	$ 154	$ 99	$ 70	$ 55

*Earnings before interest and taxes
Source: Campbell annual reports.

sellers as scallop, watercress, duck-gizzard, and ham soups. The kitchen was experimenting with other soup varieties made from pork, dates, figs, and snake.

Campbell had been successful in Mexico with spicy soups such as Creama de Chile Poblano and had captured 10 percent of Argentina's $50 million soup market within one year of introducing nine varieties of its red-and-white canned soup. A summary of Campbell Soup's geographic performance between 1991 and 1998 is displayed in Exhibit 8.

THE DALE MORRISON ERA BEGINS: MID-1997 TO PRESENT

When David Johnson's five-year contract expired and he elected to step aside as Campbell Soup Company's CEO in July 1997, the company announced that 48-year-old Dale Morrison would become its new chief executive officer effective July 15, 1997. Morrison joined Campbell Soup in June 1995 as president of Pepperidge Farm, where he was largely responsible for a turnaround of the business that had averaged 2 to 3 percent sales growth between 1990 and 1995. Prior to joining Campbell Soup's management, Morrison spent 14 years with PepsiCo, where he held management positions with both Frito-Lay and Pepsi-Cola. Dale Morrison also coordinated the merger of British snack foods companies while at Frito-Lay. Morrison held a number of positions with General Foods from 1972 to 1981, marketing such brands as Tang, Post cereals, and Kool-Aid.

David Johnson agreed to remain on as chairman of Campbell's board of directors through July 1999 from which he could aid Morrison in an advisory role. Johnson announced, "My priority is to ensure that we continue our relentless commitment to building shareowner wealth. I will assist Dale in exploring the strategies needed to achieve Campbell's vision of becoming the best consumer products company in the world."[18]

---

[18]As quoted in *Milling & Baking News,* July 8, 1997, p. 14.

Morrison's Accomplishments at Campbell Soup Prior to His Appointment as CEO

When he arrived at Pepperidge Farm, Dale Morrison initiated a number of cost-cutting programs that freed up resources and gave the division enough gross margin leeway to spend additional sums on marketing and product promotion. Such products as Pepperidge Farm Goldfish crackers and Milano cookies benefited from increased advertising and marketing innovations like Goldfish milk-carton-style packaging, which was easier for children to manage than the previous paper-bag-style packaging. Morrison also made a point of visiting all Pepperidge Farm plants and met with the company's independent distributors, whom Morrison reclassified as sales development associates. Morrison's strategies resulted in a 10 percent sales increase in 1996, a 13 percent sales increase in 1997, and a 20 percent earnings increase in both years.

In recognition of his success at Pepperidge Farm, David Johnson gave Morrison added responsibilities at Campbell Soup. Morrison was appointed president of Campbell's International Specialty Foods in November 1996, putting him in charge of Campbell's international grocery, food-service, frozen and specialty foods, and bakery and confectionery businesses.

Recent Trends in the Performance of Campbell Soup's Stock Price, 1990–2000

Exhibit 9 shows Campbell Soup's market performance relative to the Dow Jones Industrial Index and the Dow Jones composite of other food-processing companies since 1990. The company's stock performance mirrored that of many of its processed food competitors, which averaged a 30 percent decline in their share prices and had collectively seen over $160 billion in market value disappear during 1999. Some of Campbell Soup's share price decline after January 2000 was attributable to a number of class-action lawsuits brought against Campbell Soup that claimed the company misrepresented its revenue from its condensed soup sales between November 1997 and January 1999. The complaints alleged that, in an attempt to meet analysts' quarterly earnings estimates, the company claimed to have sold product to major distributors and resellers when in actuality Campbell never shipped the product to customers. When asked about the suits' allegations by a *Wall Street Journal* reporter, Campbell's chief financial officer retorted, "Campbell Soup does not make and has not made sham shipments of its products. We do not make and have not made false or misleading statements."[19]

Morrison's Strategy for Campbell Soup

Morrison's strategies to improve Campbell Soup's performance were, for the most part, a continuation and refinement of Johnson's initiatives. Morrison agreed with David Johnson that Campbell Soup should become more like Coca-Cola, with faster sales growth in international markets and a tighter focus on the core business. Morrison wanted to increase Campbell Soup Company's annual sales growth to 8 to 10 percent and believed that the company's greatest opportunity for rapid growth lay in focusing on its premium brands, which were differentiated from competing brands in terms of taste, perceived quality, and image. Morrison wanted growth to come more

---

[19]As quoted in *The Wall Street Journal Interactive Edition,* February 17, 2000.

exhibit 9   Campbell Soup Company's Stock Performance, 1990–March 2000

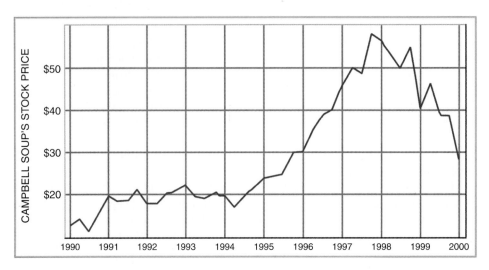

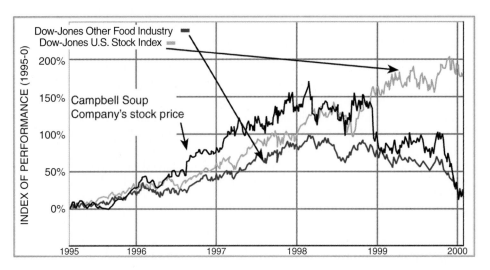

from volume increases rather than price increases and intended to allocate greater resources to advertising some of the company's more highly differentiated brands like Joseph A. Campbell premium-quality ready-to-serve soups, Pepperidge Farm Goldfish crackers, and Milano cookies. The centerpiece of Morrison's plan for boosting unit sales was to increase advertising expenditures from 3.5 percent of sales to 8 percent of sales. Morrison also launched initiatives to enhance Campbell products' differentiated image in international markets. In Japan, for example, the decision was made to upgrade the quality of its soup cans and to redesign the labels on the cans; Japanese consumers were drawn to products with high-quality packaging.

Morrison's Portfolio Restructuring Efforts   In September 1997 Dale Morrison announced the spinoff of seven low-growth businesses with combined sales of $1.4 billion—about 18 percent of Campbell Soup Company's 1997 sales. The spinoff was a carryover of strategic initiatives that David Johnson had announced in September

1996. Under the plan, Vlasic Foods International would become a stand-alone company with operations in the United States, Europe, and South America and over 9,000 employees. The new company's shares would be distributed tax-free to Campbell shareholders, and upon the completion of the spinoff the new company would be ranked 21st among 32 publicly traded food companies. Campbell's Swanson frozen food business in the United States and Canada and its frozen food lines in the United Kingdom would make up Vlasic Foods International's frozen food division. The grocery division would include Campbell's Vlasic retail and food-service products, Swift Armour meats in Argentina, Open Pit barbecue sauces, Stratford-upon-Avon's retail and food-service pickle and canned vegetable businesses in the United Kingdom, Gourmet Specialty Foods in Germany, and the U.S. fresh mushroom business.

Morrison commented at the time of the announced spinoff that shareholders would benefit greatly by a separation of Campbell Soup businesses:

> This is a watershed day for Campbell Soup Company and its shareowners. Spinning off these businesses allows us to focus on our most profitable businesses with the highest growth potential. Our core businesses have gross margins in excess of 45%. Net sales for these businesses grew 10% and earnings grew 15% in fiscal 1997. This is an outstanding platform to drive significant volume growth while continuing to deliver top-quartile earnings. The creation of this new company gives great brands like Vlasic and Swanson tremendous opportunities for growth under a dedicated management team. In both cases, shareowners will reap the rewards of highly focused companies.[20]

Some Wall Street analysts were not as optimistic that the new company would become a strong competitor in the processed-food industry. One portfolio manager suggested that the spinoff would allow Campbell to achieve higher growth rates in terms of sales and earnings, but Vlasic Foods International would find growth difficult: "Whenever a company spins off the crummy parts, it's always good for what's left. What they're spinning off didn't have the value or the growth rate of the other divisions."[21] Another analyst commented on the attractiveness of frozen food, where over the last 10 years the size of the market had declined and margin points were gained only through price cuts: "There is not going to be a mad rush to own this [new] food company. Swanson has been a stagnant brand at best, though I suppose it's a bit better than Schlitz beer."[22]

Even though the frozen foods category was highly competitive and had become commodity-like after the 1980s, Vlasic Foods International did include a number of popular brands and products. Swanson was the originator of the TV dinner in 1954 and continued to maintain category leadership with products like Hungry Man dinners, Great Start breakfasts, and Fun Feast kids' meals. Vlasic was the leader in U.S. pickle sales, with a 36 percent market share, and approximately 35 percent of Vlasic's sales came from products introduced within the previous five years. In addition, Swift was Argentina's largest exporter of beef, Open Pit was the number one barbecue sauce in the midwestern United States, Gourmet Specialty Foods was Germany's number one specialty foods company, and the company's mushroom business was the largest in the world. The new company's third- and fourth-quarter sales and earnings fell below projections, and sales of pickles and frozen foods were down about 10 percent for the year. The company's stock closed at $22¾ on the first day of trading in March 1998, but was trading in the $13 to $15 range within four months of the spinoff. The

---

[20]Securities and Exchange Commission, Form 8-K, September 9, 1997.

[21]*Knight-Ridder/Tribune Business News,* September 10, 1997.

[22]As quoted in *The New York Times,* September 10, 1997, p. D1.

exhibit 10   Vlasic Foods International's Stock Performance, by Week,
                     March 1998–March 2000

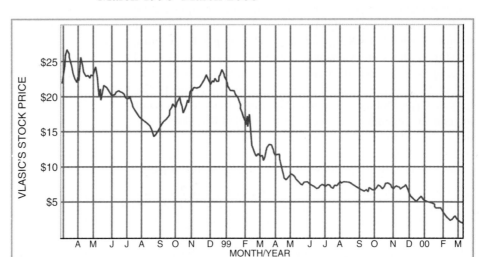

market performance of Vlasic Foods' common stock following its spinoff is depicted
in Exhibit 10.

Morrison continued to restructure Campbell's portfolio during 1998 and 1999 to
allow the company to focus on core brands and activities directly related to either product quality or image. Continental Sweets was sold to a Dutch venture capital fund in
1998. Continental Sweets made and distributed sugar and chocolate confectionery; its
facilities were located in France and Belgium. Campbell Soup also sold its European-
based Delacre premium biscuit business and Australian-based Melbourne Mushrooms
and Spring Valley beverages in 1998.

The company's Fresh Start Bakeries, a supplier of English muffins and buns to
quick-service restaurants, was sold to a joint venture between Berkshire Partners and
Fresh Start's management in May 1999. Morrison also chose to divest the company's
can-making assets to Silgan Holdings—a supplier of food cans with annual sales of approximately $1.5 billion. The can-making operations were sold for $123 million, and
the transaction included a 10-year supply agreement between Campbell Soup and Silgan that called for can purchases by Campbell totaling over $200 million each year.
The company also took restructuring charges of $262 million and $41 million in 1998
and 1999, respectively, related to streamlining its production and administrative facilities in North America and Europe. The restructuring programs merged certain Canadian and U.S. administrative functions and attempted to maximize capacity utilization
among its production facilities by combining operations whenever possible. For example, Campbell closed its Pace salsa plant in San Antonio, Texas, and shifted production of Pace products to Campbell's Paris, Texas, plant, which produced Prego
spaghetti sauce, Franco-American gravies, and an assortment of soups. Campbell Soup
management expected the restructuring program to reduce the company's operating
expenses by $221 million annually.

The spinoff and divestitures allowed Campbell Soup to implement a $2 billion
share buyback plan to repurchase 8 percent of the company's 451 million outstanding
shares of stock between 1999 and 2001. The strategy to boost earnings per share and
return on stockholders' equity was a continuation of an ongoing Johnson strategy of

repurchasing 2 percent of the company's outstanding shares annually. Morrison also retained a Johnson-devised strategy of repurchasing shares in addition to the $2 billion buyback plan to offset per share dilution resulting from incentive compensation programs.

To boost Campbell's growth potential, Morrison initiated a number of new acquisitions during 1997 and 1998. In 1997 the company purchased the remaining 30 percent of Arnott's outstanding shares for $290 million, giving Campbell 100 percent ownership of the Australian biscuit company. The company also acquired Leibig soups in 1997 for $180 million. Leibig was France's leading producer of wet soups, with annual sales of approximately $75 million. In June 1998 Campbell Soup acquired privately held Fortun Foods for $105 million. Fortun's Stockpot brand of fresh, chilled soup was distributed to restaurants, supermarkets, and convenience stores in over 20 countries and was the market leader in premium refrigerated soups, with about 50 percent market share of the rapidly growing category and annual sales of $40 million. Campbell Soup had tried unsuccessfully a number of times since the 1980s to develop freshly made chilled soup without preservatives. Fortun's manufacturing process transferred hot soup from the kettle to a vacuum-sealed bag that was then immediately refrigerated. The company's proprietary process allowed Stockpot soups to stay fresh for about 120 days.

Morrison's acquisitions and divestitures prompted a realignment of Campbell Soup divisions and business units. Morrison created a Soups and Sauces division, which included all soup and sauce brands marketed globally. The Biscuit and Confectionery division was reorganized to include all global brands of baked goods, and the makeup of the Away from Home food-service division was adjusted to include all businesses that were dedicated to supplying the growing quick-service restaurant industry. A special division titled Campbell's Other was temporarily formed to handle the details of transferring the divested businesses to the new owners and report the historical performance of divested businesses.

Morrison believed that cross-business skills transfer would be more readily achieved by abandoning Campbell's previous geographically based divisions and placing all businesses sharing common R&D, production, and marketing activities in a common division (see again Exhibit 7, which presents a comparison of business divisions and units under Gordon McGovern, David Johnson, and Dale Morrison). Exhibit 11 provides the sales and operating earnings for Morrison's divisions from 1995 to 1999. The 1995 and 1996 financial data shown in the exhibit have been reorganized to match Campbell Soup Company's divisional structure in 1997–99.

CAMPBELL SOUP IN 2000

Soups and Sauces Group

The Soups and Sauces division was Campbell's largest operating unit, accounting for about two-thirds of the company's total consolidated sales. The U.S. and international markets for canned soup were mature and possibly entering into a declining stage. The U.S. wet-soup category had grown at low single-digit rates during the late 1990s and was not expected to grow at a faster rate during 2000–2001. The maturity of the U.S. soup segment was attributable to the increased popularity of fresh foods, a 40 percent decrease in the usage of cooking soups in recipes, and an overall reduced tendency of consumers to purchase canned products. The slow growth in international markets was

exhibit 11   Sales and Earnings of Campbell Soup Company, by
Division, 1995–99 ($ Millions)

	1999	1998	1997	1996	1995
Soups and Sauces					
Sales	$4,423	$4,434	$4,156	$3,742	$3,415
Operating earnings	1,082	1,109	1,012	978	863
Biscuits and Confectionery					
Sales	1,430	1,522	1,546	1,459	1,348
Operating earnings	215	206	154	183	164
Away from Home					
Sales	507	453	459	418	345
Operating earnings	57	53	62	55	40
Other					
Sales	126	334	1,904	2,149	2,204
Operating earnings	(5)	(85)	99	150	135
Interdivision					
Sales	($ 62)	($ 49)	($ 101)	($ 90)	($ 62)

Source: Campbell annual reports.

primarily related to the preference for homemade soups in many regions. During most of the 1990s consumption of Campbell's soups grew at 2 to 3 percent annually, but U.S. consumption of Campbell's wet soups declined by about 1 percent in 1998 and by 8 percent in 1999. Campbell's worldwide soup sales grew by 3 percent during 1998, but declined by 4 percent in 1999. The company's 1997 acquisition of Liebig helped Campbell Soup increase its international wet-soup volume by 7 percent in 1999.

Campbell's market share in the condensed soup category had declined from 80 percent in 1993 to 74 percent in 1997. In an attempt to regain lost market share, the company forwent its usual 3 to 7 percent annual price increases in 1998 since much of its lost market share was being captured by lower-priced private-label brands. The level pricing failed to recapture enough lost market share to offset the impact of smaller margins on the division's 1998 revenues. In 1999 the company's U.S. sales of canned soup declined by 8 percent after Campbell management eliminated quarter-end promotions to retailers.

The division implemented a plan to increase advertising spending by 18 percent in 1998 and intended to eventually increase the advertising budget for Campbell soups and sauces from 3.5 percent of sales to 8 percent of sales. Dale Morrison believed that increased advertising was necessary to support new products and newly packaged products and to promote soup in appealing ways to children. Campbell's fastest growing soup and sauce products during the late 1990s were Swanson broths and V8 Splash juices. Swanson's 20 percent annual growth was in large part a result of new 32-ounce recloseable aseptic packaging and its positioning as a 100 percent fat-free seasoning alternative that could be used in a number of recipes. Recent product introduction V8 Splash, a beverage combining carrot and tropical fruit juices, helped the V8 brand grow by more than 10 percent in 1998, and the 1999 introduction of new packaging (e.g., kid-sized juice boxes), new flavors, and a greater availability throughout the world helped V8 Splash become Campbell's most successful new product introduction in more than a decade.

Campbell introduced additional products after Morrison became the company's CEO to improve the sales volumes of products like tomato soup. Its new 32-ounce recloseable plastic ready-to-serve Campbell Tomato Soup allowed consumers to pour a single serving or use what was called for by a recipe and then store the remaining portion in the refrigerator for later use. Campbell marketers believed that having soup in the refrigerator would lead to higher consumption since most people opened the refrigerator more often than the pantry. Campbell Soup added a line of Select Soups, packaged in metal cans, as was the company's Classic line of soups that included tomato, cream of broccoli, and cream of mushroom, but the Select Soups line included more unique varieties of soups. Select Soups used distinctive combinations of ingredients to create flavorful soups like chicken and pasta with roasted garlic—a blend of chicken, penne and rotini pasta, and vegetables with roasted garlic in a chicken broth. Campbell Soup also introduced a Soups-to-Go line of ready-to-serve microwavable single-serving bowls that achieved volume gains in 1999. Joseph A. Campbell premium-quality soups had not experienced the sales gains expected by Campbell management; the line was rebranded Simply Home in 1998 and achieved volume gains in 1999. Campbell's Chunky line was also one of the company's faster-growing lines of canned soup in the late 1990s.

Even though the company had been largely successful with its new product introductions in recent years, Campbell management still believed in David Johnson's commitment to thoroughly assessing a product's potential on the market prior to its launch. Robert Bernstock, president of Campbell's U.S. Grocery division, explained, "In the early 1990s we were launching two new, single SKU products with more than $10 million in sales a year. We're now launching more than 20 a year. Tremendous upfront discipline is the key. We spend 12–18 months in rigorous testing."[23]

Biscuits and Confectionery Group

Campbell's Biscuits and Confectionery business unit had 1999 sales of $1.4 billion and operating earnings of $215 million. The division included Pepperidge Farm in North America; Godiva chocolates in North America, Europe, and Asia; Arnott's in the Pacific Rim/Asia; and Kettle Chips in Australia. Such products as Goldfish crackers, Swirl bread, and Milano cookies helped the Biscuits and Confectionery division achieve a sales increase of 5 percent in 1998 prior to the impact of exchange rates. The division had a sales decline of 6 percent in 1999, but Godiva grew its U.S. sales volume by more than 10 percent in 1998 and made some headway in increasing penetration of European and Asian markets. Campbell management expected the business to continue to increase its strength in Asia as more Godiva retail outlets were opened in the region. The company also opened additional freestanding boutiques in shopping malls and Godiva departments in upscale department stores throughout the United States.

Pepperidge Farm continued the transformation begun by Dale Morrison in 1995 with continued increases in sales volume. The company's increased promotion of Goldfish crackers allowed sales of the product to grow 25 percent in 1996 and 40 percent in 1997. New varieties such as Goldfish Grahams contributed to sales volume increases for Goldfish products in 1999. Other market-leading Pepperidge Farm products included Milano cookies, which grew by 35 percent in 1997, Dessert Classics frozen cakes, and

---

[23]As quoted in *Prepared Foods,* September 1997, p. 14.

frozen garlic bread, which grew more than 40 percent after being moved adjacent to frozen pasta in grocery freezers. Pepperidge Farm management had established a "2 × 2" program with the objective of doubling sales between 1997 and 2000. The program called for Pepperidge Farm to achieve its growth objective by developing several innovative new products, lowering operating costs by eliminating costs that did not provide value to the customer, and purging waste.

Campbell management believed that a controlling interest in Arnott's Ltd. would yield a competitive advantage in the $3 billion Asian cookie-and-cracker market. The 132-year-old Arnott's was one of Australia's best-known food companies, had access to low-cost ingredients, and had efficient manufacturing processes. Arnott's Australian location also provided a shipping-cost advantage for products exported to the entire Asian/Pacific Rim region. The biscuit and confectionery division introduced popular Pepperidge Farm products to international markets in 1999 when Arnott's Goldfish were launched in Australia.

Away from Home Group

Dale Morrison, like David Johnson, realized the importance of Campbell's food-service unit, Away from Home, in growing corporate sales and earnings. In 2000, U.S. consumers were projected to eat approximately 46 percent of all meals away from home and spend an estimated $342 billion in restaurants. On an average day, almost 140 million meals were eaten in U.S. restaurants and cafeterias. In addition, nearly 21 percent of U.S. households used some form of takeout or delivery each day. Campbell Soup management intended for the company to make Campbell products readily available to both consumers who purchased food for home preparation and those who chose to dine away from home. Morrison believed that Campbell Soup should position itself to provide soups and other processed foods to consumers in their homes and other locations: "If you look at the U.S. soup business, you could say we have an 80% share of the condensed and ready-to-serve market, and where do we go from there? But if you look at soup consumption in total . . . we really have a 38% share. Under that frame of reference, there's real opportunity."[24]

In 1999 the sales of the Away from Home division reached $507 million—a 12 percent increase over 1998. The division provided pot pies to Kentucky Fried Chicken, soups to roughly one-third of McDonald's restaurants, and a wide variety of Prego entrees and Campbell soups to various restaurants and cafeterias. V8 Splash beverages and Pace Mexican salsas were also distributed to restaurants, delicatessens, and cafeterias. The company had introduced serve-your-own soup vending machines in convenience stores and soup kettles in college cafeterias and had also provided complete meals to supermarket delis and cafeterias that included entrees and side dishes packaged in 5.5- and 2.5-pound aluminum trays. The company also tested the popularity of soup kiosks in airports and sports arenas. Campbell's 1998 acquisition of Stockpot soups allowed the company to expand its branded soup presence in the food-service market for soups because of Stockpot's proprietary manufacturing process that allowed soups to be shipped fresh and without preservatives.

Events at Campbell Soup in Early 2000

Campbell Soup Company was ranked number four among *Fortune* magazine's 1999 and 2000 listings of the most admired food companies; it also was ranked as the third

---

[24]Ibid.

most profitable food company among the Fortune 500. However, Campbell Soup's financial and market performance fell considerably short of being rated "best in show" (a David Johnson objective). In his letter to the stockholders in the company's 1999 annual report, Dale Morrison stated his belief that even though the processed-food industry was confronted by a variety of challenges and Campbell Soup had failed to outperform the overall stock market, it was still feasible for Campbell Soup to deliver an attractive return to its shareholders:

> Campbell Soup Company's primary commitment has been, and always will be, to build shareowner wealth. For many years, we succeeded brilliantly in doing so. Lately, however, much has been said and written about the challenges facing our industry and our company—challenges relating, for example, to changing consumer habits and the pace and prospects for growth. Over the past several years, the food industry has underperformed the overall market. And as we are all aware, this year, in a painful departure from our recent track record, Campbell disappointed our investors as well. Our stock price declined 19 percent in the [1999] fiscal year. So I believe our shareowners today are entitled to ask, "What does the future hold for Campbell Soup Company?"
>
> The answer begins with our central business—soup. For millions of people, the Campbell's name is synonymous with quality, wholesomeness, and the best moments of family life.
>
> Beyond soup, we compete in categories that offer abundant opportunities to grow with changing consumer preferences and lifestyles—sauces, beverages, biscuits and confectionery. Campbell brings significant brand power to these categories with favorites like V8 and V8 Splash, Pace, Prego, Franco-American, Pepperidge Farm, Arnott's and Godiva.[25]

Mounting Problems

Despite Morrison's optimism about the company's growth prospects, Campbell's stock price continued to slide from its all-time high of $63 per share in early 1998. During the first nine months of 1999, the stock price traded mostly in the $40 to $45 per share range. Then in late fall of 1999 it began a steep slide, falling below $30 as the company was hit by (1) a series of shareholder lawsuits alleging that company documents misled shareholders about revenues, (2) a February 2000 recall of 109,000 pounds of canned vegetable soup in 13 states after consumers found long pieces of metal in the soup, and (3) forecasts of slow growth for Campbell's brands by both Wall Street analysts and Campbell's executives. Campbell Soup had reported slightly better-than-expected second-quarter earnings for the period ending December 1999, but several Wall Street analysts expected full-year earnings for fiscal year 2000 (ending July) to be $1.86, rising to perhaps $1.99 at the end of fiscal year 2001.

On March 22, 2000, Dale Morrison resigned as president, CEO, and a director of the company. He was replaced by David Johnson, the company's previous CEO, who agreed to serve while the company's board of directors searched for a permanent replacement. The closing stock price on March 22, 2000, was $29¹¹⁄₁₆, off $1⁷⁄₁₆.

---

[25]Campbell Soup Company 1999 annual report.

case 19 The Black & Decker Corporation in 2000

John E. Gamble
University of South Alabama

Arthur A. Thompson
University of Alabama

In 2000 Black & Decker Corporation was still struggling to get out from under the array of financial and strategic problems stemming from the company's $2.8 billion acquisition of Emhart Corporation in 1989. Black & Decker had long been the world's leading producer and marketer of power tools and power tool accessories. But it had begun a program of diversification in the 1980s that had produced mixed results for shareholders. The company's foray into small household appliances had been a success originally, but the small-appliance division acquired from General Electric in the early 1980s had recently been divested because of its drag on B&D's growth. The follow-on acquisition of Emhart, a conglomerate with very diverse business interests, had proved to be a significant impairment to the company's earnings and cash flow as well as a management burden, and during the past 11 years Black & Decker had achieved success in only a few of the businesses it obtained in the Emhart acquisition.

Black & Decker described itself as a diversified global manufacturer and marketer of household, commercial, and industrial products. Going into 2000, the company was the world's largest producer of power tools, power tool accessories, security hardware, and electric lawn and garden products. The company's Price Pfister kitchen and bathroom faucets subsidiary, a business acquired in the Emhart deal, had gained market share for 11 consecutive years to become the third largest brand of plumbing fixtures in North America. Black & Decker was also the worldwide leader in the market for certain types of mechanical fastening systems used in automobile assembly and in other industrial applications—fasteners had been one of Emhart's businesses as well. But while Black & Decker's business portfolio included a lineup of several competitively strong brands, the company's stock price had been a ho-hum performer

---

exhibit 1   Market Performance of Black & Decker's Common Stock, by Quarter, 1985–January 2000

(a) Trend in Black & Decker's Common Stock Price

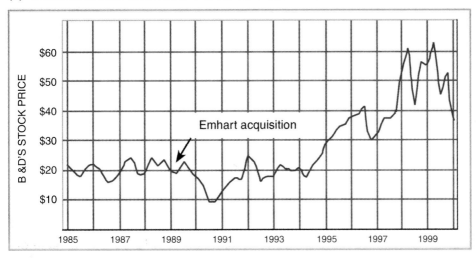

(b) Performance of Black & Decker's Stock Price versus the S&P 500 Index

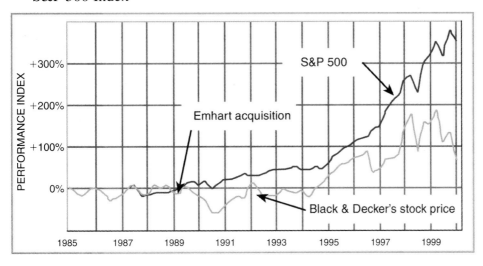

throughout the unprecedented bull market of the 1990s, substantially lagging behind the performance of well-known indexes like the Dow Jones Industrials Average and the Standard & Poor's 500 Index. A graph of Black & Decker's stock performance between 1985 and January 2000 is presented in Exhibit 1. Exhibit 2 provides an 11-year summary of Black & Decker's financial performance.

exbibit 2 Summary of Black & Decker's Financial and Operating Performance, 1989–99 (In Millions of Dollars Except Per Share and Employee Data)

	1999	1998	1997	1996	1995	1994	1993	1992	1991	1990	1989
Sales	$4,520.5	$4,559.9	$4,940.5	$4,914.4	$4,766.1	$4,365.2	$4,121.5	$4,045.7	$3,952.6	$4,313.2	$3,172.5
Operating income	536.3	(466.2)	489.3	356.9	426.1	351.9	302.7	177.1	365.2	458.1	259.2
Operating income excluding restructuring and goodwill amortization*	536.3	509.2	552.6	514.5	494.5	424.9	364.4	391.3	436.0	524.1	284.5
Income taxes	141.0	166.5	122.3	43.5	9.0	62.7	60.7	44.3	54.5	72.4	32.9
Earnings data:											
Earnings (loss) from continuing operations	300.3	(754.8)	227.2	159.2	216.5	89.9	64.1	(95.3)	16.1	19.7	30.0
Discontinued operations	—	—	—	70.4	38.4	37.5	31.1	22.0	36.9	31.4	—
Extraordinary item	—	—	—	—	(30.9)	—	—	(22.7)	—	—	—
Cumulative effects of accounting change	—	—	—	—	—	—	(29.2)	(237.6)	—	—	—
Net earnings (loss)	300.3	(754.8)	227.2	229.6	224.0	127.4	66.0	(333.6)	53.0	51.1	30.0
Total assets	4,012.7	3,852.5	5,360.7	5,153.5	5,545.3	5,264.3	5,166.8	5,295.0	5,456.8	5,829.7	6,258.1
Long-term debt	847.1	1,148.9	1,623.7	1,415.8	1,704.5	1,723.2	2,069.2	2,108.5	2,625.8	2,754.7	2,629.7
Total debt	1,243.5	1,360.6	1,862.5	1,705.8	2,351.7	2,393.3	2,564.6	2,563.8	2,870.3	3,266.2	4,057.5
Stockholders' equity	801.1	574.0	1,791.4	1,632.4	1,423.2	1,169.4	1,048.9	1,074.0	1,027.1	920.7	720.7
Capital expenditures	171.1	146.0	203.1	196.3	203.1	181.5	190.3	167.7	94.9	103.1	112.1
Depreciation and amortization	160.0	155.2	214.2	214.6	206.7	195.4	182.4	188.3	187.1	197.8	131.0
Number of employees	22,100	21,800	28,600	29,200	29,300	29,200	30,500	32,300	31,900	35,900	38,600
Number of shares outstanding	88.4	91.8	96.5	96.1	94.4	85.3	84.5	76.3	62.6	61.4	59.6
Dividends per share	$ 0.48	$ 0.48	$ 0.48	$ 0.48	$ 0.40	$ 0.40	$ 0.40	$ 0.40	$ 0.40	$ 0.40	$ 0.40

*For 1998 this figure also excludes goodwill write-off and gain on sale of businesses.

Source: The Black & Decker Corporation annual reports.

THE EXPECTATION OF BETTER TIMES FOR BLACK & DECKER

In late 1998 Black & Decker management celebrated the completion of an almost decade-long effort to divest nonstrategic businesses gained through its 1989 acquisition of Emhart Corporation and expected the company to enter a long-awaited period of growth as its entire management attention was refocused on its core power tools, plumbing, and security hardware businesses. Black & Decker's CEO, Nolan Archibald, told Wall Street analysts in early 1998 that the pending elimination of nonstrategic businesses that manufactured and marketed such products as True Temper golf club shafts and Emhart glass-making machinery would allow the company to position itself for greater growth in 1999 and 2000. "This [portfolio restructuring] will allow us to focus on core operations that can deliver dependable and superior operating and financial results."[1] However, with the exception of a brief run up to $60 per share in mid-1999, the portfolio restructuring had done little to improve the market performance of the company's securities. In January 2000 Black & Decker's common shares traded at a 52-week low and at a price below the high for 1996 and 1997. Nevertheless, management continued to express confidence that the company's streamlined business portfolio would allow Black & Decker to achieve revenue and earnings growth that the market would find impressive. In commenting on the company's year-end 1999 financial performance, Nolan Archibald said, "We are extremely pleased with Black & Decker's performance this past year, which resulted in record earnings and clearly indicates that the strategic repositioning we undertook in 1998 has been successful."[2]

COMPANY BACKGROUND

Black & Decker was incorporated by Duncan Black and Alonzo Decker in 1910 and initially produced milk cap machines and candy dippers. In 1916 the company introduced its first power tool—a portable half-inch electric drill that was eventually placed on display in the Smithsonian Institution. Over the next 40 years, Duncan Black and Alonzo Decker undertook a number of actions that established the company as the dominant name in power tools and accessories. Black & Decker introduced the first portable screwdriver in 1922, the first electric hammer in 1936, finishing sanders and jigsaws in 1953, and the Dustbuster handheld vacuum in 1978. The company expanded internationally in 1919 when it began sales operations in Russia, Japan, and Australia and opened a production facility in Canada in 1922. The company eventually became known worldwide for its power tools, particularly so in Europe. Black & Decker was managed by the two partners until they died—Black in 1951 and Decker in 1956. As managers, Black and Decker achieved growth by adding to the company's lineup of power tools and accessories and by increasing its penetration of more and more foreign markets. The company maintained a corporate growth strategy tied exclusively to product-line extensions and international expansion until the mid-1980s.

Diversification into Small Household Appliances

Black & Decker began to pursue diversification in the 1980s because of growing maturity of its core power tools business. In 1984 Black & Decker acquired General Electric's

---

[1]As quoted in *Knight-Ridder/Tribune Business News,* January 28, 1998.
[2]As quoted in PR Newswire, January 27, 2000.

housewares business for $300 million. GE's brands had about a 25 percent share of the small-appliance market and generated annual revenues of about $500 million. GE sold its small-appliance division, despite its number one market position, because of the division's low profitability. GE's strong suit was in irons and toaster ovens, where its share was close to 50 percent; sales of GE irons alone totaled about $250 million. Among the other 150 GE products acquired by Black & Decker were coffeemakers, hair dryers and hair curlers, food mixers and processors, toasters, electric skillets, can openers, waffle irons, and blenders. Also in 1984, Black & Decker purchased three European tool manufacturers to fill in product gaps and strengthen its manufacturing base; the acquisition involved a Swiss manufacturer of portable electric woodworking tools for professional users, the leading European manufacturer of drill bits, and a German producer of hobby and precision power tools.

The acquisition of GE's housewares division launched Black & Decker on a course to transform the company from a power tools manufacturer into a consumer products company. In early 1985, the firm changed its name from Black & Decker Manufacturing Company to Black & Decker Corporation to reflect its new emphasis on "being more marketing driven" rather than being merely engaged in manufacturing.

Black & Decker's CEO—Nolan D. Archibald

The chief architect of Black & Decker's foray into diversification was Nolan D. Archibald. Black & Decker hired Archibald as president and chief operating officer in 1985, shortly after the acquisition of GE's small household appliance business. Prior to joining Black & Decker, Archibald was president of the $1.7 billion consumer durables group at Beatrice Companies, where he was responsible for such business units as Samsonite luggage, Culligan water treatment products, Del Mar window coverings, Stiffel lamps, and Aristocraft kitchen cabinets. At the time he was hired, Archibald was 42 years old; he was chosen from a pool of some 50 candidates for the position and turned down offers to be president at two other companies to take the B&D job. Archibald had been at Beatrice since 1977 and was successful in engineering turnarounds in three of Beatrice's businesses. Prior to that, he had headed a turnaround of Conroy Inc.'s Sno-Jet Snowmobile business. Archibald spent two years of his youth winning converts as a Mormon missionary, was an All-American basketball player at Utah's Dixie College, became a standout player at Weber State College in Utah, earned his MBA degree at Harvard Business School, and tried out (unsuccessfully) for the Chicago Bulls professional basketball team. Corporate headhunters rated Archibald as a good strategic thinker who was personable, versatile, and sensitive to people.

Archibald's Early Successes at B&D   According to one Black & Decker dealer, prior to when Archibald took over as president in September 1985 "Black & Decker had been coasting along for quite a few years like a ship without a captain."[3] Archibald wasted little time in reorganizing Black & Decker's worldwide manufacturing operations. Within three months, Archibald initiated a restructuring plan to close older, inefficient plants and boost factory utilization rates by consolidating production within B&D's newest and biggest plants. Approximately 3,000 jobs were eliminated, including a number of high-level managerial jobs. In 1985, B&D took a $215 million write-off for plant shutdowns and other cost-saving reorganization efforts.

---

[3]As quoted in *Business Week,* July 13, 1987, p. 90.

Prior to 1985, the company had pursued a decentralized, multicountry strategy. Each geographic area had its own production facilities, its own product-design centers, and its own marketing and sales organizations to better cater to local market conditions. Over the years, this had resulted in short production runs at scattered production sites, reduced overall manufacturing efficiency, and prevented achievement of scale economies—for example, there were about 100 different motor sizes in B&D's product line. Archibald set the company on a more globalized approach to product design and manufacturing, with much greater communication and coordination between geographic operating units. Production at plants was organized around motor sizes, the number of product variations was reduced, and production runs were lengthened. From 1984 to 1989 seven plants were closed and nearly 3,000 employees were let go. Archibald also insisted more emphasis be put on quality control—during the early 1980s, B&D's reputation in power tools had been tarnished by shoddy product quality.

Meanwhile, Archibald put additional resources into new product development and redesign of the company's power tools and small-appliance lines. Archibald set a goal for the tool division to come up with more than a dozen new products each year—more than B&D had introduced in the five years before his arrival. He also created panels of dealers to suggest new products and features that consumers desired. The company introduced a number of highly successful products such as its Snakelight flashlights; a line of cordless power tools; Macho rotary hammers that could punch holes in stone, brick, and concrete; DeWalt professional power tools; and VersaPak rechargeable batteries that fit both Black & Decker power tools and household appliances.

One of Archibald's biggest marketing challenges was transferring consumers' brand loyalty for GE small appliances over to Black & Decker. Some observers believed Black & Decker would have trouble because B&D's traditional customers were men, and buyers of houseware products were usually women—as a *Wall Street Journal* article headline put it, "Would You Buy a Toaster from a Drillmaker?" B&D executives believed, however, that many women were familiar with the Black & Decker name because they bought power tools as gifts for men and because B&D had pioneered the development of household appliances powered by rechargeable batteries. Black & Decker's handheld DustBuster vacuum cleaner was the market leader, with a 45 percent share. B&D also had been marketing a cordless rotary scrub brush, a cordless rechargeable shoe shiner, and a rechargeable flashlight. Even before acquiring GE's housewares business, B&D had planned to introduce a line of cordless kitchen appliances, but gaining ample retail shelf space was often a hit-or-miss proposition. What made the GE acquisition attractive to B&D was the extra clout that being able to offer retailers a full line of housewares would have in competing for shelf space.

Black & Decker's competitors in small appliances saw the brand-name transition from GE to Black & Decker as an opportunity to gain market share that once was GE's. Sunbeam Appliance quadrupled its 1985 ad budget to $42 million because it wanted to replace GE as the best-known brand in small appliances. Norelco launched a new line of irons and a handheld can opener powered by rechargeable batteries to wrest share away from GE/Black & Decker. Hamilton Beach introduced a battery-operated carving knife. Nearly all small-appliance producers were rumored to be trying to develop cordless adaptations of irons, coffee makers, handheld mixers, and electric carving knives.

Archibald responded to the brand transfer challenge with a series of actions. Since Black & Decker had until 1987 to put its own name on all the GE products it acquired, it led off the transfer process by first putting its name on GE's innovative, expensive, high-margin Spacemaker products, which were designed to be mounted under kitchen cabinets—a line that was not as strongly identified with the GE name. Then B&D introduced a new iron (invented by GE) that shut off automatically when it sat too long or was tipped over; B&D's TV ads for the iron showed an elephant walking away from an iron that had been left on, with a tag line: "Even elephants forget." The brand transfer was accomplished product by product, in each case accompanied by heavy advertising. Under Archibald, Black & Decker spent approximately $100 million during the 1985–87 period to promote the brand transition. The company also organized a large team of brand transition assistants to hang paper tags on display models of newly rebranded products in about 10,000 retail stores across the United States—the tags stated that GE previously sold products now made by Black & Decker. Most analysts regarded Archibald's brand transfer program as successful; a Harvard Business School professor stated, "It is almost a textbook example of how to manage a brand transition."[4]

Archibald was promoted to chairman, president, and chief executive officer in 1986. He was listed among *Fortune* magazine's 10 Most Wanted Executives that year and was named as one of the Six Best Managers of 1987 by *Business Week*. By year-end 1988, Archibald was widely credited with engineering another impressive turn-around, having boosted Black & Decker's profits to $97.1 million—up sharply from the loss of $158.4 million posted in 1985. Archibald was also the recipient of the American Marketing Association's 1996 Edison Achievement Award for his accomplishments as Black & Decker chief executive.

Failed Acquisition Attempts

In early 1988 Black & Decker began an unsolicited takeover bid for American Standard Inc., a diversified manufacturer of bathroom fixtures, air conditioning products, and braking systems for rail and automotive vehicles. American Standard had revenues of $3.4 billion and earnings of $127 million in 1987 (compared to revenues of $1.9 billion and earnings of almost $70 million for Black & Decker). After several months of negotiations, the takeover effort failed and B&D withdrew from the battle.

In January 1989, Black & Decker negotiated a deal with Allegheny International to purchase its Oster/Sunbeam appliance division for about $260 million. Oster/Sunbeam was a leading manufacturer and marketer of small household appliances—blenders, can openers, food mixers, electric skillets, steam irons, and other kitchen items. However, in February, Allegheny International backed out of the sale and merged with another company instead.

The Emhart Acquisition

A month later, in March 1989, Black & Decker agreed to acquire Emhart Corporation for $2.8 billion, rescuing the firm from a hostile takeover bid. Emhart had 1988 sales of $2.8 billion, earnings of $127 million, assets of $2.4 billion, and shareholders' equity of $971 million. Emhart was a diversified manufacturer of industrial products (1988 sales of $1.6 billion), information and electronic systems (1988 sales of $654 million), and consumer products (1988 sales of $547 million). Approximately 40 percent of Emhart's sales and earnings came from foreign operations, the majority of which were concentrated in Europe. Exhibit 3 provides a profile of Emhart's business portfolio. Exhibit 4 provides data on the financial performance of Emhart's business units.

---

[4]Ibid.

exhibit 3   Emhart Corporation's Business Portfolio in 1989 (At the Time of the Company's Acquisition by Black & Decker)

Business and Product Categories	Trademarks/Names	Primary Markets/ Customers
Industrial businesses (1988 sales of $1.6 billion)		
Capacitors, audible signal devices	Emhart, Mallory, Sonalert, Arcotronica	Telecommunications, computer, automotive, and electronic components industries
Electromechanical devices, solid-state control systems, hydrocarbon leak detection systems	Emhart, Mallory, Pollulert	Appliance, automotive, and environmental controls manufacturers
Commercial door hardware, electronic locking systems	Emhart, Carbin, Russwin	Commercial, institutional building construction, and original equipment manufacturers
Footwear materials (insoles, toe puffs, shanks, eyelets, tacks, and nails)	Emhart, Texon, Aquiline	Manufacturers of footwear
Fastening systems (rivets, locknuts, screw anchors, adhesive systems, sealants, and grouts)	Emhart, Molly, Warren, Gripco, Bostik, Kelox, Dodge, Heli-Coil, POP	Appliance, construction, electronics, furniture/ woodwork, packaging, automotive, and other transportation industries
Glass container machinery	Emhart, Hartford, Powers, Sundsvalls	Producers of glass containers for beverage, food, household, and pharmaceutical products
Printed circuit board assembling machinery	Emhart, Dynapert	Electronics industry
Information and electronic systems (1988 sales of $654 million)		
Technology-based systems and services (including computer-based systems), scientific research services, program management	Emhart, PRC, Planning Research Corp., PRC System Services, PRC Environmental Management, PRC Medic Computer Systems, Nova, Stellar	Governmental units and agencies, real estate multiple listing services, group medical practices, and public utilities
Consumer products businesses (1988 sales of $547 million)		
Door hardware, including lock sets, high-security locks, and locking devices	Emhart, Kwikset	Residential construction
Nonpowered lawn and garden equipment, landscape lighting	Garden America, True Temper	Do-it-yourself homeowners
Underground sprinkling and watering systems	Lawn Genie, Drip Mist, Irri-trol	Landscape specialists, do-it-yourself consumers
Golf club shafts, bicycle-frame tubing	True Temper, Dynamic Gold, Black Gold	Golf club manufacturers
Bathroom and kitchen faucets	Price Pfister, The Pfabulous Pfaucet with the Pfunny Name	Residential and commercial construction
Adhesive, sealants	Bostik, Thermogrip	Residential and commercial construction, do-it-yourself consumers
Fasteners, staplers, nailers	Blue-Tack, POP, Molly	Residential and commercial construction

exhibit 4   Financial Performance of Emhart's Business Groups,
             1986–88 (In Millions of Dollars)

	1988	1987	1986A*	1986B
Revenues				
Industrial				
Components	$ 641.8	$ 671.9		$ 653.9
Fastening systems	640.5	638.8		576.3
Machinery	279.0	291.1		419.2
	$1,561.3	$1,601.8		$1,649.4
Information and electronic systems	653.7	438.3		39.3
Consumer	547.5	414.4		405.6
Total	$2,762.5	$2,454.5		$2,094.3
Operating Income (Loss)				
Industrial				
Components	$ 63.8	$ 65.7	$ 48.2	$ (5.4)
Fastening systems	74.8	78.7	68.3	24.8
Machinery	42.7	34.1	44.4	3.9
	$ 181.3	$ 178.5	$160.9	$ 23.3
Information and electronic systems	37.2	22.3	2.0	2.0
Consumer	84.8	68.3	60.4	51.7
	$ 303.3	$ 269.1	$223.3	$ 77.0
Corporate expense	(35.0)	(32.9)	(30.3)	(34.0)
Total	$ 268.3	$ 236.2	$193.0	$ 43.0
Identifiable Assets				
Industrial				
Components	$ 457.8	$ 472.0		$ 400.3
Fastening systems	428.4	428.2		409.7
Machinery	167.8	164.8		297.2
	$1,054.0	$1,065.0		$1,107.2
Information and electronic systems	546.7	361.3		334.5
Consumer	702.7	225.1		266.1
	$2,303.4	$1,651.4		$1,707.8
Corporate	123.2	378.5		148.9
Total	$2,426.6	$2,029.9	$000.0	$1,856.7

*1986 before provision for restructuring.
Source: Emhart 1988 annual report.

In the days following the announcement of Black & Decker's friendly plan to acquire Emhart, B&D's stock price dropped about 15 percent. There was considerable skepticism over the wisdom of the acquisition, both from the standpoint of whether Emhart's businesses had attractive strategic fit with B&D's businesses and whether B&D could handle the financial strain of making such a large acquisition. Emhart was significantly larger than Black & Decker:

1988 Financials	Emhart	Black & Decker
Sales revenues	$2.76 billion	$2.28 billion
Net earnings	126.6 million	97.1 million
Assets	2.43 billion	1.83 billion
Stockholders' equity	970.9 million	724.9 million
Long-term debt	$674.3 million	$277.1 million

The acquisition agreement called for Black & Decker to purchase 59.5 million shares (95 percent) of Emhart Corporation common stock at $40 per share—a price almost three times book value per share ($14.32). Altogether, Black & Decker had to secure $2.7 billion in financing to acquire Emhart. To come up with the funds, Black & Decker entered into a credit agreement with a group of banks that consisted of term loans due 1992 through 1997 and an unsecured revolving credit loan of up to $575 million. The loans carried an interest rate of ¼ percent above whatever the prevailing prime rate was. Scheduled principal payments on the term loans were as follows:

1992	$201,217,000
1993	274,287,000
1994	275,221,000
1995	743,923,000
1996	401,318,000

The credit agreement included covenants that required Black & Decker to achieve certain minimum levels of cash flow coverage of its interest obligations and not to exceed specified leverage (debt-to-equity) ratios during the term of the loan:

Fiscal Year	Maximum Leverage Ratio	Minimum Cash Flow Coverage Ratio
1992	3.25	1.35
1993	2.75	1.50
1994	2.25	1.55
1995 and thereafter	1.50	1.60

Note: The leverage ratio was calculated by dividing indebtedness, as defined by the credit agreement, by consolidated net stockholders' equity. The cash flow coverage ratio was calculated by dividing earnings before interest, taxes, depreciation, and amortization of goodwill minus capital expenditures by net interest expense plus cash income tax payments and dividends declared.

Other covenants in the credit agreement limited Black & Decker's ability to incur additional indebtedness and to acquire businesses or sell assets.

Black & Decker also entered into factoring agreements with financial institutions where it sold its receivables at a discounted rate to avoid waiting 30 to 60 days to collect on its invoices. The company ended its sale of receivables program in December 1997 when it became able to meet its liquidity requirements without factoring receivables.

Black & Decker recorded the excess amount of its purchase price for Emhart over the book value of Emhart's net assets as goodwill to be amortized on a straight-line basis over 40 years. This resulted in Black & Decker's having increased depreciation and amortization charges of about $45 million annually.

Initial Divestitures of Emhart Businesses

Senior management at Black & Decker realized early on that as much as $1 billion of Emhart's business assets would have to be sold to reduce B&D's interest expenses and debt obligations and enable it to meet its covenant agreements. According to accounting rules, these assets had to either be sold within a year or be consolidated with the rest of B&D assets—a move that could cause B&D to fail to meet its maximum leverage covenant. The Emhart businesses that were identified for sale within one year from the acquisition date included footwear materials, printed circuit board assembly equipment (Dynapert), capacitors, chemical adhesives (Bostik), and the entire information and electronic systems business unit (PRC). During 1989 and early 1990, Black & Decker sold the Bostik chemical adhesives division to a French company for $345 million, the footwear materials business to the United Machinery Group for approximately $125 million, and its Arcotronics capacitors business to Nissei Electric of Tokyo for about $80 million; the net proceeds from these sales were used to reduce debt. In early 1990, when the one-year period expired, Black & Decker was forced to consolidate about $566 million of the unsold assets, boosting the goodwill on its balance sheet by $560 million, raising annual amortization charges by $14 million. To keep from violating the maximum debt/equity ratio allowed under its credit schedule, Black & Decker was forced to issue $150 million in new preferred stock, $47 million of which was purchased from its 401(K) employee thrift plan when no other buyers came forward.

Throughout 1991 Black & Decker continued to struggle to meet its covenant agreements. The company divested Emhart's Garden America business unit and the Mallory Controls operations in North America and Brazil for a combined total of about $140 million. The company also sold its True Temper Hardware unit, its PRC Medic unit, and its U.S. Capacitors business for a combined total of nearly $110 million. The prices B&D got for the Emhart businesses it sold were generally below management's expectations, partly because oncoming recessionary effects reduced what buyers were willing to pay.

Nonetheless, these divestitures (described by B&D management as "nonstrategic assets") and the sale of $150 million in preferred stock, allowed Black & Decker to reduce its total debt from a peak of $4 billion following the Emhart acquisition in April 1989 to $2.9 billion at year-end 1991. Even so, Black & Decker was still hard pressed to generate enough cash to meet its debt repayment schedule, a problem compounded by the 1990–91 recession, which hit the company's tool and household goods businesses fairly hard. The company's stock price fell from the mid-20s at the time of the Emhart acquisition to a low of $11–$12 in early 1991—many observers believed that the fundamental cause of B&D's financial plight was that it had paid too much for Emhart. There was also concern about whether there was enough strategic fit between Emhart and B&D. By early 1992, the stock price had recovered to the low 20s, partly because a decline in the prime rate from 10 percent to 6.5 percent had lowered B&D's interest burden substantially. (The credit agreement pegged the interest rate B&D paid at ¼ percent above the prevailing prime rate.)

Subsequent Divestitures: 1993–96

During the next six years, Black & Decker's corporate management sought to find buyers for several nonstrategic businesses acquired as part of the Emhart deal. Three were sold between 1993 and 1996.

Dynapert   The Dynapert business unit provided automated equipment for assembling printed circuit boards to electronics customers around the world. The equipment was among the most complex computer-controlled machinery being used in any industrial application. Dynapert had two manufacturing plants (one in the United States and one in England) and sales and service facilities throughout the world. The unit had launched a total quality program and implemented just-in-time manufacturing techniques.

Sales were made directly to users by an employee sales force and independent sales representatives. Dynapert faced competition from both U.S. and foreign manufacturers. Competition centered on technological and machine performance features, price, delivery terms, and provision of technical services. The Dynapert division, which generated 1991 sales of about $180 million, had been put on the market shortly after the Emhart acquisition, and was sold two years later to Dover Corporation's Universal Instrument division for an undisclosed amount.

Corbin Russwin   Emhart's Corbin Russwin manufactured locks and door hardware for the European commercial security hardware market. The unit employed 550 people at its plant in Berlin, Germany. Yale and Valour, Inc., the British manufacturer of Yale locks, purchased the Corbin Russwin unit from Black & Decker in 1994 for $80 million. Black & Decker recorded a gain of $18 million on the combined sales of the Corbin Russwin and Dynapert units.

PRC Information Systems and Services   This segment consisted of a single business unit known as PRC, Inc., headquartered in McLean, Virginia. PRC and its predecessors had been in business since the mid-1970s. A majority of PRC's business came from contracts with various agencies and units of the federal government. Approximately 40 percent of PRC's 1991 revenues were from contracts with the Department of Defense. In addition, PRC was the leading provider of (1) online printed residential real estate multiple listing systems and (2) computer-aided emergency dispatch systems. The types of services PRC provided were highly competitive, and strategic defense expenditures were expected to decline given the improvement of foreign relations. Many of PRC's competitors were large defense contractors with significantly greater financial resources. As the Department of Defense's expenditures for weapons programs continued to decline, these large contractors were expected to bid more aggressively for the types of contract work done by PRC. PRC had also been put on the market for sale following the Emhart acquisition. In 1991, PRC had sales of $684 million and pretax operating earnings of $32.3 million. In mid-1991 B&D appointed a new person to head PRC; shortly thereafter, PRC launched an initiative to pursue new markets. The objective was to shift PRC's business mix so that half came from U.S. customers and half from overseas customers. However, PRC management had great difficulty developing new nongovernment customers and was only growing at about one-third the rate of its closest competitors under Black & Decker ownership.

Black & Decker had little success in locating interested buyers for the PRC unit until 1995, when PRC Realty Systems and PRC Environmental Management, Inc., were sold for $60 and $35.5 million, respectively. Litton Industries agreed to purchase the remaining PRC operations in 1996 for $425 million. Prior to its sale to Litton, when it appeared that finding a buyer was becoming increasingly unlikely, Black & Decker management had considered a spinoff of the unit in 1992. The spinoff was never finalized because Wall Street showed little interest in a $350 million public offering of PRC stock. PRC's 1995 sales and after-tax earnings were $800 million and $38.4 million, respectively.

Black & Decker's 1998 Divestitures

Black & Decker again initiated portfolio restructuring in 1998 when it divested its household products business and two businesses gained through the Emhart acquisition.

Household Products   Black & Decker's household products business had established itself as a worldwide leader in products used for home cleaning, garment care, cooking, and food and beverage preparation by 1990. It had the largest market share of any full-line producer of household appliance products in the United States, Canada, Mexico, and Australia and a growing presence in Europe, Southeast Asia, and Latin America. The household products division was using the worldwide distribution network and brand-name recognition that had been established by the tools division to gain greater global penetration in household appliances. However, by 1996, the company had lost substantial market share in almost every housewares product category. Its Toast-R-Ovens and irons were the only remaining Black & Decker products that held leading shares of their respective markets. (See Exhibit 5 for market shares of the major competitors by product category for 1990, 1993, and 1996.)

Like the market for power tools, the market for small household appliances was both mature and cyclical. Growth opportunities existed mainly in the form of creating innovative new products and in increasing market penetration in the countries of Eastern Europe and other developing nations where household appliance saturation rates were low. It was difficult to grow sales in the United States without introducing innovative new products since most small appliances had very high household saturation rates. In 1996 blenders were found in 80 percent of U.S. households, coffeemakers had a 74 percent saturation rate, and toasters were found in 90 percent of U.S. households. Many consumers clearly had both a toaster and toaster oven, since toaster ovens had a 42 percent U.S. household saturation rate.

Black & Decker's housewares business unit had been successful at launching new products that might entice a consumer into replacing an existing small appliance for one offering more features or better performance. The company's SnakeLight flexible flashlight was introduced in 1994 and quickly became one of the most popular small appliances ever developed by the company. In 1996 the company introduced a revamped Quick 'N Easy line of irons with a new Sure Steam system, and in 1998 it improved the glideability of its irons with a new proprietary coated soleplate. The company also introduced cordless products such as the ScumBuster, a submersible scourer and scrubber, and the FloorBuster, an upright vacuum cleaner that achieved rapid sales increases.

In late 1997 the company launched a designer line of small kitchen appliances, Kitchentools, which won five Industrial Design Excellence Awards in 1998. The Kitchentools line carried premium pricing; the stand mixer had a suggested retail price of $289.99, the thermal coffeemaker listed at $159.99, the blender was priced at $139.99, the food processor was priced at $229.99, the hand mixer's retail price was $69.00, and the Kitchentools can opener carried a suggested retail price of $34.99. Even though the Kitchentools line was praised for its quality and innovative styling, it did not sell as well as Black & Decker management had expected. The company also had some difficulty manufacturing the products and getting them to market by the planned launch date.

Black & Decker had lost substantial market share in recent years and had seen its profit margins erode despite its best efforts to maintain efficient operations. Between 1995 and 1997 the company had completely overhauled its supply chain management *exhibit 5* Unit Volume for Selected Small Appliances and Market Shares of Leading Producers, 1990, 1993, and 1996 (Unit Volume in Thousands)

Product/Leading Brands	1990	1993	1996
Can openers	6,200	6,380	6,910
Rival	33%	27%	26%
Hamilton Beach/Proctor Silex	13	15	24
Black & Decker	26	28	13
Oster/Sunbeam	11	13	13
Coffeemakers	17,740	14,390	15,000
Mr. Coffee	28%	31%	32%
Hamilton Beach/Proctor Silex	19	18	24
West Bend	—	3	9
Black & Decker	20	17	8
Food processors	4,760	1,916	1,525
Hamilton Beach/Proctor Silex	21%	19%	40%
Cuisinart	Unknown	13	18
Black & Decker	25	21	10
Oster/Sunbeam	18	19	8
Hand mixers	4,400	5,060	5,280
Hamilton Beach/Proctor Silex	14%	18%	24%
Black & Decker	34	28	15
Oster/Sunbeam	25	18	13
HPA/Betty Crocker	—	—	11
Irons	16,950	17,460	15,600
Black & Decker	50%	50%	38%
Hamilton Beach/Proctor Silex	24	30	29
Oster/Sunbeam	17	10	17
Rowenta	—	—	7
Toaster ovens	2,800	3,340	3,670
Black & Decker	57%	56%	56%
Toastmaster	13	16	17
Hamilton Beach/Proctor Silex	19	20	11
HPA/Betty Crocker	—	—	6
Toasters	8,900	9,850	10,760
Hamilton Beach/Proctor Silex	35%	50%	37%
Toastmaster	27	31	30
Rival	—	—	17
HPA/Betty Crocker	—	—	5
Black & Decker	16	13	4

Source: Compiled by case researchers from data presented in *Appliance,* April 1991 and April 1997.

to reduce finished goods inventory and improve customer service and production planning. The company had eliminated $150 million from logistics costs during that time period but still only averaged about 2 percent profit margins on its housewares products. The business unit was identified for divestiture by Nolan Archibald in January 1998 and was sold to Windmere-Durable in May 1998 for $315 million. The agreement allowed

Black & Decker to retain its DustBuster, FloorBuster, ScumBuster, and SnakeLight product lines. In June 1998 Black & Decker announced the sale of its housewares operations in New Zealand and Australia to Gerard Industries, an Australian electrical products manufacturer. The company had also sold its consumer glue gun and stapler business to Longwood Industries for an undisclosed amount in July 1998.

Recreational Outdoor Products   In 1998 B&D's True Temper Sports business unit was the leading global designer, manufacturer, and marketer of steel golf club shafts; with over a 60 percent market share in the steel shaft segment, it was three times as large as its closest rival. True Temper also manufactured graphite shafts but had a very limited market share in that segment since it focused on the premium end of the market. The division supplied more than 800 golf club manufacturers around the world, including such industry leaders as Callaway Golf, Ping, Titleist, and Taylor Made. The sales of this unit had grown at a compounded annual rate of 12 percent between 1995 and 1997. True Temper Sport's growth rate reflected the overall growth in the golf equipment industry. The unit also manufactured specialty tubing for the bicycle and sporting goods industries. Many of the bicycles and kayak paddles used by U.S. Olympians were manufactured from True Temper precision tubing.

Black & Decker sold the business to Cornerstone Equity Investors in June 1998 for $178 million. The new owners stated that they intended for True Temper to remain the leader in golf club shafts and that they intended to expand into new product categories requiring specialty tubing. True Temper's president said that the new company would develop precision tubing products for such sporting goods industries as downhill skiing and archery.

Glass-Container-Forming Machinery   In 1998 B&D's Emhart glass-container-forming machinery division was considered the global leader and offered the world's most complete line of glass-container-making equipment. Important competitive factors were price, technological and machine performance features, product reliability, and technical and engineering services. An increasing worldwide preference for plastic and other nonglass containers had led to a slowing growth rate for glass-container-forming equipment and inspection equipment. There was little seasonal variation in industry demand. Glass-container-making equipment was in 24-hour use in virtually all plants worldwide, creating a predictable need for servicing and rebuilding; nearly two-thirds of the unit's revenues came from rebuilding and repair services and technology upgrades. In January 1998 the business was identified as a nonstrategic asset that was to be divested; it was sold to Bucher Holding AG of Switzerland in September 1998 for $178 million.

BLACK & DECKER'S BUSINESS PORTFOLIO IN 2000

In 2000 Black & Decker Corporation was a diversified multinational enterprise with a business portfolio consisting of:

- Power tools and accessories for both do-it-yourselfers and professional tradespeople.
- Lawn and garden equipment.
- Security hardware for residential markets in the United States and residential and commercial hardware in certain European countries.
- Cleaning and lighting products.

exhibit 6   Black & Decker's Business Portfolio at Year-end 1999

Power tools and accessories
(1999 sales: $3.21 billion)
- Drills
- Screwdrivers
- Saws
- Sanders
- Grinders
- Tabletop saws
- Drill bits
- Screwdriver bit
- Saw blades
- Cleaning and lighting products

Hardware and home improvement
(1999 sales: $882 million)
- Lock sets
- Deadbolts

- Master keying systems
- Faucets and fixtures
- Lawn and garden care products

Fastening and assembly systems
(1999 sales: $498 million)
- Rivets and riveting tools
- Threaded inserts
- Stud welding fastening systems
- Lock nuts
- Self-drilling screws
- Construction anchors

- Plumbing products.
- Commercial fastening systems.

Exhibit 6 provides a detailed listing of the products produced and marketed by B&D in these business areas. Exhibit 7 provides 1997–99 financial performance data by business group. A brief description of each business group follows.

Power Tools and Accessories

Black & Decker was the world's largest manufacturer, marketer, and servicer of power tools and accessories. The company's products were available at almost all retail outlets that sold power tools in the United States, Europe, and other developed countries. In fact, Black & Decker products were so popular in the United Kingdom that many British do-it-yourselfers referred to home improvement projects as "Black & Deckering." Black & Decker was named as the top-performing hardware brand by 6 out of every 10 U.S. retailers included in a 1997 survey conducted by *Discount Store News*. Other brands that were highly rated by hardware retailers were Stanley, General Electric, Skil, Rubbermaid, Makita, and Dutch Boy. Black & Decker's products were also highly rated in terms of performance by consumers, and most of its products carried a two-year warranty.

Industry Growth and Competition   Demand for power tools and accessories was regarded as mature and cyclical. Volume was influenced by residential and commercial construction activity, by consumer expenditures for home improvement, and by the overall level of manufacturing activity. (A number of manufacturers used power tools in performing certain production tasks—automotive and aerospace firms, for example, were heavy users of power tools.) Worldwide sales of power tools were an estimated $10 billion in 1999. The North American market for power tools was estimated at $3.5 billion, European sales were estimated at $4.0 billion, Asia/Pacific sales were an estimated $2.0 billion, and Latin American sales of power tools were approximately $500 *exhibit* 7   Black & Decker's Financial Performance by Business Segment, 1997–99

	Power Tools and Accessories	Hardware and Home Improvement	Fastening and Assembly Systems	All Others	Currency Translation Adjustments	Corporate Adjustments and Eliminations	Consolidated
1999							
Sales to unaffiliated customers	$3,209.3	$881.8	$497.7	—	($ 68.3)	$ —	$4,520.5
Operating income before restructuring and exit costs, write-off of goodwill, and gain on sales of businesses	377.3	124.0	84.3	—	(6.9)	(42.4)	536.3
Depreciation and amortization	87.7	31.1	15.4	—	(1.8)	27.6	160.0
Identifiable assets	1,836.0	508.2	273.2	—	2,617.4	1,395.3	4,012.7
Capital expenditures	$ 109.1	$ 38.3	$ 26.9	—	($ 3.5)	$ 0.3	$ 171.1
1998							
Sales to unaffiliated customers	$2,946.4	$851.1	$463.0	$333.6	($ 34.2)	$ —	$4,559.9
Operating income before restructuring and exit costs, write-off of goodwill, and gain on sales of businesses	293.4	125.2	76.6	16.5	(4.4)	(23.3)	484.0
Depreciation and amortization	88.2	27.1	13.4	—	(1.1)	27.6	155.2
Identifiable assets	1,631.3	507.8	246.7	—	(4.6)	1,471.3	3,852.5
Capital expenditures	$ 79.1	$ 36.5	$ 16.2	$ 13.3	($ 1.1)	$ 2.0	$ 146.0
1997							
Sales to unaffiliated customers	$2,936.4	$804.8	$451.3	$718.1	$ 29.9	$ —	$4,940.5
Operating income before restructuring and exit costs, write-off of goodwill, and gain on sales of businesses	290.7	121.3	69.7	61.7	(2.3)	(51.8)	489.3
Depreciation and amortization	87.5	24.7	11.9	24.4	(0.3)	66.0	214.2
Identifiable assets	1,635.4	476.5	248.2	438.6	8.0	2,554.0	5,360.7
Capital expenditures	$ 113.2	$ 47.3	$ 15.4	$ 25.3	($ 0.2)	$ 2.1	$ 203.1

Source: Black & Decker annual reports.

million. The global market for power tools failed to grow significantly between 1997 and 1999, but was expected to grow at low- to mid-single-digit annual rates between 2000 and 2002. The industry's worldwide demand plateau during the late 1990s was attributable in large part to Asian financial and economic troubles. During 1998 and 1999 North America was the fastest-growing market for power tools as cordless and professional-grade power tools gained in popularity with consumers. Demand in Europe grew more slowly than in the United States during the late 1990s and was expected to continue to lag behind U.S. demand in the near future. Worldwide, the biggest percentage growth during the early and mid-1990s occurred in emerging Asian countries, where the use of power tools was quickly replacing the use of hand tools. Healthy demand for power tools was expected to return to Asian markets once the region had fully recovered from the effects of financial and economic instability that began in late 1997.

Market Segments   There were two distinct groups of buyers for power tools: professional users and do-it-yourselfers. Professional users included construction workers, electricians, plumbers, repair and maintenance workers, auto mechanics, and manufacturing workers. Professional users were very conscious of quality and features; they tended to buy only those tools that were durable, functional, dependable, and capable of precision. They also tended to be very knowledgeable compared to do-it-yourselfers, many of whom were first-time buyers and used power tools infrequently.

Because the needs of professional users and do-it-yourself consumers tended to be sharply different, some manufacturers had a heavy-duty professional line and a consumer/do-it-yourself line and others catered to just one of the two segments. Professional users tended to purchase their tools through jobbers, contractor supply firms, industrial supply houses, building supply centers, and some home improvement centers. Tools for the consumer segment were sold at home improvement centers, building materials centers, mass merchandisers (Sears), discount chains (Wal-Mart, Kmart), and hardware stores.

Until the late 1980s, the consumer tool segment was growing at a faster clip than the professional segment. But narrowing price differentials and a rising interest on the part of gung-ho do-it-yourselfers in professional-quality tools had, in the U.S. market, spurred demand for heavy-duty professional tools. The sales of both consumer-grade and professional-grade cordless products were also becoming increasingly popular, with a compound annual growth rate of over 10 percent during the mid- and late 1990s.

Competition   Power tool manufacturers competed on such variables as price, quality, product design, product innovation, brand-name reputation, size and strength of retail dealer networks, and after-sale service. All makers were working to bring out new products that were lightweight, compact, cordless, quiet, less prone to vibration, strong, and easy to manipulate. The major manufacturers had sales forces whose main task was to expand and strengthen the network of retail dealers carrying their line of tools. Salespeople signed on new dealers and called on major accounts—wholesale distributors, discount chains, home improvement centers, and other mass merchandisers—to win better access to shelf space in their retail outlets, help with promotion and display activities, and upgrade dealers' product knowledge and sales skills. Some manufacturers offered training seminars and provided training videos to dealers/distributors. Manufacturers that concentrated on the professional segment engaged in limited advertising and promotion activities, spending their dollars for trade magazine ads, trade shows, and in-store displays. Those that concentrated on the consumer segment, like Black & Decker, spent comparatively heavily for TV and magazine ads and also for co-op ad programs with dealers.

exhibit 8   Estimated U.S. Sales and Market Shares of Power Tool Manufacturers, 1979, 1991, and 1997 ($ Millions)

	1979		1991		1997	
	Dollar Sales	**Percent Share**	**Dollar Sales**	**Percent Share**	**Dollar Sales**	**Percent Share**
Consumer tools						
Black & Decker	$169	44.5%	$ 325	39.7	$ 460	43.1%
Sears/Ryobi	107	28.2	280	34.0	305	28.5
Milwaukee	6	1.5	4	0.5	6	0.6
Makita	2	0.5	43	5.2	32	3.0
Porter Cable	—	—	—	—	—	—
Delta	—	—	—	—	—	—
Skil	52	13.7	82	10.0	165	15.4
Others	44	11.6	86	10.6	102	9.4
Total	$380	100.0%	$ 820	100.0%	$1,070	100.0%
Professional tools						
Black & Decker	$205	42.1%	$ 125	17.9%	$ 918	36.7%
Sears/Ryobi	9	1.8	50	7.1	285	11.4
Milwaukee	89	18.2	145	20.7	436	17.4
Makita	22	4.5	160	22.9	304	12.2
Porter Cable	NA	NA	50	7.1	240	9.6
Delta	NA	NA	40	5.7	209	8.4
Skil	54	11.1	40	5.7	32	1.3
Others	109	22.3	90	12.9	76	3.0
Total	$488	100.0%	$ 700	100.0%	$2,500	100.0%
Total tools						
Black & Decker	$374	43.1%	$ 450	29.6%	$1,378	38.6%
Sears/Ryobi	116	13.4	330	21.7	590	16.5
Milwaukee	95	10.9	149	9.8	442	12.4
Makita	24	2.8	203	13.4	336	9.4
Porter Cable	NA	NA	50	3.3	240	6.7
Delta	NA	NA	40	2.6	209	5.9
Skil	106	12.2	122	8.0	197	5.5
Others	153	17.6	176	11.6	210	9.4
Total	$868	100.0%	$1,520	100.0%	$3,570	100.0%

NA = not available

Source: Compiled by the case researchers from a variety of sources, including telephone interviews with company personnel; data for 1979 are based on information in Skil Corporation, Harvard Business School, case #9-389-005.

Black & Decker's Global Competitive Position in Power Tools   In 2000 Black & Decker was the overall world leader in the world power tool industry, followed by Bosch/Skil Power Tools, a division of Robert Bosch Corporation (one of Germany's leading companies), and Japanese brands Makita and Hitachi. Other competitors were Atlas/Copco, Delta/Porter Cable, Hilti, Ryobi, and Electrolux. For most of the company's history, Black & Decker's greatest strength was in the consumer tools segment (see Exhibit 8); it was the market leader in the United States, Europe (where it had had a presence since the 1920s), and many other countries outside Europe. No other manufacturer came close to matching B&D's global distribution capabilities in the do-it-yourself segment. Makita and Ryobi were the leaders in Japan and several other Asian countries. Bosch was strongest in Europe.

In consumer tools Black & Decker's strongest U.S. competitor was Sears, which marketed tools under the Sears Craftsman label. Sears's longtime supplier of tools was Ryobi, which supplied Sears with 75 percent of its tool requirements. Skil's strength was in power saws; its 1992 joint venture with Robert Bosch Power Tools was contrived to give the two brands more clout in gaining shelf space and greater global coverage capabilities. Black & Decker's consumer-grade power tools were also carried by Sears, and the company had developed a new Quantum line of power tools sold exclusively by Wal-Mart. Quantum was an intermediate line that was more durable than typical consumer lines but did not meet the performance of the company's professional power tools. Black & Decker's Mouse sander, WoodHawk circular saws, and FireStorm drills, along with its products that used the VersaPak interchangeable battery, were among the company's best-selling consumer tools.

Although surveys showed that consumers associated the Black & Decker name with durable power tools, trade professionals viewed Black & Decker products as products for do-it-yourselfers. During the late 1980s, the company's charcoal-gray professional tools line was not seen by professional users as sufficiently differentiated from B&D's traditional black line of consumer tools. Professionals preferred tools made by Makita, Skil, and Milwaukee (a U.S. tool manufacturer with a reputation for quality, heavy-duty tools). During the 1970s and 1980s, Makita had steadily increased its share of the professional segment and by 1991 had captured 53 percent of the U.S. professional handheld power tool segment.

In 1991 B&D executives formed a team, headed by the president of B&D's power tools division, to come up with a new strategy for the professional market segment. The team elected to create an entirely new line of industrial-grade tools for professional users under the DeWalt brand, a name borrowed from a 65-year-old maker of high-quality stationary saws acquired by B&D in 1960. The team changed the tools' color from gray to industrial yellow because the latter was easy to see, signaled safety, and was distinct from other leading brands of professional power tools. Every product in B&D's professional line was redesigned based on input from professionals, dealers, and B&D engineers. The redesigned versions were all tested by professional users; every item had to meet or beat Makita's tools in user tests before going into production. The new DeWalt line was introduced in March 1992. As part of the introduction of the DeWalt line, B&D created "swarm teams" of 120 young, high-energy marketers that visited construction sites to demonstrate DeWalt tools in their bright yellow-and-black Chevy Blazers. DeWalt swarm teams also promoted DeWalt tools at NASCAR events, vocational clubs, union apprenticeship programs, and retail locations. The company intended to double the number of swarm team members in the United States between 1998 and 1999. In 1996 DeWalt swarm teams invaded Europe with a fleet of yellow-and-black Range Rover Defenders with the charge of making DeWalt a leading brand on that continent. The company also instituted a policy of offering professional users the loan of a DeWalt power tool when waiting for their equipment to be fixed at any of the company's 135 U.S. service centers. There were also DeWalt demonstration booths at each of the service centers.

Initial response to the DeWalt line was excellent. As the brand began to gain in popularity with professional users, Black & Decker developed additional DeWalt tools. In 1997, newly introduced DeWalt products were awarded two Industrial Design Excellence Awards from the Industrial Designers Society of America. The success of the new DeWalt line exceeded Black & Decker management's expectations and surpassed its

$200 million sales volume objective for 1995 by over $100 million. In 1999 DeWalt was one of the leading power tool brands for professionals and serious do-it-yourselfers.

Black & Decker was also the world leader in the market for such accessories as drill bits, saw blades, and screwdriver bits. Vermont American, Irwin Hanson/American Tool, Bosch, Freud, and Wolfcraft were B&D's closest competitors in the accessories market, but no other company had as broad a product line or geographic coverage as Black & Decker. Most of the company's growth in accessory sales was accounted for by accessory lines developed for the DeWalt brand and a line of new premium woodworking saw blades. The company intended to maintain its market leadership by expanding into more woodworking supply and industrial/construction distribution channels and continuing to introduce innovative products.

In 1998 Black & Decker launched a series of initiatives intended to strengthen its competitive position in power tools and accessories. First, it introduced a corporatewide six sigma quality program to bring about improvements in costs, defect rates, product quality, and customer satisfaction. Second, the company took a $164 million restructuring charge that involved the elimination of 2,900 positions; worldwide plant rationalization that resulted in plant closings in Canada, Singapore, and Italy; a reorganization of its European operations; and various reengineering projects in all plants. Third, it initiated a restructuring of its supply chain management to improve customer service while reducing inventories. Although Black & Decker's restructuring program cut across all business units, it was primarily focused on its global power tools business and was expected to yield more than $100 million annually in cost savings. Additional cost savings were achieved through the integration of Black & Decker's cleaning and lighting products like its DustBuster vacuum cleaner, ScumBuster wet scrubber, and SnakeLight flashlight with its power tool businesses after the sale of the housewares division to Windmere in 1998.

The April 21, 1999, exit of Joseph Galli, Black & Decker's president of its Worldwide Power Tools and Accessories group, shocked analysts and investors and caused a one-day 8 percent decline in the company's share price. Galli, age 41, was a rising star at Black & Decker and was thought to be the leading candidate to succeed Archibald as CEO. There was a widely held belief in the power tools industry that much of the DeWalt brand's success was attributable to Galli's strategic leadership and that Galli had been forced out of B&D as a result of his desire to become the company's CEO within the near future. Archibald, who had no immediate retirement plans, commented that Galli had "expressed an interest in advancing his management career to a higher level, and we have agreed it makes sense for him to pursue this goal outside of Black & Decker."[5] In June 1999 Joe Galli become president and chief operating officer of Amazon.com. Even though there was some initial concern by investors over Galli's departure, B&D's Power Tools and Accessories group continued to perform well in his absence; its sales increased by 11 percent and operating profit increased by 27 percent during the fourth quarter of 1999. The business unit's annual sales and operating profits increased by 9 percent and 29 percent, respectively, over 1998 sales and operating profits.

Lawn and Garden Equipment

Black & Decker's lawn and garden tools like Groom 'N' Edge, Vac 'N' Mulch, and LeafBuster were distributed through the same channels as the company's power tools. In addition, the buyers of B&D's hedge trimmers, string trimmers, lawn mowers, edgers, and blower/vacuums could get the items repaired at B&D's 150 company-owned service

---

[5]As quoted in the *Baltimore Sun,* April 22, 1999.

centers worldwide and several hundred other authorized service centers operated by independent owners. Where feasible, B&D's lawn and garden products had a global design. The company had recently begun to offer cordless electric string trimmers and hedge trimmers in North America and Europe. The cordless hedge trimmer could run continuously for about 30 minutes, and the cordless string trimmer could trim hard-to-reach areas from a half-acre lawn on a single battery charge. As of 2000, Black & Decker marketed its cordless lawn mowers only in Europe.

Security Hardware

B&D's security hardware business was the leader in the $2 billion global market for door hardware for homes and businesses. The company had developed good-better-best product lines that covered all major residential price points. The Kwikset brand was positioned as an affordable product targeted to do-it-yourselfers; B&D had boosted Kwikset's sales by providing retailers with a videotape that took the mystery out of changing household locks. Kwikset Plus was a midrange product, and the company's TITAN products were designed for the fine home market. TITAN NightSight handsets and deadbolts featured lighted keyways, and the TITAN AccessOne keyless entry deadbolt and handset systems allowed homeowners to use a remote control to unlock the door from as far away as 30 feet. The TITAN line also included the Society Brass Collection of solid brass designer door hardware. All TITAN products boasted a lifetime finish that was protected against tarnishing, rust, and corrosion.

This business, acquired from Emhart, had achieved significant cost savings by integrating its purchasing, distribution, and marketing activities with B&D's other consumer products businesses. B&D's worldwide distribution network was also providing the hardware group wider geographic sales opportunities. In many instances, door hardware was sold in the same retail channels as B&D's power tools and accessories. Black & Decker's restructuring and six sigma quality initiatives, begun in 1998, also affected its security hardware business—products and facilities were rationalized, high-cost operations were restructured, and automation was used where feasible. Black & Decker's major competitors in the North American security hardware market included Schlage, Weiser, Weslock, and a variety of Asian exporters. Major competitors in Europe included Williams, Assa Abloy, Cisa, Keso, and Abus.

Plumbing Products

B&D's plumbing products business, Price Pfister, had gained market share since the Emhart acquisition to become the third largest manufacturer and marketer of plumbing fixtures in North America by 2000. Price Pfister had benefited from access to B&D's retail distribution network by gaining more shelf space in home improvement centers. Price Pfister had also introduced fashionable, but affordably priced, new designs and new lines that had become popular with plumbing wholesalers and plumbing contractors. Price Pfister had increased its brand recognition through in-store merchandising activities and with TV ads using the theme "The Pfabulous Pfaucet with the Pfunny Name" in the early 1990s and "The Pfabulous Pfaucet. Pforever. No Drips, No Tarnish, No Worries" theme in the late 1990s.

Price Pfister's major competitors in the $1.9 billion North American market for sink, tub, shower, and lavatory plumbing hardware were American Standard, Kohler, Delta, and Moen. The industry had grown at a slow rate of 2 to 3 percent since 1995 and was expected to grow at a comparable rate over the next few years. Plumbing products with new styles and features were in the highest demand. Black & Decker expected new decorative faucets like Price Pfister's Georgetown and Roman lines, introduced during the late 1990s, to account for 20 percent of the unit's annual sales. Price Pfister expected to improve its performance with the addition of innovative and attractive new lines, better in-store merchandising, improved manufacturing efficiency, and better supply chain management.

Commercial Fastening Systems

Black & Decker was among the global leaders in the $2 billion fastening and assembly systems market. This business unit marketed fastening products under 26 different brands and trademarks to automotive, electronics, aerospace, machine tool, and appliance companies in the United States, Europe, and the Far East. The industry's recent growth rate had ranged between 3 and 5 percent, and future growth was expected to remain within that range. Some emerging markets did generate higher growth rates as new industries and companies emerged and plant capacity was added.

Products were sold directly to users and also through distributors and manufacturers' representatives. Competition centered on product quality, performance, reliability, price, delivery, and ability to provide customers with technical and engineering services. Competition came from many manufacturers in several countries. Major competitors included Textron, TRW, Eaton, and such regional companies as Raymond, Gesipa, Huck, and Fukui. Black & Decker was the global leader in commercial blind riveting and automotive stud welding systems, and its other fastening system categories held strong positions in various geographic regions. Black & Decker management intended to maintain its leadership in the automotive stud welding category with new product innovations. More than 30 percent of the unit's 1999 sales were accounted for by products introduced within the past five years. Black & Decker intended to improve the performance of the division through implementation of its six sigma quality initiative, reengineered operations, and plant rationalizations.

BLACK & DECKER'S FUTURE PROSPECTS

The year 2000 marked the beginning of Black & Decker's second year of operations with its streamlined portfolio of businesses following the 1998 divestiture of its small-appliance, True Temper recreational products, and Emhart glass-forming machinery businesses. Black & Decker had sold the three businesses for more than management's expected $500 million and was able to reduce operating expenses by more than $100 million annually, primarily as a result of the elimination of 3,000 jobs from its payroll. In addition, the series of divestitures had cut the company's amortization of goodwill associated with the Emhart acquisition by about $30 million annually for the next 30 years.

This last round of divestitures, coupled with the sale of businesses in earlier years, completed the divestiture of the nonstrategic Emhart assets gained in the 1989 acquisition. Price Pfister and Kwikset were two of the Emhart businesses that initially captured the attention of Black & Decker management and were now among the three remaining Emhart businesses still included in Black & Decker's portfolio. So far, the 1998 divestitures had not produced steady increases in the company's stock price, but Nolan Archibald was confident that the company's ability to focus solely on power tools and other closely aligned businesses would allow the company to begin to provide its shareholders with above-average returns.

case | 20   Robin Hood

Joseph Lampel
New York University

It was in the spring of the second year of his insurrection against the High Sheriff of Nottingham that Robin Hood took a walk in Sherwood Forest. As he walked he pondered the progress of the campaign, the disposition of his forces, the Sheriff's recent moves, and the options that confronted him.

The revolt against the Sheriff had begun as a personal crusade. It erupted out of Robin's conflict with the Sheriff and his administration. However, alone Robin Hood could do little. He therefore sought allies, men with grievances and a deep sense of justice. Later he welcomed all who came, asking few questions and demanding only a willingness to serve. Strength, he believed, lay in numbers.

He spent the first year forging the group into a disciplined band, united in enmity against the Sheriff and willing to live outside the law. The band's organization was simple. Robin ruled supreme, making all important decisions. He delegated specific tasks to his lieutenants. Will Scarlett was in charge of intelligence and scouting. His main job was to shadow the Sheriff and his men, always alert to their next move. He also collected information on the travel plans of rich merchants and tax collectors. Little John kept discipline among the men and saw to it that their archery was at the high peak that their profession demanded. Scarlock took care of the finances, converting loot to cash, paying shares of the take, and finding suitable hiding places for the surplus. Finally, Much the Miller's son had the difficult task of provisioning the ever-increasing band of Merrymen.

The increasing size of the band was a source of satisfaction for Robin, but also a source of concern. The fame of his Merrymen was spreading, and new recruits were pouring in from every corner of England. As the band grew larger, their small bivouac became a major encampment. Between raids the men milled about, talking and playing games. Vigilance was in decline, and discipline was becoming harder to enforce. "Why," Robin reflected, "I don't know half the men I run into these days."

The growing band was also beginning to exceed the food capacity of the forest. Game was becoming scarce, and supplies had to be obtained from outlying villages. The cost of buying food was beginning to drain the band's financial reserves at the very moment when revenues were in decline. Travelers, especially those with the most to lose, were now giving the forest a wide berth. This was costly and inconvenient to them, but it was preferable to having all their goods confiscated.

Robin believed that the time had come for the Merrymen to change their policy of outright confiscation of goods to one of a fixed transit tax. His lieutenants strongly resisted this idea. They were proud of the Merrymen's famous motto: "Rob the rich and give to the poor." "The farmers and the townspeople," they argued, "are our most important allies. How can we tax them, and still hope for their help in our fight against the Sheriff?"

Robin wondered how long the Merrymen could keep to the ways and methods of their early days. The Sheriff was growing stronger and becoming better organized. He now had the money and the men and was beginning to harass the band, probing for its weaknesses. The tide of events was beginning to turn against the Merrymen. Robin felt that the campaign must be decisively concluded before the Sheriff had a chance to deliver a mortal blow. "But how," he wondered, "could this be done?"

Robin had often entertained the possibility of killing the Sheriff, but the chances for this seemed increasingly remote. Besides, killing the Sheriff might satisfy his personal thirst for revenge, but it would not improve the situation. Robin had hoped that the perpetual state of unrest, and the Sheriff's failure to collect taxes, would lead to his removal from office. Instead, the Sheriff used his political connections to obtain reinforcement. He had powerful friends at court and was well regarded by the regent, Prince John.

Prince John was vicious and volatile. He was consumed by his unpopularity among the people, who wanted the imprisoned King Richard back. He also lived in constant fear of the barons, who had first given him the regency but were now beginning to dispute his claim to the throne. Several of these barons had set out to collect the ransom that would release King Richard the Lionheart from his jail in Austria. Robin was invited to join the conspiracy in return for future amnesty. It was a dangerous proposition. Provincial banditry was one thing, court intrigue another. Prince John had spies everywhere, and he was known for his vindictiveness. If the conspirators' plan failed, the pursuit would be relentless, and retributions swift.

The sound of the supper horn startled Robin from his thoughts. There was the smell of roasting venison in the air. Nothing was resolved or settled. Robin headed for camp promising himself that he would give these problems his utmost attention after tomorrow's raid.

case 21 Replacements, Ltd.: Replacing the Irreplaceable

Lew G. Brown   Kevin B. Lowe

Tony R. Wingler   Don K. Sowers

Vidya Gargeya   Kristen M. Cashman

John H. Lundin   Charles A. Kivett

All of The University of North Carolina at Greensboro

On September 5, 1997, just a little before 1:30 PM, a group of faculty members and an undergraduate research fellow from The University of North Carolina at Greensboro assembled outside the front entrance to Replacements, Ltd. The company's headquarters was located just off Interstate highways 85 and 40 on Greensboro's eastern edge. As the group waited for everyone to arrive, a steady stream of customers entered and left the company's large, first-floor showroom.

Once everyone was present, the group entered the building, and Doug Anderson, executive vice president, escorted the visitors to the second floor conference room. Waiting there was Ron Swanson, chief information officer; Scott Fleming, vice president of operations; and Kelly Smith, chief financial officer (see Exhibit 1 for Organizational Chart).

A few minutes later, Bob Page, the company's president, entered the conference room. He was casually dressed, as were all the other officers, wearing a dark blue knit shirt that bore the Replacements, Ltd., logo. Following closely behind Bob were his two miniature black and tan dachshunds, Trudy and Toby. Bob always had the two dogs with him at work, and they had free run of the executive office area. It was not unusual for them to enter and leave meetings, perhaps carrying chew-toys with them.

After introductions, Bob Page began. "I'm not comfortable making speeches, but I do like to talk about the company's history. So, I thought I would just do that as a way of helping you begin gathering information for your case."

> I was born on a small tobacco farm in Rockingham County, near the city of Reidsville. I have two brothers and a sister. We grew up working on the farm. When the time came, I went to North Carolina State University. After two years, I decided to transfer to UNC

exhibit 1 Replacements, Ltd., Organizational Chart

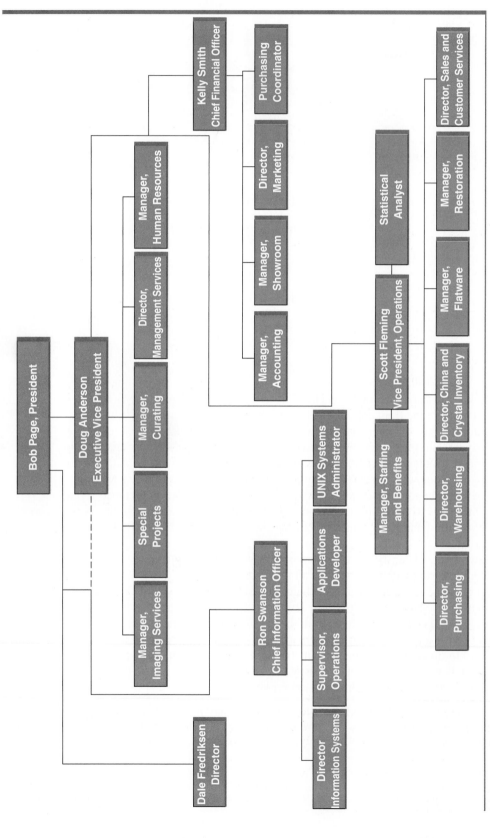

Source: Replacements, Ltd.

Chapel Hill, where I majored in accounting. After graduation, the Army drafted me. I got out in 1970, went to work for an accounting firm, and later earned my CPA.

After about four years, for some reason, I took a job as an auditor with the state of North Carolina. From the first day, I hated the job. I just didn't like politics and all the rules and regulations. I was very unhappy.

About this time, I guess to get away from my unhappiness at work, I started going to flea markets, buying and selling things on consignment. It was not unusual for me to leave work on a Friday afternoon and drive all night in order to be at a flea market, say, in Nashville, Tennessee, the next morning.

People learned about my hobby and began to ask me to keep an eye out for various things, especially china patterns. Perhaps they had broken a piece of their china and found that the manufacturer no longer made that pattern. Or, perhaps they had never had a full set and now wanted to complete it. When I got a request, I'd make a note on a 3-by-5 index card and put it in an old recipe box. When I was at a flea market and found a china pattern that someone needed, I'd buy it. When I got home, I'd drop them a line or give them a call.

I was still working for the state at this time. Word of my hobby spread, and I found myself getting more and more requests. I'd come home at night and find lots of mail and phone messages. I set up a card table in my bedroom to keep up with the paperwork. I packed orders for mailing on my kitchen floor.

By 1981, I was working late almost every night. I'd sold about $53,000 worth of china, etc., the previous year. I finally got up the nerve to quit my job with the state in March and to try to make a go of my hobby. My friends thought I was crazy to leave a good job with the state in order to sell used "dishes." But I wanted to do something enjoyable and fun. I thought I'd be better off in the long run.

The first thing I needed was more space, because I'd filled up my apartment. I rented about 500–600 square feet in a building in Greensboro. I needed some way to haul all the stuff I bought around, so I bought a used van for $3,000. Funny, I had to put up my old Toyota as collateral to buy the van. I hired a part-time college student to pack orders for me, and I did the rest. I still went on buying trips every weekend.

By September that year, 1981, I had incorporated the business as "Replacements" and bought a 2,000-square-foot building that the owner financed for me. I had several part-time employees by then, and it didn't take long to run out of space. So I started looking for another location. Zoning regulations were a real problem.

I found a place with 4,000 square feet. We filled it up in a year. This was sometime in 1982. I got two more adjoining lots, and we built a 15,000-square-foot building.

Sometime around 1986, we moved again. This time to a place with 40,000 square feet, and the company was up to 50 employees. That same year, I was nearly killed in a car wreck while on one of my trips and had to spend nearly five months in a wheelchair.

By 1989, I realized we needed more space. This time I was going to look around to find a piece of land that was big enough so that we wouldn't have to move again. Moving is such a nightmare. A friend happened to see this 87-acre parcel where we are now. I bought it, and we built 105,000 square feet. It took two teams four months to move the inventory. It was 20 miles one way from the old place. Operating during that period was also a nightmare, because you were never sure where anything was. Often a piece you needed was still at the old place, and we'd have to make a special trip just to get it.

In 1994, we expanded, adding 120,000 square feet this time. As you'll see when you tour the building, we're about full again.

Today, we have about 500 employees here and about 1,500 dealers out scouring flea markets, auctions, etc., looking for stuff they can buy and then sell to Replacements so we can then sell it to our customers. We publish a quarterly index that lists 95,000 patterns and what we will pay a dealer, or an individual, for any of the pieces in those patterns. We have four million pieces in our inventory. We also buy from manufacturers when they discontinue a pattern, and we handle current lines. We also buy silverware and flatware, collectibles, and crystal. We now get about 26,000 calls in an average week. Our sales this

exhibit 2   Replacements, Ltd., Total Sales vs. Employees

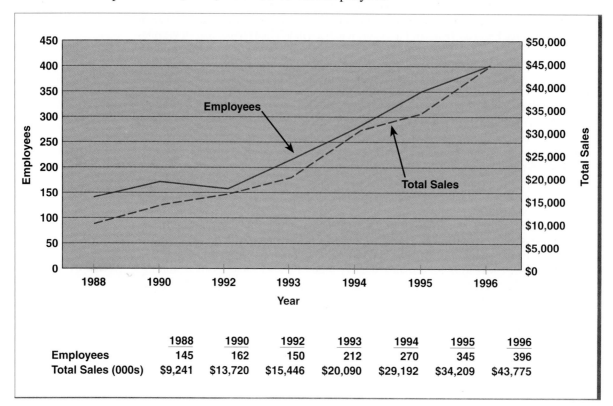

	1988	1990	1992	1993	1994	1995	1996
Employees	145	162	150	212	270	345	396
Total Sales (000s)	$9,241	$13,720	$15,446	$20,090	$29,192	$34,209	$43,775

year will be about $60 million. (See Exhibit 2.) Not bad for selling used "dishes." And we're the largest company like this in the world. Our nearest competitor has less than $3 million sales and 10 employees. We really don't have any competition.

And, I'm happy. I'm the sole owner of this business, yet I still live in the same 1,300-square-foot house I have lived in since I bought it for $55,000 fourteen years ago. I drive a seven-year-old Ford Explorer. I really enjoy helping folks find and replace that piece that broke. China, crystal, and all that is so personal. We have people come in here and bring their entire set of china and crystal. They may be going into a retirement home and don't have room for it and don't have family to give it to. They ask us to find one buyer so the set won't be broken up. And we do. I take customer calls every day. This business is all about helping people out and making them happy.

I know you folks are from the business school. We're glad you're here. We're always looking for new ideas. But, you need to understand, we don't have a business plan. We don't have a strategy. We don't have a marketing plan. We don't have budgets. We don't have much of that stuff you teach, but we've been pretty successful.

MARKETING

The Tabletop Market

Bob Page had obviously identified a large, untapped market, but no one knew just how large the market for used china, crystal, and flatware was. There were no market studies or market research reports on the market.

However, information was available on the retail "tabletop" market. *HFN* Magazine presented an analysis of the industry in its September 1997 issue. Exhibit 3 presents summary statistics from that report and information on the major manufacturers in the tabletop market. The tabletop market included dinnerware, glassware and crystal, and flatware. The dinnerware market included housewares sold by mass merchandisers (so-called "everyday" or casual dinnerware), upstairs casual (casual or everyday dinnerware with somewhat higher prices than mass market prices), and upstairs formal (including formal china). The term *upstairs* implies a higher priced, more formal item. Crystal included stemware—crystal pieces that included a base and a stem supporting the portion that held the beverage, such as a wine glass. Flatware included sterling silver, silverplate (utensils that were plated with silver), and stainless steel pieces.

The *HFN* article noted several industry trends:

- Lifestyle stores and home superstores like Linens and Things and Bed, Bath, and Beyond were responsible for much of the industry's growth.

- A move to "open stock" selling, that is, allowing customers to buy individual items rather than requiring that they buy full place settings or sets of items. Some brides, for example, were requesting just dinner plates. Some consumers were mixing formal and casual tableware.

- A continued movement from formal to casual, as evidenced by the move to more casual dress in business settings. Color had become more important in casual china.

- Baby boomers were saving for retirement and at the same time, to deal with stressful lifestyles, were eating out more often and spending more on leisure.

- In upstairs tabletop, upstairs casual dinnerware and crystal stemware were doing well, but analysts did not regard formal china as a growth opportunity. Noritake, the second largest formal china manufacturer, had targeted the self-purchase customer and the "encore" bride. Although manufacturers of formal tableware were responding to the casual trend, they were not neglecting the formal.

Marketing at Replacements

"As Bob Page often says, 'We'll try anything—once,'" Kelly Smith observed as he discussed Replacements' marketing strategy. Kelly served as the company's chief financial officer and also headed its marketing efforts. Kelly joined Replacements in 1995 after graduating from Wake Forest University with a degree in accounting, getting his CPA, and working with Arthur Andersen, Kayser Roth (a textile firm), and NationsBank.

> For example, in June 1994, the company decided to try advertising in *Parade Magazine,* the magazine that's inserted in Sunday newspapers all across the country. The people at *Parade* had been trying to get us to advertise. So, we advertised only in the west-coast edition, thinking there'd be consumers, especially in California, who'd be interested in our service; and advertising in one region would give us a chance to see how *Parade* worked. It so happened that the first ad followed a major California earthquake by only a couple of months. Apparently there were a lot of people who'd lost some or all of their china and crystal in the quake. The Monday morning following the Sunday ad, our telephones rang off the hook. We had over 3,000 phone calls that day, which at that time was really a huge volume of calls for one day. It was by far our record day. And for a long time that record stood.
>
> Just to give you an idea of how we have grown, yesterday we had—let me look at my daily call record a second—yes, we had 4,800 calls yesterday. That's a pretty normal day now.

exhibit 3   The Tabletop Industry, 1996

A. Total Market:

Category	Retail Dollar Volume	Percent of Total
Dinnerware	$1.659 billion	40.3%
Glassware and Crystal	1.706 billion	41.4%
Flatware	753 billion	18.3%
Total Market	$4.118 billion	100% +3.3% from 1995

B. Dinnerware Analysis:

Category	Retail Dollar Volume	Percent of Total
Housewares, Mass Market	$934.2 million	56.3%
Upstairs Formal	431.2 million	26.0% −2% from 1995
Upstairs Casual	293.6 million	17.7%
Total Dinnerware	$1.659 million	100% +2% from 1995

C. Crystal Analysis:

Category	Retail Dollar Volume	Percent of Total
Crystal Giftware	$455.7 million	68.1%
Crystal Stemware	175.3 million	26.2% +1.92% from 1995
Crystal Barware	38.1 million	5.7%
Total Crystal	$669.1 million	100% +5% from 1995

D. Flatware Analysis:

Category	Retail Dollar Volume	Percent of Total
Stainless Steel	$535.9 million	72%
Sterling Silver	152.0 million	20% No Change from 1995
Silverplate	65.0 million	8%
Total Flatware	$752.9 million	100% +5% from 1995

Major Manufacturers of Upstairs Tableware

1. **Lenox, Inc.** Estimated 1996 sales: $370 million. Parent: Brown-Forman, Corp. Subsidiaries: Dansk International Designs, Ltd.; Gorham, Inc.; Kirk Stieff Company.
2. **Mikasa, Inc.** Estimated 1996 sales: $372.3 million. Public company with headquarters in London.
3. **Noritake Company, Inc.** Estimated 1996 sales: $51 million. Parent: Noritake Company, Ltd. Headquarters in London.
4. **Royal China and Porcelain Companies, Inc.** Estimated 1993 sales: $30 million. Parent: Royal Worcester Spode, Ltd.; Gorham, Inc. Headquarters in London.
5. **Royal Doulton USA, Inc.** Estimated 1992 sales: $8.4 million. Parent: Pearson, Inc. Headquarters in London.
6. **Waterford Wedgwood PLC., Inc.** Estimated 1996 sales: $636.7 million. [Wedgwood Group (china) = $378 million, Waterford Crystal = $259 million.]
7. **Oneida Silversmiths Division.** Estimated 1996 sales: $270 million. Parent: Oneida Ltd. (Oneida Ltd. 1997 sales = $376.9 million, 54% of sales from consumer tableware.)
8. **Reed and Barton Corporation.** Estimated 1995 sales: $43 million. Private company with headquarters in London.
9. **Syratech Corporation.** Estimated 1996 sales: $270.9 million. Silver, silverplated, and sterling brands marketed under Wallace, International Silver, and Westmoreland brand names. Wallace Silversmiths, Inc., 1996 sales estimated at $75 million. Corporate revenues include sale of casual furniture.
10. **Durand International.** Estimated 1994 sales: $24 million. Manufactures lead crystal. Private subsidiary with headquarters in London.

Source: HFN magazine, September 1997, pp. 5–29.

I know you're interested in what I think the big issues are from a marketing perspective. Well, the first issue is how we can continue to find the right media to generate new leads, new customers. Historically, we've been space-ad driven. We've not done a lot of prospecting, direct mailing, buying lists, like a lot of direct marketing companies do. What little we've done we've found to be unsuccessful if we didn't have the names of patterns associated with customer names; that is, we know what particular patterns each customer on the list owns. We've talked to bridal stores to try to get the list of clients who bought a certain pattern when we learn that a manufacturer has discontinued that particular pattern, but we really haven't had much luck with that. The big challenge is finding the right media to help us sustain our growth rate. We know it's out there; it's just a question of finding it.

A second problem we face is having a more defined customer contact strategy. Once we get a name on file, we tend to send them quotes several times a year. We have seasonal sales and sales on select patterns. We've some general controls on this; but in theory, we could send out lots of quotes for just a little bit of inventory. We don't do any analysis of our customers' buying histories, and we rarely purge our database. We need to come up with a strategy to generate sales without spewing quotes out of our building. But, we know how important quoting is. In July 1995, we stopped quoting for a month while we converted to a new computer system; and sales plummeted. We all became sensitized to how important the quoting process is to maintaining sales growth. But I was doing some estimating just last week. If you're on file with one pattern, you'll probably get four to six mailings a year from us. If you, however, had eight patterns, you might get 48 mailings a year—and they'd all come in the same old, nice-looking envelope. So we've got to figure out what we call "smart quoting."

Target Market

Our target market is anyone who has china, crystal, sterling, or flatware patterns where they need to replace a broken or missing piece or just want to complete their set but the pattern is no longer produced. We also offer collectible items, like Hummel figurines, for people who like to collect those kinds of things.

We had a study several years ago. We determined that our typical customer was between 45 and 75 years old and was generally an affluent female. I wish I could find that study, but I can't seem to put my hands on it.

Product

I guess the first question a lot of people have is how do we get all the things we have to sell. Well, I said this is an unusual business. Unlike other retailers, we can't call up the manufacturer and say, "Send us 100 suits in assorted sizes."

The primary source of our product is the 1,500 or so active independent, individual suppliers who buy china, etc., anywhere they can find it. It might be at a flea market, an estate auction, or an antique store. The supplier can look up a particular pattern and piece in that pattern in our index to see what we'll pay for it (see Exhibit 4). Then the supplier can buy the piece for something less than what we will pay. The supplier makes money on the spread, just as we do when we sell the piece for more than we paid the supplier.

That supplier then boxes up any pieces he/she may have and sends them to us. Each morning we'll get from 300 to 500 boxes delivered to us in Greensboro—about 250,000 pieces a month. It's like Christmas every day. We never know what's coming until we open the boxes.

Once we open the box, we inspect the contents and compare them to the paperwork the supplier has completed and included with the shipment. That paperwork includes the supplier's statement as to what he/she expects us to pay. We grade the merchandise, enter it in the computer, and send it to inventory. The paperwork then goes to accounting so that we can pay the supplier. We pay the suppliers within 14 days, and sometimes sooner. Some of the suppliers just do this as a hobby. For others, it's their job. Last year we paid 61 different

exhibit 4   Sample Line from Page in Replacements' Supplier Index*

China Pattern: Noritake	N	**PLA**	**CS**	**DP**	**LP**	**SP**	**BB**	**CR**
Lilac Time	2483	13.5	1	11	9	1	.50	3
		SU	**OV**	**RV**	**PL1**	**PL2**	**PL3**	**FR**
Lilac Time (cont.)		4	2	21	24	1	41	6
		CER	**SO**	**CSS**	**GR**	**BD**	**S/P**	**TP**
Lilac Time (cont.)		7	10	17	27	23	15	45
		CP	**CV**	**DE**	**CH**	**REL**	**MUG**	**BOU**
Lilac Time (cont.)		45	49	9	33	10	10	12

Code Key

Code	Description	Code	Description
PLA	Place setting, consisting of:	**CER**	Cereal bowl (rim or coupe)
CS	Cup and saucer	**SO**	Soup bowl (rim or coupe, 7″ to 9″)
DP	Dinner plate (10″ to 10¾″)	**CSS**	Cream soup and saucer
SP	Salad plate (round, 8″ to 8¾″)	**GR**	Gravy boat with stand (1 or 2 pieces)
BB	Bread and butter (6″ to 7¾″)	**BD**	Butter dish with lid
LP	Luncheon plate (round, 9″ to 9½″)	**S/P**	Salt and pepper set
CR	Creamer	**TP**	Tea pot with lid (short and stout)
SU	Sugar bowl with lid	**CP**	Coffee pot with lid (tall and thin)
OV	Oval vegetable bowl (9″ to 11″)	**CV**	Covered vegetable (oval or round)
RV	Round vegetable bowl (8″ to 11″)	**DE**	Demitasse cup and saucer
PL1	Platter One (10″ to 13⅞″))	**CH**	Chop plate (round platter, 12″ to 14″)
PL2	Platter Two (14″ to 15⅞″))	**REL**	Relish (7″ to 10″)
PL3	Platter Three (16″ to 18″)	**MUG**	Mug
FR	Fruit/Dessert bowl (4″ to 5¾″)	**BOU**	Bouillon soup and saucer

*Figures listed under the codes for type of piece are in dollars. For example, 13.5 listed for a place setting of Noritake Lilac Time means that Replacements will pay $13.50 for a four-piece place setting consisting of a cup and saucer, dinner plate, salad plate, and bread and butter plate.

suppliers more than $20,000 each, with a few earning in the six-figure range. We want be-ing a supplier to be a reliable and stable source of income.

One problem is that, as in any business, about 20 percent of the suppliers produce about 80 percent of the product. We have a lot of inactive suppliers. We had about 3,000 suppliers two years ago. All it cost was $15 a year to be a supplier and get our index, which we publish four times a year. But it cost us $25 a year just to publish the indexes for that supplier. The index contains general information for our suppliers and lists what we will pay for every piece of every china, crystal and glassware, flatware, and collectible item. The index is about two inches thick.

So, in January 1996, we started the STAR supplier program. We raised the annual membership fee to $100. For this, the member got the indexes free, access to a special 800 number, 24-hour turnaround on quotes, electronic payment to the supplier's bank account, and a one-percent rebate on all sales to us once the supplier passed $5,000 in a year. The one percent rebate applied to all $5,000 plus the amount above that level. That program helped a little, but we still had too many people who didn't sell anything to us.

So we've just revised the program again. Now, you have to sell us at least $2,000 in the prior year in order to be a STAR supplier. If you sold less than $500, it will cost you $400 to be a member. We're probably down to about 1,500 suppliers now. They account for about 85 percent of our supply.

exhibit 5   Replacements, Ltd., Sales by Product Type

Product Type	1995	1996	1997
China	$23,280,361	$29,180,113	$34,107,173
Crystal	2,911,824	3,594,419	4,134,168
Flatware	4,986,811	6,778,454	9,097,704
Collectibles	365,474	676,207	884,495
Showroom	1,128,235	1,665,924	1,573,174
Totals	$32,672,705	$41,895,117	$49,796,714

Source: Replacements, Ltd.

About 8 to 10 percent of our supply comes from manufacturers. When a manufacturer decides to discontinue a pattern, we will buy its inventory of that pattern. The manufacturers decided about five years ago that it was cheaper to let us handle the small orders for remnants. They'll also often sell active patterns to us as they would to any other dealer with us getting a standard discount from their recommended retail price. We have active accounts with most manufacturers now. In fact, we are Noritake's biggest customer.

The final 5 to 7 percent of our supply comes from individuals. (Exhibit 5 summarizes sales by product type.) People may just walk into our showroom and sell to us. Sometimes they have inherited the items and don't want them or would rather have the money. Other times, the person is going through a divorce and wants to sell the items.

We estimate that we have about 95,000 patterns and over four million pieces of inventory. We also offer collectibles like rare figures, collectible plates, past Christmas ornaments, etc. For all our products, we offer a 30-day, money-back, satisfaction guarantee.

We also have a couple of other "products." We offer a free-pattern identification service. We have several curators who work with customers to identify patterns. Often a person doesn't know the manufacturer's or the pattern's name. They can send us a picture, tracing, or an actual piece; and our staff will conduct the research to identify the pattern and manufacturer. We also offer a flatware restoration and cleaning service and have considered offering a china repair service. We repair china now for resale, but we have never offered that service to our customers.

Price

Bob understands supply and demand so well. From the very beginning he was developing his buying-pricing model so we can buy the inventory we need, not buy the inventory we don't need, and move the inventory that we have.

Bob uses a pricing matrix that has customer groups down one axis, that is, the number of customers we have for a pattern. For example, do we have 1 to 10 customers or 11 to 20, and so forth. The other axis is the number of pieces we have in stock. At the intersection of each row and column is the percentage of the retail price that we're willing to pay for an item. So if we have a lot of customers for a pattern and not much inventory, we'll pay 50 percent of retail, which is the most we'll pay for anything. At the other end of the scale, if we have lots of inventory and not many customers, we'll only pay five percent of retail. Bob set up these parameters years ago. We continue to find ways to add layers of screening to make pricing more advantageous for us. We have minimum/maximum/absolute pricing we set for particular patterns that can override the matrix based on all sorts of factors. There may be a particular pattern that we really want, and we'll pay a certain price for items in that pattern regardless of what the matrix might say.

Pricing is a continuous process. Literally every day, Bob's setting up special pricing scales for certain patterns or groups of patterns. By changing the retail prices, we automatically change the buying prices by action of the matrix. So, if we need more dinner plates in a pattern, we can raise the retail price to reflect demand. This increases the buying price. At some price point, our buyers will seek out that pattern; or if they or others are holding that pattern, at some price they'll be willing to sell. We started getting away from the standardized pricing scales to more customized pricing about 1½ to 2 years ago. This is Bob's biggest time consumer and his most important job.

Although there'll always need to be judgment in this, we need to systematize our pricing in order to reduce the amount of fine tuning or tweaking we do now.

Place

In addition to selling directly to our customers by mail, we also operate a showroom here so customers can stop by and make purchases. Bob started a showroom several years ago. It was probably only about 200 square feet—pretty much of an afterthought. But more and more people kept stopping by, so the showroom had to grow. Now it takes 12,000 square feet, and we have about 100,000 people per month visiting it. We also offer guided tours every half hour from 8:30 AM to 8:00 PM, seven days a week, year round. Part of our showroom is our museum, which has over 2,000 unique pieces of china, crystal, and silver on display.

Promotion

I've asked Mark Klein to join us. Mark serves as our director of marketing. He's responsible for all our communications work. He directs a graphic artist, a media placement coordinator, a manufacturer's liaison, and a senior merchandising analyst who takes care of developing and placing all our ads. He also supervises our mailing operation, which involves a manager and seven employees. Before joining us last September, Mark worked 10 years with Hecht's Department Stores as a buyer of housewares, china, and furniture, and then served as a field sales representative for a furniture company for six years. He has a degree in marketing and management from Virginia Tech.

Mark, perhaps you could discuss our advertising program.

Advertising

Okay, Kelly. Our advertising's obviously very important in generating leads. We track our advertising very carefully so we can determine which are the best magazines to use for advertising.

I guess it'd be good to start by summarizing our print advertising program. I've prepared for you this table, which summarizes our print advertising program for September 1996 through August 1997 (see Exhibit 6). During this period, we advertised in 84 magazines. This table summarizes the top 14 magazines in terms of the sales dollars the advertising generated. It shows basic information on the magazine and our ad, the code our telemarketers use when they record that magazine as the source of a new customer, the "return on investment" from the ad, the cost of the ad, and the number of new sales and clients it generated in the period. We calculate the ROI measure by taking 50 percent of the total sales amount (which assumes an average 50 percent gross margin on sales) and dividing that by the cost of the ad. This figure then gives us the gross margin dollars generated for each dollar of ad cost. If this number drops below 1.0, then we drop that magazine unless there's some other factor working.

We also track sales for magazines in which we didn't advertise during the past 12 months. You see, once a person becomes a client and we include the client in our database, we designate the source of that client. Our operators ask the clients on their first call how they heard about Replacements. If a client says he/she saw our ad in the *New York Times Magazine,* then we put that code in the client's file. From then one, we credit all purchases *exhibit 6*   Advertising Analysis for Publications Where Ads Were Placed in 9/96–8/97 Period

Publication*	Code	ROI	Ad Cost	Total Sales	New Clients
Better Homes & Gardens Ad-Monthly Pub-Monthly 1½″ Listing ⅓ pg in 3/96	GB	$ 7.76	$ 62,295	$ 966,862	8,801
Colonial Homes Ad-Bimonthly Pub-Monthly ½ Pg BW	CH	$ 13.75	$ 8,444	$ 232,280	1,942
Country Living Ad-Monthly Pub-Bimonthly ⅓ Pg Masthead out May 96, 16M Classified Word Ad	CL	$ 35.40	$ 7,166	$ 507,273	4,208
Good Housekeeping Ad-Monthly Pub-Monthly 1″ Listing Remnant 7/96, 25M	GH	$ 7.91	$ 27,437	$ 433,917	3,735
Gourmet Ad-Monthly Pub-Monthly STF Calico blue starting in Dec 96 ½ Page, BW	GT	$ 6.60	$ 23,099	$ 305,065	2,002
House Beautiful Ad-Monthly Pub-Monthly ½ Page 4-C	HB	$ 8.18	$ 41,889	$ 685,364	4,526
Martha Stewart Living Ad-Monthly Pub-Monthly Vil Holly in Dec 96 issue ½ Page 4/C, 10x/yr.	MS	$ 6.27	$ 30,490	$ 382,570	5,403
New Yorker Ad-Weekly Pub-Weekly 1½″ weekly 1/6 thru 7/7/97	YO	$ 3.30	$ 54,137	$ 357,708	1,857
Smithsonian Ad-Monthly Pub-Monthly 2″ Listing/makegood 3/97	SM	$ 5.71	$ 23,709	$ 270,819	1,605
Southern Living Ad-Monthly Pub-Monthly 39 words, Prepaid Oct-Dec 97 Prepay 3 mos. 10% discount	SL	$106.87	$ 9,567	$ 2,044,962	12,122
Sunset Ad-Monthly Pub-Monthly 4-C Test ad Oct, Nov, Dec 96, JB BW ½ pg 1/12 Page, 2/97 Coach Scenes	TU	$ 10.77	$ 18,117	$ 390,238	2,668
Victoria Ad-Monthly Pub-Monthly ½ 4C in 3/96, 12M	VI	$ 6.94	$ 24,345	$ 337,898	5,286
Yankee Ad-Monthly Pub-Monthly	YA	$ 5.27	$ 27,417	$ 289,030	2,320
SUBTOTAL—All but *Parade*		$ 8.39	$ 552,346	$ 9,265,633	75,286
Parade Ad-Monthly Pub-Monthly	—	$ 2.58	$1,049,263	$ 6,246,195	89,572
TOTAL—All publications		$ 4.84	$1,601,609	$15,511,828	164,858

*Specific publications listed are the top 14 in terms of total sales. Subtotal and total figures include *all* publications.

Source: Replacements, Ltd.

exhibit 7   Source of Clients—Non-Publications 9/96–8/97

Client Source	Code	Total Sales
Antique Clubs	LZ	$ 3,380
Antique Shop	AS	462,533
C. C. M. List	GP	253,791
C. C. Lists	IQ	290,353
Department Store Referral	DQ	2,305,730
Discovery Channel—*Start to Finish*	DC	214,899
Friend or Relative Referral	FR	11,950,129
Jewelry Store—Referral	JS	613,540
Magazine Article	MG	1,456,009
Manufacturer	MF	1,880,817
M. C. C. List	MK	367,566
9/96 List	QS	537,744
NO CODE—Mail In's Letter	NC	2,452,630
Old Code—Absolute Codes	OC	2,287,369
Competition Referral	OS	841,373
Previous Customer—dropped off & came back	PC	985,375
Signs—Front of Building & Billboard	SI	1,889,706
W. D. C. List	WA	$ 1,288,942

Source: Replacements, Ltd.

that client may make to that magazine. Sometimes we may have discontinued our ads in that magazine, but we still track our sales for those customers by that magazine.

Many of these magazines also have sections where they list the advertisers in that edition and allow readers to circle a number on a card to request information from that advertiser. This information comes to us from the magazines, and we have to enter the information manually and then mail the person a Replacements' brochure. We track these inquiries and sales from the inquiries also.

"Although it's not advertising, Mark, this might be a good time to mention how we track our other client sources," Kelly interjected.

Good point. I also prepared a list of our top 16 client sources from other than publications. I took these from an overall list of about 150 such sources (see Exhibit 7). For example, if a customer calls in and says he/she was referred to us by an antique store, we would code that customer as "AS." The exhibit shows that in the past 12 months we had over $462,000 in sales to such customers. This table also shows the sales we credit to our lists, that is, lists of customers we've purchased over the years. You'll see on the exhibit a listing for the "C. C. M. List" or the "W. D. C. List." You'll notice also the listing for "Department Store Referral." Many people will go to a department store if they break a piece of china or need additional pieces. If the store doesn't carry that pattern or if it's discontinued, often the store personnel will refer the customer to us. The Discovery Channel has a show called *Start to Finish* that runs about a five-minute segment on Replacements. It's run the segment about 12–15 times over the past two years. Every time it runs, we get a burst of telephone calls. In fact, you can "see" the calls move across the country as the show airs in different time zones.

The largest total sales dollar item is the "friend or relative" entry. You can see the importance of word of mouth; but, frankly, we wonder if this entry isn't just a catch-all when our operators are busy. For example, when someone calls and indicates that she saw our ad in *American Country Collectibles* magazine, the operator may not know the code for that magazine. If not, he/she must go to another screen and scroll through a list to find the code. This takes time, and our operators are very busy. We think that in such a case it is easy just to enter the code for friend or relative (FR) and save the time and trouble of looking.

"That's right," Kelly noted. "Having our operators get accurate information is one of our biggest concerns. If they only realized how critical this information is to all our tracking."

You'll also notice (in Exhibit 7) the listings for "No Code" and "Old Code." These categories represent customers who write a letter to place an order and technically there's no other source or the customer had an obsolete (old) code. "Competition referral" represents customers who were referred to us by a competitor who could not meet their needs. "Previous customer" represents customers who at some time asked us to take their names off our lists so they wouldn't get our mailings but who subsequently called to place an order. And "Signs" represents customers who stop in our showroom because they saw one of our billboards or the signs in front of the building as they drove by.

One of the items on that exhibit listed "department store referrals." We have what we call our "Partners in Business" program. For stores that refer customers to us as a policy, we pay that store a 5 percent referral rebate based on the sales to clients it refers. We pay these rebates quarterly as long as the rebate is greater than $25. As you can imagine, however, this is another coding problem for our operators because we have about 130 of these partners.

To summarize all this, I also have a table that shows the number of phone and mail inquiries, the number of inquiries from our customer lists, the number of sales transactions from those inquiries, and the conversion ratio (see Exhibit 8). This ratio is the total number of inquiries divided by the number of sales transactions. The numbers on this exhibit represent the monthly averages for each of the last six years. The category "Customer List Inquiries" is not broken down into mail or phone, but as you can see, the great majority of our inquiries are by phone. The monthly average for customer list inquiries has grown significantly in the last two years due to several acquisitions of customer lists. When we acquire a list we also get information on the patterns each customer on the list has. Then we send each customer a quote that lists their patterns and the items we have in those patterns and lets them know that Replacements will be their new source. These mailings generate many inquiries.

When we speak of acquisitions here, we mean that we have acquired the company's mailing list and in some cases its inventory if the company is going out of business. Because of the importance of acquisitions, I also prepared this table that lists our acquisitions by year along with other information about the purchase (see Exhibit 9).

I think Kelly mentioned earlier that we are space-ad driven. We've tried a little television and radio advertising, but they just don't seem to work very well for us. We've too much information we need to communicate, and we can't seem to do it effectively in 30 seconds or a minute. Plus, we find that people need to see sample items in the ad.

For example, here's a sample ad from *Parade* (see Exhibit 10). You'll notice the line of plates across the bottom. One might assume that we just pick some sample plates for the ad, but we select each individual plate/pattern very carefully based on our inventory and the number of customers who might want that pattern. We'll have people call in who'll say that they recognize their pattern as being the fifth plate from the left in the ad. So our operators must have copies of the ads with pattern names noted so they can help the customers.

Our staff does all of the creative work in developing our ads. Until 1995, we used outside companies to do this. We think we can do it just as well; and by placing the ads ourselves, we save the 15 percent fee we'd have paid an advertising agency to do that.

Despite our focus on print ads, we're trying to get a TV ad with VISA, the credit card folks. You may remember that VISA has these ads in which it features unique or unusual businesses and notes that the establishments don't take American Express. We think we fit *exhibit 8* Average Monthly Inquiries, 1992–97 Fiscal Years

	Phone Inquiries		Mail Inquiries		Subtotal Inquiries w/o Customer List	Customer List Inquiries		Total Inquiries	New Leads Sales Transactions	Conversion Ratio
	#	% of Total	#	% of Total		#	% of Total			
1992 Monthly Average	3,815	41%	5,546	59%	9,361	—	—	9,361	4,537	2.06
1993 Monthly Average	3,968	17%	6,845	30%	10,813	11,900	52%	22,713	6,602	3.44
1994 Monthly Average	13,522	80%	3,403	20%	16,295	21	0%	16,946	8,947	1.89
1995 Monthly Average	21,249	66%	4,639	14%	25,889	6,470	20%	32,359	11,164	2.90
1996 Monthly Average	32,300	57%	4,655	8%	36,955	19,845	35%	56,800	13,234	4.29
1997 Monthly Average	29,734	46%	2,976	5%	32,710	31,755	49%	64,465	15,794	4.08

Source: Replacements Ltd.

exhibit 9 Replacements' Assets Acquisitions

Acquisition	Cost	What Purchased	Total Sales to 8/97	Number of Customers	Sales per Customer
Pre-1992					
C. H.	$ 4,500	List & Inventory	$ 128,919	2,727	$ 47.28
F. D.	4,000	List & Inventory	20,073	464	43.26
II.	Free	List	61,099	5,338	11.45
M. Z.	Unk.	List & Inventory	46,979	598	78.56
V. H.	325,000	List & Inventory	651,583	15	43,439
1993					
Mgs.	$ 25,000	List & Inventory	$ 165,371	3,562	$ 46.43
W. D. C.	14,300	List	8,904,106	123,741	71.96
C.A.	10,000	List & Inventory	124,138	3,599	34.49
1994					
Ab.	$ 125,000	List & Inventory	$ 272,331	6,859	$ 39.70
Gu.	4,500	List	44,583	2,787	16.00
C. T.	65,000	List & Inventory	419,279	11,326	37.02
1995					
C. C.	$ 10,000	List	$ 911,620	29,261	$ 31.15
A. S. G.	5,000	List	196,020	3,683	53.22
C. C. M.	240,000	List & Inventory	755,368	39,322	19.21
1996					
A. W.	$ 25,000	List & Inventory	$ 45,796	1,589	$ 28.82
He.	1,750	List	3,442	928	3.71
C. S.	683	List	53,497	2,746	19.48
C. C. X.	5,033	List & 800#	94,207	5,570	16.91
F. G.	165	List	765	659	1.16
S. H. List	11,000	List	585,178	114,348	5.12
1997					
M. C. C.	$ 200,000	List & Inventory	$ 395,539	34,548	$ 11.45
P.S.	9,000	List	42,263	4,648	9.09
W. D. S.	900,000	List & Inventory	1,450,570	82,915	17.49
P. P.	60,000	List & Inventory	35,523	1,794	19.80
TOTALS	$2,044,931		$15,408,249	483,027	$ 31.90

Source: Replacements, Ltd.

VISA's criteria, and Bob has a personal goal of getting Replacements in one of those ads. We even filmed a sample ad to show VISA. We haven't had any luck yet. VISA is also developing some radio ads with the same theme, but we're not sure Replacements will work as well on radio.

We're always looking for new home-and-shelter-type publications in which to advertise. Bob encourages us to try anything. One of the greatest things about working here is that we don't have an ad budget—so if we come up with an idea we like, we just try it. Although we don't have a budget, we spend about 3 to 4 percent of revenue on advertising. We just seem to hit that range. We could certainly spend more, but we find there is a "wearout" factor with our advertising. For example, we only advertise once a month in *Parade*. Our ad is on the page with the "Intelligence Report" feature, the second-most-read page in

exhibit 10   Sample *Parade* Ad

Source: Replacements, Ltd.

the magazine. But our space is always the same size and our ads look alike even though we change them. If we advertised every week, we'd just speed up the wear-out factor.

Personal Selling

I've mentioned our telemarketing staff several times, so perhaps I should discuss this process in more detail. We've about 70 full-time staff in this area who operate from 8 AM to 10 PM daily, year round. When we're not open, we record messages by voice mail and return the calls the next day. About 90 percent of our sales are by telephone with the remaining 10 percent occurring in our showroom. Our operators will handle about 26,000 calls a week. We have five T-1 lines into the building, each T-1 being 24 lines. Even though you have to add 24 lines at a time, we'll add a T-1 before we really need it because we want customers to be able to get in. It is rare that all of our lines are busy, but it has happened. People can also e-mail us at **ReplaceLtd@aol.com.**

The first time a customer calls our 1-800-Replace number, he/she's typically seen one of our ads and is interested in getting a free list of patterns we carry and other basic information. Our operators try to establish rapport. Our goal in that first call is to get the customer's name and address and the names of any patterns he/she owns and a particular piece request. This is critical to us knowing how to price and how to adjust our pricing matrix. As I've noted, we also record how the customer came to call us, through an ad, a referral, or however. So our goal is to get that customer on file with as much specific information as possible. Finally, our operators are supposed to conclude the call by asking if the customer has any other china, crystal, silver, flatware, glassware, everyday stoneware, etc., needs that we can help them with. This is a way to educate the customer about our other offerings. So many customers think we only carry china.

We have over 2½ million customers on file. However, one problem is that many records are so old that we are not sure if the information, such as which pieces they want, is still valid. If a customer calls in who is already on our system, the operator just punches in the customer's phone number to call up his/her information.

So, we have a standard format that our operators follow. The typical operator will take 70 to 110 calls per day. We try to hire people with telephone experience. They need the ability to sit at a desk all day and take calls. We put them through a month's training. New employees can take monitored calls in about two weeks. They have to learn the computer screens and how to work them. They'll sit and listen as an experienced person takes calls.

Because we can get bursts of calls from time to time, we've developed a system so that other staff members working in other functional areas are trained to handle phone calls and take orders. Even our managers, including Bob, do this. When someone calls, our automatic system answers before the first ring and delivers a prerecorded message. At the end of the message, the call goes to an operator, depending on which number the customer selects from the menu. The computer monitors incoming traffic, and whenever there are more than two calls in the queue, the queue beginning whenever the system answers a call, we have bells that ring in certain offices. For example, bells will ring in the accounting office, the mailroom, and other support departments. The bells also ring in several of the managers' offices like Kelly's and Bob's. A light in the telephone operators' room goes on so that an operator who's getting ready to go on a break, for example, knows to wait.

That's our standard system. We also have what we call a "Code 2." Anyone who is involved in the system can call a Code 2. They do this by announcing over the intercom that we have a Code 2.

We don't have any specific rules about when to do this. For example, we've a display on our phones that tells us how many calls are in queue and what the maximum wait time is. If I notice that there are more than three calls in the queue and wait time is 20 seconds, I'll call a Code 2. We do this over the intercom rather than with bells so that back-up staff will hear it even if they aren't at their desks.

As a result of this system, we can handle the peak-call periods. Our average wait time is *eight seconds.* If we do have calls that are blocked due to our lines being busy or customers abandon a call, we have a system that captures their phone numbers; and we'll call them the next day to see if we can help them.

We've five supervisors who monitor calls for quality-control purposes, and we produce daily reports that keep up with every detail. We know how many calls each person takes, the average talk time, and lots of other information. I noted that managers serve as Code 2 backups. Bob Page, for example, took 69 calls yesterday. That's high, but he enjoys taking the calls. It allows him, and all of us, to keep in touch with customers.

We also have a similar phone system with 20 operators in our purchasing department. These folks deal with our suppliers. We have 12 people in our customer service area, handling questions, returns, or problem orders. We're considering consolidating all three groups and using the phone system to route calls to each operator based on that operator's skills and responsibilities.

Now once a person has called, talked to an operator, and been added to the system as a new client, we'll have their patterns on file. The next day, we send that person a quote that lists his/her patterns and the prices for the pieces that we have in stock (see Exhibit 11). We send these letters first class because we found that bulk mail was too slow. We also can send just a brochure.

If the person calling wants a dinner plate in a certain pattern and we don't have that pattern in stock, we ask the customer if he/she would like to be in our "call collect first" program. That means the customer says he/she'll accept a collect call if the piece he/she is looking for comes in. We'll call them before we send out letters to other customers who're looking for that same pattern or piece. This used to be an actual collect call; but we found we were spending so much time trying to complete the collect call, so we just started paying for it ourselves. But by the customer saying he/she'll accept a collect call, we know we have a more serious customer.

When we get more pieces in on a pattern than we need to satisfy our "call collect" customers, we send out a mailing to others in the database who are looking for that pattern. These and all the other quotes we mail, with the exception of that first quote, go 3rd class bulk with about a 10-day delivery time. We have some decision rules that determine when and if we do a wider mailing.

Independent of these mailings are our "sales runs." These account for the bulk of our mailings. We group patterns into various groups to balance the size of our mailings. Based on our sales history and inventory, the computer will calculate a discount and generate sales quotes. We go through that sales cycle about five times a year with each cycle being about three weeks and each mailing ranging from 240,000 to 375,000 letters. If we still have inventory after a sales run, we may discount the item even more the next time. One to two times a year, we go through the process of quoting everybody at full price (see Exhibit 12).

exhibit 11   Sample Quote

REPLACEMENTS, LTD.
China, Crystal & Flatware • Discontinued & Active
1089 Knox Road, PO Box 26029, Greensboro, NC 27420
1-800-REPLACE (1-800-737-5223) • ReplaceLtd@aol.com

10/02/97 R01 SHEDUCR   1952

PLEASE COMPARE THIS PATTERN NUMBER AND OTHER DESCRIPTIVE INFORMATION WITH PIECES IN YOUR PATTERN. IF INFORMATION DOES NOT MATCH PLEASE ADVISE US SO WE MAY CORRECT OUR FILES.

#BWNDFCX   SHEDUCR   T010

BAHAMA SHORES DR S
SAINT PETERSBURG , FL 33705

PATTERN DUCHESS
COMPANY SHELLEY
PATTERN NUMBER 13401
DESCRIPTION RED, FLORAL BORDER
AND CENTER

THE FOLLOWING IS A LIST OF THE PIECES WE NOW HAVE AVAILABLE IN YOUR PATTERN. All pieces are subject to prior sale. For this reason, WE ENCOURAGE YOU TO ORDER BY PHONE. If ordering by mail, please fill out the quantity requested and total amount for each piece ordered in the area below, and follow the instructions found on the back of this page. Please allow 2-3 weeks for delivery.

QUANTITY AVAILABLE	PIECE DESCRIPTION	SIZE (IN INCHES)	PRICE (PER PIECE OR SET)	ENTER ORDER HERE	
				QUANTITY ORDERED	TOTAL AMOUNT
7	CUP AND SAUCER SET (FOOTED)	2 1/2	$71.95		
3	PLATE-SALAD	8 1/8	$49.95		
8	PLATE-BREAD AND BUTTER	6	$36.95		
1	CUP ONLY (FOOTED)	2 1/2	$67.95		
7	CREAM SOUP AND SAUCER SET		$108.95		
9	CUP AND SAUCER SET-DEMI TASSE		$62.95		
1	SAUCER ONLY-DEMI TASSE		$20.95		
8	BOWL-SOUP/RIM	8 1/4	$62.95		
2	VEGETABLE-OVAL	9 1/2	$137.00		

*** SPECIAL DISCOUNTED PIECES ***
*** Pieces below are discounted due to slight imperfections — discounts are ***
*** based on the condition of each piece and are taken off of our full ***
*** retail price. They are noted by the following symbols: #=25% discount; ***
*** *=50% discount; &=75% discount. Items have our full guarantee to ***
*** have NO cracks or chips and can be returned within 30 days of receipt. ***

2	CUP AND SAUCER SET (FOOTED)	2 1/2	$35.98		
6	PLATE-SALAD	8 1/8	$24.98		
5	PLATE-BREAD AND BUTTER	6	$18.48		
1	PLATTER-OVAL SERVING	16 1/2	$147.50		

*** Looking for a piece not shown above? ***
*** Ask about our Custom Hunt Program! ***

IF YOU ARE RECEIVING MAILINGS PERTAINING TO PATTERN(S) THAT ARE NO LONGER OF INTEREST TO YOU, OR IF YOU ARE RECEIVING INFORMATION ON INCORRECT PATTERNS, PLEASE NOTIFY US.

SEE REVERSE SIDE FOR TERMS AND CONDITIONS

PLEASE PROVIDE SHIPPING ADDRESS IF DIFFERENT FROM ABOVE

Name

Street Address
(No PO Box)

City   State   Zip

PAYMENT METHOD ☐ PERSONAL CHECK (make check payable to Replacements, Ltd.)

☐ CREDIT CARD (Check One)   ☐ MASTERCARD   ☐ VISA   ☐ DISCOVER

Account #   Exp. Date

Cardholder's Signature

SO WE MAY SERVE YOU BETTER, PLEASE PROVIDE THE FOLLOWING:

Day Phone (   )

FAX (   )

SHIPPING, HANDLING & INSURANCE
CONTINENTAL USA (PER TOTAL ORDERED)
$1 - $50 $7.50 $200.01 - $300 $16.00
$50.01 - $100 $9.50 $300.01 - $400 $18.00
$100.01 - $200 $13.00   over $400 $24.00
CANADA and PARCEL POST orders double above rates. International shipping not quoted upon request, they vary.

SUBTOTAL

NC RESIDENTS PLEASE ADD 6% SALES TAX

SHIPPING, HANDLING & INSURANCE

TOTAL

Source: Replacements, Ltd.

exhibit 12   1997 Sales Cycle 4—Sales Run Work Process Schedule

Group	Group's Previous Sale Ends	Sale Dates	Begin Process	Greenbar to Bob	Greenbar from Bob	Start Printing	Finish Printing	Finish Mailing	Number of Customers
11&13	6/18/97	7/16–8/7	6/24	6/25	6/27	6/30	7/6	7/7	271,568
15&2	6/25/97	7/23–8/14	6/26	6/27	6/30	7/7	7/12	7/13	239,821
1&3	7/2/97	7/30–8/20	6/27	6/30	7/1	7/13	7/19	7/21	261,169
4&5	7/9/97	8/6–8/27	7/1	7/2	7/3	7/20	7/26	7/28	313,466
6&7	7/16/97	8/13–9/3	7/21	7/22	7/24	7/27	8/2	8/4	314,709
8&9	7/23/97	8/20–9/10	7/28	7/29	8/1	8/3	8/9	8/11	317,805
10&11	7/30/97	8/27–9/17	8/4	8/5	8/7	8/10	8/16	8/18	360,137
16	8/6/97	9/3–9/24	8/11	8/12	8/14	8/17	8/23	8/25	371,760
17&14	8/13/97	9/10–10/1	8/18	8/19	8/21	8/24	8/31	9/1	375,468

Group II	Hutchenreuter Crystal—Kaysons Lenox Crystal
Group 13	Ken Kraft China—Mauser Mfg. Co. Silver (omit Mikasa & Metlox China) International Silver (Lufberry—Zephyr)
Group 15	Moncrief—Oscar de la Renta Silver
Group 2	Royal Dalton Red Wing China—Royal Saxony Gorham Silver (252H—Imperial Chrysanthemum)
Group 1	Old Abbey—Rewcrest (omit Royal Doulton) Oneida (Modjeska)—Oneida (Young Love) Rosenthal
Group 3	Royal Sealy—Sheffield (omit RW)
Group 4	Shafford—Warwick China (omit Syracuse) (omit Towle)
Group 5	Gorham Silver (Imperial—Zodiac) Waterford—Zylstra (omit Wedgwood China) Allan Adler Silver—Booths
Group 6	Wedgwood Borsumy Fine Chila—Crown Empire (omit Castleton)
Group 7	Castleton Towle Ceralene Raynaud—Englishtown Crafts
Group 8	Enesco China—Freeman (omit Fostoria)
Group 9	Fostoria Frigast Silver—Hibbard, Spencer, Bart (omit Haviland)
Group 10	International Silver (1810—Lovelace) Haviland Johnson Brothers
Group 12	Lenox China
Group 16	Noritake, Wallace Silver
Group 17	Metlox, Royal Worcester, Syracuse Oneida/Heirloom Silver (Abington)—Oneida/Heirloom Monte Carlo
Group 14	Mikasa Spode China

Source: Replacements, Ltd.

exhibit 13   Replacements, Ltd.—First Year Results of Acquisitions

Acquisition Year	Total Cost	Total New Revenue in Acquisition Year	Total New Customers in Acquisition Year
Pre-1992 (cumulative)	$ 333,500	$ 172,380	8,427
1993	49,300	2,564,436	129,045
1994	194,500	107,495	16,418
1995	255,000	434,655	66,103
1996	43,631	123,203	123,067
1997	1,169,000	1,923,895	123,905
Totals	$2,044,931	$5,326,064	466,965

Source: Replacements, Ltd.

"So you can see," Kelly concluded, "how, as I mentioned earlier, someone could get lots of mailings from us over the period of a year. This can get expensive, and we don't want to overwhelm people with quotes. So we have to work constantly on and think about our customer-contact strategy. Are there more efficient and effective ways to contact customers once we find them and get them on our system?"

FINANCE

Watching the Flow

Later, after the UNCG faculty members had left, Kelly's attention returned to the financial data on his desk. The company faced many questions ranging from how to meet space and staffing needs to the more basic question the management team had discussed informally over the past three years: Should the company plan and control its growth in a more deliberative fashion? Because Replacements' preeminent market position offered some relief from competitive pressures, the discussions focused on the market's potential and the implications of growth for various areas of the firm.

Kelly had contemplated the issue of planning growth for some time. His nature, experience, and education led him to see planned growth as essential for longer-term survival. In his professional experience, Kelly had been associated with firms that had elected to react to changing situations instead of anticipating change and identifying alternative courses of action. These "flying-blind" experiences had impressed on him the importance of proactive planning.

Though his experience with growth planning was not extensive, Kelly sensed the need for a guiding philosophy to frame the issue. Much of Replacements' recent growth had come from acquiring customer lists. As he studied the data on acquisitions (see Exhibits 13 and 14), he wondered about the benefits of growth through acquisitions—had they been good uses of the firm's resources? Given the market potential, the issue of whether to focus efforts on product and market development or on growth through acquisitions was a relevant one.

The issue of how to finance operations was also an important factor in the larger issue of long-term planning. Replacements' profit margins and healthy cash flow suggested it could benefit from including debt in the financing mix. Despite the potential of debt financing for increasing profits and performance measures such as return on *exhibit 14*   Replacements, Ltd.—Sales in Subsequent Years Derived from Acquired Lists

Year Acquired	1993	1994	1995	1996	1997	Total Sales Including Acquisition Year
Pre-1992 cumulative sales	$121,903	$ 169,218	$ 139,020	$ 150,982	$ 155,150	$ 908,653
1993		2,239,767	1,537,437	1,511,463	1,340,515	9,193,615
1994			249,840	203,378	182,402	736,193
1995				803,525	624,828	1,863,008
1996					659,682	782,885
1997					1,923,895	1,923,895
Totals by year	$121,903	$2,408,985	$1,926,297	$2,669,348	$4,886,472	

Source: Replacements, Ltd.

equity, Bob Page had consistently shunned long-term debt. The company used bank lines of credit as necessary, but the financing policy had been to be "out of the bank" as soon as possible. The aversion to debt was based on the desire to avoid outside influence and oversight regardless of the potential for boosting earnings.

Kelly felt a deliberative and integrative approach to the growth issues was integral to the firm's continued development. Members of the management team had discussed a manageable rate of growth informally, and Kelly felt it appropriate to provide specifics on the growth rate Replacements could sustain from a financial perspective (see Exhibits 15 and 16 for Replacements' financial data). Additionally, Kelly felt detailing the sustainable growth rate could motivate discussions of the benefits of using long-term debt in the financing mix. He saw contrasting the current level of sustainable growth with that provided by including some prudent levels of debt as an effective means of directing the discussions.

OPERATIONS MANAGEMENT AND INFORMATION SYSTEMS

Taking Inventory

Scott Fleming, Replacements' vice president for operations, had just left the inventory area and entered the company's first floor showroom on his way back to his second floor office. He noticed Ron Swanson, chief information officer, who had just finished talking to one of the sales associates who helped showroom customers. In the background, another group of visitors was departing on a Replacements' tour—as groups did every thirty minutes.

Scott had worked for Replacements for seven years during the 1980s. He left the company for four years before returning in 1994. Ron had joined Replacements in early 1996 as chief information officer. He brought 27 years of experience, including 20 years with county government in Iowa; 5 years with Sara Lee; and 2 years with CMI, a textile manufacturer.

"Hey, Ron!" Scott called as he waved his hand at Ron. "I was just on the way up to see if I could catch you. I've just been back in the inventory area. As you know, we had a tremendous *exhibit 15* Replacements, Ltd.—Income Statements, 1994–1997 (Fiscal Years Ending September 30th)

	Fiscal Year 1994	Percent of Sales	Fiscal Year 1995	Percent of Sales	Fiscal Year 1996	Percent of Sales	Fiscal Year 1997	Percent of Sales
GROSS SALES	$29,191,925		$34,209,290		$43,775,216		$52,150,998	
Returns and Allowances	1,327,429		1,536,585		1,880,099		2,354,284	
NET SALES	27,864,496	100%	32,672,705	100%	41,895,117	100%	49,796,714	100%
Cost of Sales	9,467,876	34%	11,387,459	35%	13,701,095	33%	16,345,752	33%
GROSS PROFIT	18,396,620	66%	21,285,246	65%	28,194,022	67%	33,450,962	67%
Salaries	1,730,479	6%	2,403,150	7%	2,905,275	7%	2,744,300	6%
Wages	3,477,359	12%	4,647,444	14%	5,789,083	14%	7,755,830	16%
Overtime	723,801	3%	940,017	3%	1,338,198	3%	1,911,367	4%
Accrued Leave	64,854	0%	111,201	0%	111,658	0%	94,095	0%
Commissions	101,989	0%	225,787	1%	41,791	0%	51,365	0%
Bonuses	96,604	0%	167,976	1%	202,032	0%	244,339	0%
Total Compensation	6,195,086	21%	8,495,575	26%	10,388,037	24%	12,801,296	26%
Unemployment Taxes	35,310	0%	40,630	0%	28,332	0%	79,233	2%
FICA	452,775	2%	615,470	2%	794,884	2%	922,148	1%
1(k) Employer Contribution	170,761	1%	217,378	1%	240,505	1%	350,655	0%
Workers Compensation	136,926	0%	148,563	0%	143,009	0%	164,507	2%
Group Insurance	643,607	2%	949,400	3%	827,184	2%	1,151,450	2%
401 K Admin. Expenses			8,660	0%	5,171	0%	3,312	0%
Section 125 Admin. Expenses			7,189	0%	2,463	0%	71,710	0%
Total Benefits	1,439,379	5%	1,987,290	6%	2,041,548	5%	2,743,015	5%
Total Benefits and Compensation	7,634,465	27%	10,482,865	32%	12,429,585	30%	15,544,310	31%

exbibit 15 (continued)

	Fiscal Year 1994	Percent of Sales	Fiscal Year 1995	Percent of Sales	Fiscal Year 1996	Percent of Sales	Fiscal Year 1997	Percent of Sales
Advertising Expense	1,110,577	4%	1,144,408	4%	1,732,440	4%	1,832,064	4%
Postage/Mailing	984,218	4%	1,551,568	5%	2,369,697	6%	2,797,134	6%
Telephone	477,404	2%	840,808	3%	804,964	2%	812,221	2%
Building Rent	400,165	1%	817,415	3%	900,000	2%	900,000	2%
Credit Card Fees	498,678	2%	590,588	2%	785,570	2%	954,801	2%
Depreciation	458,234	2%	614,112	2%	641,966	2%	789,686	2%
Operating Supplies	308,376	1%	370,575	1%	411,809	1%	473,746	1%
Utilities	160,891	1%	231,073	1%	227,696	1%	255,811	1%
Property Taxes	33,354	0%	54,262	0%	63,179	0%	67,695	0%
Packaging Materials	214,075	1%	262,546	1%	449,437	1%	595,873	1%
Printed Forms	408,916	1%	444,797	1%	488,449	1%	587,632	1%
Equipment Rent	8,701	0%	191,204	1%	342,034	1%	573,204	1%
Handling, Net	(2,105,453)	(8%)	(2,723,618)	(8%)	(1,723,072)	(4%)	(2,096,806)	(4%)
Interest Expense	17,954	0%	131,401	0%	22,936	0%	78,237	
Professional Fees							630,252	
All Other	1,615,101	6%	1,968,864	6%	652,204	2%	595,779	1%
Total Operating Income	$ 3,590,179	14%	$ 5,619,610	17%	$ 6,656,260	16%	$ 9,847,614	20%
OPERATING INCOME	7,171,976	26%	5,182,771	16%	9,108,177	22%	8,059,035	16%
Other (Income) Expense	(17,974)	0%	(1,629)	0%	33,645	0%	(92,812)	0%
Lower of Cost or Market Adjustment*	(1,819,417)	(7%)	(2,072,436)	(6%)	(3,034,060)	(7%)	1,980,476	4%
Taxes**	$ 5,334,585	19%	$ 3,108,706	10%	$ 6,107,762	15%	$ 6,171,371	12%

*Adjustment to reflect changing cost of replacing inventory.

**Replacements is a Subchapter S corp., owner pays taxes.

Source: Replacements, Ltd.

exhibit 16   Replacements, Ltd.—Balance Sheets, 1994–97

	September 30, 1994	September 30, 1995	September 30, 1996	September 30, 1997
Assets				
Cash	($ 375,198)	($ 1,447,148)	($ 104,738)	($ 437,934)
Accounts Receivable	211,687	55,580	296,872	366,892
Inventory, Net of Adjustment	9,412,126	10,484,204	13,123,100	18,156,111
Prepaid Expenses	589,364	785,119	798,343	1,066,523
Deposits	63,516	614,951	296,053	200,052
Total Current Assets	$ 9,901,495	$10,492,706	$14,409,630	$19,351,644
Computer Equipment and Software	1,495,687	1,441,437	1,604,709	1,785,108
Leasehold Improvements	1,139,830	1,332,881	1,717,359	1,817,643
Office Furniture and Equipment	733,000	1,125,775	980,615	835,647
Operations Equipment	801,168	895,837	871,504	916,524
Total Capital Assets	$ 4,169,685	$ 4,795,930	$ 5,174,187	$ 5,354,992
Accumulated Depreciation	2,392,598	(2,421,183)	2,685,836	3,052,968
Net Capital Assets	1,777,087	2,374,747	2,488,351	2,301,954
Cash Surrender Value of Insurance	93,676	115,069	133,843	176,173
Long-Term Investments	(36,996)	(39,021)	(12,236)	35,212
Fine Art Items	7,173	7,173	7,173	7,173
Total Other Assets	$ 63,853	$ 83,221	$ 128,780	$ 218,558
Total Assets	$11,742,435	$12,950,674	$17,026,761	$21,872,156
Credit Lines	$ 886,000	$ 973,000		$ 2,325,000
Accounts Payable, Trade	388,208	908,607	$ 1,389,684	1,450,395
Deferred Revenue	45	113,290	1,070,458	1,623,969
Accrued Compensation and Benefits	889,715	1,272,937	1,592,571	1,682,270
Other Accrued Expenses	51,455	9,625	6,539	102,180
Total Current Liabilities	$ 2,215,423	$ 3,277,459	$ 4,059,252	$ 7,183,814
Common Stock	20,000	20,000	20,000	20,000
Paid-In Capital	73,568	73,568	73,568	73,568
Retained Earnings	6,926,687	9,433,444	9,579,647	12,873,941
Distributions to Owner	(2,827,828)	(2,962,503)	(2,813,468)	(4,450,469)
Year-to-Date Net Income	5,334,585	3,108,706	6,107,762	6,171,371
Total Equity	$ 9,527,012	$ 9,673,215	$12,967,509	$14,688,411
Total Liabilities and Equity	$11,742,435	$12,950,674	$17,026,761	$21,872,156

Source: Replacements, Ltd.

number of shipments come in yesterday, and the pieces are beginning to work their way back to inventory. The staff is really pushed. Bob has always believed that the more inventory we have the more we can sell. But no matter how fast we grow, it seems that the inventory grows faster. I'm concerned that we need to tackle this problem strategically. I think keeping track of inventory is taxing our information system."

On an average day, Replacements' supplier network shipped 300–400 boxes via surface carriers (like UPS), resulting in the company receiving more than 50,000 pieces in an average week. In turn, the company shipped about 35,000 pieces a week to meet customer orders (see Exhibit 17).

exhibit 17   Facility Layouts at Replacements, Ltd.

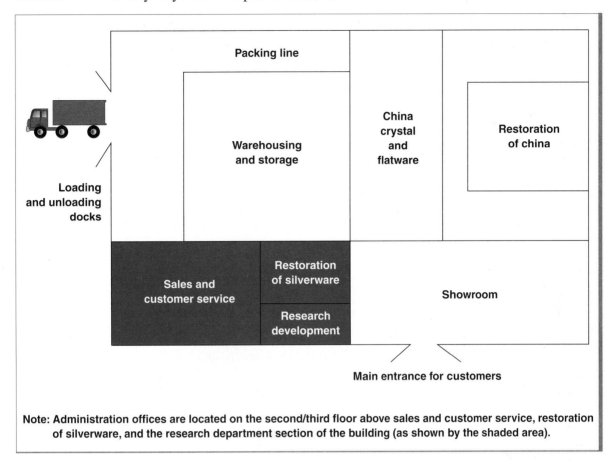

Note: Administration offices are located on the second/third floor above sales and customer service, restoration of silverware, and the research department section of the building (as shown by the shaded area).

At the beginning of any given day, the company had no listing of the items that would be delivered to its docks that day. A shipment's contents were known only after warehouse employees opened the box. Once employees opened the boxes, they used computer terminals to enter data on the pieces received. They then sent the pieces to the appropriate area (china, crystal, or flatware), where other employees carefully inspected each piece and determined the amount that Replacements would pay to the supplier for each piece. Employees then issued payment orders and sent them to the accounting department. They also assigned each piece to a specific location in one of more than 59,000 bins arranged in 16-foot-high shelves and then transferred the piece to inventory. Defective items were sent to appropriate areas for restoration and then placed in inventory.

The company stocked about 73,000 china patterns from 1,300 manufacturers; 12,500 crystal patterns from 265 manufacturers; and 9,600 flatware patterns from 439 manufacturers. The total inventory amounted to more than 4 million individual pieces.

Scott continued,

One of my concerns is that we have so many new people. They're good employees, but they don't yet know the patterns. Although they can quickly learn to find the more commonly ordered patterns, it's hard for them to find the rarer, less frequently ordered patterns. Further, I'm concerned that it is easy for a new employee who is working hard to put a piece in the wrong place. As a result, it could be lost forever! There's no telling how much lost inventory we have floating around on those shelves.

And on top of that, we estimate that about 7 percent of the items we receive are broken in shipment; and we break another 2 percent while we are handling them. So, we've got a quality problem on top of an information problem.

"I can tell you're frustrated, Scott," Ron answered. "Do you have any ideas as to how my department can help you?"

I wish I had some new ideas, Ron. Frankly, I am at my wit's end trying to solve this inventory/quality management problem without an accurate information system. And, to add to the confusion, we're unable to handle all the calls we receive from both our suppliers and customers.

Replacements received about 5,000 calls from customers and suppliers in a typical 14-hour day. About 56 salespeople and 61 purchasing employees handled most of the calls. In addition, there were more than 80 other employees, including Bob Page, who helped handle telephone calls when needed. Jack Whitley, Jr. (director of sales and customer service) felt that the company needed to add from 4 to 14 full-time employees to handle the telephone calls.

Scott lamented,

Our phone records tell us that customers abandon about 1 percent of all calls. I wish we could do something about that. That translates to more than a half million dollars in revenue! Also, many times we find that a particular item sought by a customer is not available in our inventory. However, in all likelihood a supplier could find that item within a few months. But, we have no system in place by which we can correlate the receipt of that item to the earlier customer request. I really have no idea how much money we may be losing on that account.

History of Replacements' Information Systems

The earliest system used to remember customers' names and patterns was simply Bob Page's handwritten 3-by-5 file cards. After about three years, the manual system was unable to keep up with the growth in customers and inventory.

In 1985, Replacements purchased a Data General (DG) minicomputer. The installation automated both the china and flatware inventory and the customer list.

In 1987, Replacements hired an internal programming staff to develop both batch and data-entry functions to support the company's operations. This group subsequently developed the first online systems, which were referred to as "green screen-COBOL-interactive" systems.

In 1993, the company installed the first local area networks (LANs), and PCs began to replace the terminals. Even though the PCs possessed computing capability, they employed a "terminal emulation" interface that used only a small portion of their total capability. Eventually, the DG system grew to 300 terminals, with 220 of them being PCs.

Later in 1993, the DG system's scalability (the ability to increase the system to meet demand) became an issue. Replacements' management decided to look into two alternative solutions:

1. Expand the existing, proprietary DG platform by changing to the UNIX operating system using Oracle database software.

2. Move to a more "open" system of Hewlett-Packard hardware with the UNIX operating system and Sybase database software.

Both options required a database conversion from the old INFOS database management system. Replacements hired an independent consulting firm to supply the project manager for the projected conversion. The task of translating the database structure from the hierarchical INFOS database to the relational Oracle database proved more difficult than the consulting firm had projected. The initial implementation date was delayed over nine months. During this period, many of the development staff left Replacements. After eighteen months of working to convert the database, the management team decided to implement the new system immediately. Managers had considered different cut-over approaches; but the main problem was that only one computer was available, and it could only run one operating system and database at a time. The team decided that an immediate cut-over from the old to the new system would happen over a long holiday weekend—"Tomorrow we go live!" That holiday weekend was the July 4th weekend, 1995.

Problems riddled the changeover from the start. The new systems lost recently entered orders. Critical inventory updates failed. Important data was lost somewhere in the system. The new system "came apart," and system users rapidly lost confidence in its precision and reliability. In some instances, when a customer called to place an order, the order taker would frequently run back into the warehouse to verify the existence of the inventory before confirming the order. Because of the problems with lost orders, some orders were handwritten and hand filled to insure inventory availability and delivery. One executive remarked, "This came as close as anything to completely destroying the business."

Eventually the new system became more reliable, and the employees became more confident in its ability to reflect inventory and to execute necessary transactions accurately. During this period, Replacements' programmers found lots of errors in the programming modules. This revelation made the managers realize that they needed to be more proactive in their system's design and development.

It took the internal programmers almost a year to repair the system installed on July 4, 1995. By then, they had also implemented a limited fail-safe system that provided redundancy in the system by providing for the operation of major functions if the primary system failed. The backup system did not have the capability to run the entire operation, but it would prevent a total shutdown. In order to keep the vital operations functioning, the group decided that the system would suspend noncritical operations in the event of a primary computer failure.

Toward the end of 1995, managers decided that they needed to take a more strategic view in the information systems area. A six-month search ensued to select a chief information officer (CIO). The search resulted in the hiring of Ron Swanson as Replacements' first CIO in May 1996. At this time, most of the information systems' staff were new on the job also. The information services provided consisted of basic maintenance only (keeping what was running operational).

After five months on the job, CIO Swanson submitted his initial vision of what was needed. The report, entitled, "A Proposal for Strategic Direction," recommended a change in hardware platform, a change to a new financial system, a change to database servers, and a change in application development tools. As a result, Replacements developed a new financial system on the IBM AS400; moved to a Microsoft NT Server on a 10/100 megabit local area network to provide access to data and images pertaining to china and flatware; and implemented Powerbuilder, a comprehensive application development tool. A new call center was implemented to enhance the capacity for handling incoming calls. Replacements also began leasing rather than purchasing hardware.

Systems in Place—Late 1997

Replacements' information systems fell into two categories: processing equipment and telecommunications equipment. The processing equipment included the following hardware and applications: (see Exhibit 18).

exhibit 18 Replacements, Ltd., Network Diagram

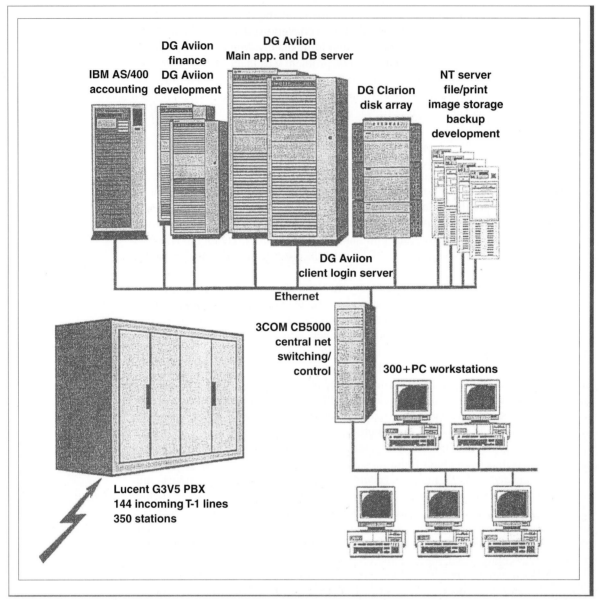

Source: Replacements, Ltd.

- Two Data General (DG) Aviion 9500s configured with multisymetric arrays of processors (12 ea. 50 mhz Motorola CPUs), 1 gigabyte of RAM, sharing a 72 gigabyte Clarion Disk Array (RAID) configured as servers in a client/server architecture. One DG was dedicated as an Oracle database server handling the customer, supplier, and inventory databases; the other DG was used as an application server doing the "workhorse" applications: retail sales and quoting, customer service, purchasing, inventory receiving, and operations tasks. Both systems were rapidly approaching their functional limits. Management needed to decide on future upgrades of and applications for these systems.

- One IBM AS400 operating J. D. Edwards financial systems, which interfaced with the Oracle database server once per day to update the open purchase orders to the large corporate china and flatware suppliers.
- Two NT workstations operating the shipping–package processing. The system weighed the parcel, calculated the shipping, and sent the data to a printer to create a label and to a COBOL application that generated manifests for both UPS and the U.S. Post Office.

Replacements relied on MicroFocus COBOL for its applications and had in excess of 1,000,000 lines of COBOL code. Some managers wanted to replace COBOL programming with something more effective.

The telecommunications equipment handled both voice and data communication with customers and suppliers. The communication equipment included:

- Lucent Technologies Definity G3 PBX, which operated call management, call accounting, Audix (voice mail and internal call switching), and CMS (call management system) software to handle the call volume.
- A switched Ethernet 10/100 megabit data communications network employing a fiber backbone between the wiring closets and Category 5 copper cabling from the closets to the desktop.
- One NT server that operated OnTool fax server software. Incoming faxes were viewed and forwarded via e-mail, and outbound faxes were generated at each individual's workstation.

IS Challenges

Replacements faced many questions and challenges in the information systems area. How could the functional areas integrate their operations, and how could the systems insure the data collected was current and accurate? What upgrade path should the company take to enhance the performance of the major processors (DGs and IBM)? Could operations and marketing help to design a more effective system to support their needs? Did Replacements have the information architecture to guide its processing and application decisions into the 21st century? In which IS competencies should Replacements invest? Should IS merely support the other functional areas at Replacements, or were there some areas where IS should take the lead?

HUMAN RESOURCES AND ORGANIZATIONAL BEHAVIOR

Waiting in Line

Doug Anderson was standing in a *slow*-moving line at a "fast-food" restaurant. As the line inched along, his shoes disconcertingly sticking to the gummy floor, he watched the employees' apparent ambivalence toward their customers. Doug reflected on how far the service ideals of these employees were from those espoused in the restaurant founder's autobiography. He pondered the problem of increased organizational size and the role of human resource policies in creating this distance between vision and reality. He resolved that his company must maintain the "Spirit of Replacements" despite tripling the number of employees in the past four years and despite the coming growth.

Doug had been with Replacements for four years. As executive vice president, he was Bob Page's "right-hand man," charged with seeing that what Bob wanted got done. Doug had earned a business degree in 1969 from The University of North Carolina at Chapel Hill and had worked for Blue Bell Corporation, now VF Corporation, for 17 years in human resources. Following a series of leveraged-buyout-driven, downsizing initiatives at Blue Bell, he accepted a position as the first American that the Japanese firm Konica hired for its U.S.-based film-manufacturing operations. There, he served as head of human resources and public relations. After four years with Konica, he chose to open his own consulting firm. Replacements hired Doug to perform an executive salary survey; and a few months later, he joined the firm.

As Doug reflected on his experience in the fast-food restaurant, he wondered,

> When I came, we had 150 employees. Everybody knew everybody, and you really didn't worry much about a system. But when you get in the 450 range, communication gets difficult. If everyone had the same wage grade, 450 employees would still not be too much of a problem. But with 450 employees, 80 of those taking sales calls alone, and prospects for continued rapid growth, I am no longer sure if the current approach is appropriate. When in a company's growth do you need to get more procedural? How do you institute new work systems in an organization where department heads recoil at the mere mention of a process that has even a hint of bureaucracy? If we believe in documenting performance, and clearly we do, then why not document how we handle a call, certify an employee skill, or determine compensation increases?

The "Spirit of Replacements"

Employees used the phrase "Spirit of Replacements" to capture the attitude that serving the customer was more important than mechanistic operating procedures, job titles, or organizational turf battles. The company did not define customers as dollars but as individuals who each deserved the highest service level possible. Day-to-day resource allocations were driven by what was fair, what was logical, and what made sense for the customer in the context of the moment.

Doug Anderson summarized the philosophy by noting that, "Values drive the system, the system does not drive the values, but common sense supersedes the values. The customer does rule here. We are about *actions,* not plaques and mission statements. The Spirit is the meat, the glue. People know if you are sullen. I don't care how many units you produce, we want people who care and that this caring flows through to the customer's impression of the company. Some people come in with the expectation that if they do not violate a handbook regulation, then you can't talk to them about their actions. We do not believe in that here."

Making the spirit operational required a high energy level and a highly flexible workforce. It also required a very high level of workforce commitment. The company asked employees to "see" when extra work was required and to step up to that need. Replacements operated 365 days a year because it was often on holidays or weekends that customers had the opportunity to think about their need for replacement pieces, or additional china, or their desire to complete a silver service. Thus, Replacements often experienced peak demand at times when many businesses did not operate. It was at these peak times that the spirit was most prevalent.

Doug continued,

> We do not want to be like other companies. We do not use terms like *organization* or *company,* or *report to.* We do not want to say, "Attention shoppers! It is time to go home." We want people to see the work and step up to do it. Everyone does not work every holiday, but

we are always asking managers to volunteer. Every holiday that I have been away, I have this nagging feeling that I have in some way let Bob down. When there is a forecast of snow, you look for who hangs in there the rest of the day and who gets up early the next day to insure he/she arrives on time. Because, you know what? It's not snowing in California, and that customer expects to be served. We never forget these things [committed employee actions].

But for the true believers, this high commitment, high involvement workplace was highly motivating. One employee referred to working at Replacements as "like playing on the Internet—you sit down to do one thing and three hours later you look at your watch and way, 'Wow, is it that late already?'"

Recruitment, Selection, Training, Compensation, and Turnover

Recruitment   Replacements recruited primarily through local newspaper advertisements and word of mouth. The company had no nepotism rules beyond the prohibition of direct-report relationships. It made every effort to place employee relatives in separate departments, although this was not always possible. The company's reputation for paying above-average wages, providing a high involvement workplace, and having progressive policies toward same-sex domestic relationships was an asset to its recruiting efforts.

Selection   Replacements primarily used the interview process and an assessment of prior work history in making its selection decisions. It used the interview method extensively because most employees came with little or no job knowledge, making attitude an important selection variable. The company did not have the luxury of hiring trained employees away from competitors, because there weren't any competitors. Though there were a number of entrepreneurs with some relevant knowledge, their importance as suppliers precluded bringing them in house. Hiring clerks who sold china in retail stores was also of limited value because they were generally only familiar with 100 or so current patterns of the 95,000 patterns that Replacements sold.

The interview included a realistic job preview for the applicant. Doug believed job previews served the candidate well because no one ever left saying, "I didn't know it would be this way."

Interviewers focused on identifying enthusiastic employees who were willing to be flexible. The company valued enthusiasm because, although the technical side of the business was not complex, the volume of products required a passion for the business. Experience indicated that employees who lacked enthusiasm were probably going to leave, whereas an enthusiastic worker had a much higher probability of achieving high performance.

Doug observed that,

The catalyst for the effectiveness of the training is whether people care about the business or not. If you are interested in baseball cards you will learn baseball cards. If you don't care, it's going to be a struggle. We kind of like what we do, or at least those who do well here do. If this is nothing more than a job, nothing more than *dishes,* then they can memorize some things, but they are not what we want. That is where we have turnover.

The challenge of selecting those who would adopt and embody Replacements' values was vexing. The company found that a business that needed to operate day and night and on holidays and weekends required a level of employee commitment that many employees in the 1990s did not have. Yet this level of commitment was what the customer expected. Finding employees who would place customer needs above their own was difficult.

> If I could find a consultant who could help me measure, give me the formula . . . not for whether people care, I can determine that, it may take a week but I can determine that . . . but who will take the values that we believe in and carry those out to 200 calls. We don't set rules here, every case is so different. . . . Bob values flexibility deeply and values are what allow for consistent service delivery under flexible conditions. . . . So [in selection decisions] . . . *How do I know that you are the one?* . . . Finding people who want a piece of this, who will be on fire here, is the greatest challenge . . . deciding *whom* to hire is just critical.

Training   Replacements trained new employees intensively during a 90-day probationary period. Supervisors met with new employees weekly and gave formal feedback. At 30, 60, and 90 days, the company provided employees with quantitative performance indicators. Training emphasized "training them our way" with a focus on serving the customer and continuous improvement. One element of the continuous improvement approach was an emphasis on providing feedback, both positive and negative. The feedback process permeated the organization as a training mechanism, and Bob Page drove the process by declaring that he was never satisfied with how well Replacements served its customers. Though negative feedback might occasionally engender conflict, Doug pointed out that the attitude toward the importance of feedback was simply that, "Conflict or not, the company must excel in serving the customer, so we will do what needs to be done. We simply have got to fix it [what is wrong]."

Replacements adopted a policy of cross-training employees in order to avoid service delays or peak-period staffing problems in each department. The flow of work through the organization was often referred to as "chasing the bubble." If incoming shipments were especially large for several days, "bubbles" occurred in receiving, then grading, and then inventory stocking. If sales were especially strong for several days, the "bubble" appeared in customer service (answering phones), then pulling inventory, then packing, and then shipping.

Volunteerism was one method for cross-training. Because of the "bubble," employees volunteered to help out in departments experiencing a bottleneck and effectively became cross-trained. Supervisors using volunteers were counseled to give those employees work at which they could be successful so as to encourage future volunteerism and to make their cross-training experience a positive one.

> Eighty percent of what we do can be done with manual skills and enthusiasm for learning. About 20 percent requires some specialized knowledge. So give the volunteers the 80 not the 20. Because we give feedback, we need to make sure that feedback is given in something that they have a chance to succeed in. Otherwise volunteerism will be avoided because people won't seek opportunities for lots of negative feedback. Thus the manager has an incentive to make sure that it is a good experience.

Supervisors conducted appraisals for compensation purposes annually with occasional six-month review for employees who were really "showing us some stuff." Seeing job descriptions as too constraining, the company measured performance against job guides consisting of three or four "bullet" statements that outlined the major job requirements. Supervisors gave informal developmental appraisals daily or weekly through the emphasis on feedback.

Supervisors provided a global rating of performance and then ranked their employees from highest performer to lowest performer with rationales for why they ranked them where they did. Though supervisors used a traditional dimensional performance appraisal instrument for feedback, the global rating/ranking system drove the compensation decisions Bob Page made (a process described in more detail later). Bob's perspective was that you could write all you wanted on an appraisal instrument, but what is a "3" versus a "4," anyway? Bob wanted to know which employee was best and why. He simply did not have the time to read ratings and rationales for multiple dimensions of each employee's performance. Bob then directly linked this rating to rewards asking: If he/she is the best, why isn't he/she making the most?

Replacements informed employees of their ranking within quartiles, but it did not provide feedback in any formal way as to what the employee needed to do to move into the next quartile. Supervisors often "power ranked" the dimensions of quantitative performance with qualitative measures prior to determining global ratings. These qualitative categories included company commitment, concern and respect for others, cooperation/adaptability, and problem solving/initiative. Ultimately, however, to satisfy his analytical bent, Bob Page wanted hard data. He then would apply his own power ranking to the intangibles, as a way of acknowledging that "attitude is half the battle."

Compensation   Replacements' policy was to pay above-average wages at lower organizational levels and competitive or above-average salaries at upper-management levels. Above-average wage levels increased the selection pool and reflected the desire to select and retain employees who would embody the "Spirit of Replacements" and reach higher productivity levels.

"Our expectations are up here," Doug emphasized, raising his hand above his head. "Our reward system is up here [again, raising his hand]. We don't expect people to perform miracles, we just expect them to care enough to give more than most people choose to give their employers."

To encourage employee flexibility, Replacements' compensation system incorporated the notion of skill-based pay. The company regarded an employee who could perform multiple jobs as being much more valuable and added an additional $.25 to $.50 *per skill* to hourly pay rates for those employees. Because the employee acquired these skills through the volunteer system, the method for determining whether the employee had acquired the new skill was relatively informal. Basically, the employee earned a skill-based pay increase when the department head in a particular area said, "Hey, that guy Kevin does a good job when he comes over to help us out with [skill]."

Acknowledging the informality of the system, Doug observed,

> Employee compensation for skills is somewhat like most of the business—we take an honest appraisal and run with it. We do not have a very sophisticated instrument. An employee could say, how do you know if I have the skills or not. . . . We may be too subjective about that. But we do have a tracking report, who can do what . . . so people at least know that we value skill acquisition and that we try to keep up with it. Still, once the employee is designated as having acquired the skill, it's not clear how often they would have to use it to continue to have it incorporated into their hourly wage. . . . We would welcome some wage and salary guidance along those lines.

Informal rewards were also an important motivator. Given Bob's strong persona, many employees coveted his attention, Doug noted.

> Bob is the star, the Michael Jordan of Replacements, and the reward structure includes the level of interaction with Bob. One VP left because it ate at him that he had less access to Bob than some other employees. But one does not gain Bob's favor by trying to gain Bob's favor. Bob's favor is gained by exemplary commitment to the customer and only by extension to Replacements, Ltd.

Some who did not get an above-average level of interaction with Bob and other senior management employees charged favoritism. On the charge of favoritism, Doug readily admitted,

Yes, we do [play favorites]. Who upper management speaks to are those that love to be here. They are the ones we interact with the most. I think that is only natural. This combination of monetary compensation and informal rewards serves as a powerful motivator for the "right type" of employee. . . . We say thank you a lot. But at the end of the day, you still have to put the money where your mouth is.

Management reviewed salaries each October. Supervisors presented quartile rankings with supporting quantitative data to Bob. Bob reviewed each of the 450 salary increases personally, adjusting them upward or downward based on his interpretation of the supervisor's appraisal and his personal assessment of that employee's performance. Replacements' employees also received a Christmas bonus, generally ranging from $1,000 to an amount known only to Bob. These Christmas bonuses were solely subjective on Bob's part, determined without formal supervisor input. Occasionally, some employees would argue that this procedure for determining merit and Christmas bonuses was not fair. It then fell to Doug Anderson and other senior managers to educate them on how they might be misinformed regarding the fairness issue. Most senior managers were comfortable with this "education" responsibility because they believed Bob was extremely fair and logical in his decision processes.

Turnover   Turnover rates had been a consistent source of concern. Despite requiring little or not industry experience, paying above-average wages, and offering considerable opportunity for increasing task variety through a high involvement volunteerism culture, Replacements experienced "more turnover than you might predict."[1] For some, learning the breadth of product line might be a barrier. For others, the level of commitment required to embody the "Spirit of Replacements" might cause them to leave. The most frequently given reason for leaving in exit interviews was, "Well, I'm leaving because you are never satisfied—no matter what I do, it is just never enough!" It seemed to Replacements' long-term employees that people who left for this reason had failed to grasp the essential element that made the company a unique place to work.

The people who left here, who were not a selection mistake, missed the point. They never should have tried to satisfy us. . . . Bob tells them going in that we will never be satisfied . . . that constant struggling to better satisfy the customer is on-going. . . . I guarantee if you do 1,000 boxes today I am going to praise you and tell everyone about it. But, I am going to want you to do 1,100 tomorrow, and *why aren't you doing it*? Not that we want to embarrass or place undue pressure, but we want to probe how you can do your job better to make the next record. The goals have meaning only within satisfying the customer. . . . 1,100 means that someone got their package quicker.

The organization took turnover seriously, and those who had the "Spirit of Replacements" had a feeling of personal rejection when people resigned.

When people leave saying, "I do not want to work Saturdays," it hurts our feelings. When you feel the way we do, and you invest the time to communicate why this is such a unique place to work, it hurts our feelings when you want to leave. It's not personal, but [when you leave] we just do not want to talk to you, really.
       It is such a personal thing. Sometimes when we hire the wrong leaders, they feel like we need some guidance, that we ought to chill out. You can debate what is a fair expectation

---

[1]Turnover rates were 37 percent (148 employees) in 1996 and 36 percent (186 employees) in 1997.

of a person's commitment, but we only want 400–500 people . . . *this is not a national movement!* We've had only 2 dismissals in 2 years—most get the idea independently.

The company had recently initiated two innovative programs in response to turnover caused by burnout and by a relatively tight local labor market. The first program, known as the "30 for 40" program, targeted employees who would be willing to work 30 relatively unpopular hours (nights, weekends, and holidays) in exchange for 40 hours of pay. These employees typically were trained in and performed one job in an area that had consistent demand for employees during these hours (e.g., customer service). Employees in this program did not work a set shift; instead, the company provided them some flexibility in scheduling their 30 undesirable hours. The program appealed to moonlighters and mothers with small children whose spouses were available for child care during these times.

The second program, known as the "super part-timer" program, paid a 33 percent wage premium ($12 versus $9, for example) in exchange for the employee being willing to rotate among four designated jobs. This allowed the company some flexibility in giving employees in those areas a break when volume was high and the volunteerism system failed to provide sufficient support or taxed the stamina of those who would normally volunteer. Management believed that both of these programs were very successful.

Nondiscrimination toward Gay/Lesbian Employees

Replacements was the first company in North Carolina to offer same-sex partner benefits and to apply nepotism rules to same-sex partners. The early move toward offering gay/lesbian benefits may be attributed in part to Bob Page's sexual orientation. Having experienced considerable discrimination as a gay man in the Southeastern United States, he developed a strong distaste for discrimination in any form. Replacements personnel policies had been labeled "progressive," "liberal," and "gay friendly" and were consistent with Bob's philosophy that discrimination in any form was unacceptable. Replacements stated that its ethical standards did not promote homosexuality. Instead, they promoted the right to protection from discrimination for all employees.

> Bob is not pro-gay. He is antidiscrimination. We never promote homosexuality. The only thing we are promoting is the right to discrimination protection. What Bob wants is some sort of basic acceptance. An "in-your-face," gay-pride sort of environment is inappropriate. We are not into quotas. . . . We are just saying do not discriminate.

Though the company did not develop "gay-friendly" policies in an effort to attract gay or lesbian employees and customers, these policies had created business opportunities and problems both internally and externally. A customer participating in the Replacements' tour or browsing in the showroom might happen upon a framed cover page highlighting Bob Page, gay businessman, or an award plaque designating Bob Page as "Gay Entrepreneur of the Year." Although it was quite common for companies to display the achievements of their CEOs, the "discovery" that the owner was gay elicited varied reactions. Some customers reacted with indignation and left. Others felt a closer bond with the company. Some simply admired the founder's courage to be open and take a stand, while others were curious or indifferent. Although the thought of displeasing a customer was anathema to Replacements, the company was willing to risk losing customers if it was a consequence of doing what it thought was the right thing.

Doug pointed out one advantage Replacements had.

Our position creates a number of marketing opportunities. The gay/lesbian population is somewhat hidden, but large and very loyal. When gay/lesbian individuals learn we are supportive, they are more likely to send their business this way, because so many [other] companies disassociate themselves.

When a controversial "coming out" episode of the network show *Ellen* was scheduled to air on network television, a number of large corporations bowed to pressure to remove their commercial sponsorship. In this void, Replacements decided to "do the right thing." It developed a short commercial describing the company that included a trailer stating: "The employees of Replacements, Ltd., both gay and straight, are proud to stand against discrimination, on any front."

Despite the relatively innocuous nature of the statement, only two local affiliates (Raleigh, North Carolina, and Washington, D.C.) of several solicited along the eastern seaboard were willing to run the ad. Despite the relatively low exposure, the company got a number of letters supporting the commercial.

Internally, having a reputation for being gay/lesbian friendly both attracted and repelled some potential job applicants. On the positive side, many highly qualified employees were attracted to the company.

Our recruiting efforts are aided by coverage of the company in the gay/lesbian publications such as *The Advocate,* and the knowledge among gay/lesbian professional groups, that this is a "safe place." Many times, that alone can get us some very talented people. Here they can be free to serve the customer and not worry about factors unrelated to the company influencing their career. . . . You simply cannot underestimate how attractive that feature is to some. To affiliate with Bob and his leadership in this area. . . . But do not confuse gay friendly with gay preference. One employee once boasted that his job was safe because he was gay. . . . That gentleperson was eventually displaced.

On the negative side, Replacements' selection pool was unquestionably reduced through a process of self-selection. Though this impact had not been quantified, the organization was aware that a certain percentage of the population was not comfortable with and even fearful of alternative lifestyles. Just as some people would self-select themselves out of organizations based on racial composition, some potential employees would self-select themselves out of a gay/lesbian-friendly organization.

Replacements instructed all managers to tell the potential employee that the owner was gay and that the organization did not tolerate discrimination on any basis, including sexual orientation, before they made an offer to anyone. The company implemented this policy after an employee overheard a manager trainee state that if he had known when he came in that the owner was gay and that a number of employees were gay or lesbian, he would never have taken the job. Doug noted that due to this disclosure in the offer process, the issue of sexual orientation rarely came up in the day-to-day workplace.

CORPORATE STRATEGY

Finding Respect

Bob Page looked out his window toward Interstates 85/40. It was snowing heavily—very unusual for the first week of December in North Carolina. It was Friday, and everyone was exhausted but energized by the last two weeks' hectic activities. Sales on

Monday reached a record high of $417,000, smashing the previous one-day record of $286,000 set just a year ago on December 5, 1996. Tuesday's sales had topped $375,000.

A reporter from *The Wall Street Journal* had visited Replacements earlier in the week and made several follow-up telephone calls about an article that the paper would publish in late December. An issue of *Southern Living* that included an article on Replacements had just hit the newsstands. The president of Wedgwood USA and a representative from the office in England had come to see him. Five years ago, Bob had gone to England to see someone at Wedgwood only to be stood up. Now, it was Wedgwood that approached Replacements.

Trudy, one of his two dachshunds, interrupted his thoughts, begging for a dog treat. Her puppies would arrive in three weeks. Several employees had already adopted them and, like their parents, they would come to work every day.

He had never envisioned it being like this. He had thought that he would be lucky to have six employees. Now there were 500 people in the Replacements family, 50 hired in the last two months. He'd known there was demand, but he'd never dreamed how much demand there was.

> It's not something that business school professors would want to hear, but we really don't talk about the bottom line. That would almost never come up in a conversation here. Our philosophy is that we do the things that we believe in and the bottom line will take care of itself. We take care of our customers.
>
> I think that just by doing the things that we're doing today, sales are going to continue to grow. The articles in *Southern Living* and in *The Wall Street Journal*—that's exposure. More and more people find out about us, yet half of our business still comes from word of mouth.
>
> There are dozens and dozens of companies that've started up since I started Replacements, but they're still on a level like when I operated out of my attic. We recently bought out a competitor in Washington state, and its entire inventory and office furniture fit in two tractor trailers. We ship out two tractor-trailer loads of merchandise daily.
>
> We've established an impeccable reputation with our suppliers. They know that they can trust us to send them their money. I've heard some horror stories that when they've sent someone else something it would take them six months to get their money. In other cases, I've heard that the company said that it was going to pay one price and after they have shipped it the company said, "Well we're not going to pay that." I think that our real focus on computers and our index have made us different. We have one competitor who was sending out letters to our suppliers asking them to get our index but not let us know what they were doing. On certain items they would pay $2.00 or $5.00 per piece more—but then told the suppliers not to ship anything without telling them.
>
> We recently purchased the mailing list of one of our former competitors. It also wanted to sell its inventory, but it had such depth in the pieces that it had. It had a fifty-year supply of cups and saucers in one pattern! What we look at is buying a lot of different pieces, but not in huge amounts. They just kept accumulating pieces, but it was their buying system that didn't work for them. They might pay $15 for a cup and saucer and then they would automatically pay $15 for the dinner plate because the system was so rigid. We may be paying $1 for the cup and saucer and $25 for the dinner plate based on demand or how much inventory we already have.
>
> Our customers can't find the product anywhere else. Some of our patterns are more than 100 years old. We couple that with the level of customer service that we provide. What would it take for a substantial competitor to emerge? Money, experience, a customer list, inventory, and a period of time. At this time, I'm not really concerned about competitors, because if someone had all the money in the world, they wouldn't have the inventory. We have the largest stockpile in the world of discontinued products. It would take a competitor a period of time to accumulate the inventory.

When we put out our indexes, the first ones to buy them are our competitors. Of course, a lot of our competitors sell a good portion of their inventory to us. They don't have the client base that we do. It has taken us all these years to accumulate 2½ million customers. You couldn't do that overnight. If you had all the customers, what would you sell them? Now we have made lots of mistakes over the years. For example, we were buying a pattern called "Sylvia" from a German manufacturer. It turned out that Sylvia was a shape, not a pattern, and now we have 25 patterns with a Sylvia shape. This is something that was listed in our book, and if someone brought a piece in we would buy it—but it wasn't what we thought we were buying. These are the kinds of things that other people are going to have to learn, too. We have knowledge here that nobody else would have. And we keep documenting things. We have over 2,200 old Noritake patterns, forty years old or older. When we publish our book, it's just going to be a killer book. This is doing a service to the world.

We are constantly adding patterns. We computer-image hundreds of patterns a week. We'd love for our customers and suppliers to have access to this knowledge. We have suppliers who fax things in here or bring a piece in or try to describe it over the phone. If they had access to some of this knowledge, it would make it easier. Here is an example of a pattern to which we have assigned a number. For our purposes, it is an identifiable pattern. This would save on our own research time. We may also want to have customers place their own orders.

We entered the silver business because we kept getting more and more requests from people asking why we didn't handle silver, too. And, of course, we already had our mailing list. It's fairly cost effective to add silver. With our supplier base, we just had to let them know we were in the silver business. It was a natural expansion of our business . . . all tableware.

Refurbishment is a business that we want to do at some point when we get caught up ourselves. We have a large new kiln that we're operating; and in the last couple of weeks, we have gotten fire polishing for beveling stemware. We lost some pieces before we perfected that. There's a lot of experimentation involved. With the china patterns, we keep records of the temperature to fire various patterns, which patterns we can fire, and which we can't. We get better at what we do as time goes on. We have the ability to launch the business now, but we are processing so many things that we already bought but can't sell until we refurbish. If someone came in right now, we could do it—but we don't have the manpower. It's very time consuming, and it's a real art.

I went to England four or five years ago to meet with people from Wedgwood, and the man who I had an appointment with was out of town. Now, they want us to be their worldwide distributor for closeouts. The president of Wedgwood USA and another man from England were here. They approached us about this arrangement—we did not approach them. They have their own matching center for recently discontinued patterns (patterns discontinued within the last 5 years). They shared information with us on the total sales of various patterns in all markets. They gave us a breakdown of sales by those patterns in the U.S., U.K., Japan, and Australia. They want to sell us all the company's discontinued inventory, and they would refer to us all the customers who are looking for discontinued merchandise. We would supply that from the United States.

Over the years, we've bought thousands of pieces of stemware from Lenox crystal in recent patterns that have been out of production for three or four years. We had such demand that they'd produce those just for us. They also have produced some of their china patterns for us if they still had some of the decals to decorate the pieces. Once they've discontinued patterns, they'll sell them out to us because they want to dispose of them. They also have outlet stores, but we sell more Lenox pieces than all their outlet stores combined.

Back four or five years ago, we had a dip in employee morale. I'd say that now our employee morale is way up there. Everyone's working really hard. And we have people who're really thrilled to be here. It's really great. It's demanding, very demanding; but it's positive adrenaline for the most part. I really enjoy it.

I still try very hard to know everyone by name. I'd know 95 percent of them. We've got so many new ones. I get a picture of everybody, and they fill out a questionnaire giving a little bit of information about themselves, what attracted them to Replacements, and what's the most interesting thing about them. I took these home last night. In my spare time, I look at their pictures and read their comments. When we had 25 employees, I knew everybody and their brothers and sisters. I miss some of that, but I am still very close to a lot of people here. I like to think that this is my extended family.

It's our real intent to take care of our people. We've higher expectations of our employees than most places. Right now, they're overworked because it's our busy season. I think that people either love it here, or they hate it. Typically, people who just want a job won't be here long. We have others who just couldn't think of working anywhere else. They just love being here. And it's a very diverse group. For example, there's a guy who we hired down in imaging who's a vegetarian and is really new-wave looking. But he wrote the nicest little thing. He started working here through a temporary agency. And he wrote that this is the neatest job that he'd ever worked at or heard about, and he had been looking for over a year. He's very enthusiastic about being here. We want people who are really glad to be here. We feel like attitude is the most important thing.

There's a learning curve. The new employees train for two or three weeks out in the warehouse before they ever have anyone on the phone, and then they are not proficient at what they do. It takes six months to a year to really get familiar with the products, and still they wouldn't have the depth of knowledge needed to put that customer on file and send them a list. There are so many times that I get a customer on the phone and think that if somebody else in phone sales had gotten that customer that they'd not be able to talk them through and get the information to put that customer on file and send them a list. I'm able to talk them through because of my product knowledge. Right now our employee is just looking at a computer screen; it will be very educational when we get pictures on the screen and he or she can see what the product looks like.

The thing I love to do is to go to flea markets and antique shops and buy things. What would I do if I didn't own Replacements? I love what I do. I really enjoy it. I'm overworked right now. I enjoy going out in the warehouse and working. I go out there every day. And, of course, I do a lot of the identification. There were 750 pieces of mail today. Some days there are 1,100 or 1,200, so it was fairly light today. I go through and I can identify up to one-half of the pieces that come in. I love to take sales calls. I get ideas from everything I do, whether it's the mail or sales calls. If I'm out of town for a few days, I can hardly wait to get back. I'm always ready to get back.

The Kimpton Hotel and Restaurant Group

Armand Gilinsky Jr.
Sonoma State University

Richard L. McCline
San Francisco State University

When your strategy is deep and far reaching, then what you gain by your calculations is much, so you can win before you even fight. When your strategic thinking is shallow and nearsighted, then what you gain by your calculations is little, so you lose before you do battle. Therefore it is said that victorious warriors win first and then go to war, while defeated warriors go to war first and then seek to win.

—Sun Tzu, "The Art of War"

At 8:30 AM on June 3, 1999, Steve Marx, vice president of hotels for the Kimpton Hotel and Restaurant Group, Inc., left the office of Thomas La Tour, president of Kimpton. The hour-long breakfast meeting in the company's San Francisco headquarters had been bittersweet. On the previous day, Marx had accepted an "irresistible" offer from Jonathan Tisch, president of Loews Hotels, to manage its hotel operations based in New York City. Marx had wrestled with the decision but recognized that, professionally, he almost *had* to accept the offer from Loews. La Tour understood the dilemma and, with regret, accepted Marx's resignation and two-week notice. The two men anticipated a continuation of the friendship that had characterized their relationship from the beginning. The personal aspect of the decision was as difficult for Marx as the professional component had been. He, his wife, and their 10-year-old son loved living in the San Francisco Bay area and were not thrilled about the prospect of relocating to the New York metropolitan area.

Over the past six years, Marx and La Tour had built the ninth largest hotel management company in the United States, with groupwide revenues per available room (RevPAR) approaching $125 per night and occupancy rates an estimated 85 percent, placing it in the top tier of all U.S. hotel management companies. (RevPAR is a key industry benchmark that really indicates how one makes money in the hotel industry.) Since is formation in 1981, Kimpton Group (KG) had, by 1999, grown into a $250 million hotel company with 5,308 rooms and 5,325 employees, among which 40 staff

This case was presented at the 1999 meeting of the North American Case Research Association in Santa Rosa, CA.

managed its hotel division alone. In early 1998, La Tour had said publicly that he expected the growth pattern of opening three new hotel properties a year to continue "indefinitely." Whereas seed investment capital had originally come from some 200 loyal investors contributing $100,000 apiece, more recently a partnership with the Crow family in Texas provided a $300 million development fund to acquire new hotel properties. The company was privately held.

At 51 and now in his 26th year in the industry, Marx had previously worked his way up at Hilton to become a manager of several hotels. He then left Hilton in the late 1980s for London to manage Trusthouse Forte's hotel properties in the United Kingdom. Just before their son was born, Marx and his wife relocated to Monterey, California, where he managed a Doubletree hotel for three years before being headhunted by KG in 1992.

Prior to his 3:00 PM, June 3, 1999 meeting with his two senior direct reports, David Martin, director of operations, and Jeff Senior, vice president of hotel sales and marketing, Marx reflected on the several key strategic issues that he thought the senior management team would need to address in the near future. Among the strategic choices that he thought would require attention were (1) determining the feasibility of acquiring new properties in new markets on the East Coast and in the South; (2) evaluating the near-term potential to gain additional revenue by developing and adding new services such as Internet connectivity and related products; and (3) the pros and cons of developing product branding to increase market identification, using perhaps the Hotel Monaco as the flagship brand. Additionally, Marx would encourage the senior managers to consider how much longer Kimpton could continue to capitalize on the benefits of the rapidly closing "window" in the real estate market. Historically, Kimpton has prospered by purchasing and renovating buildings at a discount in strategic nationwide locations that matched Kimpton's niche segment. Aggressive national growth could potentially create a strong base of resources and core competencies to support an eventual long-term growth strategy of diversification and globalization. In the short term, maybe some forms of valued-added services could be added to the marketing mix to win the battle for more discriminating customers in a highly competitive marketplace. The hotel industry in general had been slow to enter the boutique niche, and Kimpton currently enjoyed a substantial edge in experience in developing value-added services for guests. Another potential strategic choice could have the Kimpton team focus on the individual brand equity of each hotel and embrace the entry of new boutique competitors into the competitive set, since they would help create and grow the category, in essence giving the "boutique category" the credibility necessary to generate long-term profitability and growth.

Marx would caution Senior and Martin that any future strategy would have to be guided by founder Bill Kimpton's original formula for acquiring undervalued assets:

> We are proud of our value engineering, construction, and design. We make very few mistakes. Kimpton doesn't build hotels from the ground up. We buy buildings and renovate them, primarily undervalued assets in downtown, urban locations. We try to outperform other hotels in our particular segment and create value for our owners.

Equally important, Marx would remind his executive team, is that the important strategic decisions that must be made must also uphold the company's mission of "getting and keeping guests, keeping and developing employees." He felt personally responsible for having developed an organization and management style to attract professional managers from other hotel chains to Kimpton. Martin and Senior were part of his recruited talent and would be expected to take increasingly more highly visible roles in determining the company's destiny after Marx's departure.

As the meeting began, Marx reflected on the Kimpton Group's rapid growth and strategic positioning within the hotel industry:

> Five or six years ago we made a conscious decision to grow. Life is growth; you can't ever stay where you are. Our investors see us as the future of the industry, as we have created a category and become a dominant player in that category. We offer personal, intimate service to our guests, people who live in an increasingly impersonal world. We provide five-star service at a four-star price. We need to become the most unique "four-diamond" hotel in each market we serve. That's our niche, and we welcome imitators because they validate what we're doing.

Since Marx joined the company, KG had grown from 14 hotels and restaurants in San Francisco to 23 boutique hotels and 24 upscale and popular restaurants in major cities such as San Francisco, Portland, Seattle/Tacoma, Chicago, Denver, and Salt Lake City. Two new properties, Serrano Hotel and Hotel Palomar, were scheduled to be opened in San Francisco in summer 1999. A list of KG's leading hotel and restaurant properties is provided in Exhibit 1.

THE U.S. HOTEL INDUSTRY

Global issues, changing industry fundamentals, increasing volatility in the capital markets, and a general unease with the direction of the economy created opportunities for Kimpton to aggressively expand nationally while its competitors were scrambling to refocus. For hotels, managing supply and demand was a top priority for decision makers. Since the hotel industry's recovery from the recession of the early 1990s, it had changed from the fragmented, high-growth state that dominated the 1980s to the fierce competitive environment of the late 1990s. As the industry approached the millennium, demand for hotel rooms increased by 3.1 percent in 1997–98 over 2.5 percent in 1996–97, while RevPARs also grew by 5.3 percent and 3.5 percent, respectively, according to Smith Travel Research. Exhibit 2 provides a summary of the generally upward trends of occupancy rates and RevPARs for the 1994–98 period. Exhibit 3 provides time series data on occupancy and average daily revenue trends in the U.S. lodging industry.

The American Hotel and Motel Association had forecast that both business and tourist travel would increase during the early 21st century, and that more than 1 billion people would be traveling worldwide by 2006, when international tourism dollars were projected to total more than $7.1 trillion. The United States would continue to be the first choice for tourists, attracting almost 50 million for 1999 alone. Employment was also expected to rise, with estimates of 1.89 million people working in the tourism industry by 2005, according to the U.S. Department of Commerce's *1998 Census of Service Industries.*

KG's competition in the full-service hotel segment included many well-known brand names such as Hilton, Hyatt, Marriott, Promus (Doubletree), and Starwood (Sheraton and Westin brands). For the year ending December 1998, revenues rose at Hilton by 35 percent, Promus by 25 percent, and Marriott by 20 percent. In 1998 RevPARs at these hotels demonstrated the continued strong recovery of the industry from the recession of the early 1990s, rising by 8 percent at Hilton, 6 percent at Promus, and 6 percent at Marriott. This upsurge in business made its way to the bottom line. Hilton's earnings before taxes and other nonoperating income rose by 75 percent; Promus's corresponding earnings rose 25 percent and Marriott's by 18 percent, according to *Moody's Industry Review* on January 22, 1999. Operating profit margins for some of the more profitable companies reached a high of 35 percent in 1997, according to *Moody's.* Selected 1998 operating results for the top 10 publicly traded U.S. hotel

exhibit 1 Kimpton Group Hotels and Restaurants as of June 1999

	Date Opened	Number of Rooms	Number of Seats
San Francisco			
Clarion Bedford Hotel at Union Square	April 1981	144	—
Hotel Vintage Court/Masa's	April 1983	107	100
Galleria Park Hotel/Perry's Downtown	June 1984	177	133
Juliana Hotel	September 1985	106	—
Villa Florence Hotel/Kuleto's Italian Restaurant	May 1986	180	176
Monticello Inn	October 1987	91	—
Puccini & Pinetti	June 1995	—	160
Prescott Hotel/Postrio	April 1989	158	150
Carlton Hotel	June 1989	165	—
Splendido	November 1989	—	150
Cartwright Hotel	January 1990	114	—
Tuscan Inn/Café Pescatore	July 1990	221	—
Harbor Court Hotel/Harry Denton's	April 1991	131	176
Hotel Triton	October 1991	140	—
Kuleto's Trattoria	September 1993	—	200
Sir Francis Drake Hotel	April 1994	417	—
Scala's Bistro	January 1995	—	200
Hotel Monaco/Grand Café	June 1995	201	260
Serrano Hotel	June 1999	236	—
Hotel Palomar/Fifth Floor	August 1999	198	75
Portland			
Hotel Vintage Plaza/Pazzo Ristorante	May 1992	107	200
Fifth Avenue Suites Hotel/ Red Star Tavern & Roast House	May 1996	221	200
Seattle/Tacoma			
Alexis Hotel	September 1982	109	—
The Painted Table	May 1992	—	100
Hotel Vintage Park/Tulio	August 1992	127	156
Hotel Monaco Seattle/Sazerac	August 1997	189	185
Sheraton Tacoma Hotel/Broadway Grill	May 1984	319	170
Chicago			
Hotel Allegro/312 Chicago	March 1998	489	244
Hotel Monaco Chicago/Mossant	November 1998	193	174
Denver			
Hotel Monaco Denver/Panzano	October 1998	189	244
Salt Lake City			
Hotel Monaco Salt Lake	July 1999	—	—

Source: The Kimpton Group.

corporations are presented in Exhibits 4 and 5. A brief overview of the strategies and competitive tactics of the three largest competitors is shown in Exhibit 6.

Some industry observers commented that the hotel industry's outlook remained uncertain. Joseph Tardiff, an analyst writing in *U.S. Industry Profiles, 1998,* reported that across the nation, room supply grew by about 4 percent in 1998 after 3.5 percent growth in 1997. In the July 1998 edition of *Lodging,* a leading industry trade publication, Smith

exhibit 2   U.S. Lodging Industry Supply and Demand, 1994–98

| % Change in Supply | | | | | % Change in Demand | | | | |
1994	1995	1996	1997	1998	1994	1995	1996	1997	1998
1.0	1.5	2.8	3.4	4.0	3.0	1.7	2.3	2.5	3.1

Sources: Bear Stearns & Co., Smith Travel Associates Research, Coopers & Lybrand LLP.

exhibit 3   U.S. Lodging Industry Occupancy and Average Daily Rates, 1991–99

	1991	1992	1993	1994	1995	1996	1997	1998	1999 (1st quarter)
Occupancy %	61.8	62.6	63.5	64.7	65.0	65.1	64.5	64.0	59.4
% change	(1.7)	0.8	0.9	1.2	0.3	0.1	(0.6)	(0.5)	(4.6)
Average daily rate	$58.10	$58.90	$60.50	$62.80	$65.80	$69.90	$75.20	$78.60	$81.90
% change	0.2	1.4	2.8	3.8	4.7	6.2	5.3	3.5	3.3

Sources: Bear Stearns & Co., Smith Travel Associates Research, Coopers & Lybrand LLP.

exhibit 4   U. S. Lodging Industry Rankings by Revenues, Fiscal Year 1998 ($ Millions)

Company Name	Latest Revenues
Sodexno Marriott Services, Inc.	$12,034
Hilton Hotels Corporation	5,316
Starwood Hotels & Resorts	4,700
Trump Hotels and Casino Resorts	1,399
Host Marriott Corporation	1,147
Promus Hotel Corporation	1,038
MGM Grand, Inc.	828
Red Roof Inns, Inc.	351
Prime Hospitality Corporation	341
Sunterra Corporation	338

Source: "Hotels and Motels," *Moody's Industry Review,* January 22, 1999.

Travel Research forecast that demand growth would average 2.4 percent through the year 2000. Analysts also cautioned that room supply growth would average 3.2 percent, raising fears of oversupply, declines in occupancy rates, and probable diminution of growth rates in RevPAR as well as industrywide profitability. Industrywide profits had risen by 20.5 percent from 1997 to a record $17.6 billion in 1998, and were forecast by Smith Travel Research to increase to $19.2 billion in 1999 and $21 billion in 2000, respectively. To partially offset the prospect of oversupply in the industry, some hotel companies (e.g., Marriott) were said to be pursuing diversification into retirement facilities and time-share programs, according to Bill Scatchard, publisher of *Hoteliers' Infosource.*

exhibit 5   Financial Ratio Data for Top 10 Hotel Chains (Ranked by Fiscal Year
1998 Revenues)

Company Name	Return on Capital	Return on Assets	Current Ratio	Operating Profit Margin	$ Revenues per Employee
Sodexno Marriott, Inc.	10.13%	5.30%	.88	6.03%	$61,713
Hilton Hotels Corporation	3.73	3.19	1.07	11.21	87.147
Starwood Hotels & Resorts	12.40	7.70	.50	7.62	36,154
Trump Hotels	nmf	nmf	1.55	10.23	12,580
Host Marriott Corporation	0.80	0.72	10.43	35.05	n/a
Promus Hotel Corporation	4.52	4.01	.55	17.72	25,317
MGM Grand, Inc.	9.47	8.24	.94	23.08	126,219
Red Roof Inns, Inc.	2.91	13.15	.71	25.05	60,517
Prime Hospitality Corporation	2.36	2.16	.76	26.64	50,147
Sunterra Corporation	3.23	2.83	4.67	15.89	81,445
Marcus Corporation	5.32	4.68	.43	17.16	48,000
Industry averages	4.00%	5.90%	1.00	2.99%	$62,343

nmf = not meaningful figure
n/a = not available
Source: "Hotels and Motels," *Moody's Industry Review,* January 22, 1999.

exhibit 6   Major Lodging Companies' Strategies

Marriott	Hilton	Promus
• Price segmentation • Customer segmentation • Global presence • Time-share segments • Senior care—bought senior living Forum Group, now largest operators of senior housing • Brand management • Selling non-industry-related businesses • Selling hotels that do not match strategy • Acquisitions in midpriced segment • Acquisition of small hotel companies	• Price segmentation • Customer segmentation • Global presence • All-suites segment • Gaming—now industry leader in facilities • Brand management • Acquisition of full-service hotels • Global expansion in midpriced segment • Electronic marketplace • Employee training in quality improvement	• Price segmentation • Customer segmentation • Global presence • Time-share segments • All-suites segments • Merger with other large hotel leader • Brand management • Partnership with food producer (Dole) • Sponsorship of sporting events • Restructuring of management in early 1999

Sources: www.mariott.com, www.hilton.com, www.prnewswire.com, May 12, 1999.

Ted Mandigo, an industry observer quoted in *Hotel & Motel Management,* felt that
location was the key to success: "Finding a good location in a commercial district is an
excellent way to enter a market. Many such opportunities have already been exploited.
The operator looking for undervalued assets that can be turned into boutique hotels will

exhibit 7   Hotel Industry Growth, 1990–98

Year	Number of Hotels	% Growth	Number of Rooms	% Growth
1990	30,114		3,206,454	
1991	30,384	0.9%	3,234,673	0.8%
1992	30,516	0.4	3,249,699	0.5
1993	30,727	0.7	3,270,864	0.6
1994	31,152	1.4	3,306,304	1.1
1995	31,808	2.1	3,354,970	1.5
1996	32,851	3.3	3,455,087	2.9
1997	34,225	4.2	3,588,072	3.8
1998	35,013	2.3	3,662,524	2.1

Source: Smith Travel Associates Research.

need a sharp pencil to avoid buying bargain properties that do not create a situation of oversupply." Other critical success factors appeared to determine a firm's ability to remain competitive in the hotel industry. At the basic level, hotel owners strove to create a level of service that attracted and retained customers. The "experience" of staying at a particular hotel facility was intended to have a lasting and memorable effect if a hotel was to be distinguished from the competition.

The trend, noted in the *1994 Atlas of the American Economy,* toward hotel property and management consolidation, posed several threats for owners of small and midsized hotel chains. As the larger firms continued to grow and expand their operations, it became easy to expand beyond economies of scale factors and create an oversupply, driving down room rates. This threat was heightened during economic downturns and could significantly affect both the overall occupancy rate in the industry and profitability. In the early 1990s there was a notable and steady increase in the number of establishments, according to Smith Travel Associates (see Exhibit 7). The result was a surplus of rooms and low occupancy rates. High operating expenses diminished profit margins considerably in years with low occupancy rates, especially given that hotels had to keep room rates down in such years as well. The predictable outcome was that record losses were experienced by the industry during a period of oversupply (e.g., full-service hotels with significant departmental expenses particularly experienced this loss history). The occupancy rates for limited-service hotels were not significantly different from those of full-service hotels, according to Smith Travel Associates. This suggests why some large corporate hotel operators in the late 1990s were emphasizing a more limited-service facility that had lower operating costs yet retained good customer traffic and operating gross margins. Exhibit 8 presents 1995 data on hotel real estate selling prices and estimated costs of replacement per room.

Perhaps the most profound change in hotel industry strategy arose from the dramatic shift of hotel properties from private to public ownership. The volume of investment dollars for the hotel industry was significantly greater in the late 1990s than it had been historically. Banks, insurance companies, finance companies, equity investors and real estate investment trusts (REITs) entered the hotel industry with aggressive parameters as they perceived that the market oversupply had begun to dissipate. The latter instrument, REITs, which emerged in 1991, had become a major source of low-cost capital that fueled growth and construction in the hotel industry. Starwood Lodging had used REITs as a vehicle to acquire Westin Hotels and Sheraton Hotels from IT&T. The availability of low-cost capital became an especially important factor for the larger players in the industry, who moved increasingly toward consolidation via acquisition *exhibit 8*　Hotel Real Estate Selling Prices and Estimated Costs of Replacement, 1995

Lodging Segment	Average Selling Price per Room	Estimated Cost of Replacement per Room
Budget	$11,804	$25,000–30,000
Economy—limited service	20,538	30,000–35,000
Economy—full service	19,239	35,000–50,000
Midmarket—limited service	42,244	35,000–50,000
Midmarket —full service	42,117	45,000–70,000
Luxury—limited service	65,174	80,000–150,000

Source: National Hotel Realty Advisor.

of other chains, according the Smith Travel Associates. However, the lowering of barriers to entry allowed disproportionate levels of new supply in the industry.

Aging of the baby boomers also emerged as a significant demographic factor. Seventy million Americans were moving into their midlives (over 50) and were expected to seek greater comfort and choose service over price in their choice of hotels. In the late 1990s, other emerging trends in the hotel industry included (1) the introduction of limited-service suites; (2) additional emphasis on higher-value-added business-related amenities such as data ports for laptops and interactive Web TV sets in rooms; (3) automation of labor-intensive functions via information technology; (4) development of extended-stay or "residence-style" hotels and time-share projects; (5) reduction in marketing expenses and long-term operating costs via standardization and branding of properties.

In spite of the many changes in the hotel industry, comments made by Kimpton executives suggest that, in addition to location, the factors still considered critical to success in the hotel industry include:

- Low-cost purchases of land or buildings.
- Greater latitude in product/service offerings at comparable profit margins.
- Customer service.
- Effective utilization of technology.
- Brand loyalty.
- Employee training and development.
- Complementary services.
- Revenue management systems.
- Clean and comfortable lodging.
- Strategic alliances.
- Convenience in making reservations.
- Access to growth capital.
- Value-added services.

The Boutique Hotel Niche

As the millennium approached, the emerging boutique or small luxury hotel niche began attracting new entrants, both large and small. For example, Starwood Hotels & Resorts announced in late 1998 that it was launching a new "W" line of boutique hotels with fewer than 400 rooms in an attempt to replicate the Kimpton formula for success.

Based in White Plains, New York, Starwood Hotels & Resorts managed, owned, and operated such branded properties as St. Regis and the Luxury Collection (luxury hotels), Westin (upscale full-service), Sheraton (full-service), and W (boutique full-service hotels for business travelers). It had sold its Caesars World properties in early 1999. Starwood's meteoric yet troubled rise had been guided by chairman Barry Sternlicht (German for "starlight"), an aggressive dealmaker who snatched ITT from Hilton Hotels. Sternlicht owned about 5 percent of the firm. In 1999 the company abandoned its paired-share real estate investment trust structure for a standard corporate structure with a property-owning REIT subsidiary; Starwood Hotels & Resorts Worldwide managed the operation of the properties. A 21-story W Hotel opened across from the Moscone Convention Center in San Francisco in April 1999. Despite heavy debt and the high costs of integrating operations acquired during the whirlwind buying spree that preceded the change in its structure, in mid-1999 Starwood announced that it planned to expand into Latin America.

The other national player in the boutique hotel category, according to a July 1999 story in the *San Francisco Examiner,* was New York hotelier Ian Schrager (formerly co-owner of the Studio 54 disco). Schrager ran the Royalton in New York, the Mondrian in Los Angeles, and had purchased the Clift Hotel in San Francisco for $80 million in June 1999. The Clift was undergoing a $25 million facelift prior to its reopening in October 1999.

Boutique hotels accounted for about 15 percent of San Francisco's estimated 31,000 rooms. In San Francisco, KG was the recognized market leader, with 67 percent of the city's boutique hotels, according to analyst Anwar Elgonomy of PKF Consulting. Chip Conley's Joie de Vivre Hotels enjoyed 20 percent of the San Francisco market, and Yvonne Lembi-Detert's Personality Hotels on Union Square, with four properties, had 12 percent of the market. Other operators split the remaining 1 percent. "It's a very specific group of people [boutique hoteliers] are going after: well-educated professionals," Elgonomy said recently in an interview in the *San Francisco Examiner,* "people who don't like generic activities. People who don't like Starbucks."

Chip Conley, president of Joie de Vivre, a $40 million chain of 14 boutique hotels and motels in the San Francisco Bay area, commented on the boutique lodging niche in an April 1999 interview with Neal Templin in the *Contra Costa Times*:

> The question is whether the big boys will have the agility to handle the boutique market. We look for aging hotels with "good bones"—good elevators, plumbing and electrical systems—and bad images. We spend our money on things that get a lot of bang for the buck. Our strategy is to make our Hotel del Sol a national brand by buying a portfolio of motels around the country and converting them to the same concept. There's a huge collection of 1950s and 1960s hotels waiting to be fixed up. Our next project to open will be a boutique camping resort south of San Francisco where guests will rough it in tents but still be able to order up caffé lattés after their hikes in the woods. It is aimed at the sort of people who buy sport-utility vehicles even though they rarely drive off-road. They can feel like they're connected with nature while not getting their hands dirty.

One reason San Francisco spawned so many boutique hotels is that it had had a big inventory of older hotels that could be cheaply acquired and converted. Analyst C. Jay Scott, of Scott Hospitality Services in San Francisco, noted, "Boutique hotels don't work everywhere. They work only in downtowns that are still vibrant relative to business and leisure travel markets. It's a concept that has been well received by the marketplace. Why try to continually reinvent yourself when you have a concept that works?"

As property values in San Francisco soared, KG's competitors were increasingly building all-new developments, which, in the opinion of Kimpton executives, were both more risky and less profitable than conversions. By contrast, most of the KG's hotels were converted buildings that had been built for other purposes. In the words of Jeff Senior, KG's director of marketing:

> Our lowered asset investment requires a lesser average rate to be successful. In other words, it costs us less, so we can charge less and still be as much or more profitable than our competitors. In reality, any full service hotel in markets we compete within is a competitor, including Sheraton, Westin, Hyatt, Starwood, etc. Other competitors include other boutique providers.

According to Bill Scatchard, publisher of *Hoteliers' Infosource,* the baby-boomer generation was attracted to the boutique style hotel that Kimpton Group pioneered. The brightly trimmed decor with a hint of European luxury appeared to capture the taste of this lucrative segment. In general, the market appeared to favor properties that offered a fun atmosphere in an intimate surrounding. One hotel manager at the Kimpton Group suggested that his organization was one of two or three companies that had responded to this boutique hotel niche very well. This general manager, keenly aware of Kimpton's prominence in the San Francisco market, took a more global perspective. He emphasized the relative smallness of the company's presence overall and described the Kimpton Group niche in the hotel industry colorfully: "We're like a pimple on the ass of an elephant."

The Kimpton Organization

The Kimpton Hotel and Restaurant Group consisted of a family of 23 boutique-style hotels and 24 unique and often independently successful restaurants. Its hotels ranged in size from 91 to 483 rooms, and a typical hotel had between 100 and 200 rooms. KG's destination restaurants, each with its own local following, were located in the same buildings as the hotels.

Founder William Kimpton, now 63, bought his first hotel in 1981. Kimpton was born in Kansas City, Missouri, and in his schooldays was hampered by what he now believes was dyslexia. He noted that he did not learn to read until he reached high school. He struggled academically but was encouraged by his family to continue schooling. Kimpton earned a bachelor of science in economics from Northwestern University and was a graduate of the renowned University of Chicago Lab School. Prior to starting the Kimpton Group in 1981, Kimpton served for three and a half years as director and vice president of Lepercq de Neuflize, an international investment banking firm. During his stint at Lepercq, Kimpton participated in negotiating, structuring, and overseeing the projects of Lepercq de Neuflize. Preceding Lepercq, Kimpton was a partner in Shuman, Agnew & Co., Inc., in Belvedere, California, where he was responsible for project finance. Other experiences that helped shape his acumen for project financing included almost four years as a manager with Lehman Brothers (now Shearson–Lehman Brothers American Express, Inc.) in its San Francisco office. This assignment in San Francisco followed his three years as an associate for Lehman Brothers in its Chicago office.

Bill Kimpton's approach to the hotel industry was based on his prior career as an investment banker. Kimpton began his foray into the hotel industry by structuring a highly creative investment strategy for the Helmsley Hotel organization. He worked with Harry Helmsley (now probably best known for the exploits of his controversial wife, Leona Helmsley, the "Queen of Mean") to raise seed money for the $23 million renovation of the New York Palace Hotel. Through that project Kimpton became known for his imaginative approach to raising investment capital. Kimpton also handled the financing for the exclusive Kapalua Bay resort in Maui and brought in the Rockefeller family's RockResorts to manage the property.

Bill Kimpton recalled that he wanted to get into a business "that sells sleep, because sleep has high [profit] margins." He combined his bottom-line focus with a unique feel for offering value and comfort with a "personality" in all the Kimpton Group properties. He imprinted on his hotel and restaurant management team a flair for being different yet profitable. "My theory is, no matter how much money people have to spend on big, fancy hotels, they are intimidated," Kimpton said recently. "The psychology of how you build restaurants and hotels is very important. You put a fireplace in the lobby and create a warm, friendly restaurant and the guest will feel safe."

Bill Kimpton, by 1999, had served as chairman and chief executive of KG since its inception. Although he was by then no longer intimately involved in day-to-day management, Kimpton's entrepreneurial style was still very visible in the organization. His style was very personal, and he practiced a decentralized approach to decision making since the early days of the corporation. Following his entrepreneurial flair, each property emphasized guest room comfort rather than high overhead amenities such as fancy water fountains, ornate lobbies, or excessive brass and glass.

Guest rooms were tastefully decorated in cheerful colors with elegant bedspreads and thick carpeting, perhaps reflecting Bill Kimpton's trademark multicolor sweaters. Each room was meant to feel like a comfortable guest room in a friend's luxury home and was complete with good lighting; a stocked honor bar/refrigerator; and direct-dial phones with extralong cords to reach the bed, the desk, and other parts of the room. Hotel lobbies were furnished with the emphasis on comfort, not on waiting, and each had a cozy fireplace.

KG's strategy was to create each hotel as a stand-alone "personality" that appealed to its own unique customer group. The hotels shared a common upscale theme and appearance but priced the rooms below the full-service hotels such as Marriott or Hilton. A European style was visible in almost every KG property. Kimpton's aggressive expansion in San Francisco made it very difficult for other chains to find low-cost property in commercial locations that could compete on both price and amenities found at the KG properties.

A high degree of personalized service and numerous complementary amenities were also the hallmark of KG's hotels. Some KG hotels were testing a system to provide arriving guests with "desk-less" check-in via use of cellular and digital communications technology. Doormen were equipped with headsets and could escort new guests directly to their rooms without the usual paperwork and waiting around, considered to be some of the most unwelcoming experiences of tired travelers who just want to get into their rooms. Most hotels featured some or all of the following complementary services: limousines to the financial district, wine served in the lobby each evening, continental breakfast, and coffee and tea available throughout the day. Most hotels also offered same-day valet and laundry service, room service and express check-out with on-site parking. According to Kimpton executives, all of these services were provided at room rates that averaged 25 to 30 percent lower than comparable hotels in the same markets. Indicative of the success of KG's strategy was its annual occupancy rates, which averaged 85 percent over the group, compared to the industry average, which hovered between 68 and 75 percent, depending on the geographical market segment served.

Human Resources

Hotel general managers were strongly encouraged to innovate and provide their specific property with a personality that separated it from the other properties in KG's portfolio.

Senior management practiced reciprocal communication and was very reluctant to impose anything other than customer-related service standards on each property.

Nanci Sherman, general manager of the Hotel Monaco in San Francisco, confirmed this approach:

> Most of our general managers have a hotel background, but like me are refugees from patriarchal companies like Hilton, Disney, and Ritz-Carlton. People come to Kimpton because they see there's another way. Why is it that in 200,000 hotels around the world that the staff meet every Tuesday and Friday for two hours but no changes ever take place? We built our business around the 2 percent that rarely occurs, not on the 98 percent that happens regularly. We really want to look good. Very rarely do we (as industry people) want to take risks. Building a group culture starts with who we are as people: giving, teamwork, friendship, and confidence. People who get rewarded and promoted here are team players. But you can't run a highly bureaucratic, top-down management style anymore, even in a conservative industry like the hotel industry. That's a major reason why our staff turnover rate has been 18–21 percent over the past two years, far below the average rate of 50 percent in the industry. Low turnover rates are absolutely essential to us, because the hotels with the lowest turnover rates have the highest financial performance, particularly in the tight labor markets that we are experiencing now.

Each hotel manager and line staff member attended "Kimpton University," a program of in-house classes on front-desk service, housekeeping, finance and record-keeping, and corporate wellness. In keeping with KG's philosophy of the "gracious host," general managers poured wine for guests at the cocktail hour each night. It was on these occasions that feedback on amenities and service was most readily obtained on a firsthand basis. Feedback from guests was systematically gathered via comment cards in guest rooms. Some of its hotels were experimenting with using interactive TV in guest rooms to obtain comments at check-out. The company also had hired Pannell Kerr Foster (PKF), a San Francisco-based consulting firm, to obtain quality control information using "phantom guests." Executives were also considering the use of focus groups to obtain feedback about the efficacy of current and planned future service offerings. KG observed a "sundown rule," in that each general manager must respond to a guest's comments on their stay by the end of the business day.

KG hired people whose "light had been hidden under a bushel," according to Jim McPartlin, general manager of the Prescott Hotel in San Francisco and the citywide manager for KG's San Francisco Hotels. "We encouraged the operating managers to 'be different' and think 'outside of the box,'" said McPartlin. "The incentives are there, as we can earn up to 25 percent bonus on our salaries, paid out quarterly. Our typical wage percentage of sales is about 22 percent, of which 70 percent is 'raw' wages and 30 percent are benefits. We also have a 'Circle of Stars,' an employee luncheon once a month, where employees who are recognized by guests for outstanding service can win prizes in a 'Wheel of Fortune'–type game," he added.

KG did not have a formal organization chart. According to David Martin, the director of hotel operations:

> Perhaps this is because we try to create an entrepreneurial atmosphere. We hire managers who have the guts to make decisions. Internal competition—creativity—that we label as entrepreneurial is healthy, as long as it's in the customer's best interests. We must meet minimum customer standards. There's sort of a Maslow's hierarchy almost. We gotta be clean, personable, and offer quick service.
>
> We offer a "fireside chat" once a quarter, where we put Steve [Marx] on the firing line with the hotel general managers. He gets people to express their needs. We've challenged Steve on many occasions. We talk about real issues that are important to managers.

"Mongoose" Strategy

Since its inception in 1981, KG had followed a so-called mongoose strategy—named after the ferretlike animal that successfully kills poisonous animals by circling them until they tire, at which point it dives in quickly and finishes them off. Before the company successfully bought its Bellevue property, Kimpton bid $10 million and was outbid by investors who paid $15 million, according to the *New York Times* on January 16, 1994. The company watched the property for seven years until it was able to pick up that property from those owners for $5 million. Similarly, the firm bought the Sir Francis Drake property for $19.5 million, although the property had been on the market eight years earlier for $60 million. If a property possessed the three attributes of uniqueness in character, location, and design potential, it became a target for the patient capital of the KG and its co-investors. Each new property was typically financed by 60 percent equity and 40 percent debt, considered low leverage in the hotel industry.

In the San Francisco market, which by 1999 included 15 semiluxury hotels and 16 destination restaurants, KG began with the Bedford Hotel in 1981, which was followed by the Vintage Court, the Galleria Park, the Juliana, and so on until the firm controlled some 2,000 rooms in its home market. As a point of reference, the Hilton, which towered in the skyline of San Francisco, had almost as many rooms as the entire collection of KG properties in that city. Other properties were located in Seattle, Tacoma, Portland, Denver, Chicago, and the soon-to-be-opened Hotel Monaco in Salt Lake City.

By mid-1999, KG was considering expansion to the East Coast and had begun looking at properties in New York, Boston, and Washington, D.C. "It's time to start looking outside the West Coast," Bill Kimpton recently told the *San Francisco Examiner.* "It's difficult to find a building that hasn't already been worked over. We'd love to be in New York. We'd like to be in San Diego. We're going into Vancouver [in spring 2000]."

Customer Targets

The KG avoided targeting the 10 percent of customers who wanted absolute luxury. Nor was it after the backpacking student. Rather, KG had sought to serve the 50 to 60 percent of the market that was looking for "comfort and value." In 1994, Bill Kimpton summarized his approach quite succinctly in the *New York Times*: "We sell sleep, while corporation lodging [full-service hotels] is in the entertainment business because of all the extras it has to offer." Guests at those other hotel facilities paid for the meeting rooms, the ornate lobbies, the fabulous water fountains, the unused restaurants, and other services that most would never use. A hotel, according to KG's philosophy, should relieve a traveler of his or her loneliness. It should make guests feel "warm and cozy," Bill Kimpton told the *Chicago Tribune* in 1998. This vision shaped the organization's approach to the hotel industry in general and to its markets in particular.

In discussing KG's success, Steve Marx spoke of a "customer intimacy" that gave "personality" to each one of its properties. This focus on service details resembled the attention to cost details that characterized the property acquisition process for which KG had become noted.

According to Jeff Senior:

> How do we build brand equity? Classic brand management. We need to rely on the power of the individual hotel brands, a core premise in our niche/boutique hotel segment. We need to focus on the product positioning, ensuring uniqueness and legitimate competitive advantage; product and service delivery consistency with the positioning; distribution focus against the highest-yielding channels for our target; and performance management to ensure desired results are achieved, appropriate corrective action taken, and strategic revisions evaluated in

an ongoing manner. We compete within the deluxe category in urban markets . . . both reflecting much higher barrier to entry.

The target market for KG included both business and tourist travelers who were looking for a unique, intimate, and personal hotel experience. International guests represented about 11 percent of KG's total. The amenities offered by KG properties bordered on luxury but provided each guest with a clearly recognized bargain compared with the upscale chains such as Hilton or Marriott.

Restaurant Operations

Each of the restaurants that KG operated had a separate entrance and a separate identity from its hotel location. The company took pains to avoid having its restaurants perceived as "hotel restaurants." Niki Leondakis, vice president of restaurant operations for KG and six-year veteran of the organization, said that hotel restaurants were the antithesis of what her company did best. "The minute that we become a hotel-restaurant," Leondakis added, "that's death. A hotel-restaurant has a stigma: overpriced [and offering] poor service." KG strove to offer dining patrons a "handcrafted" experience—something that gave character and personality. "[We] want our guests to feel they're getting something they can't get anywhere else," commented Leondakis.

Jeff Senior commented:

> When I came to Kimpton less than a year ago, we were already structured with a separate restaurant division. While the downside is a duplication of resources to support the respective businesses, the upside is a focus on the core competencies of each business and the key drivers of profitability. The result: we have profitable restaurants and profitable hotels.

Following this strategy, each KG restaurant was custom-made for each property and market location. Each restaurant was allowed to run independently and to exist with renowned chefs including Julian Serrano (at Masa's), Wolfgang Puck (at the Postrio), and Gionvanni Perticone (at the Splendido). According to KG's San Francisco city manager Jim McPartlin, "We create freestanding restaurants that actually make an operating profit, around 5 to 15 percent versus the break-even margins at typical hotel restaurants."

Each of the KG-managed restaurants was individually themed and offered a variety of food styles, price ranges, and ambiences. Many of the restaurants featured exhibition kitchens and counter seating that made them user-friendly for single guests who wished to dine alone. "Our restaurants are run by restaurateurs," said Leondakis. "We provide service to the hotel, but our restaurants are more than a food and beverage outlet. We are a profitable, independent, and separate business."

In December 1998, a Smith Travel Associates report on the U.S. lodging industry noted that, on average, 73 percent of a hotel's revenue came from rooms, 20.6 percent from food and beverage, and 6.4 percent from minor operations such as telecommunications, space rentals, and other miscellaneous sources. KG depended on its restaurants to deliver extra perceived value to customers, much as the full-service hotel with much higher room rates would. The most obvious cross-marketing between the restaurant and hotel operations occurred when restaurant customers visited the restroom and inevitably had to walk through the lobby of the hotel. Diners would, hopefully, spread the word about the little boutique hotel that they had "discovered" while having a terrific dinner.

Thus, KG helped pioneer the strategy of a stand-alone restaurant as a lure to get word-of-mouth advertising for its hotels. However, other chains, such as Fairfield Inns by Marriott, Hilton Garden Inn, and Microtel were known to be operating some of their properties under a strategy very similar to the Kimpton Group's approach of attracting travelers by being closely associated with a world-class restaurant. A potential concern for all using this strategy is that there is a limited pool of quality chefs willing to work within the structure of a corporation, especially when the strong suit of the corporation is the hotel division.

The Future

As with most business situations, past success could turn out to be a double-edged sword for KG. A recent collaboration with the Trammel-Crow investment group made funds more or less readily available for property acquisition and rapid growth. Yet, it was not clear that KG's strategy could be easily transferred to other markets. KG needed to decide on its desired growth rate and how it could manage growth without losing the uniqueness and decentralized culture that its senior management held in high regard.

According to PKF, the San Francisco-based hotel and real estate research firm, the projected profitability of the industry could, by the year 2000, reach the highest in at least a half-century. Gross margins could exceed 30 percent, fattening returns on investment and permitting aggressive expansion by KG into untapped markets.

Still, KG has insisted that the organization does not do deals just to do deals. By 1999, the group was managing almost 4,000 rooms in increasingly far-flung locations. Although privately held, KG executives revealed that revenues had grown by an estimated 10 to 20 percent per year in the past six years. The organization had been generating a consistent 15 to 20 percent return for its investment partners, all high-net-worth individuals including movie stars Paul Newman and Harrison Ford, as well as members of the Getty family. The level of return also exceeds the 13 percent return on investment target set by the Crow family.

In order to continue to differentiate itself from the competition, in 1999 KG added new amenities in its guest rooms such as telephones that easily accommodated laptop computers, easy chairs, desks with large work surfaces, and improved lighting. Technological trends that may affect the competitive landscape of the hotel industry included the emerging use of "smart cards" to replace cash and capture unique preferences of the hotel guest. Technology similarly made hotel-specific Web sites and bargain-hunting at sites like www.priceline.com almost ubiquitous within the industry.

According to Jeff Senior, KG was experiencing difficulty entering the Internet age:

> Fear of technology and systems is serious around here. The infrastructure does not exist. We have only one management information system person in this entire organization. We're not using e-mail. Our high technology is voice mail.

Also in 1999, KG began to emphasize on-site revenue management systems. This information would help general managers decide what each part of their operation contributed to profitability, which, in turn, would help senior executives at the group level to understand the potential for increasing internal efficiencies. Additionally, information access improvements were expected to give each property general manager a sense of decentralized decision making in spite of living under a corporate umbrella.

Strategic Meeting at KG: Afterthoughts

Before the 3:00 PM meeting with David Martin and Jeff Senior ended, Marx had an opportunity to explore with them the range of strategic choices that he thought were critical to the continued success of KG. Looking back after that meeting, Marx noted:

There are people in integral positions in this organization who remain "small thinkers" and who are afraid to step up to the plate. Our greatest fault is that we're sometimes not ready to put our money where our mouth is. That's a real danger. From the top, you've got to send a signal that it's okay to take risks, that it's (sort of) okay to fail. Mind you, we have made very few mistakes. Still, we have to be more careful about seducing ourselves that every market is the right place for our hotels. The problem is the fragility of the tourism economies in other cities, making it difficult to expand into new markets.

We're sort of disorganized; I know we like to kid ourselves about how "seat-of-the-pants" we are, and we say we're strategic but we're really very tactical. This is typical of the hotel industry. We are trying to be strategic in what really is a tactical industry. We need to decide where we're going in the future. You can't have two sides of an organization in conflict. We have tension that is unnecessary, sort of a push-pull between those managers that advocate returning to what we used to be and those that advocate changing into what we're going to become. Even Bill [Kimpton, the founder and chairman of the Kimpton Group] is torn.

We need to preserve our philosophy to enable a general manager to imprint their personality on an individual hotel. We need to continue to go to great lengths to attract and nurture people who believe that their success is also the success of the company. Always stay in touch with line employees. I actually want to hear bad news. Be unreasonable. Set unreasonable expectations. And always be really hands-on with our owners. These are hallmarks of what we do.

After the afternoon meeting with Martin and Senior, Marx wondered to what extent his successors could cope with the changing dynamics in the hotel industry and at the same time continue the open management philosophy and participatory decision-making style that had served KG so well during his tenure. The strategic choices to be made now fell—at least, temporarily—on Martin and Senior's watch. He wondered in what direction they would take KG and which issues they would make their priorities.

bibliography

Allen, J. L. "San Franciscan Making More Room at Inns." *Chicago Tribune,* March 18, 1998.

Anderson, R. *Atlas of the American Economy.* Washington, D. C.: Congressional Quarterly, 1994.

Armstrong, D. "Keeping Hotels Hot." *San Francisco Examiner,* July 18, 1999, p. B1.

"Front Desk." *Lodging,* July 1998, p. 16.

Garfinkel, P. "Bed & Breakfast? No, Bed and Dinner." *New York Times,* January 16, 1994.

Higley, J. "Kimpton Group Broadens Its Horizon." *Hotel & Motel Management* 213, no. 13 (July 20, 1998).

"Motels and Hotels." *Moody's Industry Review,* January 22, 1999.

"Ratings of Hotels & Motels." *Consumer Reports,* July 1998, p. 17.

Scatchard, B. "Occupancy Was Down Last Year." *Hoteliers' Infosource* 7, no. 1 (January 1999).

Smith, R. A. "Lodging Outlook Survey for the Year Ending December, 1998." Smith Travel Associates Research, www.hotel-online.com, May 16, 1999.

Tardiff, J. C. *U.S. Industry Profiles.* New York: Gale Research, 1998.

Templin, N. "Eccentric Sells: S. F. Firm Finds a Profitable Niche with Boutique Hotels." *Contra Costa Times,* April 17, 1999, pp. C1–C2.

U. S. Department of Commerce. *Census of Service Industries.* 1998.

case 23 Brithinee Electric in 1999: Raising the Standards

Harold Dyck
California State University–San Bernardino

Sue Greenfeld
California State University–San Bernardino

As teenagers, identical twins Wallace Jr. and Don Brithinee helped when their father, Wallace Sr., started Brithinee Electric in 1963. Back then, the entire business consisted of repairing electric motors. Providing first-rate service to customers with critical motor repair needs became the primary mission and business of Brithinee Electric. On occasion, meeting the turnaround times desired by customers meant working around the clock. Hard work eventually earned the twin brothers PhDs in mathematics from the University of California–Riverside by the time they were 23 years old, and helped lay the foundation for the cultural values and success of the firm in the succeeding decades. Brithinee Electric had won an assortment of industry and manufacturers' awards, which were proudly displayed in the lobby of the company's offices. At the entrance to the company's conference room were pictures of Wally and Don Brithinee with a number of distinguished political figures, including former head of the Joint Chiefs of Staff, General Colin Powell, and former British prime minister Margaret Thatcher.

Brithinee Electric repaired industrial motors, distributed motor/control devices, and designed and built control panels, primarily for municipalities and other businesses. In 1988 this Colton, California, firm commemorated 25 years in business, had 23 employees, and brought in $4.6 million in revenue; that same year, a case study about the firm appeared in three strategic management textbooks.[1] At that time, the company had an implied mission based on quality and service, but did not have a formal mission statement. The most pressing issues facing the company then included employee development, job rotation, overdependency on the "Brithinee boys," and whether to undertake a major expansion. The company was located in the "Inland

---

[1]S. Greenfeld, "Brithinee Electric," in Smith, Arnold, and Bizzell, eds., *Business Strategy and Policy* (Boston: Houghton-Mifflin, 1991), pp. 180–200. Also in Stahl and Grisby, eds., *Strategic Management for Decision Making* (Boston: PWS-Kent, 1992), pp. 368–87, and Dess and Miller, eds., *Strategic Management,* (New York: McGraw-Hill, 1993), pp. 393–410.

exhibit 1   Brithinee Electric's Mission Statement

Brithinee Electric

Our mission:

to delight our customers by delivering products and services of superior quality, thereby raising their expectations.

Empire," about 50 miles directly east of Los Angeles; the expansion then under consideration would have meant building a new facility to service customers in the San Diego area.

Eleven years later, in 1999, Brithinee Electric had grown to 50 employees and $6.7 million in revenues. The company had decided against expanding into the San Diego area. It had weathered a recession, struggled through the loss of a $1-million-per-year customer, coped with mounting competition in its industry, improved employee training through more formalized methods, worked through the job rotation issues encountered earlier, and solved most of the dependency issues. The Brithinee brothers had developed a formal mission statement centered on "enabling the customer." This had led to an effort to encourage and empower the company's multiethnic employees to "provide literature, materials, specifications, and some learning opportunities for our customers." The company had recently added the words "Brithinee Electric . . . Raising the Standards" to its "Customer Bill of Rights" (see Exhibits 1 and 2).

In 1999, Brithinee Electric had a different set of challenges. Competition in selling electric motors was now considerably stronger than it had been in the late 1980s. Moreover, customers wanted more sophisticated control devices than used to be the case. Wally and Don believed that for Brithinee Electric to grow and prosper in the years ahead they would need to resolve several strategic and organizational issues: How could an independent motor rewinding shop like Brithinee Electric best position itself against its rivals, many of whom were substantially larger? What could Brithinee Electric do to distinguish itself from its competitors? Could Brithinee successfully position itself as a high-quality service provider when a number of its customers didn't seem to appreciate the need for or the value of high standards for motor repair? What organizational changes, if any, did the company need to consider making? Exhibit 3 presents the company's current organizational chart.

COMPANY HISTORY

Wallace Brithinee Sr. started Brithinee Electric in 1963 after two previous ventures did not work out. The earlier ventures proved to be a springboard for getting into the business of repairing industrial motors. Wallace's young sons, Wally and Don Brithinee, worked alongside their father in starting and developing the fledgling company, gradually learning the rewinding business.

In 1970, when Lincoln Electric, a large manufacturer of electric motors, came out with an appealing low-priced motor, the Brithinees made a strategic decision to become distributors for Lincoln's new product line. Taking on the Lincoln line allowed *exhibit 2*   Brithinee Electric's Customer Bill of Rights

---

CUSTOMER BILL OF RIGHTS

At Brithinee Electric, we believe both the customer and the supplier of electrical hardware and service will benefit if the purchase decision is an informed one. Assert your rights as customer by getting to know your vendor's business practices. Get maximum value by comparing the vendor's commitment as well as the price.

As a customer of Brithinee Electric, you have the right to expect:

RELIABILITY
- Stable workforce
- Work references
- Sound financial condition
- Environmental responsibility

QUALITY
- Qualified personnel
- Documentation
- Pride in workmanship
- Best available technology

COMMUNICATION
- Before and after tests reports
- Prompt and accurate quotations
- Product and service alternatives
- Accurate itemized invoices

COMMITMENT
- Service
- Investment in technology and our facility
- Investment in inventory
- Problem solving

BRITHINEE ELECTRIC
. . . *Raising the Standards*

Brithinee Electric to offer its customers the choice of repairing or replacing a malfunctioning motor. By 1972 Brithinee Electric had seven employees and enough business to feel optimistic about the future, so it built a 10,000-square-foot facility to house the business. The company's facilities were expanded to 16,750 square feet seven years later. By 1980 Brithinee Electric had 23 employees. In 1982 Wally and Don Brithinee took over management of the business when Wallace Sr. decided to retire.

In 1987, Brithinee had about $4.5 million in revenue, about 75 percent of which came from selling its Toshiba and Baldor lines of electric motors and about 25 percent of which came from motor repair work. Building customized electric control panels was a new venture with one full-time employee, but control panel sales were not yet large enough to be listed as a separate revenue category in the company's financial statements. Brithinee's main emphasis was in motors for water pumping and treatment areas, rock crushing, cement facilities, and the food industry, including wineries and breweries.

MOTOR REPAIR AND ENERGY EFFICIENCY

Various government agencies and utilities in the United States and Canada estimated that the use of electric motors in various types of equipment and appliances accounted for close to 70 percent of total electrical energy consumption, roughly equivalent to the energy consumption of all passenger automobiles. Just as proper maintenance and repair practices had a positive effect on reducing an automobile's gasoline consumption, proper maintenance and repair practices had a positive effect on the electric motor efficiency. A poorly repaired electric motor could end up using significantly more electricity than was

exhibit 3   Brithinee Electric's Organization Chart

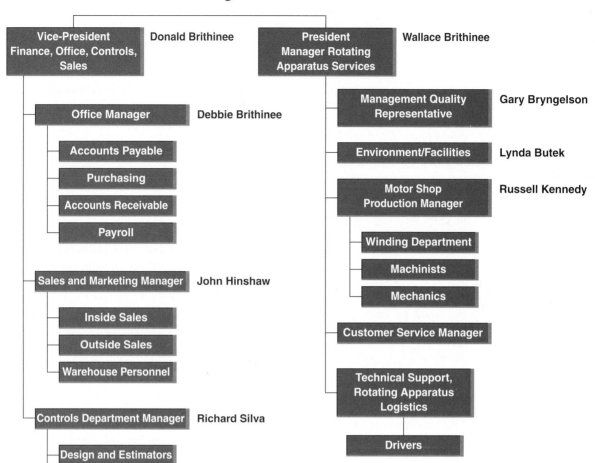

necessary. Most industrial users of electric motors were aware that using properly repaired electric motors not only improved the reliability of electric-powered equipment but also helped reduce their costs for electric power.

When Iraq invaded Kuwait in August 1990, threatening Western oil supplies, legislators in the United States and Canada passed more stringent requirements mandating greater electric motor efficiency. Noting that the horsepower of electric motors repaired far exceeded the horsepower of newly sold electric motors, regulators studied the repair process for electric motors as well as the purchasing practices of industrial firms. While considering draconian measures such as licensing schemes or even the banning of motor repair in favor of replacement with new, energy-efficient models, the sentiment for less government intervention led to voluntary-compliance programs to improve electric motor repair practices in ways that would boost efficiency and reduce electricity consumption. Wally Brithinee, as the chairman of the Engineering Committee of the Electrical Apparatus Service Association (EASA), had led the development of a set of standards and guidelines for repair of electric motors that met most of the regulators' concerns. These standards and guidelines subsequently became the building blocks for the motor repair industry, ushering in a new set of best practices in electric motor repair. Brithinee's adherence to these new standards was used as a marketing tool to attract new customers and win business away from rivals.

In addition to seeking to reduce U.S. dependency on foreign oil, the U.S. government had signed two climate-change treaties and agreed to pursue actions to reduce greenhouse gas emissions. Since fossil-fuel power plants were large contributors to such emissions, any actions that increased the efficiency of electric motors and dampened electricity consumption helped meet greenhouse gas emission standards. Hence, heightened environmental concerns were adding to the pressure to improve electric motor repair practices.

BRITHINEE ELECTRIC IN THE 1990S

In 1991, Brithinee Electric experienced its first significant decline in revenues. The company "hit a brick wall," says Don Brithinee. The U.S. economy went into a recession, which Brithinee weathered with some pain. Through no fault of its own, the company lost a $1-million-per-year customer because the customer's equipment could not accommodate the change in the size of the variable frequency drive that Brithinee was supplying. Brithinee's total revenue declined further in 1992 before turning upward again. But it was not until 1996 that revenues exceeded the level achieved in 1990. Brithinee was proud that no one was laid off during the downturn, though some employees were asked to take accumulated vacation time.

In 1992, Brithinee made three changes to enable it to handle the rebuilding of large quantities of locomotive motors from General Motors' Electro-Motive Division (EMD) and to expand inventory space. First, the company acquired a 13,000-square-foot building (called the 680 Building due to its address) about 100 yards south of the old site. This building cost $495,000, and another $141,000 was spent for remodeling. Second, $500,000 of inventory was moved out of the main building into the new building, the winding machine shop areas were enlarged, and special floor space was dedicated to EMD motor repair activities. Third, the company established more stringent quality procedures than had previously existed.

Acquiring the 680 Building pushed Brithinee Electric in a new strategic direction: designing and building control panels. Previously, Brithinee had dabbled in making control panels, but making customized control panels became a significant part of the business in order to broaden the company's revenue and customer base and avoid being too dependent on one customer or product category. The decline in aerospace and defense in the early 1990s taught many Southern California businesses not to have all their eggs in one basket. Expanding into control panels was a "Y in the road," according to Don Brithinee. "It is a different beast . . . It's a cleaner operation . . . It's not a repair operation at all. It is an assembly of new electronic components." As part of this new focus, Brithinee hired Richard Silva in 1992; Silva was instrumental in attaining Underwriter Laboratories (UL) certification for the company. UL certification paved the way for Square D and Telemecanique, both subsidiaries of French multinational Groupe Schneider, to become major new customers.

Lynda Butek, the environmental/facilities coordinator, who worked directly for Wally Brithinee, was responsible for the 1992 installation of a closed-loop aqueous parts washer for loads weighing up to 20,000 pounds. The installation improved efficiency by eliminating the need to dispose of large quantities of water from a washdown area. Exhibits 4 and 5 show Brithinee's current facilities.

exhibit 4   Layout of Brithinee Electric "620 Building" (Facility for Manufacturing Electric Motors and Headquarters Office)

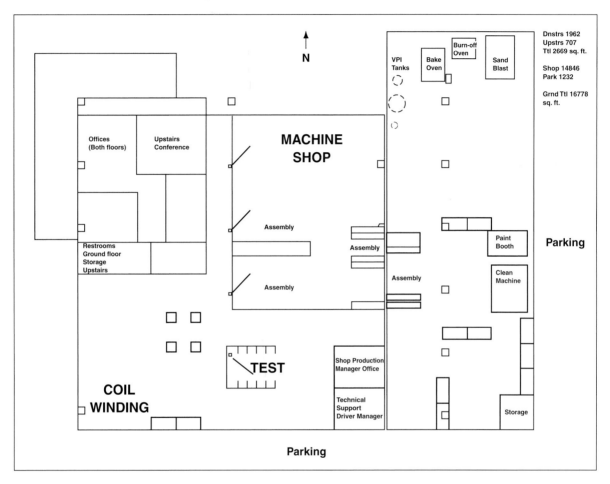

Wally described the circumstances surrounding the $315,000 renovation of the original 620 Building in 1997, stating that the reason for the remodel was

> to control the environment in the manufacturing area, and to make it reflect the quality of the products produced there. In that regard, we had specific goals and tasks. One was to reduce noise and increase the desirability of the eastern third of the building as a work area. That area has certain processes with air handlers and pumps that generate audible noise. These include the paint booth exhaust; the sand-blast cabinet and dust collector; and the parts washer, with its array of pumps. We evaluated all the lighting in the building and greatly increased it . . .
>
> At the same time, controls were centralized so that it would be easy to reduce lighting and electrical consumption when personnel were not in the work area. During the remodel, we added insulation with value of R-30 and covered the ceiling with a white plastic sheath. That moderated temperatures, further reduced noise, and increased the effectiveness of the light. The effects were dramatic.
>
> Shop offices were enlarged, allowing better supervisory control at the plant floor. A laser printer was added, with fax-modem, and the shop offices became much more efficient. There was far less cause for drivers, delivery persons, and shop personnel to come

exhibit 5   "680 Building" Layout

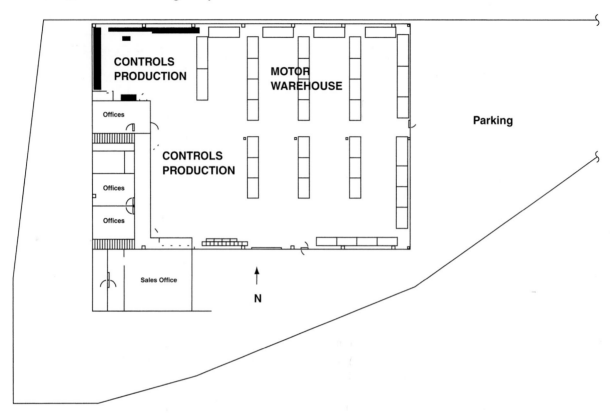

into the business office. The offices of this building were redone to eliminate the large, open office area. As we had grown, the open area seemed to create many distractions to the tasks at hand and to offer sound interference for telephone conversations.

The conference room that existed was reshaped and enlarged, and today is fitted with a table for executive meetings. The decor has been completely redone from its early 1970s look to a more modern look.

Brithinee was installing a vacuum pressure impregnation (VPI) tank as an integral part of the company's repair capabilities. The closing of other motor repair shops in Southern California had resulted in an increase in larger motors coming into Brithinee for repair, creating the need for equipment to handle the larger stator and rotors on such motors. Putting in the new VPI tank required digging a 10- to 12-foot pit and getting various environmental protection permits.

Brithinee primarily relied on personal selling to establish and cement relationships with customers. It also was the beneficiary of word-of-mouth advertising from satisfied customers. In late 1997, the company hired Cyd Sandefur as an assistant to Don Brithinee to work on advertising and other special projects.

Brithinee's revenues in 1998 were $6.99 million; 43 percent came from motor repair work, 26 percent came from motor sales, and 31 percent were from custom-made control panel sales. While 11 years ago the company's accounting system provided separate itemized statements for repairs and sales, in 1999 there was a single consolidated statement. This system made it easy to move people from one area to another without making significant accounting changes but it provided less detailed information concerning specific labor charges to each different activity—motor repair, motor sales, and custom-made control panel sales.

THE INDUSTRY ENVIRONMENT FOR MOTOR SALES AND MOTOR REPAIR

Throughout the 1980s, sales of new electric motors grew at a 20 percent average compound rate. As the industry moved into the 1990s, growth slowed and the market matured, motor prices came down, and electric motor reliability went up. Features became user-friendly. Many types of electric motors became more standardized and more widely available from a variety of sources. By the late 1990s, competition had heated up to the point that 12 out of 13 of Toshiba's top distributors of variable-frequency drives (inverters) were selling fewer new motors. According to Don Brithinee, "What changed was better competition from some premium brand names." As Brithinee Electric lost market share to competing brands, the company's revenues from new motor sales dropped, contrary to management's expectations.

The introduction of electric motors with variable-frequency drives greatly changed the market by increasing motor system efficiency, reducing energy consumption, and changing repair requirements. Variable-frequency drives introduced high-voltage pulses, thousands each second, into the motor windings, resulting in partial discharge and corona. This produced highly corrosive ozone and charged particles that eroded the organic insulation from the windings. These problems increased the costs to rework a motor. Previously, insulation life could be 10 to 12 years without a failure, but with the new electronic frequency drives, wire failures could occur within a few hundred hours of operation.

The Engineering Committee for EASA had met with researchers from various electrical testing laboratories and with the suppliers making the various components of motor windings to make sure they understood the nature and costs of the repairs, to try to identify all the causes of the increase in winding failures, and to explore why the new motor inspection procedures and analysis used in the past were not working. Motor repair firms wanted to stay on top of what progress, if any, was being made in developing more resistant insulation materials.

The development of a microprocessor-controlled variable-frequency drive created opportunities for improved process control as well as improved energy efficiency of the driven system. With the more stringent energy-efficiency requirements mandated in the Energy Policy Act of 1992, motor manufacturers were redesigning electric motors. The design changes generally included increasing the active materials in the stator and rotor. In the stator (the part that is usually rewound) the active materials being used were laminated steel sheets ("core iron") and copper wire. In the case of copper wire, designers had increased the cross-section of the conductor, while reducing the length of the wire and cutting winding resistance. But in so doing, these design changes usually resulted in increased difficulty for coil insertion (trying to stuff more copper into a very crowded frame and core). Thus, motor repair firms needed thinner, tougher, slicker insulation in order to maintain the energy efficiency of the motor and withstand the harsh electrical environment that variable-frequency drives entailed.

The EASA Engineering Committee, chaired by Wally Brithinee, had brought all of these issues to the attention of Du Pont's Nomex and Kevlar researchers and marketers in Richmond, Virginia, as well as key industry suppliers of wire (Essex Group, Phelps Dodge) and resins (P. D. George Company). Additionally, the committee had met several times with the Technical Subsection of the NEMA Motors and Generators Committee in an effort to strengthen the information ties between manufacturers and the repair industry. All this had produced guidelines for motor rewinding that provided both an energy-efficient rewind as well as a winding that could give long life in the variable-frequency applications, using materials that were readily available.

Wally Brithinee's experiences in chairing the EASA committee helped him understand how the company could improve its motor repair practices to better address the maintenance problems that users were having, especially as concerned winding an "inverter-duty" motor. The repair process changes the company had implemented had been well received, enhancing the company's stature with several motor manufacturers. In a growing number of instances, the company's windings on repaired motors were proving superior and longer lasting than the windings on brand-new motors.

The Exit of Several Rivals from the Southern California Market

In 1999 Brithinee Electric confronted weaker competition in motor repair than it had in the late 1980s. Several large manufacturers with repair shops had withdrawn from the Southern California market. Don Brithinee observed, "The playing field is a lot more level when we are competing with another independent company than with the captive business of a major manufacturer. That has brought some positive changes for us because we don't have the pressure of competing with some of the majors." Some of the area closures included the 30,000-square-foot facility of Swiss-based ASEA Brown Boveri, located 30 miles to the west of Brithinee Electric. General Motors' Electro-Motive Division had closed its motor repair facility in Los Angeles, while Reliance Electric had shut its shop in Anaheim. Westinghouse had been gone for a number of years, and General Electric's facility no longer did rewind work and did very little repair work on high-voltage motors. The last big captive shop in the area was a McGraw-Edison facility that had recently been purchased by MagneTek and then resold to Eastern Electric, which was operating with a much smaller staff. The closing of the shops of the major manufacturers had boosted opportunities for small independents like Brithinee. Don and Wally were unsure exactly why the "big boys" had left the market but were eager to capitalize on what they saw as an opportunity to fill the gap left by the closings and pick up new customers.

Trade Association Participation and Regulatory Affairs

As part of Brithinee Electric's commitment to educating and raising the expectations of their customers, Wally Brithinee and Lynda Butek had cultivated leadership roles within EASA. Wally chaired the EASA Engineering Committee and Lynda had become chair of EASA's Environmental Affairs Committee, recently renamed the Governmental Affairs Committee. Lynda was also on the Insurance and Safety Committee of EASA. Lynda believed that being closely involved with EASA activities "really helped the business from a technical standpoint." Wally and Lynda's committee work had helped Brithinee gain access to the latest and best information about new materials and technology. Plus, it had afforded them the opportunity to initiate and maintain contacts with wire, insulation materials, and equipment manufacturers.

In addition, Brithinee Electric worked closely with several regulatory agencies, including the South Coast Air Quality Management District and the Air Resources Board of California, to help streamline regulations. There were several agencies in California with overlapping jurisdictions, but the agencies did not appear to coordinate and collaborate with each other. Every year Lynda filled out three sets of forms with basically the same information for three different state agencies. In one instance, Lynda was forced to spend half a day preparing a report documenting that Brithinee owed $6.95 for particulate matter emissions (e.g., sulfur oxide, methane, hydrogen oxide, 1.1.1 trichloroethane, and carbon monoxide). Lynda questioned the reasonableness of all the regulations and procedural requirements of the three agencies and was working to figure out how to best streamline the processes to minimize repetition and how to gather the information with the least work disruptions. She believed that "California is still the toughest state to get permits in." Regulatory developments in California were closely watched by regulatory agencies in other states, with several environmentally conscious states sometimes following California's lead in establishing regulatory requirements for emissions and waste disposal. In reflecting on the company's involvement with EASA and various agencies, Wally was uncertain how to best influence government regulatory policies and whether there was anything he or EASA could do to minimize agency overlap and duplication of effort for the industry. He thought there ought to be a role for EASA in lobbying state and federal agencies to become more business-friendly while also protecting the environment.

OPERATIONS AT BRITHINEE ELECTRIC

Motor Repair

Brithinee repaired motors up to 1,000 horsepower, 4,000 volts, and 5 tons in weight. According to Wally Brithinee, "95 percent of all motors 200 horsepower and above can be expected to be repaired once in their lifetime." The motor repair process began when incoming electrical motors were received. Using contract drivers and its own fleet of trucks, Brithinee picked up and delivered customers' motors; some customers brought motors in to the shop for repair. Incoming motors underwent initial inspection and testing before being dismantled. The core was tested and the old windings were burned off in a temperature-controlled oven. Then a second core test was performed. The motors were rewound with new quadruple-build or inverter-duty magnet wire. Connections were made and a preassembly inspection performed before additional assembly and final testing. Approximately 70 percent of the motor was used in the remanufacture; most of the rest was recycled. The motors Brithinee repaired were able to maintain energy efficiency within 0.5 percent of what the motor was originally designed to achieve when new. The final step in the repair process was to prepare the motor for shipping and delivery to the customer. Brithinee did not repair motors on a customer's site due to liability, the difficulty associated with burning off the old windings, the use of chemicals, and the equipment needed to rewind, assemble, and bond the new wire inside the industrial motor (see Exhibit 6).

Motor Repair Workflow   Russ Kennedy, production manager since 1988, oversaw the workflow from start to finish. He made the work assignments and scheduled the repair process so that customers' motors could be returned and put back into service in a timely fashion. Kennedy documented the conditions of incoming motors using one of three digital cameras and stored the images electronically on a Macintosh.

exhibit 6   Activity Sequence for Motor Repair

1. Receipt	7. Rewind & Connect
2. Initial Inspection & Test	8. Pre-Assembly Inspection
3. Dismantle	9. Assembly
4. Core Test	10. Final Test
5. Burn Out Old Windings	11. Prepare for Shipping
6. Core Test	12. Ship

The use of digital cameras had improved the process tremendously over previously used Polaroid pictures. Benefits included lower costs, more flexibility, more views of each motor, and electronic file handling capability. Having digital pictures associated with work orders had decreased the number of misunderstandings with workers and customers. For example, one customer, after delivery of a repaired motor, thought a part was missing; the digital pictures of the motor in the company's file were used to clear up the problem of the missing part.

Brithinee had designed process flow charts for the jobs it did for GM's Electro-Motive Division because the procedures were more standardized for these types of motors than most of the other motors that it serviced. These procedures instituted for the GM jobs included calibration of all measuring instruments. Some aspects of the flow charts developed for GM's work had proved useful for other motor repair work and were incorporated into the company's motor repair process.

Workers went to Kennedy's office to pick up their repair assignments—with the photos attached to the work order. Motors at various stages of repair were stored in bins that were labeled both alphabetically and numerically. Supposedly, every job had a storage location home, but with three shifts and uneven pallet sizes, there were times when workers would put a motor or some of its parts "wherever," and finding them could become an Easter egg hunt. The motor repair area contained several motors that had been left for repair as far back as 1995. Customers who did not have sufficient funds to get their motors repaired immediately sometimes just left them with Brithinee indefinitely. Although Brithinee had cleared out a significant number of these older jobs, management was still pondering the issue of how long it should provide service to customers by storing their motors gratis versus when it should start charging them for storage service.

A typical repair could range from $600 to $7,000. When a motor came in for repair, an estimate of the repair costs was prepared and provided to the customer by fax or phone; customer authorization to proceed was required before Brithinee initiated the repair process. Work was scheduled at a daily production meeting where the day- and night-shift production and customer service team discussed work in progress and promised delivery times. At that time, the team determined the priority for open jobs and discussed what work would be performed during the night shifts. Each workstation was equipped with EASA-created laminated charts showing the acceptable tolerance values to allow the workers to compare the fit of each part. Various agencies recommended that motor owners patronize repair facilities using EASA guidelines and standards.

Work orders were color-coded: green for go, red for stop, and orange for a "hot" rush job. Orange jobs went to the head of the queue. An orange-coded priority job could preempt another job, "by the minute," according to Russ Kennedy. He cited a rush-order case where the city of Riverside didn't have water for 10 city blocks and

Brithinee Electric worked through the night to complete the rush job. Customers paid a premium for overtime on orange-coded jobs. Jobs might be assigned by workers' ability. Repairs on a hot rush job from a very big customer sometimes began before a repair quote had been accepted, causing consternation in the accounts receivable department. Kennedy did not want procedures to hold up emergency work. One of Wally Brithinee's goals was to reduce the company's overtime costs (though not necessarily on orange-coded rush jobs, where customers expected to pay for emergency work). Three-fourths of the costs of repairing a motor were labor costs; one-fourth went for parts and materials.

Plant Layout Issues and Outsourcing Potential   With 75 to 110 work orders open at any one time and 18 workers on the day shift, 5 on the swing shift, and 3 on graveyard shift, there was seldom a time when a worker was idle. Occasionally a machine might be idle if workers were pulled off to work on a rush job. At one point the company encountered frequent bottlenecks in the shop floor area; thinking that more space would remedy the problem, Brithinee hired a consultant to redesign the plant layout. After conducting interviews and studying ways to reorganize the layout to get a better workflow, the consultant concluded that the company did not need more space and recommended a different plant layout. The basic problem of work frequently crossing paths as the repair process moved from department to department was corrected by relocating and widening aisles, adding electrical outlets and lighting, and redesigning each workstation. Hazardous repair operations were relocated to a different area.

Other operating problems included work stoppages that occurred when work crews ran out of propane gas because no one was assigned the task of monitoring the gas level on a regular basis. This problem was addressed by having a propane gas vendor make regular deliveries. Russ Kennedy was looking at whether there were any other tasks that could be outsourced, thereby freeing worker time for motor repair work.

Customer Reports   Beginning in 1993, Brithinee Electric began providing customers a previously internal computer report on why a motor fails and the state of the motor when it arrived and when it left the shop. This report explained what Brithinee found, how the motor tested when it came in, and how it tested when it went out. Included were such items as vibration, resistance of the winding, and types of bearings installed that provided a baseline for the motor's performance. Brithinee decided to share this information with its customers as a value-added service and as a way of raising customer expectations about the caliber of Brithinee's expertise and capabilities. Wally explained, "We don't expect [the customer] to even ask for what they really need . . . With our training and outreach programs through the Department of Energy, [we ask ourselves,] 'How do you get the user of electrical motor systems to develop or purchase a good system—for both efficiency and reliability?'"

Lynda Butek added, "Brithinee Electric has always had a reputation for quality . . . and that reputation has tripled in the last 9 to 10 years. Wally has instituted a very rigorous testing and reporting system for our customers that they didn't even know they wanted." She indicated that at first customers appeared to pay little attention to the report, but "now you try not to send it and you get a phone call. 'Where is my report? I need my report!'" Some customers had even begun expecting such reports from Brithinee's competitors when they sent them motor repair work.

Customized Motor Control Panels   Customized control panels involved building industrial integrated systems and dealing with programmable logic controllers, motor controls, and variable frequency drives. Brithinee did not consider itself to be either a mass producer or a low-price leader in providing custom control panels; rather, it saw this market niche as a value-added service it could provide. From one employee in 1987, this department had grown to eight employees in 1999. Sometimes the workload for control panels was heavy, necessitating "borrowing" up to nine people from the repair side to complete a project. Brithinee specialized in drives and soft-start applications that reduced stresses associated with each motor start, and increased the longevity of the motor. Depending on the complexity, motor control panels could cost $1,000 to $10,000 in labor time to design. Brithinee sometimes charged separately for designing the control panel and related software and for manufacture.

When Brithinee hired Richard Silva as controls department manager in 1992, one of his first assignments was to establish the procedures necessary to manufacture control panels meeting standards prescribed by Underwriters Laboratories (UL), specifically UL Standard 508 and, later, UL Standard 845. Panels carrying UL certification signaled that the product met accepted safety standards in its construction, thereby reducing the risk of liability. According to Richard Silva, "It legitimizes you . . . It has been real good for our business. It has opened doors, and been a plus for us."

It was Brithinee's practice to "overdesign" a product in order to guarantee product performance. Brithinee used a larger size wire and would dip it in tin to lessen problems associated with heat. Brithinee also investigated where the panel would be installed and serviced, including exposure to heat, moisture, wind, and other environmental conditions. One panel shipped to the United Arab Emirates was designed with parts that would be available locally should the need arise. The company's goal was to make sure its panels worked the first time and every time thereafter. If a panel failed, the company's reputation suffered and it had to incur the cost of sending someone to fix the problem.

Silva worked closely with several large companies to meet UL Standard 845 in building control panels. Square D found Brithinee's control panel operations very flexible and responsive to its requests. Brithinee could build control panels faster than Square D's own plant. Richard Silva explained the distribution pattern: "Brithinee is a subcontractor to Square D, who sells the product to a distributor, who sells it to an electrical contractor, who will sell it to the general contractor, who actually is providing the control panel to the municipality or utility company." Square D supplied Brithinee with some control panel parts.

Candace Winn, Square D's Oceanside, California, plant manager, described their relationship with Brithinee as "unique." She said, "We talk to them all the time on the phone three to six times a day . . . They have a real knack for educating the customer." She was confident that repairs by Brithinee were done correctly and almost considered them to be a sister company. David Whitney, a senior sales engineer at Square D who called on industrial-type end users in Orange County and part of Los Angeles County, characterized the Square D–Brithinee relationship as more like a partnership than a customer-supplier relationship. David remarked, "There is a lot of trust and shared information . . . Brithinee has a lot of product expertise. They will see what our customers want and design it for them."

Brithinee used AutoCAD software to design control panels on the computer and shorten the time it took to bid on projects. Once a project bid was accepted, it typically took four to six weeks to build a control panel. The longest lead time was needed for acquiring the metal structure that housed the electrical components. Building the control panel might take only a week or two.

In scheduling a control panel job, Richard planned for unexpected delays, but the control panel department took special pride in knowing that they had so far met all the deadlines for shipping their products. Richard stated, "We have never, ever, ever missed a ship date. Never. We will never miss a ship date . . . I have been here Saturday and Sunday to make a ship date . . . It is important to us. You are only as good as your reputation." He went on to say that the UL 508 directory looked "like a telephone directory," adding that Brithinee was among only 20 companies in the United States with UL 845 certification. Most were very large corporations like Siemens, Allen-Bradley, and Square D. The limited number of companies with UL 845 certification had elevated the company's visibility in the industry and helped it attract more business.

Several Brithinee employees told the case researchers that motor repair costs were fairly well known and manageable but that a good system for determining the labor costs and profit on control panels had so far eluded them. Richard stated, "Labor has been a real problem. Until recently, we did not have a good way to keep track of accounting hours." Sometimes Brithinee would not know for six months whether they had made money on a job. For bidding on a job, Brithinee based its cost estimates on historical data, but the unique and variable nature of each job made it difficult to estimate costs accurately. Richard was pondering how to develop a way to track the costs of building control panels so as to make better bids and increase the profitability of this part of the company's operations.

ISO and EASA Q Certifications

The International Organization for Standardization (ISO) had created worldwide guidelines to promote higher-quality engineering designs and product manufacturing practices in a variety of industries. The ISO 9000 concept took off in the early 1990s and helped manufacturers to implement a number of quality improvements. Manufacturers that met ISO standards had formal systems in place to produce their products in a consistent manner. Most large manufacturers of motors like Toshiba, General Motors, and Square D were ISO 9000 compliant. There were three levels of ISO 9000 certification, referred to as 9001, 9002, and 9003. (However, a forthcoming revision in ISO certification was expected to have only one level.) The most rigorous of the three ISO standards, ISO 9001, meant a company had certification in design, engineering, and manufacturing; ISO 9002 signified qualification in just manufacturing. The popularity of ISO 9000 certification among manufacturers and the recognition that it provided made Don and Wally Brithinee wonder if ISO certification could make their company more visible and more competitive in the electrical apparatus industry. David Whitney at Square D believed that Brithinee would be smart to attain ISO certification since many big customers, like Boeing or General Motors, inquired about a vendor's quality control programs and sometimes used ISO certification as a way to screen possible vendors. Whitney said, "It certainly helps to be able to say, 'We are working with customers with ISO.'"

The Electrical Apparatus Service Association (EASA) had initiated a related standard, the EASA Q. Lynda Butek asserted that this standard "is *more* than the ISO 9002 . . . [It is 9002] plus specific procedures only having to do with motor rewind. It also includes a customer satisfaction audit of certain selected customers, which the ISO 9002 does not have." The EASA Q was put together by the Technical Services Committee of EASA, chaired by Wally Brithinee. Russ Kennedy said he supported industry movement toward EASA Q and ISO 9002 because it "makes my job easier with the documentation. Procedures are being implemented that everyone's following. It helps change the mind-set of a 20-year mechanic to conform to today's standards and regulations . . . It's a great adventure we're in right now. It makes work very interesting, and these guys [the Brithinee brothers] are behind it."

On the other hand, it was not clear that meeting ISO 9002 standards at Brithinee was strategically important given the company's UL certification. Candace Winn, at Square D, said it was the UL certifications that distinguished Brithinee from other control panel makers. Of the three certifications—UL 845, ISO 9002 and EASA Q, the UL 845 was "drastically important," she claimed. The pressure for achieving ISO 9002 certification was internally driven by the two brothers, although Wally readily admitted, "It is not a big market issue here in Southern California." Don Brithinee agreed: "Most of our customers are not terribly concerned about [our being ISO 9002 certified] . . . For our size business, it doesn't seem to be an expectation. We have virtually no external pressure from our customers to become ISO certified. The principal benefit will be the internal side, the savings associated with going through the process of developing these systems." Wally and Don did acknowledge that GM's Electro-Motive Division used ISO 9000 certification as a qualifying screen when selecting new vendors (but continuing to get business from GM was not contingent on Brithinee's meeting new ISO standards). While ISO certification often helped a company compete in foreign markets, none of Brithinee's motor repair work came from customers in foreign countries due to the high cost of transporting heavy industrial motors. It was, however, economically feasible to make and ship custom control panels to foreign customers; Brithinee had not pursued this possibility because it lacked knowledge about the opportunities that might exist and because it made more sense to concentrate its resources on serving local area customers.

The company's goal was to achieve ISO 9002 certification in 2000, but Wally and Don acknowledged that while the company was working on a number of fronts to meet the necessary requirements, it was "still a ways off." Getting there in 2000 might not be realistic. Their hope was that the company's attaining ISO 9002 certification would awaken customers' interest in having their work done by a quality-conscious vendor and that the added reputation that accrued to Brithinee from ISO 9002 certification would translate into a competitive edge over rivals.

Efforts to Improve Internal Administrative Procedures and Practices

Don Brithinee was interested in developing better ways to detect and prevent errors in any and all aspects of the company's operations. He said, "Every point seems to be a spot in which we can make savings." He recited an instance where Brithinee had sold a vehicle and verbally canceled the cellular telephone service associated with that vehicle. The provider stated that it did not need anything in writing to cancel the telephone number. Debbie Brithinee wrote a memo to staff members to watch out for further charges that might come through on that telephone number. Sixteen months later, the company discovered it had been charged $70 a month for a telephone number that had zero calls on it. The vendor refused to refund the money. Don was contemplating whether it was worth the time and energy to change cellular telephone vendors or whether the company's procedures were basically at fault and should have been tight enough to reveal the error much sooner.

Another costly error occurred when the employee preparing the bid on a large customized control panel inadvertently made a mistake in handling the spreadsheet and deleted a line containing 18 percent of the materials in the final cost estimate. The mistake, which was not discovered until too late, wiped out the profits on the project. The error unfortunately occurred on the largest control panel job Brithinee had ever done.

Wally and Don believed that one of the greatest benefits of achieving ISO 9002 certification might ultimately prove to be the internal savings associated with improving the company's administrative procedures and eliminating clerical errors such as those just described.

Brithinee's Value Chain, Relationship Marketing, and Advertising

In 1999, Brithinee Electric was very alert to ways to add customer value to the activities it performed and was working with its suppliers in this respect as well. In earlier periods, Brithinee did not place much strategic emphasis on value-added assembly, but this had changed. The contract with EMD Locomotive provided one value-added dimension in the repair shop. Most of Brithinee's motor sales in the late 1980s were off-the-shelf packages made by Toshiba and Baldor and for which it was an authorized distributor. But over time Brithinee Electric found that having only one location and a relatively small volume of sales made it tough to compete against multioutlet discount houses that entered the market in the early 1990s and had greater sales volumes and buying leverage with manufacturers. Brithinee discovered that it was in better position to compete for the business of customers wanting customized electrical apparatus products and services such as sophisticated motor control panels. Brithinee had the expertise and capabilities to tailor-make certain types of electrical products to customer specifications, giving it the ability to add value through its own internal activities and deliver something to buyers other than a standard package stocked by a variety of electrical suppliers.

Brithinee applied the principles of relationship marketing whenever the opportunity presented itself. For instance, Brithinee worked closely with David Whitney at Square D to better satisfy Square D's customers. According to Whitney, "My customer may be a water district and I may ask where they get their motors repaired and suggest to the customer that they contact Brithinee." And when a Brithinee customer could profit from using Square D products, Brithinee suggested the customer get in touch with Dave Whitney at Square D.

Two outside salespeople generated business by calling on customers and identifying new prospects, whether in the repair area, sales, or control panels. Brithinee's competitors sometimes referred a customer to Brithinee when they could not fulfill a customer's request, and Brithinee reciprocated. Bill Gaborko, at C&M Electric, a small local competitor, did not repair large motors and referred those customers to Brithinee. Brithinee sent customers wanting repairs on single-phase motors to C&M.

Brithinee was exploring new ways to generate sales in order to run all three shifts at full strength and to increase revenues and profit margins. John Hinshaw, the sales and marketing manager, said, "Getting a new customer is the most expensive part of the business." His goal was to grow and maintain the business primarily with existing customers but to also search out new customers. One source of leads was business starts in the Inland Empire. Using a Dun and Bradstreet "Marketplace" CD-ROM set, the company had identified hundreds of prospects with profiles similar to its current customer base. Brithinee had learned that a number of its repair customers did not know the company could provide customized motor control panels and that some control panel buyers were unaware of the company's motor repair capabilities.

Hinshaw expressed a belief that the computer-generated repair report accompanying each particular job had been instrumental in raising the expectations of current customers. Those customers now required the same information from Brithinee's competitors. He also felt that the UL certification was the most important one in generating sales locally, especially for the control panel side of the business. He observed, "For electrical safety, UL is it."

***exhibit* 7**   Selected Balance Sheet and Income Statement Data for Brithinee Electric, 1988–98

	1988	1989	1990	1991
Balance sheet				
Assets				
Current assets	$1,278,365	$1,644,500	$1,551,245	$1,229,799
Fixed assets less accumulated depreciation	121,739	82,625	139,922	193,562
Other assets	14,716	14,716	14,716	7,876
Total assets	$1,414,820	$1,741,841	$1,705,884	$1,431,238
Liabilities and Shareholders' Equity				
Current liabilities	$356,096	$563,656	$332,276	$328,377
Long-term liabilities				
Shareholders' equity	1,058,724	1,178,184	1,373,607	1,102,860
Total liabilities and shareholders' equity	$1,414,820	$1,741,841	$1,705,884	$1,431,238
Income statement				
Gross income	$4,836,401	$5,372,555	$5,643,979	$4,530,838
Cost of goods sold	3,349,853	3,766,378	3,751,243	3,013,072

*Projected.

As part of the company's effort to reach out to a new customer base, Don Brithinee and Cyd Sandefur had been attending a marketing class at a local community college to help them create presentation material for seminars and to learn other ways Brithinee could gain recognition with potential customers. Don and Cyd had given a number of presentations to groups of customers and EASA meeting attendees concerning such topics as how to hook up and safely use industrial motors, how to make the equipment run better, and how to do maintenance planning. Wally said, "Customers are better customers when they know what we do." Don and Cyd had also toyed with the idea of pursuing customer accounts in Arizona and Northern California because there were carrier services that guaranteed overnight delivery. Cyd said the company was still in the infancy stage of its marketing outreach efforts and was looking for further steps to take to grow its business.

Accounting and Information Technology

In 1999 Deborah Brithinee was responsible for Brithinee's general ledger and other types of accounting. Prior to marrying Don Brithinee and coming to work at Brithinee Electric, Deborah had worked for 17 years in accounting, purchasing, and trust operations in a county government, overseeing a $70 million budget. Periodically, she helped on special projects before becoming Brithinee's office manager in 1990. Exhibit 7 presents an 11-year overview of Brithinee's financial statements.

In 1998, Brithinee introduced a new 401(K) profit-sharing plan after company-wide meetings and a vote by employees. Previously, the company had paid annual year-end bonuses tied to company profitability into a guaranteed retirement fund managed by the company. With the 401(K) plan, Brithinee paid into each employee's fund monthly. Contributions were based on a percentage of each employee's salary rather than being linked to year-end profits, as had been the case with the prior plan. Deborah indicated that "our financial statements look very different month-to-month than they did in prior years . . . It was a big step for us to go into the 401(K)." Employees

1992	1993	1994	1995	1996	1997	1998*
$1,105,523	$997,596	$1,125,322	$1,195,479	$1,269,494	$1,501,129	$1,446,709
271,273	223,745	293,329	240,558	363,180	406,165	441,091
2,087	6,896	6,896	6,896	1,093	2,004	1,951
$1,378,883	$1,228,238	$1,425,546	$1,442,933	$1,633,767	$1,909,299	$1,889,752
$540,978	$376,593	$378,799	$292,863	$305,465	$550,758	$351,239
	28,079	19,036	26,708	36,106	27,662
837,905	851,644	1,018,668	1,131,034	1,301,593	1,322,434	1,510,850
$1,378,883	$1,228,237	$1,425,546	$1,442,933	$1,633,767	$1,909,299	$1,889,752
$4,405,211	$4,968,783	$5,127,066	$5,995,404	$5,696,261	$6,490,431	$7,037,731
3,045,850	3,260,598	3,344,487	3,854,561	3,525,998	4,370,105	4,483,012

*Projected.

were fully vested in the 401(K) the first day they began work. The two advantages, as Wally saw it, were (1) the employee awareness of the plan throughout the year and (2) employees' control of their own retirement funds. But the disadvantage to Wally was the lack of an obvious tie to the company's performance; he explained, "How do you get the employee to understand a tie-in between his or her performance and the company's performance? If they [the employees] are to succeed, the company needs to succeed."

A major accounting issue was how to track and measure the labor costs associated with control panel projects. "We don't do cost accounting," stated Deborah Brithinee. "In the repair shop, we have done considerable analysis on what goes into a repair . . . We have a handle on that. But in the control panel area, it's very, very difficult to get a handle on that. That's what we're working on now." Deborah was trying to determine what different systems would capture information to solve this problem. She was certain the company needed better methods for addressing the sometimes-dramatic differences between initial cost estimates and actual costs incurred in building the control panels. The big problems were in the labor cost estimates and changes in the prices of parts between the time the estimate was made and the work was done. Customer design changes could also complicate the process. Deborah suspected that the company needed to overcome its reluctance to adjust original estimates as a result of materials price changes and customer design changes. Tracking purchase orders was another problem area, according to Cyd Sandefur, who did the tracking manually. She said that "things change in the middle of the project. Something will be quoted in the bid that doesn't work." Making substitutions typically entailed renegotiating with suppliers for parts and prices.

Don said, "We don't have an integrated system for our order entry and accounting." While Brithinee had purchased some custom software to reduce paperwork and streamline processes, it had not yet been installed on the system and implemented. The goal was to reduce the amount of hours devoted to accounting, but no plan to do this was in place.

In the information technology area, Don stated, "We enjoy our computers . . . We probably have 30 computers scattered around . . . versus only one or two 10 years ago . . . This is a big plus." The company had both Macintosh and Windows NT-based machines operating on the same network. The company allowed both types of machines to be used for entering orders, sending mail, accessing data files, and exchanging data on the company's local area network (LAN). The LAN was connected to the Internet, but Brithinee did not yet have its own Web site. Don explained, "I don't find that most of the customers we deal with would find their way to us through [a Web site] . . . not yet." Brithinee hoped to find lower-cost ways of reaching out to new and existing customers, but didn't believe a Web page would serve this purpose very well. Wally had created spreadsheets that tracked progress of work orders through the shop; he said, "Computers for us are a shop tool. It is not universally acknowledged that you would put computers in the shop area."

Personnel Issues

Brithinee Electric's commitment to helping customers out with emergency repairs had attracted a lot of emergency repair work and fostered a high-pressure work environment driven by trying to meet tight time deadlines. To respond to the problem of being worn down by "always being in a panic mode" and to create a less stressful organizational climate, Brithinee had contracted with a psychological consultant and added second and third shifts. In 1996, the industrial psychologist began testing applicants and looking at ways to improve the work climate. Don Brithinee explained, "We have been trying to put together a company of more like-minded people. We have managed to remove some personnel who were a problem for us . . . This has made the organizational environment more pleasant and conveyed a better image to our customers and even our vendors." Brithinee had done personality profiles of job applicants and, with their permission, existing employees. Profiling had helped management better understand why certain personalities worked well together and why some were better suited to the company's work environment. The consultant's work had led to the development of a preferred profile that was used to screen job applicants. According to Russ Kennedy, "We want people to fit . . . the Brithinee profile." The profiles of existing employees had been used as a basis for reassigning some personnel; so far, the results had been quite satisfactory.

Brithinee had also instituted drug testing as part of its job applicant screening process and a no-tolerance drug use policy. Personnel found to be using illegal drugs were dismissed. The dismissal of one employee for drug use had boosted morale in the shop (the individual had crashed a truck and was a disruptive force on the shop floor). One employee described the management style at Brithinee as "very forgiving" when errors or mistakes were made.

The hiring of additional personnel with the right characteristics to staff the second and third shifts had alleviated attrition problems associated with employee burnout. Moreover, the new employees fit the Brithinee profile and seemed to work well together. To help add workforce flexibility, the company had hired three or four "all-purpose, no-purpose" entry-level people who were moved from task to task as needed. According to operation manager Russ Kennedy, "We have grown on all fronts . . . [and now] we take emergencies more in stride."

Brithinee Electric suffered from some common people-management problems associated with the growth of small, family-owned businesses. Longtime employees who had once worked side by side with Don and Wally sometimes had difficulty following the chain of command and going through the new managers who had been brought in. The industrial psychologist had improved matters by redefining job descriptions, creating better-documented employee manuals, and helping Wally and Don communicate better with each other. Wally remarked that he was sold on the value of using a psychologist to help managers better understand their staff and adopt a team approach. Pay increases were determined by Don and Wally, who factored in profitability, labor market conditions, and the value of the individual to the company. Employees were not automatically granted annual pay raises.

Growth and the Future

As the Brithinee brothers looked to the future, they knew the company faced a challenge trying to grow revenues by 10 to 15 percent annually in an industry predicted to shrink by 2 percent per year. They were uncertain whether to keep the company focused on expanding its existing electric motors sales, motor repair, and control panels departments or whether to branch out and diversify into other areas. Predicting what areas would offer the best growth opportunity was difficult. For example, since 1988 the rewinding portion of the company's business had grown 180 percent. Wally said, "I would have never expected that . . . We've never been good at predictions here." Brithinee Electric forecast its earnings only one year at a time, but the consultant had suggested setting longer-term goals and making longer-term financial forecasts.

In speculating on future business opportunities, Wally noted that the water industry nationwide was expected to spend $40 billion in upgrades of water and waste-water treatment facilities in the near future, a significant part of which was expected to involve converting the associated electric motors to variable frequency drives. He said, "Upgrading fits our controls arena. This is our greatest potential area for growth." Brithinee could readily accommodate growth by expanding its second- and third-shift skeleton crews into fully staffed crews. However, expanding repair capabilities for handling larger size motors would require extensive capital investment. Wally said, "Everything would have to be upsized to another level greater than what we have." It was unclear where the capital for such upgrades would come from.

There was room to expand the shop facilities if necessary by acquiring a vacant lot of about five acres between the two current buildings. According to Lynda Butek, it was a strange piece of property because it also wrapped around the back of both buildings and a cul-de-sac, and extended to the next street. At the moment, though, it was not clear whether the property would be best used for expansion of the warehouse, a parking lot, a bigger control panel area, or another building equipped to handle more repair work. Aside from how to grow, there was the issue of what to do about ISO 9002 certification and whether company emphasis on quality would pay off in the eyes of the company's existing and prospective customers.

Finally, as the Brithinee brothers approached celebration of their 50th birthdays, the issues of retirement and succession were not too far down the road. Don and Deborah Brithinee had one child, Nicole, age 10, while Wally remained single. The brothers carried substantial life and disability insurance policies on each other.

bibliography

Electrical Apparatus Service Association, Inc. (EASA). "Understanding A-C Motor Efficiency." Pamphlet, 1994.

———. "How to Get the Most from Your Electric Motors." Pamphlet, 1997.

———. "EASA AR 100 1998 Recommended Practice." Pamphlet, 1998.

Greenfeld, S. "Brithinee Electric." In *Business Strategy and Policy,* ed. Smith, Arnold, and Bizzel. Boston: Houghton-Mifflin, 1991, pp. 180–200. Also in *Strategic Management for Decision Making,* ed. Stahl and Grisby. Boston: PWS-Kent, 1992, pp. 368–87. Also in *Strategic Management,* ed. Dess and Miller. New York: McGraw-Hill, 1993, pp. 393–410.

Nailen, Richard L. "Building a Service Company's Numbers with Higher Mathematics." *Electrical Apparatus,* December 1997.

"You Got It Off the Ground and Flying, Now How Do You Safely Land It?" *Los Angeles Times,* December 16, 1998, p. C8.

case 24 The Roccoco New York Hotel

Anna S. Mattila
The Pennsylvania State University

The following customer complaint letter was submitted by a first-time customer at the Roccoco New York Hotel. Tony Richards, the general manager, had called a meeting with his executive committee to ponder the situation facing the hotel. The director of operations, Sylvia Jenkins, the human resource director, Paul Gordon, and the director of marketing, Nancy Wheeler, were glancing through the letter as Mr. Richards explained that, unfortunately, this customer encounter typified what many clients experienced during their stay at the hotel. Two members of the executive committee, the food and beverage director and the head of the engineering department, were absent due to a mandatory fire drill taking place in the main kitchen on snowy January 2, 1998.

To Whom It May Concern,

I stayed at your hotel last week and was disappointed in my overall experience. I travel to the city often and will probably not return to your hotel. I would, however, like to express my discontentment with the service I received.

As I sat in the bar waiting for my cocktail to be delivered, I became more and more frustrated with the service I had received since my arrival the day before. Upon booking my reservation, I was kind of wary about what I was in for. After all, I had not heard too much about this brand. It was not like going to a Hilton or Marriott where I know what type of service and atmosphere to expect. Needless to say, I was pleasantly surprised with the grand atmosphere at this hotel. It can be described as an oasis in the heart of Times Square. The lobby area is small, yet elegant and quaint. It is the type of hotel where I can feel comfortable entertaining my clients and holding negotiations. It is big enough to provide privacy, yet cozy enough to deliver a personalized type of service. Automatically, my expectations of service soared as I admired the care and beauty of the rooms and public areas. No detail has been left unfinished. Unfortunately, my expectations were quickly shot down as reality set in.

After an extremely long journey from halfway across the world, I was more than looking forward to a hot shower and warm bed. I checked in at about 6:00 PM on a Wednesday evening. Upon arrival, the doorman welcomed me graciously and collected my bags. I took the elevator to the lobby area to check in. I approached the desk and stood there for what seemed like an eternity before either of the two girls standing there acknowledged my existence. Finally, one of the girls looked up from her paperwork and, as if I were interrupting her, asked me if she could be of assistance. I gave her my last name and told her I had a reservation. She confirmed my room number, handed me my key, and in no time I was on my way—I could not wait. Upon entering the room, I noticed that there were two beds and a horrible smoky smell. I had asked for a king bed, nonsmoking. I immediately called down to the front desk. The girl who answered seemed a bit annoyed and said that I could return to the lobby, as she would try to accommodate my needs. With that, I went back to the elevator, down 20 floors and finally back to the front desk. She half-heartedly apologized for the inconvenience, gave me another key, and once again, I was on my way.

I waited nearly a half an hour before the boy at the entrance came up with my luggage. He placed my very expensive carryon piece in front of the door (to hold it open) and proceeded to take in the rest of my bags. He informed me about the amenities available at the hotel. You know, the usual—minibar, complimentary shoeshine, 24-hour room service, exercise room, and so on. With that, he smiled and wished me a pleasant stay. I wondered if he even knew my name or realized that I was upset with the time it took my luggage to arrive (not to mention the fact that my carryon piece had doubled as a doorstop).

After unpacking and settling in, I picked up the room service menu. It was pretty limited, but I was very tired and was not about to go out for a bite to eat. The girl who answered the phone knew who I was. Quite impressive, as I had only been there for about two hours: "Good evening, room service, this is Cary, how may I help you, Ms. Bressner?" The meal was delicious, although it arrived nearly an hour after I ordered it—the girl who took my order said it would be up in 25 minutes. After finishing my meal, I called back down to room service to tell the girl that I would leave my tray outside the door. Finally, with all that I had been through that day, it was almost midnight before I was finally able to get some rest.

The following morning, I stepped out of my room and almost onto the very same room service tray; it was right where I had left it the night before. That evening, upon checking out, the girl asked me if she could assist me in making reservations for a future trip to the hotel. I politely declined and told her that my stay was not a pleasant one. She apologized and wished me a good evening. As I walked away from the desk, thinking of what my stay had been like, I knew that I would never return.

I liked the hotel; in fact, it is definitely nicer than most of the Marriotts or Hiltons I had been to and the price was very reasonable for NYC. However, I do not think I will return. It is something about the service—it is definitely not what I had expected. Your staff should work on their attitudes and attention to detail. Very few were really friendly, and even fewer seemed interested in my happiness. I hope this situation is rectified, as you have already lost at least one guest.

Sincerely,

Laura Bressner

As the executive committee reviewed the hotel's performance, Tony Richards addressed the critical questions. "What can we do to avoid problems on this type in the future? How can we improve the level of service quality in our establishment? We need to do something to ensure that occupancy levels will remain high despite the rate increases imposed by our financial situation. Why don't we brainstorm to get some ideas? Nancy, what do you suggest from the marketing perspective?"

Nancy Wheeler responded, "Well, given the resistance to rate increases from our current guests, I feel that we should focus on attracting new customers. Weekends are clearly a problem for us; the occupancies drop to a mere 50 percent on most weekends. By offering attractive packages, we could get more leisure travelers to stay with us. Because we have such a high proportion of Asians in our client mix, I suggest that we get into Web marketing. We could place ads on Asian air carriers' sites or on Netscape or Yahoo! so that, when people are seeking travel information regarding New York City, they get an immediate exposure to our hotel. I have done some data searching, and the current monthly cost on travel sites is about $12,000."

"I hate to disagree with you, Nancy, but our main goal should be to satisfy our existing customers," Paul Gordon asserted. "Look, the data from our customer satisfaction surveys and the ever-increasing pile of complaint letters that I have in my office clearly indicate that our current guests are not happy. Or, have a look at the shopper report summary (see Appendix 1). I think that we should put our efforts into developing a service recovery policy. My informal talks with our front-line employees indicate that they feel lost with our operating manuals. They have to deal with upset customers without having the power to do anything about their complaints. At the moment, a supervisor's signature is required for any service recovery effort. I can just imagine how our guests feel about paying over $200 a night and having to wait for someone's approval to get a complimentary welcome drink because the room is not ready. In many cases, further referral to the department head is needed, causing unseemly delay and further guest irritation. These things should be handled on the spot by our customer-contact employees."

Sylvia Jenkins, the director of operations, joined the discussion. "Empowering the front line to deal with service failures is a good idea in theory, but how do you control the money involved? Free meals and free stays represent lost revenues, and I do not believe that our cash position is such that we could afford a dip in revenues. Moreover, as you know, we are in the process of hiring new food and beverage employees, and this additional expenditure will have an impact on our bottom line."

MANAGEMENT BACKGROUND

Tony Richards's first exposure to the hospitality business had come 25 years ago working as a busboy in his father's family restaurant. During college, he had worked summers at various resorts on Cape Cod. After graduating with an undergraduate business degree, he spent three years working for an insurance company in Hartford, Connecticut. His heart kept longing for the hustle and bustle of hospitality, and he then decided to return to school to earn a master's in hospitality management. After college, he worked for Bristol Hotels, mainly opening new properties for the fast-growing hotel chain. Since he had joined the Roccoco hotel two years ago, Tony had been working vigorously to bring the revenue stream to its optimal level while controlling costs and increasing demand. As a result of these efforts, the Roccoco New York Hotel realized its first positive cash flows in 1997.

The general manager hired a new food and beverage manager, Mr. Jean-Pierre Pottier, at the end of 1996. His dynamic character, combined with a prestigious culinary degree from Cordon Bleu in Paris, had made him successful in revamping the hotel's restaurant business. Jean-Pierre's reputation for superb banquets and creative menu concepts had resulted in a 22 percent increase in food sales during the past 12 months. Room service sales, in particular, had gone up by 50 percent since 1996.

Paul Gordon, the current director of human resources, had worked for Holiday Inns in the corporate training position for 15 years prior to joining the Roccoco Hotel six months ago. His wife had been relocated to New York City, and Paul was looking forward to a more stable family life. The hotel's former HR manager had implemented sizable budget cuts for employee training and hiring practices, and these efforts had indeed showed a positive impact on last year's bottom line. In the past, newly hired employees had completed a two-week formal training program, but this procedure had been replaced by a more cost-efficient, on-the-job "buddy" training system. In addition to on-the-job training, each new employee received the hotel's 500-page operations manual, which explained company policies for each department. The hotel had lost many of its middle managers to competitors over the past three years, but these positions had been left vacant to improve the bottom line.

The director of marketing, Nancy Wheeler, had joined the Roccoco Hotel nearly a year and a half ago. Her previous job as a middle manager of a mega-convention center had familiarized her with group business travel. Summarizing the situation facing Roccoco, she reported: "There is perceived guest resistance to higher rates, requiring our hotel to have a competitive edge when compared to similar hotel properties and hotel brands."

Sylvia Jenkins, the director of operations, was an old-timer at the Roccoco Hotel. In fact, she had been with the hotel over ten years and had personally seen the transformation from a typical mid-priced Restwell Inn to a quaint boutique hotel. Sylvia started her career as a housekeeper and worked her way up to a rooms division manager within the Restwell Corporation. When she was offered her current position five years ago, she gladly accepted. Sylvia strongly believed in "management by walking around" and was constantly fixing problems throughout the hotel.

PROPERTY OVERVIEW

The Roccoco was a full-service, 30-story boutique hotel with 305 rooms. Boutique hotels were relatively small, well-staffed properties that offered upscale, high-end and ample amenities. Corporate buildings, restaurants, shopping, and the theater district surrounded the Roccoco Hotel. The Times Square location was, however, less desirable than Central Park or the Upper East or West Side. Amenities offered included a full-service restaurant overlooking Times Square, a wine bar, a cocktail lounge, and 24-hour room service. The lobby was small and quaint, perfect for the business traveler who preferred a private, relaxing atmosphere. In addition, amenities such as complimentary shoeshines, coffee delivery with wake-up calls, and entertainment services were available to all guests.

In terms of meeting business travelers' needs, the property lagged behind the competition. Meeting facilities were limited to less than 2,000 square feet, and there was no business center. The guests could, however, request a personal fax machine in the room. The guest rooms themselves offered great convenience for computer and modem hook-up and had plenty of workspace.

Formerly a Restwell Inn, the Roccoco group purchased and reflagged the property in the early part of 1993. More than 25 million dollars was allocated to renovate the hotel. Because no structural upgrades were needed, all of the capital was used to enhance the property's appearance. The general manager contracted a famous New York City artist to design an art-deco lobby area, restaurant, and guest rooms. Marble and fine cherry woods replaced the original décor. Massive statues and fine, imported furnishings created a lavish environment, and a restaurant and a lounge area were created on the main lobby level.

COMPETITION

The New York City hotel market was fiercely competitive. (The 1996–97 statistics on the overall New York market are shown in Exhibit 1. For information on Manhattan rate structures, refer to Appendix 2.) There were two main competitive sets (see Exhibit 2). The Sheraton, Crown Plaza, Guest Suites, and Millennium were all relatively large *exhibit 1* New York Area Hotel Market—Selected Properties

| Year | Occupancy | | Room Rate | | Annual Room Supply | | Annual Room Demand | |
	Current Year	Prior Year	Current Year	Prior Year	Current Year	Prior Year	Current Year	Prior Year
1996	81.9%	76.2%	$158.45	$144.60	2,533,794	2,328,794	2,075,177	1,744,469
1997	84.1%	81.9%	$176.90	$158.50	2,637,125	2,533,700	2,217,822	2,075,177

exhibit 2 Competitive Set Report

1996	Occupancy	ADR	REVPAR	Competitive Set I
Roccoco	79.8%	$167.13	$133.38	Sheraton
Competitive Set I	83.3%	$166.53	$138.72	H. I. Crown Plaza
Competitive Set II	84.1%	$176.95	$148.90	Marriott
				Guest Suites

1997	Occupancy	ADR	REVPAR	Competitive Set II
Roccoco	83.1%	$174.86	$145.30	H. I. Crown Plaza
Competitive Set I	86.5%	$169.65	$146.75	Millennium
Competitive Set II	85.1%	$184.23	$156.82	Guest Suites
				Leonardo Davinci

Source: Smith Travel Research. This information is taken from a sample of eight area hotels and general demand patterns. RevPar stands for revenue per available room. ADR refers to average daily rate.

properties that catered to a different clientele, as the properties offered a less personalized atmosphere and larger public areas; however, their geographic location and price similarity had enabled them to control a large portion of the market. A nearby property owned by the Roccoco group, previously considered a major competitor, had evolved into a support system for the Roccoco. Since becoming part of the same global distribution system, all overflow from the second property, which ran at full occupancy most of the year, was diverted to the Roccoco. The Sheraton had completed its renovation at the end of 1997; every guest room was now equipped with ergonomic chairs, in-room data ports, voice mail, and a Hewlett-Packard Office Jet Printer/fax/copier machine. The Sheraton was expected to increase its room rates to $240 per night within the next three months.

Perhaps the Roccoco's primary competitor was the Leonardo. Located only blocks away, this 178-room property offered its guests a more personalized and superior stay. Amenities such as fresh flowers in the rooms, standardized bath amenities (i.e., bubble bath), slippers, and fruit baskets were among the items all guests could expect. In evaluating the quality of the property and service at the Leonardo, even Roccoco's management admitted to the property's inherent superiority. One guest who had previously stayed at the Leonardo described it as, "The perfect place to stay—anywhere in the world. The staff there knows what you need even before you do. It is amazing. Every luxury you could expect, right in the heart of New York's finest. They even know your name before you introduce yourself. I do not know how they do, they just do."

CUSTOMER PROFILE

Because of its boutique orientation, the hotel attracted guests looking for a quiet, convenient place to stay. The property's mix was 70/30 between business and leisure guests. Accordingly, weekday occupancy levels were much greater than weekend, with little seasonal variation. Many of the hotel's business clients were mature, that is, between the ages of 45 and 65. They preferred to stay in the same hotel and quite often the same room. This had contributed to the property's repeat customer base of nearly 60 percent. Unfortunately, the customer retention rates had been consistently dropping over the past few years, as the repeat base had declined by about 10 percent in reaction to the hotel's increase in room rates (see Appendix 3A). To induce high response rates, Mrs. Wheeler had revamped the hotel's customer satisfaction instrument (see Appendix 3B). Many of the clients, up to 40%, were international travelers. With the hotel's luxury reputation in Asia, about 80% of the international guests came from this market. Customer satisfaction data indicated that Asian business travelers were particularly unhappy with the level of service provided by the Roccoco staff.

EMPLOYEE OVERVIEW

The Roccoco had approximately 250 employees. Because of the hotel's relatively small size and the complex labor market in the New York area, staffing issues posed a major problem. This hotel was a nonunion property in a market where approximately 96 percent of hotels were unionized. Thus, in order to keep the union out of the hotel, pay and benefit packages were slightly higher than union standards. The property realized an annual turnover rate of approximately 10 percent, although the industry standard for first-class hotels was 45 percent. Average seniority was 3.7 years, with 10–15 percent of the employees remaining from when the hotel was a Restwell.

Despite this seemingly low level of turnover, employee satisfaction was quite low. Morale and culture had been compromised through the shifts in management and the ambiguous nature of policies, procedures, and management support (see Appendix 4). In terms of management, turnover was extremely high. In fact, the current general manager was one of five who had been at the property since it opened. With the exception of Ms. Jenkins, the rest of the members in the executive office were also relatively new to the property (hired within the past two years). Ms. Jenkins was often heard to repeat the following phrases to her employees: "You should have seen this place before renovation took place . . . all the furniture and fixtures were getting worn out . . . really shabby. But look at it now; what a beauty this hotel has turned out to be. We should all be proud of it."

FINANCIALS

Although occupancy levels remained high and the New York market was booming, the Roccoco was struggling. In the first three years of operation, the property realized a net loss of nearly $12 million annually. This loss had since been reduced to approximately $1 million per year. The property showed its first positive cash flow in 1997. With this in mind, the management team had calculated that the rates must be increased by an additional 30 percent over the following two years.

In light of the relatively low ADR (average daily rate), the property had not realized its revenue goals. Guests had been paying a room rate that was, on average, $30.00 less than the projected $205.00 ADR budgeted for 1998. Additionally, many guests paid current rack rates (published, nondiscount rates) of $205 to $305 (the differentiation in rates can be accounted for by differences in weekend–weekday demand patterns). These mostly non–New York City residents would need to believe they were receiving value with personalized service and attention to detail that was worth the additional $30 over current rack rates (see Appendix 5).

A comparison of Roccoco's profitability against industry standards (ratios and publications published by consulting firms) showed that the level of gross operating income (income before fixed charges) was about 2 to 4 percentage points below the average for comparable properties. While Tony Richards acknowledged that opportunities for marginal cost-cutting might exist, these efforts might well conflict with the need to provide higher levels of service quality. For example, in a previous board of directors' meeting two months ago, one of the owners of the hotel had suggested that management should get rid of the hotel's full-service restaurant or its labor-intensive 24-hour room service. The executive committee strongly objected to this cost-cutting plan because reputable food service operations form an integral part of any upscale property's image and prestige value.

WHAT TO DO!

The slowly drifting snow had turned into a heavy mix of snow and rain by 5:30 PM. The traffic would be chaotic in a couple of hours, so Mr. Richards decided to call it a day. He would draft a letter of apology to Ms. Bressner the first thing in the morning. Driving home that night, he started to think about the board of directors' meeting scheduled for next Friday. "What can we do to add value to the guest experience? How can we enhance guest satisfaction? Should we aim at new target markets to increase occupancy levels? I need to have my recommendations ready by Friday."

appendix | 1   Roccoco Hotel Sample Executive Summary— Shopper Survey, September 1998

- The High Stars Consulting Company is a leading international firm specializing in quality management programs in the hospitality industry.
- The executive summary is based on the experience of four shoppers who stayed at your property for three nights during the week of September 15.
- Shoppers are trained by the corporate office to pay attention to the following areas: speed of service, cleanliness of the property, handling of special requests, and overall employee attitudes.

Reservations

- All reservationists with whom we spoke were polite and professional; however, one reservationist addressed us by first name, although a full, simple name had been provided.
- Inconsistent offers of smoking versus nonsmoking rooms and mention of the 6 PM check-in time.

- Only one on-site reservationist extended thanks or other words of appreciation, simply waiting for the caller to thank them, to which they would respond, "You are welcome."

Arrival

- Immediate, friendly assistance curbside with "Welcome to the Roccoco."
- During an evening arrival, prompt processing, but when arriving at the hotel at 2 PM, the room was not ready until 3:22 PM.
- The complimentary drink while waiting for the room to be ready never arrived.
- Baggage delivery was slow, requiring 18 to 51 minutes.
- Upon delivering of the luggage, the bellman made no introduction to the room's features, nor any other information.
- An on-arrival message was handled effectively.

Departure

- During one check-out, we were not asked if we enjoyed our visit, nor asked about late charges, nor specifically thanked.
- The folios were correct except for some minibar charges.
- When questioned a charge on our folio, the cashier explained that he needed to talk to his supervisor. We waited for 10 minutes for any action; at the end the charge was removed.

Concierge

- The concierge staff seems to be a genuine strength of the hotel. They seemed well trained, considerate, and thorough.
- Excellent assistance about local dining options was readily available. Restaurant A was one of the six options provided, not recommended either more or less enthusiastically than any other restaurant.
- A FedEx package arrived at the hotel at 9:52 AM, but we were first notified of this by a written message under the door at 1:15 PM. No message light was used, and there was no offer to deliver the package to us.

Telephone

- Unusually long delays in answering of inside and outside telephone lines.
- In one instance, a wake-up call was requested but never received.
- During the survey, we received a voice mail from a front-office manager that was actually addressed to another guest.

Housekeeping

- During the survey, rooms #243, 480, 115, and 755 were occupied.
- Rooms 243, 115, and 755 were generally very clean, although a rumpled hand towel was left on the bed in #115.

- During remakes in #480, there was incomplete attention given to restocking of guest supplies.
- Housekeeping staff consistently honored posted DND signs and was polite and smiled frequently when interacting with or passing guests.
- Responses to special requests were 23 minutes for an iron and 10 minutes for a DND sign.

Room Service

- Breakfasts were served in 45 and 37 minutes, far exceeding the estimated time of 20 minutes.
- During dinner, the order taker failed to mention any dinner specials.
- The ordering process was affected by numerous call-holds and by considerable background noise.

Restaurant A

- During all meals, the host staff seemed absolutely intent on getting guests' names recorded in the logbook, although they made no use of the name once learned.
- The breakfast buffet had a particularly imaginative impression, and all products were fresh and appetizing.
- One dinner was a poor experience from start to finish, and the dining-room manager did not seem able to control the situation.
- Impolite hostessing, greeting, and inaccurate seating, possibly resulting in our getting someone else's table. The hostess was overheard to interrupt some guests trying to speak to her, saying abruptly, "I will be with you in a minute," and command other guests to "wait over there."

Lounge Bar

- Four out of our five visits resulted in poor performance from staff.
- On Tuesday night, service at the bar counter was hectic and available to only those who were assertive.
- The server pick-up area was incredibly untidy, yet guests often walked through this area.
- When we were escorted to a table, it was unclean. The server appeared not to notice that some guests at the same table had coasters while others had none.

appendix | 2   Manhattan Lodging Report, Average Daily Rates

	YTD November 1997	YTD November 1996
Manhattan	$171.39	$154.43
Hotel Type		
Deluxe	309.22	288.31
Luxury	236.32	208.38
First class	176.30	157.28
Convention	182.11	167.91
Affiliation		
Chain	176.96	165.78
Independent	205.39	189.50
Size		
Less than 200 units	167.04	154.59
201–500 units	184.12	173.53
501–1,000 units	204.67	186.53
More than 1,000 units	170.63	161.79

Source: Coopers & Lybrand, LLP.

appendix | 3A   Roccoco Hotel

An Analysis of Customer Satisfaction Survey Results, 1997			
Process Area	**Delighted**	**Satisfied**	**Dissatisfied**
Overall stay	32%	55%	13%
Room	54	40	6
Front-office service	20	68	12
Room service	19	50	31
Physical property	68	22	10
n = 547			

Source: Company records.

An Analysis of Customer Retention Rates, 1997	
Chance of Return	**Percentage of Guests**
100%	18
80	12
60	29
40	24
20	14
0	4

Source: Company records.

appendix|3B Sample Guest Survey

Hotel Roccoco New York

1. Please rate your experience with us by circling the number that best describes your feelings about the various aspects of your stay.

How did you feel about . . . ?	1 = delighted	2 = satisfied	3 = dissatisfied
Overall stay	1	2	3
Condition of your guest room	1	2	3
Service at the front desk	1	2	3
Room service	1	2	3
Condition of lobby and other public areas	1	2	3

2. On a scale from 0 to 100%, how certain is it that you will return to this hotel?

0%	20%	40%	60%	80%	100%
Chance that I'd come back					Chance

3. Your primary purpose of visit: 1 = business   2 = pleasure

4. How many times have you been a guest at this hotel?   1   2   3   4+

COMMENTS

Please give us any other comments you feel would help us:

_____

_____

_____

_____

_____

Please place this survey in the envelope provided. Seal the envelope and bring it to the front desk upon departure. Thank you.

appendix|4

Results of Roccoco Employee Survey (non-managerial employees)	
1 = strongly disagree, 7 = strongly agree	Mean
1. I have to do things that I think should be done differently.	4.8 (1.2)
2. There is a lack of policies and guidelines to help me.	4.0 (1.4)
3. I work under guidelines that are inconsistent with other guidelines for doing my job.	2.5 (.9)
4. I often get work to do without being given the right materials, training, or direction.	4.3 (1.3)
5. I do not know if my work will be acceptable to my supervisor.	4.3 (1.2)
6. I have to work under vague directives from management.	4.4 (1.1)
7. I know what is expected of me.	4.8 (1.8)
8. I receive clear guidance on how to resolve customer complaints.	2.5 (.6)
9. I work on unnecessary things.	2.3 (1.5)
10. I am allowed to perform work in a way that suits my own style and approach.	2.4 (1.5)
11. I have to ignore guidelines in order to do my job.	2.4 (1.3)
12. I receive clear guidance on how best to serve the guests.	2.1 (.8)
13. I receive clear guidance on how much time to spend on the various aspects of my job.	4.5 (1.5)
14. I receive clear guidance on how to plan and organize my daily work activities.	4.6 (1.4)
15. I receive clear guidance on where to get assistance in doing my job.	4.3 (1.2)
16. I receive clear guidance on the extent to which I can bend the rules to satisfy customers.	1.8 (1.0)
17. I receive clear guidance on how to operate hotel information systems.	4.7 (1.6)
18. I often receive incompatible requests from two or more people at work.	3.8 (.9)
19. The guests and management often expect different things from me.	5.1 (.5)
20. I often have to bend the rules to satisfy the guests.	5.3 (.6)
21. I receive clear, planned guidelines for doing my job.	2.3 (1.5)
22. I know what my responsibilities are.	4.8 (.9)
23. I know how to fulfill my work responsibilities.	5.1 (1.1)

Source: Company records. All the employees of the Hotel (excluding middle and top management) were surveyed in January 1997. *n* = 239. The standard deviations are in parentheses.

Results of Employee Satisfaction Survey (all employees)	
1 = very dissatisfied, 7 = very satisfied	Mean
1. your overall job	4.3 (1.2)
2. your fellow workers	5.1 (.8)
3. your supervisor(s)	4.2 (1.5)
4. hotel policies	3.1 (.7)
5. the amount of pay you receive	4.5 (1.3)
6. your opportunities for advancement	3.9 (1.3)
7. your hotel's customers	5.4 (.9)
8. the resources you have to do the job	5.1 (1.4)
9. the training you receive	3.5 (.6)

Source: Company records. *n* = 247. The standard deviations are in parentheses.

appendix|5 Roccoco New York Hotel, Statement of Income and Cash Flow after Debt Service

	1996	1997
Occupancy	79.8%	83.1%
Average Daily Rate	$ 167.13	$ 174.86
Revenues		
Rooms	14,847,386	16,176,487
Food & Beverage	2,534,920	3,235,297
Other	724,263	808,824
Total Revenues	**$18,106,569**	**$20,220,608**
Departmental Expenses		
Rooms	$ 5,493,533	$ 5,500,005
Food & Beverage	2,332,126	2,911,768
Other	579,410	582,354
Total Departmental Expenses	**8,405,069**	**8,994,127**
Total Departmental Profit	**$ 9,701,500**	**$11,226,481**
Undistributed Operating Expenses		
Administrative & General	$ 2,715,985	$ 2,729,782
Marketing	1,357,993	1,415,443
Energy	905,328	950,369
Property Operation & Maintenance	1,176,927	1,213,236
Total Undistributed Expenses	**6,156,233**	**6,308,830**
Income before Fixed Charges	**$ 3,545,267**	**$ 4,917,651**
Fixed Charges (*Insurance, Prop. Taxes . . .*)	**$ 1,267,460**	**$ 1,314,340**
Income before Debt Service Depreciation & Taxes	**2,277,807**	**3,603,311**
Debt Service	**3,183,777**	**3,183,777**
Cash Flow after Debt Service	**($ 905,970)**	**$ 419,534**

case | 25 Developing a Global Mind-Set at Johnson & Johnson, 1998

Vladimir Pucik

International Institute for Management Development

In 1998, Johnson & Johnson (J&J) was the world's most comprehensive manufacturer of health care products. It was composed of more than 180 operating companies worldwide with three major business segments for consumer, pharmaceutical, and professional markets. In the late 1980s, its total revenue was close to $10 billion, but it more than doubled to $22.6 billion in 1997, generated from sales activities in more than 175 countries (refer to Exhibit 1).

The company's sales were evenly distributed between the United States and the rest of the world, but only one-third of profits were earned abroad, compared to one-half of corporate profits almost a decade before—a consequence of several recent U.S. acquisitions. By 1997, Europe accounted for 26 percent of J&J's total sales and 28 percent of operating profit. The Western Hemisphere (not including the United States contributed 9 percent to the total sales, and J&J's sales in Africa, Asia, and the Pacific region accounted for 13 percent of sales (refer to Exhibit 2). Over the same decade, the company's number of employees grew from 83,500 to 90,500 and the percentage of J&J's total workforce outside the United States had grown from half to two-thirds.

Before 1998, Johnson and Johnson had been organized around its operating companies established mostly on a country level (in some countries, J&J was represented by more than one operating company, and some companies operated in more than one country). The legacy of commitment to decentralized management was still evident in the company's customer-related functions. Marketing, sales, and country management functions remained largely decentralized. However, support functions such as finance, human resources, and information technology were increasingly shared among operating companies, and in an effort to streamline activities and reduce costs, J&J was moving toward a regional and global approach.

Prepared with the support of Cristina Duffy, Research Associate, as a basis for class discussion rather than to illustrate either effective or ineffective handling of a business situation. Copyright © 1999 by IMD—International Institute for Management Development, Lausanne, Switzerland. Used with permission.

exhibit 1   Regional Sales as a Percentage of Total J&J Sales

	1989	1997
Africa	1.1	1.2
Asia	8.9	11.6
United States	50.0	51.9
Europe	27.6	26.3
Western Hemisphere (not including United States)	12.4	9.0

Source: Johnson & Johnson.

exhibit 2   Number of J&J Employees per Region

	1989	1997
Africa	1,985	1,568
Asia	9,449	11,962
United States	37,465	42,946
Europe	19,939	23,581
Western Hemisphere (not including United States)	14,258	10,447
Total number of employees	83,096	90,504

Source: Johnson & Johnson.

GLOBAL PLATFORMS

Due to the high cost of formulating new drugs, the company's pharmaceutical business segment had always used centralized research shared among operating companies worldwide. Johnson & Johnson consumer and professional businesses were pursuing a similar approach in a large portion of their value chains. J&J was seeking to utilize fewer company resources by implementing coordinated strategies, for example, a single, common marketing strategy for a given region rather than several different marketing tactics.

Johnson & Johnson's three business segments were subdivided into franchises, which could best be described as loose federations of individual products integrated across the company's three major operating groups. This integration was achieved through the company's new global platforms, defined as groupings of product franchises unified by use. J&J's new global platforms included such product franchise groups as wound care, skin care, women's health, and urology. The wound care global platform, for example, included a full range of Band-Aid products in the consumer business segment, and all types of surgical dressings in the professional business segment.

By 1998, the company's strategy had shifted from individual product-based operating companies to the new global platforms and integrated franchise management.

This shift to global platforms included shared marketing functions within geographic regions, consolidated production, and streamlining of product offerings to eliminate cost duplication. As recently as five years ago, J&J had marketed as many as 75 formulas for baby shampoo worldwide, but the product line had been streamlined to just a few formulas for differing hair types in world markets. Standardization of products within franchises allowed the company to make changes quickly to keep pace with global competition.

Consolidated production figured prominently in J&J's shift to global platforms. For example, rather than maintaining separate production facilities for different European markets, the company had started producing all its shampoo products for the European region at a single efficient plant in Italy. Globally, the company's Ethicon franchise (part of worldwide sutures platform) provided goods to Latin American markets from J&J's main facilities in Scotland, and Ethicon Brazil provided catgut and certain raw materials to Asia and Africa.

Before the shift to global platforms, individual manufacturing plants had been like silos of production activity—acting separately and producing different formulas. But the reduction of trade barriers and shipping costs in the era of globalization had increased opportunities to export, which allowed J&J to maximize plant capacities and increase efficiency.

J&J top management recognized that to compete in today's marketplace the company had to be nimble and agile and guided by a global mind-set, defined by Allen C. Anderson, J&J's vice president of education and development, as "the ability to think globally and act locally, and to understand the impact of worldwide strategies." The company's global approach, fueled by the reduction of trade barriers and unification of regional markets, required more communication among employees, an increased emphasis on matrix management, and more shared responsibility between managers worldwide.

GLOBAL HUMAN RESOURCES STRATEGY

With the ongoing globalization of J&J businesses, the firm's human resources management had also become increasingly global. The external forces of globalization created new business opportunities for increased efficiency through global integration in R&D, production, and marketing, but were also reshaping the opportunities and challenges in human resource management.

The unification of the EU labor market and the decline in barriers to labor mobility facilitated the movement of J&J employees within EU countries, both influencing staffing decisions and broadening career opportunities. At the same time, the shift to global platforms created new human resource challenges and expectations of the skills and competencies required from J&J managers in a globally integrated business environment. J&J managers also had to be able to share responsibility with J&J managers in other parts of the world, and the compensation system was intended to mirror this shared responsibility.

Johnson & Johnson's human resources organization reflected the company's recent changes in business strategy. J&J's regional human resource vice presidents spanned the globe, with one human resource vice president for each of the company's three business segments in Europe, three human resource vice presidents in the Asia Pacific region, and two in Latin America. The 28 human resource vice presidents in the United States represented each of J&J's companies operating in the United States and were equivalent in scope of responsibilities to human resource directors in Johnson & Johnson's international operations. In 1997, all of the company's human resource vice presidents and directors had met to develop J&J's worldwide human resource strategic plan, which centered all management education and development initiatives around the company's Standards of Leadership developed in 1996.

Standards of Leadership

The company's Standards of Leadership had helped make leadership relevant to J&J employees by identifying 60 specific behaviors that contributed to business results (refer to

Exhibit 3). These behaviors were grouped into categories: Customer/Marketplace Focus, Innovation, Interdependent Partnering, Masters Complexity, and Organizational and People Development. They were inextricably linked to the philosophy expressed in the well-known J&J Credo.

The J&J Credo (refer to Exhibit 4), which was periodically reviewed and updated, defined the company's view of its responsibility to customers, company employees, communities in which J&J operated, and finally, company stockholders. The values that underpinned Johnson & Johnson's Credo influenced how the company conducted its business. Upon this foundation, J&J's Standards of Leadership guided all aspects of the company's human resource function, from providing a basis for candidate assessment to evaluating managers' performance and potential.

International Recruitment

J&J's Standards of Leadership provided a basis for assessing an individual's potential fit with the company and helped the interviewer ask the right questions during the recruitment process. In the cast of upper-level management positions, candidates' previous international experiences were assessed, and their savvy regarding the global mind-set was evaluated through questions on cultural diversity. For lower-level managers, a global mind-set was not considered immediately necessary; to rise to a leadership position, the candidate was expected to acquire his mind-set on the job.

However, recruiters did examine entry-level candidates' résumés for evidence of a global orientation. Candidates who had taken advantage of educational exchanges outside their home countries were of interest to J&J, and those who had undertaken internationally focused degree programs in another country were actively pursued by J&J's international recruiters. For example, an Italian student studying for an MBA at the International Institute for Management Development (IMD) in Switzerland might well have been considered a prime prospect for an international management career with J&J.

J&J's international recruiters, based at J&J headquarters in New Jersey, sought candidates form the top U.S. and European MBA schools for J&J's overseas companies. Each year, the operating companies sent requests to international recruiting with the number of MBAs they were seeking and descriptions of the positions they needed to fill. J&J international recruiters then made campus visits seeking suitable candidates from among the world's most competitive MBA programs.

J&J's international MBA recruitment programs included the Leadership Development Program Europe and the Asia Global Managers Program. The Leadership Development Program Europe focused on top MBA students in Europe. Usually, these graduates were not placed in their home countries, but rather in other European countries in which they were authorized to work. This program required that candidates be multilingual and mobile, since after their initial assignments of 12 to 18 months in one country, they were likely to be moved to other European countries. During their initial assignments, new hires in this program were assigned development mentors who worked with them to improve their management skills.

The Asia Global Managers Program recruited Asian candidates from top U.S. and European MBA programs. J&J international recruiting manager Dina Da Silva explained: "After interviewing with the international recruiters, candidates were referred to top management for further interviews. Once selected the new hires were trained for approximately 18 months in the U.S. and Asia, always outside their home countries." Training consisted of broad, multidisciplinary overview assignments that helped define the type of position for which the new hire was best suited. After the training period, new hires were placed in Asia, usually in their home countries or in other countries in which they were authorized to work and had language fluency. The company's experience had

exhibit 3   Standards of Leadership

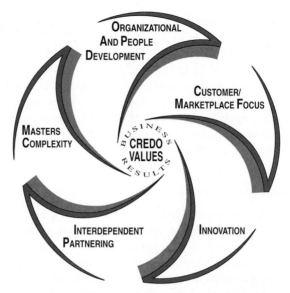

STANDARDS OF LEADERSHIP

Johnson & Johnson

CREDO VALUES/BUSINESS RESULTS	
Credo Values	**Business Results**
Behaves with honesty and integrity	Cash flow
Treats others with dignity and respect	Cost effectiveness
Applies Credo values	Customer satisfaction
Uses Credo Survey results to improve the business	Environmental/safety responsibility
Balances the interests of all constituents	Income growth
Manages for the long term	Market share
	New product flow
	People development
	Product quality
	Productivity
	Regulatory compliance
	Volume growth

"Credo values represent the foundation stone upon which leadership is built. Certainly within Johnson & Johnson you cannot be a good leader if you don't believe in and try to live up to the Credo."

Ralph S. Larsen, Chairman and Chief Executive Officer

"Business results are in the center of the model because all five leadership competency areas influence business results."

Clark H. Johnson, Vice President, Finance

shown that placing new hires in their home countries for initial assignments often of-fered the best environment for career growth and development.

The company was satisfied with the success of these international recruitment pro-grams, and the numbers of new hires through the programs had increased substantially

exhibit 3   (continued)

CUSTOMER/MARKETPLACE FOCUS

Creates Value for Customers

Projects a sense of passion about customers

Recognizes the range of customers and their needs

Serves as the voice of the customer

Uses customer-perceived value as the key criterion for the design of current and future products and services

Focuses Externally

Analyzes market forces and positions Johnson & Johnson to capitalize on opportunities

Seizes the advantage of being first

Benchmarks competitive practices and performance

"Our raison d'être, as the French say, is the customer. We tend to forget that we do not have any role to play if the customer is not there. Its place in this model is a way of reminding everyone that this is what we're here for."

Christian Koffmann, Worldwide Chairman, Consumer & Personal Care

INNOVATION

Forges a Vision of the Future

Visualizes and communicates the future

Develops strategies for growth

Inspires others to commit to the vision

Executes vision and strategy

Fuels Business Growth

Acts and encourages others to be entrepreneurial

Finds and exploits new opportunities

Takes risks and manages them intelligently

Demands the pursuit of stretch goals for self and others

Promotes Innovation and Continuous Learning

Generates and encourages creative ideas

Finds new ways to do things better and faster

Challenges and encourages others to challenge the status quo

Transfers ideas and successes across boundaries

Promotes quality improvement as a value and as process

Finds new ways to use technology more effectively

Learns from personal and organizational experiences

"Our whole business is built on innovation and the ability to move rapidly ahead with new therapies, to be the first in a new treatment category. It is a key element of the Johnson & Johnson history and future, and a key competency of leaders within our company."

Robert N. Wilson, Vice Chairman, Board of Directors

INTERDEPENDENT PARTNERING

Builds Interdependent Partnerships

Cooperates across functions, business units and geographic boundaries

Leverages technology, products, and services across boundaries

Establishes mutually beneficial objectives; clarifies roles and accountabilities with partners

Fosters open communication with partners

Communicates commitment to the success of the partnership in both words and actions

"We can no longer afford to be independent silos, not worrying about what's happening on your left or right or with other sister companies or other departments. It just isn't going to work that way as the environment is changing. We need to do things differently and interdependent partnering is a very important part."

Ronald G. Gelbman, Worldwide Chairman, Pharmaceuticals & Diagnostics Group

(continued)

exhibit 3   (*continued*)

MASTERS COMPLEXITY	
Manages Complexity	**Implements Positive Change**
Thinks analytically and acts decisively	Recognizes and communicates the need for change
Thrives in uncertain circumstances	
Knows when to act and when to wait	Embraces non-traditional ideas and practices
Makes the complex clear and compelling	
Builds consensus and impacts outcomes with limited authority	Engages in constructive conflict
	Drives the change process
	Teaches and encourages others to deal with change

"As our business lives get more complex and we enter new businesses, we'll have to have a compass in the forest of all the information that comes at us every day and this model includes the leadership skills to handle it."

James T. Lenehan, Worldwide Chairman, Consumer Pharmaceuticals & Professional Group

ORGANIZATIONAL AND PEOPLE DEVELOPMENT	
Creates an Achievement Environment	**Develops People for Optimal Performance**
Challenges and motivates people to reach their highest potential	Fosters the continuous professional development and career growth of a diverse workforce
Creates an environment that encourages risk taking	Provides challenging work assignments and development opportunities
Promotes the business value of diverse perspectives, ideas, backgrounds, styles and cultures	Identifies and champions high potential talent as a Johnson & Johnson resource
Fosters organizational flexibility	Coaches and mentors future leaders
Sets clear performance standards and holds people accountable for results	Requires people to expand their capabilities, knowledge and skills
Values, recognizes, and rewards the achievement of others	Functions as both team player and leader
Promotes teamwork	

"Our company is all about a large group of people engaged in a common endeavor. There's nothing more important than making our people better and better at what they do and at who they are."

Roger S. Fine, Vice President, General Counsel

"The organizational part is just as important. We need an environment in each of our business operations that encourages, fosters, and develops the kind of business activities and leadership we need to grow the business."

Russell C. Deyo, Vice President, Administration

Source: Johnson & Johnson.

over the last decade. By 1998, the programs were bringing in an average of 90 new hires a year, with about 45 in training at any given time.

Management Development

J&J's emerging regional and global strategies required managers to develop new skills to support the integration of company's business segments. These skills included partnering *exhibit 4*   Johnson & Johnson's Credo

We believe our first responsibility is to the doctors, nurses and patients, to mothers and fathers and all others who use our products and services. In meeting their needs everything we do must be of high quality. We must constantly strive to reduce our costs in order to maintain reasonable prices. Customers' orders must be serviced promptly and accurately. Our suppliers and distributors must have an opportunity to make a fair profit.

We are responsible to our employees, the men and women who work with us throughout the world. Everyone must be considered as an individual. We must respect their dignity and recognise their merit. They must have a sense of security in their jobs. Compensation must be fair and adequate, and working conditions clean, orderly and safe. We must be mindful of ways to help our employees fulfill their family responsibilities. Employees must feel free to make suggestions and complaints. There must be equal opportunity for employment, development and advancement for those qualified. We must provide competent management, and their actions must be just and ethical.

We are responsible to the communities in which we live and work and to the world community as well. We must be good citizens— support good works and charities and bear our fair share of taxes. We must encourage civic improvements and better health and education. We must maintain in good order the property we are privileged to use, protecting the environment and natural resources.

Our final responsibility is to our stockholders. Business must make a sound profit. We must experiment with new ideas. Research must be carried on, innovative programmes developed and mistakes paid for. New equipment must be purchased, new facilities provided and new products launched. Reserves must be created to provide for adverse times. When we operate according to these principles, the stockholders should realise a fair return.

Source: Johnson & Johnson.

with colleagues, sharing responsibility with managers in other units, cross-border communication, and matrix management, along with a broad global perspective and international experience. J&J's Anderson said, "To develop these skills in J&J managers, the company depended largely on on-the-job training."

J&J's new corporate structure based on global franchises promoted on-the-job training for employees, which the company viewed as 80 to 85 percent of an employee's overall development. Since J&J believed formal education and training could be difficult to apply directly to employees' jobs, development programs utilized on-the-job learning to develop managers, both individually and in the context of their organizational roles. Cross-functional teams in global franchises were one potential source of hands-on training, which strengthened global franchises and enhanced employees' matrix management skills.

Formal Training Programs   J&J also provided formal training programs to support leadership development. In the late 1980s, J&J sponsored in-company management development programs at Northwestern University in Chicago (for North American employees), the University of California at Berkeley (for the Asia-Pacific region), and IMD in Switzerland (for Europe). J&J had also developed relationships with several other universities in the United States and the United Kingdom; however, since more and more training programs were being developed in-house, most of these relationships had disappeared.

After gaining experience through the earlier outside programs and opting not to invest in physical institutes of its own, J&J had developed in-house formal training programs which it viewed not only as more cost-effective but also more flexible in teaching employees as needed and where needed. As Anderson reported, "Essentially, J&J had decided to build its own management program to take on the road as needed, which could be tailored for different regions and thereby minimized travel costs by bringing training to the most cost-effective location." In recent years, the company had offered an Advanced Manager Program in Antwerp for European employees and a smaller program in Sao Paulo and Miami for the South American region.

Ethics Training

As J&J grew from a $1 billion company with fewer than 10,000 employees in 1970 to a $23 billion company with over 90,000 employees in 1998, much of this through acquisitions, it had been challenged to maintain a high level of ethics in accordance with the long-standing Johnson & Johnson credo. Dedicated to upholding J&J's ethics standards, top management considered the Credo to be the "heart and soul" of their leadership, and took ownership of ethics development throughout the company. J&J's human resource personnel recruited individuals who shared Johnson & Johnson's values and then developed these new employees around J&J's Standards of Leadership.

Adhering strictly to the company's ethical values throughout the global organization was difficult, considering the varying cultures of acquired companies and the varied countries in which J&J did business. To help employees deal with the variety of complex ethical issues that they might encounter in the company's extensive international operations, J&J's training organization had developed a case-based education program called "Ethics Toolkit" to help managers worldwide learn how to uphold the company's values regardless of prevailing cultural norms. Ethics Toolkit training examined front-line ethics situations (such as third party payments), taught managers ethical decision-making processes, and advised them whom to turn to for help and advice when ethical gray areas arose (refer to Exhibit 5).

Stretch Assignments

In order to accelerate development of high-potential managers, J&J used "stretch assignments" designed to extend a manager's range of skills by providing new challenges and career opportunities. Stretch assignments were the basis of J&J's succession planning, which focused on building dynamic leadership.

For example, the company might assign a manager who had performed particularly well in one turnaround situation to another turnaround assignment. However, J&J was aware of the limitation this could place on the employee's career development, and preferred to find an assignment in which the manager could gain additional experiences and skills. Still, international assignments were, by definition, well suited for a stretch.

Global Coordination and Development Programs

The key J&J global coordination and development programs were the executive development programs and executive conference sessions.

The objective of the executive development program was to help managers develop global mind-set through action learning. These high-impact programs, which were designed for high-potential managers, were driven by business needs (business issues addressed during the program were selected by each company's operating committee). Cross-border work groups, members of which were nominated by each company group chairman, were assigned to spend three weeks in the field abroad working on solutions for business issues and then present specific recommendations for action.

J&J's executive conference sessions were convened by global franchise leaders, who selected key franchise managers from around the world (usually numbering around 40 to 50 but as many as 130) and determined which specific business to address. Over a custom-developed session that lasted several days, the group worked to resolve specific business issues within the franchise with participants from across the globe. Executive conferences provided opportunities for managers to broaden their global perspectives by working with colleagues from other regions, deepen the communication channels and relationships among franchise members, and advance partnering between employees and shared responsibility between managers. To demonstrate senior management *exhibit 5*   Ethics Toolkit (Sample Case)

Applying Credo Values in the Real World—A Diagnostic Survey Case: The Fine Line between Custom and Corruption

You are the new general manager of Utopia, a recently acquired subsidiary that does business in a country with a tradition of corruption. It is customary for businesses to make payments and gifts to government officials. You have been briefed by the company's legal counsel about the Credo's statements about good citizenship and about the Foreign Corrupt Practices Act (a U.S. law that makes the company criminally liable for improper payments to foreign officials). When you meet with the management to tell them that some of the practices they are used to may not be acceptable to the company, the reaction is disdain. One manager says flatly, "You don't understand what it takes to do business in this part of the world. If you can't make the traditional payments to politicians and bureaucrats we will be out of business within a year." You know that other U.S. companies try to avoid the problem by hiring independent expediting firms who take care of all the details and shield management from direct knowledge or involvement. You ask an executive to make a list of the kinds of payments they are talking about. Each of the following was on the list and you are to determine whether you will permit continuation of the payments.

1 = Yes—there is nothing legally or ethically wrong with this action.

2 = Yes—this may not be proper elsewhere but it is acceptable under local standards.

3 = Yes—if the amounts are relatively small. Tell your people to proceed with caution.

4 = No—it is not consistent with Credo values or the Company's worldwide reputation.

5 = No—don't even think about it; this is foolish and probably illegal.

1 2 3 4 5 When acquiring permits to ship good internationally, it is customary to pay an unofficial service fee to the official in charge equal to 10 percent of the permit fees that go to the government.

1 2 3 4 5 When goods arrive from outside the country they must go through customs. It can take months to get release of the goods and the custom official exercises broad discretion in assessing duty. Officials are given monthly "gifts" during visits to the plant.

1 2 3 4 5 When the electricity goes down, state-employed electrical workers expect to be "tipped" for performing their services. The more you tip, the faster the service.

1 2 3 4 5 One of Utopia's largest customers is a state-run medical facility. It is customary to provide the buyers with free products, trips, and cash.

1 2 3 4 5 The Minister of Health serves on the Company's "advisory council." A substantial fee is paid. The Company benefits from preferential treatment from the Ministry.

1 2 3 4 5 During busy times one has to "tip" the train ticket agent to get a ticket.

1 2 3 4 5 Occasionally, the local police stop Company vehicles for real or fictitious traffic violations. Employees are reimbursed for payments to avoid having the truck impounded.

Source: Johnson & Johnson.

commitment to managerial development, executive committee members actively participated in executive conferences.

International Mobility

Johnson & Johnson consistently worked to balance its use of in-country talent and expatriates. Since the 1980s, the number of expatriates had decreased, primarily to reduce costs. In addition, expatriate compensation packages had been reduced in recent years, making expatriate assignment less glamorous to many managers. However expatriate assignments were still used when in-country talent was unavailable, or for the cross-cultural development of managers. Expatriate assignments were usually to a single country for a limited time period, although some expatriate managers moved from one foreign country to another.

J&J's reduction in the use of expatriate managers had achieved significant cost reductions without diminishing the effectiveness of the organization. Still, maintaining the balance between using in-country talent and providing opportunities for cross-cultural experience through expatriate assignment remained a constant challenge. Expatriate assignments were often learning-driven, rather than solely driven by the demand for a manager in a foreign location, and were intended to develop managers' global mind-sets and international experience. Limiting the use of expatriate assignments to these development goals reflected the company's traditional preference for using in-country talent.

International experience was considered extremely important for young J&J managers, and international assignments were encouraged early in managers' professional careers. Ideally, the company tried to assign managers internationally when they were in their late 20s and early 30s, since young families usually relocated more easily than those already established in communities and schools.

Johnson & Johnson also found that a global mind-set was more readily adopted when managers were fairly young. To increase the likelihood of success of managers on international assignment, the company also worked to find challenging employment in the company for spouses in dual-career couples.

The International Recruitment and Development Program (IDP), J&J's broader umbrella development activity, also included career development programs for employees worldwide. Each year, the IDP moved 70 to 80 current J&J employees from different parts of the globe into one or two year assignments in the United States. Since each operating company had to pay for the program, and accordingly had to justify the expense, the recurrent choice of the IDP program to develop managers reflected the value it provided. The company was pleased with this success: roughly the same number of participants took part in 1998 as 10 years before, and the program had an excellent retention rate.

J&J had also launched a special program to globalize high-potential employees from the United States. A formalized structure which can best be described as a "reverse IDP" program was used to give young U.S. employees international exposure to prepare them for full time international experience. Each year, 5 to 10 U.S. employees sere sent abroad for up to 18 months for development purposes. These employees set out with clear individualized objectives specifically based on their own development requirements and the company's business needs. During the overseas assignment, the employee was expected to gain international experience through exposure to different cultures, markets, and products.

For example, a high-potential employee responsible for corporate compensation in the United States might have been assigned for 18 months to work in corporate compensation in Belgium. After the assignment was completed, the employee returned to the United States. J&J arranged work authorizations for employees in this program, since temporary assignments for current employees were easier to arrange than permanent assignments for new hires. Cost issues were always a factor in this program as well, since moving families, arranging spousal employment, and overall expatriate support were costly. This program was relatively new, and the company was watching the results closely to see if demonstrated success warranted expansion of the program.

Preparing for a Global Future

J&J top management believed that, from the point of view of doing business on a worldwide scale, leaders are leaders, no matter where. Having found commonalties among excellent managers around the globe, the company was fine-tuning its global franchise corporate strategy.

J&J was also constantly searching for new methods to develop crucial cross-cultural business skills and to provide international management experiences that were driven by business needs. Anderson explained, "Rather than just providing classroom cross-cultural training, or arranging an international experience—which often amounted to picking up managers and moving them to foreign countries for a short time, only to have them then come back to sit at the same desk, unable to fully utilize their cross-cultural experience—J&J was focusing on increasing the opportunities for bringing managers together to work on specific business issues."

Through this international work integration, managers both developed cross-cultural management skills and accomplished business tasks. By partnering with international colleagues to solve specific operational problems, managers also developed the ability to share responsibility with others, improve cross-border communication, and operate in an international matrix organization. The company believed this hands-on approach was well suited to prepare managers for future global management activities because it supported global coordination while developing managers' international management skills.

case 26

Motorola: Ethical Challenges in a Multicultural Environment

E. Brian Peach
The University of West Florida

Kenneth L. Murrell
The University of West Florida

In June 1999 Christopher Galvin, Motorola's CEO, wrote a memo to all Motorola employees concerning the company's continuing commitment to its code of business conduct and the ongoing efforts to get "Motorolans" worldwide to live up to the highest possible ethical standards:

> As we continue to focus on the future, we are changing many things in the corporation. However, we will never change or compromise our high principles—our superb business ethics and the dignity and respect we hold for the individual. This week, I met with the team responsible for revising and reissuing Motorola's code of business conduct. The updated code has been well researched and embodies insights of small group discussions with Motorolans around the world. You will hear more about it soon.
>
> The code is an important milestone in the Motorola Ethics Renewal Process, which has engaged us over the last few years. During that time, we established ethics committees and ethics compliance officers worldwide in our vigorous commitment to live up to the highest possible standards. We have always considered trust to be our competitive advantage and we continue to demand ethical behavior throughout the Corporation. Adherence to our code of business conduct ensures that we will disappoint neither ourselves nor the world.
>
> We are committed to behave honorably at all times when conducting business. Global implementation of our code is challenging because cultures, morals, value systems and business ethics standards vary widely from country to country. To address this, we have established an active, open, participative process where Motorolans worldwide can discuss how to determine right and wrong in various situations. Our process, which has been in place for years, is powerful, exciting and right. It will be expanded and re-emphasized over the next few months through training and employee communications, including Motorola's Intranet.

Financial support for this project was provided by a grant from the Shell Corporation, and a University of West Florida Research Grant. Copyright © 2000 by the case authors.

exhibit 1 Motorola's Revenues and Workforce Size, 1930–99

Year	Sales	Employees	Sales/Employee
1930	$ 287,256	—	—
1940	9,936,558	985	$ 10,088
1950	177,104,669	9,325	19,000
1960	299,065,922	14,740	20,300
1970	796,418,521	36,000	22,100
1980	3,098,763,000	71,500	43,340
1990	10,885,000,000	105,000	103,670
1998	29,398,000,000	133,000	221,000
1999	30,931,000,000	121,000	255,600

Source: Company annual reports.

Motorola had a long legacy of honorably and ethically conducting its business worldwide, and Christopher Galvin wanted to continue the company's tradition. But as Galvin and others at Motorola had come to recognize, this was easier said than done given that the company had over 121,000 employees scattered across company operations in nearly 100 countries.

COMPANY BACKGROUND

Founded in 1928 as the Galvin Manufacturing Company, Motorola manufactured radios for cars, developed home and police radios, and during World War II developed the walkie-talkie. The company's name was changed to Motorola in the 1940s. During the 1950s and 1960s, Motorola emerged as pioneer in developing semiconductor-related products and became a leading commercial provider of semiconductors for sale to other manufacturers. Motorola introduced computer microprocessors and high-capacity telephone systems in the 1970s and 1980s. It became a world leader in the cellular telephone and wireless communications industry during the 1980s and 1990s. Motorola initiated a companywide six sigma quality program in 1979 and won the Malcolm Baldrige Quality Award in 1988, the first year the award was given.

In 2000, Motorola was one of the world's leading providers of wireless communications; semiconductors; and advanced electronic systems, components, and services. Its major equipment businesses included cellular telephones, two-way radios, paging and data communications products, personal communications products, automotive products, defense and space electronics, and computers. Motorola semiconductors powered communication devices, computers, and thousands of other products. Exhibit 1 shows long-term trends in Motorola's revenues and workforce size.

Motorola competed in industries noted for extraordinarily intense competition, the exit of formerly significant competitors, and rapidly changing technology. Remaining on the cutting edge of technology was often insufficient—firms had to anticipate and lead the changes in technology. In addition, Motorola competed against some of the strongest and most competitive global firms in the world, including Intel in microprocessors, the leading Japanese firms in semiconductors, and Nokia and Ericsson in cellular telephones. Two of the seven arenas the Japanese government had targeted for development support as critical industries of the future were semiconductors and communications—the very industries in which Motorola derived most of its revenues and earnings.

Motorola's revenues tripled from approximately $10 billion in 1990 to almost $31 billion in 1999, but its 1996–99 bottom-line performance did not match its rapid growth and profitability during the 1990–96 period (see Exhibit 2). Rapid technology gains and product innovations by Motorola's rivals in wireless communications, combined with a downturn in demand for semiconductors and pagers and an economic meltdown in parts of Asia, contributed to a stunning reversal of fortune for Motorola in 1998. In two years, Motorola had gone from being a firm respected around the world for cutting-edge technology and six sigma quality to being a company bombarded by criticism for its management style, its lagging digital cellular phone technology, its focus on a wireless-equipment technology that only covered half the U.S. market potential, and its poor quality and performance in some of its product areas (which resulted in loss of customers). But, to Motorola's credit, things began to turn around in late 1999, with the company reporting full-year earnings of $817 million in 1999 versus a loss of $962 million in 1998 (after restructuring charges of $1.93 billion).

AN OVERVIEW OF MOTOROLA'S BUSINESSES IN 1999

Cellular Phones

Motorola invented the cellular phone and had excelled at improving analog technology, making its phones ever smaller and more feature-rich. Although dominant in the area of analog technology, Motorola made some missteps and errors in judgment during the 1995–98 period. In one instance, trying to maintain its high margins, Motorola attempted to leverage its dominant market share and limit wholesale sales to a few companies—a move that antagonized many of its major customers.[1] But its biggest error was continuing to put its emphasis on analog technology at a time when rivals were racing forward with advances in digital cellular technology. This mistake was compounded by the company's banking on a single digital technology. Globally, three competing digital technologies were being developed and in use: time division multiple access (TDMA), which was six times as fast as analog technology; code division multiple access (CDMA), which was three times as fast as analog; and global standard for mobile communications (GSM), which was two to three times as fast and was the primary system used in Europe and Japan.

Motorola had elected to abandon its early efforts on TDMA, where it had a technological lead, to concentrate on CDMA, which it viewed as having greater market potential. This decision prevented Motorola from competing for customers that used TDMA and also resulted in Motorola's losing the business of carriers that used CDMA (such as AT&T) and that therefore wanted equipment capable of interfacing with both analog and digital systems. Dual compatibility was necessary for carriers to provide national coverage, since most carriers had CDMA systems in some geographic locations and TDMA systems in other geographic locations. National coverage equipment was provided by Nokia, which had introduced a cellular phone that worked on analog networks and both CMDA and TDMA digital networks.[2]

---

[1]Daniel Roth, "Burying Motorola," *Fortune*, July 6, 1998, p. 28.
[2]"Sales Surge for Wireless Makers," *The Wall Street Journal*, February 8, 1999.

exhibit 2   Motorola's Financial Highlights, 1994–99

	Years Ended December 31					
	1999	**1998**	**1997**	**1996**	**1995**	**1994**
Operating results						
Net sales	$30,931	$29,398	$29,794	$27,973	$27,037	$22,245
Manufacturing and other costs of sales	22,652	20,886	20,003	18,990	17,545	13,760
Selling, general and administrative expenses	5,045	5,493	5,188	4,715	4,642	4,381
Restructuring and other charges	(266)	1,980	327	—	—	—
Depreciation expense	2,182	2,197	2,329	2,308	1,919	1,525
Interest expense, net	155	216	131	185	149	142
Total costs and expenses	29,763	30,722	27,978	26,198	24,255	19,808
Net gain on Nextel asset exchange	—	—	—	—	443	—
Earnings (loss) before income taxes	1,168	(1,374)	1,816	1,775	3,225	2,437
Income tax provision (benefit)	351	(412)	636	621	1,777	877
Net earnings (loss)	$817	($962)	$1,180	$1,154	$2,048	$1,560
Net earnings (loss) as a percent of sales	2.6%	(3.3)%	4.0%	4.1%	7.6%	7.0%
Per share data (in dollars)						
Diluted earnings (loss) per common share	$1.31	$(1.61)	$1.94	$1.90	$3.37	$2.66
Diluted weighted average common shares outstanding	624.7	598.6	612.2	609.0	609.7	591.7
Dividends declared	$0.480	$0.480	$0.480	$0.460	$0.400	$0.310
Balance sheet statistics						
Total assets	$37,327	$28,728	$27,278	$24,076	$22,738	$17,495
Working capital	4,087	2,091	4,181	3,324	2,717	3,008
Long-term debt	3,089	2,633	2,144	1,931	1,949	1,127
Total debt	5,593	5,542	3,426	3,313	3,554	2,043
Total stockholders' equity	$16,344	$12,222	$13,272	$11,795	$10,985	$9,055
Other data						
Current ratio	1.33	1.18	1.46	1.42	1.35	1.51
Return on average invested capital	3.9%	(6.2)%	8.4%	8.4%	16.7%	17.5%
Return on average stockholders' equity	5.0%	(7.6)%	9.4%	10.0%	20.2%	21.1%
Capital expenditures	$2,684	$3,221	$2,874	$2,973	$4,225	$3,322
% to sales	8.7%	11.0%	9.6%	10.6%	15.6%	14.9%
Research and development expenditures	$3,438	$2,893	$2,748	$2,394	$2,197	$1,860
% to sales	11.1%	9.8%	9.2%	8.6%	8.1%	8.4%
Year-end employment (in thousands)	121	133	150	139	142	132

Source: Motorola annual reports.

Lack of a competitive digital product also hurt Motorola in Asian markets. Motorola had spent 20 years developing and cultivating Asian markets and dominated the markets for two-way radios and pagers across most of the Asian-Pacific region; the region accounted for 20 percent of Motorola's revenue in 1997. In Japan, after spending considerable energy penetrating the market and attaining a 25 percent market share in

1995, Motorola's lack of digital phones working on GSM had reduced its market share to 3 percent in 1998. In Thailand, one of Motorola's top three Asian markets, Motorola lost its lead and fell behind Nokia and Ericsson. At year-end 1998, Nokia had 40 percent of the Thai market.[3] In China, Motorola lost its dominant position in the cellular phone market when China adopted GSM instead of CDMA, allowing Ericsson and Nokia to move in and control approximately two-thirds of the market by mid-1998.[4]

By 1998, the lack of a competitive digital cellular phone was really beginning to hurt Motorola. The company continued to dominate sales of analog phones, but these were now only 15 percent of worldwide sales. In 1998, Motorola had only a 20 share of the $28 billion global market for wireless telephones.

Wireless Technology Equipment

Motorola was a major supplier of wireless system infrastructure products—the support equipment that made pagers, two-way radio systems, and cellular phones work. Motorola had excellent base station equipment that sent and received signals from mobile phones. However, it had problems developing a reliable switching system. Digital systems offered a great many new capabilities and features, and digital switches were required to make many of the new digital services possible. Because many customers preferred to purchase a complete system infrastructure solution from a single supplier, between 1990 and 1999 Motorola lost a number of customers and contracts because of the poor switching capabilities of its digital equipment. By 1998, Motorola's market share had dropped to 13 percent versus Lucent's 38 percent share.

Satellite Systems

The Iridium Network   Motorola was a major backer and developer of Iridium, a satellite-based worldwide phone network that allowed users to make and receive calls anywhere in the world. Iridium was intended to be an anywhere, anytime communication device for people needing global mobile communications services. Iridium management had predicted that the network would garner a 40 percent share of an anticipated 12 million users by 2002, and projected that it would generate revenues of over $2.5 billion by the year 2000.[5] However, technical and construction problems delayed introduction of Iridium to consumers, and major problems were encountered. Iridium users found the handsets to be bulky and hard to work. In addition, the handsets required a clear line of sight to the satellites, which precluded their use in buildings and other obstructed sites. User costs were high—the Iridium handset itself cost $3,000, and airtime charges ran $2 to $7 per minute.

By mid-1999, although more than $5 billion had been invested in Iridium, there were only 10,000 subscribers (barely a fifth of the expected number) and revenues were a meager $1.45 million, well short of covering operating expenses and a $400 million annual debt service.[6] Iridium filed for Chapter 11 bankruptcy in August 1999.

---

[3]"Thailand: Motorola Undertakes a Marketing Drive," *Nation*, October 27, 1998.

[4]"Motorola Expands Operations in China," *The Wall Street Journal*, June 12, 1998.

[5]Roger Crockett, "How Motorola Lost Its Way," *Business Week*, May 4, 1998, pp. 140–48.

[6]"High Wireless Act," *Forbes*, June 4, 1999.

Motorola had set aside a reserve of $740 million to cover its exposure in case Iridium was unable to restructure its debt and avoid bankruptcy. Meanwhile, three more hand-held mobile phone services serving the rural areas of Latin America, Africa, and Southeast Asia were expected to be launched in 2000–2001, intensifying competitive pressures on Iridium.

Teledesic   Motorola was a 26 percent owner of Teledesic, a low-earth-orbit (LEO) satellite network originally intended to begin operations in 2002. Other owners included billionaires Bill Gates of Microsoft and Craig McCaw of McCaw Cellular Communications (now part of AT&T), who each had a 21 percent stake in Teledesic; Saudi investor Prince Alaweed Bin Talal, with 11 percent; and Boeing, with 4 percent. Teledesic planned to have 288 LEO satellites and was designed to support millions of simultaneous users. Teledesic's business plan was to provide business users with Internet access at speeds up to 2,000 times faster than a dial-up modem.

In May 1999, Motorola shifted several hundred engineers from the Teledesic project, and rumors flew that Motorola was rethinking its support for Teledesic given its problems with Iridium. The satellite rocket launch industry had experienced a rash of satellite launch failures, and this raised concerns about possible increased costs for projects such as Teledesic in establishing its LEO network.[7] In July 1999, contracts were finalized for Motorola to build most of the satellites to be used in the Teledesic network. Cost estimates were revised to $9 billion, and the expected service date was moved to late 2003.[8]

Semiconductors

In mid-1999, Motorola was the third largest semiconductor manufacturer in the world, trailing Intel and NEC. Motorola's semiconductor business was organized around 23 decentralized product groups with responsibility for 82,000 commodity products. The groups were said to be reluctant to share designers or designs with each other. Each group had its own fabrication and systems design libraries and submicron laboratories. Believing that the future of embedded chips was evolving rapidly toward whole systems on a chip, Motorola's semiconductor group had recently changed its product emphasis, dropping generic products and moving to differentiated lines. As part of a plan to get out of low-end chip manufacturing, Motorola laid off over 17,000 employees and sold the commodity component of its semiconductor division for $1.6 billion in cash.

Recent Management Actions to Turn Motorola Around

CEO Christopher Galvin took a number of actions in 1998 to reverse Motorola's market share losses and return the firm to profitability. He reorganized Motorola into three major enterprises and replaced the heads of a number of divisions. The objective was

[7]Joanna Glasner, "Motorola Wavering on Teledesic"
(www.wirednews.com/news/news/business/story/19758.html), May 19, 1999.

[8]Joanna Glasner, "Motorola on Board for Teledesic"
www.wired.com/news/news/business/story/20655.html).

to reduce interdivision competition, encourage sharing of ideas, reduce development costs, and coordinate actions between Motorola's business units. He also instituted a bonus system for top executives based on companywide performance, rather than division performance, to encourage cross-unit cooperation and collaboration.

MOTOROLA'S CORPORATE CULTURE AND MANAGEMENT STYLE

Motorola's culture was grounded in its two "key beliefs" of "constant respect for people" and "uncompromising integrity," a long tradition of participative management, decentralized business divisions and groups that operated with considerable independence, a strong and pioneering commitment to six sigma quality, a technology-engineering orientation, and a deep commitment to operating honestly and ethically.

The Roots of Motorola's Culture

Motorola's ethical culture began with founder Paul Galvin's personal code, which had its roots in the ethical milieu of the small-town U.S. Midwest in the early 1900s. Whether accurately or not, this era is regarded by many as one of integrity and honesty in business dealings. Galvin's code was institutionalized as the "Key Beliefs of Uncompromising Integrity and Constant Respect for People." Motorolans believe that the value they place on these key beliefs is demonstrated by their everyday work habits and is measured by the sacrifices they have made to uphold them over the years.

The consistency of ethical behavior in the performance of business tasks is a critical aspect to understanding Motorola's approach to ethical behavior. Paul Galvin's son, Bob Galvin, who in turn became the company's chief executive and dominant figure from 1956 to 1990, declares that "there is no such thing as situational ethics"[9] and he also believes that you cannot predict or specify every situation and ethical challenge. Thus, the approach is to provide an ethical posture that enables Motorolans to act ethically when confronted with an unexpected or unfamiliar challenge. Just as culture provides members of a society a set of standards for their behavior in all aspects of their life, Motorola's two key beliefs provide Motorolans standards for their behavior across cultures in their accomplishment of business-related tasks.

Since 1973, Motorola has published and periodically updated a document entitled "For Which We Stand: A Statement of Purpose, Objectives & Ethics." Initially it was a response by Bob Galvin to what he perceived to be unfair criticism of American industry, where many were labeled with the sins of a few.[10] It is both notable and typical of Motorola that "ethics" would be a prominent part of a statement of purpose. The document was revised several times over the succeeding years, but the last revision, published in 1996, contained the same emphasis on integrity and ethics and could be

---

[9]Interview with author.

[10]Corporate Public Relations, Motorola, Inc., "For Which We Stand: A Statement of Purpose, Objectives & Ethics," October 1973.

exhibit 3 Motorola's Fundamental Objective, Key Beliefs, Key Goals, and Key Initiatives (Referred to by Motorolans as the Total Customer Satisfaction Card)

Our Fundamental Objective (Everyone's Overriding Responsibility): Total Customer Satisfaction
Key Beliefs—How we will always act
• Constant Respect for People
• Uncompromising Integrity
Key Goals—What we must accomplish
• Best in Class
People
Marketing
Technology
Product: Software, Hardware, and Systems
Manufacturing
Service
• Increased Global Market Share
• Superior Financial Results
Key Initiatives—How we will do it
• Six Sigma Quality
• Total Cycle Time Reduction
• Product, Manufacturing and Environmental
• Profit Improvement
• Empowerment for All, in a Participative, Cooperative, and Creative Workplace

Source: Company documents.

readily found in all parts of Motorola throughout the world. This document was incorporated in 1999 into the revised "Motorola Code of Business Conduct."

Motorola's Key Beliefs

Motorola has an informal, first-name-only culture that stresses the role and importance of individual employees. As noted earlier, Motorola has two key beliefs: constant respect for people and uncompromising integrity (see Exhibit 3). Both beliefs originated with Motorola's founder, Paul Galvin. Galvin consistently demonstrated a concern for people and integrity in business; his concerns ran so deep and were so strongly evident in his actions and behavior that they became ingrained in company practices during its early years. Motorola was recognized as a family-friendly place to work and for emphasizing a balance between work and family. The family orientation and the faithfulness with which the company lived up to its core values were prime reasons that Motorola was named to the *Fortune* list of the 100 best companies to work for in 1997.[11]

---

[11]"The 100 Best Companies to Work For," *Fortune*, January 12, 1998, p. 94.

Numerous Motorola employees had worked for the company many years. Employee longevity was reflected by the fact that in 1997 most of the employees hired in 1952 celebrated their 25th anniversary at Motorola.

Folklore and Stories   Part of Motorola's culture was rooted in stories about Paul and Bob Galvin, and in some of the company's policies and practices. Aspects of the culture included the following:

- In Motorola's early days, the company experienced serious financial struggles. Despite the almost overwhelming challenges, Paul Galvin kept all the regular employees on the payroll.
- In the 1950s Motorola withdrew from a potentially profitable contract in a foreign country because there were payments that had the appearance of a kickback.
- Paul Galvin initiated a policy of treating female employees fairly and with respect decades before sexual harassment issues became a matter of general concern and legislation was passed. The policy was continued by Bob Galvin. One oft-told story concerned Bob Galvin's visit to a Motorola manufacturing facility where he observed women working on the assembly lines. He expressed concern about what Motorola should do to protect the women from offensive behavior and harassment, making it clear that such behavior would not be tolerated. One senior official was dismissed for failure to enforce the behavior standards that Bob Galvin set forth.
- Several stories illustrated how, when the choice was money or ethics, Bob Galvin always went with ethics. Others were more about him as a role model. One person told about a meeting where Bob Galvin gave a 10-minute speech shortly after he had a heart bypass operation. He was very tired, but later in the meeting, when he saw women standing in the crowded room, he went around gathering chairs for them and gave up his chair so a woman could be seated.
- Motorola has an official policy of refusing to supply customers with any materials that would be used in making land mines.
- Motorola has a long-standing policy that no employee with over 10 years service can be fired without prior approval of the CEO.

Decentralization and Management Style

Paul Galvin had a highly participative management style that had become embedded in the company's culture. In the late 1980s and early 1990s, Motorola had a strong three-man office of the chief executive and a highly decentralized organization structure that placed operating and strategic authority at the business-unit level. While such functions as strategic planning, finance, human resources, legal, ethics, and quality were centralized at the corporate level, full authority to develop business strategies was delegated to the heads of Motorola's business units. Motorola's decentralized approach to running its different businesses and divisions was both a strength and a weakness. Divisions headed by strong managers operated as virtual fiefdoms, pursuing their own agendas and priorities. Divisions were often not cooperative or responsive to the requests and needs of sister divisions, prompting one outsider to label them "warring tribes."[12] The

---

[12]Crockett, "How Motorola Lost Its Way."

lack of cross-division collaboration was said to allow "stovepipe thinking." There were cases where divisions became so preoccupied with their own business issues and problems that they took little note of the rapidly changing nature of the global marketplace (unless it bore directly on the division's own business). Division autonomy and independence tended to result in strategies and behavior that appeared best for the division and that sometimes were contrary to the competitive interests of Motorola as a whole.

But case researcher interviews with Motorola insiders indicated that this characterization might be overblown, Motorola's organizational structure was basically relational, not hierarchical. While Motorola did have general managers with considerable authority over a particular business or group, most of life within Motorola consisted of collaborative relationships. Motorola made a practice of giving managers cross-functional tasks and assignments outside of their formal job descriptions. As a consequence, it was customary for Motorolans to have and use a network of contacts across the company that made the company's informal structure almost as influential as its formal structure. Moreover, the company's strong emphasis on ethical standards created trust between co-workers and promoted a good basis for information sharing and cooperation across departmental boundaries.

Technology-Engineering Climate

Another characteristic of Motorola's leadership culture was its engineering base. Motorola competed in industries with rapidly advancing technologies and high-velocity product innovation. Most of Motorola's key executives were well versed in technology, and over time the company had developed a high level of technological and engineering expertise. For many decades, Motorola had demonstrated an ability to stay on the cutting edge of technological advances. Going into the 1990s, however, some observers viewed Motorola's technology- and engineering-based culture as a liability in a world they saw as increasingly driven by marketing.

Other Motorola critics saw the company's top executives as insular and tradition bound. In 1998, 67 percent of Motorola's top executives had been with the company for more than 20 years.[13] Internally, this was viewed by many Motorola leaders as a source of strength and cohesion; externally, it was viewed by critics as evidence that Motorola was inbred and out of touch at the top.

The Ethics Component of Motorola's Culture

Motorola's ethical standards were set forth in its code of business conduct. Over more than five decades, company officials had issued interpretations and clarifications of the code to further communicate to all Motorolans what behaviors were expected and what behaviors were prohibited. The company's ethical standards were deeply ingrained in the Motorola culture. Respect for and appreciation of the company's high ethical standards were widely shared among employees and managers.

Top executives at Motorola had an unwavering conviction that maintaining high ethical standards was not only the right thing to do but also good business. This conviction extended to both countries where business was conducted in a manner that matched Motorola's ethical standards and countries where it was not. Motorola executives believed that the company's stance against bribery, extortion, and "lubricating

---

[13]Rick Tetzeli, "And Now for Motorola's Next Trick," *Fortune*, April 27, 1997, p. 122.

fees" (fees paid to local officials to speed needed actions) reduced costs in the long run and that Motorola's reputation for ethical behavior made it a desirable business partner. Other benefits they saw included higher morale, a higher level of mutual trust among Motorolans, and greater trust between Motorola and its customers and vendors. Case researcher interviews revealed a general opinion among Motorolans that the company's long-standing commitment to ethical behavior set a good example for other firms to follow in those foreign-country markets where corruption and questionable ethical behavior were still common. Motorolans took pride in the fact that the company's strong focus on providing quality products at competitive prices while conducting its business honorably showed to the world that a company could succeed in global markets without resorting to unethical or questionable acts.

ETHICS IN THE GLOBAL MARKET ARENA

Ethical standards, of course, vary widely in countries across the world. Each region of the world has its own interpretations of what is ethical and what is not, and many countries have implicit and explicit standards for appropriate business practices both at home and around the world. In the United States, the passage of the Foreign Corrupt Practices Act (FCPA) of 1977, prohibiting a variety of unethical actions and imposing severe sanctions for violations, had heightened the need of U.S. companies to exercise due diligence in how they did business anywhere in the world. Some of the actions considered illegal under the FCPA were considered acceptable business practices in parts of Europe, Asia, Africa, and Latin America.

But economic globalization was beginning to drive greater homogeneity of what was ethical and what was not. Whereas in the 1970s and 1980s it was hard to get government or business leaders to acknowledge that corruption existed, by the mid-1990s there was open talk about corruption and discussion of ways to curb it. The United Nations had begun to issue statements supporting the criminalization of bribery and extortion and to express concerns about various types of "facilitating payments." Bribery and extortion could range from passing a few dollars to a poorly paid border guard to gain exit from a country, to agreeing to the monetary demands of local government officials in return for their issuing the necessary permits to conduct business or open factories. Extortion payments were a permissible legal business expense for many European firms but were illegal for U.S. firms. Facilitating payments to expedite services of one kind or another were fairly widespread in many countries; but because they did not entail requests for actions that weren't ordinarily expected, they were acceptable under the FCPA. The United Nations Center on Transnational Corporations had put together a sample code of conduct to provide guidance on ethical conduct.

In Europe, the Organization for Economic Cooperation and Development, which had 29 European nations as members, adopted an accord in 1997 that called for firms in member countries to conduct business according to rules that were similar to those governing U.S. firms.[14] In Latin America, where bribery and other forms of corruption had long been common in business, there had been some movement by national leaders to curb such practices—the Interamerican Convention Against Corruption was adopted by the Organization of American States in 1996. The Caux Round Table, an international group of business leaders from the United States, Europe, and Japan that

---

[14]Paul Blustein, "Major Nations Agree to Ban Trade Bribery," *Los Angeles Times,* May 24, 1997, p. D1.

was formed in 1986 to foster international business relations, published a set of "Principles for Business" that advocated corporate responsibility for ethical concerns and business practices.[15]

In 1993, an organization called Transparency International began an effort to reduce corruption by encouraging nations to pass laws and anticorruption programs. Transparency International conducted an annual survey of businesspeople, risk analysts, investigative journalists, political analysts, and the general public to determine perceived corruption levels for various countries. In 1999, the five countries perceived as least corrupt were Denmark, Finland, Sweden, New Zealand, and Iceland. The five countries perceived as having the most corruption were Nigeria, Tanzania, Honduras, Paraguay, and Cameroon.[16]

MOTOROLA AND ETHICS IN A GLOBAL ENVIRONMENT

For much of its history, Motorola was unyielding in its definitions of what constituted ethical behavior and what did not. Virtually no official exceptions were made for any reason. As Motorola began to expand into foreign countries, company executives were adamant that its key beliefs and code of business conduct should be applied evenhandedly across the board everywhere it operated and that the well-defined ethical behaviors the company had always expected of Motorolans had to remain intact. But such strict black–white interpretations placed a mounting burden on Motorolans in foreign countries. In complying with the company's ethical expectations, Motorola managers and employees sometimes found themselves doing things they considered "business suicide" of one form or another. For example, many Motorolans in Japan knew that their Japanese counterparts expected them to participate in the gift-giving rituals so much a part of the Japanese culture. Yet, if Motorolans did participate in such rituals in direct violation of the company's code of business conduct, they were subject to dismissal and to feelings of guilt. Similar problems surfaced elsewhere. Growing numbers of Motorolans began to point to conflicts between Motorola's traditional ethical expectations and what were acceptable business practices and ethical standards in the countries where they operated.

Adjusting Ethical Standards and Interpretations to Make Room for Cultural Diversity

Over a period of time, Motorola executives came to the conclusion that there were legitimate circumstances in which the company's strict ethical requirements ought to permit some room for responsiveness to local customs, business practices, and ethical standards. Motorola began taking one of four stances when conflicts arose. One stance was to make no adjustment in expectations. The remaining three stances involved situations in which some responsiveness and modification in expectations appeared reasonable and appropriate without compromising basic principles; in these cases, company policy was to (1) make minor adjustments in its ethical expectations to respond to local

---

[15]See the Caux Round Table Web site (www.cauxroundtable.org).

[16]See the Transparency International Web site (www.transparency.de). The current Corruption Perceptions Index is at www.transparency.de/documents/cpi/index.html.

standards, (2) make major adjustments to be responsive to local standards, or (3) make global adjustments.

Enforcing Ethical Behavior Expectations without Adjustment to Local Conditions

One area where Motorola stood fast and refused to adjust its ethical behavior expectations to meet local standards was payment of bribes. Paying money to government officials or customers to gain a contract was clearly out of bounds at Motorola no matter what the local circumstances might be. Motorola executives believed this strict policy had served the company well. To make their point, they told the story of a time when Motorola had constructed a large and expensive factory and was ready to begin production, but a local official was in control of operating permits and the official would not issue the permit without a bribe. The choice was to either pay the official or experience a very expensive delay in opening the plant. Motorola elected to wait, and as word spread in the local community over a period of several months that Motorola wouldn't pay bribes, the necessary permits were issued.

Motorola also enforced a strict policy worldwide for not allowing Motorolans to enter into procurement arrangements with family members or be a party to any such negotiations, despite the fact that doing business with companies owned by family members is common practice in countries such as Russia and China.

In instances where senior management concluded that no adjustment in its ethical behavior expectations could be allowed, company officials met with the affected Motorolans to justify its expectations and/or explain why responsiveness to local standards should not be accommodated. Such meetings helped clarify the company's code of business conduct, reinforce the appropriateness of the company's behavioral expectations, and gain stronger employee acceptance of both the code and the company's ethical expectations of Motorolans.

Making Minor Adjustments to Respond to Local Standards

Historically, Motorola's prohibition against paying bribes had been extended to include accepting or giving gifts in any form to government officials, suppliers, customers, or other business associates. In some cultures, however, gift giving was a fundamental part of the business relationship. In Japan, it was considered an offense not to accept and give gifts in business. In a move to establish a behavior expectation that remained true to its overall ethical philosophy yet responsive to local standards and sensitivities, Motorola adopted an ethical expectation for Japan that permitted limited gift giving and acceptance under well-defined conditions. For example, there were cost and time-of-year limitations on gifts, and any gift to a Motorolan had to remain on display in the recipient's office rather than becoming his or her personal property.

Another area where adjustment was deemed appropriate was Motorola's long-standing policy against paying agent's fees (perceived as similar to bribes). In numerous countries where Motorola operated, it was common to engage the services of an agent when a firm was unfamiliar with a country's conventions, rules and regulations; agents introduced company officials to local government officials and businesspeople and helped a firm avoid violating local rules or customs. It was difficult if not impossible to do significant business with the government in Saudi Arabia without being properly introduced. After a time, Motorola determined it would agree to the payment of agent's fees, provided they were a relatively small amount of the total contract value. In the Middle East, where agents played a critical factor and demanded substantively larger payments, Motorola approved such payments on a case-by-case basis after taking steps to ensure that the payments were comparable to local practice and none of the money was used as a bribe or other illegal payment by the agent. Under the FCPA, it is illegal for U.S. firms to pay an agent if the firm knows that part of the payment will be used as a bribe.

Making Substantive Adjustments to Respond to Local Standards

On occasion, Motorola encountered situations where responding to local standards and customs required "substantive" adjustments in its ethical expectations or a different interpretation of what constituted a fundamental conflict with its key beliefs. For example, Motorola had historically rewarded outstanding individual performance as part of its "constant respect for people" belief, but in Malaysia the culture valued group rewards. To accommodate the Malaysian preference for group-based rewards, Motorola allowed one of its plants in Malaysia to shift to a group-based performance evaluation and compensation. Given Motorola's cultural tradition of rewarding employees for outstanding individual performance and the strong tie this practice had to Motorola's belief in constant respect for people, agreeing to group-based rewards in Malaysia was indeed a substantive adjustment. To combat any perception that this adjustment comprised or posed fundamental conflict with its key belief, in 1992 Motorola added a fifth key initiative ("Empowerment for all, in a participative, cooperative and creative workplace") to its Total Customer Satisfaction Card.

Substantive adjustments were also made in cases where local officials asked for monetary payments from Motorola. While bribes were never paid, Motorola did work to achieve a creative solution within the boundaries of its key beliefs and ethical principles. In a country where Motorola had a large production facility, local officials indicated that some critical services such as police or fire protection might not be available unless funds were transferred. Further investigation revealed that the officials intended for the funds to be used to improve the equipment and boost the caliber of local government services. Motorola decided to donate communications equipment in support of the government effort to better serve the local community.

Making Global Adjustments

Global adjustments occurred when Motorola extended what was a local adjustment to a number of different locales. The most significant instance of global adjustment was taking place in the company's reward structure, where there was a growing shift from individual incentives to group-based incentives. A number of Motorola plants in varying locales had been granted permission to shift to group-based incentives. The preference for group-based rewards in these locations had begun to affect management thinking more globally as the company shifted to the use of more team-based production and design units where group-based incentives worked well.

THE CHALLENGES POSED BY MOTOROLA'S RAPIDLY GROWING MULTICULTURAL WORKFORCE

When Motorola's activities were confined primarily to the United States, its growth involved new employees of relatively similar backgrounds. Maintaining a homogeneous culture and ethical posture was relatively straightforward. However, as Motorola sought to preserve and apply its ethical tradition in the face of global expansion, it faced a complex array of new cultural challenges.

During the 1990s, Motorola added 50,000 employees drawn from cultures around the world. Half of the company's 121,000 employees were in locations outside the United States. In 1999, its employees spoke more than 50 different home languages and belonged to as many or more cultures. Motorola's employee base resided in hundreds of subcultures based on region, dialect, gender, class, wealth, education, occupation, religion, age group, and other variables. In addition to the diversity among its employees, Motorola's supplier and customer base was already multicultural and becoming more so.

The addition of 50,000 new employees in less than 10 years posed a big challenge to Motorola in terms of assimilating such large numbers of new employees into its culture and instilling Motorola's core beliefs and ethical posture. Rapid workforce expansion meant that there were proportionally fewer experienced employees to help indoctrinate new employees in Motorola's culture and to help with the process of continuously reinforcing the company's key beliefs and ethical expectations. The employee influx problem was complicated further by the fact that the new employee pool consisted of people coming from not only a variety of countries and cultural backgrounds but also from other companies—Motorola recruited many of its new employees from jobs at other corporations. These new employees often had developed ethical practices based on societal or company cultures that were quite different from Motorola's. Historically, Motorola had assigned experienced managers to its new subsidiaries and business divisions who acted as mentors and role models and transmitted the Motorola philosophy of doing business. In both the 1980s and 1990s, the company's rapid growth, coupled with the retirement of many senior Motorolans of various nationalities who knew Motorola's ethics well, had depleted the pool of experienced, culturally aware managers available for new assignments. Still another factor compounding the problem was Motorola's efforts to flatten the organization structure, empower employees, and further involve them in decision making in their areas of responsibility. These changes in roles and relationships put enhanced responsibilities on each Motorolan to understand and support the values of the corporate culture.

Responding to the challenges of a rapidly expanding multicultural workforce, Motorola's senior leadership initiated and supported a number of programs to help all Motorolans operate with high ethical standards. One step was to reinstitute use of the Total Customer Satisfaction Card (Exhibit 3) which had been used in the 1940s and 1950s. The card was translated into all the needed languages and provided to all Motorola employees worldwide; the hope was that they would keep the card in their possession at all times and refer to it frequently. A second step was the development and execution of the Motorola Ethics Renewal Process (MERP).

The Motorola Ethics Renewal Process

In 1995 Motorola's board of directors asked a group of very senior retired Motorola officers to look into the status of ethics understanding and compliance around the world. The team spent about a year interviewing people both inside and outside Motorola and produced a recommendation to the board that an "ethics renewal process" be created and rolled out across the corporation. The board concurred with the proposal, and the Motorola Ethics Renewal Process (MERP) became the focal point for disseminating, maintaining, and modifying Motorola's ethical posture. Board members agreed to put their full weight behind the MERP initiative, and several personally participated in the process.

Responsibility for implementing and executing MERP was assigned to the human resources department rather than to legal personnel. A unit was formed to ensure ethics compliance; its charge was to be proactive rather than reactive. According to Motorola executive Glenn Gienko, "From the start, the objectives were to establish an honest dialogue on concerns about ethical compliance, ethical values and the code of conduct." A book providing information about ethics, along with a set of real-life cases, was prepared for use in training discussions and ethics workshops.[17] The cases presented real-world ethical dilemmas faced by Motorolans, along with commentaries by ethics experts on the issues that were raised. The cases were designed to bring to the surface what was keeping people awake at night, things they couldn't easily discuss with co-workers. The majority of ethical questions were local, making local workshops an essential part of MERP.

The rollout process was structured to build higher levels of participation from all regions of the world and eventually from all levels of the organization. The first MERP workshop was successfully piloted in 1996, and workshops were held in additional regions throughout 1997–99. Establishing MERP meant answering everyday questions and developing an escalation process for major problems; it also meant making ethical issues a part of local management's everyday decision-making process. Workshop sites were selected without regard to whether a country might be experiencing unusual levels of ethical problems. Management emphasized that the workshops were not a search for possible violations or violators. By mid-1999 the process had involved Motorola employees in Africa, Canada, the Caribbean, Central and Eastern Europe, China, France, Japan, Korea, Latin America, the Middle East, Mexico, the United Kingdom, and Southeast Asia.

However, the chief purpose of MERP was not to be a platform for teaching ethics or business conduct. Rather, it was to help Motorolans at all levels in all countries make ethically appropriate business decisions every day and to get them to take ownership and accountability for Motorola's key beliefs and ethical values. MERP was intended as a vehicle to (1) allow open and honest exchanges of ethical questions across businesses and regions; (2) make dialogues about ethics and values as common as discussions about quality, cycle time, or customer satisfaction; and (3) encourage employees to discuss and debate the most sensitive aspects of remaining ethically steadfast in daily behavior.

Ethics Committees   Part of the comprehensive MERP involved creating local, country, and regional ethics committees to be responsible for promoting a culture that embodied Motorola's key beliefs and for providing a forum to openly discuss issues surrounding these beliefs and the code of business conduct. Regional/country committees included senior managers from the region/country as well as other appointed members. Ethics committees were expected to address (and hopefully resolve) procedural issues, questions of interpretation, and the appropriateness of particular local exceptions. They had no responsibility for conducting investigations.

---

[17]R. S. Moorthy et al., *Uncompromising Integrity: Motorola's Global Challenge* (Schaumberg, IL: Motorola University Press, 1998).

When tough issues emerged that could not be resolved at the local level, the ethics committee structure provided a way for major problems and issues to work their way up the ladder to final resolution. In 1999, final authority for setting "big-issue" ethical standards still remained a corporate function, but handling specific case-by-case interpretations of the code and local exceptions had been largely decentralized to the regional, country, and local ethics committees. The establishment of ethics committees continued Motorola's move away from corporate absolutism and put in place a decentralized structure for determining when and under what circumstances corporate ethical expectations should be adjusted to fit local customs and business practices. Greater reliance on ethics committees for such determinations meant that senior corporate executives and the CEO could concentrate their full attention on handling major ethical issues and leading the ethics compliance process.

Ethics Compliance at Motorola

In Motorola's early years, the procedures for ethical enforcement were straightforward. The code of business conduct was clear and provided a list of "thou shalt nots." Possible breaches of the code were investigated by the human resources, legal, or finance departments. Any requests for exceptions or exemptions from the code were referred to the chief legal officer. But as Motorola began to expand its operation to countries around the world, it became increasingly impractical to set worldwide ethical standards for every situation from corporate headquarters and to enforce them in the same strict fashion in light of all the cultural diversity.

In 2000, compliance was considered the responsibility of all Motorolans at all levels. Supervisors at all levels were charged with enforcing ethical standards and ensuring compliance to company's code of business conduct. However, three of Motorola's functional departments—human resources, legal, and finance—had important roles in monitoring compliance, investigating complaints, and reporting problem areas. All three departments had representatives on the ethics committees that had been created as a part of MERP. Complaints and allegations of ethical misconduct from parties outside Motorola were received by the company's legal department; the department's investigative team was headed by a former U.S. attorney. Human resources also had investigators to look into internal allegations of ethics violations. Finance, through the auditing function, monitored financial activity for possible ethical violations. Over time, as potential violations were investigated and sanctions were meted out where violations had occurred, the compliance effort contributed to the storytelling that reinforced the fabric of Motorola's ethical culture.

Some authority to approve country-specific variances from the code of business conduct was delegated to regional managers. For example, say that in China either a local ethics committee or the national ethics committee determined that a variance to currently stated Motorola policies was appropriate. A recommendation would be made to the Asian regional manager for approval of a variance. If the Asian regional manager concluded that the variance did not compromise Motorola's Key Beliefs and did not violate either U.S. or local laws, then a variance for China could be authorized.

If a local or national issue had ramifications for conduct in other countries or parts of the world, then the issue was passed up to the regional and corporate level ethics committees. Recommendations for global variances had to be approved at the corporate level and were reviewed by the CEO.

THE ONGOING ETHICS COMPLIANCE CHALLENGE AT MOTOROLA

In interviews conducted with senior managers, the case researchers pressed on the issue of what types of ethical violations the company's investigative forces were currently encountering. Company officials stressed that Motorolans were complying with the company's code of ethical conduct in good faith and that violations were usually unintentional and occurred in "gray areas." They provided the following examples to give a sense of the type of problems being encountered:

● An Asian government official wanted a "scholarship" for his son. Motorola had programs where it provided scholarships, but the awards were never in response to such types of requests for aid. In this case Motorola determined that the government official's request involved paying tuition fees and was unacceptable.

● It came to Motorola's attention that a particular distributor who had obtained Motorola products was avoiding tariffs in a country by trucking them through a remote border post. This distributor was not officially connected to Motorola, and the Motorola products the distributor had obtained had changed hands several times after leaving the authorized Motorola distributor. The matter was referred to an ethical committee. The committee determined that the distributor's actions were a fairly common occurrence, and now that Motorola had knowledge, this violated the key belief of uncompromising integrity. Motorola directed its authorized distributor to no longer sell to this chain of buyers.

● A salesperson was working with a lobbyist to sell equipment to a municipal government. The lobbyist suggested an action that raised the salesperson's concerns about ethical propriety. In accordance with company policy, the salesperson went to his supervisor for approval. The supervisor also had concerns and went up a level to seek approval from a manager. The manager was heavily preoccupied with other business and gave the OK. During an annual audit, the auditor challenged the expenditure. The subsequent investigation determined that all three should have known that the action was unacceptable, and all three were disciplined.

● Entertainment expenses were an area rich for possible violations. Motorola sponsored a number of events, such as the Phoenix Open, to which current and potential customers were invited. But to guard against ethical violations the circumstances for an invitation were restricted. The restrictions for governmental customers were more strict than for business customers. Guest lists for all Motorola-sponsored events had to be cleared through Motorola's legal department.

● Agent's fees were cited as a constant compliance and enforcement problem. In the Middle East, many of Motorola's potential customers were extraordinarily wealthy. Thus, for an agent to maintain contacts, it required a very high lifestyle, and exceptions might be made for higher than "normal" agent's fees. Such exceptions were made very carefully. In China, it was critical to have an effective agent to make introductions. Despite their importance, Motorola worked hard to find effective agents who charged reasonable fees; the company did not authorize above-normal payments.

● When the Chinese government brutally suppressed student demonstrations in Tiananmen Square, Motorola had to decide whether to pull out or continue doing business in the country. Given the substantial financial investment Motorola had in China, and the size of the potential consumer market, some observers questioned the ethical standards Motorola used to decide to remain in China. Motorola's leaders issued statements saying that they carefully considered the options and decided that Motorola could have a more positive impact on China by remaining, and that many innocent people in China would be severely hurt if Motorola departed. In interviews conducted for this case, it was reiterated that there were many reasons for remaining in China, but a primary reason was the belief of Motorola's leaders that increasing the free flow of information would facilitate reforms. By manufacturing and supplying telecommunications equipment and improving the telecommunications infrastructure, Motorola could act as a change agent and in the long run help shape the society and its values.

- While it was a common practice for salespeople to buy tickets to events, a violation occurred when a salesperson unwittingly purchased tickets from what turned out to be a government agency, which was prohibited.

- Motorola officials cited a case where taking aggressive action to uphold ethical standards resulted in unexpected and undesirable consequences. Another Western multinational firm operating in a country where Motorola had operations reported one of its employees to local authorities for stealing. The police came, arrested the individual, and shot him on the spot. The incident had the effect of making Western firms doing business in this country reluctant to report employee theft. They were caught between letting a crime go unreported or taking action that might result in punishment out of proportion to the crime being committed.

MOTOROLA AND ETHICS: THE VIEWS OF COMPANY INSIDERS

The case researchers' interviews revealed a clearly discernible ethical attitude and demeanor among the top managers at Motorola. Ethical behavior was considered a given. The typical attitude was that Motorola's two key beliefs had "stood the test of time in all different cultures." Bob Galvin, the current chairman of Motorola's executive committee, said that a lot of people across the world believed that their traditions were different from those in other countries but in fact "all people value honesty, values, and fair compensation." Jack Bradshaw, Motorola's chief ethics compliance officer, made the comment that "ethics is good business" because "people like to work for an ethical company." The opinion was expressed that a company with high ethical standards attracted employees who had high ethical standards and wanted to work in an ethical environment. One vice president with Latin American heritage and work experience said that working in an ethical company "allows me to sleep at night." A manager noted that Motorolans were rarely asked to pay bribes or kickbacks because of the company's well-known reputation for not engaging in such practices—a condition that made ethics enforcement at Motorola easier.

While most managers interviewed agreed that Motorola' strong enforcement of ethical standards had cost it some business and some time in penetrating certain markets (there were stories of a lost contract here or a lost opportunity there), there was a strong consensus that in the long run Motorola got more business, even in countries with varying levels of corruption. Several reasons were given. First, buyers knew Motorola had high standards and that customers would get what they paid for because the price did not include allowances for bribes or kickbacks. One senior manager cited a case where a customer was offered $2 million to go with another supplier; the customer declined because it wanted to deal with an honest company. Second, a government official that contracted with Motorola did not have to be concerned about being charged with graft because it was well known that Motorola could not be bought and did not pay bribes.

Ethics at Motorola as Seen by Outsiders

The case researchers interviewed a sampling of people who conducted business with Motorola, either as suppliers or customers. Those interviewed were of the opinion that Motorola's employees as a rule tried to abide by the code of business conduct and to serve as ethical role models. But they expressed concerns about whether Motorola's conduct in certain situations reflected high ethical standards, and they related instances where they believed Motorolans had violated the company's code of business conduct.

One challenged Motorola's willingness to forgo profit to maintain its ethical posture. The individual commented that Myanmar had had riots that were suppressed similar to those in China in Tiananmen Square. Motorola had pulled out of Myanmar but remained in China, where it had substantially greater investments.

One consultant who had an association with Motorola extending over 20 years told the case researchers that Motorola had an ideal image of itself and the expected behaviors for its employees but that the actions of its 121,000 employees covered the spectrum of ethical behavior. This person expressed a belief that Motorolans in different countries held different interpretations as to what constituted ethical behavior and was allowable under the code. He also spoke of occasions where he had observed Motorolans engaging in actions he perceived as contrary to the code of business conduct. While he thought that the Motorolans in question may have believed they were acting within the code's parameter, he believed they were violating the code based on his familiarity with the company and its ethical expectations.

Several interviewees cited instances where lower-level Motorolans experienced conflict between the restrictions of the code and requirements of their job. When asked about the oft-stated beliefs of senior leaders that code violations were certainly rare exceptions rather than the rule, the responses varied. One source felt top managers could become somewhat disconnected from reality; the source said the practice of executives traveling to Asian countries in first-class or business-class cabins and being whisked through customs to waiting limousines did not mirror the travails of lower-echelon Motorolans. The source said that when lower-level Motorolans were in a dusty airport late at night in an insecure city with a departing airplane their only possible transportation, a few dollars as a "tip" were treated as an acceptable violation of the code.

Other interviewees also told of having observed occasional minor violations but contended that, at the corporate level, Motorola did not make concessions and that as a group Motorolans were likely to act ethically. One told the story of a Motorolan in India who refused to pay a bribe to keep the power at his residence from being turned off—stating to officials that Motorolans did not pay bribes. In another story, in Bangladesh, which was cited in the interview as a country noted for corruption, a Motorolan would not pay bribes to import critical items necessary for the operation of his office. He also told local officials, "Motorolans do not pay bribes." Eventually he got what he wanted and felt gratified that even in a country with high corruption one could work ethically.

Motorola's Response to the Comments of Outside Observers

When Motorola's managers were apprised of the foregoing comments, they responded, in essence, as follows:

1. Yes, we know that some Motorolans will occasionally feel their health or safety is threatened and pay sums of money or surrender items to value to extricate themselves from the situation. What outside observers may not know is that such cases are reported to supervisors and documented by Motorola. A number of examples in Eastern Europe and Asia were cited. Such actions were not considered a violation of the code because the company's key belief of constant respect for people took precedence over uncompromising integrity. They cited a statement by Bob Galvin: "Do not be embarrassed by embarrassment."

2. In response to the contention that interpretations of ethical conduct varied across cultures, Motorola managers indicated that varying interpretations were the motivating force behind MERP. MERP was designed to clarify ethical behavior in local terms and involve and empower local Motorolans in the ethical process.

3. Even senior managers flew business class, and the use of corporate drivers and vehicles was for security reasons.

case 27 Levi Strauss & Company

John E. Gamble
University of South Alabama

In 1999 Levi Strauss & Company was the world's largest branded apparel manufacturer and second largest manufacturer and marketer of blue jeans. Levi's 501 button-fly jeans, introduced in the 1800s, were available in 108 sizes and 20 different finishes and fabrics, and were the best-selling brand of blue jeans in the United States during 1999. The company also manufactured and marketed the L2, Silver Tab, and Red Line brands of blue jeans; Dockers khakis; and Slates men's dress pants. Dockers was the leading brand of khakis in the United States, and Slates was the best-selling brand of dress pants in department stores.

Levi Strauss & Company (LS&C) was widely regarded as a leader in promoting corporate social responsibility. It was active in advocating ethical labor practices in the apparel and textile industries and helping communities in North America, Europe, and Asia respond to critical societal issues. Each year during the 1990s, LS&C had awarded more than $20 million to programs that addressed AIDS prevention and care, economic empowerment of low-income people, youth empowerment, and social justice programs that attempted to eliminate racial prejudice and discrimination. The company had received numerous awards for its social responsibility efforts from such organizations as the U.S. Centers for Disease Control, Volunteers of America, Harvard University, the United Nations, and the U.S. Department of Commerce. The company's employee benefit plan was ranked number one by *Money* magazine in 1992, and *Fortune* magazine listed Levi Strauss 15th on its 1996 list of the 100 best companies to work for. LS&C management stressed building an organizational culture that empowered and fairly rewarded employees.

However, in 1999 the company's declining competitive position in its core jeans business was of considerable concern to CEO Robert Haas and other company managers and shareholders. Even though Levi's was still the best-selling brand of blue jeans, the company's share of the U.S. men's jeans market had declined from 48.2 percent in 1990 to 25.0 percent in 1998. Its overall share of the jeans market had fallen from 30.9 percent in 1990 to 14.8 percent in early 1999. Company revenues had declined from $6.9 billion in 1997 to $6.0 billion in 1998. Analysts estimated that Levi's plummeting sales and market share had driven the value of privately held Levi Strauss shares down by nearly 45 percent since 1996.

In an effort to reverse its deteriorating competitive position, the company announced it would close 11 of its 22 plants and cut nearly one-third of its workforce in

North America. In Europe, Levi Strauss said it would close three plants and trim its workforce by 20 percent. The announcements triggered alarm among the company's suppliers and in the communities where the affected plants were located. Several long-time fabric suppliers indicated that the Levi Strauss plant closings would force them to lay off many of their employees. Merchants in the small towns where LS&C plants were targeted for closure expressed concern that the lost jobs would hurt local economies.

COMPANY HISTORY

Levi Strauss was born in Buttenheim, Bavaria, in 1829 and came to New York in 1847 to join his brothers Jonas and Louis, who had preceded him in immigrating to America. Jonas and Louis had established a successful dry-goods business and eventually brought all three of their siblings to New York to work in the store. Levi became a skilled salesman and merchant under the tutelage of his brothers during his first five years in America. In February 1853 Levi left New York to go sell supplies to the multitude of miners lured to California during the gold rush. He packed such goods as thread, scissors, yarns, and bolts of canvas with him for his two-month voyage to California, which would take him down the Atlantic coast, through the Panama Canal, and then north up the Pacific coast to San Francisco.

Levi Strauss's independent venture into the dry-goods business met with a rocky start; the young man found it difficult to sell many of the items brought from New York to stock his new store. Strauss had hoped to sell canvas to miners to use to make tents but was largely unable to find a market for the heavy, durable fabric. Legend has it that at some point during his first year in San Francisco, a lamenting Strauss was approached in a saloon by a stranger who suggested that Strauss use the unsellable canvas to produce rugged pants for miners. Strauss believed that the idea had promise and began producing and selling canvas "waist overalls" to area miners. Strauss's garments quickly gained in popularity, providing the basis for a thriving wholesale dry-goods business and work-clothes manufacturer. The evolution from waist overalls to the blue jeans of today began when Strauss soon ran out of canvas and switched to denim fabric. Rivets were added in 1873 to reinforce the pants' pockets, and in 1886 the now-familiar Levi's Two Horse Brand leather patch was sewn to the back of the waistband. The 501 designation was given to the pants in 1890, belt loops were added in 1922, the red tab was added to the back pocket in 1936, and in 1960 waist overalls were renamed jeans.

Levi Strauss was the company's chief manager until his death in 1902; his four nephews inherited Levi Strauss & Company. A large number of Levi Strauss's heirs have since held management positions with the company throughout its history, including chairman and CEO Robert D. Haas, a great-great-grandnephew of the company's founder. Between the early 1900s and World War II, the company's jeans became the uniform of hardworking miners, factory workers, farmers, and ranchers. Levi's jeans became fashionable as well as functional in the 1950s when Marlon Brando and James Dean helped make Levi's a must-have brand for teenagers. The popularity of Levi's jeans continued to rise through the 1960s and 1970s before ebbing somewhat in the early 1980s. Blue jeans regained their popularity in the mid- to late 1980s and at the onset of the 21st century continued to be among the most frequently worn pants by teens and young adults in the United States and many other parts of the world.

OWNERSHIP STRUCTURE AND GOVERNANCE

Levi Strauss & Company was a private company controlled by heirs of the founder until 1971, when it offered shares to the public to finance its growth and diversification moves into such new apparel businesses as rainwear and wet suits. Levi Strauss's heirs retained control of the company through the collective voting rights of their shares. In 1985, confronted with the potential threat of hostile takeover, the family chose to initiate a $1.6 billion leveraged buyout (LBO) to again take the company private. The LBO resulted in 94 percent of the company's shares coming under the control of Levi Strauss's 203 descendents. Four percent of the shares were held by a company employee stock ownership plan and 2 percent of the remaining were held by outside investors led by F. Warren Hellman, a distant relative of the controlling Haas family.

Further ownership changes occurred in 1996 when members of the Haas family began to quarrel about the company's dividend policy and other potential uses of its $1 billion cash balance. Robert Haas, Warren Hellman, previous Levi Strauss & Company CEO Peter Haas Sr., and Peter Haas Jr. initiated a deal that would buy back all employee shares and the shares of discontented Haas family members. Employees and family members were initially offered $189 per share—a price established by a valuation analysis conducted by Morgan Stanley—but then offered $265 per share when advisers to disgruntled family members valued the stock at $315 to $387 per share. Thirty percent of the company's shares were repurchased through the buyout at a price of $4.3 billion. All shares were placed in a trust that was controlled by the four men who organized the buyback. The four trustees possessed all voting rights concerning company business issues and were required to approve any subsequent sale of Haas-family-member shares and were the only shareholders allowed to name successors as trustees. The trust was structured to remain in force for 15 years or until Robert Haas ceased to be a trustee, or unless two-thirds of the company's shareholders voted to alter the trust. Haas called the trust an insurance policy that "would allow the company to remain private and family-owned for years to come."[1] Exhibit 1 presents a list of LS&C's top 10 shareholders prior to the 1996 buyback.

In a Securities and Exchange Commission filing describing the company's ownership restructuring, it was noted that Robert Haas, Warren Hellman, and an investment banker and a company attorney who both played key roles in the buyback were allowed to purchase shares valued at nearly $90 million for $250,000 in return for organizing the buyback. At the $265 per share buyback price, Robert Haas received shares worth about $70 million, while Hellman and the other two men received shares worth a total of about $17.5 million. Employees who were required to sell their shares to the trust were promised a bonus roughly equal to each employee's 1996 annual compensation if the company's cumulative cash flow reached $7.6 billion by 2001. CEO Haas stated that if the company's cumulative cash flow between 1996 and 2001 was less than $7.6 billion, employees would receive a proportionately smaller bonus.

---

[1]"Levis Strauss Offers $265 a Share in Stock Buyback Plan," *Los Angeles Times*, February 10, 1996, p. D1.

exhibit 1   Levi Strauss & Company's 10 Largest Shareholders as of January 1995

Shareholder	Relationship	Total Shares (in millions)	Percent Ownership	Value of Shares (in billions)
Robert D. Haas	Great-great-grandnephew of Levi Strauss	4.2	8.0%	$1.1
Peter E. Haas Sr.	Robert Haas's uncle	11.5	22.3	3.1
Josephine B. Haas	First wife of Peter Haas Sr.	5.7	10.8	1.5
Peter E. Haas Jr.	Son of Peter Haas Sr.	4.5	8.6	1.2
Estate of Walter A. Haas Jr.	Robert Haas's father	4.3	8.2	1.1
Rhoda H. Goldman	Sister of Peter Haas Sr. and Walter Haas Jr.	3.7	7.1	0.9
Miriam L. Haas	Second wife of Peter Haas Sr.	3.0	5.7	0.8
Margaret E. Jones	Daughter of Peter Haas Sr.	2.9	5.5	0.8
Daniel E. Koshland Jr.	A Haas cousin	2.9	5.5	0.8
Frances K. Geballe	Sister of Daniel Koshland Jr.	2.7	5.2	0.7

Source: "Levi's Bold Plan for Reorganization," *San Francisco Chronicle,* February 13, 1996, p. C1.

In addition, if cumulative cash flows exceeded $7.6 billion, the employee bonuses would be increased.

Robert D. Haas—Levi Strauss & Company's CEO

Robert D. Haas was among a long line of Haas family members to hold high-ranking management positions with Levi Strauss & Company. Robert Haas's grandfather Walter Haas Sr. was the company's president between 1928 and 1955; his father, Walter Haas Jr., was president between 1958 and 1970; and his uncle Peter Haas Sr. was president between 1970 and 1981. Robert Haas began his career with Levi Strauss & Company in 1973 and held positions as marketing director and group vice president of Levi Strauss International, director of corporate marketing development, senior vice president of corporate planning and policy, president of the operating groups, and LS&C executive vice president and chief operating officer before being promoted to CEO in 1984 and named chairman of the board in 1989. Robert Haas was also the president of the Levi Strauss Foundation, a member of the Conference Board, and former director of the American Apparel Association.

Prior to joining LS&C, Haas was elected to Phi Beta Kappa and was valedictorian of the 1964 University of California–Berkeley graduating class. After then spending two years with the Peace Corps in Africa, Haas received an M.B.A. degree from the Harvard School of Business in 1968. Robert Haas was a White House Fellow under the Johnson administration for two years before joining consulting firm McKinsey & Company as an associate between 1969 and 1972.

When Haas became CEO in 1984, Levi Strauss & Company was troubled, with declining sales and market share. The company's profits had fallen by over $160 million in recent months as Levi Strauss lost market ground to designer jeans brands like Calvin Klein and Guess. Haas began a major overhaul of the business by divesting noncore businesses, creating a flatter organizational structure, cutting the workforce by one-third, and investing heavily in new product development, marketing, and process

exhibit 2   Levi Strauss & Company Sales and Operating Income,
1962–98

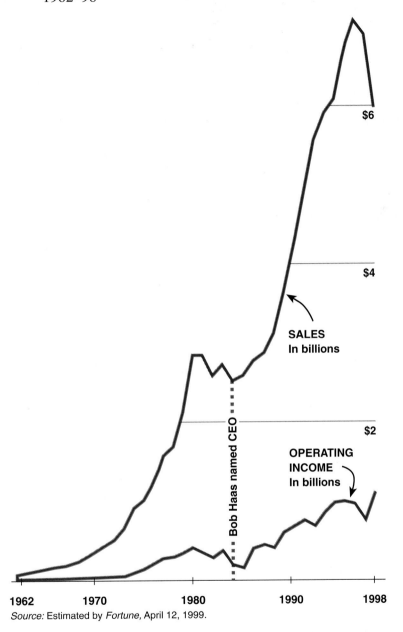

Source: Estimated by *Fortune,* April 12, 1999.

improvements. In 1985, Haas engineered the LBO to protect the company from an un-
friendly takeover during its recovery period. By 1989 the company's sales had increased to $3.6 billion (a 31 percent increase over 1985 sales), and its profits grew by
500 percent between 1985 and 1989, to a record $272 million. The company regained
its market-leading position with a 48 percent share of the U.S. jeans market in 1990.
Exhibit 2 present s graph of Levi Strauss & Company's estimated sales and operating
earnings between 1962 and 1998.

Robert Haas was instrumental in shaping the company's policies regarding its treatment of employees, its expectations for ethical business practices by suppliers, community involvement, and other issues concerning corporate social responsibility. Haas thought that after the turnaround the company could focus on its corporate values and social mission: "I said, let's fix the business issues first, but as soon as we have our business back on track we have to attend to our culture, because that's the glue that unites us, the beacon that guides our actions."[2] Robert Haas believed that the company's culture should promote ethical decision-making and that when making business decisions company executives should take into account the well-being of all stakeholders, not just shareholders. Haas said, "The key thing is that we try to look at our decisions from as many different points of view as we can. We look at the impact on the community, on the people involved."[3]

"ASPIRATIONAL MANAGEMENT" AT LEVI STRAUSS & COMPANY

Even though the company was forced to reduce its workforce by nearly 12,000 employees and close over 40 manufacturing and distribution facilities worldwide during its 1984–89 turnaround, Haas ensured that terminated employees were offered generous severance packages; these included 90 days of notice pay, one week of severance pay for each year of service, three months of health benefits beyond the 90-day notice period, job counseling, and relocation assistance. When labor leaders criticized the company's relocation of its production to such offshore locations as the Dominican Republic and Costa Rica, where hourly wages ranged between 30 cents and $1.00, Haas conceded that there were "no simple answers" but emphasized that "we are in business to make a fair profit" and that "we are not a government entity."[4]

The severance package LS&C offered to displaced workers was an illustration of how the Levi Strauss Mission, Vision, Aspirations, and Values Statement affected management decisions at the company (see Exhibit 3). Robert Haas orchestrated the development of the first such statement in 1987 when he saw a need to define the shared values that should guide the company's management and workforce. The values embodied in the document called for mutual trust and respect among management and employees and a commitment to strong ethical standards, teamwork, diversity, and empowerment. The Mission, Vision, Aspirations, and Values Statement guided strategic decisions, company operating policies, and company practices and, in management's view, promoted a corporate culture that recognized the demands of balancing a job and family.

The statement, for example, set the tone for how the company dealt with job responsibilities, performance appraisal, and training and resulted in personnel policies that provided employees with paid time off and leaves of absence for vacations, illness, medical appointments, or other personal emergencies. All LS&C employees were eligible for some type of incentive pay and were offered what *Money* magazine called the

---

[2]"How Levi's Trashed a Great American Brand," *Fortune,* April 12, 1999, p. 86.
[3]"Keeping a Shiny Corporate Image," *San Francisco Chronicle,* January 29, 1990, p. B1.
[4]Ibid.

exhibit 3   Levi Strauss & Company's Mission, Vision, Aspirations, and Values (as revised in May 1999)

Mission

The mission of Levi Strauss & Co. is to achieve and sustain commercial success as a global marketer of branded apparel.

Vision

Through a relentless focus on consumers, innovation, and people, Levi Strauss & Co. will be the world's foremost authority in casual apparel.

Aspirations

All LS&C employees aspire to be part of a winning organization built on the strong foundation of accomplishments, traditions, and values that we have inherited and that continue to lead us to commercial success.

Values

Our values guide our success, unite us, and make LS&C unique.

- **Integrity and Ethical Behavior**
  Honesty, promise-keeping, fairness, respect for others, compassion, and integrity guide our conduct and actions, even when we are confronted by personal, professional, and social risks or economic pressures.

- **Commitment to People**
  We want LS&C to be known as a great place to work—a place where satisfaction grows out of the contributions we make and that offers opportunities for professional growth.

- **Diversity**
  We value and utilize the varying backgrounds, experiences, knowledge, and talents of all of our employees. Our global workplace will reflect the ethnic, cultural, and lifestyle diversity within the communities where we do business.

Behaviors

Our behaviors will support the achievement of the company's Mission, Vision, and Aspirations.

- **Be Innovative**
  We will be innovative and embrace new and exciting ways of thinking. Innovative products, marketing programs, and business practices are the keys to our success.

- **Take Informed Risks**
  We will take informed risks that enable each of us to create new opportunities and to challenge established business practices.

- **Be Decisive and Results-Oriented**
  We will act decisively to assess and act swiftly on opportunities that will contribute to our commercial success. Our decision making will be results-oriented and guided by our strategic business vision and our values.

- **Seek Leverage**
  We will work together, actively exchanging ideas and information throughout the company, in order to achieve our business goals. Successful teamwork involves using the knowledge and opportunities created by our global presence.

- **Be Accountable**
  We will set clear and measurable responsibilities for individuals and teams, and will hold each other and ourselves accountable for the success of the company.

- **Recognize Results**
  We will recognize and reward superior contributions to our business success. We will also acknowledge our failures and shortcomings, and respond quickly with any necessary corrective actions.

Source: Levi Strauss & Company, www.levistrauss.com/about/vision.html.

exhibit 4   Highlights of the Levi Strauss & Company Employee Benefit Plan

- Health and dental insurance for employees, unmarried partners, and dependents. (Levi Strauss & Company was the first *Fortune* 500 company to offer medical and dental benefits to employees' unmarried partners and their dependents.)
- Vision plans.
- Life insurance.
- Accidental death and dismemberment insurance.
- Short- and long-term disability.
- 50 percent company-matched retirement plans.
- Time off with pay.
- Paid holidays.
- Three to seven weeks of annual vacation time.
- Child care subsidies.
- Friday afternoons off.
- Incentive pay for employees at all levels of the organization.

Sources: Levi Strauss & Company Web site and press releases.

United States' best employee benefits program in 1992. Exhibit 4 lists some of the traditional and less commonly offered benefits provided by LS&C to its employees.

Levi Strauss & Company's compensation was among the highest in the apparel industry, with hourly rates of pay that ranged from $8 to $10 per hour and incentives for hourly employees like sewing machine operators as well as incentives for management. The company's Global Success Sharing Plan, announced after the 1996 LBO, promised all employees a onetime bonus roughly equal to their 1996 salaries if the company accumulated excess cash flow of $7.6 billion between 1996 and 2001. The bonus would cost the company as much as $750 million, but Robert Haas believed the expense was worth it. Haas commented that the company's managers, shareholders, and workforce were "all in this together" and that a large lump-sum bonus could make a difference in the lives of LS&C employees since it was so difficult for hourly employees to accumulate wealth.[5] Some industry analysts questioned why the company would promise such a large bonus while others in the industry were trying to reduce expenses to better compete against rivals relying on contract manufacturers located in low-wage countries. Robert Haas rebutted his critics by suggesting that Levi Strauss & Company was "a company that zigs when other companies zag."[6]

Haas believed that the company's efforts to compensate employees fairly and provide them with flexibility and participation in decision making would lead to a stronger resource base and set of competitive capabilities. In a *Harvard Business Review* interview, Haas explained how the aspirations statement was a melding of the "hard stuff" with the "soft stuff" and why the company's values were crucial to its competitive success:

> If companies are going to react quickly to changes in the marketplace, they have to put more and more accountability, authority, and information into the hands of the people who are closest to the products and the customers. That requires new business strategies and

[5]"Levi's Pot o' Gold," *Business Week,* June 24, 1996, p. 44.
[6]"Levi Strauss Offers to Pay a Dividend to Workers," *New York Times,* June 13, 1996, p. D4.

different organizational structures. But structure and strategy aren't enough. This is where values come in. In a more volatile and dynamic business environment, the controls have to be conceptual. They can't be human anymore: Bob Haas telling people what to do. It's the ideas of a business that are controlling, not some manager with authority. Values provide a common language for aligning a company's leadership and its people.

The passivity and dependence of traditional paternalism—doing what you're told—doesn't work anymore. People have to take responsibility, exercise initiative, be accountable for their own success and for that of the company as a whole. They have to communicate more frequently and more effectively with their colleagues and customers.

The Aspirations encourage and support the new behaviors we need. For example, in an empowered organization there are bound to be a lot more disagreements. Because we value open and direct communication, we give people permission to disagree. They can tell a manager, "It doesn't seem aspirational to be working with that contractor because from what we've seen, that company really mistreats its workers." Or they can say, "It may help us conserve cash to be slow in paying our bills, but that company has been a supplier for a long time, and it's struggling right now. Wouldn't it be better in terms of the partnership we're trying to create with our suppliers to pay our bills on time?"[7]

Levi Strauss & Company attempted to make its Mission, Vision, Aspirations, and Values Statement an important part of the company's culture by covering leadership, employee empowerment, diversity, and ethical decision making in a three-part, 10-day course called Leadership Week. Haas had formed 80 task forces to study and make recommendations concerning the company's policies related to overseas labor practices, work-and-family issues, and diversity in the workforce. Managers were encouraged to practice and nurture the behaviors outlined in the statement and were trained in how to do so during the Leadership Week course. The company's compensation plan for management made one-third of managers' bonuses, raises, and other financial rewards contingent on their ability to manage in a style and manner that promoted deeper commitment to the company's mission, vision, aspirations, and values. Haas stated that the company could also ingrain the aspirations and values into its culture by encouraging managers to be explicit about their vulnerabilities and failings, talk about the bad decisions they've made, and talk about the limitations of their own knowledge. Haas also suggested that promotions were not in the future of managers who did not improve their ability to manage aspirationally.

LEVI STRAUSS & COMPANY'S PARTNERSHIPS WITH SUPPLIERS AND RETAILERS

As with the company's relationships with its employees, Haas also believed that the company needed to structure its supplier network to reflect LS&C's values and to emphasize long-term relationships. In the past, Haas said, the company maintained a large number of suppliers in order to promote strong price competition among suppliers: "The old way of thinking was, if you had enough different suppliers, the competition for your business would force them to drive their prices to the lowest possible point and to maintain the highest possible quality."[8] Haas believed that partnerships between the company and its suppliers would improve the overall quality of Levi's products and

---

[7] "Values Make the Company: An Interview with Robert Haas," *Harvard Business Review,* September–October 1990, p. 329.

[8] "Robert Haas' Vision Scores 20/20," *Industry Week,* April 2, 1990, p. 19.

allow the company to provide better service to its customers through more timely deliveries. Haas also believed that it was important to treat the company's retailing customers as partners by providing assistance in point-of-sale program support and a strong national advertising program plus the availability of information systems that aided retailers in improving inventory management and purchase ordering. In summarizing the importance of the company's supplier and customers partnerships, Haas suggested that Levi Strauss was forced to "change the way you look at things—your retailers and your suppliers as partners. If they're not successful and profitable, then we go down the tubes over time."[9]

Robert Haas also oversaw the development of the company's Global Sourcing and Operating Guidelines, drafted in 1991 and approved by the company's board of directors in 1992 to ensure ethical business practices on the part of LS&C suppliers. The guidelines called for LS&C's overall evaluation of the country-specific external issues beyond the control of individual business partners (e.g., health and safety issues and political, economic, and social conditions) to help the company assess the risk of doing business in a particular country. Levi Strauss managers could avoid suppliers and other potential business partners that were located in what were deemed to be high-risk countries where unethical or inhumane business practices were likely to occur. The Global Sourcing and Operating Guidelines also created terms of engagement that approved business partners were expected to adopt and follow. If LS&C determined that a business partner was in violation of the terms of engagement, it could withdraw production from that factory or require that the contractor implement a corrective action plan within a specified time period. Contractors were aware that if they failed to meet the corrective action plan commitment, Levi Strauss would terminate the business relationship. The Global Sourcing and Operating Guidelines' terms of engagement are presented in Exhibit 5.

LS&C's terms of engagement and its close relationships with suppliers helped improve the working conditions of those around the world who worked in factories where Levi's products were made. The company's supplier-monitoring program revealed that in Bangladesh several underage girls were working in two suppliers' factories. After a discussion of the situation, the suppliers agreed to discontinue hiring underage workers and to release existing underage workers from their job responsibilities but continue to pay a salary to the girls as long as they attended school. Levi Strauss & Company agreed to pay for the girls' tuition, books, and school uniforms until the completion of their education when their jobs would again be available at the factory if they desired to return. LS&C also negotiated safer work environments for workers employed by offshore suppliers and encouraged suppliers to offer medical treatment to employees and their families and find ways for employees to further their education.

LEVI STRAUSS & COMPANY'S COMMITMENT TO ADDRESSING BROAD SOCIAL ISSUES

The company's social mission and commitment to bettering the lives of others could be traced to its founder, who used his influence and wealth to benefit such charities as orphan homes, homes for the elderly, the Eureka Benevolent Society, and the Hebrew Board of Relief. Levi Strauss also provided funding to the California School for the Deaf and endowed perpetual scholarships at the University of California–Berkeley. At the time of Strauss's death, the San Francisco Board of Trade passed a special resolution noting his contributions to the community:

---

[9]Ibid.

exhibit 5   Levi Strauss & Company's Global Sourcing and Operating Guidelines' Terms of Engagement

1. **Ethical Standards**

   We will seek to identify and utilize business partners who aspire as individuals and in the conduct of all their businesses to a set of ethical standards not incompatible with our own.

2. **Legal Requirements**

   We expect our business partners to be law abiding as individuals and to comply with legal requirements relevant to the conduct of all their businesses.

3. **Environmental Requirements**

   We will only do business with partners who share our commitment to the environment and who conduct their business in a way that is consistent with Levi Strauss & Co.'s Environmental Philosophy and Guiding Principles.

4. **Community Involvement**

   We will favor business partners who share our commitment to contribute to improving community conditions.

5. **Employment Standards**

   We will only do business with partners whose workers are in all cases present voluntarily, not put at risk of physical harm, fairly compensated, allowed the right of free association and not exploited in any way. In addition, the following specific guidelines will be followed:

   Wages and Benefits: We will only do business with partners who provide wages and benefits that comply with any applicable law and match the prevailing local manufacturing or finishing industry practices.

   Working Hours: While permitting flexibility in scheduling, we will identify prevailing local work hours and seek business partners who do not exceed them except for appropriately compensated overtime. While we favor partners who utilize less than sixty-hour work weeks, we will not use contractors who, on a regular basis, require in excess of a sixty-hour week. Employees should be allowed at least one day off in seven.

   Child Labor: Use of child labor is not permissible. Workers can be no less than 14 years of age and not younger than the compulsory age to be in school. We will not utilize partners who use child labor in any of their facilities. We support the development of legitimate workplace apprenticeship programs for the educational benefit of younger people.

   Prison Labor/Forced Labor: We will not utilize prison or forced labor in contracting relationships in the manufacture and finishing of our products. We will not utilize or purchase materials from a business partner utilizing prison or forced labor.

   Health & Safety: We will only utilize business partners who provide workers with a safe and healthy work environment. Business partners who provide residential facilities for their workers must provide safe and healthy facilities.

   Discrimination: While we recognize and respect cultural differences, we believe that workers should be employed on the basis of their ability to do the job, rather than on the basis of personal characteristics or beliefs. We will favor business partners who share this value.

   Disciplinary Practices: We will not utilize business partners who use corporal punishment or other forms of mental or physical coercion.

Evaluation & Compliance

All new and existing factories involved in the cutting, sewing, or finishing of products for Levi Strauss & Co. must comply with our Terms of Engagement. These facilities are continuously evaluated to ensure compliance. We work on-site with our contractors to develop strong alliances dedicated to responsible business practices and continuous improvement.

Source: Levi Strauss & Company, www.levistrauss.com/about/code.html.

The great causes of education and charity have likewise suffered a signal loss in the death of Mr. Strauss, whose splendid endowments to the University of California will be an enduring testimonial to his worth as a liberal, public-minded citizen and whose numberless unostentatious acts of charity in which neither race nor creed were recognized, exemplified his broad and generous love for and sympathy with humanity.[10]

Many LS&C CEOs, including Robert Haas's father, grandfather, and uncle, continued the founder's commitment to social causes. Walter Haas Sr. established the Levi Strauss Foundation as an independent charitable organization in 1952 to support nonprofit organizations that addressed important social or community issues. Throughout the 1990s the company donated more than $20 million annually to fund nonprofit organizations in more than 40 countries. Walter Haas Jr. initiated Community Involvement Teams (CITs) in 1968 to provide employees with time off from work to take an active part in their communities through volunteerism. The CITs were promoted further by Peter Haas during his tenure as CEO, and in 1984 the White House presented Levi Strauss & Company with the President's Volunteer Action Award for Corporate Volunteerism for its support of employee community volunteer efforts. In 1999 LS&C employees had established over 100 CITs worldwide to donate time to projects as diverse as refurbishing homeless shelters to teaching computer skills to women in prison.

Levi Strauss & Company offered and promoted a variety of employee-giving programs in addition to Community Involvement Teams. The company awarded volunteer service grants to organizations where LS&C employees volunteered or served as board members. The company also matched employees' contributions to all types of nonprofit organizations and held campaigns to encourage employees to donate money to their favorite charities or disaster relief drives.

Robert Haas held a deep personal interest in many social issues and maintained and extended company's policy of providing funding to organizations that addressed what he saw as critical societal issues. Robert Haas was awarded Volunteers of America's Ballington and Maud Booth Award for Distinguished Service to Humanity in 1993 for his leadership in shaping Levi Strauss & Company's commitment to philanthropy and community service. He received an award from the United Nations for his commitment to improving the lives of LS&C employees and was recognized for his commitment to developing awareness of such social issues as racism and AIDS prevention and care.

Haas was frequently called on to make speeches on business ethics and once distributed AIDS leaflets to employees outside the company cafeteria. The U.S. Centers for Disease Control's National Business and Labor Award for Leadership on HIV/AIDS was presented to LS&C in 1997 in large part because of Haas' commitment to AIDS education. Robert Haas also encouraged employees to volunteer time and raise funds for community projects related to their interests and directed ample funding to the Levi Strauss Foundation which provided grants worldwide to organizations dedicated to such causes as social justice, AIDS awareness, youth empowerment, and economic empowerment.

Examples of programs funded by the Levi Strauss Foundation included Project Change which was launched in 1991 as an ongoing program to combat cultural beliefs and social norms that perpetuated discrimination in Albuquerque, New Mexico, El Paso, Texas, Valdosta, Georgia, and Knoxville, Tennessee. In 1998 President Clinton made Levi Strauss & Company the first recipient of the Ron Brown Award for Corporate Leadership in recognition of Project Change's efforts to promote social justice and end institutional racism. OCCUR was another social justice program funded by Levi

---

[10]Levi Strauss & Company—Biographies. www.levistrauss.com/about/bio_founder_downey.html.

Strauss that allowed the Japan Association for the Lesbian and Gay Movement to expand its peer-based telephone counseling services and begin a media campaign to promote positive images of lesbian and gay people. Levi Strauss also funded a youth empowerment program that allowed 100 youth from low-income and racial minority backgrounds to write short cultural diversity articles that were to be printed in various Canadian newspapers. In Mexico, LS&C funded an organization made up of university students and prostitutes that included AIDS workshops for prostitutes, their partners, and their clients. The president of the organization commented that Levi Strauss had made it "possible for these women to determine how to best stop the spread of HIV in the community—and to actually implement the program themselves."[11]

LEVI STRAUSS & COMPANY'S DECLINING SALES AND MARKET SHARE IN ITS CORE JEANS BUSINESS

Even though Levi Strauss & Company had reemerged during the 1990s as the leader of the jeans segment of the apparel industry, as 2000 approached it was again confronted with falling corporate sales and earnings resulting from the rapid decline its blue jeans business. The company's 1998 sales total of $6.0 billion was 13 percent lower than 1997's $6.9 billion total, and its market share in the jeans category had fallen from its 1990 high of 30.9 percent to 14.8 percent in 1999. The blue jeans segment of the apparel industry had grown by 6 to 8 percent in 1995 through 1997 and by 3 percent in 1998, but beginning in late 1997 LS&C began to lose sales to more stylish designer brands like Tommy Hilfiger and Polo and better-priced private-label brands offered by The Gap, Old Navy, J.C. Penney, and Sears. A retail analysis suggested that "Levi Strauss was zagging when the world was zigging"[12] as it failed to introduce new styles that appealed to consumers aged 15 to 24, who accounted for the largest percentage of blue jeans purchasers. Some analysts and competitors doubted that Levi's declining market share would be short lived, since appealing to the 15-to-24 age group was so important to the apparel industry. An executive at VF Corporation, the jeans segment leader and maker of Lee and Wrangler jeans, stated, "It's very important that you attract this age group. By the time they're 24, they've adopted brands that they will use for the rest of their lives."[13]

Robert Haas conceded that the company had missed trends like wide-legged pants, baggy jeans, and cargo pockets, but suggested that at the time the company was overly concerned with growing its newer Dockers and Slates brands: "When you try to take on too many things, you are not as attentive to the warning signs."[14] Levi's inability to introduce styles that appealed to teens was reflected in a Teenage Research Unlimited survey that found only 7 percent of teens in 1998 viewed Levi's as a "cool brand" and focus group results that pointed out that teens viewed Levi's as a brand more suitable for their parents or older siblings than teens. Levi's inability to keep its styles fresh was suggested to be in part related to the company's consensus management style and a

---

[11]Levi Strauss & Company Giving Program description,
www.levistrauss.com/community/HIVAIDSstudy.html.

[12]"Levi's Is Hiking Up Its Pants," *Business Week,* December 1, 1997, p. 70.

[13]Ibid.

[14]Ibid.

management team that was characterized as "insular, paternalistic, and quite frankly, a little smug" by the president of a retail sector marketing research firm.[15]

A J. P. Morgan Securities analyst stated that LS&C managers were "still resting on their laurels at bit" and were ultimately responsible for "a brand that is really stale right now" and "doesn't have any momentum." The analyst also commented that Levi's had "not been able to aggressively move into the new trends" and that "they are definitely not being as hip as some of the new brands we've been seeing that focus on what the kids want."[16] Levi Strauss & Company's former president suggested that strategic decisions at the company were difficult to make: "[Some managers say,] 'Our objective is to be the most enlightened work environment in the world.' And then you have others who say, 'Our objective is to make a lot of money.' The value-based people look at the commercial folks as heathens; the commercial people look at the values people as wusses getting in the way."[17] LS&C's previous chief financial officer claimed that "it was very difficult to be responsive" at the company because of the "principled reasoning approach" promoted in the company's leadership courses that called for consensus decisions: "Unless you could convince everyone to agree with your idea, you didn't have the authority to make a decision."[18]

A previous head of marketing who left the company in 1998 after a 20-year tenure suggested that Levi's problems had been building for years but were ignored by some executive level managers: "A big brand like Levi's is an aircraft carrier. You can turn the engines off and the actual speed of the carrier will not slow perceptibly for a long time. With the Levi's brand we gradually dialed down our propeller speed and the carrier kept moving. People up on the deck said, 'We're still moving fast!' But those down in the engine room said, 'Whoa! We're going to be dead in the water!'"[19]

The president of a major Levi's retailer suggested that Robert Haas was partly to blame for the company's falling sales during a time when rival apparel manufacturer Gap had increased its market value from $7 billion to over $40 billion: "Typically in apparel you have merchants, men like [Gap CEO] Mickey Drexler. I'm not sure Bob Haas has ever been trained to be a merchant. I'm not sure he's even been in a store, waiting on customers, talking to them so that he could hear them say, 'Why are the legs on those jeans so tight?'"[20] Expressing similar concerns, a former Levi's executive stated, "Bob is very smart. But then the question is 'What's he smart at? Is he smart at running an apparel company?' I think that's an open question."[21]

Many longtime Levi's retailers complained that the company's inability to introduce new styles that appealed to teens and young adults caused sales decreases for retailers as well as the manufacturer. In noting that Levi's declining popularity had contributed to Sears' 4 percent decline in men's apparel sales during 1998, the company's chairman and CEO stated that "we've suffered because of our excessive dependence on Levi's."[22] In addition, Levi's declining sales also affected suppliers adversely.

---

[15]Ibid.

[16]"Bad Day at Levi's: 11 Plants to Close, Costing 5,900 Jobs," *WWD,* February 23, 1999, p. 1.

[17]"How Levi's Trashed a Great American Brand," p. 86.

[18]Ibid.

[19]Ibid., p. 85.

[20]Ibid., p. 84

[21]Ibid.

[22]"Bad Day at Levi's: 11 Plants to Close, Costing 5,900 Jobs," p. 1.

The manager of a company that had been a supplier to Levi Strauss for more than 50 years was forced to lay off 400 employees when its orders ceased from Levi Strauss.

TURNAROUND EFFORTS AT LEVI STRAUSS

Levi Strauss & Company first took steps to correct its acknowledged cost disadvantage in 1997 by closing 11 of its 37 North American factories and eliminating 34 percent of its North American workforce. Each of the 6,395 displaced workers received eight months' severance pay, paid health insurance for 18 months, and up to $6,000 for education, relocation expense, or job training. Laid-off employees were also awarded a $500 bonus when they found a new job and would still be eligible for the Global Success Sharing Plan bonus. In addition, the Levi Strauss Foundation announced plans to grant nearly $8 million over a three-year period to the eight communities affected by the plant closings. Levi Strauss & Company also announced that 1,000 salaried positions in the United States would be eliminated during 1997.

In 1999 the company reacted to its declining sales and market share by bringing in new outside managers, hiring a new advertising agency, announcing new styles and subbrands of jeans, and announcing that 11 of its remaining 22 production facilities in the United States and Canada would be closed. The plant closings would eliminate over 5,000 of Levi Strauss & Company's 19,900 employees in North America. In Europe Levi Strauss would close three factories and eliminate over 1,500 of its 7,500 jobs on that continent. The plant closings announced in March 1999 and plant closings announced in November 1997 that had previously eliminated 6,400 LS&C jobs were expected to improve the company's cost-competitiveness. The production lost to the plant closings would be outsourced to offshore contractors.

The company's 1999 severance package included eight months' notice pay, up to three weeks' severance pay for each year of service, outplacement and career counseling services, medical coverage for up to 18 months, a $500 transition bonus, and up to $6,000 to offset education or retraining expenses, business start-up costs, or relocation expenses. Like the workers who were laid off in 1997, workers laid off in 1999 were still eligible for the Global Success Sharing Plan bonus. Even though the company's severance package was among the industry's most generous, some employees believed that it would be difficult to find jobs in the small, economically depressed towns where Levi Strauss plants were located. The Levi Strauss Foundation committed up to $5 million to ease the social and economic impact of the plant closings in the 11 affected communities. Merchants in towns like Johnson County, Tennessee, where a Levi Strauss plant closing would increase the county's 18 percent unemployment rate, were skeptical of the success of the financial aid offer and suspected that the plant closings would reduce the sales of all goods and services in the community. A local barber commented, "It's sad, boy. I think it's going to hurt everything. It's got to if you lose that many men and women."[23]

---

[23]"Levi's Plant Closing Is Latest Economic Hardship to Hit Johnson County," Associated Press State & Local Wire, March 22, 1999.